Women
and the
American
Labor Movement

Women
and the
American
Labor Movement

From Colonial Times to
the Eve of World War I

Philip S. Foner

THE FREE PRESS
A Division of Macmillan Publishing Co., Inc.
NEW YORK

Collier Macmillan Publishers
LONDON

The Free Press
A Division of Macmillan Publishing Co., Inc.
866 Third Avenue, New York, N.Y. 10022

Collier Macmillan Canada, Ltd.

Library of Congress Catalog Card Number: 79-63035

Printed in the United States of America

printing number
1 2 3 4 5 6 7 8 9 10

Library of Congress Cataloging in Publication Data

Foner, Philip Sheldon
  Women and the American labor movement.

  Bibliography: p.
  Includes index.
  1. Women in trade-unions — United States — History.
  2. Women — Employment — United States — History.   I. Title.
HD6079.2.U5F65   1979   331.88   79-63035
ISBN 0-02-910370-3

80-1972

To Roslyn

Contents

Preface and Acknowledgments   ix

1. Colonial and Revolutionary America   1
2. In the Factories   20
3. In the Trades   38
4. The Battle for the Ten-Hour Day   55
5. A New Era Dawns   80
6. Black Women before the Civil War   98
7. The Civil War   109
8. The National Labor Union   122
9. Workingwomen's Associations   141
10. The Long Depression   163
11. The Knights of Labor   185
12. The American Federation of Labor, 1881–1894   213
13. The American Federation of Labor, 1894–1900   235
14. The Turn of the Century   256
15. The Socialist Party and Socialist Women   270
16. Birth of the National Women's Trade Union League   290
17. The League Begins Its Work   303
18. The Waistmakers' Revolt   324
19. Repercussions of the Garment Workers' Uprising   347
20. New Unionism in the Garment Industry   374
21. The Wobblies and the Woman Worker   392
22. Rebel Women and the Free-speech Fights   413
23. The Lawrence Strike   426
24. Little Falls, Paterson, and Other Struggles   440
25. Wages and Working Conditions   459

26. *The League, the IWW, and the AFL*   470
27. *On the Eve of World War I*   487
     Notes   501
     Bibliography   576
     Index   601

Preface and Acknowledgments

As long ago as 1922 Arthur M. Schlesinger, Sr., in *New Viewpoints in American History* pointed out our need for an intensive study of American women. Research in women's history is in full swing today. Scholars have been investigating the history of the American women's movement in its various phases. In published and unpublished studies, monographs and interpretative essays, overall accounts of the American women's movement from a political, social, and cultural standpoint have been appearing in increasing number.

Workingwomen, however, do not loom large in the new scholarship dealing with the American women's movement just as they do not occupy an important place in most histories of the American labor movement. While women are not new to the American work force, their role in this capacity has been largely neglected. In the more than fifty years since Alice Henry published *Women and the Labor Movement* (1923) and Theresa Wolfson issued *The Woman Worker and the Trade Unions,* only one new study has appeared, the 1977 work by Barbara Mayer Wertheimer, *We Were There: The Story of Working Women in America,* which runs from colonial times to 1912.

For the most part historians of women and the American labor movement have relied on standard printed sources. But today there exist many repositories throughout the United States that house materials relevant to workingwomen. Prominent among them are the Arthur and Elizabeth Schlesinger Library of the History of Women in America, formerly the Women's Archives, at Radcliffe College, Cambridge, Massachusetts, the Sophia Smith Collection at Smith College, Northampton, Massachusetts, the Manuscripts Division of the Library of Congress and the National Archives in Washington, D.C., the Tamiment Institute Library at New York University, and others. The use of these repositories have resulted in several doctoral dissertations on workingwomen leaders and on organizations which throw new and valuable light on the history of women and the labor movement. This volume is vastly indebted to the important collections in these and other repositories.

Anyone today who writes labor history knows that it means more than the history of organized labor and that the history of working-class experience must go beyond emphasis on workers on the job and in their collective organizations and actions. But we most certainly do not know all we need to know about workingwomen and the American labor movement, and we cannot content ourselves with glorifying inchoate dissatisfaction while at the same time underemphasizing organized resistance. This resistance, moreover, is a fitting answer to the tendency to view women's past as one of undifferentiated subjection and passive victimization, in short, a chronicle of failure.

Women have been active in their own behalf since the earliest days of the factory system, often against what must have seemed insurmountable odds. Far from being passive, many women were militant and aggressive in their attempts to improve their working conditions. In a number of important industries, it was the militancy and perseverance of women workers that laid the foundations of trade unionism. This in the face of the double obstacle of employer–public hostility and the indifference of most male-dominated unions.

In analyzing the history of American workingwomen, I have tried to take into account both their status as women and their status as workers, and tried to understand the ways women's experiences as workers were different from those of men. Throughout, too, I have sought to point up the unique experience and problems of black women in the work force, both as slaves and as free laborers.

Nevertheless, it is impossible to separate the story of workingwomen from that of working men and from major events in social, economic, and political history that had profound effects on changes in women's work, as well as from changes going on in American society generally. Therefore, after reexamining the appropriateness of traditional periodization in the history of workingwomen, I have decided to follow the conventional marking of time-periods. In doing so, I have sought to identify a "woman's issue" within a larger historical content.

The present volume begins with colonial America and ends on the eve of the First World War. The second volume will carry the story from World War I to the present.

A work of this nature would have been impossible to produce without the kind cooperation of many libraries, historical societies, institutions and individuals. I owe a deep gratitude to the staffs of the libraries of Radcliffe College, New York University, University of Illinois, Tamiment Institute of New York University, Northeastern University, University of Maryland, University of Chicago, University of Texas, Austin,

University of California, Berkeley, University of California, Los Angeles, University of California, Santa Cruz, University of Pennsylvania, Georgetown University, Northwestern University, Columbia University, Lincoln University, Wayne State University, Detroit, University of Florida, Gainesville, University of Delaware, University of Wisconsin, Madison, University of Wisconsin, Milwaukee, Catholic University of America, Boston Public Library, New York Public Library, Library of Congress, Newberry Library, Chicago, Library Company of Philadelphia, Lynn Public Library, Detroit Public Library, Augusta Public Library, Cohoes Public Library, San Antonio Public Library, New Orleans Public Library, New York State Labor Library, State House Library, Boston, American Institute for Marxist Studies, New York, Tennessee State Library and Archives, American Federation of Labor Library, Library of Trade Union Women's Studies, Cornell University, Amalgamated Clothing Workers of America Library, United States Department of Labor Library, Rhode Island Historical Society, New Hampshire Historical Society, Maryland Historical Society, Pennsylvania Historical Society, Illinois Historical Society, and State Historical Society of Wisconsin.

I owe sincere thanks to Ken Lawrence of the Deep South People's History Project and to Ron Benson, Millersville State College, for kindly furnishing me with copies of several important documents. Lislotte Gage of the University of Hannover, Germany, Carl Gersuny of the University of Rhode Island, Robert E. Snyder of Syracuse University, Josephine Pacheco of George Mason University, Linda Nyden, and Linda Steinberg kindly furnished me with copies of their own work in the field.

Portions of the manuscript have been read, and valuable suggestions offered, by Sally M. Miller and Ted Werntz. My brother Henry Foner read the entire manuscript and helped in many ways to make this book possible. I owe him a special debt of gratitude.

Women
and the
American
Labor Movement

1
Colonial and Revolutionary America

CAPTAIN JOHN SMITH once wrote of colonial America: "Nothing is to be expected thence by labour." In Virginia, Massachusetts, and Pennsylvania, there were no fabulous cities ripe for looting like those visited by Cortés and Pizarro. Whatever wealth there was in North America had to come from the hard labor of mining, cutting down forests, planting and harvesting crops, and constructing buildings, roads, and bridges. America would bring great profits, the Virginia Company assured prospective investors during the winter of 1616–1617, as soon as there were "more hands" in the New World to exploit its resources.[1]

But where would these hands come from? The Indians could be captured and sold as slaves, but they died too quickly in bondage, and those who survived were inclined to escape to their tribes and then return with reinforcements to pay their respects to their former masters by taking their scalps as souvenirs.[2]

The colonizing companies looked to Europe for laborers, not gentlemen of taste and refinement who would rather "starve for hunger than lay their hands to labour"[3] but men who would explore new territory, clear lands, battle Indians, and maintain permanent and profitable settlements. However, they were convinced that as long as the men were single, they would never establish anything more than temporary camps. The colonizers therefore believed that if permanent communities were to be founded, women were essential.

Unlike the Spanish colonizers, most Englishmen in the American colonies did not seek to redress the imbalance of males by making sexual partners of Indian women. To be sure, Pocahontas, the favorite daughter of chief Powhatan, married the widower John Rolfe of Virginia. But this was unusual. In the main, the few Englishmen who had contacts with Indian women were trappers and traders on the frontier. Generally

1

Englishwomen were imported to fill the need for wives and domestic workers.[4]

In order to attract women settlers, several of the colonizers offered inducements to any married man who brought his wife, children, and servants to the colony. In the case of Maryland, for example, Lord Baltimore offered a hundred acres for each male settler, 100 for his wife, 50 for each child, 100 for each manservant, and 60 for each womanservant.[5]

Single women were also encouraged to come to the colonies. At first any woman who emigrated received the same acreage prescribed for her male counterpart. (In this way several single women in early colonial history obtained large tracts of land.) However, promoters usually sought to lure women to the colonies by promising them that they would soon find "copulative matrimony."[6]

It has been estimated that the "colonial workman commanded real wages which exceed[ed] by from 30 to 100 per cent the wages of contemporary English workmen."[7] The high price of labor brought both poor and married women to colonial America. In return for passage to the New World, most of them bound themselves out for a period of years as indentured servants, signing contracts with merchants and shipmasters in Europe to do "any work in which the employer shall employ them" for five to seven years. Some of them—the "redemptioners"—signed no indenture or contract in Europe but were allowed a certain number of days after arriving in America in which to arrange payment for their passage. Both groups of indentured servants were described in notices appearing in the colonial press. One such notice, in the *Pennsylvania Evening Post,* read: "Just arrived in the Ship Ann. Capt. Fortin, from Bristol, a number of healthy men and women servants, whose times are to be disposed of by William Fisher, Esq. and Son, or said captain on board, at Arch Street wharf."[8] Another, from the *Maryland Gazette,* read: "Just arrived—to make their own bargains, for the payment of ten guineas, amount of passage. Upwards to one hundred men and women as redemptioners."[9]

Not all the women sold at auction had come to America of their own free will. Some were prisoners (or the wives of prisoners) sentenced to labor in the colonies because of some trivial offense. In 1739 a shipload of 115 convicts, including 31 women, was sent from England to Maryland.[10] Others who came without being consulted were children who had been kidnapped in London, Bristol, or Liverpool by agents called "menstealers," "crimps," and "spirits." The largest group of those who came against their will were, of course, Africans, brought to America in chains.

While indentured servants were an important source of labor in some colonies, they could not meet the growing demand for labor because of their limited term of bondage. Increasingly, therefore, the colonists turned to slavery. Blacks could be impressed into lifetime bondage more easily than whites, and once enslaved, their color made it difficult for them to run away and mingle in strange surroundings. More important, black slavery could be justified by the ideology of racism. A black skin connoted both evil and inferiority; blacks were said to be destined for slavery by the "Curse of Ham" and the "Curse of Cain." They were pictured as savages and infidels from a barbaric, dark continent without a civilization, and enslavement was actually considered an improvement in their way of life. As Winthrop Jordan points out: "Slavery could survive only if the Negro were a man set apart; he simply had to be different if slavery were to exist at all."[11] The same rationalization was applied to black women.

The first group of twenty Africans brought to Jamestown, Virginia, in 1619 were indentured servants, not slaves. But between 1660 and 1682, throughout the colonies, court decisions, special laws, and codes transformed the black servant into a slave. The slave codes generally provided that blacks were to be slaves for life, that their children were to inherit their mothers' status, and that Christian baptism would not automatically assure freedom. They also prohibited marriage between whites and blacks and forbade bondsmen to acquire or inherit property, to hold secret gatherings, to be parties to contracts or suits, to marry legally, or to engage in certain trades. Violators were punished by a variety of means—fines, imprisonment, whippings, and even death.[12]

During the seventeenth century, the number of black slaves grew slowly. By 1700 there were probably no more than 25,000 in all of colonial America. Thereafter, growth was rapid because of the expansion of tobacco, rice, and indigo plantations in the South. It did not take the landowners long to realize that slavery was well suited to plantation agriculture and to the Southern economy generally. Slave labor could be maintained at a subsistence standard of living. And while it was a criminal offense for an indentured or free woman to bear children out of wedlock, this was not a crime for a slave woman, who could not be legally married and whose children were viewed solely as added property for the master.[13]

An advertisement typical of many that appeared frequently in the colonial press read: "To Be Sold—a healthy negro wench about twenty-eight years old. She is now pregnant, and will be sold with or without the child she now has who is about three." The following advertisement makes it blatantly clear that black slave women were considered no different from other property: "To Be Sold: A negro wench and three girls aged from three to eleven, a wagon, horses, hogs and cattle. Terms are to be three years credit."[14]

By 1770 there were about half a million black slaves in the colonies, constituting about 20 percent of the colonial population. The plantation

system, based principally on tobacco, rice, and indigo, was well established in the five Southern English colonies—Maryland, Virginia, North
Carolina, South Carolina, and Georgia. Black slaves made up over 36
percent of the population in these colonies—220,000 out of 609,000.[15]
The largest proportion of them were plantation field hands. Male and
female slaves labored side by side. Hector St. John de Crèvecoeur, who
emigrated from France in 1754 and settled in the New World, wrote of
them:

> They have not time, like us, tenderly to rear their helpless offspring, to nurse
> them on their knees, to enjoy the delight of being parents. Their paternal
> fondness is embittered by considering that if their children live, they must
> live to be slaves like themselves; no time is allowed to them to exercise their
> pious office, the mothers must fasten them on their backs, and with this
> double load follow their husbands into the field.[16]

The use of the word "husbands" when referring to slaves, while not
unusual in the colonial period, is misleading. The prevailing conception
of slave marriages and families in nearly all the colonies was expressed in
1767 by Daniel Dulany, a judge in a Maryland court, who ruled that
slaves were incapable of marriage. "A slave," he observed, "has never
maintained an action against the violation of his bed. A slave is not
admonished for incontinence, or punished for fornication or adul-
tery."[17]

A small number of female slaves in the South were members of the
master's household staff, and their proximity to his family gave them
certain privileges. The children of these slave women were allowed to
enter the owner's house at will. And domestics who were assigned to
cooking, spinning, and weaving could always obtain additional quantities
of food and clothing for their own use. Still, one should not exaggerate
these privileges. Like the field hands, the household workers and personal servants were viewed simply as investments in capital and items of
commercial exchange, much the same as livestock.

In the Northern colonies, on the other hand, large landholdings
were uncommon, and economic life was diversified. The important elements were industrial production, shipbuilding, seagoing commerce,
and small farming. Most Northern slaves, therefore, were either domestic servants or artisans. Female slaves were used as cooks, laundresses,
nursemaids, or waitresses.[18]

The punishment of slaves specified in the slave codes of the Northern
colonies was a good deal less harsh than in the Southern colonies. Only
in New England, however, was the slave recognized both as a human
being and as a piece of property. Indeed, blacks there, like whites, were
guaranteed the basic legal rights of Englishmen. Whether slave or free,
they were able to marry. If slaves, they had to have the consent of both

owners. In all other respects, slave weddings in New England were no different from those between free white persons.

The marriage of a slave to a free woman, however, did not bring freedom to the husband. Nor did marriage ensure that black families would remain intact. Children could be and often were sold apart from their parents. A typical advertisement in the *New England Weekly Journal* of May 1, 1732, listed a "likely negro woman about 19 years and a child of about six months of age to be sold together or apart." The memorial of a group of Boston blacks to the Massachusetts legislature in 1774 told more about the effects of slavery on the black family than scores of articles about how slaves in that colony enjoyed rights denied blacks in other colonies:

> We are deprived of everything that hath a tendency to make life even toler-
> able, the endearing ties of husband and wife we are stranger to for we are no
> longer man and wife than our masters or mistresses thinks proper married
> or unmarried. Our children are also taken from us by force and sent miles
> from us where we seldom or ever see them again to be made slaves of for life
> which sometimes is very short by reason of being dragged from their
> mother's breast. By our deplorable situati_n we are rendered incapable of
> showing our obedience to Almighty God. How can a slave perform the duties
> of a husband to a wife or parent to his child? How can a husband leave
> master to work and cleave to his wife? How can the wife submit themselves to
> their husbands in all things? How can the child obey their parents in all
> things?[19]

Indentured servants, unlike black slaves, knew that they would someday be free, but as long as they remained in bondage they too were at the mercy of their master or mistress, who owned their labor twenty-four hours a day, seven days a week. Like the slaves, the servants were chattel and could be bought and sold. They had no property themselves except that allowed them by their masters. Disobedience and attempts to escape were severely punished, although not as harshly as was the case for a slave, who might be killed or, if a male, castrated. While stories of inhuman cruelty to white servants were quite common, nevertheless, unlike slaves, they had personal rights to life and contract rights to a minimum standard of living, nor could their children be sold from them. They were able to bring suit to enforce their contract rights, and the courts would comply, even to the extent of freeing them outright. Only in Massachusetts did a slave have the right to bring suit against a master, and even here, more often than not, this right was little more than academic.[20]

Female indentured servants were constantly guarded by their masters and mistresses to make certain that they did not engage in illicit sexual relations, which could result in childbearing, loss of service during pregnancy, and permanent damage to their health. (However, many servants had to be equally constantly on guard against their masters' sexual advances.) Still, since indentured servants were prevented by law from marrying without their masters' consent, some masters encouraged illicit sexual relations on the part of the female servant, and then compelled her, after bearing her child, to work additional years for having committed the crime of "bastardy."[21]

Both servants and slaves ran away from their masters, sometimes even together. A notice in the *Pennsylvania Gazette* of October 8, 1747, read: "There went away with Ann Wainright, white servant, a Negro slave woman belonging to June Bailard." More often male and female servants fled together, in which cases the man usually fetched the higher reward, as the following advertisement illustrates: "$8 reward—two servants, James Goddard and Elizabeth Condon, ran away from William Cromwell. $2.00 for her, $6.00 for him. Both have three more years to serve."[22]

Runaway indentured servants, whether male or female, generally did not command so high a reward as runaway slaves, whose return usually brought between $30 and $50. These differences are not hard to understand. The indentured servant's time of service was limited. Even if he or she was returned, the master could expect only a few more years of labor. The slave, however, was personal property for life. An absconding female slave could also cost her master the loss of several decades of labor in the form of the future slave children she would be expected to bear. Small wonder, then, that the slave's master went to great lengths, advertising his loss in several newspapers, even in other states, and offering lucrative rewards to get back his property.[23]

Because of their color, it was harder for slave women to escape recapture than for white servants. Nevertheless, many attempted flight not just once but several times. "Ran away before" and "an old offender in this way" were often part of advertisements for black slave women. Some told of female slaves who had escaped in order to be near a husband or lover, sold to a distant buyer. Advertisements also reveal the harsh punishments that servants and slaves, especially the latter, suffered at the hands of their masters. For example: "Runaway—a negro woman named Nanny. Several marks on her occasioned by whippings. But one tooth in her upper jaw." "Runaway—a negro wench named Rachel. She has scars on her neck and right elbow and has been branded on the neck with the letter R."[24]

Slaves had other ways of resisting bondage besides flight. Some deliberately damaged their tools, disabled work horses and mules, or poisoned wells or their master's food. Some committed thefts, set fire to barns, and ruined stored crops by other means. Some slaves murdered their masters and overseers.[25]

In 1712 rebellious slaves in New York City—men and women, blacks and Indians—set fires and killed those whites who rushed to put out the flames. Governor Hunter sent a detachment of troops against the out-numbered rebels, who retreated to hide in the woods or in the town. The next morning the militia was dispatched to search for them. Six of the rebels, including two women, committed suicide, and one killed his wife and then himself. The rest were captured. Twenty-five slaves were con-victed, and all were sentenced to death. Of these, six, including a preg-nant woman, were reprieved by Governor Hunter. The others, women as well as men, were speedily executed. The suspected leaders were horribly tortured before they were put to death. The governor described the inhuman punishments inflicted on men and women alike: "Some were burnt others hanged, one broke on the wheel, and one hung alive in chains in the town, so there has been the most exemplary punishment inflicted that could be possibly thought of."[26]

Slave women did the same work in the fields as men, and female indentured servants worked in the fields along with menservants. But there was a distinct difference between the sexes in the other form of bound labor in the colonies—apprenticeship. This system provided a technical education and room, board, and clothing for children who were bound out either by parents or by overseers of the poor. Once apprenticed, the child's labor belonged to the master as fully as did that of a servant. Even visits to their own parents could be forbidden, and the free-time conduct of apprentices was subject to the same restrictions that applied to adult servants or slaves.

Male apprentices were taught a variety of trades, including apothe-cary, victualer (cook), bricklayer, goldsmith, sailor, ship carpenter, sail-maker, cordwainer (shoemaker), cooper, leather dresser, and tailor. But poor women were apprenticed chiefly to serve as household maids and were seldom taught a trade. They ended their apprenticeship with the prospect of either continuing as paid household servants or getting mar-ried. In the latter case, their choice of husband was limited by the fact that they had no dowries to bring to their marriage.[26]

In the colonial cities, there were thousands of free workers who worked for wages, including artisans, mechanics, journeymen, dock-workers, and merchant seamen. Until the very eve of the War for Inde-pendence, however, unfree labor—slaves, indentured servants, and apprentices—constituted a high percentage of the urban work force.[27] Estimates for Philadelphia, for example, indicate that in 1775 there were at least as many slaves, apprentices, and indentured servants in that city as there were free wage-earning laborers and journeymen: 800 to 900 male and female indentured servants, 600 to 700 male and female slaves, and 1,500 to 2,000 male and female apprentices.[28]

In her seminal study *Working Life of Women in the Seventeenth Century,* Alice Clark showed how women in England had once belonged to craft guilds, as widows worked in their late husbands' jobs, had professional standing as midwives, and acted with power of attorney in lieu of their husbands, but had by the end of the seventeenth century lost these positions. As far as the New World was concerned, this transformation still lay in the future. The colonial housewife, living in a labor-scarce, underdeveloped country with a shortage of women, still had access to any occupation she wished to pursue. To be sure, the vast majority of women were absorbed in domestic responsibilities. But in colonial America, such work was demanding and important and brought with it both high status and self-esteem. (A somewhat similar situation prevailed on the frontier well into the nineteenth century.) Woman's role as a household manager was basic to colonial society. There was little room for the ornamental middle-class woman in the preindustrial family, where most of the clothing and other goods that were needed were produced by women and children in the home. Under such conditions, moreover, a large family was an asset, and "women's reproductive work, as well as her productive work, was valued."[29]

While homemaking was the sole employment of most free, white women in colonial America, an important minority was employed outside the home. They ventured into the world of the marketplace not because time hung heavy on their hands—the arduous tasks of running a colonial household left few idle hours—but, in most cases, out of financial necessity. Many craftsmen who owned their own shops lived marginally; they had to take out short-term loans, and, during a period of recession, they were in constant danger of ending up in debtor's prison.[30] To cut expenses, the wives of tradesmen often helped in their husbands' shops. This was the age of the artisan, and the lack of formal education did not hinder a woman's success as a storekeeper or artificer. Though often illiterate, a wife was able, by close association, to acquire both business experience and technical skill,[30] and if she were lucky enough to have had a loving and conscientious father who, in the manner of Cotton Mather, taught her bookkeeping "and such other arts relating to business, as may enable her to do the man whom she may hereafter have, *good and not evil all the days of her life*,"[31] so much the better. In any case, most wives learned enough of their husbands' trades to continue on alone if they were left as widows with large families to support. The community needed their products or services, and idleness was frowned upon in a society where there was always more work to do than hands to do it. If the widow remarried, she usually kept the enterprise going under her new name. Women who did not inherit shops sometimes began their own. Spinsters or recent widows who found themselves suddenly penniless and who were unable or unwilling to depend on relatives often sought to support themselves.[32]

Whatever the reasons, there was nothing in the social or economic code of colonial America to prevent a woman from working outside her home. Indeed, local poor laws encouraged single women to work rather than become recipients of tax-funded relief. While the number of women artisans and others engaged in business never exceeded a small percentage of the female population, they were a very significant group. Female artisans in Philadelphia worked as silversmiths, tinworkers, barbers, bakers, fish picklers, brewers, tanners, ropemakers, lumberjacks, gunsmiths, butchers, milliners, harnessmakers, potash manufacturers, upholsterers, printers, morticians, chandlers, coachmakers, embroiderers, dry cleaners and dyers, woodworkers, staymakers, tailors, flour processors, seamstresses, netmakers, braziers, and founders. The list may even be longer, for as Frances May Manges points out, "[m]any an artisan functioned quietly and was never referred to in the newspapers."[33]

In New York, Boston, and Baltimore, as well as in the smaller towns, women artisans and merchants made or sold everything from dry goods and groceries to china, furniture, and hardware. This was especially true after 1760, with the growth of the population and the extension of the market for many items of home manufacture. Women commonly ran taverns and coffeehouses. Others were carpenters, cabinetmakers, braziers, soapmakers, cutlers, and ropemakers. Some were even blacksmiths. The hardier of these occupations had been inherited from deceased husbands, but their widows seem to have taken over such work quite matter-of-factly.[34]

Women were equally active on the professional level, and for the same reasons: a shorthanded country could not disdain womanpower, and in colonial times these occupations required little education. Women frequently taught in the common schools; nurses and midwives had more patients than they could handle, and they and other women did a flourishing business by offering their services as doctors and healers. However, some portent of the future, when medicine came to be dominated by professional training and excluded women, is to be found in the fact that rich women were beginning to have their babies delivered by male doctors rather than by the local midwives, even though the presence of a male at a delivery was considered by many to have "sullied the chastity and tainted the purity of the clients."[35] Because of the alarming frequency with which mothers, both rich and poor, died in childbirth, these women were prepared to risk shocking their neighbors in order to have their babies brought into the world by doctors. Unfortunately, the inscriptions on tombstones indicate that the doctors were no more successful than the midwives in halting the rising maternal mortality rate.[36]

While the range of occupations of colonial women who worked outside the home is impressive, by far the largest number of such women were involved in some facet of the clothing trade, as seamstresses, tailoresses, and laundresses—occupations long associated with work in the home. Poor women and free black women especially tended to gravitate toward laundering, since it required little or no investment. The black washerwoman was a common sight in all colonial towns and cities. The only other jobs available to most free black women were house servant and cook.[37]

Poor white women had equally limited choices, but they at least had the right to do something about improving their working conditions. What may be the first effort of workingwomen to organize for such a purpose is revealed in the following advertisement in the *New York Weekly Journal* of January 28, 1734, inserted by a group of white maid-servants:

> Here are many women in this town that these hard times intend to go to service, but as it is proper the world should know our terms, we think it reasonable we should not be beat by our mistresses' husbands, they being too strong, and perhaps may do tender women mischief. If any ladies want servants, and will engage for their husbands, they shall be soon supplied.

In colonial times women, as later (and even now), did not usually receive the same wages as men. James Galt was paid £100 a year as keeper of the hospital for the insane in Virginia, but his wife got only £25 as matron. A study of workingwomen in Newport, Rhode Island, reveals that female laborers in that city (whether free, indentured, or hired-out slaves, and regardless of race) were paid approximately 30 percent less than the lowest paid unskilled, free, white male workers, and 20 percent less than hired-out male slaves.[38]

Several women in colonial America have come down in history as feminists of a sort. Margaret Brent appeared before the Maryland Assembly in 1647 to request a seat in that body. When the delegates refused, she "protested against all proceedings in this present Assembly unless she may be present and have vote as afores'd."[39] Anne Hutchinson—"a woman of ready wit and bold spirit"—began sometime during 1636 to challenge the church ruling that barred a woman from teaching and held private Thursday meetings of women at her house in Boston to discuss the preceding Sunday's sermon for the benefit of those who had been unable to attend. Before long she was adding interpretations and comments of her own and criticizing the ministers. When the sessions also began to attract men and became more popular than the public worship, Hutchinson precipitated a controversy in the Massachusetts Bay colony, comparable only to the witchcraft mania a generation later. It ended in her banishment.[40]

The action of these pioneers had no effect on the legal status of colonial women, which continued to be determined by the tradition of the British common law, with certain modifications compelled by America's pioneer conditions. According to its precepts, a woman ceased to exist if she married, for she and her spouse became one flesh and the flesh was his. She was no longer responsible for her debts or even for her personal actions. She had no legal control over any property, whether inherited or earned. In most colonies, married women could conduct business in the courts as agents for their husbands, but in Maryland even this right was revoked in 1658. The husband had the right to chastise his wife physically as he did his children and servants, and he had exclusive rights to any property she might have owned as a single woman, to her dower, and to any wages or property that might come to her while she was his wife. In short, like slave and servant women, married women, whether rich or poor, were legal nonentities.

Unmarried women, both widows and spinsters, enjoyed a much better status. They were considered competent to own land, to enter into contracts and deeds, to write wills, to execute estates, to bring suit and be sued, and to engage in business enterprises on their own account. But there was great social pressure on women to marry, so that there were few spinsters, and widows usually remarried within a year. The poor laws prescribed compulsory labor for the poor, so that an impoverished widow who was unable to get a new husband might be bound out to serve as a domestic.

A woman whose husband deserted her or failed to provide for her was in a double bind, because if she went out to work, her earnings belonged to her husband. Although for a time in the seventeenth century divorce laws were relatively liberal, it later became practically impossible for a woman to obtain alimony, regardless of the cause of the marital dissolution.[41] Small wonder that a contemporary poem by a woman complained:

> Custom, alas! doth partial prove,
>   Nor gives us equal measure;
> A pain for us it is to love,
>   But it is to man a pleasure.
>
> They plainly can their thoughts disclose,
>   Whilst ours must burn within:
> We have got tongues, and eyes, in vain
>   And truth from us is sin.
>
> Men to new joys and conquests fly,
>   And yet no hazard run;
> Poor we are left, if we deny,
>   And if we yield, undone.
>
> Then equal laws, let custom find,
>   And neither sex oppress;
> More freedom give to womankind
>   Or give to mankind less.[42]

Still, in times of political turmoil, colonial women played an active role. Several vigorously aided their husbands in the revolt Nathaniel Bacon led against the planter aristocracy in 1646. The rebellion, said the report of the king's investigators, sprang "from the poverty and uneasiness of some of the meanest whose discontent renders them easier to be misled." Bacon's army was described by a contemporary as "rabble of the basest sort of people, whose condition was such, as by a change could not admit of worse." He was shocked to hear the female participants talk "of sharing men's estates among themselves," and even more shocked to learn of the involvement of lower-class women in the uprising. One was so active that she was specifically exempted from the general pardon passed by the Virginia Assembly at the end of the hostilities.[43]

Just as Nathaniel Bacon was the "torchbearer" of the American Revolution, so the women in Bacon's Rebellion were the "torchbearers" who lit the way for the Daughters of Liberty of that epochal upheaval.

By 1763 a number of cities in the colonies had become commercial and manufacturing centers, although the manufacturers in these cities had to await release from British mercantilist restrictions before they could develop. Under the British mercantile policy, the American colonies existed solely for the purpose of increasing the profits of British manufacturers, merchants, and landlords. To assure that the colonies would not become an economic threat to the home industry, and to prevent the New World from becoming a power in its own right, the British rulers would not, for example, permit the colonies to set up furnaces or forges or to ship iron, wool, or woolen cloth from one colony to another. The colonies were forced to send their commodities either to England alone or, if they were destined for a non-British port, to England first. They could only import goods produced in England or goods sent to the colonies by way of England.

Commercial traffic between England and America had been disrupted during the Seven Years' War of 1757–1763. Furthermore, the British had been forced to rely on the colonies to supply many of the goods and services needed to support the American theater of war. The London merchants, alarmed by reports of the considerable growth of manufactures in the colonies during the war, began to dump large amounts of British manufactured goods on the American market, flooding it with textiles, linens, hats, shoes, metal goods, and luxuries of all sorts.

These efforts to reestablish the ante-bellum mercantile model in America inevitably worsened relations between the mother country and the colonies. Adding fuel to the fire was the fact that restraints on American economic development were intensified precisely when Americans were being subjected to a series of measures that not only were arbitrary and illegal but also threatened the very existence of their civil liberties. The Sugar Act of 1764, the Stamp Act of 1765, the Quartering Act of 1765, the Townshend Acts of 1770, the Tea Act of 1773, and the "Intolerable Acts" of 1774* were all part of a series of "obnoxious measures" passed by Parliament, which Americans believed were designed to fleece them and reduce them to a state of total dependence. They did everything they could to force the repeal of these measures and to defeat what they came to view as a vast conspiracy against liberty in America.[44]

Apart from the areas of tobacco cultivation in Maryland and Virginia, the protests against Britain centered in the cities, where they were spearheaded by extralegal organizations generally known as the Sons of Liberty. While the leaders of the Sons of Liberty were recruited from among master craftsmen, merchants, and professional groups, and the membership included professional men, lesser merchants, and even local officials, the rank and file were mechanics, tradesmen, carpenters, joiners, printers, shipwrights, smiths, caulkers, ropemakers, masons, and other artificers. The rank-and-file workingmen of the Sons of Liberty were always more radical than the merchant-professional leadership and pushed both the leadership and the Revolution forward. "It was the mechanics," notes Alfred P. Young, "who in effect nullified the Stamp Act, provided the means of coercion to effect nonimportation, took the lead in direct action against the British army, provided the muscle for the 'Tea Parties,' and in the final crisis, exerted pressure from below for independence."[45]

The Sons of Liberty was an all-white, all-male organization. While blacks participated in crowd actions during the Revolutionary decade,[46] all of the Revolutionary bodies, including the Liberty Boys, remained closed to slaves, free blacks, indentured servants, and women. Associated with the Sons of Liberty, however, was an organization called the Daughters of Liberty. Its members helped put teeth into the nonimportation agreements—a chief weapon in the struggle against British policies—by boycotting English goods. The Daughters of Liberty joined the battle against the Tea Act, refusing to drink tea under any circum-

*The Sugar Act provided for an increased duty on all white sugar imported from the West Indies and banned the importation of rum from the same source. The Stamp Act required everyone in America to pay stamp duties on periodicals, pamphlets, commercial paper, and legal documents, including marriage contracts. The Quartering Act provided that Royal troops were to be garrisoned in the colonies—even in colonists' homes—at colonial expense. The Townshend Acts levied new duties upon tea, lead, paper, and painters' colors. The Tea Act gave the East India Company a monopoly on the sale of tea directly to the colonies and enabled it to eliminate American wholesale merchants. This led to the famous Boston Tea Party of December 16, 1763, and to the "Intolerable Acts," which closed the port of Boston until such time as compensation was paid to the East India Company for tea destroyed.

stances. When a festival of the Daughters of Liberty was interrupted by a man who denounced the Revolution, the women emulated some of the crowd actions of the Sons of Liberty by seizing the intruder, stripping him to the waist, and, lacking tar and feathers, covering him with molasses and the downy tops of flowers.[47] The *Newport Mercury* of December 9, 1765, reported in all seriousness that since marriage licenses required stamps, "the young ladies of this place are determined to join hands with none but such as will to the utmost endeavour to abolish the custom of marrying with licence."

Although the Daughters of Liberty accepted the custom that a woman should not appear in a public gathering and speak, they did challenge other customs. They passed spirited resolutions condemning Parliament's interference with the liberties of Americans and commending the work of the Sons of Liberty. The male organization welcomed their help. "With the ladies on our side we can make every Tory tremble," they announced. On one occasion, the Boston Sons of Liberty passed a resolution thanking their female associates in Providence for their firm stand in defense of American rights.[48]

During the resistance to the Townshend measures of 1767, artisans formed societies called "Lovers and Encouragers of American Manufacturers." Advertisements appeared in the press announcing homespun products for sale, and items such as "Liberty umbrellas" were advertised as the product of home craftsmanship. A widely circulated appeal addressed to the Daughters of Liberty read in part:

> First then throw aside your high top knots of pride
> Wear none but your own country linen.
> Of economy boast. Let your pride be the most
> To show cloaths of your make and spinning.[49]

The Daughters of Liberty responded by devoting themselves to spinning and weaving and passing resolutions pledging not to patronize merchants who broke the nonimportation agreements. In Boston, William Molineaux, a leading member of the Sons of Liberty, organized the women into spinning bees, or contests, which created "remarkable records."[50]

At times, the Sons and Daughters of Liberty acted in concert. A broadside posted in Boston read:

> WILLIAM JACKSON
> an importer, at the Brazen Head,
> North Side of the Town House, and opposite the town-pump, in Corn-Hill, Boston.
> It is desired that the SONS AND DAUGHTERS OF LIBERTY, would not buy any one thing of him, for in so doing they will bring disgrace upon themselves, and their posterity, forever and ever.
> AMEN.[51]

The unity of the mechanics of the Sons of Liberty with their wives, sisters, and other female relatives in the Daughters of Liberty was a significant aspect of the revolutionary struggle, and their contribution to its success was of the utmost importance.[52] During the War for Independence, while their menfolk were fighting in the Continental Army, the Daughters of Liberty spun cloth and made shirts for the soldiers. But much of their time was spent trying to keep their children and themselves alive in the face of soaring prices. The inflationary trend had started with the outbreak of the war as the value of Continental currency dropped and merchants took advantage of the wartime scarcity to raise prices to exorbitant levels. While a few speculators continued to get rich, many, including the soldiers fighting the war, went hungry. "Four months' pay of a private will not procure his wretched wife and children a single bushel of wheat," complained one soldier. Another echoed: "Few of us have private fortunes: many have families who are already suffering everything that can be received from an ungrateful country. Are we then to submit to all the inconveniences, fatigue and dangers of a camp life, while our wives and children are perishing for want of common necessaries at home?"[52] Joshua Huntington, who had left Yale just before graduation to join the army, graphically described the tribulations of the soldiers, criticizing the Connecticut legislature for failing to pay the soldiers or to provide for their families:

> Not a day passes my head, but some soldier with tears in his eyes, hands me a letter to read from his wife painting forth the distresses of his family in such strains as these: "I am without bread, and cannot get any, the Committee will not supply me, my children will starve, or if they do not, they must freeze, we have no wood, neither can we get any—pray come home."[53]

In some states laws were passed to control prices but were rarely enforced. In Boston a mechanic calling himself "Joyce Jr."—a name he took from the original Edward Joyce who had arrested King Charles I—advertised for other patriots "to carry into execution the act of this state to prevent monopoly and oppression." Abigail Adams, writing to her husband, John, described how a band of five hundred, composed largely of working-class women, followed Joyce Jr., "who was mounted on horseback with a red coat, a white wig, and a drawn sword, with drum and fife following." This band "carted" five terrified "Tory villains" outside the town limits of Boston, overturned the cart, and warned them not to return to the city. Joyce Jr. advertised his gratification that his warning to the shopkeepers had reminded at least some of them of their duty to sell at fixed prices. Abigail Adams also described how a group of Boston women treated a merchant who had hoarded coffee:

> A number of females, some say a hundred, some say more, assembled with a cart and trunks, marched down to the warehouse and demanded the keys which he [the merchant] refused to deliver. Upon which one of them seized

him by his neck and tossed him into the cart. Upon finding no quarter, he delivered the keys when they tipped up the cart and discharged him; then opened the warehouse, hoisted out the coffee themselves, put it into the trunks and drove off.[54]

During the war, the British promised freedom to all slaves who deserted their masters for British service. Thousands of bondsmen and bondswomen quit slavery for freedom behind British lines. It is estimated that more than 65,000 slaves went over to the British, and that Virginia alone lost thirty thousand. On the other hand, five thousand to eight thousand blacks served in the Continental army, and countless others made valuable contributions to the patriot cause as military laborers. Black women, usually slaves, served with the American army as nurses and cooks. General William Smallwood wrote to the president of the Maryland Council: "I shall be glad that the sale of two Negro women . . . might be suspended. Their services will not only be valuable to me, but will promote the good of the service as they will supply the place of soldiers—who other ways must be necessarily employed in my kitchen."[55]

Three women fought in combat on the patriot side during the war. Margaret (Molly) Corbin, a farm laborer who followed her husband into the Continental army, went into action beside him during the battle of Fort Washington on November 15, 1776, firing a two-gun battery. When he fell mortally wounded, she kept serving his gun until she herself was severely wounded, one arm nearly severed and part of her breast mangled by three bursts of grapeshot. The Continental Congress voted "Captain Molly" a pension on July 6, 1779, decreeing that she should receive "during her natural life or the continuance of said disability the one half of the monthly pay drawn by a soldier in the service of these States . . . and one complete suit of clothes or the value therein in money." For the rest of her life, she drew medical and commissary supplies from West Point.

Margaret (Molly) Hayes, another farm laborer, also followed her husband to war. During the Battle of Monmouth, on June 28, 1778, with the temperature soaring close to 100 degrees, she brought pitcher after pitcher of cool water to the troops from a nearby spring, thereby acquiring the name "Molly Pitcher." On one of her trips, she saw her husband wounded. Grasping a rammer staff from his hand, she fired the cannon until the end of the battle. General Washington issued her a warrant as a noncommissioned officer. Although she received state honors, "Molly Pitcher" was never awarded the army pension to which she was entitled.

The third woman to serve was Deborah Sampson Gannett, an enlisted soldier in the Continental army. Left fatherless at the age of five, she was bound out for five years' labor as an indentured servant. When her indenture ended, she determined to serve her country. Disguised in a man's clothing, she made her way to the town of Uxbridge, Massachusetts, where, using the alias "Robert Shurtleff," she enlisted in April, 1781. She served with the Fourth Massachusetts Regiment through months of hard fighting at White Plains, Tarrytown, and Yorktown. She was always seen in the forefront of every action and suffered both sword and bullet wounds. Fearing that her sex would be discovered, however, she made light of her injuries. On the march north after the Battle of Yorktown, she succumbed to a fever in Philadelphia. She was carried, unconscious, to the hospital, where her secret was discovered, but it was kept by the doctor until she was discharged.

For her service to the nation, Deborah Sampson Gannett received pensions from both the federal government and the state of Massachusetts. After her death, her husband became the first American to be granted a pension as a soldier's widower. At the time of the award, the Congressional Committee on Revolutionary Pensions paid the following tribute to the indentured servant who became the only woman to enter the ranks of the Continental army as a common soldier: "The Committee believes they are warranted in saying that the whole history of the American Revolution furnishes no other similar example of female heroism, fidelity and courage."[56]

It is significant that one of the results of the victory in the War for Independence to which the "female heroism" of this indentured servant contributed was the end of indentured servitude itself. Thousands of indentured servants obtained their freedom through enlistment in the army, and the traffic in such servants ceased during the war years. A meeting of New York citizens on January 24, 1784, called for the abolition of the "traffic in white people, heretofore countenanced in this state, while under the arbitrary control of the British government," because such traffic was contrary "to the idea of liberty this country has so happily established." While the importation of servants continued after the war, indentured servitude eventually disappeared, partly as a result of the Revolution.[57]

The War for Independence resulted in some concrete gains for blacks as well. Many who had served in the American or British forces secured their freedom. Others were liberated by their masters, influenced by the ideology of the Revolution. By 1804, largely as a result of this ideology (although the hostility of white workers toward the competition of black slaves also played a part), all the Northern states and the Northwest Territory had finally abolished slavery, either by immediate emancipation, as in Vermont, New Hampshire, and Massachusetts, or by gradual emancipation. The terms of emancipation were that children born of slave mothers were freed after an apprenticeship lasting from eighteen to twenty-eight years, during which time the slaveowners were entitled to the unpaid services of the blacks.[58]

For women as a whole, the American Revolution may have created an "illusion of change," in Joan Hoff Wilson's phrase. There is no denying the fact, for example, that women were excluded from the Declaration of Independence—even after the famous plea of Abigail Adams that the patriots should pay "particular care and attention" to the ladies.[59] But one change was not an illusion. Even before the outbreak of overt resistance to British policies in 1763, New England households had become the center of what has been called "proto-industrialization" as women increasingly produced goods in their homes to be sold in the market. The Revolutionary boycotts after 1763 heightened this trend. Then, during the war, the demands of the military establishment, putting less of a premium on quality and more on quantity, led to the rise of the early piecework factory system. By mid-1776, four thousand women and children in Philadelphia were spinning for local textile plants under the "putting-out system."*[60]

The American Revolution exerted a powerful influence on succeeding generations of American workers, men and women alike. By the 1820s and 1830s, the Fourth of July had become fixed as the working-class day of celebration. It was a day of parades, banquets, and festivals, a day for remembering the contributions of the Revolutionary mechanics and artisans and for renewing the Spirit of '76. Nor were the Revolutionary working-class women forgotten. It was about them that the mechanics of Fall River, Massachusetts, sang in their song "Independence Day," written to the tune of "Yankee Doodle":

> Again we hail the day's return,
>   That gave us independence,
> And freedom's fires, that warmed our sires,
>   Still glow in their descendants.
>
> Then let us sing till welkin ring,
>   When freedom's friends assemble,
> And deal such blows upon her foes,
>   As made her foemen tremble.
>
> And while we have to cheer us on,
>   The smiles of female beauty,
> We will not yield till victory's won
>   And we have done our duty.[61]

It was not just on the Fourth of July that the Revolutionary working-women were remembered. The Mechanics' Association of Fall River

---

*Under the "putting-out," or "domestic," system, merchant-employers "put out" materials to producers, who usually worked in their homes or sometimes in workshops. Finished products were returned to the employers for payment on a piecework or wage basis. The "putting-out" system differed from the handicraft system of home production in that the workers neither bought materials nor sold products. It brought the first widespread industrial employment of women and children. The "putting-out" system was generally superseded by the factory system.

publicly acknowledged in August, 1844, that just as the Sons of Liberty would not have succeeded in their resistance to British oppression without the Daughters of Liberty, so they could not have triumphed over their employers without the aid of the Ladies' Mechanics' Association of Fall River, "whose members remind us of the Daughters of Liberty of revolutionary days":

> We owe much of our success to their efforts in our behalf. Without their timely encouragement and assistance, many of our members would have given up the contest as hopeless. But when the opposition was arrayed against us, with all their unholy weapons, when defeat seemed to stare us in the face, the wives, and mothers, and daughters of the mechanics have come forward to our aid, and bid us persevere in our work of reform. Mechanics, may we never forget their works of beneficence.[62]

More important is the fact that the workingwomen of those years viewed themselves as descended from "the heroines of the Revolution" whose spirit and militancy they invoked in their own struggles for higher wages, shorter hours, and better working conditions.

2

In the Factories

FROM THE BEGINNING of the young Republic, women and young girls were viewed as the main labor source for the emerging factory system in textiles. When Secretary of the Treasury Albert Gallatin reported in 1810 that the eighty-seven cotton mills in operation or about to begin operation in the United States needed a labor force of about 500 men and 3,500 women and children, political economist Tench Coxe, known as the father of the American cotton industry, rejoiced that the great increase of "female aid in manufactures . . . prevents the diversion of men and boys from agriculture."[1]

New England textile mills provided the first big opportunity for large numbers of women to work outside the home in nondomestic work. At first they were recruits from the town poor rolls, orphans, and widows. But by the 1820s and 1830s thousands of young women had left the farms to enter factories in the company towns of New England.[2]

The first of these towns was Pawtucket, Rhode Island. In 1790 Samuel Slater, an English mechanic, introduced the spinning machine into the production of cotton textiles in America. The British refused to export their machines and jealously guarded against the copying of their plans, but Slater stored away the details of the new devices in his memory and came to the United States in the hope of finding sponsors to start a cotton spinning mill. He succeeded in Rhode Island, where the rich Quaker merchants William Almy and Moses Brown supplied the capital. Slater drew up the plans of the Arkwright spinning machine from memory and turned them over to David Wilkinson, a Pawtucket blacksmith, who in 1790 built the first Arkwright machinery to be successfully operated in the United States. A year later several such machines were producing satisfactory yarn.[3]

The Pawtucket spinning mills not only were based on an English invention but also copied the English system of labor. Young children constituted the principal labor supply. Samuel Slater's first nine operatives were seven boys and two girls under twelve years of age. In 1820 half of the factory workers were boys and girls "of the tender age of nine and ten years," who worked twelve to thirteen hours a day for wages ranging from 33 to 67 cents a week. A typical advertisement of the period appeared in the Rhode Island *Manufacturers' and Farmers' Record* of May 4, 1820: "Wanted—a family of from five to eight children capable of working in a cotton mill." When Josiah Quincy, the New England educator, statesman, and reformer, visited a textile mill in Pawtucket in 1801, the owner pointed with pride to the number of children at work. By keeping out of mischief and not wasting time playing games, he said, these children were serving God as well as aiding their families. Quincy, however, was not impressed by this eloquent defense of child labor, writing: "But an eloquence was exerted on the other side of the question more eloquent than his, which called us to pity these little creatures, plying in a contracted room, among flyers and cogs, at an age when nature requires for them air, space, and sports. There was a dull dejection in the countenances of all of them."[4]

By 1812 there were forty spinning mills in Rhode Island with thirty thousand spindles, and thirty mills in Massachusetts with eighteen thousand spindles. However, these early mills were small; even the Slater factories employed only twenty-five to fifty young women or children to tend the spinning machines. Weaving was still done in the homes on hand looms, "worked by the farmers' wives and daughters of the countryside." Under such an arrangement, the development of the factory system was limited; in 1810 twenty times as much cloth was produced by household manufacture as by America's few cotton mills.[5]

But a major transformation was about to take place, a transformation that was to introduce the first modern factory in America and with it the beginnings of urban industrialism. The man largely responsible for this was Francis Cabot Lowell, a successful importing and exporting merchant.

During the years 1810–1812, Lowell took a trip through the British Isles. In the course of his stay, he investigated the textile industry in England, Scotland, and Ireland. He noticed two developments. One was the recent invention of the power loom, which enabled spinning and weaving machines to be placed under one roof. The other was the harmful effects that the factory produced on both its operatives and its environment. In the English mill towns the poor were packed in slums, with families living and sleeping in one room. Such overcrowding inevitably produced a high death rate. Lowell was quick to realize that the combination of spinning and weaving in one place would increase the profits from textiles, but he also understood that duplication in America of the horrors of Lancashire would only serve to intensify the opposition to industrial growth.

When he returned to Boston, Lowell engaged the services of a talented mechanic, and together they constructed a workable power loom. Twelve Boston merchants put up first $100,000 and later $400,000 more to convert Lowell's loom into a profitable industry. The Boston Manufacturing Company was incorporated in 1813 to produce cotton, woolen, and linen cloth, although only cotton was ever fabricated. Two years later the first power loom in the United States was patented by Lowell and his brother-in-law, Patrick Tracy Jackson. By this time the factory was operating in Waltham, Massachusetts, manufacturing cotton textiles in a mill in which, for the first time, all the machinery was power-driven. The production workers were not whole families, especially children, as they were in the Rhode Island system, but rather adult females.[6]

The decision of the Boston Associates (as the founders came to be known) to employ adult females in preference to whole families was partly due to the fact that the equipment at Waltham was too complicated to be operated by children. (In Lancashire, too, technological problems barred children from employment at the power looms.) If the labor of children could not be used, the cheap labor advantage of the family system was lost.[7] But another significant reason was the need to overcome the argument that the factory system would bring in its wake an impoverished, vice-ridden, ignorant laboring class as it had in the Old World, and that this would constitute a threat to a democratic republic. In any event, having elected to employ hundreds of farm girls in their mill, the Boston Associates had to decide how such a work force was to be accommodated. Clearly Yankee farmers would not send their daughters into the factories if they became known as breeding places for sin and corruption. Nor would the community permit the invasion of a large number of youthful maidens to become a regular work force without the assurance that they would not be tempted into a life of vice.

The answer lay in the famous system introduced by the Boston Associates: boardinghouses under the direction of matrons, usually widows, who represented the company and its interests in enforcing strict adherence to the regulations. The girls were required to reside in the boardinghouses, and the doors were locked at ten o'clock at night. The girls were also required to be constant in their attendance at religious worship. As the Reverend Henry Miles, a Lowell clergyman and an enthusiastic propagandist for the corporation, pointed out: "The sagacity of self-interest as well as more disinterested considerations, has led to the adoption of a strict system of moral police." Without "sober, orderly, and moral" workers, profits would be "absorbed by cases of irregularity, carelessness, and neglect."[8]

On top of providing for company housing and house mothers and the establishment of proscriptive rules and regulations—all in order to ensure a labor force for its large-scale operations—the Boston Associates found it necessary to introduce the payment of wages in money rather than, as previously, in scrip and to shun the establishment of company stores. Here, too, it was economic rather than moral considerations that dictated the decision. The girls employed at Waltham, provided with room and board by the company, did not spend any substantial part of their earnings within the community. Instead, they sent a large portion home to help their families. Therefore, they had to be paid in currency that was good anywhere, not merely at a company store.[9]

This unique system, first introduced in Waltham, came to full flower in Lowell. Factory expansion at Waltham was limited by the water-power capacity of the slow-flowing Charles River, and so, after completing the third mill on that site in 1820, the Boston Associates sought other locations on swifter streams. The farming community of East Chelmsford, at the junction of the Concord and Merrimack rivers, some 25 miles from Boston, was selected. With the Pawtucket Falls providing motive power and with Boston close by and connected by the Middlesex Canal, the area held great promise. The land was purchased from local farmers in 1821, and construction of the first mills began two years later. The Merrimack Manufacturing Company, made up predominantly of the original Waltham group, was created for the new venture. This time, the plans called not for a single mill but for an entire community. The community of East Chelmsford was renamed Lowell after Francis Cabot Lowell, who had died in 1817.

The town of Lowell grew rapidly. By December, 1823, the Merrimack factory was constructed; two new mills went up in 1828, another in 1830, three more in 1831, and still another in 1835. Between 1822 and 1839 nine cotton textile companies were formed. The population of Lowell mushroomed, from 200 in 1820 to 17,633 in 1836 and over 30,000 in 1845. In 1835 the Boston & Lowell Railroad was opened.

The success of the Lowell mills (its dividends rarely fell below 10 percent) led to their expansion, with their accompanying boardinghouses, throughout New England. The mills in Manchester, Dover, and Nashua in New Hampshire, and Chicopee, Holyoke, and Lawrence in Massachusetts all followed the Lowell pattern. Outside New England, in the 1820s, two other companies—one at Whitestown, New York, and one at Pittsburgh—were begun, also combining the process of producing cotton textiles under one roof with the employment of "factory girls" (as they were called and as they called themselves) who lived in company boardinghouses.

In most cases these new textile enterprises were financed by the profits first amassed at Lowell and Waltham. In fact, many were established by men who were connected with the Boston Associates—the Jacksons, the Abbots, the Appletons, the Lawrences, the Bootts, and the

Lowells—a close-knit group, holding tightly to patents and controlling blocks of corporate stock. As absentee owners, these capitalists rarely visited the factory towns they had created.[10] The mills were operated for them by managers who lived at the site of the factories and were in actual charge of production. These agents, the Boston capitalists acknowledged, were "gentlemen selected for their offices, not on account of any mechanical knowledge or experience in manufacturing, their training before their appointments having been wholly mercantile or professional, but for their executive ability, their knowledge of human nature, their ability to control large numbers of operatives, and their social standing."[11]

Who were the female operatives of this and other Lowell mills? From his detailed study of the work force in the Hamilton Manufacturing Company, one of the large mills of Lowell, Thomas Dublin concludes:

> The mill workforce was remarkably homogeneous with regard to sex, nativity, age, and residence of operatives. It was composed overwhelmingly of young women recruited from the surrounding New England countryside and residing in company boarding houses.
>   More than 85 percent—881 of 1030—of those employed in the mills of the Hamilton Company in July 1836 were female . . . and less than 4 percent of the overall work force was foreign-born.[12]

The "factory girls" were, in the main, farmers' daughters who came from the rural districts of New England, by stage or baggage wagon, usually recruited by agents of the corporation. They came to the city of spindles for a variety of reasons—to earn money with which to buy finery and save for the future, to help their fathers eke out an existence, or to assist a brother in furthering his education. Many came because they were smitten by what was known as "Lowell fever," attracted by the educational opportunities provided by the Lowell library (begun in 1825 with a contribution of $500 by the corporation), the Lyceum (built at company expense, which offered twenty-five lectures per season for a price of 50 cents), and night school courses. (These educational facilities were also supported by community taxes.) "We had all been fairly educated at public or private schools," recalled Lucy Larcom, a mill operative who became a writer, "and many of us were resolutely bent on obtaining a better education."[13] Although circulating libraries were encouraged, reading in the mills themselves was strictly forbidden. But the Lowell operatives "pasted their spinning frames with verses to train their memories," and "pinned up mathematical problems in the 'dressing room.'"[14]

Under the Waltham system, enlarged upon at Lowell, work in the mill was organized according to the steps in producing cotton fabric. In the basement the large water wheel turned. The first floor held the carding room, where raw cotton was cleaned and brushed. Men tended the carding machines and boys carried the carded slivers of cotton to drawing frames, tended by women, which further stretched and turned the cotton. This was taken by elevator to the second floor, where it was spun into yarn. Adult women tended spinning machines, fixing threads when they broke, while girls from ten to fifteen years old worked as doffers. On the next floors, the yarn was woven into cloth by power looms, also tended by women. The large machines were crowded in rows extending the length of the room. Every room had a male overseer and a second hand, who assisted him. The sexual division of labor in the mill was clear: men held all the supervisory positions and the machine-tending jobs in picking and carding.* They also worked as skilled mechanics in the repair shops. Women worked in all the machine-tending jobs after carding.

Each male worker established his wages by negotiations, and they were in keeping with prevailing rates in the region for skilled or unskilled labor. In the case of women, however, there was no firmly established going rate. Wages were set at a level that was high enough to induce young women to leave the farms and stay away from competing employment, such as household manufactures and domestic service, but low enough to offer the owners an advantage in employing women rather than men and to compete with the unskilled wages of the British textile industry. Thomas Dublin's study of the Hamilton mill in Lowell reveals that women who had been in the mill for three to six years made only half of what was earned by men who had been there a comparable time.[15]

Men were generally paid by the day, from 85 cents for an operative to $2 for an overseer. Women were paid on a piecework basis, averaging between 40 and 80 cents daily. In the late 1830s the female factory operatives of Lowell earned about $1.75 a week after deduction for board, which came to about $1.45 a week.

The boardinghouses were crowded with fifty or sixty young women who slept ten or twelve in a room, two in a bed, and ate in a large communal dining room. The factory operative was awakened before dawn by the bell that called the workers to the mills. She worked in a tall, narrow, badly ventilated building. The windows were rarely opened because overseers wanted to preserve the humidity they thought would keep the threads from breaking. Seth Luther, a bitter critic of factory life in the 1830s, described how in some New England mills "the windows

---

*In the operation of picking, a pick of weft (threads which lie widthwise) is laid between the two sheets of warp (lengthwise threads) and pushed a desired distance.

   Carding is the process used in the preparation of fibers for spinning into yarn. The operation removes many impurities and very short fibers.

have been nailed down and the females deprived of even fresh air, in order to support the 'American System.'"[16] The operative worked twelve or thirteen hours a day. She started before seven in the morning in winter and before five in the summer, and stayed at work until seven at night, with a half hour break for breakfast and another half hour for midday dinner. Children had frequent rest periods, but they, too, had to be in the mill for twelve to fourteen hours a day and rarely had a chance to attend school.[17] A Lowell factory song of 1835 complained of the pernicious mixture of smoke from the oil lamps and cotton dust in the dank air and the incessant noise of the machine:

> It was morning, and the factory bell
> Had sent forth its early call,
> And many a weary one was there,
> Within the dull factory wall.

> And amidst the clashing noise and din
> Of the ever beating loom,
> Stood a fair young girl with throbbing brow,
> Working her way to the tomb.[18]

Factory life demanded workers who would submit to factory discipline. There was a set of rules, enforced by the overseer, who acted as both work supervisor and moral policeman in the mill. Seth Luther widely publicized the following "Conditions on which help is hired by the Cocheco Manufacturing Company, Dover, New Hampshire" and which every mill operative had to sign before entering employment. They included an agreement to work "for such wages per week . . . as the company may see fit to pay"; to be subject to all the fines imposed; to allow 2 cents each week to be deducted from wages "for the benefit of the sick fund"; not to leave the company's service "without giving two weeks notice of our intention, with permission of an agent, and if we do, we agree to forfeit to the use of the company, two weeks pay"; "not to engage in any combination, whereby the work may be impeded, or the company's interest in any work injured"; and also to agree "that in case we are discharged from the service of the company for any fault, we will not consider ourselves entitled to be settled with, in less than two weeks from the time of such discharge." Luther sarcastically described the conditions as "much like the handle of a jug, all on one side."[19]

Factory women could be dismissed for "immoral conduct," drinking, smoking, failure to attend public worship, lying, "suspicious or bad character," "unauthorized absence," "boarding off the corporation without leave," expressing dissatisfaction over wages, levity, hysteria, impudence, or simply not being liked by a particular overseer. In September, 1830, Elizabeth Wilson was discharged from the Hamilton Manufacturing Company for being a "devil in petticoats." Any woman who was discharged or left a mill before the expiration of the year without permission had her name placed on a blacklist that was circulated through all the mill towns. One weaver was discharged by her overseer because she had left her loom to wash her hands and two threads had broken in her absence. Although this was her first infraction, her name was placed on the black list.[20]

Beginning with President Andrew Jackson's visit in 1833, there was a steady procession of dignitaries—both Americans and foreigners—to Lowell, the showcase of industry. Ignoring the long hours, low wages, and poor working conditions, the distinguished visitors were impressed by the pianos in some boardinghouses and by the Lowell Lyceum. They drew an image of American factory towns that contrasted the cultured and disciplined life they saw in Lowell with the degradation, vice, and wretchedness of British Manchester.[21] Although this picture was far from accurate, in the 1830s there were still some compensations for factory work. Life was more easygoing than it was to become in the decades that followed, when wage cuts, speedups, and even more rigid supervision became the norm. Women could still—with permission— take time off to visit their homes in the country and return to work in the mills. And most of them left permanently after four or five years. At work and in the boardinghouses, the women formed a close, supportive community, helping new arrivals make the adjustment to mill town life. Moreover, the work gave the women a taste of economic independence, offering them an opportunity to earn their own cash wages at a time when most women were still on the farm or working in other trades or domestic service, where the wages were even lower.

Unfortunately, even these compensations did not exist for the women who worked in the mills of southern New England (Rhode Island and Fall River, Massachusetts), in Philadelphia, and in some of the middle states. There, they still labored under the English system, in which whole families were hired and child labor predominated. In 1831 children under twelve constituted 40 percent of those employed in the Rhode Island mills; at about the same time, the *Mechanics' Free Press,* a labor paper published in Philadelphia, said of the cotton factories of that city that "the principal part of the help . . . consists of boys and girls . . . from 6 to 17 years of age."[22] A public appeal by the workers of Manayunk, a factory district near Philadelphia, pointed out that in England the terrible condition of the children working in the factories had at least been somewhat improved as a result of investigation. Here, however, nothing had been done for their children, who were "oppressed as much as those in the English factories." Children who had to enter the factories at an early age were "reared in total ignorance of the world, and the consequence . . . is the inculcation of immoral and often times vicious habits, which terminates in the disgrace of many . . . in the public prisons." If the factories worked reasonable hours at decent wages, the appeal went on, the children could be placed in a public school, "but situated as they are, and reared in ignorance, they are made the tools of political as well as avaricious men, who lord over them as does the southern planter over his slaves."[23]

Workers in a Maryland mill complained of being paid off "with depreciated paper after there is from four to five months' wages due." They complained further about being paid with notes on the company store, "which reduces us to the disagreeable necessity of paying whatever price the extravagance of the storekeeper may think proper to demand."[24]

The hours of work in the mills were long, and the workers were haunted by fear of deductions from their wages or even discharge if they were late. Women and children in the mills of Paterson, New Jersey, had to be at work at 4:30 A.M. Yet it was said to be a common thing in that city "to see little children, and some of very tender years, at daylight in the cold of winter season, running through the snows and storms with a crust in their hands, lest by being a few minutes too late they should incur the displeasure of their employer and get discharged."[25]

From the earliest days of the factory system, women workers fought oppressive conditions. Their struggles took the form of individual acts of defiance and work stoppages in the mills (called "mutinies" by the companies) in order to express their discontent over rules, wages, and fines.* But there were also strikes in which the women "turned out" and conducted their struggles in public, combining a battle against the tyranny of the factory owners with one that challenged the accepted middle-class bounds of female propriety. One writer states:

> It required some spirit for Yankee "young ladies" to brave public opinion in order to develop strike tactics at this early period. . . . It was felt that young women should not march about the streets, making a spectacle of themselves. And yet, in spite of disapproval they were prepared to do this in order to protect their standards whether it was conventional or not.[26]

From 1824 to 1837, at least twelve strikes took place in textile factories in which women were the main participants or played the leading role. Most of these early strikes ended with the women returning to work in defeat and the leaders discharged and blacklisted; in only a few cases were they able to win their demands. Again, most of the early organiza-

---

*In his study of discharges at the Hamilton Manufacturing Company, one of the leading Lowell mills, Carl Gersuny (1976) notes that in the first ten months of operation (May, 1826–March, 1827), there were thirty-four dismissals and "most of them seemed directed toward defiance and encouraging defiance to authority" ("'A Devil in Petticoats'" and "Just Cause: Patterns of Punishment in Two New England Factories," *Business History Review* 50 (Summer, 1976): 134, 136, 138.

tions connected with the strikes proved to be temporary. But word of these strikes spread through reports in the commercial and early labor press. The strikers' courage and imagination, together with their collective spirit, inspired others to act, and even when they were not successful, they succeeded in raising serious questions about woman's so-called "place."

The first strike of factory workers, and the first time women workers participated in the activities of a labor organization, occurred in May, 1824, at Pawtucket. About one hundred female weavers joined with male workers to protest a wage reduction and an attempt to increase the working hours. The women strikers met separately from the men. The *Patriot,* published in nearby Providence, reported that "the meeting was conducted, however strange it may appear, without noise, or scarcely a single speech." The *Providence Gazette* appeared to be so startled by the event that it could merely report, on June 2, 1824: "A difficulty has originated in Pawtucket, in consequence of a resolution of the owners of cotton manufactures to lower the wages and increase the hours of labor of the persons in their employment." It predicted, however, that "the mutual interests of the parties, if it has not already, doubtless will speedily suggest the means of settlement." A week later, the *Gazette* announced that the "means of settlement" proposed at a meeting of the manufacturers was for the "female weavers" to agree to the extension of the working day by one hour and the reduction of their wages, from $2 a week to $1.50, over and above their board. Since even with this reduction they would be receiving what "was generally considered to be extravagant wages for young women," the manufacturers felt that their proposal was more than fair. The "female weavers" disagreed, but after a week's strike, they were forced to return on the employers' terms. A fire broke out in the mill, however, early on the morning of June 1, and an account of the 1824 strike points out that such fires were often deliberately set by workers in their opposition to mill owners' policies.*[27]

In the summer of 1828, the children of Paterson, New Jersey, including a large number of girls, marched out of the cotton mills after the mill owners tried to change their dinner hour from 12 to 1. "The children would not stand for it," said one observer, "for fear if they assented to this, the next thing would be to deprive them of eating at all."[28] The parents supported their children, and, joined by carpenters, masons, and machinists, the children extended their strike to include a demand

---

*Kulik sees the strike as part of the community's resistance to an invasion by the factory system—a resistance "intermittently punctuated by conflict over water rights, taxes, work routine, and the recording of factory time." The strike itself, he insists, can only be understood "in the context of a long tradition of local resistance to textile mills and mill owners." (Gary Kulik, "Pawtucket Village and the Strike of 1824: The Origins of Class Conflict in Rhode Island," *Radical History Review,* 17 [Spring 1978]: 5–6.)

for a ten-hour day. The militia was called out to quell the disturbance, and the strike ended when the owners reestablished the 12 o'clock dinner hour. But the strike leaders were dismissed. That same fall, in a strike of spinners in the vicinity of Philadelphia, a strikebreaker was prevented from working by the children, and he brought an action against them on the ground of assault. The outcome of the suit against the children is not known.[29]

The first all-women factory strike took place at the Cocheco mill in Dover, New Hampshire, in December, 1828. The "turnout" was triggered by the corporation's attempt to impose a series of new "obnoxious regulations," including fines of 12½ cents for even a minute of lateness, the introduction of the blacklist, and a ban on talking at work. Years later, a citizen of Dover who knew the strikers recalled: "There were exactions on the part of the corporation that the independent spirit of the fair spinners and weavers could not brook. . . . One fine morning the mills were idle. Every operative was out, leaving the overseers to run them alone."[30] Preceded by a band, the strikers paraded through town "with flags and inscriptions." They shot off gunpowder and asked: Who among the Dover girls could "ever bear, the shocking fate of slaves to share?"[31]

The *National Gazette* of Philadelphia conceded that the "grand public march of the female operatives" in Dover exhibited "the Yankee sex" in a new and unexpected light, and, after commenting with some amusement on the objection to the ban on talking at work, observed in the same spirit: "By and by the governor may have to call out the militia to prevent a gynocracy."[32] The militia was not called out, but the company did advertise for "better behaved women" to replace the strikers. The outcome is not clear, but it is reported that the "offensive rules were withdrawn."[33]

In 1829 the Dover women in Mill No. 2 turned out again after the agent had nailed the windows closed to maintain the humidity, and one of the girls had fainted. They returned after management agreed that the windows would be opened partway.[34] That same year the Richmond Company at Taunton, Massachusetts, reduced the wages of the women in the weaving department. One of these weavers was Salome Lincoln, the first known female preacher in the United States. Her biographer wrote that the factory girls, including Salome, indignant at the wage cut,

> bound themselves under an obligation, not to go back into the mill, until the former prices were restored; and this not being granted, they formed themselves into a procession, and marched through the streets, to the green in front of the Court house. . . . They were in uniform,—having on black silk dresses, with red shawls, and green calashes. They then went into a hall near the common, in order to listen to an address. Salome was selected as the orator of the day. She then took the stand, and in her own peculiar style,

eloquently addressed them at considerable length, on the subject of their wrongs; after which they quietly returned to their homes.

Like most of the other strike actions of this period, the protest of the weavers ended in defeat. The women returned to the mill and resumed their work at the reduced wages. But not so Salome Lincoln, who "manfully refused to violate her word; but chose rather, to leave business— and break up all the social and religious ties she had formed than to deviate from the paths of rectitude. After this she never worked in the factory again at Taunton, but sought employment elsewhere, and was successful." It may be that Salome Lincoln's search for employment elsewhere was caused by her having been blacklisted because of her leadership role in the strike.[35]

These strikes of the 1820s were small when compared with the turnouts that took place in 1834 and 1836. There were several reasons for the difference. For one thing, the late 1820s and early 1830s saw the growth of labor protest all over the country, along with the rise of a labor press along the entire Atlantic seaboard and in the interior, which spread the news of these protests and of the conditions that sparked them. Skilled workers not only organized themselves in trade unions and went on strike for higher wages and a shorter workday, but in several cities unions of various trades joined together in central labor associations. In 1831 the New England Association of Farmers, Mechanics and Other Workingmen was formed—the first labor organization in American history to attempt to unite skilled mechanics, factory workers, farmers, and common laborers in one group. In 1834 the first national labor federation in America, the National Trades' Union, was organized.[36]

Soon after its formation, the New England Association appointed lecturers to spread the doctrine of trade unionism to the factory women. Its most effective champion of the rights of the women mill workers was Seth Luther, "the Tom Paine of the labor movement."[37] Luther was born in Rhode Island in 1795, the son of a Revolutionary soldier. He had a common-school education, worked in the cotton mills and as a house carpenter, and became intimately acquainted with the evils of the new factory system. During the summer of 1832, Luther delivered a series of speeches from Boston to Portland, Maine, in which he charged that the manufacturers had betrayed everything the American Revolution stood for and condemned them for attempting to construct a new repressive aristocracy. Luther's *Address to the Working Men of New England* quickly ran through three editions and was a topic of discussion among all American workers, including the factory women.

The mill workers were especially impressed with Luther's charge that the vast campaign publicizing the virtues of the American factory system represented an equally vast deception. He pictured the daughters of the mill owners "gracefully sitting at their harp or piano, in their splendid dwellings, while music floats from quivering strings through perfumed and adorned apartments, and dies with gentle cadence on the delicate ear of the rich"; all the while "the nerves of the poor woman and child in the cotton mill are quivering with almost dying agony, from excessive labor to support this splendor." After describing the low wages, long hours, and barbarous work rules in the "prisons of New England called cotton mills," Luther declared: "We do not believe there can be a single person found east of the mountains who ever thanked God for permission to work in a cotton mill."

So long as these conditions existed, Luther argued, the American Revolution remained unfinished, and it was the duty of all workers, skilled and unskilled, mechanics and factory workers, men and women, to fulfill the promise of the Declaration of Independence, with its thesis that "all men are created equal." He called on all these workers—the source of all wealth—to unite and demand a just return for their labor.[38]

At the first convention of the National Trades' Union in 1834, Charles Douglas, the other outstanding figure of the early New England labor movement, echoed Luther's condemnation of conditions in the cotton mills and of the exploitation of the female manufacturing operatives in America. He accused the Lowell mills, so highly praised as a "Garden of Eden," of being instead establishments where four thousand women had to endure "a life of slavery and wretchedness."[39]

These attacks on the factory system, including the Lowell showcase, spread within the mills themselves and supported the women workers' own experiences.[40] Then, in 1834, the factory owners, facing higher prices for raw cotton and increased competition from England, tried to reduce costs through wage cuts, speedups, and new oppressive rules. The result was a series of strikes in many mill towns.

In February, 1834, between seven and eight hundred women struck the Cocheco Manufacturing Company in Dover, New Hampshire, after they were informed that their wages would be reduced to meet the "unusual pressure of the times." Gathering at the local courthouse, they resolved never to return to work at reduced wages. They expressed anger at the fact that those "who are least able" were forced to bear the burden of "the unusual pressure of the times" while the wages of "our overseers and agent are continued to them at their former high rate." They further resolved: "However freely the epithet of 'factory slaves' may be bestowed upon us, we will never deserve it by a base and cringing submission to proud wealth or haughty insolence." They then voted to spread the news of their strike to their sisters in other factory towns, and called upon all New Hampshire papers "opposed to the system of slavery attempted to be established in our manufacturing establishments" to publish their resolutions.[41]

The *Dover Gazette* quickly complied, and, after noting that the resolutions were adopted "without a single dissenting voice," characterized them as "highly creditable" to the "Factory Girls of this town": "They . . . breathe a spirit of Liberty and Republican Independence worthy of the descendants of the heroes and patriots of the Revolution—rightly entitling them to the proud appellation of DAUGHTERS OF REPUBLICAN AMERICA."[42]

Whether or not, as one paper reported, the Dover strikers formed a trade union, their turnout certainly demonstrated clear planning and an attempt to win the support of both other workers and the general public. One paper reported that there was "unqualified approbation" of the strikers' "propriety and decorum" because "instead of forming processions and parading the streets to the amusement of a crowd of gaping idlers, they have confined themselves for the most part within their respective boarding houses."[43]

The company, however, did not share in the "unqualified approbation" and began advertising for strikebreakers. It asked for "five hundred females" to work under a new set of regulations aimed at preventing any future resistance. In an early version of the "ironclad oath," the new girls were required to pledge not to join a union or to take any collective action at the price of forfeiting wages owed them.[44] The strikers responded with their own announcement warning other women not to seek work in the factory because there were already enough operatives ready to produce cotton cloth but not willing to consent to "a reduced tariff of wages." The *Dover Gazette* not only published the strikers' response to the appeal for strikebreakers but also urged every "friend of liberty" in the nation, and especially those of "the stronger sex," to come to the strikers' assistance. The paper encouraged the women to hold out: "Though their prospects may appear gloomy, they have only to persevere, and they will inevitably succeed."[45]

In the end, however, the strike was lost. Nevertheless, the Dover girls refused to return to the factories and went back home instead. They had already prepared for such a contingency by raising a fund "to defray the expense of those, in returning to their homes, who may not have the means at their command."[46]

That same month—February, 1834—eight hundred Lowell female operatives also turned out to protest a proposed 15 percent reduction in their wages. This strike was not a spontaneous outburst but was planned in advance. Even before the formal announcement of the wage cuts, rumors had caused the women to meet together, and a mill agent observed with some surprise that at these meetings, they were making threats "with a truly Amazonian spirit." After the wage reduction was announced, the same agent noted that the operatives had appointed "a directress and voted to be governed by her in all cases." When this spokeswoman voiced her protest at the wage cut and refused the suggestion that she leave the mill with an honorable discharge, she was fired.

The agent reported: "She declared that every girl in the room would leave with her, made a signal, and . . . they all marched out."[47]

The strikers paraded through the streets of Lowell, visiting the various mills and attempting to induce others to join their protest. Their "directress" was reported to have "mounted a pump and made a flaming Mary Wollstonecraft speech* on the rights of women and the iniquities of the 'monied aristocracy,'" which produced such a powerful effect on her sisters that they resolved "to have their own way if they died for it." They then endorsed a petition calling on their fellow operatives to "discontinue their labors until terms of reconciliation are made." Their petition concluded with a pledge "not [to] go back into the mills to work unless they receive us all as one." If anyone did not have enough money to transport her back home, she would be "supplied."[48]

In a statement of principles accompanying the petition that the strikers circulated among their fellow operatives, they declared:

UNION IS POWER

Our present object is to have union and exertion, and we remain in possession of our unquestionable rights. We circulate this paper wishing to obtain the names of all who imbibe the spirit of our Patriotic Ancestors, who preferred privation to bondage, and parted with all that renders life desirable—and even life itself—to produce independence for their children. The oppressing hand of avarice would enslave us, and to gain their object, they gravely tell us of the pressure of the times, this we are already sensible of, and deplore it. If any are in want of assistance, the Ladies will be compassionate and assist them; but we prefer to have the disposing of our charities in our own hands; and as we are free, we would remain in possession of what kind Providence has bestowed upon us, and remain daughters of freemen still.[49]

However, before this appeal, with its reflection of the Spirit of '76, could take effect, the strike was over. Within a few days, the striking women returned to work or went home to their farms.†[50] But Lowell was to remember this first strike for a long time.

In October, 1836, the Lowell female operatives again went on strike—this time against an increase in the price of room and board in the company boardinghouses. Since there was no accompanying raise in wages, this amounted to a new pay cut of 12½ percent. This time, however, the strike involved over fifteen hundred operatives (compared to

---

*Mary Wollstonecraft, Anglo-Irish pioneer in the women's liberation movement, published *A Vindication of the Rights of Woman* in 1792, challenging the idea that women exist only to please men and proposing that women receive equality.

†The *Man* reported that twelve hundred additional women signed the pledge (Feb. 22, 1834). But there is no other evidence that any but the original eight hundred were involved in the strike.

eight hundred in 1834), and the turnout lasted much longer. Although the women gradually returned to work at reduced wages or left for home, the mills ran at far below capacity for several months.[51]

As in 1834, the strikers held marches and large open meetings. As they paraded in their strike demonstrations, they sang this to the tune of "I Won't Be a Nun":

> Oh! Isn't it a pity that such a pretty girl as I
> Should be sent to the factory to pine away and die?
> Oh! I cannot be a slave;
> I will not be a slave,
> For I'm so fond of liberty
> That I cannot be a slave.[52]

This time, the strikers formed the "Factory Girls Association" to coordinate strike activities, and its membership reached 2,500. They also formed committees from the several mills to raise funds for "those who have not the means to pay their board" while on strike. Their resolutions informed the manufacturers that they would not receive communications except through their officers. They were "daughters of freemen" and would not permit corporation tyrants to dominate their lives. "As our fathers resisted unto blood the lordly avarice of the British ministry," they announced, "so we, their daughters, never will wear the yoke which has been prepared for us." They would rather die in the almshouses, they proclaimed, than "yield to the wicked oppressions attempted to be imposed upon us."[53]

The strike was finally broken after the women had been evicted from their boardinghouses and had run out of funds. But the mills continued to feel the effect of the walkout for several months, for the strikers, lamented one mill agent, had succeeded in shutting down production "as effectually as if all the girls in the mill had left."[54]

Other factory women followed "the example of their pretty sisters at Lowell." When the women of Amesbury were ordered to tend two looms at the same pay, they stopped work, proceeded to the Baptist vestry, elected officers, and adopted resolutions pledging that "under a forfeit of five dollars," they would not go back until the speedup was abandoned. "The agent," reported the *Boston Evening Transcript,* "finding them determined to persevere, sent a written notice that they might come back." The strike was victorious.[55]

The high degree of organization displayed in these strikes in Dover, Lowell, and Amesbury was not followed up with a stable labor organization. As long as the operatives could escape the factory system by returning home to their farms, there was not a strong enough motive for them to maintain more than temporary associations. To be sure, the employers took no chances; they discharged strike leaders for "mutiny" and forwarded their names to other manufacturers to prevent them from getting jobs elsewhere. They knew that even the temporary associations formed by the strikers indicated that the factory workers were moving in the direction of trade unionism.[56]

This trend was also evident in two other strikes of the period. The first occurred in the Schuylkill Factory Company of Manayunk, Pennsylvania, where male and female workers formed a "Manayunk Working People's Committee" and drafted resolutions protesting the long hours of labor ("from 5 o'clock in the morning until sunset, being 14 hours and a half") and a proposed wage cut. In the spring of 1834, the workers went out on strike when the company threatened to close the factory unless they agreed to a 25 percent wage reduction. Five weeks into the strike, the company offered to reduce the cut to 15 percent. A large meeting of the strikers chose a committee of two women and three men to draft resolutions calling on the workers to stand firm in their commitment to each other and to hold "beneath contempt" any man or woman who would return to work at the proposed lowered wages. The strikers sent committees to Philadelphia and New York to raise money, particularly for the "widows and orphans who had been unable to save anything from their miserable earnings." Although the outcome of this strike is unknown, the women in Manayunk turned out in 1835 and again in 1836, and were reported to be "forming societies to protect themselves from the rude grasp of avarice."[57]

Even children in the factories learned the value of associations, and in Paterson, New Jersey, when they struck again in the summer of 1835, they were better organized. The strike started on the eve of the Fourth of July, already established by American labor as *its* day, with the objective of reducing the workday in the factory from thirteen and a half to eleven hours and nine hours on Saturday, ending the practice of paying wages in scrip, and also putting a halt to excessive fines and extra work without pay. The strike spread rapidly to twenty cotton mills, and the children—boys and girls—paraded regularly through the streets of Paterson, appealing for support.[58]

Toward the end of the month, the parents and guardians of the fifteen hundred striking children formed the Paterson Association for the Protection of the Working Classes and sent out a plea for support from other workers. The call was publicized in the labor press, and funds began to arrive. Some sympathizers gave weekly donations.[59] "An Operative" sent the following note with her contribution:

There is not a parent in the country whose mind is not perverted, whose sympathies are not destroyed, whose feelings are not corrupted, and in whom is not deadened every generous impulse of nature, but will pray to heaven in so holy a cause; and rejoice that there is still a distant prospect of these children being released from the cruel bondage of their unnatural taskmasters.

After arguing that the condition of the factory child was worse than that of the Southern slave, since the former was forced to work "three hours per day longer than is required from the slaves of the south or felons in our prisons," the writer urged the children to stand firm, and, together with the other factory workers, to resolve to tell "these cotton lords . . . that it is our labor alone that supports every other class in the community, maintains the state, and upholds every institution and energy of the country, and that we are determined to be no longer gulled out of the blessings that we alone produce." The operative added the following postscript: "N.B. While I was writing the above I was half asleep, for the long time system deprives me of time to write or think, unless I take it out of the time my Boss allows me to sleep, so you will please make any corrections you think wanted." To this, George Henry Evans, the editor, replied: "We saw no corrections of consequence in the above letter to make, and therefore have made none. We wish that many of our legislators had as much good feeling and good sense in their whole career as this single letter evinces."[60]

Newark workers responded to the appeal from the Paterson Association by setting up a committee to raise funds and by sending another committee to investigate conditions in Paterson. The investigators reported that conditions in the Paterson mills "belong rather to the dark ages than to the present times, and would be more congenial to the climate of his majesty, the emperor and autocrat of all Russias, than this 'land of the free and the home of the brave,' this boasted asylum for the oppressed of all nations." The mechanics of Newark urged the child strikers to stay out until they won, and promised continued financial support.[61]

Heartened and sustained by money and encouragement from workers in a number of cities, the strikers held out for two months. They returned when the mill owners agreed to reduce the workday by one and one-half to two hours. The work week was to be sixty-nine hours, twelve hours a day for the first five days and nine hours on Saturday.[62]

The severe Panic of 1837, which forced mill closings and caused widespread unemployment among workers, brought an end to the period of early protest of the women in the factories. But "the rising of the women" of this period was to be only the beginning.

3

In the Trades

WE HAVE ALREADY SEEN that in 1824 women participated in the first factory strike along with men. A year later there occurred the first strike in which women alone participated. This was the strike for higher wages of "the Tailoresses of New York." While we do not know much about the events leading up to the strike,[1] we do know a great deal about the conditions that caused it.

Women in Jacksonian America had few rights and little power. Their role in society was sharply limited. While propertyless white men were becoming part of the electorate, women were denied the vote; their property rights were restricted, and they were excluded from most trades and professions.[2] In particular, they were systematically eliminated from medical practice. Although most of the colonies' original healers were women (a tradition that existed in England and Europe until the execution of some 4 million "witches" from 1749 to 1755 effectively thinned the ranks of female health practitioners), by the end of the Revolutionary War a male medical elite had begun to band together against women through a complex campaign for licensing and other legislation, harassment, restrictive medical school admission policies, propaganda about the alleged biological frailty and emotional instability of women, and the repeated assertion that women's proper sphere was home and hearth. By the 1820s all but three states had set up licensing requirements for midwives that made medical school a prerequisite, and no women were admitted to regular medical schools. Except for a brief resurgence of women healers ("irregular" doctors) during the Popular Health movement in the second half of the nineteenth century, women were all but excluded from the field until the early 1900s.[3]

In short, in Jacksonian America, women were largely confined to the domestic realm, where their duty was to be submissive and patient and to cultivate and spread virtue. While men could be both competitive and aggressive as they dealt with the harsh reality of the worlds of business and politics, women, from their place in the home, were supposed to provide the soothing, taming, and gentle energy that would help ensure harmony and social order—a counterpoint to the "ruggled individualism" that accompanied the rise of industrial capitalism and westward expansion.[4]

The "cult of true womanhood"—the belief that women are mysteriously but definitively different from men and can realize their womanliness only in the uniquely female role of bearing and nurturing children—was spread through a host of popular novels, sermons, etiquette books, manuals, and new ladies' magazines.[5] Women were counseled to be submissive and good-natured, to avoid politics, and to concentrate their energies on domestic tasks. These tasks were said to have their own political importance.[6] Thus, while not participating directly in political life, a woman was described as performing her civic duties through her role as "the Republican mother" who raised and educated the nation's children and was therefore responsible for preserving the civic virtues.[7] Said *The Lady at Home,* a popular book of the day: "Even if we cannot reform the world in a moment, we can begin by reforming ourselves and our households. It is woman's mission. Let her not look away from her own little family circle for the means of producing moral and social reforms, but begin at home."[8]

Thus, while industrialization brought lower-class women into the factories as unskilled labor, middle-class women were excluded from the newly formed professions by both prejudice and cultural restraints. Paradoxically, however, they had more leisure time than women in any previous generation. The tasks that had been assigned to them in colonial society—the manufacture of food and clothing, the education of children, home nursing, and medical care—were now institutionalized outside the home. Many of them, therefore, turned their energies to reform activities and literary pursuits.[9]

What of the thousands of poor women who could not stay at home and cultivate virtue—unmarried or orphaned young women, widows who had to support themselves and their children, and wives whose husbands could not work because of illness? They simply had to work.

During the colonial period, nearly all clothing not intended for home use was either made to order or sold by the person who made it. What turned women sewers into wage workers was the development of ready-made clothing and the wholesale trade. The demand for cheap, ready-made clothing came largely from the army and navy and from Southern slaveholders. Producing cheap clothing for Southern slaves proved to be a profitable enterprise for Northern capitalists. The growing industry, centered in New York, Philadelphia, and Boston, was further aided by the tariffs imposed on imported clothing in 1816 and

1828. By 1835 "every country village within 100 miles of New York became as busy as a beehive with tailors and tailoresses."[10]

Most of the work was done either at home or in small shops, called "slop shops," under miserable conditions. The name derived from the waterfront shops in the eastern seaboard cities that catered to the clothing needs of sailors waiting for their ships to leave. In these shops women produced on demand shirts and pants made of sturdy fabric. Since payment was at a piece rate, there was terrible pressure on the workers to increase their output by toiling longer hours. Meanwhile, agents for the shops traveled about the countryside distributing cut parts of the garment to women who assembled them at home. They played off the out-of-town sewers against the women in the city shops to keep rates low. Little skill was required for most of the work, and the women were deliberately kept unskilled by the employers. It was difficult to gain access to the better-paying, more highly skilled sections of the trade, such as dressmaking and millinery. Apprentices were compelled to keep sewing and were not taught the art of design.[11]

In 1828 Matthew Carey, an Irish immigrant who had amassed a fortune in Philadelphia's publishing business and had devoted himself to philanthropy, began a crusade on behalf of working women, especially tailoresses and seamstresses. In pamphlets, essays, and letters to the press, he revealed the wages and conditions of women sewers. But even Carey did not fully grasp the stark reality of the situation. In an 1831 pamphlet he estimated the average wages of sewing women at $1.25 a week, whereupon a committee of these women notified him that earnings were usually $1.12½ a week and often fell below that figure. In his revised publication, Carey revealed that a skilled sewer, constantly employed, working early and late, could make no more than nine shirts a week. Since two-thirds of her pay went for rent, this would leave her only 40 cents—or 6 cents a day—for food, clothing, fuel, and other necessities. A woman who had children or a sick husband to look after and thus could not put in full time might have 4 cents a day to meet her needs.[12]

Women in Boston made even less than those in Philadelphia. In 1830 the average weekly wage for a fully employed woman was the same in both cities, but rent in Boston was higher, with rooms generally costing $1 a week. In New York City, the situation was even worse. A physician in that city who saw many of these women as patients wrote: "To say that the wages paid by clothing store keepers to seamstresses are inadequate to their support is but a cold and imperfect statement of the truth." He found women making duck trousers for a store "at FOUR CENTS A PAIR; and cotton shorts at SEVEN CENTS A PIECE." When he asked the women if they could live on such pay, the answer was in one word: "Impossible!"[13]

A tailoress described her plight and that of her sisters in a letter to the press:

> Only think of a poor woman, confined to her seat fifteen hours out of twenty-four to make a pair of ... pantaloons, for which she receives only twenty-five cents. And indeed, many of them are not able to make a pair in much less than two days. ...
>
> Only think of twelve and a half cents for making a shirt, that takes a woman a whole day, if she attends to any other work in her family. There a poor soul must sit all day in this dark weather, and burn candles half her time, and injure her health, to lay in coal for the approaching winter. How shall she clothe her poor children, or even feed them at this rate? Yet there are many poor women of my acquaintance, that are placed in the disheartening situation I have mentioned; and many of them are widows, with a number of children. And the tailors scold us when we bring home the work, and some of them say the work is done ill, and then take out half the price, or give us nothing if they think fit, and at the same time they sell their clothing much dearer than they did some time ago, and God help us, we have to submit to the injustice.[14]

Matthew Carey appealed several times to rich ladies and gentlemen to provide relief by hiring these women at higher wages. He protested: "I have known a lady to expend a hundred dollars on a party; pay thirty or forty dollars for a bonnet, and fifty for a shawl; and yet make a hard bargain with a seamstress or washerwoman, who had to work at her needle or at the washing tub for thirteen or fourteen hours a day to make a bare livelihood for herself and a numerous family of small children."[15] "A Working Woman" was even blunter. She used the term "beating-down ladies" to describe "these fine people" ("who never had a care in their minds [but] to make their parties equal to those of their associates, and their dress more recherché"), because they were constantly "beating down" prices and helping to aggravate the poverty of the seamstresses.[16]

The low wages paid to seamstresses (as well as to domestics and washerwomen) forced them to face "the alternatives of begging—applying to the overseers of the poor—stealing—or starving." We might add another," wrote philanthropist Carey, "but we forbear."[17] That other option was prostitution. In 1835, a year after it was founded, the New York Female Moral Reform Society reached the conclusion that many of the city's poor workingwomen, even though they were basically moral, were being forced to turn to prostitution because of ruthless economic exploitation.[18] The New York *Daily Sentinel,* the first daily labor paper in the United States, reached the same conclusion:

> What wretched, wretched state of things is this which confronts our working women! How the miserable sufferers endure it, or in what way they procure

bread and water for their support, God only knows. That many of them, after struggling for years against honest pride, at last become inmates of the work-house, we have daily evidence. That some, maddened to despair by the utter hopelessness of living reputably in comfort, should stoop to the last, most degrading of resorts for support, and fit themselves to become inmates of the Magdalen Asylum [for prostitutes], can we wonder?[19]

While the New York tailoresses began as early as 1825 to try to find a way to combat the anguish, desperation, and powerlessness that characterized their lives, it was not until six years later that their efforts took the form of sustained activity. On February 11, 1831, the New York *Daily Sentinel* carried two items relating to women who worked with the needle. One, simply called "Facts," read: "A Tailor in Chatham street, who advertises for 'twenty or thirty' seamstresses, offers the applicants, for making shirts, *seven cents* each. Oak wood is *five dollars* a load." The other, headed "Meeting of Tailoresses," reported that "from two to three hundred females" had met in Mott Street "to form an association for the purpose of taking measures for bettering their conditions." The report also revealed that the tailoresses had agreed to form an association and had chosen one committee to draft a constitution and another to come up with a plan of action. There had also evidently been some discussion of a strike, since a correspondent who was present reported that many women who had families to support and who depended entirely on their labor to do so had indicated that they would not be able to hold out long enough "to make the stand effectual, unless they were provided for," as a result of which it was decided to raise a fund to support people in such circumstances.[20]

The United Tailoresses' Society of New York, as the new organization was called, met weekly. At one of its early meetings, the society aroused considerable attention because Mrs. Lavinia Wright, its secretary, had raised the issue of women's rights. The *Boston Evening Transcript* paid no attention to the conditions that prompted the tailoresses to form their union, but it was quick to condemn Wright's "clamorous and unfeminine" declaration of the rights of women, which, according to the newspaper, it was "obvious Providence never destined her to exercise." The *Transcript* advised the tailoresses to confine themselves to "their scissors and pincushions, their tape and foot stoves."[21]

Despite such objections, the United Tailoresses' Society continued to meet, and discussions of the rights of women continued to take place at the meetings. "Let us turn a deaf ear to the slanders of our enemies, for enemies we have, no doubt," boldly declared Sarah Monroe, a leader of the society, at one of its meetings. "If we are true to ourselves and each other, they cannot harm us." While she did not minimize the difficulties they faced, she urged her sisters not to be discouraged: "If we do not come forth in our own defense, what will become of us? . . . Let us trust no longer to the generosity of our employers; seeing that they are men in whose heads or hearts the thought of doing justice to a fellow being never seems to enter." Only by organizing themselves and standing up boldly for their rights, she went on, would they be able to secure for themselves "an adequate and permanent reward" for their labors. And she concluded:

> It needs no small share of courage for us, who have been used to impositions and oppression from our youth up to the present day, to come before the public in defense of our rights; but, my friends, if it is unfashionable for the men to bear oppression in silence, why should it not also become unfashionable with the women. Or do they deem us more able to endure hardship than they themselves?[22]

In June, 1831, the United Tailoresses' Society of New York prepared its own list of wages and declared that its members would not work for less than the amounts listed. When the employers rejected the new scale, the United Tailoresses, sixteen hundred strong, went out on strike. They continued to hold out through June and July, combating "difficulties from which men might have shrunk."[23] Their struggle was ridiculed in the commercial press, which echoed the employers' argument that since women, unlike men, were "exempt" from the need to support families, their demand for wages similar to those of men was ridiculous. The society's secretary responded:

> Now this is either a sad mistake, or a wilful oversight; for how many females are there who have families to support, and how many single men have none, and who, having no other use for the fruits of their employers' generosity, they, childlike, waste it, while the industrious mother, having the care of a helpless offspring, finds (with all the economy she is necessitated to practice) the scanty reward of her labors scarcely sufficient to support nature![24]

The labor press, led by the New York *Working Man's Advocate* and the New York *Daily Sentinel* (both edited by George Henry Evans), carried editorials and correspondence offering the striking tailoresses both support and advice about how they might win. One suggestion was to call "a meeting of the male population" to propose a boycott by the men trade unionists of all tailors who had not accepted the United Tailoresses' wage scale. Another urged a campaign against the use of prison labor and the labor of people in almshouses, which undercut the wages of seamstresses and tailoresses. Still another was that the members of the society collect funds by subscription among themselves to set up a cooperative store, which would provide employment at "liberal wages," with sick pay and retirement benefits for the subscribers. One correspondent urged the society to present a petition to the ministers of all churches asking them to "plead their cause with the people" and take up collections for the strikers. "Then," he concluded, "it will be seen who are and who are not friends of the widows and orphans, and of suffering, unprotected females."[25]

Unfortunately, the advice produced little in the way of funds, and the male trade unions showed little interest in the suggestion of a boycott of employers who refused to accept the proposed wage scale. Nor did an appeal to clergymen produce any results. "Where now are you disinterested philanthropists," asked the *Daily Sentinel* angrily, "your Magdalen people, who make such a wonderful display of reclaiming two or three dozen females from vice, while *two or three thousand,* at this present moment, are unable to obtain the necessaries of life by honest industry?"[26] But, as before, the appeal fell on deaf ears. The result was that when the society's members resolved to "adhere steadfastly to their own bill of prices" and sent a committee of three to inform the employers of this determination, the employers refused to make any concessions whatsoever. On July 25, 1831, the tailoresses voted to return to work and to "draw up an Address to the public stating their reasons for adopting this course."[27]

In this address, the society described the hardships and inadequate wages that had compelled its members to strike and announced that, despite the defeat, they would continue to meet and would even launch a cooperative clothing establishment. But that project never became a reality, and the last heard of the organization was the following announcement in the New York *Daily Sentinel* of September 5, 1831: "The monthly meeting of the United Tailoresses' Society to be held this Monday evening at 7 o'clock at Congress Hall, corner of the Bowery and Hester Street. Phebe Scott, President; Louisa M. Mitchell, Secretary."

Baltimore's trade unions were more inclined to help the tailoresses and seamstresses of that city than were their counterparts in New York. When the sewing women organized the Female Union Society of Tailoresses and Seamstresses of Baltimore on September 20, 1833, drew up a bill of wages, and voted to strike on October 1 if their demands were not met, they received assurances of support from the city's unions. The Baltimore journeymen tailors called a special meeting to aid the women in their strike.[28] Unfortunately, because of a scarcity of reports in the contemporary press, we do not know the outcome of the strike or even what happened to the Female Union Society. But the men and women workers of Baltimore retained a unified front. In September, 1835, the United Men and Women's Trading Society, a joint organization of men and women workers, came into existence in that city.[29]

In 1832, after four years of incessant campaigning on behalf of higher wages for women workers in Philadelphia, Matthew Carey was forced to concede that his appeals had gone largely unheeded and abandoned the cause as "impracticable." So indeed it seemed until 1835, when the workingwomen themselves began to organize. In June, 1835, eighteen women met and planned a large meeting for all workingwomen of the city. They invited Carey to preside, and he eagerly accepted, acknowledging in doing so that he had naively believed that all that was needed to improve conditions for workingwomen was to "excite public sympathy" for their sufferings. He had, he admitted, been "miserably mistaken," but he hoped that now, through their own struggles, the workingwomen would gain the success they deserved.[30]

The meeting was attended by an overflow crowd of about five hundred workingwomen from all the sewing trades and several others as well. Several clergymen and philanthropists were also present, but no trade union of men workers was represented. After speeches describing "the injustices and oppression of the poor, honest, and industrious working women of Philadelphia," the women formed the Female Improvement Society for the City and County of Philadelphia—the first citywide federation of workingwomen that embraced women from several trades. Committees were chosen from each trade to draw up wage scales. At the next general meeting, other committees were charged with submitting the new wage demands to the employers and publicizing the names of those who acceded. A special committee was appointed to protest the low pay received by women for sewing army clothes and to call upon the Secretary of War to remedy the situation.[31]

The secretary replied that he could do nothing more than submit the petition to the commissary general of purchase, writing that, while the government did not wish to oppress the "indigent but meritorious females employed in its service," the issue was one of "much delicacy," since it was "so intimately connected with the manufacturing interests and the general prices of this kind of labour in the city of Philadelphia."

The standard for "this kind of labour" was determined by the Provident Society, one of Philadelphia's charities, which paid seamstresses 12½ cents a shirt. Both private employers and the U.S. War Department consequently paid the same wage for the work. So when the seamstresses pleaded in their petition that such a price reduced them "to the degradation of pauperism," the Secretary of War could defend the practice by arguing that he was doing only what charitable institutions were doing, and it was not proper for him to disturb the existing structure. Fortunately, a number of employers were not so sensitive, and the women did win a series of wage increases.[32]

Women shoebinders were among the groups of women workers who united to fight for improved conditions in these early years. Although the factory system and modern machinery were still to affect the making of shoes, the trade was undergoing important changes. In 1800 the household served as the basic unit of shoe production. The master shoemaker (and head of the household) purchased the leather and supervised production in a small shop called a "ten-footer" behind his family's cottage. Working under him were a group of (usually younger) journeymen who brought their own kits of tools with them and received from the master not only wages but room and board, firewood, and clothing. Within the master's house, his wife and daughters, working as binders, hand-stitched the upper part of the shoe. His sons, serving as apprentices and entrusted with a variety of odd jobs, completed the work team.

By the 1830s household shoe production had given way to the central shop. The master, who had fashioned his finished goods on customer order or else sold them to a small shopkeeper, had fallen victim to his supplier and distributor. Merchants with access to credit and an eye to expanding markets created a new production system. While household manufacture remained important, the merchant-owned central shop was becoming dominant in the field. Skilled cutters prepared leather for the merchant. Rural and village women and girls hand-stitched uppers for him. Journeymen bottomers, who owned little more than their tools but still retained essential skills, tacked the upper to the sole. They worked for the merchant but labored at home or in "ten-footers." The merchant's delivery wagons would bring the leather to the women to be sewn, and the merchant marketed the finished product.[33]

Massachusetts was a center for shoemaking, with Lynn at its hub. As early as 1829 there were 1,500 women binding and trimming shoes in Lynn, and, as the demand for lower-priced shoes grew, women from all the surrounding villages became shoebinders.[34] Women shoebinders were paid on a piecework basis, often in scrip redeemable at certain dry goods stores. At first the wages in Lynn were comparatively high, but by 1833 they had begun to fall, and the women decided to do something to maintain their standards. The *Lynn Record* of January 1, 1834, heralded the New Year with a story under the startling head: "The Women Are Coming."

> Alas for the Shoe Manufacturers! We tender our sympathy and condolence but in vain. It is all over with you! You may as well strike your flag, and give up the ship, first and last. The powers that be are against you. *Men* may commence an enterprize and become disheartened—they put the hand to the plough, and look back. Not so, the women—they know no defeat. We would as soon invade the armies of Philip of Macedon, as theirs, and with more hope of success. *We intend to be on the popular side*—on the side of *power*, right or wrong, and therefore cannot help you. Our advice is: agree with your adversary quickly. The women want money and must have it—you must give it to them, *that* you must: and you may as well make no bones of doing it at once, as to have your bones broken, and do it afterward.

In a more serious vein, the *Lynn Record* went on to report that about a thousand women had gathered in convention at the Friends' Meeting House in Lynn, and at this gathering, "probably the largest ever held in

New England," they had formed the Female Society of Lynn and Vicinity for the Protection of Female Industry. In a manifesto to the public, they insisted that it was only just that "equal rights should be extended to all—to the weaker sex, as well as to the stronger," that the "disadvantages which nature and custom have entailed upon females, as to the common transactions and business of life; are sufficiently great of necessity, without the addition of others, which are unnecessary and unjust." Hence they had been "driven by necessity to seek relief, impressed with the belief that women as well as men have certain inalienable rights, among which is the right at all times of 'peaceably assembling to consult upon the common good.'" Despite the concession to the prevailing opinion as to the relative strength of the two sexes, the *Lynn Record* correctly noted that the demand for equal rights for women was very advanced for the time and that probably no other meeting place would have tolerated such a stand. But at the Friend's Meeting House "the *liberty of speech* is not all on one side, the women, as well as men are here permitted to *speak out.*"

The constitution of the Female Society provided for quarterly meetings, established a relief fund and quarterly dues of 12½ cents, and provided for a wage scale to be voted on quarterly. Every member had to agree to work only at the agreed-upon wages, and members could be censured or expelled for violating this pledge.[35]

Once organized, the women shoebinders of Lynn went out on strike for a new wage scale. Two days after the strike began, the women of Saugus, "encouraged by the example of the ladies of Lynn," formed their own organization. The 125 members adopted the wage demands of their Lynn sisters, presented them to their employers, and won their acceptance.[36] But the Lynn manufacturers responded to the demand of the Lynn women with the cry that to raise wages would ruin the town. The women replied: "We can only say that we regard the welfare of the town as highly as anyone can do; and that we consider it to consist, not in the aggrandizement of a few individuals, but in the general prosperity and the welfare of the industrious and laboring classes."[37]

The Lynn strike continued for over two months. In March the Female Society announced that most of its demands had been agreed to, and the shoebinders returned to work under a new wage scale. Apart from the militancy and solidarity of the women strikers, their victory was aided by the fact that they were fully supported by the men's Cordwainers' Union, whose members raised funds for the strike and agreed not to work for any shoe manufacturer who did not meet the women's demands. Perhaps as a token of its gratitude, the Female Society chose two men to serve as its delegates to the Boston Trades' Union, the city central labor organization. But the society was not represented for long; by June, 1833, it was reported to be facing difficulty in maintaining its existence, with most of its members again working "under price" or not paying dues.[38]

The women shoebinders and corders of Philadelphia were able to maintain their organization after they organized and struck. In March, 1836, five hundred corders and binders formed the Female Boot and Shoe Binders Society, and even though they were not organically united, they struck together with the men's cordwainers' union for a rate advance. Denouncing the "detestable machinations of the employers to crush a suffering class of females," the journeymen announced: "Although they may forget they have mothers, we have resolved to take them [the women] under our protection, to flourish or sink with them." Even if they won their own demands, the men declared, they would not return to work until the women had won theirs. They formed a committee to solicit donations for the corders and binders and urged all unionists to "join their sisters in the holy cause of bettering their conditions."[39]

The *National Laborer,* Philadelphia's leading labor paper, urged full support of the women strikers and, in appealing to "trade unionists to come manfully forward to their succor," observed admiringly, "They well deserve generous aid, for they have stood out boldly for their rights, with an unanimity the other sex might truly be proud of."[40] Contributors to the strike fund included the shoemakers of Wilmington, Delaware, and the hand loom weavers of Philadelphia. Matthew Carey raised money and spoke in behalf of the strikers. The outcome of the strike is unknown, but it must have ended in some victory, since in June, 1836, the Female Boot and Shoe Binders Society published its constitution and invited all binders and corders to join this "large and growing society."[41]

There are other examples, in this period, of rampant exploitation of women wage earners—those making straw hats, cigars, and artificial flowers, as well as umbrella sewers and bookbinders—and of the attempts of these women to organize against it. Unfortunately, because of lack of records, we know little about these early efforts. Few lasting organizations of women workers emerged in this period. The women's associations were even shorter-lived than the male trade unions of the period, generally coming into existence during a time of struggle and fading after a strike was won or lost. It was an experience that was to be repeated many times throughout American labor history.

Despite the frequent defeat of hopes and the temporary nature of these first associations, the efforts of women workers to organize themselves into protective organizations during this time are significant. They are closely connected with the general rise in American labor activity, and the tactics used by women workers were similar to those employed by unions in other trades. Like their brothers, fathers, husbands, and sons, they met, drew up wage scales, and pledged not to work for any employer who would not agree to pay the wages being demanded. A committee would usually present the wage scale to the employers, and other committees would publicize the women workers' case to the public. By the time women workers organized, these had already become tried and tested methods of the trade unions. As the sewing women of Baltimore put it at their first meeting in September, 1833: "We know of no method so likely to procure us relief as that which has of late been successfully practiced by the mechanics of this city."[42]

Still, the painful truth is that the major reason women workers were so late in organizing compared with men is that the early trade unions, with few exceptions, were hostile to women workers, viewing them as a competitive threat instead of as potential allies, and refused to organize them. Thus, in the main, women were compelled to organize themselves.

The first trade unions were set up by skilled craftsmen who converted their mutual aid societies, organized to assist members in time of illness, to ones that could conduct struggles for higher wages and shorter hours. Their members were workers in a single craft, often working in a small shop and performing most of the work required to produce a product. But the 1790s marked both the beginnings of a national market and the rise of the merchant capitalists who furnished credit and materials to local producers and put pressure on them to increase their production. The small shops with skilled craftsmen producing for a local market soon gave way to larger shops with more and more workers and with one employer, manufacturing for markets in the South and West. As competition for these markets increased, employers reduced wages and increased working hours. They also divided workers into teams in order to speed up the work through specialization and division of labor. And they began to replace adult men with young boys and girls and adult women to do the work at one-fourth or one-half the men's wages.

The early trade unions fought vigorously against the growing division of labor and tried to prevent the hiring of more and more apprentices and unskilled workers who "will work for what they can get." As they saw it, the more women workers hired, the more the wages of the skilled male workers would suffer. They saw the women as part of a reserve of cheap labor being used against them, and they often blamed the women instead of their employers for their plight.

Thus the first trade unions, established in the 1790s, were for men only.* So, too, were the Democratic-Republican societies, in which the early trade unions were active. While the societies, in advancing the

---

*The Philadelphia Benevolent Society stated in its 1802 constitution that "women as well as men may become subscribers to the *Benevolent Society* and every member shall have an equal voice in questions relative to the management thereof." (*Rules and Regulations of the Philadelphia Benevolent Society* [Philadelphia, 1802], p. 23.) But when the male craftsmen who belonged to the society organized their specific unions, they all excluded women.

cause of Jeffersonianism, regularly toasted "the fair daughters" of America, none of these fair daughters was invited to join.[43]

From refusing to include women, the early trade unions moved to exclude them from the trades. In 1819 the Journeymen Tailors of New York went out on strike to keep master tailors from hiring women. In the printing trade, unions took similar action: the Typographical Society of Philadelphia forced one printer to renounce a plan to hire women compositors, and the printers of Boston joined together to drive "the girls from the business of setting type."[44]

The introduction of machinery intensified the trend toward division of labor. Skilled craftsmen were increasingly confronted with machines that could do their work in less time and robbed them of the advantage they had enjoyed over unskilled workers. Since women and children were the first to be hired to tend the machines in the new factories, many male workers associated "female labor" with the developing factory system and the cheapening of the value of skilled labor. This was made clear in the 1819 walkout of New York journeymen tailors against the use of seamstresses in their profession. They insisted that since women possessed inherently inadequate abilities, their labor insulted the trade. Here is how one such tailor explained it in a letter to the New York *Evening Post:*

> A journeyman tailor not above the level of mediocrity cannot make a superfine plaincoat to pass the ordeal of criticism—much less many other garments that might be named; yet this very man can make waistcoats and pantaloons and that, too, with more judgment and solidity than a woman can; *hence* we infer that women are incomplete, and if incomplete, they ought to disclaim all right and title to the avocation of tailor.[45]

In their pursuit of self-esteem, the mechanics upheld their dignity by refusing to work side by side with women. Although revolutionary changes in transportation and technology had greatly altered the usual patterns of labor, many skilled craftsmen saw the entrance of women into the job market as the major source of their problems. They tended to the view that women belonged in the home, where they would be supported by male workers, and not in the world of trades and industry, where they added "unfair competition." A strike declaration of 1809 argued that American society had an overriding obligation to provide its workingmen with sufficient compensation for their labor so that their wives and daughters would not have to work.[46]

The *Mechanics' Free Press* of Philadelphia devoted considerable space to the argument that women should remain at home, and it became an ardent supporter of the "cult of true womanhood." One of the articles, entitled "Female Society," pointed to the proper role women should play:

The advantages of female society are numerous, and extend themselves over almost every custom and every action of social life. It is to social intercourse with women, that men are indebted for every effort they make to please and be agreeable. . . . In our sex, there is a kind of constitutional or masculine pride which hinders us from yielding, in points of knowledge or of humor, to each other. Though this may be designed by nature for several useful purposes, yet it is often the source, also, of a variety of evils, the most dangerous to the peace of society; but we lay it entirely aside in our connections with woman. . . . Hence we may rest assured, that it is the conversation of virtuous and sensible women only, that can properly fit us for society; and that by abating the ferocity of our more irascible passions, can lead us on in that gentleness of deportment distinguished by the name of humanity. The tenderness we have for them softens the ruggedness of our nature.[47]

It is a measure of the contradictory attitude toward women held by many male workers of the period that in 1829 the Mechanics' Union of Trade Associations of Philadelphia, the first city central labor body in the United States and the sponsor of the *Mechanics' Free Press,* invited Frances Wright to deliver the Fourth of July address to the workers of its city. Wright, a young Scottish woman, was one of the first to speak about women's rights and thus was an outstanding example of what the "cult of true womanhood" was against. For days thereafter, the workingmen of Philadelphia (and later those in other cities who read the address) echoed her concluding statement that, valuable as the Declaration of Independence was, it would not serve the interests of the American people unless it was rewritten to add certain guarantees to its basic principles; namely, that each child had a natural right to a free education, each man and woman to the fruits of their labor, and each aged person to retirement in comfort: "Until this oversight be rectified, the revolution we this day commemorate will be incomplete and insufficient, the 'declaration' contained in this instrument will be voided."[48]

But since Frances Wright, although an ardent champion of labor, was not herself a workingwoman, she did not pose a threat to the skilled craftsmen who had invited her to address them and who published and distributed her Fourth of July speech. In any case, the fact is that for several years after they were founded, the early labor papers ignored the workingwoman. In 1830, three years after the *Mechanics' Free Press* was launched, "A Working Woman" complained to the Boston *Working Man's Advocate:*

You come out to support and advocate the rights of Working Men, their wrongs are trumpeted from paper to paper, from city to city, from the "Literary Emporium" to the "Ancient Domain." Thus far you are right. "This ought ye to have done, and not leave the other undone." Know ye not that a large portion of the females of our country come under the denomination of Working Women—that they are oppressed and injured as deeply as are the Men?

George Henry Evans was so struck by this complaint that he reprinted the letter in his New York *Daily Sentinel* and vowed to devote space in his papers to correcting the omission.[49] The *Daily Sentinel,* the *Working Man's Advocate,* and the *Man*—all edited and published by Evans in New York—devoted considerable space to the conditions and activities of workingwomen, supported them editorially, and opened their columns to correspondence from workingwomen and their sympathizers. Among the causes Evans promoted was the establishment in New York City of a "Women's Library," to be composed "of the writings in favor of women, and books best calculated to improve the minds and disposition of females."[50]

Evans even went so far as to challenge the prevailing view of the male trade unions that women should not be allowed to enter new trades. He supported Matthew Carey's idea of increasing the number of occupations open to women in strong words:

> And these [occupations] are much better paid than any which we self-styled lords of the creation have hitherto left to the gentler sex. We are quite willing to flatter women, to profess love and devotion for them, to call them angels and fifty other foolish names; but we are not willing, it seems, to let them share with us those profitable employments which are perfectly adapted to their sex's strength. It is very true that such changes in female labor might tend to lower men's wages, and still more to overstock occupations already more than supplied with hands. But such an argument ought not to weigh as a feather in the balance. If we are to suffer, let us suffer equally and together.[51]

Other labor papers did not go that far, but they did begin to pay more attention to workingwomen. The *National Laborer* of Philadelphia argued that *special* attention must be paid to these workers: "There is no portion of the community whose condition demands our immediate attention more than the female operatives of this country."[52]

The more enlightened approach of the labor press of the 1830s helps to explain the greater support of women workers by male trade unionists during that decade. It also helps to explain the fact that one of the labor parties of the period—the Association of the Working People of New Castle, Delaware (a community with a labor paper alert to the problems of workingwomen)[53]—even demanded the enfranchisement of women.[54]

As we have seen, when factory workers organized and "turned out," their actions were publicized and supported by workers in other trades. In much the same spirit, the cigarmakers of Philadelphia resolved during their ten-hour strike in 1835 that the wages paid to "females engaged in segar making is far below a fair compensation for their labor." They invited the females "in a body to strike with us."[55] And, as we have seen, the Philadelphia men's Cordwainers' Union struck together with the female corders and binders and resolved to take the women "under our protection to flourish or sink with them."

It can be argued that however supportive these male trade unionists were, they appeared to have shared the sexist attitudes of the time that the women were weaker, gentler, and more dependent, and needed male protection. It can also be argued that in these (and other) cases of male supportive help, women were firmly established in the occupations, so that the men had everything to gain and nothing to lose by helping them win better conditions. But however imperfect the motives may have been, these instances of cooperation disprove the view that *all* male trade unionists of the period were hostile to women workers.[56]

This is not to say that even the more enlightened male trade unionists took a consistent position on the issue of workingwomen. While many expressed concern that if women continued to operate under existing oppressive working conditions, the effect on their own health and that of future generations would be harmful to the nation, they still felt that if women were to enter trades where conditions were better, performing work then done by men, "wages would gradually sink to almost nothing."[57] To their minds, the solution was for workingwomen to return to the home. Thus, the president of the Philadelphia Trades' Assembly appealed to working women in 1835 to unite and "form a female traders' union" to battle for higher wages and shorter hours, until they succeeded in working only half as long as they did at the time. At that point there would be more work for men to do, and since they would be paid better for this work,

> ultimately you will be what you ought to be, free from the performance of that kind of labor which was designed for man alone to perform. Then will you who are wives be able to devote your time to your families and your homes; then you will be able to attend to the cultivation of your mind, and impart virtuous instruction to your children; then you will be able to appreciate the value and realize the blessings of the connubial state. And you who are unmarried can then enjoy those innocent amusements and recreations, so essential to health, and qualify yourselves for the more sober duties of wives, mothers, and matrons.[58]

These often contradictory attitudes toward women workers of the period came to a head at the third convention of the National Trades' Union in 1836. There the Committee on Female Labor presented the first trade union report in American history dealing with women workers. It recommended that men admit women workers into their unions or encourage the women to form separate unions, with "one auxiliary to the other," so that "in case of difficulties they [the women] would be governed by their [the men's] laws and receive their support." It also called upon the convention, "from feelings of humanity," to "recommend to the different Unions the propriety of assisting with their advice and influence, the female operatives throughout the United States, in ameliorating their present unhappy situation, under the female system of labor." But the committee saw these actions only as temporary necessities to "curb the excess before we destroy the evil." Its main point was that the existing system of employing women was a blot on the "escutcheon on the character of American freemen, [which] if not checked by some superior cause . . . will entail ignorance, misery and degradation on our children, to the end of time." The solution for women and the nation was inherent in the nature of women: "The physical organization, the natural responsibilities, and the moral sensibility of women, prove conclusively that her labors should be only of a domestic nature." Unfortunately, the report went on, women were "very blind as to their real interest," and imagined that efforts to destroy the vicious system under which they were forced to leave the home were "destructive to their interest." It was therefore necessary to educate such women, and indeed all workingwomen, to understand that under existing conditions the woman

> in a measure stands in the way of the male when attempting to raise his prices or equalize his labor; and that there her efforts to sustain herself and family are actually the same as tying a stone around the neck of her natural protector, Man, and destroying him with the weight she has brought to his assistance. This is the true and natural consequence of female labor, when carried beyond the necessities of the family.

Thus, the report, which opened with the most advanced position of any trade union movement of that era, closed with the exposition of a backward attitude that women continue to confront today. The Committee on Female Labor urged male trade unionists to "act the part of men" and seek the gradual destruction of the "unnatural policy of placing females in a different element from that designed by nature."[59]

In 1834 Seth Luther, perhaps the most enlightened labor leader of the period on the issue of women workers, pointed out: "It is quite certain that unless we have the female sex on our side, we cannot hope to accomplish any object we have in view."[60] Few workingmen of the period were ready to take the necessary steps to achieve such an alliance of workingpeople. But whatever the attitudes of male workers, women would continue to enter the work force in increasing numbers and would continue their attempts to organize themselves into protective organizations.

4

The Battle for the Ten-Hour Day

THE ECONOMIC CRISIS OF 1837 dealt a devastating blow to American trade unionism. Production practically came to a standstill, and thousands upon thousands of workers were thrown out of jobs. With one-third of the working class unemployed and most of the others working only part-time, the trade unions of the 1830s found it impossible to keep their heads above water. One after another, local societies, city centrals, and the national trade unions passed out of existence, taking with them the first labor newspapers.[1]

Throughout the Northeast, mills closed down as the words of a bitter song rang through the region:

> "The mill has shut down! Good God, shut down!"
> It has run at loss this many a day.
> Far worse than flood or fire in the town
> Will be the famine, now the mill has shut down.
> But to shut mills down is the only way,
> When they run at a loss, the mill owners say.
> God help the hands to whom it meant bread!
> With the mill shut down they'd better be dead![2]

When the mills reopened in the early 1840s, there emerged both a new type of factory operative and a new form of struggle against oppressive conditions. Before the crisis, most factory women came from the nearby farms, and their earnings in the factories were not their sole means of support. They could leave whenever they desired. Under these circumstances, their demonstrations were bound to be more in the nature of temporary, short-lived outbursts than sustained trade union activity. But in the 1840s a more or less permanent working class gradually began to emerge in the factories. A good many New England farmers had lost their farms during the depression of 1837–1840. "As the New England farms disappeared," writes Norman F. Ware, "the freedom of the mill operatives contracted. They could no longer escape. . . . A permanent factory population became a reality."[3] Or, as a contemporary labor journal emphasized in the summer of 1845, the workers in the mills were composed "of a large share of poverty's daughters whose fathers do not possess one foot of land, but work day by day for the bread that feeds their families. Many are foreigners free to work . . . according to the mandates of heartless power, or go to the poor house, beg or do worse."[4]

Once the female factory operatives became the primary wage earners in the family, they became fully committed to improving their conditions systematically rather than through brief "turnouts." The factory operatives of Lowell, Manchester, Dover, Nashua, Fall River, and Waltham, already famous for their cultural and literary activities, were now to earn a new reputation. They were the ones who, in the mid-1840s, formed the first trade unions of industrial women in the United States—the Female Labor Reform Associations—and furnished the first women trade unionists of note in this country: Sarah G. Bagley, Huldah J. Stone, and Mehitabel Eastman.[5] By their ability, militancy, and hard work, these women leaders won the respect of the men who led the New England labor movement. They served as delegates to labor conventions and, along with men, became officers of regional labor organizations. They moved about the towns and villages of New England, soliciting subscriptions for the labor press, and they played a leading role in the great struggle initiated by the male operatives of Fall River for a ten-hour day. They gave impetus, as well, to a number of other important reforms, including the emancipation of slaves, the abolishment of capital punishment, and temperance. Moreover, these militant mill workers were among the real pioneers in the movement for women's rights. They were pressing for full citizenship for women, through voice and pen, at precisely the same time that Elizabeth Cady Stanton, the Grimké sisters, Susan B. Anthony, and other middle-class women were active, and they used many of the same arguments.

During the 1840s newspapers, magazines, and foreign travel books continued to paint glowing pictures of life in the Lowell mills, stressing the point that, unlike the workers in the manufacturing plants of Europe, those in the Lowell mills were living in a veritable paradise, cared for more as "pupils at a great seminary than as hands by whose industry profit is to be made out of capital."[6] Even Harriet H. Robinson, the famous Lowell mill operative, in her reminiscences, described what she called the "bright side" of the existence led by the women factory workers in Lowell. However, she conceded at the end: "Undoubtedly there might have been another side to this picture, but I have described the side I knew best."[7] What she may have meant was that factory work had a "bright side" compared with conditions in the rural communities from which the young women had moved, and in other occupations where conditions were even worse—a point that a number of scholars have recently stressed in arguing that the favorable contemporary accounts of life and work in the factories should be taken seriously.[8] But in the contemporary literature on the "Lowell System," there never was "another side." The entire emphasis was placed on the "Beauty of Factory Life." It was summed up in a poem entitled "Song of the Factory Girls" (published at the mill owners' expense):

> Oh, sing me the song of the Factory Girl!
> So merry and glad and free!
> The bloom in her cheeks, of health how it speaks,
> Oh! a happy creature is she!
> She tends the loom, she watches the spindle,
> And cheerfully toileth away,
> Amid the din of wheels, how her bright eyes kindle,
> And her bosom is ever gay.
>
>   . . . . .
>
> Oh, sing me the song of the Factory Girl!
> Whose fabric doth clothe the world,
> From the king and his peers to the jolly tars
> With our flag o'er all seas unfurled.
> From the California's seas, to the tainted breeze
> Which sweeps the smokened rooms,
> Where "God Save the Queen" to cry are seen
> The slaves of the British looms.[9]

Ironically, by 1845 workers in the oft-maligned English system labored four to six fewer hours a week and had two more holidays a year than the Americans, and most British operatives were required to tend fewer looms.[10] Ironically, too, for several years the female operatives themselves helped to propagate the myth of New England's factory paradise. The young women in the Lowell mills formed "improvement circles"—little clubs in which they produced sketches, essays, and short tales modeled on those in the popular periodicals of the day. The circles were fostered and encouraged by both the clergymen of Lowell and the mill owners, who looked with favor upon their employees' devoting themselves to culture rather than to complaining about their conditions in the mills and acting to remedy them.

Out of one of these little clubs emerged the *Lowell Offering*. Under the supervision of Reverend Charles Thomas, pastor of the Second Universalist Church, four small quartos of sixteen pages each, containing the literary efforts of factory operatives, made their appearance at irregular intervals between October, 1840, and March, 1841. The major emphasis in these issues was to dispel the notion that factory work was degrading and that the mill operatives were exploited.

Soon the *Lowell Offering* was attracting national and international attention. Another improvement circle in Lowell, guided by the Reverend Thomas Thayer, pastor of the First Universalist Church, began a rival publication in April, 1841, called the *Operatives' Magazine.* Unlike the *Offering,* it did not advertise itself as exclusively female but "solicited communications from the operatives of both sexes." Printed by William Schouler, an agent of the mill owners, the *Operatives' Magazine,* like the *Offering,* had no intention of criticizing factory conditions or urging the factory operatives to unite to change them. In August, 1842, Schouler became the proprietor of the *Lowell Offering* and united the *Operatives' Magazine* with that more famous publication.

Still another magazine that espoused the escapist outlook of factory operatives was the *Olive Leaf, and Factory Girls' Repository,* published in Cabotville, Massachusetts.[11] But the *Lowell Offering,* with Harriet Farley and Harriot F. Curtis, both former mill operatives, as coeditors, advanced the view most clearly. It carried the words "A Repository of Original Articles Written by Females Employed in the Mills" and for several years was accepted as the voice of the mill workers. William Scoresby, a visitor from England, called it "the ninth wonder of the world, considering the source from which it comes." Charles Dickens, in his *American Notes,* referred to it as the "first clear notes of real life in America."* An American returning from England reported: "The *Lowell Offering* is probably exciting more attention in England, than any other American publication. It is talked of in the political as well as literary world." And in France, Adolphe Thiers solemnly proclaimed to the Chamber of Deputies that the magazine proved that in a democracy, labor could possess a mind and soul as well as a body.[12]

At the height of its fame, the tone of the *Lowell Offering* was set by Harriet Farley. One of ten children of a Congregational minister in New Hampshire, she had had to seek work at the age of fourteen to help support the family. After working at straw plaiting, binding shoes, tailoring, and other trades, she had entered the Lowell mills and joined an improvement circle. She first won attention in December, 1840, when the *Lowell Offering,* then edited by Abel C. Thomas, printed her reply, signed "A Factory Girl," to an attack by transcendentalist Orestes A. Brownson (in his magazine *Boston Quarterly Review*) on textile mill owners and their exploitation of factory labor. Brownson observed: "We

---

*Dickens added: "Of the merits of the *Lowell Offering* as a literary production, I will only observe, putting entirely out of sight the fact of the articles having been written by these girls after the arduous labors of the day, that it will compare advantageously with a great many English Annuals."

know no sadder sight on earth than one of our factory villages presents, when the bell at break of day, or at the hour of breakfast or dinner, calls out its hundreds of thousands of operatives." Factory work, he wrote, was enough "to damn to infamy the most worthy and virtuous girl." Farley defended the mill owners, attacking Brownson as a "slanderer," and called work in the textile mills "one of the most lucrative female employments." Her defense of the corporations came to the attention of Amos Lawrence, Lowell textile magnate, and in the fall of 1842 he assisted her financially so that she could leave the mill and devote herself to the editorship of the *Offering.* A year later Harriot F. Curtis joined her as coeditor.[13]

It was not long before the factory owners sent a written tribute to the editors, praising the "worthy enterprise" in which they were engaged.[14] For the editors of the *Lowell Offering* were not in the least concerned with wages, hours, and working conditions. As stockholders multiplied and greater profits were demanded, the wages of the Lowell operative were reduced more and more and a speedup of work and a longer day became the rule. "Since 1841," declared the *Lowell Advertiser* of October 28, 1845, "the operatives' wages have been cut down twice directly, besides being cut down indirectly by requiring them to do at least 25 percent extra work." The operatives, tending as many as three looms, worked indoors for long hours daily, pausing only for two hastily gulped meals. They were off only on Sundays and on four holidays during the year. Even Saturday evenings were denied them—the boardinghouses refused to allow lamps to be lighted so that the girls would retire early in preparation for church on Sunday. Moreover, Lowell set the pattern for all mills using the Waltham system, and agreements existed among employers to follow the wage rates and production speed of the machines adopted at Lowell.[15]

But none of this found its way into the pages of the *Lowell Offering.* "We could do nothing to regulate the price of wages of the world," wrote Harriet Farley. "We would not if we could, at least we would not make that a prominent subject in our pages, for we believe there are things of even greater importance." As for hours and working conditions, these were matters over which workers had "no control." Improvements would come as a result of the kindheartedness of the factory owners, who would "in their own good time introduce the ten-hour system, and will not this be a noble deed?"[16]

What were the "things of even greater importance"? All that really mattered, said Farley, was to "elevate, instruct and purify the mind and soul of the workers; to give them an outlet for the spiritual and emotional needs of the soul; to provide them with sweetness and light." Let the factory girls, therefore, continue to meet in improvement circles where they could read and study. Armed with learning and culture, they could protect themselves from the crushing power of the machine, which dehumanized the worker and robbed her of dignity and self-assurance. At the same time, they would prove to the world that there was "Mind Among the Spindles" and that a factory girl was the equal in learning and culture of the lady who stayed at home in leisure and comfort and did not soil her hands with work. As long as the mind and the soul were free, what did it matter what happened to the body? The philosophy of the factory girls should be that of the Apostles: "Having food and raiment, let us be therewith content."[17]

Writing of Harriet Farley's editorship of the *Lowell Offering*, Norman F. Ware points out that she "began by defending the operatives against attacks that were levelled at the corporations, and finished by defending the corporations at the expense of the operatives."* Nor did contemporary labor reformers fail to recognize this. They criticized the *Offering*'s editor for being deferential to employers and indifferent to the real needs of the factory operatives. When, they asked, would the *Offering* begin to reflect the real problems of these workers?[18]

However, the factory operatives themselves remained silent, no doubt influenced by the prevailing view that it was not fitting for mere female employees to question a magazine supported by the men who owned the mills. It was Sarah G. Bagley who broke this silence. She initiated a public debate that made it widely known that the world-famous magazine did not meet with the approval of all the female operatives it was supposed to represent.

Bagley, the first woman labor leader in American history, was probably born in Meredith, New Hampshire, and received a common-school education before moving to Lowell in 1836. She was employed in the Hamilton Manufacturing Company for six and a half years, and then in the Middlesex Factory, for about two years. For four of her eight years as a weaver, Bagley conducted a free evening school after working hours for the factory women, who were so eager to acquire an education that they were called the "culture-crazy girls."[19]

Bagley joined the Lowell Improvement Circle and wrote articles on the "Pleasures of Factory Life" for the *Lowell Offering*. As wages declined, working conditions deteriorated, and especially as the speed of machine operations increased rapidly, she became increasingly discontented with conditions in the mills and began to contribute articles to the *Offering* that were critical of the corporations. Later, denied access to this timid magazine, she voiced her anger at an Independence Day rally in 1845

---

*An anthology of the *Lowell Offering* which does not offset Norman J. Ware's evaluation is in Benita Eisler, ed., *The Lowell Offering: Writings by New England Mill Women (1840–1845)*, Philadelphia and New York, 1978. Several issues of what is called *New Lowell Offering*, produced at the University of Lowell by women students, faculty, and staff, have appeared since the Spring of 1977.

at Woburn, Massachusetts, attended by two thousand workingmen. When one of the speakers praised the *Offering,* Bagley took the platform and, according to the reporter for the *Lowell Advertiser,* "made some statements . . . which will do much to correct the impression abroad that it is the organ of the 'Factory Operatives'—stating that she had written articles in relation to the condition of the operatives, and their insertion had been invariably *refused!*"[20]

Bagley's attack on the *Offering* was widely reported, and Harriet Farley promptly responded through Schouler, the editor of the *Lowell Courier,* denying that she had ever rejected any article by Bagley. If any had been refused, Farley declared, it must have been while Mr. Thomas was in charge of the *Offering.* This started a debate between Bagley and Farley in the columns of the *Lowell Express* in which the mill operative challenged the editor to cite one article she had published that was critical of corporation policies and conduct. When Farley refused, Bagley called her a "mouthpiece of the corporations" (August 7, 1845). On this note the debate ended, but undoubtedly Bagley's attacks won support among the factory operatives. Late in 1845, despite assistance from the corporations and their agents, the *Offering* died for lack of support. Bagley greeted the news with the statement: "Peace to its slumbers, and if it should ever witness a morn of resurrection, may it be prepared to take a high stand among the redeemed as the bold defender of the rights of the people."[21]

Even before the *Lowell Offering* surrendered to the attacks of factory operatives, the women had acted to set up their own magazines and periodicals. In 1842 a fortnightly periodical, the *Factory Girl,* saw the light of day in New Market, New Hampshire. It was edited by men, but they were assisted "by several operatives of undoubted ability," and most of its contents were by young factory women. In 1842 the *Wampanoag, and Operatives' Journal* came into existence in Fall River, Massachusetts, edited by Frances Harriet Whipple.* In 1844 the *Factory Girl's Garland,* published by a man but edited by female factory operatives, appeared in Exeter, New Hampshire. Exeter was also the site for the *Factory Girls' Album and Operatives' Advocate,* which began publication in 1846. Although published by a man, it too was edited entirely by "an association of females who are operatives in the factories, and consequently qualified to judge the wants of those whose cause they will advocate."[22]

On November 7, 1845, the *Voice of Industry,* originally published by

---

*Frances Harriet Whipple, a native of Rhode Island, became active in the movement led by Thomas Dorr for a more democratic suffrage in that state, and was also a leading figure in the Rhode Island antislavery movement, writing poetry for the cause. Whipple's interest in labor is indicated by the fact that in addition to editing the *Wampanoag, and Operatives' Journal* during its year of existence (1842–1843), she was also the author of a pro-labor novel, *The Mechanic* (1841).

William F. Young in Fitchburg, Massachusetts, but now issued in Lowell, carried the notice:

> We cordially invite the Factory Girls of Lowell, and the operatives and working people generally, whether they agree with us or not, to make the *Voice* a medium of communication; for it is your paper, through which you should be heard and command attention. The press has been too long monopolized by the capitalist non-producers, party demagogues and speculators, to the exclusion of the people, whose rights are as dear and valid.

So many factory operatives made the *Voice* their "medium of communication" that it soon came to be known as "the factory girl's *Voice*." In May, 1846, the paper was taken over entirely by the young women in the factories.[23]

These new periodicals carried their share of genteel poetry, stories, and advice on general conduct, but they also spoke out vigorously in defense of the factory operatives and their efforts to improve their conditions. Moreover, through their columns, the young women began to demolish the myth of the "Beauty of Factory Life" in letters, articles, and poetry describing the actual conditions in the mills. Liberal papers like the *Manchester Democrat* also opened their columns to letters and articles from factory operatives describing the conditions they faced in the mills. "What Are We Coming To?" asked Octavia in the *Factory Girl* of March 1, 1843:

> I can hardly clear my way, having saved from four weeks steady work, but three hundred and ninety-one cents. And yet the time I give to the corporation, amounts to about fourteen or fifteen hours. We are obliged to rise at six, and it is about eight before we get our tea, making fourteen hours. What a glorious privilege we enjoy in this boasted republican land, don't we? Here am I, a healthy New England Girl, quite well-behaved bestowing just half of all my hours, including Sundays, upon a company, for less than two cents an hour, and out of the other half of my time, I am obliged to wash, mend, read, reflect, go to church!!! &c. I repeat it, what are we coming to?

Other letters told of girls who, "scarcely paid sufficient to board themselves," were forced to abandon their virtue to obtain favors. They told of managers who, finding the girls "languorous" in the morning, conceived the "brilliant" plan of forcing them to work on empty stomachs. They told of wage reductions of 40 percent in mills earning enormous profits; of workers forced to accept their wages in scrip, which meant a loss of about 50 percent in the value of these wages. Many letters complained of the unbearable speedups and pointed out that whereas ten years earlier the girls had tended two looms, making from 216 to 324 picks a minute,* they were now forced to tend four looms, making 480

---

*The process of pushing the pick the desired distance from the last one inserted previously.

picks a minute, "the increased work being done by labor and the profit going to capital." The letters protested vehemently against the blacklist system employed by all corporations to terrorize the factory workers and the "curse" of the premium system, under which bonuses were given to overseers and second hands (assistant overseers) who were able to get more work out of the operatives. A special target were the widely circulated reports telling of factory women who had accumulated sufficient savings to move west and purchase farms. "An Operative" replied:

> In the first place our average amount of wages is two dollars per week; then allowing for every day's labor, without sickness, and without rest, we have, at the close of the year, one hundred and four dollars. Out of this sum, for the "preservation of health," we must be supplied with comfortable clothing, suitable for toil with constant wear and tear; not to put on to merely loll upon sofas. No small amount is paid out for the mere article of shoes; for this running six times a day back and forth from the mill to our boarding houses, over stone sidewalks, takes off our *soles*. Then come rubbers, umbrellas, shawls, bonnets, &c., for everyday use; and this is not all;—we are required by our corporation rules to attend church regularly, and if we comply, a pew rent is added to our expenditures, of about five or six dollars. And what church is there in the city that would receive us upon their velvet cushions in our mill attire? Not one, I believe, could be found. Then comes the expense of a better suit, a Sunday garb, to appear decent in the eyes of the community. And to follow it out and really not to be niggardly or mean, we must contribute to the various *professedly* charitable objects of the day.

"How long," she asked, "do you think it would take us to become independent at this rate, go out west and buy us farms?"[24]

In addition to demolishing the romance of factory life, the operatives used these publications to point out that it was impossible to take a neutral position "while manufacturers and operatives were diametrically opposed in their pecuniary interests." This note of class-consciousness was sounded in many forms, including poetry and what was called "New Definitions":

> Overseer—A servile tool in the hands of an Agent; who will resort to the lowest, meanest and most groveling measures, to please his Master, and to fill the coffers of a soulless Corporation.
>
> Operative—A person who is employed in a Factory, and who generally earns three times as much as he or she receives.
>
> Contemptible—For an overseer to ask a girl what her religious sentiments are, when she applies to him for employment.
>
> Oppressive—To make two men to do the work of three, without making any addition to their wages.[25]

The importance of the factory magazines cannot be overemphasized. Workers smuggled them into the mills, and they were read eagerly and passed along. These magazines stimulated the type of resistance described in the *Factory Girls' Album* of September 19, 1846:

Dialogue of a Lowell girl with the overseer of a factory:—"Well, Mr. Buck, I am informed that you wish to cut down my wages?" "Yes, such is my determination." "Do you suppose that I would go into that room to work again, at lower price than I received before?" "Why, it's no more than fair and reasonable, considering the hard times." "Well, all I have to say is, that before I'll do it, I'll see you in Tophet, pumping thunder at three cents a clap!" It is needless to say that she was not invited to resume her duties.

Behind such resistance were the first unions of female factory workers—the Female Labor Reform Associations.

The first and most important Female Labor Reform Association was organized in January, 1845, in Lowell, Massachusetts, by twelve workers in the cotton mills. Within six months, its membership had grown to five hundred and was rising steadily. "Our numbers have been daily increasing," said its president and one of its founders, Sarah G. Bagley, in May, 1845, "our meetings generally well attended, and the real zeal of the friends of equal rights and justice has kindled anew."[26]

The constitution of the association, adopted at the January, 1846, meeting, reflected the operatives' desire to improve factory conditions and their quality of life. It pledged to work for the ten-hour day and for improvements in sanitary and lighting conditions in the textile factories. It called upon all the operatives "to throw off the shackles" that prevented them "from rising to that scale of being for which God designed us," and required every member to pledge herself "to labor *actively* for reform in the present system of labor."

The association at first relied on moral suasion to gain its goals, but it declared in its 9th Article: "The members of this Association disapprove of all hostile measures, strikes and turn outs until all pacific measures prove abortive, and then that it is the imperious duty of everyone to assert and maintain that independence which our brave ancestors bequeathed us, and sealed with their blood."[27] Representatives of the Lowell association attended mass meetings of factory women in the mill towns of Manchester, Dover, and Nashua, New Hampshire. In each of these places, Female Labor Reform Associations were organized. The Lowell union also contacted factory women in western Pennsylvania, and they soon formed the Female Labor Reform Association of Allegheny and Pittsburgh.

An appeal from the Lowell association, addressed to all working-women in America, urged them to organize for the struggle for a better life. It was necessary, it said, to have "a complete union among the worthy toilers and spinners of our nation": "By organizing associations and keeping up a correspondence throughout the country, and arousing the public mind to a just sense of the claims of humanity we hope to roll on the great tide of reformation until from every fertile vale and towering hill the response shall be echoed and reechoed: Freedom—Freedom for all!"[28]

The Lowell Female Labor Reform Association did not achieve a nationwide organization of working women, but it was the first and probably the only mid-nineteenth-century association to organize women workers outside a local area. Its influence even extended to workingwomen in the trades.

The factory magazines and the *Voice of Industry* devoted most of their attention to the conditions of the factory operatives and to efforts to improve them, but they were not indifferent to the problems of other workingwomen. On August 28, 1845, the *Voice of Industry* announced: "We are publishing a series of articles from the *New York Tribune* upon the state of 'female labor' in that city, which develop a most deplorable degree of servitude, privation and misery among this helpless and dependent class of people." The articles revealed that while these workingwomen were living "half fed, half clothed, and half sheltered [in] cooped up, ill-ventilated cellars and garrets, [their] ill-rewarded and slavish toil [had] raised to lordly wealth, a herd of merchants and speculators who add nothing to the real wealth of the country."* The *Voice* urged these "terribly exploited women" to emulate their sisters in the factories by organizing to improve their conditions. It was delighted to report a series of strikes of seamstresses, and commented: "We hope the rebellion will sweep the whole country. . . . Shame upon man when weak and friendless women were compelled to appear before the public and give tongue to their wrongs." The *Voice* was especially pleased to report the formation of the Female Industrial Association of New York as another of the Female Labor Associations of the period.

The New York Association was organized at an 1845 meeting attended by seven hundred women who were determined to win better wages "by appealing to the public at large and showing the amount of their suffering." Noting that a speech by Elizabeth Gray (subsequently elected president) signified the emergence of an articulate spokeswoman for "suffering female workers of New York," the *Voice* approvingly quoted her statement that the Association was open to all, "for only by a firm cooperation could they accomplish what they are laboring for."[29]

The Female Industrial Association of New York did include representatives of almost all the women's trades: tailoresses, plain and coarse sewers, shirtmakers, bookfolders and stitchers, capmakers, straw workers, dressmakers, crimpers, and fringe- and lacemakers. The preamble to the association's constitution stated:

*The *Tribune* articles, entitled "Labor in New York: Its Circumstances, Conditions and Rewards," were probably the most detailed picture of white working women in any ante-bellum city. Beginning with an examination of the status of the ten thousand seamstresses in the city, the articles went on to deal with straw braiders, artificial-flower makers, shoebinders, bookfolders, bookbinders, map colorers, curled-hair manufacturers, dressmakers, huckster women, milliners, umbrella and parasol makers, and domestic servants (*New York Tribune*, Aug. 18, 20, 22, 25, 26, 28, 29; Sept. 3, 5, 9, 11, 13, 15, 16, 17; Oct. 4; Nov. 8, 11, 18, 1845).

> Whereas, the young women attached to the different trades in the city of New York having toiled a long time for a remuneration totally inadequate for the maintenance of life, and feeling the truth of the gospel assertion that "the laborer is worthy of his hire," have determined to take upon themselves the task of asserting their rights against unjust and mercenary employers.[30]

The *Voice* carried only one other report on the Female Industrial Association of New York. On September 4, 1846, it noted that President Elizabeth Gray had conceded at an association meeting that the organization had met with little response from the public to its pleas for justice, and that the employers had refused to meet with association representatives or to make any changes in the conditions of the working women.

But the campaign of the Female Industrial Association of New York to convince the public of the need for reform was insignificant in scope compared with that conducted by the various Female Labor Reform Associations of the factory girls, and especially by the Lowell association. To further this work, the Lowell association appointed a committee to expose and counteract the false impressions created by the newspapers and corporation apologists. "The Press," Sarah G. Bagley declared, "takes every effort to slander our efforts and ridicule our operations." When the labor weekly *Voice of Industry* was in financial difficulty, early in 1846, the Lowell Female Labor Reform Association purchased the press and type and continued the publication with Bagley as chief editor. Forced to work fourteen or more hours a day in the mills, Bagley and other association members could not continue to issue the paper by themselves and had to turn it over to a man. But the association's officers still continued on the publishing committee and conducted speaking tours among mill workers and mechanics throughout New England to solicit subscriptions for the *Voice of Industry*.[31]

The Lowell Female Labor Reform Association also made its point of view known through the "Female Department" of the *Voice of Industry*, the first newspaper column edited and produced by workingwomen. The "Female Department," directed by Bagley, featured articles and poetry on a wide range of subjects of interest to women and regularly carried notices of meetings of the association. Under its masthead of the "Female Department" appeared the words, "As is Woman, so is The Race." Some of the articles, letters, and poetry in the column were written by men, including James Russell Lowell and John Greenleaf Whittier, but most of it was by women, for, as Bagley pointed out in the "Introductory," it had been deemed advisable to have a medium "devoted to the females of our country and through which they shall be heard." She also emphasized: "Our department devoted to woman's thoughts will also defend woman's rights, and while it contends for physical improvement, it will not forget that she is a social, moral, and religious being. It will not be neutral, because it is female, but it will claim to be heard on all subjects that affect her intellectual, social or religious condition."[32]

The Lowell association also established an "Industrial Reform Lyceum" to discuss controversial subjects ignored by the regular town lyceum. It organized fairs, May parties, and social gatherings at which copies of the *Valentine Offering*, a collection of articles and poems written by factory women, were sold. One of its most important activities was the publication and distribution of a series of "Factory Tracts," which were "to give a true exposition of the Factory system and its effects upon the health and happiness of the operatives." Written by the mill women, the tracts did more perhaps than any other publication to expose the myth of the factory paradise of New England. In "Some of the Beauties of Our Factory System—Otherwise Lowell Slavery," a mill operative who signed herself "Amelia" described in detail the long, tedious hours, the speedups, the low wages, the tyrannical boardinghouse system, and the blacklisting in the factories, and then asked: "Now, reader, what think you? Is not this the height of the beautiful and are not we operatives an ungrateful set of creatures that we do not properly appreciate, and be highly thankful for such unparalleled generosity on the part of our employers?"[33]

But "Amelia" was not content merely to expose the evils of "Lowell slavery." She called upon her sisters "for action—*united and immediate action.*" Her plea was not in vain. Not only did more operatives join the association, but when the Massachusetts Corporation in Lowell ordered weavers to tend four instead of three looms, and at the same time reduced wages one cent for each piece of work, the association called a meeting of the factory women to protest this order. The workers drew up a pledge resolving that they would not tend a fourth loom unless they received a wage increase in ratio to the increased work and that any worker who signed the pledge and then violated it should have her name published in the *Voice of Industry* as a traitor to the working class. Every weaver who worked for the corporation signed the pledge, and not a single girl violated the agreement. The company was forced to rescind its order.[34]

"Amelia" was also the author of "The Summons," one of the most widely published of the many songs and poems by members of the female labor reform associations. It went in part:

> Ye children of New England!
>   The summons is to you!
> Come from the workshop and the field,
>   With steadfast hearts and true.
>
>   . . . . .

'Tis mockery in the sight of God,
    To say that land is blest
Where millions bow beneath the rod
    Of tyranny oppressed.

For bread, where famished children cry,
    And none their want supplies—
Where toiling thousands live and die
    In ignorance and vice.

Then in the name of God come forth,
    To battle with the foe;
Nor stay ye till our hands have laid
    Each proud oppressor low.[35]

The chief "oppressor" was the mill owner, but there were many others in American society who had to be fought. Some operatives charged the abolitionists with taking a stand against slavery in the South while ignoring what they considered worse slavery in the factories of the North.*[36] But most factory women disagreed, and, indeed, they became known as the "Pretty Friends of the Slave."[37] "Should We Keep Quiet About Slavery?" asked "A Factory Girl," and she answered in a resounding negative. Another expressed the same idea in a poem:

Hast thou ever asked thyself
    What is it to be a slave?
Bought and sold for sordid pelf,
    From the cradle to the grave!

After describing the daily humiliations and sufferings inflicted upon slaves, especially women, she concluded:

Such is slavery! Couldst thou bear
    Its vile bondage? Oh! my brother,
How, then, canst thou, wilt thou dare
    To inflict it on another![38]

The Lowell Female Labor Reform Association participated officially in antislavery meetings and circulated antislavery petitions among the factory women.[39] The female associations also aided the drive to bring

---

*Such an attitude was expressed in the concluding verse of a poem, "The Factory Girl" published in the *Voice of Industry,* Dec. 11, 1845, describing the death of a factory woman from starvation:

That night a chariot passed her,
    While on the ground she lay;
The daughters of her master
    An evening visit pay—
Their tender hearts were sighing,
    As negroes' woes were told;
While the white slave was dying,
    Who gained their father's gold!

relief to the starving peasants of Ireland during the tragic potato famine and became active in the movement to abolish capital punishment. The temperance organizations in the mill cities were made up largely of the factory women.[40] The female operatives became associated, too, with the Utopian Socialist movement organized by the followers of Charles Fourier in America; Sarah G. Bagley was elected vice-president and Mary Emerson, another official of the Lowell Female Labor Reform Association, secretary of the Lowell Union of Association.*

When the Lowell Female Labor Reform Association announced the launching of its "Female Department" in the *Voice of Industry,* it pointed out bluntly: "Our department devoted to woman's thoughts will also defend woman's rights." This it did throughout its existence, as did the other publications that carried the writings of the factory operatives. In its entire publication history, the *Offering* carried only one article devoted to the issue of women's rights, and even Harriet H. Robinson, a champion of the *Offering,* conceded that the approach in that article was a timid one.[41] While the single article in the *Offering* touched delicately on the need for greater status for women in society, the author warned her sisters not to move too far from their "proper sphere," lest they risk losing "the grace of their own sex" without acquiring any of the superior qualities of the opposite sex. But the militant factory girls insisted that women had the right to aspire to every place in society occupied by men and condemned the entire establishment of laws and customs that prevented them from doing so.[42] The *Lowell Offering* and the other genteel publications of the factory women viewed marriage as a means of escape from the laboring class—especially marriage to the rich son of a mill owner[43]—but the militant factory women cautioned against marrying men of money who were spoiled by their upbringing and had no true understanding of the needs of workingwomen. Marriage to a working-class man was considered preferable, but in any case, the factory women were advised not to marry the first eligible man who came along but rather to make certain that the prospective husband would be as attentive to and respectful of their rights once married as he was during courtship. In "Rights of Married Women," an "Indignant Factory Girl" condemned the entire structure that caused a woman "to lose her individuality" in marriage, and insisted that if men and women could not function as true equals in the marital state, it would be better that each

---

*The basic concept of Charles Marie François Fourier (1772–1837), French Utopian Socialist, was the Phalanx, around which a new social order would grow. His movement was known in the United States as Associationism, and his followers included Albert Brisbane and Horace Greeley. Among significant colonies incorporating Fourierite principles were Brook Farm and Hopedale. For the influence of Fourierism on the American labor movement in the 1840s, see Philip S. Foner, *History of the Labor Movement in the United States* (New York, 1955)1: 174–78.

"live a life of heroic isolation in calm self-reliance." For the woman, it was "better than submission," she wrote, concluding:

> No relation is true that *makes* one soul subservient to another, none is true which does not rather tend to the elevation and equalization of both parties. The same lie which reveals itself in slavery, is at the bottom of our marriage institution,—the governing of one nature by its loss to the will of another, and they must both pass under the renovating hand, now that they have been bared to the marching eye of this Age.[44]

Practically every argument put forth by the middle-class women's rights pioneers was advanced in the publications of the militant factory women. In addition, they contributed a working-class point of view. Thus, they insisted on equal pay for men and women performing the same work. One wrote: "If a certain amount of labor is performed, it can make no difference by any manner of rational reasoning, by whom the labor is done. It is folly to argue that labor performed by females is not in every respect done as well as by men, and there is no earthly reason why they should not receive as much." There was only one principle that should prevail in a democracy:

> The labor of one person ought to command the same price as the labor of another person, provided it be done as well and in the same time, whether the laborer be a man or woman. A thousand of type, properly set in a stick and deposited on a galley, a thousand stitches in a waistcoat, by a girl, are worth as much to a master tailor or printer, as if the work be done by a man,—and ought to be paid as well.

There was even a pioneer proposal for what is now called affirmative action: "Those who have employment fit for women, to bestow, ought to give them preference; for there are fewer occupations of which they are capable, and they need help and encouragement more than men."[45]

A prominent Lowell physician, who signed himself "Spectator," published a series of articles sneeringly criticizing the factory women for forming labor reform associations and agitating for women's rights instead of properly educating themselves to function as women had always operated—as "the power behind the throne," manipulating men to get from them what they wanted and compelling them to do as they wished. A member of the Female Labor Reform Association, signing herself "Operative," took on "Spectator" and challenged the entire concept of the "power behind the throne," arguing:

> Man forms our customs, our laws, our opinions for us. He forms our customs, by raising a cry against us, if he thinks we overstep our prescribed limits. Woman is never thought to be out of her *sphere,* at home; in the nursery, in the kitchen, over a hot stove cooking from morning till evening—over a wash-tub, or toiling in a cotton factory 14 hours per day. But let her for once step out, plead the cause of right and humanity, plead the wrongs of her

slave sister of the South or of the operative of the North, and even attempt to teach the science of Physiology, and a cry is raised against her, "out of her sphere."

Not so with man, she went on; he could fill any position, and everything he did was accepted as "within the range of man's sphere." Pointing specifically to the disfranchisement of women, she noted: "Man forms our laws, and by them we must abide, although we have no voice in making them," and she added: "Man forms our opinions, for he has the keys of knowledge in his own possession. Our colleges of education are founded expressly for him—and all offices, scientific, as well as political, military and ecclesiastical, man fills." She asked why all the offices in public institutions were filled by men; why men got paid more for the same work that women did; why women were deprived of the opportunity to guide the nation as well as men. "Will 'Spectator' tell?" she inquired, and went on to observe: "I think I have proved that the 'power behind the throne' is powerless."

With respect to "Spectator's" suggestion that the factory girls educate themselves properly, she commented briefly:

> I would sincerely thank "Spectator" for marking out for us a course of study, and would be happy to pursue it, if I had books and *time* to peruse them—but my excuse must be that I am still an
>
> OPERATIVE.[46]

Much has been written about the middle-class women of the 1840s who defied convention by traveling about for various causes of the period and who, in the process, advanced the movement for women's rights. But not enough has been said about the pioneer women labor leaders who performed the same function at the same time. In their letters to the *Voice of Industry* relating their travels to various towns and villages to collect subscriptions for the labor paper, Sarah Bagley, Huldah Stone, and Mehitabel Eastman described the hostile reaction of middle-class men who charged them with being "unfeminine."[47] But they refused to be intimidated; on the contrary, they used the criticism to advance the cause of women's rights. Reporting an attack upon her by a middle-class man who was infuriated when "*a female*" dared to approach him with the request that he subscribe to the *Voice of Industry,* Huldah Stone wrote to the various female labor reform associations:

> There, my sisters, now will you not hang your heads in disgrace, and abandon the cause of equal rights at once and forever? "Why," said he, "no man that has any *influence,* or that is of any use to the cause will take it. Females are out of *their place* while soliciting names to a working man's paper."... From my very soul I *pity* such a man—one who holds the female sex in such low estimation as to make such an assertion.... I suppose he is one of those who would wish to have "*the woman*" a domestic animal, that is, know-

ing just enough to cook his victuals, mend his feetings, rock the cradle and keep the house in order; and if she wished for any further information, why she must ask her Lord and Master! An *equal* she must not be. She must not engage in any great and noble enterprise to benefit her own and the other sex, *even* if she could accomplish twice as much as a man, for she would be "out of place." She must not dare go forth . . . to labor in order to sustain a paper devoted entirely to the interests of the thousands of females who are toiling beyond anything which their physical natures can endure, in close, unhealthy atmospheres, and to hard working laborers who receive just enough to keep soul and body in the same latitude, for fear of getting out of place![48]

The women labor leaders who advanced the cause of women's rights in various towns and villages were ignored by the educated women of leisure on whom the early feminist movement depended. Hence the mill women sent no delegates to the 1848 Woman's Rights Convention at Seneca Falls, New York, and those who met there did not speak on the most immediate economic issues of concern to these exploited working-women. Yet when they read the Declaration of Sentiments adopted by the Seneca Falls convention in the *New Era of Industry* (successor to the *Voice of Industry*), particularly the list of impositions upon woman by man, beginning with the fact that he had never permitted her "to exercise her inalienable right to the elective franchise," as well as the assertion that women "do insist upon an admission into all the rights and privileges which belong to them as citizens in the United States," the mill women must indeed have felt that the convention spoke for them, too. Through the journal known as the *Factory Girls' Voice* they declared: "We rejoice in that convention as a significant indication of the tendencies of this age."[49]

Like the middle-class women of the period, working-class women found it difficult to obtain respect from middle-class men. But they did gain it from working-class men, as Bagley, Stone, and Eastman noted in their letters. Mill superintendents ordered Stone out of the factories, but the men working in the mills received her cordially and subscribed to the paper. An agent forced Eastman to leave when she tried to sell subscriptions to the men at work, but, she reported, he "could not extend his authority any further and I went on with my business and was well treated throughout the premises."[50] To be sure, workingmen had the same interest in advancing the labor reform cause, especially the ten-hour day, as did the women, and they were fully aware that the organizations the pioneer women labor leaders represented gave the cause great impetus. Nevertheless, their response to the working-class women stood in sharp contrast to the reaction of middle-class men to middle-class women activists of the time.

The issue that, more than any other, united workingwomen and workingmen of the 1840s was the struggle for the ten-hour day. Many mechanics had gained the ten-hour day during the 1830s, but the New England workers had not shared the gains of the shorter workday movement of the preceding decade, and many of those outside of New England who had won the ten-hour day had lost it during the years of the economic crisis.[51] The vast majority of workers—male mechanics and female operatives alike—still worked twelve to fourteen hours a day. A fourteen-hour day was in many cases a twelve-and-a-half-hour working day when two mealtimes were deducted. Nevertheless, there were operatives who worked a full fourteen or fifteen hours a day, and those women who did not live in boardinghouses and had to shop for food and cook meals had to spend additional hours in their second, unpaid job.[52]

Advocates of the ten-hour movement of the 1840s developed a philosophy of their own to justify their demand and win public support, vividly expressed in the magazines and periodicals issued by or in behalf of the factory operatives. In letters and articles, the factory women emphasized the fact that because of the physical and mental effects of the existing hours of labor, the average worker could not expect to live long or hope to devote energies to anything but endless toil.[53]

Some ten-hour advocates even regarded the lessening of the hours of labor as "the primary social step" toward the achievement of a new social order. As the workers became more enlightened, they reasoned, they would grasp more clearly the necessity of putting an end to the existing economic system and would join eagerly in the crusade for a cooperative society. Still, if we were to select a single statement that summed up the position of the advocates of the ten-hour day, the following by Huldah Stone (who, incidentally, expressed the view in 1845 that *eight* hours should be the normal working day), would do as well as any:

> Is it really necessary that men and women should toil and labor twelve, sixteen, and even eighteen hours, to obtain the mere sustenance of their physical natures? Have they no other wants which call as loudly for satisfaction as those? Call ye this *life*—to labor, eat, drink and die, without knowing anything, comparatively speaking, of our mysterious natures—of the object of our creation and preservation and final destination? No! 'tis not *life*. It is merely existing in common with the inanimate and senseless part of creation.[54]

"I verily believe," replied one mill owner, "there are a large number of operatives in our cotton mills who have too much spare time now." To reduce the working hours, he went on, "would increase crime, suffering, wickedness and pauperism." When workers refused to accept this argument and continued to insist on a ten-hour day, the capitalists struck back viciously with discharges and blacklists. Corporation agents threatened to blacklist all women who joined the Lowell Female Labor Reform Association and with it the crusade for the ten-hour day. Sarah Bagley wrote: "Deprive us, after working thirteen hours, of saying our lot is a hard one! We will make the name of him who dares the act stink with every wind."[55]

Ten-hour advocates differed with respect to the methods to be employed to secure the shorter workday. Some called for a huge campaign to convince legislators that incessant toil was inconsistent with the health, happiness, and liberty of the laborer and the welfare of the community and that laws should be passed restraining employers from hiring workers for more than ten hours a day. Others believed that groups of workers should concentrate on achieving agreement with their employers and establishing the ten-hour day in their own shops or factories. Still others favored the adoption of methods used successfully by workers in England in their struggle for shorter hours. This plan of action, popularized by John C. Cluer, an English weaver and labor organizer who had come to this country early in the 1840s, included three points: first, a convention of workers and manufacturers to discuss and agree on a program for the reduction of working hours; if the convention failed, a petition campaign to the legislatures; and finally, if that method also failed to bring results, a general strike, or, as it was popularly called, a "Second Independence Day." The general strike would take place on July 4, with all New England workers declaring their "independence of the oppressive manufacturing power."[56]

In the main, however, the movement for the ten-hour day depended on legislative action. In 1840 the ten-hour system had been established for federal government employees by executive order of President Van Buren. To do the same thing for employees of private concerns involved the state legislatures that had chartered them. The problem was to organize enough mass pressure to overcome the control exercised over the legislatures by the corporations.

How much pressure would be needed was graphically illustrated in 1842 and 1843, when the Massachusetts legislature ignored petitions for a ten-hour day forwarded by mill workers. In the fall of 1844, however, a new labor organization—the New England Workingmen's Association—came into being, which gave vigorous support to the crusade for a shorter workday.[57] Sarah Bagley represented the Lowell Female Labor Reform Association at the 1845 convention of the new association. Nor was she just a silent delegate; she delivered a forceful appeal for joint activity of men and women workers for the ten-hour day. Conceding that there were those who disapproved of such conduct by a woman, she declared: "For the last half a century, it has been deemed a violation of woman's sphere to appear before the public as a speaker, but when our rights are trampled upon and we appeal in vain to legislators, what shall we do but appeal to the people?" Were "the daughters of New England" to be told again by the powers that were that "they have no political rights and are not subject to legislative action"? "It is for the workingmen of this country to answer these questions— what shall we expect at your hands in the future?" In short, it was for the delegates to answer the question of whether or not their sisters and daughters should also enjoy the blessings of shorter hours, even though they could not vote.

The members of the Female Labor Reform Association claimed "no exalted place" in the labor movement, said Bagley, but wished, "like the heroines of the Revolution . . . to furnish the soldiers with a blanket or replenish their knapsacks from our pantries." In behalf of the union of factory women, she presented the Workingmen's Association with a silk banner on which was inscribed the motto: "Union for Power—Power to bless humanity."[58]

Despite her modest claims, the male delegates to the convention knew enough about the militant and inspired leadership of Sarah Bagley to elect her vice-president of the association—the highest position occupied by a woman in the labor movement anywhere in the world at that time—and to assign her the leading role in the campaign for the ten-hour day.* In the months that followed, the drive for the ten-hour day—sparked by the Lowell Female Labor Reform Association and the *Voice of Industry* and headed by Bagley—blanketed the mill towns with petitions. Thousands of signatures, most of them of workingwomen, were obtained.[59]

Upon receiving the petitions, the Massachusetts House of Representatives' Committee on Manufacturing decided to hold hearings. Its chairman, William Schouler—proprietor of the *Lowell Courier,* an important backer of the *Lowell Offering,* and a leading spokesman for the corporation—informed the petitioners, most of them women, that they would have to appear to testify in defense of the ten-hour day, "or we shall be under the necessity of laying it aside." Evidently he was confident that "maidenly modesty" would prevent the militant factory women from appearing in public before a legislative committee in the statehouse in Boston—but he quickly discovered that he had underestimated their militancy. When the committee hearings opened, Bagley and other operatives were on hand, and their testimony provided a dramatic picture of the working life of a female factory operative. One operative's testimony was described in part as follows:

---

*Two other leaders of the Female Labor Reform Associations were elected officials of the New England Workingmen's Association: Huldah J. Stone as recording secretary and Mehitabel Eastman as secretary.

She complained of the hours for labor being too many, and the time for meals too limited. In the summer season, the work is commenced at 5 o'clock a.m., and continued till 7 o'clock p.m., with half an hour for breakfast and three-quarters of an hour for dinner. During eight months of the year, but half an hour is allowed for dinner. The air in the room she considered not to be wholesome. . . . About 130 females, 11 men, and 12 children work in the room with her. . . . Thinks that there is no day when there are less than six of the females out of the mill from sickness. Has known as many as thirty.

Despite the overwhelming evidence presented by witnesses of the pressing need for a ten-hour day, the report of the investigating committee, written by Schouler, was opposed to any legislation. It insisted that "a law limiting the hours of labor, if enacted at all, should be of a *general nature;* it should apply to individuals or copartnerships as well as to corporations." It conceded that there were abuses in the factory system but expressed confidence that these could be eliminated without legislation, for "here labor is on an equality with capital, and indeed controls it, and so it ever will be while free education and free institutions exist." The report concluded by asking that "the petitions be referred to the next General Court."[60]

When the report was made public, Harriet Farley timidly rebuked the committee. Calling the petition to the legislature both "proper and dignified," she went on to ask: "Might not an arrangement have been made which would have shown some respect to the petitioners, and a regard for the ease and comfort of the operatives?"[61] The *Lowell Advertiser* criticized Farley for her restraint and charged the committee with inconsistency in conceding the existence of abuses while at the same time insisting that it was not up to the legislature to deal with them. As for the statement that labor was "on an equality with capital," it asked:

Why do not laborers reform the abuses of which they complain, instead of applying for protection to a Legislature that tells them that they are abused, but that the Legislature can't help them? Why does capital take the Lion's share and compel the laborers to put up with the Jackal's? . . . Capital is the Lion! and the terms he imposes *must* be submitted to.[62]

The *Voice of Industry* and the Lowell Female Labor Reform Association charged that the petitions had been rejected because the committee had been bought by the corporations. When William Schouler later ran for reelection to the legislature, the Lowell association denounced him as "a corporation machine or tool" and urged the male workers to defeat him. When the returns were in, the association published a resolution expressing its "grateful acknowledgement to the voters of Lowell" for "consigning William Schouler to the obscurity he so justly deserves."[63]

While the campaign for a ten-hour law was going forward in Massachusetts, the factory women in western Pennsylvania, members of the

Female Labor Reform Association of Allegheny City and Pittsburgh, were so incensed by legislative stalling that they decided to take matters into their own hands. On September 15, 1845, five thousand workers went on strike for the ten-hour day. They held out for almost a full month, at which point some of the women, desperate, decided to go back to work. But they did not remain at work long. Strikers went from factory to factory, broke open the gates, seized the workers at the machines, and dragged them outside. At the largest of the mills—Blackstock's factory—they were joined by the "men's auxiliary." An on-the-spot reporter for the *Pittsburgh Journal* describes what happened at Blackstock's:

> They [the factory girls] were now in full force. A whole legion of men and boys accompanied them as auxiliaries, to be used in case they were required. Thus prepared, flushed with conquest... they marched to *the scene of the great struggle*—the Battle of Blackstock's.
>
> On their arrival, they saluted the enemy with three shouts of defiance and a universal flourish of sticks and bonnets. After a minute or two spent in reconnoitre, they moved forward in a solid column of attack, on the... pine gate of the yard.
>
> In a moment the gate was forced open. But the defenders were determined on a heroic defence, and the assailants were thrown back and the gate again closed. A second time the assault was made with a similar result.
>
> Both parties now took time for breath, and opened negotiations. The factory girls demanded the instant expulsion of the girls at work. The people inside obstinately refused the terms, and both parties again prepared to decide the matter by the uncertain chances of the field.
>
> "They say they won't—let's try again!" and encouraging each other with loud cries, the legions marched to the imminent breach. For a moment, the combat was a doubtful one. The garrison made a stubborn resistance—but what could you expect from pine boards?... The gate gave way—"hurrah! hurrah!," and in a moment the yard was filled, the fortress was taken by storm, and the garrison were prisoners of war.

The following day the same paper carried this report:

> We are informed that the manufacturers have expressed a great deal of dissatisfaction with reference to the conduct of the Police, on Monday, during the disturbances. It seems to us that this is unjust. It was utterly impossible for any ordinary police force to have maintained order. There were hundreds of male friends of the operatives standing round—ready to interfere whenever it should become necessary... "let 'em hit one of them gals if they dare, and we'll fetch them out of their boots!" said a grim double-fisted fellow on our right, while they were breaking open Blackstock's.[64]

Although the male workers supported the women strikers, they did not, as in the 1830s, regard the women as too fragile to be able to conduct a militant struggle by themselves. The "factory Amazons," as the

Pittsburgh Journal described them, broke down the fences and walls barring them from those who continued to work and won their strike by themselves. The men stood around waiting to help if needed.

The sight of hundreds of women daring to break open the factory gates and toss out the strikebreakers by sheer force so antagonized conservative middle-class groups that the factory women found it impossible to gain public support. The employers were adamant, contending that they could not decrease working hours as long as New England mills continued to operate on a thirteen- or fourteen-hour basis. They promised, however, that the moment the ten-hour day was instituted in the New England mills, they would introduce it in Pennsylvania.

The Pittsburgh workers then turned to their sisters and brothers in New England and urged them to intensify their fight for the ten-hour day, assuring them that in western Pennsylvania arrangements had been made "for continuing the warfare." Upon receiving this plea, the Lowell Female Labor Reform Association invited John C. Cluer to discuss his plan for a ten-hour day at their meeting. Cluer outlined his three-stage idea and was "enthusiastically received."[65]

In conjunction with the New England Workingmen's Association, the Lowell Female Labor Reform Association once again circulated petitions, once again gathered thousands of signatures, and once again presented them to the legislature. Once again, too, the petitions were rejected. Now completely infuriated, the Lowell association set July 4, 1846, as the day for a general strike for the ten-hour day. But the movement received little support. The fact that five thousand workers in western Pennsylvania had been unable to gain a victory despite their militant struggle discouraged many workers in New England, and the idea faded away.[66]

The petition crusade for a ten-hour law continued in Massachusetts, but the Senate committee appointed to consider the petitions once again advanced the principle that a ten-hour law applicable only to corporations would be unjust. Although it admitted that the legislature had the power to define the number of hours that should constitute a day's labor, the committee insisted that "it could not deprive the citizen of [the right to make his own] contract." Furthermore, it went on, any restriction would "injure business, and the result will be, the laborer is sure to suffer."[67]

Only in New Hampshire was the petition crusade for a ten-hour law successful. There, the campaign gained thousands of petition signatures under the leadership of Mehitabel Eastman, the factory operative who was president of the Manchester Female Labor Reform Association, a coeditor of the *Voice of Industry,* and secretary of the New England Workingmen's Association. The signatures were backed up by mass meetings sponsored jointly by the Female Labor Reform Associations of Manchester, Dover, and Nashua, and the male operatives and mechanics.[68]

In urging the enactment of a ten-hour law, the legislative committee in New Hampshire argued that a shortening of the workday would be advantageous to the employers, for they "would realize a greater profit, even in less time, from laborers more vigorous and better able to work, from having had suitable time to rest."[69] Evidently the New Hampshire employers were not entirely convinced by the logic of this argument, for, at their insistence, clauses were inserted into the statutes permitting employers to draw up special contracts with workers for more than ten hours. Even before the laws were passed, employers submitted these contracts to their workers and informed them that they had the alternative of signing and continuing to work or refusing to sign and going jobless. They also threatened to blacklist the workers who refused to sign.

In spite of the terror of the blacklist, the workers fought valiantly to preserve the ten-hour laws by agreeing among themselves not to sign the special contracts. A mass meeting held on August 24, 1847, in Manchester's City Hall was described as "filled to overflowing with the factory girls prominent among those in the large audience." Female and male operatives alike pledged never to sign the special contracts, and the *Manchester Democrat* editorialized: "The meeting illustrates that both male and female operatives are capable of uniting effectively for a common cause."[70]

But the workers in New Hampshire were unable to maintain their pledge. The power of the corporations was too great. Workers who refused to sign were discharged, and when they went elsewhere to seek employment, they found all doors closed to them.[71]

In 1847 a ten-hour day became law in England without any provisions for special contracts permitting a longer workday. It was not until 1874 that a comparable law was passed in Massachusetts! Little wonder, then, that the Lowell Female Labor Reform Association, pointing to the difference in the situations of the factory worker in monarchical England, with its ten-hour day, and democratic America, with its fourteen-hour day, declared bitterly that "the fourteen hour system of Labor, adopted in the American Factories . . . makes the system of Factory Life and labor but little better than physical assassination."[72]

5

A New Era Dawns

By 1847 it was clear that the petition campaign for a ten-hour day was a failure. Massachusetts had refused to pass a law, and even though New Hampshire had enacted such legislation, it was made meaningless by the provision enabling employers to compel their workers to sign contracts agreeing to work longer. The female factory operatives voiced their determination to continue the struggle in their letters, articles, and poetry, such as the following:

> Try again! Try again!
> Heart and hope should never wane;
> Fear not the bold aggressor,
> Heed ye not the stern oppressors;—
> Try again! Try again![1]

During the 1850s the workers of Massachusetts did indeed try again to secure a ten-hour law. This time the workingmen rather than the workingwomen constituted the majority of the petition signers, and it was they who led the movement. When a meeting was organized in Lowell in October, 1853, for the proposed legislation, it attracted fifteen hundred men and only two or three hundred women. In the 1840s the figures had been just the opposite; the women in the mills had both led the petition drive and dominated the meetings. In 1853 about 75 percent of the work force in the Lowell mills was female, but women made up less than 25 percent of the attendance at this rally.[2]

One reason for this was that by 1853 the Female Labor Reform Associations had become a thing of the past. On February 13, 1846, the *Voice of Industry* announced that "The Magnetic Telegraph is now completed from this city of Boston; and will be in successful operation in a few days." It commended the "democracy" of Paul R. George for selecting Sarah G. Bagley as superintendent in Lowell. Thus Bagley became the first woman telegraph operator in the United States. But her absence from the mills and from active involvement in the Lowell Female Labor

Reform Association was keenly felt. Mary Emerson, who replaced Bagley as president of the association, had neither the experience nor the ability to maintain the organization in the face of the setbacks it suffered in the petition campaigns for the ten-hour law.[3]

In any case, the trend was now away from militancy. In January, 1847, the name of the Female Labor Reform Association was changed to the "Lowell Female Industrial Reform and Mutual Aid Society," and its aim was to appeal to the "self-love" of the factory girls and to "their higher nature." Through enlightenment and education, the factory operatives, "doomed to eternal slavery," would be brought together to end a "state of society which debases the masses to a level with the serfs of the old countries."[4]

The Lowell Society and the Female Labor Reform Associations in New Hampshire sent delegates to the New England Labor Reform League (formerly the New England Workingmen's Association), and at a convention held in Lowell in March, 1847, several of the female delegates engaged in a heated debate over the so-called "Beauty of Factory Life." But the general tone of the discussion was on the need for enlightenment.[5] However, more than enlightenment was needed to cope with the power of the corporations. By March, 1848, the New England Labor Reform League had gone out of existence. The Female Labor Reform Associations of Lowell, Fall River, Manchester, Dover, and Nashua also disappeared at about the same time.[6] Only the Pennsylvania society remained in existence, and there the factory women maintained their militant spirit. One reason may be that in the Pennsylvania labor movement the influence of middle-class utopian reformers was negligible. Such reformers, who were especially influential in New England, played down the need to struggle for immediate demands and emphasized a fundamental change in the structure of society or in the ownership of the land as the solution for all the ills facing the working class. While the militant factory girls, under the leadership of Sarah G. Bagley, had shown an interest in the Utopian Socialism movement, they had not neglected the struggle for immediate improvements. After Bagley's departure and the failure of the ten-hour petition, middle-class utopian reformism gained the upper hand in influencing the leaders of the Lowell Female Labor Reform Association.[7]

The situation was quite different in Pennsylvania. After that state passed a ten-hour law in 1848 similar to the one enacted in New Hampshire, corporations in the Pittsburgh area tried to force factory workers to sign special contracts permitting their employers to extend the working hours beyond ten a day. When the workers refused to comply, employers closed their factories and announced that they would not reopen them until the workers signed contracts permitting a twelve-hour day. They also threatened to move their machinery out of the state.

This was early in July, 1848. Three weeks passed and still the workers held out. Finally, toward the end of the month, about a hundred desperate workers agreed to sign the contracts and returned to work. But the employers rejoiced too soon. Once again the workers marched in to drive out the strikebreakers. Women strikers, armed with axes, began to hack away at the factory gate "with true Amazonian vehemence and vigor." Unable to cut their way into the yard because of the iron supports on the gate, they stormed the gate, tore off the boards, fell upon a detachment of Allegheny police, and captured the factory. The strikebreakers were forced to leave their benches and marched out with the strikers.[8]

Many of the women strikers were arrested and brought to trial, charged with destroying property. During the trial they made it quite clear that their aim had not been to seize the factory but rather "to get our rights." Elizabeth Haggerty, secretary of the Female Labor Reform Association, added: "We went to get the girls out; we went to get them out the best way we could." Mary Fulton, president, Haggerty, and twelve other members of the association were found guilty and sentenced to jail. The employers claimed that the strike had already caused "serious injury to the whole community by deterring new investments and inducing withdrawal of some already made,"[9] and were now confident that the strike was over.

They were mistaken. The strike continued until August 28, when the companies were compelled to abandon their effort to force the workers to sign special contracts. The ten-hour day in the textile mills of western Pennsylvania became a fact—but the workers were forced to accept a 16 percent reduction in wages. The battle to raise wages to the previous level continued, and in 1849 the mill workers experienced a double satisfaction. For one thing, the wage cut was restored (without a strike), and, in large measure because of their militant struggle, the ten-hour law was amended and the proviso for special contracts dropped. The Pennsylvania law declared ten hours to be a legal day's work in textiles, bagging, and paper mills—period.[10]

Even before this, however, the Female Labor Reform Association in the Pittsburgh area had passed from the scene, and soon thereafter the factory magazines and the *Voice of Industry* ceased publication.[11] "What has become of the girls?" asked one woman who had been impressed by their writings and activities. "I would like to know what has become of the girls that used to write for the *Voice?*"[12] The answer was that with no organizations or publications to express their grievances and unite them to resist oppression, many of them no longer found mill work tolerable and left. Some returned to their homes. Others left for the West. Still others went to their graves, the victims of byssinosis, or brown lung, a pulmonary affliction caused by the inhalation of cotton dust. A letter from a factory girl who stayed in the Lowell mills to one who had escaped began:

> With a feeling which you can better imagine than I can describe do I announce to you the horrible tidings that I am once more a *factory girl*. Yes, once more a factory girl seated in the short attic of a Lowell boarding house with a half dozen of girls seated around me talking and reading and myself in the midst, trying to write to you, with the thoughts of so many different persons flying around me that I can hardly tell which are my own.

She had returned home and decided never to go back to the mills, but events had forced her to change her mind and again become a factory worker. "Ah! me I rue the day," she practically sobbed.[13]

With the disappearance of the magazines and periodicals that had challenged and doomed the *Lowell Offering*, Harriet Farley attempted to regain her former audience. The *New England Offering*, her new enterprise, began publication in April, 1848, soliciting the support of the operatives for a magazine "to be wholly written by females who are or have been employees in mills." Probably convinced by her previous experience with the *Offering* that she could not entirely exclude material of a "controversial nature," Farley opened her columns to bitter attacks by the factory women on the evils of slavery in the South, but she still would have nothing to do with the complaints about the "wage slavery" of the mills. Since she received a small stipend from Amos Lawrence, one of the mill magnates, she was certainly not inclined to question the benevolence of the factory owners, and the *New England Offering* carried much material that was reminiscent of the earlier pieces in the *Lowell Offering* on the "Beauty of Factory Life." Only once did Farley venture to raise the possibility that Lowell might not be a "workers' paradise," when she criticized the indifference displayed by the author of an article on "The Rights and Duties of Mill Girls" in dealing with the tragic effect of wage cuts on the operatives. Even then, Farley assured the operatives that the economic crisis responsible for the reductions would soon end and that wages would be restored by the benevolent "humanity of Abbott Lawrence, the Lowells, and others of our most influential capitalists."[14]

Farley soon discovered that her efforts to portray the "Beauty of Factory Life" met with little response from the operatives, and in 1850 the *New England Offering* also ceased publication. The young women who remained in the mills and who had previously repudiated the *Lowell Offering* were not interested in supporting its carbon copy.

But these women were now a declining force in the mills. The proportion of immigrants in the Lowell work force was increasing year by year. In the Hamilton Company, for example, the percentage of immigrants increased from 39 to 62 over the course of the 1850s, and by 1860 the Irish made up almost half of the mill work force.[15] The immigrant women and the increasing number of children in the mills were not yet ready to challenge the power of the corporations. "Even had the more experienced Yankee operatives chosen to protest," Thomas Louis Dublin concluded, "it is likely that the Irish would have been recruited to take their places."[16] (In 1852 striking Yankee operatives at the Amesbury-Salisbury mills were replaced by Irish newcomers.)[17] Immigrant workers from famine-ridden Ireland needed jobs and a steady income immediately, both of which the mills could offer, "and they were less likely than Yankee operatives to be concerned with the specific wage levels or working conditions"—at least for the time being.[18]

The era of the magazines by and for factory operatives and of the Female Labor Reform Associations was over. Yet it had not all been in vain. The magazines and the associations had united the factory workers and created a community movement for betterment and a tradition of organization. Except for Pennsylvania, they had not produced the ten-hour day, but in some Massachusetts factories hours were reduced from thirteen to eleven, and in New Hampshire many factories instituted a workday of ten hours and fifty minutes, although at the same time speeding up production.[19] Moreover, the magazines and the associations had given considerable impetus to the movement for women's rights.

The spirit that had animated the militant factory women of the female labor reform associations was to resurface among the foreign-born women in the mills. In February, 1859, three hundred to five hundred women spinners at the Tremont, Suffolk, and Massachusetts mills in Lowell, all immigrants according to contemporary accounts, and many of them Irish, turned out for higher wages after the mills had reduced operations because of the general depression and had cut piece rates. The strikers represented only about 5 percent of the ten thousand mill operatives, and their turnout had little effect. Nevertheless, the first labor protest in the textile mills involving foreign-born women made it clear that "no longer could the Irish be counted on to be a docile, tractable labor force."[20]

The spirit of the 1859 strike was the spirit of the militant factory women of the 1840s, and, as we shall see, it was to reappear frequently in the decades after the Civil War.

Immigrant women were entering other areas of gainful occupation in the 1850s. They had no choice. Both the *New York Times* and the *New York Tribune* estimated that a moderate income for a family of four in the early 1850s was approximately $11 a week.[21] But many men and women earned far less. In order for their families to survive, wives and daughters often had to supplement the income of the head of the household, and many widowed households depended on women as the main breadwinner. Both married and widowed households often had to take in boarders.[22]

In general, young unmarried women in immigrant families worked outside the home while married women maintained their functions as wives and mothers by working within the home. The wives of German and Irish tailors often worked together with their husbands at home. The introduction of the sewing machine in 1846 and of the foot treadle in 1851 led eventually to the production of ready-made clothing in factories and workshops outside the home, but in the early years homework continued, with the tailor or seamstress buying or renting a machine from a contractor. The women also had to pay for thread and needles and for machine repairs. Early sewing machines frequently got out of control, tearing the fabric; and, as Barbara M. Wertheimer points out, "contractors, of course, charged the sewers of each torn garment, and these women lived in constant fear of accidents."[23]

Both immigrant and American-born women of the 1850s were subject to the generally depressed conditions prevailing in what were categorized as "women's occupations": domestic and personal service, including hotel maids, waitresses, and cooks as well as personal servants, housekeepers, and laundresses; the sewing trades, including dressmakers, seamstresses, tailoresses, cap- and vestmakers, milliners, and artificial-flower makers; upholsterers; bookbinders; and cigarmakers—occupations already overcrowded before the arrival of the immigrants.*

From contemporary newspapers and government reports, we have been able to piece together a general picture of mid-nineteenth-century conditions in these occupations. On at least two points all are in agreement: (1) women in these trades were paid half of what men received for comparable work,† often because it was assumed that women's wages were part of a family wage (an assumption that often did not correspond with reality); and (2) women's wages rose little during the 1850s and in some trades actually declined. Real wages sank as the cost of living soared. The *New York Tribune* estimated an increase of 50 percent in the cost of provisions in New York City between 1843 and 1850, while the

Major Occupations in Which Women Were Found, 1850

Occupation	Number of Women
Domestic service	330,000
Clothing	62,000
Cotton textiles	59,000
Teaching	55,000
Shoemaking	33,000
Wool textiles	19,000
Millinery	8,000

From Stanley Lebergott, *Manpower in Economic Growth* (New York, 1964), p. 520.

†In a study of crafts in Newark, New Jersey, Susan E. Hirsch concludes that the wages of women "ranged from two-fifths to two-thirds that of men in the same craft." She adds: "In the 1850s the school board paid female teachers exactly half the salary of male teachers." (*Roots of the American Working Class: The Industrialization of Crafts in Newark, 1800–1860,* Philadelphia, 1978, p. 39.)

Citizen stated that in 1854 alone fuel prices rose over 30 percent. The depressions of 1853–1854 and 1857, combined with seasonal and irregular employment, left all workers' incomes far below the minimum suggested as necessary by the newspapers of the period. Women fared the worst. During the depression of 1857, the *Philadelphia Evening Bulletin* concluded that "all things taken into consideration, the lot of the woman who has to labor for her living is actually harder in the United States than in any other civilized country in the world."[24]

Some unionized workers increased their wages by periodic strikes in the early 1850s, although even their wages hardly kept pace with the rising cost of living.[25] But very few of the "women's occupations" were unionized, and the trade unions of the 1850s were exclusively craft unions composed of skilled mechanics. Unskilled workers found it almost impossible to join these unions, and several of them, such as the printers, hotel waiters, shoemakers, and tailors, excluded women from both the unions and the trades. A few unions allowed the wives or daughters of members to work in shops controlled by them, but, as was the case in the Journeymen Cordwainers' Union of New York City, they insisted that the male member "should be held responsible for the acts of the woman."[26]

Under these circumstances, one of the few ways women were able to break into the trades with strong unions was by accepting employment as strikebreakers in the hope of being retained after the strike was settled. At least one union learned from these experiences the folly of excluding women from membership and accordingly revised its previously hostile attitude toward workingwomen. The Journeymen Tailors' Union of Cleveland called upon the very women it had excluded to assist its members during a strike and to join the walkout. "Some of the employers in the tailoring business," went the appeal, "have refused the demands of the men, on the ground of being able to hire the sewing women at their own prices. Therefore, Ladies, *Strike for your Rights!*" The ladies struck, but they reminded the men that one good turn deserved another. Thereafter, the Cleveland Tailors' Union allowed women to join.[27]

With very few exceptions, and in sharp contrast to the attitude of the men in the New England labor movement in the 1840s, the craft unions of the 1850s were hostile to women in industry, even more so than during the period from 1790 to 1837. In fact, the unions in the 1850s did not even bother to examine the issue of women in industry, as the National Trades' Union of the 1830s had done, but simply took it for granted that it represented an "evil" that had to be combated.[28]

Thus, once again, the women in the trades were compelled to "go it alone" in the attempt to achieve improvement in their conditions. And the need to do so was desperate. "A woman," the *New York Tribune* stated, "may be defined to be a creature that receives half price for all she does, and pays full price for all she needs. . . . She earns as a child—she pays as a man."[29]

In 1853 the *Tribune* investigated the "Needle Women of New York" to see if conditions had improved any since its 1845 investigation. There was some improvement: thousands of milliners, dressmakers, and other needle trades workers who had averaged $2 a week in 1845 now earned between $3.50 and $6. But nothing had changed for the seamstresses and tailoresses. Shops located in the lower wards of Manhattan that gave out piecework to seamstresses paid 8 cents and often as little as 4 cents per shirt. Since finishing three shirts was a hard day's work, the *Tribune* estimated that some needlewomen, considering the time spent in obtaining and returning goods and other trips to secure their pay, could conceivably be earning as little as 50 cents for an entire week's labor. There were hundreds of tailoresses and seamstresses whose annual income was estimated to be approximately $91.[30]

New York was by no means the only city in which seamstresses and tailoresses toiled for unbelievably low piece rates. The same was true in Boston, Philadelphia, Cleveland, Chicago, and Cincinnati.[31] A Report of a Committee on Arrangements for a mass meeting of the seamstresses of Cincinnati held in April, 1853, pointed out: "They say they must work on at what the shops will give them. If they have no work this week, before the next they will become so much embarrassed, they can never *'retrieve their fortunes.'*" The report told of women who supported themselves and their children by "making pantaloons at 15 cents a pair, and [who] could earn but 30 cents per day."[32]

At a meeting a week later, the seamstresses agreed on a bill of prices and appointed a committee to visit the employers to get their assent to the new scale. This apparently failed, because a week later a mass meeting was held and the following resolutions were adopted:

> *Resolved,* That we form a Society, to be called "The Seamstresses' Association"; that we pledge ourselves to stand firmly together, in want, in sickness, and in health; and that we recommend the Seamstresses in Fulton, Columbia, Covington, Newport and others, to adopt this resolution.

> *Resolved,* That we form a depot for giving out work; that those who are sick be attended to immediately, and those who are out of employ be recommended to call on those who will give the bill of prices for their work.[33]

By the end of the next month, the seamstresses had set up a store in the Mechanics' Institute in which they sold garments they had made. By July those seamstresses who were still working in the shops were also demanding a ten-hour day. Although it is difficult to determine how many seamstresses were supporting the association or its bill of prices, the venture seems to have been proceeding fairly well.[34] The end came in September, apparently as a result of internal quarreling and friction.

On September 17, 1853, the *Cincinnati Enquirer* reported that the Seamstresses' Association had met for the purpose of suspending its president "for an alleged defalcation," and that the "jealousies . . . [and] paltry meanness of some of its members" had resulted in the decision to cease operations. The paper observed with a trace of sadness: "When this Association was established, it was done to benefit that respectable class of this community known as seamstresses. Much good has been done by it, and if the Society could have conducted itself well, much good might have been done." Many years were to pass before the Cincinnati seamstresses would once again organize to better their conditions.[35]

More successful and longer-lasting associations were established in Philadelphia and New York. The Philadelphia press carried the following appeal on February 16, 1850:

> To the Humane: A Petition from the Tailoresses of the City and County of Philadelphia.—The winter is upon us, and distress and want stare us in the face. By reason of the low prices for which we are obliged to work, many of us are found at the midnight lamp and until daybreak, at the needle, labouring for a pittance which is scarcely sufficient for the necessities of the summer season. . . .
>
> Ladies, we appeal to you to aid us, and to represent our case. Gentlemen, women whom Almighty has placed under your care, now present themselves before you and implore your succor. Raise for us funds, in any way that you think proper, and secure them as you please. Most of the clothing which you wear passes through our hands, but very little does it profit us. Help us to help ourselves. Give us but justice—favour we ask not—and then Rosines, and Magdalens, and children's prisons may want inmates! . . . The funds required to maintain these institutions are far more than enough to start us in our enterprise, and we believe that there is no other way to secure for us a fair compensation for our labor. We do not propose to undersell the tailors, nor to increase the cost of any garment, nor in any way to disturb trade; we only wish to sell our own work, in order that the reward of industry may reach the hands which accomplish the task.

"We are industrious and willing to work," the petition emphasized, "but paid as we are, we cannot get enough to support life." It had been adopted at a mass meeting held on February 15, 1850, at which it had been decided that the only solution for the women workers was to organize an "Industrial Union," a cooperative establishment for the manufacture and sale of clothing made by Philadelphia's tailoresses.[36]

The Tailoresses' Industrial Union was immediately endorsed by George Lippard, a socialist and the founder of the radical Brotherhood of the Union.[37] With the funds obtained in response to the public appeal, a store was opened at 121 South Second Street on April 13, 1850. Tailoresses were taught to manage the enterprise, while a committee of sympathetic men and women operated it; goods were manufactured and sold to the public. Soon a second cooperative store was set up at 90 Walnut Street. After six months the committee in charge of management reported that it was succeeding in training tailoresses "to become their own factors, and thus to realize the profits as well as the prices of their work; this latter being, in general, rated so low, as nearly to preclude all hope of ever attaining competence, when deprived of its profits." They urged continuing support of the enterprise and reminded the people of Philadelphia that apart from moral considerations, such support was "of vital consequence to the material well-being of the whole community," for it was essential that "that large class now represented, the *mothers of so great* a proportion of its future citizens, should be protected and encouraged in well-doing:—that their honest industry should find its deserved reward; and that the compensation which is to require their toil should be commensurate with their necessities."[38]

Supported by a group of reform-minded women led by Lucretia Mott, Philadelphia's foremost antislavery and women's rights advocate, the Industrial Union prospered, paying out more than $4,000 during the first two years of its existence to the tailoresses for making garments—twice what they would have received from employers.[39] The Industrial Union remained in existence until the economic crisis of 1857, when, along with a number of other Philadelphia enterprises, it went bankrupt.

New York's Cooperative Clothing Store was established by the Shirt-Sewers' Co-Operative Union after an appeal for public support in the *New York Tribune* of July 31, 1851. The appeal included a quotation from Thomas Hood's "Song of the Shirt," the great British poem first published in this country in the Fall River *Mechanic* on December 7, 1844:

> Oh, men, with sisters dear!
> Oh, men, with mothers and wives!
> It is not linen you are wearing out,
> But human creatures' lives.[40]

The response was immediate. A public meeting was called, the shocking scale of wages paid the sewing women was again disclosed, funds were collected, and a cooperative store was set up. Business flourished, and contrary to predictions in the trade press, the enterprise survived. By the summer of 1853 the Cooperative Clothing Store was pointed to as "among the successful combinative efforts at work in New York City."[41]

The cooperative establishments of sewing women in several cities were able to exist because of support from liberal and philanthropic middle-class men and women. They had no support from the craft unions of skilled workers. To be sure, the Philadelphia Tailoresses' Industrial Union sponsored lectures on the labor question and elected delegates to the National Industrial Congress,[42] but by the time the tailoresses had formed their Industrial Union, the National Industrial Congress was dominated by middle-class reformers, and few, if any, trade unions were represented in it.[43] In Philadelphia itself, the Industrial Union was unable to establish relations with any of the craft unions, all of which were totally indifferent to any but skilled male workers.[44]

The outstanding example of working-class unity of men and women during this period came in the winter of 1859–1860, when the largest strike in United States history before the Civil War, involving at least twenty thousand men and women shoe workers, began in Lynn, Massachusetts, and spread throughout New England.

During the depression years of 1837–1842, there was little connection between the men cordwainers and the women shoebinders. But influenced by the unity of male and female operatives in the cotton mills, the Lynn cordwainers in 1844 invited the women to attend their meeting. The *Essex County Whig* hailed the decision: "This is just what is wanted. The presence of women will aid the cause more than anything else. They are interested in this movement and should be represented at the meetings."[45] On January 4, 1845, the *Awl*, organ of the Journeymen Cordwainers' Society of Lynn, called for even greater unity of men and women shoe workers: "The woman binder ought to unite with the journeyman in carrying on the great work of labor reform. The interests of the Awl and the Needle are one. They both point to the same thing. They are brother and sister, and should work together in perfect harmony." That year a Producers' Cooperative was established in Lynn by the cordwainers and shoebinders, but it was short-lived.

During these developments, the manufacturing of shoes was still more or less what it had been in the 1830s: household manufacture was still important, and the putting-out (or domestic) system was still dominant. Rural and village women and girls still hand-stitched uppers for the merchant while the journeymen bottomers retained their skills as they tacked the uppers to the soles. They still worked for the merchant who controlled the trade and set wages and conditions. How oppressive these conditions were, even in the preindustrial period of shoemaking in the 1840s, is revealed by the fact that in 1850, Lynn health officials reported that the life expectancy of Massachusetts shoemakers was far lower than that of Massachusetts farmers—forty-three as contrasted with sixty-five years.

But worse was still to come. Starting in the 1850s, the factory with its mechanization brought about changes in the shoe industry, just as it had already done in textiles. Large-scale factory production in the shoe industry began in 1852 with the utilization of the sewing machine, invented six years earlier, for stitching on the upper portion of boots and shoes. The sewing machine drew women into the factories, and the hand workers were largely replaced by female machine operators: binders, stitchers, basters, and gummers. Workshops still turned out shoes along with the factories, and skilled journeymen were still important. (The McKay stitcher, with its power pegging machinery, was not introduced until 1862.) But the handwriting was on the wall for the skilled shoemaker.[46]

In 1860 the workshops and factories of Lynn produced 4½ million pairs of women's and children's shoes. Still, the wages of the shoe workers had been sharply reduced. While the cost of living rose, wage cut followed wage cut. After a reduction in the fall of 1859, men were earning $3 a week. Wages for women were even lower, many women earning as little as $1 a week for as much as sixteen hours of work a day.[47]

The horror of what the factory system portended for Lynn was brought home starkly on January 10, 1860, when news reached the city that because of faulty construction, the Pemberton Mill of Lawrence, built in 1853, had collapsed, killing five hundred women and men operatives. In sermons the following Sunday, Lynn's ministers refused to attribute the mill disaster to an "Act of God" but instead put the blame on the mill owners' greed in failing to provide adequate safety precautions for the workers and to supervise the hasty construction properly. Were the shoe workers in Lynn's factories to face the same fate? The words of the song "The Fall of the Pemberton Mill" sent a shudder through Lynn.

> Not a moment's warning, I presume
> Of their impending, awful doom;
> The Pemberton Mills came tumbling down
> With souls five hundred to the ground.
>
> Through Lawrence streets, by old and young,
> The awful cry of fire was rung.[48]

On February 1, 1860, the *Lynn News* reported a meeting of shoemakers "to take measures to secure an advance upon the present low rates of wages." The paper expressed its sympathy: "We certainly think that something ought to be done to secure to the workmen full compensation for their labor. They are the true wealth of this city, and one dollar taken from their just earnings is so much taken from the value of our real estate, from the revenue of our city government, and from the appropriation for educational purposes."

When the manufacturers turned down the workers' request for higher wages and refused to meet with their committees, the workers chose Washington's Birthday, 1860, for the beginning of the strike, in the hope that "his history of patience and endurance, may inspire every one that has pledged his honor to persevere in the cause so vital to themselves and their families." The *Lynn News* reported that the shoe workers had enthusiastically supported the decision to strike, and again expressed support: "When we place ourselves in their position, we can sympathize with all their trials, and feel the justice of all their demands."[49]

Two weeks later, the women binders and stitchers of Lynn joined the strike. At a mass meeting held before their decision to strike, a list of prices for various kinds of work presented by a committee of women workers was discussed and a canvassing committee was appointed to enlist all female workers. Another meeting held the following evening was so well attended that many could not get into the hall. Alonzo G. Draper, one of the leading figures in the strike, assured the women that the outcome of the struggle depended on their decision, "for if the ladies refused to bind and stitch, the bosses must either accede to the strikers' demands or go out of town." He urged the women to join the strike, "unless they could secure a permanent advantage by compelling the manufacturers to sign their list of prices." Draper's plea was endorsed by a Mrs. Greenleaf, described by one reporter as a "Jewish shoebinder, member of the canvassing committee." The reporter wrote: "She considered their cause as a sacred one and precisely similar to that of the Jewish patriarchs who left Egypt because they were obliged to work for nothing and furnish their own materials."

After some discussion, the binders voted to strike on March 7, 1860, if the new price scale was not accepted, and to mark the decision with a great procession. They also voted to invite the Lynn City Guard and Light Infantry to escort the procession. Before adjourning, the meeting appointed committees to visit Swampscott, Salem, Marblehead, Danvers, Ipswich, and other towns to "invite the binders of those places to join the strike and sign the pledge of adherence to the list of prices."[50]

Despite his sneering tone at the militant spirit displayed at the meeting, the reporter for the *New York Times* could not help expressing admiration for the women shoe workers:

> Every one of the fifteen hundred women at the meeting pledged herself to turn out, and to urge her friends to do the same. Draper was not mistaken in calling this the decisive step. Woe to the scab, be it male or female, who appears in the streets of Lynn henceforth. No unkindly greeting will be uttered, no act of violence perpetrated, but what is worse, withdrawal of all sympathy, either in word or deed, by the determined female strikers.

Later, after meeting with the "Female Committee," the *Times* reporter wrote that they had reached the decision to have the "girls call upon the scabs and endeavor to inoculate them with their own love of freedom, and tell them that the treatment they might expect from their old friends would be worse than the small-pox."[51] A special "Scab Committee" was appointed to visit homes in the different wards to make certain that no one was strikebreaking "by binding or gumming, or finishing on the sly."[52]

Elsewhere in the shoe towns, the women workers joined enthusiastically in the struggle. Many a reporter who observed the spirit of the women strikers was convinced that the strike could only end in victory. Thus, a correspondent for the *New York Herald* wrote from Marblehead, Massachusetts: "The women are talking about taking part in the strike—and what the Marblehead women undertake they are bound to succeed in accomplishing." He wrote of the women strikers in Lynn: "They assail the bosses in a style which reminds one of the amiable females who participated in the first French Revolution."[53]

Yet mingled with the reports commending the spirit of the women strikers were repeated comments that their conduct violated the cultural code that women should not venture beyond the kitchen hearth and church pew. Editorial writers thundered that the shoemakers' strike was living proof of the demoralizing influence of the women's rights movement. Were not these female strikers asserting that they were struggling for equal pay for equal work? Surely, socialism would be the next step![54] Ironically, unlike the factory women of Lowell and Manchester, the female shoebinders of Lynn showed little interest in the political and legal aspects of the women's rights movement. Their activity appears to have been confined to the economic sphere. The male strikers responded by organizing a "vigilance committee" to make certain that only those reporters who wrote of the "female strikers with respect" would be permitted to attend their meetings. The women strikers endorsed this action and voted not to admit reporters to their open meetings who "misrepresented or burlesqued" them.[55]

Reporters had predicted that the women strikers' procession on March 7 would "be the feature of the strike," and so it was. For a week before the scheduled date, after it had become clear that the employers had rejected the women workers' new price list, Lynn, Marblehead, South Reading, Saugus, and Swampscott came alive with the painting of banners and the enrollment of female strikers. On Tuesday morning, March 6, a delegation of Lynn women shoe workers presented a banner to the strikers' Executive Committee on behalf of all the women who had voted to join the strike. On one side, the banner bore a likeness of Washington and the words: "With the spirit of '76 we hope to gain the day. Perseverance is our motto. We all unite in the grand strike to aid our friends and brothers." On the reverse side was a painting of two hearts united with the words: "The strikers. Let our hearts beat as one, in the spirit of '76. Stand firm, and victory is sure."

In presenting the banner, Ellen Darlin, one of the strike leaders, denounced the "avarice of the manufacturers who, in their haste to be

rich, have abridged the wages of the workers, until they are now not only
in danger of losing the fruits of their past labors, but of being reduced to
a condition little superior to that of bond slaves." She concluded: "And
not only are the wages of the workmen abridged, but those of the work-
women are also reduced far below a just compensation. These things
have forced us into action, against our inclinations, and we rejoice to see
that the workmen have taken a stand against such oppression."

Accepting the banner on behalf of the men strikers of Lynn, David
N. Johnson declared: "May we ever regard it as an emblem of woman's
interest and devotion in every worthy cause—for I express no unmean-
ing compliment when I say that without woman's sympathy and cooperation, no noble work was ever consummated. May your hopes and ours
be realized."[56]

A leading speaker at the mass meeting held on the eve of the procession was Reverend Thomas Driver, the city's black preacher. He told the
women that he "always liked the looks of the Lynn girls, but now he was
proud of them." He knew their condition and was convinced that they
were "worse off than the slaves in the South." He reported that he had
recently visited nine slave states, had witnessed the evils of slavery, and
had become a "confirmed Abolitionist." But, he added: "I find there are
white as well as black slaves; there are slaves in this state and in this city
worse, far worse, in their condition than the black slaves at the South.
The only difference is that they can't sell you. Thank God for that!"
These remarks created a "great sensation," and Reverend Driver was
wildly applauded,[57] as was the canvassing committee, which reported to
the meeting that 1,711 signatures had been obtained in support of the
bill of wages and that all would strike.[58]

"The great feature of Wednesday, March 7, was the women's procession," began an account in the *Lynn Weekly Reporter*. The parade was
scheduled to start at ten o'clock in the morning, and by the first break of
light, a deputation of men and women strikers, firemen, and military
from Marblehead, South Reading, Swampscott, and Saugus arrived in
Lynn. At eight o'clock a driving snowstorm set in, and by ten the streets
seemed impassable. But, nothing daunted, the procession began on
time, and, escorted by a detachment of musket-bearing militia and the
Lynn Cornet Band, eight hundred women strikers started at Lynn
Common and marched for several hours in the falling snow past the
central shops on Lynn's major thoroughfares. At the head of their procession, they carried a banner with the inscription: "AMERICAN LADIES
WILL NOT BE SLAVES. GIVE US A FAIR COMPENSATION AND WE LABOUR
CHEERFULLY."

Other banners, representing the different wards, carried the slogans:
"Our Union is Complete: Our Success Certain!" "Weak in Physical
Strength but Strong in Moral Courage, We Dare Battle for the Right,

Shoulder to Shoulder with our Fathers, Husbands, and Brothers!" "We
Scorn to Labor For Half Prices!" "May Revolution Never Cease While
Tyranny Exists!" "We Strike For Our Rights!" A banner carried by Ward
7 bore a poetic slogan:

> We could not live and pay our fare,
> When binding shoes at one cent a pair.

The women strikers were followed by male strikers, who marched in
the order of their wards, and then by delegations from the other shoe
towns. A female drummer accompanied the Marblehead delegation of
men and women strikers "and excited great enthusiasm." At the common, the procession broke up and the women moved to the Lyceum
Hall, where a collation had been prepared by sympathetic citizens.

Despite the stormy weather, the whole vicinity of the common had
been densely packed with people and carriages, and at least ten
thousand people witnessed the parade. "The demonstration appears to
have given the highest satisfaction, and is very properly regarded as a
great success," the Lynn *News* concluded.[59]

Ten days later, the women again paraded in Lynn, this time in the
sunshine. Delegations from Salem, Marblehead, Newburyport, and
other towns joined them, while the fire companies of Lynn, Marblehead,
and several other shoe towns marched along. Ten thousand strikers
paraded that day in a procession almost two miles long, and many
thousands more, including schoolchildren who had been dismissed for
the day, lined the way.

There were five processions in all, and each time the spirit of the
strikers remained firm. The employers tried to break the strike by
threatening the German and Irish workers that the state legislature
would deprive them of the vote. The German workers of Natick met and
unanimously resolved: "That neither the fear of losing our political influence nor the threats of our would-be masters will deter us from
adhering to the rules of the Natick strikers until the battle is fought and
victory won." The German shoebinders adopted a resolution supporting
the stand taken by their husbands and fathers and also resolved "to
uphold the cause of the battle of justice against oppression."[60] Although
most of the strikers were descendents of eighteenth-century rural and
village Yankees, the immigrant shoe workers identified with them and
the spirit of earlier American struggles for freedom.

In response to an appeal by the Lynn employers, State Attorney
General Phillips came to the shoe town and convinced the mayor to call
out the militia and the Boston police to quell minor disturbances. The
workers massed at the railroad station and greeted the Boston police
with jeers, hisses, and shouts. Eight thousand people were there, and the
women strikers carried banners reading, "Go Back Home," "You Are

Not Wanted Here," and "No Outside Police." The town officials who had called in the militia and police were later voted out of office.[61]

Community support for the strikers was widespread. Hungry men and women were fed at collations, and, over the objections of the employers, the Overseers of the Poor dispensed wood and coal to the strikers—"to those even who refuse to go to work when they could earn from $1.50 to $2.00 per day," wrote an indignant employer who was having no success in recruiting scabs.[62]

Nowhere was support for the strikers more in evidence than among the clergy. When a group of manufacturers informed Reverend Charles C. Shackford, pastor of the Second Congregational (Unitarian) Church, that they expected him to deliver a sermon criticizing the women strikers for defying St. Paul's injunction that women should be passive and silent, he told the group that he believed them to be in the wrong and urged them to accept the strikers' demands.* Father John Strain also refused to condemn the women strikers, and advised "every Catholic shoemaker not to lift a hammer while the Yankees were standing out for higher wages; and if any of the Yankees did not remain firm, to influence them, if possible, to be true to the objects of the strike." And Reverend Driver spoke out again and again for the strikers, telling his congregation: "You, my colored brethren, know how to sympathize with labor unrequited. The poor journeyman is the bird picked. He is now the cider juice in the press under the screw."[63]

The Lynn strike attracted nationwide attention, and meetings of support were held in New York and Philadelphia by sympathetic workingmen and workingwomen. Abraham Lincoln and Stephen Douglas, then competing for the presidency, commented on it. Douglas blamed the strike on the "irrepressible conflict" doctrine of William H. Seward, with its "inflammatory attack" on the rights of property in slaves. Lincoln, on the other hand, declared in his New Haven speech of March 6, 1860: "I am glad to see that a system of labor prevails in New England under which laborers can strike when they want to, where they are not obliged to labor whether you pay them or not. I like the system which lets a man quit, when he wants to, and wish it might prevail everywhere. One of the reasons why I am opposed to slavery is just here."[64]

But the strike was taking its toll of the strikers. On April 10, after thirty manufacturers had signed a written agreement advancing wages over 10 percent, more than a thousand workers—men and women— went back to work. The employers involved refused to recognize the unions that were organized during the strike, while other manufacturers

---

*St. Paul's exact words were: "Let your women keep silence in the churches: for it is not permitted unto them to speak; but they are commanded to be under obedience, as also saith the law. And if they will learn any thing, let them ask their husbands at home: for it is a shame for women to speak in the church" (1 Cor. 14:34–35).

refused either to recognize the unions or to sign written agreements. Some of the strikers held out for another week or two, but they finally returned to work without written agreements. After all the workers had gone back, they held a mass meeting at which they announced that their principal objective—a fair remuneration for their labor—had been achieved and that, having formed a permanent association for the protection of their interests during the strike, they would continue the struggle until the owners recognized their organization. And although they did not invite the binders or other women shoe workers into their association, they expressed gratitude to them for their faithfulness to the labor cause and announced their determination to work jointly with them and any organizations they might form.[65]

It was less than a decade later that the Knights of St. Crispin came into existence, and the shoebinders organized an auxiliary organization—the Daughters of St. Crispin—which was the first national union of women workers. Each Washington's Birthday, the Knights and Daughters of St. Crispin held picnics and parades to mark the anniversary of the great New England Shoemaker's Strike of 1860.[66]

So it was that the decade of the 1850s opened with the passing of the era of the militant factory women of the textile industry and closed with the beginning of a new era of militant factory women of the shoe industry.

6

Black Women before the Civil War

IN THE YEARS following the American Revolution, many Americans, including even some Southerners, believed that the Spirit of '76, combined with the economic stagnation in tobacco, rice, and indigo planting, would bring about the disappearance of slavery in the South. But in 1793 Eli Whitney invented the cotton gin, and with the rise of the factory system in textiles, there was such a steady increase in the demand for cotton that the planters began to remove the acreage from other crops and enter the cotton market. There was an equally steady growth in the appetite for slaves. By 1800 they were selling for twice the price of 1790. Not even the prohibition of Congress against the importation of slaves from Africa after 1807 could keep cotton from becoming king. With big money to be made from planting cotton with slave labor or from breeding slaves for sale to the planters, the plantation system spread westward and slavery became solidly rooted in fifteen Southern states. By 1860 these states contained four million slaves.

The vast majority of these slaves consisted of field hands. Most of them worked on small, family-operated farms, although many worked on large plantations. The system impartially exploited both groups as unpaid workers, and with similar evenhandedness, it treated black slave women as savagely as black men. But slave women suffered an even worse exploitation. While they performed the same duties on farms and plantations as the men, upon them fell the added burden of childbearing and childrearing. Overseers and owners punished them as severely as men, without regard to pregnancy or motherhood. And the South took for granted the white man's right to exploit and abuse black slave women sexually.* It compelled black women to breed slave children for the

---

*There is increasing evidence, however, that white wives felt a good deal of jealousy and even occasional sympathy for the slave woman.

98

master's profits; at the same time, it held them and their daughters available whenever and for whatever purposes the master or overseer cared to use them. And if their daughters were beautiful, they could also be sold at fancy prices as concubines.[1]

The forced separation of parents and children at slave auctions was one of the cruelest features of slavery. The following, related by Josiah Henson, is only one of many examples:

> My brothers and sisters were bid off first, and one by one, while my mother, paralyzed with grief, held me by the hand. Her turn came and she was bought by Isaac Riley of Montgomery County. Then I was offered.... My mother, half distracted with the thought of parting forever from her children, pushed through the crowd while the bidding for me was going on, to the spot where Riley was standing. She fell at his feet, and clung to his knees, entreating him in tones that only a mother could command, to buy her baby as well as herself, and spare to her one, at least, of her little ones.... This man disengaged himself from her with ... violent blows and kicks.... I must have been between five and six years old.[2]

Black women who worked in their masters' homes as cooks, chambermaids, nursemaids, and seamstresses were better off than the field hands—they at least could count on table scraps to supplement their meager diet. And in 1860 more than five thousand slaves, most of them women, were engaged in nonagricultural work in Southern cotton and textile mills. One cotton mill in Alabama employed one hundred slaves, three-fourths of whom were women. Similar mills existed in Georgia, North Carolina, Mississippi, and Florida. Slave women also worked in turpentine camps, in sugar refineries, in food and tobacco processing, in rice mills, in foundries and saltworks, and in mines (where they pulled trams), and as lumberjacks, ditch diggers, and even construction workers, laying track for Southern railroads.

The work week for slaves on farms and plantations was six days, from sunup to sundown, which in summer months could mean as many as sixteen hours a day. If orders were plentiful, they would work seven days a week. They lived in shanties and cooked over an open pit in the middle of the floor. There was practically no such thing as medical care for them. Pneumonia, typhus, tuberculosis, scarlet fever, diphtheria, dysentery, and other diseases were quite common. Here and there, owners would erect a clinic near the factory, but even when they did, it was invariably crowded and dirty, and the maternal and infant mortality rates were scandalously high.[3]

While both black men and women suffered under slavery, Eugene Genovese has pointed out that "the women field hands generally had a longer day than their men.... In addition to the usual work load, the women had to cook for their families, put the children to bed, and often spin, weave, and sew well into the night." Genovese quotes an ex-slave who recalled his mother returning exhausted from the field and having to cook for her husband and children. The son wrote, "Lots of times she's so tired she go to bed without eatin' nothin' herself." Fannie Moore of South Carolina told an interviewer: "My mammy she work in de field all day, and piece and quilt all night.... I never see how my mammy stand such hard work."[4]

In Southern cities, where women made up a majority of the slave population, slave women enjoyed greater freedom than those on the plantations and were able to establish contacts with free blacks more easily. City slaves could also escape more easily, but a slave woman, with her ties to her children, was less able to take advantage of this condition.[5]

Survival under slavery necessitated a certain amount of accommodation. Yet the fact is that for two centuries black slave men and women struggled by every conceivable means to gain their freedom. Rather than put up with brutal treatment, some black women killed their masters or overseers. They quickly learned that as blacks they did not have the same right to defend themselves as white women. This is illustrated by the case of Celia, a slave whose master repeatedly forced her to have sexual intercourse with him although she had been pregnant for some months and was ill. On the night of June 23, 1855, Celia warned her master that she was very ill and threatened to hurt him if he did not cease forcing her to have sex relations. When he ignored the warning and attacked her, Celia killed him.

During August, 1855, Celia was formally indicted for murder by a Callaway County (Missouri) grand jury. Her court-appointed attorneys cited a Missouri statute of 1845 that stated that "any attempt to compel any woman to be defiled by using force, menace or duress is a felony," and implied that any woman who defended herself in such a case, even to the extent of committing murder, would be judged innocent. The attorneys insisted that the words "any woman" embraced slaves as well as free white women and asked the jury to find Celia not guilty on this ground. The court, however, rejected this interpretation of the statute and instructed the jury to disregard the section cited because it did not cover slave women. Celia was found guilty of murder in the first degree.

When, two days later, the attorneys for the defendant filed a motion asking the court to set aside the verdict and grant the defendant a new trial, the motion was immediately overruled, sentence was pronounced, and Celia was ordered to be executed by hanging on November 16. The Supreme Court of Missouri denied Celia's subsequent appeal, but the execution was delayed until after the birth of her child. On December 13, 1855, the day after the child was born, Celia was taken from her prison to the gallows and hanged.[6]

Small wonder, then, that black women who killed their masters or overseers for violating them sometimes committed suicide. Others fled to nearby swamps and forests or tried to escape to the North and freedom.

Although attempts were numerous, slave escapes were rarely successful. Most runaway slaves returned voluntarily from their brief escape to the woods, usually driven by hunger, or else they were hunted down and returned to their masters. The absence of sheltered places of refuge, the vast distances to be covered, the slave's ignorance of geography, as well as his illiteracy, isolation, lack of knowledge, and high visibility, made successful escape difficult, to say the least. Yet, despite these obstacles, some slaves did succeed in escaping. They did so through tremendous courage and endurance, traveling at night over hundreds of miles of hostile territory, hiding in swamps and forests, as they made their way slowly to freedom.[7]

One of the most dramatic escapes was that of a young slave woman who had herself boxed up in Baltimore in the winter of 1857 and conveyed as freight to the depot, to be shipped to Philadelphia. William Still, a free Philadelphia black who was secretary of the city's Vigilance Committee and who compiled a remarkable record of assisting escapees, described what happened next: "Nearly all one night the box remained at the depot with the living agony in it, and after being turned upside down more than once, the next day about ten o'clock it reached Philadelphia." When the lid was pried off, the slave woman was discovered in the straw. After three days in bed, she told how she had survived the ordeal. "She had a pair of scissors with her, and in order to procure fresh air she had made a hole in the box, but it was very slight. How she ever managed to breathe and maintain her existence, being in the condition of becoming a mother, it was hard to comprehend." After she recovered, the Underground helped her settle in Canada.[8]

Perhaps the most ingenious escape was that of Ellen Craft, who, with her husband, William, devised a bold plot to achieve freedom. Ellen was fair enough to pass as white, and they decided to escape by having her act the part of the master while William posed as her servant. Ellen cut her hair short, wore clothing stolen from her master, and, to disguise her beardless face, muffled it in a shawl, pretending that she was suffering from severe toothache. They knew that they would have to register at hotels in the course of their travels, but neither could write—so they placed Ellen's hand in a sling. Anticipating queries, they concocted the story that William's young master was terribly ill, traveling North in search of medical care. To make the story even more plausible, Ellen wore dark glasses, limped slightly, walked slowly with a cane, and was said to be almost totally deaf. In this way, hotel clerks and strangers could be discouraged from prolonged conversation.[9]

The two started out from Macon, Georgia, on December 21, 1848, and arrived safely in Philadelphia on Christmas morning. Free blacks and white abolitionists afforded them shelter and taught them to read and write. Boston gave them a home, and Theodore Parker, the antislavery Unitarian minister, performed a legal marriage for them.

William Lloyd Garrison's antislavery weekly, the *Liberator,* celebrated the bold escape in its issue of January 12, 1849, and the story became known all over the North. The slave hunters then began a concerted search for the Crafts, and when Congress passed the new Fugitive Slave Law in 1850, the search was intensified. Agents representing the Macon owners appeared in Boston to begin legal proceedings. Protected by the Boston Vigilance Committee while arrangements for passage were being made, the Crafts finally departed for England. Lord Byron's widow helped to facilitate their education, and they raised a family in their new life of freedom. After the Civil War, the Crafts returned to Georgia, purchased a plantation, and established an industrial school for black children.[10]

A number of black women who escaped from slavery to the North spent a good deal of their time and much of their limited means seeking to locate and purchase the freedom of members of their family. This was a difficult undertaking. The system made the sale and resale of slaves an economic aspect of human bondage, and it not only separated members of the same family but frequently changed their locations. Escaped slaves found no detectives to hire to help them locate their parents or other relatives, nor did any records exist for them to examine, while whites, outside of the antislavery committees, could not be expected to offer much help. Many escaped slaves in the North also found it difficult to locate other members of their family who had run away to freedom, since the first thing a fugitive slave did upon reaching the North was change his or her name, and since fugitives of the same family often escaped to different states or cities. The anguish of a black mother seeking her son after both had escaped from slavery was revealed in a letter from Fredreick Douglass to a white antislavery Philadelphia woman, who had written to the black abolitionist for aid in finding her son:

> It will give me pleasure to serve you and your friend in bringing mother and son together so far as I am able. At present I am totally ignorant of the young man's whereabouts—but I have several acquaintances in different parts of the country from North Carolina of whom I will gladly make enquiries—and should any trace of him reach me, I will gladly inform you of the facts. It is, however, exceedingly difficult to find colored people from the South. They change their names—and conceal their origin for obvious reasons. I have been looking for a friend of mine from slavery this 10 years—and in a measure, know how to sympathize with your poor friend in search of her son.[11]

And when they did succeed in locating members of their family still in slavery, the escaped slaves had to begin a series of negotiations to try to purchase them. This usually involved a long correspondence with the slaveowner while the prospective purchaser was saving funds to meet the required price. Following a visit to Cincinnati in the 1830s, the white abolitionist Theodore Weld wrote:

There are scores of black women here who work day and night taking in washing or in domestic service so as to acquire the means to purchase relatives still in bondage. One paid $800 for her husband; another $400 for her mother; still another $500 for her daughter. It takes years of unceasing toil for such purchases to be consummated, but it is in this way, I learned, that mothers, daughters, fathers, husbands, and sons were reunited.[12]

One black woman, herself a fugitive from slavery, helped her aged parents and brothers gain their freedom, not by purchasing them but by returning to the South and bringing them out secretly. During a decade of such missions, she made nineteen forays into the South to lead many scores of fellow blacks from the bondage of slavery to freedom in the North. She was, of course, the legendary Harriet Tubman, the "Moses" of the Underground Railroad during the years before the Civil War.

After her own escape from slavery, Tubman determined to return to the South to rescue her aged parents, her brothers, friends, and any other slave who would follow her to freedom. She engaged a Northern assistant to write to a free black in Maryland who could read and write and who was willing to help slaves escape. The letter contained a code passage with a biblical reference: "Read my letter to the old folks," it went, "and tell my brothers to be always watching unto prayer, and when the good old ship of Zion comes along, to be ready to step aboard."

In all, Harriet Tubman rescued about three hundred slaves herself and inspired many others to escape. By 1856 there was a price of $40,000 on her head in the South. It was a source of great pride to her that she had "never lost a single passenger" on the Underground Railroad. She always carried a pistol, with which she spurred on fugitives who were about to give up, telling them, "You'll be free or die."[13]

Many free black women worked in the South, for even when the husband worked, his income was insufficient to support the family. Black women worked as cooks, laundresses, housekeepers, and peddlers. In general, they were confined to the menial, servile occupations. They could not join together to form trade unions, and they were excluded, as were black men, from any unions that did exist in the South.

Like the black man, the free black woman occupied a degraded social position in the South. She had to carry identification papers at all times to prove that she was not a runaway slave, for, except in Louisiana, color created the presumption that a black was a slave, and the burden of proof of freedom, by certificate of freedom or otherwise, rested on the blacks. At any time, a white person could demand proof of her status as a free black, and even if her papers were in order she was subjected to scorn and humiliation. She faced the constant danger that some unscrupulous white person might steal her registration certificate and sell her into slavery as a fugitive.

Her testimony was not admissible in courts of law in cases involving white persons. By 1835 black women had lost all rights to free assembly in most Southern states and were forced to obey curfews at night. The law prevented them from entertaining or visiting slaves, and if a free black woman was charged with violating a law or committing a crime, she was subject to trial anywhere in the South before the same kind of court that was provided for slaves. While her testimony was not acceptable in court against that of a white person, a slave could be used as a witness against her. Thus, she lived in constant fear of being enslaved for infractions of any of the multitude of regulations that dominated her life as a black, as well as of being kidnapped, deprived of her freedom papers, and sold as a slave.

In spite of the most rigorous efforts of the masters to keep their slaves in ignorance, the blacks very often managed to learn the fundamentals of education by clandestine methods. Susie King Taylor described her own underground education received from another black woman while she was a slave: "We went every day about nine o'clock with our books wrapped in paper to prevent the police or white persons from seeing them. We went in, one at a time, through the gate into the yard to the L kitchen, which was the schoolroom. . . . After school we left the house the same way we entered, one by one."[14]

Before the 1840s and 1850s, black male workers in many Northern cities had monopolized the occupations of longshoremen, hod carriers, whitewashers, coachmen, stablemen, porters, bootblacks, barbers, and waiters in hotels and restaurants. This was changed radically by a huge influx of white immigrants, particularly after the Irish famine in 1846. The unskilled Irish, in particular, pushed the blacks out of these occupations, depriving many black males of employment. In November, 1851, the *African Repository* noted that in New York (as well as in other Eastern cities), it was no longer possible to see the black "work upon buildings, and rarely is he allowed to drive a cart of public conveyance. White men will not work with him."[15]

Black male workers found that not only did whites refuse to work with them, but employers, fearing retaliation, would not hire them. No wonder Carter G. Woodson and Lorenzo B. Greene concluded in their study of blacks as wage earners that "without a doubt many a Negro family would have been reduced to utter destitution had it not been for the labor of the mother as a washerwoman." It was the black washerwoman in most Northern cities who supported her family on a bare minimum subsistence while her husband sought in vain for any kind of work.[16] Black abolitionist physician James McCune Smith described "The Washerwoman" in a series of sketches of black New Yorkers at work:

Saturday night! *Dunk!* goes the smoothing-iron, then a swift gliding sound as it passes smoothly over starched bosom and collar of one of many dozen shirts that hang round the room on chairs, lines and every other thing capable of being hanged on. *Dunk! Dunk!* and that small and delicately formed hand and wrist swell up with knotted muscle and bursting veins!

The apartment is small, hot as an oven, the air in it thick and misty with the steam rising from the ironing-table. In the corners, under the tables, and in all out-of-the-way places are stowed tubs of various sizes, some empty, some full of clothes soaking for next week's labor. . . . *Dunk! Dunk!* goes the smoothing iron. The washerwoman bends again to her task. Her mind is far away in the South, with her sisters and their children who toil as hard but without any pay! And she fancies the smiles which will gladden their faces when receiving the things she sent them in a box by the last Georgetown packet. *Dunk! Dunk! Dunk! Dunk!!!* goes the iron, this time right swift and cheerily. Oh Freedom! Her tired muscles forget all weariness. The iron flies as a weaver's shuttle, shirts appear and disappear with rapidity and at a quarter to twelve, the groaning table is cleared, and the poor washerwoman sinks upon her knees in prayer for them, that they also may soon partake of that freedom which, however toilsome, is so sweet.[17]

Most black women in the North in eighteenth-century America did various types of domestic work. The Revolution, the abolition of slavery, the rise of the factory system—none of these had caused any significant change in their occupations. By mid-nineteenth century black women remained effectively locked into the same types of occupations. Of 4,429 black women workers in Philadelphia in 1848, 1,970 were washerwomen, 496 were seamstresses, and 786 were domestic workers. The rest were hairdressers, milliners, midwives, nurses, servants, cooks, and ragpickers. An 1859 survey found that more than eight out of every ten black workingwomen in Philadelphia labored as domestic servants. The 14 percent who worked as seamstresses accounted for nearly all the skilled workers among the black female force. There were no black women employed either in the cotton mills of Philadelphia or in any other factory in the community.[18]

The same situation existed in all Northern cities, and Sharon Harley notes the "conspicuous absence of black female workers in the newly formed factories, many of which employed more females than males. . . ."[19] No black women worked in the New England textile mills, and when black minister Reverend Thomas Driver told the women shoe strikers in 1860 that he had "always liked the looks of the Lynn girls," he knew that not a single black woman member of his congregation was then or had ever been among the female shoe workers.[20]

But being confined to servile jobs was only one of the many disabilities facing black workingwomen in the North. Everywhere they were segregated by law and custom and were subjected to constant discrimination. There were black pews in the churches, black seats in the courtrooms, black balconies in the theaters, and separate and inferior schools for black children. Blacks were forced to live in the worst neighborhoods and were excluded from many public omnibuses, most streetcars, and the cabins of steamers (although they were permitted to travel on the exposed deck). They were even buried in separate graveyards. Evidence of the American belief that "God himself separated the white from the black" was to be found everywhere—"in the hospitals where humans suffer, in the churches where they pray, in the prisons where they repent, in the cemeteries where they sleep the eternal sleep."[21]

The transportation problem was an especially serious one for the black workingwoman. Her exclusion from theaters and concert halls did not cause hardship, but how was she to get to work when blacks could not use the public transportation facilities? In 1859 streetcar lines operated by horses were introduced into Philadelphia. Of Philadelphia's nineteen streetcar and suburban railroad companies, eleven refused to admit blacks to the cars. The other eight reluctantly allowed them to ride but forced them to stand on the front platform with the driver, even when the car was half empty, and even though it might be raining or snowing. Quite often during a wintry blizzard, black washerwomen, even those in their seventies and eighties, found themselves forced to stand outside on the platform of a totally empty car. In many parts of Philadelphia, blacks seeking transportation had to walk or hire an expensive carriage—a situation that continued until 1867, when the state legislature compelled the companies to end segregation against blacks on the streetcars of Philadelphia.[22] A similar condition prevailed in New York, Cincinnati, Washington, D.C., and other cities.

Only a few trade unions permitted white workingwomen to join their ranks before the Civil War, but no unions permitted the black worker, skilled or unskilled, male or female, to be a member. In 1835 the *National Trades' Union,* official organ of the labor body bearing the same name, explained that blacks could not belong to unions of white workers because they were inherently inferior to whites and were actually tools of employers, hired in order to hinder the growth of unions and keep white workers oppressed. The National Industrial Congress did admit black delegates to its 1851 convention—the same convention that seated delegates from the Philadelphia Tailoresses' Industrial Union. The Mechanics' Assembly of Philadelphia raised no objection to the tailoresses' delegates, but it so resented the admission of blacks that it voted to sever all ties with the Industrial Congress.[23] For its part, the Tailoresses' Industrial Union, like all trade unions or cooperative associations of white women workers before the Civil War, recruited no black women into membership.

Confined by racism to the most menial of women's occupations and excluded, along with black men, from all trade unions, free black workingwomen could do little to improve their status. "How long shall the fair daughters of Africa be compelled to bury their minds and talents beneath a load of iron pots and kettles?" asked Maria Stewart, the first black woman to speak in public and probably the first to become publicly active in behalf of black workingwomen. Addressing the newly formed Afric-American Female Intelligence Society in Boston in 1832, she pointed out the need to provide opportunities for black women to find better employment than as washerwomen and domestics and urged them to unite and build a store of their own, selling the products of their work directly to the consumers.[24] But nothing came of this proposal. Twenty-two years later, when he drew up a plan for an American industrial school for blacks, to be established in Pennsylvania, Frederick Douglass emphasized the need to upgrade employment for black women. "A prominent principle of conduct will be to aid in providing for the female sex, methods and means of enjoying an independent and honorable livelihood." Unfortunately, the plan for an industrial school never materialized.[25]

All women in pre–Civil War America suffered discrimination, inferior rights, and indignities, and white workingwomen suffered economic exploitation as well. But black women suffered more discrimination than any other group in American society. White workingwomen were discriminated against as women and as low-paid workers. Free black workingwomen were discriminated against as blacks, as women, and as low-paid workers. The slave woman, of course, experienced complete degradation. Frederick Douglass put it masterfully on the eve of the Civil War:

> We hear much about the wrongs of married women, the wrongs of single women, and about the inadequate wages paid to women, and the deficient representation of women in public life—about the wrongs perpetrated against her in excluding her from the pursuit of the most lucrative branches of trade; we admit it all, and lament it all, and yet we may ask: what are these wrongs, how trifling, how as the small dust of the balance when compared with the stupendous and ghastly wrongs perpetrated upon the defenseless slave woman? Other women suffer certain wrongs, but the wrongs peculiar to woman out of slavery, great and terrible as they are, are endured as well by the slave woman, who has also to bear the ten thousand wrongs of slavery in addition to those common wrongs of woman. It is hard to be underpaid for labor faithfully performed; it is harder still not to be paid for labor at all. It is hard that woman should be limited in her opportunities for education; it is harder still to be deprived of all means of education. It is hard for the widow only to receive the third part of her deceased husband; it is harder still to be a chattel person to all intents and purposes. It is hard only to enjoy only a qualified right to one's children; but it is harder still for a woman to have no rights which white men are bound to respect.[26]

Most of these women survived the brutality of slavery while conducting a consistent struggle against the system, ranging from slave rebellions to sabotage and passive resistance. While this struggle did not at any time take the form of trade unionism, there are few pages in the story of America's workingwomen that are more important than the battles of black slave women against their bondage. They were to carry this tradition into the post–Civil War labor movement.

7

The Civil War

FOLLOWING THE CIVIL WAR, President Lincoln wrote of the part women had played in making the Union victory possible: "I have never studied the art of paying compliments to women; but I must say, that if all that has been said by orators and poets since the creation of the world were applied to the women of America, it would not do them justice for their conduct during this war."[1]

Lincoln included in his tribute the workingwomen who had filled the places left vacant by men who had departed for the battlefront, as well as all others who had played an increasingly important role in the production of goods during the war years. Because of the shortage of male workers and the wartime industrial expansion, over 100,000 new jobs had been available for women in factories, sewing rooms, and arsenals. Women accounted for a substantial proportion of national production in the 1860s; in St. Louis as many as one in three wage workers were women. There were 270,897 females employed in manufacturing in 1860, and 358,950 in 1870.[2]

An increasing number of women were making their way into new trades and occupations. In 1862 General Francis Elias Spinner, treasurer of the United States, advised the incumbent Secretary of the Treasury, Salmon P. Chase: "A woman can use scissors better than a man, and she will do it cheaper. I want to employ women to cut Treasury notes." Chase agreed that if female labor was as competent as male, *and considerably cheaper,* Spinner's plan made a good deal of sense. Spinner thereupon hired a few young women as "temporary clerks." In 1864 Congress appropriated money specifically for the salaries of these women. But the appropriation set a maximum of $600 a year for female clerks, while male clerks earned from $1,200 to $1,800 a year.[3]

Private employers drew the appropriate conclusions and began to hire women in print shops, telegraph offices, department stores, and light manufacturing. The introduction of the cigar mold, which eliminated the need for both skill and strength in twisting and breaking filler leaves, "opened the way for the women cigarmakers to leap, between 1860 and 1870, from 731 to 21,409 (eight times the number of men in the trade)."[4]

"Woman's field of labor in this part of the country has been very greatly enlarged during the past eight or ten years," the *New York Times* reported early in 1869, "and it is annually extending to embrace occupations, trades and professions heretofore considered as closed to them." The paper went on to note that the extension began with the war and was accelerated by the fact that in both New England and the middle states, women between the ages of fifteen and thirty so outnumbered men of the same age group that there were some 250,000 "young women who must support themselves and who cannot reasonably look forward to any matrimonial alliance which will relieve them of this inevitable necessity."[5]

There was one point that all surveys of the Civil War era emphasized: "Women are wanted—in fact are preferred to the men—at the wages they receive." Women in both government and private employment during the war years were paid no more than 50 percent of the wages men received for the same work, and it was predicted that, if the trend continued, men's wages would be brought down to the level of women's by the end of the war.[6]

This prospect compelled the labor movement to take greater interest in women workers and to pay more attention to the improvement of their conditions. This did not come about automatically. When the trade unions began to revive from the shattering impact of the Panic of 1857, the secession crisis, and the calls for war volunteers, and began to rebuild their membership, their first reaction to the increase in the female work force was the traditional one.[7] "We will resist," said the secretary of the Journeymen Tailors' Association of St. Louis, "any attempt to introduce female apprentices by encouraging them to leave service and other employments more congenial to girls than mixing with men in a workshop from morning to night."[8] The labor press, whose rise both accompanied and advanced the revival of the trade unions, at first supported this traditional attitude. *Fincher's Trades' Review* of Philadelphia, the leading labor weekly of the Civil War era, agreed with the prediction that the employment of women in the trades at half the pay men received would soon result in depressing the wages of workingmen. The male workers currently in the armed forces, it argued, "will esteem it a poor reward for all their sacrifice, to find (when the war is over) every avenue choked by their wives and daughters at half paying prices."[9]

It soon became clear to trade unionists and labor editors alike that this attitude was misguided. The wives and daughters (and widows) of the workers in the armed forces were being compelled by soaring prices to enter any available avenue of work just to stay alive. It was fruitless to lecture these women to the effect that their proper role was that of homemaker. If wages in the trades were not to sink to the level of women's wages, as predicted, it was necessary for the men to bring the women into trade unions and raise their wage standards. The *Boston Daily Evening Voice,* the only daily labor paper of the period, editorialized:

> Women, and working women especially, know nothing of getting up and organizing unions, and much as they may feel the need of protective organizations, they do not know how to begin the work. If it were but well begun for them, it is not to be doubted that they would zealously sustain them. We would respectfully urge upon the men who are active in the labor movement to devote the necessary time to assisting working women in this important activity. Apart from the justice of our appeal on humanitarian grounds, there is a selfish motive involved, since if the women are helped to organize and raise their wages, the menace of low wage competition may well diminish.

However, the paper went on to emphasize, this competition would not disappear totally "until the wages of men and women doing the same work are made equal, and the barbarous idea that sex not work should determine the reward of labor is completely eliminated." The *Voice* concluded by observing that in asking male trade unionists to aid the workingwoman "we do not imply her inferiority"; rather, the paper was simply acknowledging the fact that "society has doomed her to an inferior position, and insufficiently equipped her with the knowledge and experience to take the initial steps to defend herself from exploitation."[10]

Fincher's Trades' Review admitted that its initial suggestion for solving the problem of competition by workingwomen was unrealistic and endorsed the *Voice's* call for men trade unionists to help workingwomen organize and for equal pay for equal work.

The labor weekly began a campaign to convince men that "a more just compensation of female labor" was the surest road to the maintenance of wage levels. At the same time, it appealed to workingwomen:

> There is but one road to travel—but one way to seek redress. The workingwomen must follow in the wake of the workingmen. Let each trade organize, distinct from all others, from which delegates can be sent to a General Trades' Assembly, where *all* can be represented in a recognized head, and from which can emanate a call for wages for women equal to that of men, for the establishment of the principle that the labor should be rewarded equally regardless of sex.

The *Review* assured the workingwomen that the workingmen would help them in this endeavor, "for no person claiming to be a *man* would shrink from any duty assigned him in such a cause."[11]

During the Civil War, both the *Boston Daily Evening Voice* and

Fincher's Trades' Review made equal wages for men and women an issue.
(They were occasionally joined by the St. Louis *Daily Press*.)[12] The *Voice*
and the *Review* published and endorsed the speeches on this issue by
Anna E. Dickinson, the noted antislavery orator. In "Woman's Work and
Wages," Dickinson, speaking as "a woman and a worker" (she was a
teacher), began by condemning the "vulgar prejudice" against "work
and workers," reminding her audience: "Work is the everlasting, enduring granite upon which rests the world." This prejudice against work
created the view "that the proper place for a woman was the home," and
therefore her work was never valued as equal to that of men. In words
that did not endear her to feminists, she declared, "I grant that the
sweetest and noblest bliss that a woman can feel in the world is that which
is enjoyed by the married woman and mother, and when those who carp
at women's working for a living will provide the lonely and unemployed
with husbands, I will stop talking upon the matter, and not till then."
The low wages paid to women, she noted, were often justified on the
grounds that a woman had only herself to support, in contrast to a man,
who presumably supported a family. But in a number of industries—
textiles, for example—few families could enjoy a subsistence income
unless every member worked. In that case, why should not the wife
receive the same wages as the husband for doing the same work? It was
simply not true that the "great reason" for giving men more than women
was that "men had somebody else dependent on them":

> Here stands a man with no one but himself to support, and he is paid
> $1600 a year; and here is one, with a wife and two children, and he is paid
> $1600 a year; and there is one with cousins, and uncles and aunts, and a
> countless number of children, and he is paid $1600 a year; and here stands a
> woman, with father and mother, and perhaps a husband to support, and she
> is paid $750 a year. The case simply stands thus: he is paid $1600 because he
> is a man, and she $750 because she is a woman.

She then proceeded to relate her own experience when seeking employment. She had applied to a country school for a teaching post and
was told that "$26 is what we have paid when a man kept the school, but
in the case of a woman we only pay $16."* She refused the job: "Not one
cent would I lower the price, for the principle of it. I afterwards suffered
for employment, and for weeks walked the streets in vain search of work,
but I would not undervalue my work—would not do work at a reduced
price because I was a woman."
Dickinson called upon all women teachers to take a similar stand and

---

*This was an important reason for the feminization of teaching. By the time of the Civil
War, women made up two-thirds of the teaching force of the country. The "Yankee
schoolmarm" guided the common school of the North, receiving a good deal less than the
man she replaced. (*Report of the U.S. Commission of Education* [Washington, D.C., 1868], pp.
649–50.)

urged them also to do what they could to make sure that the education children received emphasized that "woman should have an equal chance with man": "[Do] not teach the boy that industry and ambition is honorable, and teach the girl that work is a disgrace. Take the impediments out of her way and give her the same pay for the same work; and then, if she fall by the wayside, let her fall."[13]

Fincher's Trades' Review featured Dickinson's speech in its column "The Workingwomen" and called upon all male trade unionists to study it and endorse her call for equal wages, since "the cause of labor is the same with both sexes as it is in all countries and for all time."[14] The *Boston Daily Evening Voice* not only featured the speech on its front page, calling it "an unanswerable argument for woman's equality with man in the employment of life," but also urged teachers to follow the example Dickinson had set:

> The greatest recommendation that we ever heard of Miss Anna Dickinson is that she refused to do a man's work as teacher for less than a man's pay. We would to God that the noble women of this old Commonwealth would all come to a similar resolution. There ought to be a general strike among female teachers. Go to Texas, Colorado, Oregon, take up land, raise cattle, dig gold, cultivate the earth; you can do it as well as men if you only determine to learn to shoot; give up the softness that makes you slaves to the injustice of men; die rather than let others grow rich from robbing you, and the end will be that justice will be awarded to your deserts.

"The real remedy," the *Voice* prescribed, "will be found in union—a matrimonial one with teachers of the other sex, or a protective one among female teachers by themselves."[15]

Serious as the problem of the female teachers was, it was the plight of the sewing women that demanded the most immediate attention. Their wages were so low that many were actually starving. Girls engaged in sewing umbrellas in New York earned $3 a week by working from 6 A.M. to midnight. Tasselmakers, who made $6 a week in 1853, made about $4 in 1863 by working from 6:30 A.M. to 10 P.M. In March, 1864, sewing girls who made underwear earned about 17 cents for a twelve-hour day, while girls who made cotton shirts received 24 cents for a similar day's work. And from these wages the employers deducted the cost of needles and thread. Meanwhile, the price of spools, like all prices during the war years, had risen—from 4 to 10 cents.

The sewing women were further victimized by the contract system, under which the government paid a contractor a certain price per dozen for sewed garments. The contractor's profit obviously depended on what he paid to have the garments made. Thus, what he took from the starving sewing women went into his pocket. Then, too, as David Montgomery points out, hundreds of thousands of seamstresses, umbrella sewers, mantuamakers, and milliners in the cities suffered competition "from the weekly wagonloads of needlework put out by contractors to the wives and daughters of neighboring farmers." They suffered, too, from the competition of the sewing machine. At the outbreak of hostilities, 38,000 Singer and Wheeler sewing machines were in factory use, but by the end of the war, the number had risen to 63,000. The shirt that had taken fourteen hours to make by hand now took one hour by machine.[16]

No wonder the plight of the sewing women seemed so hopeless. In October, 1863, the umbrella sewers of New York City and Brooklyn formed a union and struck for an extra 2 cents for each umbrella cover sewn. Many employers gave in, but others held out, and the organization was too weak to bring the strike to a successful conclusion. The following month the New York women shirtmakers also went on strike for an increase, but despite their militancy, their struggle was also unsuccessful.[17]

In reporting these strikes, *Fincher's Trades' Review* expressed admiration for the sewing women's spirit but pointed to the failures as proof of its argument that workingwomen needed the assistance of the more experienced male unionists.[18] The argument hit home, and late in November, 1863, a mass meeting of workingwomen held in New York City received the cooperation of many workingmen's unions in the city, with several men sharing the platform with the women. Most of these unions later voiced their approval of the resolution adopted by the meeting, which recommended that "an organization be commenced for the purpose of uniting the working women of the City of New York in a movement for increasing the prices now paid them for labor."[19] The same unions also voted to give financial assistance to the organizing drive.

The Working Women's Union of New York City was modeled after the Workingmen's Union, and (with the women's consent) Daniel Walford of the latter organization was assigned to serve as temporary president to help the women's union get off the ground. "The Work Goes Bravely On," *Fincher's Trades' Review* headed the news of the first activity of the new women's union—its formation of the Sewing Women's Protective and Benevolent Union. The SWPBU combined benevolent features with trade union principles. Fifty cents was charged for an initiation fee and 25 cents a month for dues. In case of sickness or unemployment, the member received $3 a week. But the organization's chief purpose was to enable women "to obtain fair remuneration for their labor." "We have organized," declared Ellen Patterson, recording secretary, "to improve our social conditions as far as possible and in no case to allow employers to reduce our wages, and, lastly, as soon as we have the numbers and the funds, to have an advance of wages and shorter hours." After nine months of existence, the sewing women's organization reported that it had "many members and considerable money in hand."

The funds had been accumulated through initiation fees, dues, picnics, and "other means . . . appropriate to woman's sphere."[20]

In its issue of September 17, 1864, *Fincher's Trades' Review* carried the text of a petition sent by the Working Women's Union to Secretary of War Stanton, pointing out that the price of "women's labor had been reduced more than thirty percent since the breaking out of the rebellion" and asking him to authorize the quartermaster general to increase the price of female labor "until it shall approximate the price of living." It also asked that the government so modify the contract system "as to make it obligatory upon all contractors to pay Government prices," ending the practice under which thousands of women whose husbands, fathers, and brothers "have fallen on the battlefield, are making army shirts at six cents apiece." "We do not ask charity," the petition concluded; "we come to you as American women, many of whom have sacrificed the dearest treasures of their hearts on the altar of freedom."

Nothing came of this moving document, but the Working Women's Union was not discouraged. On January 17, 1865, it held a spirited mass meeting in New York City. A number of male trade unionists, including a delegate from Britain, addressed the meeting, pledging their organizations' support. William Harding, president of the New York Trades' Assembly, assured the workingwomen that the city's central labor body was ready to aid them, asking in return only that they convince their gentlemen friends who did not belong to a trade union to join. "If they do not join," he said, "then have nothing to do with them, and tell them you do not wish to associate with any gentleman who refuses to aid in a movement calculated to benefit his fellow-man."

Eighteen new members were admitted to the Working Women's Union at this meeting. As they were being sworn in, the members formed a ring around them, singing:

> "Welcome sisters, to our number,
>   Welcome to our heart and hand;
> At our post we will not slumber,
>   Strong in union we shall stand."

Miss M. Trimble, the union's president, then addressed the new members, saying in part: "This chain which you now behold is a bond of that union that should always exist among working women. Remember that union is power; a good many can help one when one cannot help the many. Behold, the chain is now broken that you may be added as another link." Both new and old members closed the meeting by singing:

> "No angry passions here should mar
>   Our peace, or move our social band,
> For friendship is our beacon star,
>   Our motto, union, hand in hand."[21]

Harding's pledge that the Trades' Assembly would assist the workingwomen was fulfilled. Financial contributions were made to the Working Women's Union, and Harding himself visited the Journeymen Tailors' Union and discussed the importance of opening its membership to women in the trade. In June, 1865, the union passed the following resolution: "*Resolved,* That each and every member will make every effort necessary to induce the female operatives of the trade to join this association, inasmuch as thereby the best protection is secured for themselves as well as for the female operatives."[22]

On the heels of the developments in New York, the Working Women's Relief Association of Philadelphia was formed to organize dressmakers, milliners, arsenal workers, clothing workers, and women employed in stores and manufacturing of all kinds. The association issued an address to the public setting forth in detail the injustices done to women in every area of labor, based on the information contained in the replies to a questionnaire sent to workingwomen, and calling for support for these oppressed workers. It presented a petition to the Secretary of War asking that prices for government work be advanced until they would approximate the cost of living, and that many more women be given their work directly from the government "without being swindled by contractors." The petition met with partial success; the Superintendent of the Arsenal informed the association that from one thousand to two thousand more women would thereafter receive work directly from the government, and that an advance of 20 percent in prices paid for work would go into effect immediately.[23]

On January 24, 1865, a delegation of Philadelphia workingwomen employed in the arsenal, members of the Working Women's Association, met with President Lincoln and presented him with a list of grievances. Lincoln called the quartermaster general and, in the presence of the delegation, told him: "I shall consider myself personally obliged if you can hereafter manage the supplies of contract work for the Government made up by women so as to give them remunerative wages for their labor."[24]

Fincher's Trades' Review hailed the "grateful news" from Washington and advised other women engaged in government work to call their plight to the President's attention.[25] A month later, under the heading "Wrongs of Sewing Women," it published the news that "the sewing women of Cincinnati have addressed the following memorial to President Lincoln":

To His Excellency, Abraham Lincoln, President of the United States:
The undersigned wives, widows, sisters and friends of the soldiers in the army of the United States, depending upon our own labor for bread, sympathizing with the Government of the United States, and loyal to it, beg leave

to call the attention of the Government, through his Excellency the President, to the following statement of facts:

1. We are willing and anxious to do the work required by the Government for clothing and equipping the armies of the United States, at the prices paid by the Government.

2. We are unable to sustain life for the price offered by contractors, who fatten on their contracts by grinding immense profits out of the labor of their operatives. As an example, the contractors are paid one dollar and seventy-five cents per dozen for making gray woolen shirts, and they require us to make them for one dollar per dozen. This is a sample of the justice meted out to us, the willing laborers, without whom the armies could not be promptly clothed and equipped.

We most respectfully request that the Government, through the proper officers of the Quartermaster's Department, issue the work required directly to us, we giving ample security for the prompt and faithful execution of the work and return of the same at the time required, and in good order.

We are in no way actuated by a spirit of faction, but desirous of aiding the best government on earth, and at the same time securing justice to the humble laborer.

The manufacture of pants, blouses, coats, drawers, tents, tarpaulins, &c., exhibits the same irregularity and injustice to the operative. Under the system of direct employment of the operative by the Government, we had no difficulty, and the Government, we think, was served equally well.

We hope that the Government, in whose justice we have all confidence, will at once hear us and heed our humble prayer, and we will ever pray, &c.[26]

Sewing women set up unions and/or cooperative workshops in Baltimore; Boston, Woburn, and Worcester (Massachusetts); Troy and Buffalo (New York); Detroit; and Chicago. In all cases, these were "protective associations" established with the assistance—and sometimes even at the initiative—of union men, who helped the women draw up resolutions of protest and gave financial support to the associations that emerged. In the case of the Buffalo union, the male unionists joined the women's picket lines when several sewing women were discharged for belonging to the union.[27]

One of the most interesting of the sewing women's unions was organized in Detroit, on the heels of a meeting held on November 21, 1864, and was described as "the largest public meeting of workingmen and women that ever occurred in Detroit." The speaker was Richard F. Trevellick, president of the Detroit Trades' Assembly and shortly to become president of the International Union of Ship Carpenters & Caulkers. A considerable portion of his address was devoted to the plight of workingwomen. So vivid was his description of their sufferings that the *Detroit Tribune* reported that "the audience were frequently moved to tears."

Tears were not enough, Trevellick insisted. The answer was for the workingwomen to follow the pattern set by the male workers of Detroit and for the men to assist them in this activity:

> One year ago, the laboring men of this city received $1 per day—now they get $2. Why was this? Because they had been taught the benefits of union. They had banded together for protection, and by stoutly maintaining their rights, had succeeded in gaining their point. Does anyone suppose they could have done this without union? Not a bit of it.

Workingwomen would never gain their point unless they did the same.[28]

Early in 1865 the Sewing Women's Protective Association of Detroit was organized and announced a scale of prices by which all employers would have to abide or face retaliation. Trevellick described how the "retaliation" operated:

> All the trades unite for this purpose, and when a case of oppression of sewing women is made known a committee from the Trades' Assembly calls upon the offender and demands redress. If the demand is not complied with every trade is notified, and the members all cease trading at the obnoxious establishment. Sentinels are placed around notifying people of the facts, and in every case the offender is brought to terms.[29]

The association also established a cooperative workroom, so that the fruits of the women's labor would go to them "instead of going into the capacious pocket of the capitalist." The Detroit Trades' Assembly paid the rent for the hall and donated eight sewing machines. The *Boston Daily Evening Voice* was so enthusiastic over this venture that it pleaded: "Let such unions be formed among sewing women everywhere. They are sure to succeed if they are in real earnest as spunky women know how to be."[30]

Already the leading labor spokesman for black-white labor unity, the *Voice* added the hope that black sewing women would be invited to join these unions.[31] Its plea, however, fell on deaf ears. None of the workingwomen's unions of the Civil War years made any effort to recruit black women, even though they were the most exploited of the women who worked. Not only did they receive even less pay than the starvation wages meted out to white workingwomen, but they also faced greater risk of discharge and frequently the danger of personal violence from resentful white coworkers.

Early in 1863 bloody riots broke out between black and Irish workers in Cincinnati, Detroit, Brooklyn, New York, and other cities. Several black workingwomen were attacked and beaten severely. In July of that year, riots against the draft in New York City, Newark, Troy, Hartford (Indiana), and elsewhere were converted into violence against blacks. Everywhere, blacks were attacked and even murdered, and their homes were sacked and burned. Many were driven out of their jobs, in a number of cases despite years of service, and many employers, fearing mob attacks, simply refused to employ black workers at all.[32] In September, 1863, William J. Watkins, a black lawyer, wrote in the *Christian Recorder*, the official organ of the African Methodist Episcopal Church: "Since the commencement of the rebellion, the spirit of caste has become tenfold more virulent and powerful than before. Colored men and women are being driven out of vocation after vocation. The determination of the white man is to starve us out."[33]

Fincher's Trades' Review condemned the draft riots but insisted that those involved represented only a small part of the working class. This was small comfort to the blacks who were unable to find work and were even afraid to walk on the streets lest they be lynched. The *Review* did nothing to rally support for these innocent men and women of the working class. For that matter, while it devoted considerable space to the plight of workingwomen, it never once referred to the problems facing black workingwomen. Even though the *Review* waxed indignant over the protest of middle-class Philadelphia women against having to ride on the streetcars with workers, whose clothes gave off "an offensive odor," it never expressed any criticism of the fact that black workers could not even ride on most streetcars of the city—no matter how they were dressed.[34] Obviously, to the labor press and the trade unions of the Civil War era—including those favored by white workingwomen—blacks were either not part of the working class or, if they were, had no rights.

At the same time that efforts were being made to organize white workingwomen into unions, another type of women's organization was coming into being. It owed its existence to a suggestion from a New York workingman to Moses S. Beach, editor of the New York *Sun,* that he investigate the bondage of the starving seamstresses of his own city. During the last two months of 1863, Beach turned the columns of his newspaper over to workingwomen, who proceeded to pour out their tales of woe. "A great many of us work girls are perishing with cold this winter," wrote one of them.

> The majority of sewing girls in large establishments are working in garrets in high buildings, without a particle of artificial heat. Some of us are obliged to come from a long distance, from Brooklyn, Jersey City, and uptown in this city, in cold rain storms, and are obliged to sit down in wet clothes, with feet and fingers benumbed with cold. In many cases, our dresses are frozen stiff before night which is very injurious to our health, and in reality a number die early by consumption, through heavy colds engendered in these establishments.

Other women complained of low rates of pay, brutal treatment by foremen, fraudulent apprenticeships, and, most important, nonpayment of wages.[35]

Moved by these stories, Beach called upon the workingwomen of

New York to attend a meeting at the Military Hall. A survey of the hoop-skirt makers, shirt sewers, vestmakers, sewing machine operators, press feeders, silver burnishers, photographers, and umbrella sewers who crowded into the hall revealed that the average wage was between $2 and $3 a week. A committee of workingwomen was appointed to consult with a committee of men to devise means of securing relief.[36]

The committee's report led, early in 1864, to the formation of the Working Women's Protective Union to examine the petitions of seamstresses and domestic workers and to take action in cases of "remediable grievances"—that is, clear cases of fraud, such as nonpayment for work done and the practice of deducting a considerable portion of wages for so-called imperfect work.[37] The Protective Union made efforts to train women in many new occupations to prevent overcrowding in some trades and to teach seamstresses who worked by hand to run a sewing machine, work for which the pay was higher, but it placed special emphasis on its success in providing legal protection for workingwomen. Largely as a result of the union's activity, a law was passed providing for the imprisonment of employers guilty of failure to pay wages to workingwomen. (The law did not end the abuse entirely because employers could get around the penalty by transferring their businesses to their wives or other women.) Those who made deductions from wages for supposedly imperfect work were threatened with prosecution, and by 1870, this threat alone was enough to force the employers to pay wages in full. In 1880 the Protective Union's treasurer reported that the organization had settled 27,292 disputes since 1867, and that fully twenty thousand of them had been settled out of court. A total of $24,647.49 had been recovered, with the average recovery amounting to $3.38. No woman was ever charged for these legal services. The Protective Union also provided occupational training and found jobs for several thousand women.[38]

The labor press praised Beach, and other philanthropists who supported the Protective Union, among them Judge Charles P. Daly, Mr. and Mrs. William E. Dodge, and Mrs. Russell Sage. The Union was criticized, however, for making no attempt to deal with the workingwoman's major problems, other than outright fraud. The *Boston Daily Evening Voice,* after praising the Protective Union for establishing, with donations from middle-class citizens, a library of about four thousand volumes to which every workingwoman in New York had access at a nominal charge, went on: "Very well: and an excellent preparation for the next step, which shall establish and maintain the prices the women should receive for their work and the number of hours they will consent to be employed. Till they do this they will have but little time and not much money to patronize their library.[39]

Neither in New York nor in other cities where they were established

(Chicago, Detroit, and St. Louis) did the protective unions encourage women to join trade unions. Since they relied mainly on sympathy to obtain what was "due to the otherwise defenseless ... working women," they could not accomplish much in the way of securing better wages and shorter hours, even for those women who were placed in occupations.* Yet it cannot be said that the trade unions of workingwomen established during the war years accomplished very much in that direction either. In the summer of 1867, the New York *Sun* ran a series of articles on the workingwoman in New York, which painted a very depressing picture. Despite the Protective Union and the trade unions for workingwomen there were still some fifty thousand young women working from Monday morning to Saturday night for no more than $5 a week. These female laborers were trying to avoid a life of vice while struggling with abject poverty. In New York it was a losing battle, since board could not be obtained for less than $3 a week, and conditions drove many of them to the "solution" of prostitution.[40]

The Working Women's Protective Unions remained in existence until the 1880s, but the workingwomen's trade unions of the war years either vanished before the war's end or were barely able to keep their heads above water.[41] Having stimulated the formation of these unions, *Fincher's Trades' Review* and the *Boston Daily Evening Voice* sought an explanation for this development and came up with what might be called the theory of "Spasmodic Sympathy for Working Women." According to this analysis, stable, lasting unions, which were difficult to establish and maintain in any case, were especially so for workingwomen, most of whose occupations were terribly overcrowded. Only when organized men assisted them could they make gains; indeed, they had won improvements in New York, Philadelphia, and Detroit when such assistance was forthcoming. But the employers, even when compelled to make these concessions, relied on the fact that the male unionists' sympathy for workingwomen would be merely temporary and transitory. The employers were confident that they would soon retrieve what they had been forced to grant and that the workingwomen, powerless once more, would "again relapse into the servitude of unrequited labor."

Nevertheless, the labor papers felt that the experience of the war years was not wasted, for a foundation had been laid for the cooperation of workingmen and workingwomen for their mutual advantage. They voiced the hope that in the postwar years, the labor movement would succeed in building a more permanent structure on this foundation.[42]

---

*In one instance the New York Protective Union did cooperate with a women's trade union. That was in the fall of 1864, when it endorsed the petition of the Working Women's Union of New York to Secretary of War Stanton and requested the press to publish it or publicize the fact that women "are making army shirts at six cents a piece." (*Fincher's Trades' Review*, Sept. 17, 1864.)

8

The National Labor Union

IN THE WINTER of 1864–1865, as victory for the Union forces seemed imminent, the demand arose that workingwomen should make way for the returning soldiers by quitting the jobs they had filled during the war years, replacing men who had left for the front, and should prepare, instead, to marry. It was claimed that the men returning from the front would provide a stabler labor force than women who were working only temporarily and would sooner or later leave to marry and raise families. A group of workingwomen in Ohio, faced with the threat of loss of their jobs, met the argument head on. "Whom are we to marry when so many have died in the cruel war?" they asked in a letter to the *Boston Daily Evening Voice*. "And what about those of us who gave our husbands to die for the country?"

> To hear some very proper persons discourse upon woman's sphere and influence, one would imagine that all women are blessed with comfortable homes, having nothing to do but cultivate amiability and gladden the hearts of those to whom they are bound by the ties of relationship.
>
> Many are shocked that we should insist on trying to keep our occupations, and charge us with masculinity. Perhaps it would be more feminine to fold our hands and starve in graceful indolence; or pass through life an object of charity.[1]

Unfortunately, logic had little effect. When the war ended, in April, 1865, the veterans of the Union Army became the army of the unemployed. Immediately, female clerks in Washington began to be discharged, and private employers, faced with a sudden cessation of war contracts, followed the pattern set by the government. With so many unemployed men looking for work at any wages, the advantage of cheaper female labor disappeared, at least for the time being.[2]

The *Boston Daily Evening Voice* pleaded in vain that since "so few avenues are open to women," they should be retained wherever they could work as efficiently as men: "We believe the welfare of the country depends as much, to say the least, upon the elevation of woman as upon the elevation of workingmen." Nor was it only the nation's welfare that was at stake, but its morality as well. For what alternative was there for so many women, suddenly thrown into the ranks of the unemployed, except "total moral ruin"?[3] But the only response to this plea was the accumulation of daily reports of "increasing numbers of unemployed females."[4]

Except for the *Boston Daily Evening Voice,* not a single labor journal spoke out against the indiscriminate discharge of workingwomen to make room for returning war veterans. Indeed, it seemed that most men and most trade unions still regarded women workers as nothing more than irritants who threatened to drive down wages by taking jobs at substandard rates when they should have remained at home, and who were now aggravating the difficulties created by postwar unemployment. Apart from a local here and there, virtually every trade union still refused to admit them to membership.

Nevertheless, the immediate postwar years did bring some startling changes. Workingwomen did not just wait for men to approve of their presence or assist them but organized themselves. Even ballet dancers in New York City met in November, 1865, "to discuss the feasibility of a strike," and resolved to demand a raise in their pay from $5 to $9 a week. When they were turned down, they struck until they won their demand.[5] One group of workingwomen in particular won the admiration and respect of male unionists by their militancy and effective organization. They were the laundresses of Troy, New York, who contributed the next important woman labor leader after Sarah G. Bagley to American labor history—Kate Mullaney.

Laundry work had long been one of the lowest-paying occupations for women. In 1829 a Philadelphia laundress was reported to be receiving $10 for washing eight dozen articles of clothing a week, less the cost of soap, starch, fuel to heat the water, and replacement of buttons. In the 1850s, steam laundries made their appearance in the hotels of New York, and as machinery began to take over the work of individual washerwomen, laundresses' rates fell still lower.[6]

Troy, New York, where the detachable collar was invented and introduced in the 1820s, rapidly became the center for the manufacture of collars and cuffs for men's shirts and of shirts and ladies' blouses that carried detachable collars. But washing, starching, and ironing the collars and cuffs were as important as making them, and several hundred Troy women were engaged in the processes involved: washing with soap; bleaching with chloride of soda; adding dilute of sulfuric acid to further bleach the collars; and again washing in suds; boiling; rubbing and rinsing; bluing and rolling; starching (with thin starch to be followed by a thick starch); drying; and finally ironing.[7] An 1865 description of

Troy told of the laundresses whose daily work required them "to stand over the washtub and over the ironing table with furnaces on either side, the thermometer averaging 100 degrees, for wages averaging $2.00 and $3.00 a week." This they did for twelve to fourteen hours a day![8]

One of these Troy women was Kate Mullaney, and some time during the summer of 1865, she brought together about two hundred of the laundresses to form the Troy Collar Laundry Union. The immediate issue that sparked the meeting was the introduction of starching machines, which were scalding hot to handle and which cut prices for starching almost in half.[9]

Not far from where the laundresses met secretly were the offices of the local unions of the Iron Molders' International Union and the Sons of Vulcan (skilled iron puddlers). Both organizations had become defunct early in the war but had been revitalized, had grown steadily, and had won agreements that satisfied their members' demand for higher wages. "Why not follow this example?" the fiery Kate Mullaney asked her sisters. The laundresses responded. By the beginning of 1866, the union had succeeded in increasing their wages to $8 to $14 a week, although their workday remained twelve to fourteen hours long. By this time the laundresses had gained a reputation among male unionists as "the only *bona fide* female union in the country." Respect for the Troy laundresses mounted when the labor press in April, 1866, carried the story that the female union had contributed $1,000 to the striking molders of their city. The Troy Trades' Assembly showed its respect by inviting the union to affiliate, and even added a whole section of books relating to women to its Labor Free Library and Reading Room.[10]

Laundresses made labor history in 1866 in still another way. The Jackson (Miss.) *Daily Clarion* of June 24, 1866, carried on its front page the text of a startling "Petition of the Colored Washerwomen" to the mayor, informing him that "the subject of raising the wages" had been considered at a meeting on June 18 and the following resolution unanimously adopted:

> That on and after the foregoing date, we join in charging a uniform rate for our labor, that rate being an advance over the original price by the month or day the statement of said price to be made public by printing the same, and anyone belonging to the class of washerwomen, violating this, shall be liable to a fine *regulated by the class.* . . .
>   The prices charged are:
> $1.50 per day for washing
> $15.00 per month for family washing
> $10.00 per month for single individuals

The petition is historic; it represents the first known collective action of free black workingwomen in American history, as well as the first labor organization of black workers in Mississippi. The editor of the *Daily Clarion,* hardly able to believe his eyes, responded to the black washerwomen that he regarded "the agitation as ill-timed, unfortunate and calculated to injure instead of better their condition." He assured the white community that it need not believe black women of Jackson capable of such audacity:

> We believe it originated with one or two Northern adventurers who have come here to fill their pockets at the expense of the ignorant negro, under the pretense of philanthropy and benevolence. Whether one of the said adventurers presided at the conclave of the washerwomen, we are not advised, but he acted as their amanuensis, and it is said the petition comes up in his writing.[11]

The editor was soon to see evidence that the tradition of organizing to reduce their grievances, begun by the black washerwomen of his city, would be picked up by black workingwomen throughout the country.

In 1866 there was another first in the history of workingwomen: for the first time a national labor federation pledged support to all workingwomen.

It will be recalled that in 1836, the National Trades' Union, the first national labor federation, had denounced the employment of women outside the home. In 1864 an attempt was made to establish a national labor federation—the International Assembly of North America—but it failed. At the founding convention in Louisville, however, the trade unionists expressed support for workingwomen, but only for women sewers, and even then it was on the ground of labor's moral responsibility to "the poor, the helpless and the oppressed of the weaker sex."[12] While this was a definite advance from the attitude of 1836, it was still a very short step. Two years later a new effort at forming a national labor federation was more successful, and the position on women workers was far more advanced. To be sure, of the seventy-seven delegates representing thirteen states and the District of Columbia who met in Baltimore on August 20, 1866, to create the National Labor Union, none was a woman or represented an organization with a large female membership. But the women workers did have their champions among the men present in Baltimore—such as Richard F. Trevellick of Detroit and Andrew C. Cameron of Chicago. William H. Sylvis, cofounder of the National Labor Union and the foremost labor leader of the era, was their leading advocate.

Sylvis, though lacking formal education, had risen to the position of president of the Iron Molders' International Union in 1863 and had transformed the union into the largest and most effective trade union of the period. During his frequent organizing tours throughout the country (on the meagerest financial resources), Sylvis obtained a firsthand picture of the sufferings of workingwomen as well as a healthy respect for their contributions to the labor movement, wherever they were permitted to make them. He attended the great picnic of the Troy Trades' Assembly to raise money for their library and reading room, and in a letter to *Fincher's Trades' Review* he emphasized that it was the working-women who had made its success possible. He hoped thereby to convince the "old fogies" in other cities to begin making common cause with workingwomen.[13]

Like most other male trade unionists of the period, Sylvis believed that while it was the duty of organized labor to protect female workers, women did not basically belong in the labor force and should return to "the domestic circle." If women had to leave their exalted position as wives and mothers, he believed, it should be for the trades that were traditionally women's occupations, where they would not compete with men. This was his chief motivation in behalf of the sewing women.

But Sylvis learned from the class struggle, in which he believed devoutly, and his opinions changed. Although he never completely gave up the belief that the presence of women in the labor market was a violation of the natural social order of things, he saw only too clearly that the number of workingwomen had increased greatly during the Civil War and that even though many had been discharged at the war's end, they were in industrial life to stay. If the wage standards of the mechanics were to be defended, all women workers, and not just the sewing women, had to be organized into unions and their wage standards equalized with those of the men.

Sylvis went even beyond this approach to the understanding that none of labor's broader objectives could be achieved without the cooperation of workingwomen. He had come to the conclusion that trade unions by themselves could not solve the problems of the workers under capitalism. The inability of the Iron Molders' Union to preserve its gains in the face of postwar depression and unemployment led Sylvis to search for new ways to solve the problems of workers. He began to emphasize the need to broaden the constituency of the labor movement to include both blacks and women, to establish international labor solidarity, to encourage independent political action by labor, and to form producers' cooperatives in order to replace the existing wage system with a more equitable social order. To achieve these goals, the cooperation of the workingwoman was essential, especially if she gained the right to vote: "How can we hope to reach the social elevation for which we all aim without making women the companion of our advancement?"[14]

Under Sylvis' influence, the National Labor Union adopted a progressive approach toward women workers. The 1866 convention pledged "individual and undivided support to the sewing women, factory operatives, and daughters of toil," and made it clear that in so doing, it was not acting solely out of sympathy with the workingwomen but also in the self-interest of the male workers. An *Address of the National Labor Congress to the Workingmen of the United States* tackled the issue of "Female Labor." It conceded that "prejudices" existed against the employment of women, but insisted that the position of the laboring classes on the issue had been "grossly misrepresented." It was natural that male workers had objected to the introduction of female labor "when used as a means to depreciate the value of their own." The employers' action, under the pretext of "disinterested 'philanthropy,'" was intended not so much to elevate woman as to achieve "the degradation of man," by bringing "the labor of one . . . into competition with another." Declaring boldly that the time had come for a clear statement of labor's stand on the issue, the *Address* went on:

> We claim that if they are capable to fill the positions now occupied by the stronger sex—and in many instances they are eminently qualified to do so—they are entitled to be treated as their equals, and receive the same compensation for such services. That they do not is *prima facie* evidence that their employment is entirely a question of self-interest, from which all other considerations are excluded. Why should the seamstress or female factory operative receive one-third or one-half the amount demanded by and paid to men for the performance of the same work? Yet that such is the case, is a fact too well established to require corroboration.
>
> We trust, therefore, that the workingmen of America will protest against this iniquitous system, and lend their powerful influence to effect a reform, and in no manner can they do so more thoroughly than by aiding in the formation of those labor associations in which experience has demonstrated their own safety lies.[15]

Implementation of the address was left to the various trade unions. Only one union responded—the Cigar Makers' International Union. The CMIU was organized in 1864 with a constitution that prohibited both women and blacks from membership. Meanwhile, as we have noted, the large-scale introduction of molds for the forming of cigars (formerly the most important aspect of skill involved in cigarmaking) brought large numbers of women into the trade. At first the male cigarmakers reacted to this threat in fairly typical fashion: in 1866 they debated whether or not they should allow women to work in union shops, with the majority arguing that they should be eliminated from the industry and sent back home where they belonged.[16] But in 1867, in response to the twin pressure of competition from female labor and the action taken by the National Labor Union, the cigarmakers amended their constitution. A third factor may well have been the fear of independent organizing by women. During the war the Lady Segar Makers in Providence had unionized, and in September, 1864, they voted to boycott a nonunion employer.[17] The possibility that similar unions of women might be established outside the control of the Cigar Makers' International Union may have helped convince recalcitrant members that they ought to change their union's constitution. Whatever may have motivated the action, the fact is that the CMIU was the first national union to admit women to membership, and it went the whole way by permitting blacks to join as well. It is not clear whether the women and blacks were to be organized into separate locals or integrated with the existing membership. Nonetheless, the action taken by the Cigar Makers International Union in 1867 was a pioneer step in the organization of both women and blacks.[18]

The National Labor Union's 1866 pledge to workingwomen may have made little impact on the male unionists of the country, aside from the cigarmakers, but it did pave the way for an alliance between the labor and women's rights movements. Although this alliance was of brief duration, it had important repercussions on both participants.

The women in the alliance were feminists led by Elizabeth Cady Stanton and Susan B. Anthony. In the immediate postwar atmosphere, Stanton and Anthony, along with other woman suffragists, expected that they would be rewarded for their wartime patriotism and for having suspended their suffrage demands for the duration by being included in the expansion of the franchise, along with ex-slaves. They envisaged the emergence of the movements for black suffrage and women suffrage as a united front coalescing in a single demand for universal adult suffrage. A movement did arise to achieve this goal. In May, 1866, the American Equal Rights Association was organized with the aim of securing the suffrage for black men and all women. Frederick Douglass was chosen as one of the three vice-presidents, and both Stanton and Anthony were active in its leadership. The association launched a campaign to petition Congress, then in the process of molding the Fourteenth Amendment, to include suffrage of women and black men.

But it soon became clear—at least to male abolitionists, black and white, to most black women, and to some white feminists—that it would be impossible for both women and black men to gain the ballot at this stage. Radical Republicans were engaged in a difficult struggle with President Johnson and his allies, prominent among whom were the former slaveowners, for a meaningful freedom for the ex-slaves. They became convinced that to advocate woman suffrage would not only further complicate their already difficult task but would also guarantee defeat of their effort to enfranchise the freedmen. They were able to convince a number of feminists, Lucy Stone among them, that suffrage for the black men should take priority, and that the struggle for woman suffrage should be delayed until the former was obtained, after which a campaign for the right of all women to vote could get under way.[19]

But Stanton and Anthony and the women they influenced refused to go along. Instead, they broke with their former allies in the abolitionist camp and launched an independent movement, hoping to gain new support for their efforts to achieve the immediate enfranchisement of women. Whether or not they acted in the best interests of their own cause by breaking with the abolitionists is a matter of some disagreement among historians,[20] but there is no disputing the fact that the split in the feminist movement led Stanton and Anthony to look elsewhere for allies. This search for support had two direct consequences. One was the beginning of feminist attention to the cause of the woman worker in an effort to create a mass base of working-class feminism. The other was their search for coalition with the labor movement, through the National Labor Union, by means of which the feminists could more readily come into contact with workingwomen and, at the same time, create a new political party to support the woman suffrage cause. The fact that this could only be done through the defeat of the Republican Party, and with it the Radical Republican program of Reconstruction, was a matter of no concern to the Stanton-Anthony group. Even further, they were prepared to ally themselves with the bitterest racist enemies of black suffrage, if necessary. to accomplish their aims. Included among these was an eccentric railroad promoter and financier, George Francis Train, a well-known white racist, who now became a champion of woman suffrage. To Train, this latest cause was a convenient weapon to be used against the specter of black domination, which, in his terms, would reduce American society to the level set by "ignorant negroes."[21]

None of this troubled Stanton and Anthony. On the contrary, when Train offered them financial backing for a newspaper to be called *The Revolution,* through which they could build a new constituency for woman suffrage, they eagerly accepted. As early as November, 1866, Anthony had said that the "working women of the country are with us. Say to them that with the ballot in their hands, they can secure equal pay for their work, and the demand for the ballot will be as strong as that of the black man today."[22] With the split developing in the suffrage movement, the workingwomen became even more important to Anthony, and she looked to the new publication as a means of transforming her rhetoric into action.

The first issue of the *Revolution* came off the press on January 8, 1868, and ten thousand copies of the sixteen-page weekly were sent throughout the country under the frank of James Brooks, the proslavery, Copperhead Democratic Congressman from New York. The magazine announced that it was devoted to principle, not policy: to suffrage, irrespective of color or sex; to equal pay for equal work; the eight-hour day; the abolition of party despotism; currency reform; unrestricted immigration; and the regeneration of American society. Its slogan was "Down with politicians, up with people." On the day the *Revolution* made its publishing debut, Train left for England, where he was arrested and imprisoned for pro-Irish activities. Thereafter, the paper depended almost entirely on the resources of Anthony and Stanton, particularly the former. Having read themselves out of the abolitionist-feminist coalition, they were unable to obtain any assistance from that quarter. But by advocating an eight-hour day and equal pay for equal work, and by calling attention to women's substandard wages and supporting unions and strikes, they were able to gain the support of the labor press and of a number of the leaders of the National Labor Union—especially Sylvis, Cameron, and Trevellick.[23]

The NLU leaders were impressed by the argument, emphasized in every issue of the *Revolution,* that without the ballot workingwomen would never be able to resolve the two major disadvantages from which they suffered: inequality of wages with men and inability to enter the trades and professions. Not only would the vote serve to dignify both woman and her labor, but it would enable her to back up her economic struggles with political action—to battle with both hands and not with one tied behind her back. The editors of the *Revolution* argued that both men and women workers suffered from the oppression of capital and that both were defrauded of their "just dues." But in the struggle to redress their grievances, workingwomen were victims of a disability not shared by their fellow sufferers: lack of access to the ballot box.[24] To Sylvis, Cameron, and Trevellick, who were already envisioning an independent labor party, the *Revolution's* editors pointed out that "all their efforts of self-extraction and elevation" would be for naught if they did not include workingwomen in their plans.[25]

The NLU leaders were also impressed by the attention paid to their organization by the *Revolution.* At the time the paper was launched, the NLU was foundering, partly because of an economic recession during 1867 and 1868. With the elevation of Sylvis to the NLU presidency and the return of prosperity in mid-1868, the federation began to flourish. An indefatigable organizer, Sylvis spread the NLU's message throughout the country, and the *Revolution* reported his progress with delight, noting that he had "visited nearly all the cities, towns, and villages in the United States, attended hundreds of meetings, public and private, and made the acquaintance of many hundred thousand workingmen." Sylvis was portrayed as the prototype of the new labor leader—a man who combined remarkable organizing talent with a broad vision of the labor movement as the vanguard for all the oppressed. The *Revolution* analyzed and then endorsed every one of the NLU planks: the eight-hour day, land reform, opposition to monopolies, producer and consumer cooperatives, currency reform, and support of trade unionism. "The principles of the National Labor Union are our principles," the editors proclaimed. "We see on the surface of this great movement the portent of bright days and hear a voice that shall be heard by all the

people's servants in Washington, and by the selfish, hard-hearted op-
pressors everywhere." It hailed the commencement of "the contest between labor and capital," and confidently predicted that the NLU would
lead the entire working class, women included, in the impending struggle.[26]

The unsuccessful attempts of the *Revolution*'s editors to win support
for woman suffrage from the Republican Party leadership served to
further cement their ties with the NLU leaders, who were themselves
turning against the Republican Party, which they identified as the political party of the class responsible for the oppression of the urban industrial workers. In Sylvis' words, the new "money" power made no
distinctions—sexual, racial, or any other—in exploiting its victims: "The
working people of our nation, white and black, male and female, are
now sinking to a condition of serfdom." To defeat this money power and
end its control over the national government required the defeat of its
political tool and agent, the Republican Party.[27] As Ellen Carol Dubois
points out: "Stanton and Anthony criticized the Republican Party on
different grounds but they shared with labor a rejection of its claim to be
'the party of progress.'"[28] Hence their readiness to support and campaign for the Democratic Party, the party of the former slaveowners, if it
would incorporate their demands into its platform.[29]

But both the *Revolution* editors and the NLU leaders were unsuccessful in their efforts to get the 1868 Democratic convention to adopt their
respective positions—for woman suffrage, in the case of Stanton and
Anthony, and, in the case of the NLU spokesmen, for the eight-hour
day, a greenback currency system, the granting of public lands to actual
settlers rather than to corporations, and the speedy and noninflationary
payment of the national debt. While the platforms of both petitioners
met the same fate, for the women suffragists it had not been a wasted
effort. During the Democratic convention, they met with leaders of the
National Labor Union and arranged for Sylvis and other spokesmen to
contribute articles to the *Revolution* on the need for a labor-centered third
party.[30] For its part, the *Workingman's Advocate*, official organ of the NLU,
carried a series of articles in September, 1868, by "Mrs. M. Wynkoop,"
urging "the wives of workingmen" to concern themselves with extra-
domestic activities. The articles included tributes to the "woman's rights
women" and their "noble mission." They urged workingmen's wives to
apply the same devotion to the cause of labor reform as the "woman's
rights women" had given to the suffrage:

> You, wives of the working men, have a great work before you. If you will be
> persuaded to do it earnestly and well, our millionaires on the one hand, with
> their vast hoarded treasures, that have been wrung out of the flesh and
> nerves of the masses; and our wearied men and women on the other, with
> worn out bodies and broken spirits, who are ready to lay down their burden

of life, almost as soon as they have taken it up, will be only in the history of the past.*[31]

The *Revolution* began publishing its call a month before the 1868 NLU convention met, inviting unions and all organizations that worked for the "amelioration of the condition of those who labor for a living" to attend.[32] Susan B. Anthony was determined to have women represented, and she succeeded. When the congress convened, the only women who requested delegate status were those whom Anthony had brought with her: Mary Kellogg Putnam, Mary McDonald, Elizabeth Cady Stanton, and Anthony herself. Anthony came with credentials from the Working Women's Association #1, an organization she had formed in the offices of the *Revolution* just a week before the congress "for the purpose of doing everything possible to elevate women and raise the value of their labor." Its membership consisted of the women typesetters and clerks employed by the *Revolution,* together with Stanton, Anthony, and Mary McDonald. However, Stanton came to the NLU representing not the Working Women's Association but the Woman Suffrage Association of America, another organization that was put together for the convention. Mary Kellogg Putnam, daughter of Edward Kellogg, the monetary reformer, came as a representative of Workingwomen's Association #2, which Anthony also set up. Mary McDonald represented the Women's Protective Labor Union Association of Mt. Vernon, New York, likewise organized just before the congress.† Thus outfitted with hastily prepared credentials, the "Sentimental Reformers" (as David Montgomery calls them) descended upon the NLU Congress in New York City on September 21, 1868.[33]

The Committee on Credentials seated Anthony, Putnam, and McDonald without protest, despite the fact that none of them was really a workingwoman. However, when Stanton presented credentials from the Woman Suffrage Association, the committee decided to refer the matter to the entire assembly on the ground that it was not a labor organization. During the discussion, those who opposed the seating of Stanton, mainly delegates from the building trades, argued on this ground. They also made it clear, however, that their real target was the

---

*With the advice of Eugene V. Debs to "get the railroaders' wives interested in the Brotherhood," Ida Husted Harper wrote a monthly column from 1883 to 1894 ("The Woman's Department") in the *Locomotive Firemen's Magazine,* official organ of the Brotherhood of Locomotive Firemen, which Debs edited. Ray Ginger, *The Bending Cross: A Biography of Eugene V. Debs* (New Brunswick, N.J., 1949), p. 31; Nancy Barker Jones, "A Forgotten Feminist: The Early Writings of Ida Husted Harper, 1878–1894," *Indiana Magazine of History,* 73(1977): 79–101.

†"Despite its title," Ellen Carol Dubois notes, "the Mt. Vernon Association was made up of property-owning women who demanded the right to vote on the basis of their role as taxpayers." ("A New Life: The Development of an American Woman Suffrage Movement, 1860–1869" [Ph.D. dissertation, Northwestern University, 1975], p. 203.)

issue of woman suffrage. Sylvis argued for seating Stanton, hastening to add that doing so would not constitute an endorsement of women's suffrage. He paid tribute to her as "one of the boldest writers of her age . . . [who] has done more than anybody I know to elevate her class and my class, too, and God knows they need elevation." Anthony spoke in Stanton's defense, directing her argument to those who opposed woman suffrage: "She considered that the improvement of the condition of woman was only to be accomplished through the means of giving them the ballot. Hence the Woman Suffrage Association of America, more than any other, had for its object the amelioration and elevation of the women who work for a living."

Many trade unionists were persuaded by her speech, and when the question was put, Stanton was seated by a vote of forty-five to eighteen. The next day, however, eighteen delegates representing the building trades threatened to leave the convention if her delegate status was allowed to stand. To prevent a split in the NLU, the congress engineered a compromise. It refused to rescind Stanton's credentials, but passed a resolution asserting that in admitting her as a delegate, the NLU "does not regard itself endorsing her particular ideas, or committing itself to the position of Female Suffrage." Still another defeat was suffered by the suffragists when the delegates rejected a recommendation of the Committee on Female Labor, headed by Anthony, that their resolution should include the phrase "secure the ballot."[34]

Yet the remainder of the report by the Committee on Female Labor was truly historic. It urged the extension of eight-hour demands to women workers, equal pay for equal work, and trade unions for working women. It also encouraged women "to learn trades, engage in business, join our labor unions, or form protective unions of their own, and use every other honorable means to persuade or force employers to do justice to women by paying them equal wages for equal work."[35]

When the report (without any reference to the ballot) was adopted by the congress, the National Labor Union became the first labor federation in world history to vote for equal pay for equal work. Indeed, to Karl Marx, this stand made the NLU one of the most significant organizations in the world labor movement. Thus, he wrote to a friend in America:

> Great progress was evident in the last Congress of the National Labor Union in that among other things it treated working women with complete equality—while in this respect the English, and the still more gallant French, are burdened with a spirit of narrow-mindedness. Anybody knows, if he knows anything about history, that great social changes are impossible without the feminine ferment. Social progress can be measured exactly by the social progress of the fair sex.[36]

In many ways, as Marx pointed out, the women had been treated "with complete equality." They had been granted delegate status at a national labor assembly, and only in the case of one had there even been a dispute over the credentials; the women had participated in every phase of the congress. Nor had they limited themselves to feminist issues—they had spoken at length on resolutions relating to strikes, currency reform, and political action. Anthony and Putnam had been appointed to the resolutions committee, and the subject of workingwomen had been frequently discussed. In his keynote address, President Whaley had spoken at length about the problems of workingwomen and about the necessity of raising their wages so that the general wage level could be uplifted. He called for equal pay for equal work and for trade union encouragement and assistance to women's labor organizations. Vice-President Jessup, himself from New York, reported favorably on Anthony's recent efforts to organize workingwomen in New York City and said that the workingwomen's associations she had formed had a "good prospect of success." The convention had mandated a committee to report on female labor, appointed Anthony its chairperson, and included Jessup among its members, as an indication of the importance it placed on the issue. Finally, the convention commended Kate Mullaney, president of the Collar Laundry Union of Troy, for her "indefatigable efforts" on behalf of female laborers, and appointed her special assistant secretary to correspond with workingwomen and coordinate national efforts to form workingwomen's associations.*[37]

The convention also moved toward the creation of an independent, labor-based political party and adopted a platform for the party that included a pledge of "undivided support for sewing women and daughters of toil in this land." Anthony had strongly supported the formation of an independent labor party because, she argued, Democrats and Republicans alike were in the hands of finance capital. She predicted "that they will never propose or bring about any measure for workingmen of real permanent benefit."[38] Despite the convention's coolness on the issue of women's suffrage, Stanton and Anthony were convinced that with Sylvis and most of the NLU's other leaders actively supporting independent political action by labor, they would soon endorse suffrage for women in order to strengthen the ranks of the new labor party.[39]

Most of the women who attended the convention were deeply impressed. In their minds, the very seating of women delegates marked "a new era in Workingmen's conventions," while the appointment of Mullaney to organize workingwomen proved that "the recognition of woman

*Kate Mullaney was also elected second vice-president of the NLU, but the action had to be annulled because the first vice-president came from the same state. It is not clear if she attended the convention, since she is not listed among those given delegate status.

[was] to be future policy of the National Labor Congress." Evaluating the convention for the *Revolution*, Stanton wrote that the men of labor "have inaugurated the grandest movement of the century." And now it was clear that workingwomen were to be part of that movement![40]

It was not so clear whether black workingwomen would be included. At no point in the discussions on workingwomen was there a single reference to black women. However, the delegates had elected Sylvis president, and in his letters to the *Working Man's Advocate* while on an organizing tour for the NLU, Sylvis told of black workers, mostly men but some women, too, organizing unions in Baltimore, Mobile, Charleston, Savannah, and Philadelphia and engaging in militant strikes. He warned those unions that declared strikes in protest against the employment of black workers that their "fanatical bigotry" jeopardized the future of the labor movement, for it was "impossible to degrade one group of workers without degrading all." Besides, he pointed out, labor must realize that the black man now had the suffrage in the South, would soon gain it in the North, and would even hold the balance of political power in the nation: "If we can succeed in convincing these people to make common cause with us ... we will have a power ... that will shake Wall Street out of its boots." It did not require much imagination, he declared, to picture the consequences for the American working class if women were enfranchised in addition to black men, and if they joined in the crusade against Wall Street. Such a development, Sylvis insisted, was now overdue. "Why," he asked, "should women not enjoy every social and political privilege enjoyed by men? The time, I hope, is not far when universal suffrage and universal liberty will be the rule over the world."[41]

In December, 1868, Sylvis and the Executive Committee of the NLU met in Washington, D.C., and, in a precedent-shattering action, extended a formal invitation to all persons interested in the labor movement, regardless of color or sex, to attend the annual convention in Philadelphia the following August.[42] The national labor federation, which had already seated four women as delegates in 1868, was to mark a new era by seating nine blacks in 1869. None of the black delegates was a woman, and the nine black male trade unionists voted unanimously with the majority of the delegates to prevent the seating of a white woman delegate—Susan B. Anthony.

The issue came to a head when Anthony's credentials as a delegate from the Working Women's Association were challenged by John Walsh of Local #6 of the National Typographical Union, on the familiar ground that the association was not a *"bona fide* labor organization," plus the new charge that Anthony had "striven to procure places for girls from which men had been discharged"—in other words, had acted as a recruiter of strikebreakers. He supported his charges with details of

Anthony's activities during a printers' strike, and with a letter from Augusta Lewis detailing her unfortunate experiences in the Working Women's Association. (Both events are discussed in the next chapter.) The dispute came to the floor, where Anthony, permitted the right to respond to the charges against her because she had been a delegate to the 1868 congress, admitted the charge relating to the printers' strike and justified her action by the statement that this was the only way women could get experience in the trade: "The result was that some forty or fifty girls served with Gray and Green* and others, during a few months while the strike was in progress."[43]

Anthony's chief champion was Austin Puett, an Indiana attorney, and he did her cause more harm than good by dismissing with contempt the trade unionists' anger over strikebreaking. He proclaimed his faith in the universal equality of rights and his hope that everyone would "enter upon the grand platform of competition, and I do not care whether he is a 'rat' or a mouse." This was too much for Delegate Walsh to stand, and he declared angrily that Puett had not only demonstrated a total ignorance of trade union principles but "convinced me that he is not a workingman or he would know what a 'rat' is." Walsh also favored "Equal rights for all," he said, but not for "a rat or a renegade." He then went on to voice a typically sexist sentiment that had nothing to do with the issues at hand. "The lady goes in for taking women away from the wash tub," he cried, "and in the name of heaven, who is going there if they don't? I believe in a woman's doing her work, men marrying them, and supporting them."[44]

In her final defense before the convention, Anthony raised the feminist argument. She insisted that the real reason her seating was opposed was that women did not have the right to vote. If women had the franchise, they would be respected, admitted to the trades, and treated with equality. "All women in this country are under the power of men," she concluded. "We ask for a change, we ask for a change."[45]

It took three days for the delegates to reach a decision—a clear indication that there was no simple issue involved in the conflict over Anthony's credentials. Actually, the first vote was fifty-five to fifty-two in favor of her admission. Anthony concluded that these "55 men felt they were voting for Woman Suffrage."[46] This was an exaggeration; the fifty-five men were voting to keep the alliance between the National Labor Union and the woman reformers from breaking apart.

In the end it took a threat by the printers to withdraw to bring about Anthony's exclusion. A day after the first vote, the Typographical Union said bluntly that it would pull out of the congress if Anthony's credentials were accepted. Andrew Cameron tried to work out an acceptable

*Gray and Green was the job printing firm that printed the *Revolution*.

compromise but failed, and the second and final vote was sixty-three to twenty-eight to reject Anthony's credentials and eject her from the convention.[47]

A number of the delegates told the press that Sylvis, who had died less than a month before the convention, might have been able to find an amicable solution. The *American Workman,* a Boston labor paper, agreed. Sylvis, it maintained, would have had the issue fought out in the New York Typographical Union and not at the NLU convention. It was also convinced that "it was a narrow spirit which sought to entrap her in the meshes of technical quibbling, or hold her amenable in open convention to the rigid rulings of local trade-unions."

Sylvis may have been free of such a "narrow spirit," it went on, but unfortunately many male unionists were not. Some still believed women to be inferior to men and mentally and temperamentally unfit to vote. Others believed that suffrage was only incidental, and that in advocating equal pay for equal work, the NLU had "acknowledged all the correlative rights of women, including property and suffrage." Still others maintained that it would take too long to secure female suffrage and insisted that "our business is with those who are already voters." The *American Workman* concluded, "He must be a short-sighted person who cannot see that labor reform needs the support of the women of the country, irrespective of their views upon the matter of the ballot."[48]

The editor of the Boston labor paper was also troubled by the fact that "the colored delegates, whose cause she [Anthony] has so long advanced, were as a unit against her admission—a fact which I cannot understand."[49] The editor obviously did not know that Anthony had cut her ties with blacks several years before the NLU convention and had increasingly antagonized them by her willingness to ally herself with any group, no matter how racist, so long as it would give lip service to woman suffrage. These relations degenerated still further when she increasingly criticized the granting of the ballot to the "brutish and ignorant Negro man" and argued that woman suffrage would serve as a bulwark against "Negro rule" in the South.[50]

It should be noted that not all women were excluded from the 1869 NLU convention. Martha Wilbridge, from the Excelsior League of Massachusetts, was admitted and placed at the head of one of the important committees. Even a devoted friend of Anthony's praised the convention for having declared itself in favor of the principle that women deserve to be dealt with "as worthy of recognition on terms of the fullest equality."[51]

Several female delegates, including a white—Mary A. S. Carey—were admitted to the founding convention of the Colored National Labor Union, which opened in Washington, D.C., on December 6, 1869. However, the delegation from Newport to the Rhode Island State Labor Convention, which chose delegates for Washington, included a woman only after a letter of complaint was received from "A Colored Woman of Newport." She said she "was much disappointed in that all your deliberations, speeches and resolutions, which were excellent so far as the men are concerned, the poor woman's interests were not mentioned, or referred to." She then asked a pertinent question:

> . . . are we to be left out? we who have suffered all the evils of which you justly complain? Are our daughters to be denied the privilege of honestly earning a livelihood, by being excluded from the milliner, dressmaker, tailor, or dry goods store, in fact every calling that an intelligent, respectable, industrious female may strive to obtain, and this merely because her skin is dusky? These privileges are all denied colored females of Newport. However well they may be fitted for other positions, they are compelled to accept the meanest drudgeries or starve. . . .
>
> Therefore the colored women of Newport would ask your meeting and Convention that is to assemble next Monday to remember us in your deliberations so that when you mount the chariot of equality, in industrial and mechanical pursuits, we may at least be permitted to cling to the wheels.

Chastened by this deserved rebuke, Newport's black workers set up a committee, which nominated "a lady to represent the city of Newport in the coming State Convention."[52]

On the second day of the Colored National Labor Union's convention, a tax of $2 was proposed to be levied on each delegate to cover expenses. When Mrs. Colby, delegate from the District of Columbia, asked "if the ladies were to be included in the persons taxed," she was told that "there was no distinction to be made on account of race, sex, or color." However, since it was felt that female delegates might not be able to afford so steep a tax, the tax for all delegates was reduced to $1, and the principle of equality was retained. Shortly thereafter, Isaac Myers, who was to be elected first president of the union, introduced a resolution urging, among other points, that the new labor organization dedicate itself to carrying out "the learning of trades and professions by our children without regard to sex." After this proposal was adopted, Mrs. Carey, the white female delegate from Detroit, addressed the convention at considerable length on the issue of "the rights of women and the justice of their recognition by the sterner sex." At the conclusion of her remarks, the chairperson of the Committee on Female Suffrage offered a resolution that the new organization, "profiting by the mistakes heretofore made by our white fellow citizens in omitting women as co-workers in such societies," should cordially include black women in the invitation to further and organize cooperative societies. The committee report made it clear that in that body's opinion, "no subject bearing upon the industrial relations of the colored people to the community requires more earnest consideration." The report suggested that the solution to the plight of the women workers lay in "organized effort, whether in associations with men or in societies of their own." It recommended that women "learn trades" and engage in whatever honorable callings would have a tendency to "enlarge their sphere and influence of labor." The report expressed confidence that once women had demonstrated their willingness to form associations, they "could not fail to impress upon the sterner sex the importance of removing all barriers to the full recognition and success of woman as an important industrial and moral agent in the field of human activities and responsibilities."

The convention unanimously adopted the resolution and report submitted by the Committee on Woman's Labor. The Colored National Union thereby took, in several respects, a stronger stand in defense of equal rights of women in industry and trade unions than its white counterpart. Yet the *Revolution* failed to inform its readers that the black labor delegates had taken this advanced position in favor of equality for women workers.[53]

When the *American Workman* said that the *Revolution* had remained "constantly in support" of the NLU since the 1868 congress, it was exaggerating the case. In truth, the Stanton-Anthony journal's enthusiasm for the NLU had begun to wane even before the 1869 congress. In contrast to its active campaign to recruit women for the 1868 NLU meeting, the *Revolution* carried only one notice, without comment, about the 1869 convention.[54] Four women associated with the *Revolution* had attended the 1868 congress; only Anthony went to the 1869 convention, and even she had to be persuaded by NLU representatives that despite the death of suffragism's strongest ally in the organization— William H. Sylvis—it was still worth her while to attend.[55]

The point is that Stanton and Anthony were interested in the labor movement mainly as a force to advance the cause of woman suffrage, and even their work among workingwomen was centered on building a new base for the suffrage movement. The experience at the 1869 NLU congress convinced the *Revolution*'s editors that an alliance with the labor movement to advance the woman suffrage cause was nothing but an illusion. Stanton, never as enthusiastic about the possibilities of that alliance as Anthony, wrote that the National Labor Congress' action "has proved what the *Revolution* has said over and over again, that the worst enemies of woman's suffrage will ever be the laboring masses of men."[56]

But not many workingwomen shared this attitude. Their faith in the National Labor Union as a vehicle through which they might redress their grievances was still strong enough in 1870 for the Massachusetts Working Women's League and the Working Women's Labor Union for the State of New York—the only two statewide organizations of female workers established in the post–Civil War period—to place themselves "under the protection of the National Labor Union." The founding convention of the New York Working Women's Labor Union, held in

March, 1870, adopted a series of resolutions denouncing the fact that women and children had to work longer than ten hours a day, deploring strikes "except as a last resort toward the maintenance of our rights," endorsing the cooperative movement "as the true way in which the wealth of the country can be more equally distributed," urging the creation of a paper "devoted to our interests as *bona fide* working women," and calling for the establishment of a Labor Exchange in New York City to help women procure employment. Finally, the convention appealed directly to the workingmen of the nation through the National Labor Union "to come forward and aid us in this work of reform ... as we believe our interests are identical and our objects are one."[57]

Two men active in the NLU—Alexander Troup and William J. Jessup—were present at the convention and conveyed the appeal to the NLU congress, which thereupon urged male unionists to respond to the appeal and "welcome [women] entering into just competition with men in the industrial race of life."[58]

Four women delegates were present at the 1870 and 1871 conventions of the National Labor Union. In 1870 Mrs. E. O. G. Willard of the Sewing Girls' Union of Chicago was elected second vice-president. A year later, Mrs. Willard, representing the Working Women's Union of the same city, was reelected.[59]

The National Labor Union never took a stand in favor of woman suffrage before it passed into history in 1873, but it did reaffirm its position in favor of economic rights for workingwomen, including their right to receive equal pay with men for equal work. The 1871 congress put it in these words: "*Resolved,* That this organization cheerfully recognizes the right of women everywhere to learn and engage in any profession, trade or occupation which they may desire, and that for any certain amount of work they should receive the same pay as men."[60]

9

Workingwomen's Associations

ON SEPTEMBER 18, 1868, a *New York Times* report on the "Working Women's Association" began with this description:

> A meeting of ladies was held yesterday at noon, in the office of the *Revolution* newspaper in Park Row, for the purpose of organizing an association of workingwomen, which might act for the interests of its members, in the same manner as associations of workingmen now regulate the wages, &c., of those belonging to them. Mrs. Elizabeth Cady Stanton and Miss Susan B. Anthony were present, together with Mrs. MacDonald, a woman suffrage advocate from Mount Vernon, and a number of other ladies, conspicuous among whom were several still in girlhood, and of unusual comeliness and intelligence.

The *Times* also reported a dispute between Stanton and Anthony and one of the young ladies "of unusual comeliness and intelligence," twenty-year-old Augusta Lewis, who worked on "the newly-invented type-setting machine." When Anthony stated that the object of the meeting was the organization of an association "to elevate women and raise the value of their labor," Stanton insisted that there was need for only one type of organization—a women's suffrage association with the aim of obtaining the ballot. No disfranchised class had power, she maintained, and the ballot would be "the salvation" of workingwomen as it already was for workingmen, and even for black men. Thereupon, Anthony modified her original suggestion and seconded Stanton's proposal that the organization be called the Working Women's Suffrage Association.

However, Augusta Lewis objected, insisting that "women's wrongs should be redressed before her rights were proclaimed." She warned that to include the word "suffrage" in the name "would couple the association in the minds of many with short hair and bloomers and other vagaries." She believed that workingwomen should be brought together to improve their economic conditions, "after which they could be indoctrinated with suffrage or any other reform." Stanton replied that this

141

was "placing the cart before the horse," while Anthony expressed pity for workingwomen, like Augusta Lewis, who did not understand that "the ballot was the fulcrum by which they could gain their ends." But those "young ladies who were present who were workers" sided with Lewis, and the body voted to adopt the name "Working Women's Association." Furthermore, all of the officials were workingwomen. The president, Anna Tobitt, was the wife of an independent printer and worked in her husband's shop; the three vice-presidents—Susie Johns, Augusta Lewis, and Emily Peers—were young typesetters; and Elizabeth and Julia Brown, who were elected secretary and treasurer, respectively, worked as clerks in the office of the *Revolution.* Anthony, it will be recalled, had been elected the association's delegate to the 1868 NLU congress, but only after she had assured the members that her object there would be not only to agitate for suffrage but also to seek recognition for women as members of men's societies, and "gain for them the same wages as men for the same work."[1]

The New York press hailed the decision to drop the word "suffrage" from the association's name as a sign that the feminists were finally becoming practical. The *New York Times* (which insisted on calling the association the "Working Women's Protective Union" until the secretary of that older organization protested) warned that the women's rights agitation was "now very formidable where it was a few years ago simply ridiculous." Now that Stanton and Anthony understood the need for women to obtain "a recognition of their rights as laborers rather than as citizens," it declared, they would seek for women through their new organization goals similar to those associated with organizations of workingmen.[2]

Anthony was amused by the inference that she had abandoned feminist goals in working with the Working Women's Association. Speaking at Cooper Institute on November 5, 1868, to an audience of several hundred workingwomen, she made it abundantly clear that the organization's aim was "the doing of the Women's Rights." "Excuse me, audience," she quipped to the delight of the listeners. "I beg your pardon. No one would believe that the cloven foot of Woman's Rights was tamped upon the undertaking if I had not stated so."[3]

Anthony herself commented that she had grudgingly agreed to the deletion of the word "suffrage" from the name of the Working Women's Association only because she did not wish to push the workingwomen "beyond what their present mental state sanctioned." Thus, it is not surprising that in the platform of the Working Women's Association, which was made public for the first time at the Cooper Institute meeting, the "cloven foot" of women's rights was obscure. There was no reference to suffrage. Nor did President Dickinson mention it in her two-hour speech. Rather, she emphasized that the Working Women's Association had a dual mission: (1) to make labor honorable for women; and (2) to train women to enter various trades and professions so that they would not be forced to join "the vast sisterhood of the needle" who were compelled to toil "eight, ten and twelve hours daily earning from three to five dollars a week."[4]

The platform of the Working Women's Association began: "The workingwomen today, like those of the past, belong to the large class of manufacturing and distributing producers, and as such are entitled to recognition and adequate remuneration in the great army of the world's work." However, it went on, because of a lack of a "just estimate" of women's work, no definite wages had ever been fixed in the departments of women's special industries, and this had given rise to various abuses, particularly "the oppression of workingwomen by corrupt and avaricious employers," which caused "poverty, misery and death." "Hence the necessity of association in order that we may attain enlightened views, devise plans for cooperation, and establish our position on an equitable basis."

The association would seek initially to refute the concept that honest labor was "a disgrace and scourge" and to create among all workingwomen the feeling that they should be "proud of the name which distinguishes them from the multitude of idlers and dependents." Next, it would attempt to train workingwomen to become expert in their chosen fields, "gaining that perfection of skill that secures self-approval, commands respect, and guarantees success." In addition, it would provide an opportunity for social life so that workingwomen, after their "exhausting toil," could experience an "interchange of sentiment and cordiality" in place of the isolation they were ordinarily compelled to endure: "As it was 'good and pleasant for brethren to dwell together in unity,' so it was equally good for sisters who are engaged in a common cause to meet in friendly conference." Meetings would take place at least once a month for the purpose of "mutual exchange, encouragement and improvement." Finally, while it would be "unwise as well as futile" for the association to attempt to right at once "all the wrongs to which workingwomen are subject," the platform operated on the principle that "in union there is strength," and "agitation of thought is the beginning of wisdom." It therefore recommended that the Association be a

> ... Central Workingwomen's Union and that at our monthly meetings, we not only strike hands in friendship, but solicit from competent persons hints, maxims, addresses, heroic songs, whatever will awaken and direct our thought, and give us wisdom for future action and attainment. Furthermore, we recommend the formation of a fund for the benefit of members in sickness and misfortune, and for carrying out such plans as many from time to time offer for bettering the condition of workingwomen.[5]

In the years before the Civil War, and particularly from 1780 to 1835, feminists had sought to associate virtue with those areas of activity commonly thought to be degrading and demeaning—home and family—and "to include a role in the civil and public sphere among women's rights and prerogatives."[6] Out of this came a sense of woman's power and potential and a genuine sense of sisterhood. Now this focus was to be applied to workingwomen. Through the Working Women's Association, women's work would be associated with value and dignity; the women would be uplifted and dignified both in the public's eye and in their estimation of themselves, and they would gain a sense of sisterhood, which would be used to redress their grievances. The exact means were left vague, perhaps because the feminists who sponsored the association did not want to reveal their still firm belief that it was only through the ballot that workingwomen could attain their goals. This conflict in methods was to mount in intensity and eventually destroy the association. But for the moment, it did not loom as an important issue.

The association's immediate task was to draw women into unions, and the aim of one of its early meetings was the organization of a women's typographical union. The battle goes back at least as far as 1853, when newspapers in New York City tried to break the power of Local #6 of the National Typographical Union by hiring women during a strike and teaching them to set type. The publishers justified their action with noble words about assisting the emerging women's rights movement and providing "a real practical way of enlarging the sphere of female labor." The NTU scored the newspaper publishers for "base hypocrisy" in pretending concern "for the amelioration of the conditions of woman" and labeled the device as "put on to conceal their designs to depress the liberty and reduce the wages of the males." In a long resolution it blasted the idea "that any benefit can accrue from taking women from the sphere of action God (as is evident from her physical and mental qualities) designed her to occupy.... The purity of woman should be guarded with care, and surely contact with the world in the same method that man finds necessary would have a very pernicious effect upon her morals." It would also, of course, have a depressing effect on the wages of male printers, and would soon "render it a necessity on the part of both man and wife to labor all week for about in the aggregate the same compensation that is at present paid to the male for his services."[7]

But the argument that women printers would lower the wages of men in the craft was nothing but a smokescreen behind which the union and its members tried to hide their sexist attitudes. This became clear during the first strike of printers against the hiring of women typesetters. Interestingly enough, this occurred on the *Lily*, the paper published by Amelia Jenks Bloomer, the dress reformer and women's rights and temperance advocate. Bloomer was the first woman to edit and publish a paper. When the *Lily* was launched in New York City in 1853, she had been forced to reject the pleas for employment of women typesetters because she did not own the press on which it was published. With the removal of the *Lily* to Mount Vernon, Ohio, in 1854, Bloomer now had her own type, and she sought to make an arrangement with the printers to enable her to employ a woman typesetter as an apprentice. Bloomer guaranteed that once the apprenticeship was finished, the woman printer would receive equal pay with the men and that their wages would not be reduced in the slightest. Thus there could be no complaint that Bloomer was using a woman to undermine male printers' wages.

Accordingly, Mrs. Bloomer hired Mrs. C. V. Lundy of New York as an apprentice typesetter on the *Lily*. But she was unable to find a single male printer in Ohio who would instruct her. When Bloomer insisted that Lundy learn to set type by practicing on her paper, the printers struck not only the *Lily* but also the *Western Home Visitor* of Mount Vernon, in which Bloomer's husband owned a partial interest. Mrs. Bloomer refused to budge and was supported completely by her husband and the other owners of the *Western Home Visitor*. Both papers continued to appear because Mrs. Lundy laboriously set the type for the two journals. Soon, three women and a journeyman printer from Columbus, Ohio, who instructed them, began to work in the offices of both papers. The result was a triumph for Mrs. Bloomer. She reported joyfully that four women and three men were putting out both papers, and "working together peaceably and harmoniously. It does our heart good to see the happy change which had been wrought in the office by this attempt to crush woman's efforts in her own behalf.... Woman's cause is upward and onward, and all the puny efforts that man may make to stop it will be like attempting to blow back the rushing wind with a breath."

A firm believer in equal pay for equal work, Bloomer was happy to report that the women and one male printer were receiving the same wages and that these wages were as high as any paid to union printers anywhere in Ohio. All that was needed to fill her cup of happiness was for the printers' union to initiate the women printers in her office as members.[8]

That hope was not to be realized for several years. Still, the practice of employing women printers increased during the Civil War. According to the National Typographical Union, there were two hundred women setting type in New York City in 1868, constituting between 15 and 20 percent of all workers in the printing trades. Other women were used as typesetters during strikes and in nonunion shops, particularly in the book and job printing plants, and especially outside of Manhattan.[9]

Despite the growing use of women strikebreakers during the war years, it was not until 1867 that the Typographical Union reconsidered its policy with respect to women workers. Local No. 6 sponsored a motion to permit women to join, "provided that they receive a compensation for their labor equal to that received by male printers." As a mechanism for achieving the integration of women into the union, the proposal was without any practical force. It included no provision for the active recruiting of women as members and it placed the responsibility for raising women's wages to the men's level on the women themselves. Clearly, the union's aim was less to organize the unorganized women than to improve its public image, which had suffered from "the assertion, constantly made use of by enemies of our organization, that Typographical Unions are opposed to, and use all means to prevent, females from working at the business." Nevertheless, the majority of the delegates found even this proposal too radical and defeated it.[10]

Late in 1867 Local No. 6 called a strike against the New York *World* because its owners had been directing their employees to set type for the *Brooklyn Eagle,* whose union printers were on strike for higher wages. As others had done before them, the *World*'s owners turned to women as replacements for the striking typesetters, to be trained on the job. They responded in large numbers to this rare opportunity to learn a skilled trade; the *World* later asserted that it had trained over one hundred women.[11] Ten months after the strike began, the *World* and Local No. 6 reached a settlement. As part of the agreement, the *World* dismissed the women typesetters, allegedly for incompetence. Despite "every opportunity to learn," the employers asserted, the female compositors could not spell, could not space, could not read untidy manuscripts, shirked their duties, and produced messy copy. The *World* maintained further that it had found places for as many of the women as it could in good conscience recommend in the job and book printing industry, where the requirements—and the wage scales—were significantly lower.[12]

The woman typesetters angrily challenged the *World*'s assertion that their incompetence was responsible for their dismissal and that women were constitutionally unable to set type as well as men. They insisted that they had reported to work early, had not shirked their responsibilities, "no matter what time of night it might be," and, far from being incompetent, had had to clean up after some of the sloppy male printers who were still on the job.[13]

To the *Revolution,* the strike on the *World* was of major significance, so the eyes of all editors were focused on its progress. The paper urged the women not to abandon their jobs as strikebreakers but rather to hang on and learn as many skills as they could.[14] It described the *World*'s charges justifying their dismissal as a "wet blanket" hiding the real cause, which, the *Revolution* maintained, was contained in a letter it printed from a San Francisco female compositor, protesting her treatment at the hands of the union:

> I found the proprietors of all the offices willing to give me employment, but the Typographical Union refused to permit me to work, the members threatening to leave any office where a lady might be employed. . . . I did not

wish to work for any less but asked for an exception to be made in my case or to admit to me into the Union. My request was treated with contempt.

The lesson drawn by the *Revolution*'s editors was that female enfranchisement was imperative. "This is the case all over the country, both with women and negroes, ignored ever in printers' unions," they argued.* "Now what is the reason? Only this, they are disfranchised classes, hence ignored in the world of work."[15]

This editorial was published just a week before the meeting that led to the formation of the Working Women's Association.† Not only were there several typesetters among the young women who joined Stanton and Anthony in forming the association, but two of them—Augusta Lewis and Emily Peers—had worked at the *World* during the strike. While these workingwomen welcomed the suffragists' assistance in organizing, they were not convinced that the vote was the only way to improve their situation. After all, they knew from experience that it was the economic power of Local No. 6 that had forced the *World* to fire the women it had hired during the strike.[16]

Once the Working Women's Association was established, the female typesetters turned their attention to concrete ways of improving their status. The first proposal was to establish a "cooperative female printing office." Such a shop had been organized by women typesetters in San Francisco as a reaction to their exclusion from union-controlled offices, and it seemed to be prospering.[17] William Tobbitt, husband of the association's president and himself the publisher of a newspaper, offered the use of his shop to the women typesetters, and when Anthony promised to print the *Revolution* in the proposed shop, the women printers voted to go ahead with the proposal to form a cooperative printing office. A committee was appointed to call meetings of the typesetters to discuss the proposed organization and to draw up the bylaws.[18]

The formation of the Working Women's Association, the meetings held to form an organization of women typesetters, and the hatred expressed there by the women printers against Local No. 6's policies and practices, combined with their readiness to help break the union's strikes—all finally drove the Typographical Union to action. The independent organizing efforts of female compositors constituted a powerful threat that finally convinced the Typographical Union to admit women.

---

*The reference to blacks and the printers' union is to the widely publicized case of Lewis H. Douglass, son of Frederick Douglass, who was forced out of the Government Printing Office because, being black, he was not permitted to join the International Typographical Union. Since only union members could work in the office, he was discharged. See Philip S. Foner, *Organized Labor and the Black Worker* (New York, 1974), pp. 28–30.

†It is clear who initiated the meeting, but it is likely that the *World* strike and the firing of the women who replaced the strikers brought the female typesetters together with the editors of the *Revolution,* and the idea of an association followed naturally.

It was a similar threat that had earlier resulted in the Cigar Makers becoming the first national union to admit women.

Representatives of Local No. 6 therefore attended a meeting of the Working Women's Association and sought to appear as friendly as possible to the female compositors. The *Revolution* carried the following exchange:

> Mr. Alexander Troup, a delegate to the National Labor Congress from Typographical Union #6, denied that the association of which he was a member was in hostility to female compositors. If the female compositors will work together with members of the Union, they will get equal remuneration for their labor.
>
> Miss Peers—Will the union allow ladies to join their ranks as members?
>
> Mr. Troup—I never knew of any woman applying for admission. I can speak for Mr. McKenchic, the present foreman of the *World* and President of the National Typographical Union as being in favor of women working at case with equal rights and privileges as the men. But he is not in favor, nor am I, of women coming in to undermine the prices paid to men.
>
> Miss Anthony—How much is the initiation in this union of yours?
>
> Mr. Troup—One Dollar.
>
> Miss Anthony—Oh, that is not much. I guess our girls can stand that. *(Laughter).*
>
> Miss Peers to Mr. Troup—Will you take my initiation fee now, if you please?
>
> Mr. Troup—Yes, of course I shall; and will propose you as a member.

Then and there, Peers gave Troup her dollar and challenged him to make good on his pledge.[19]

On October 12, 1868, the Women's Typographical Union was formally organized, with Augusta Lewis as president and Emily Peers as secretary. Although the new organization was called a "union," it appears that it was intended as both a trade union and a producers' cooperative, which was not unusual in the labor movement in the post–Civil War era. Nor was it intended to replace the Working Women's Association, which was to remain open to women of diverse trades for the consideration of all possible remedies for aiding working women.

Anthony addressed the union's first formal meeting with these words of encouragement:

> Girls, you must take this matter seriously now, for you have established a union, and for the first time in woman's history in the United States, you are placed, and by your own efforts, on a level with men as far as possible, to obtain wages for your labor. I need not say that you have taken a great momentous step forward on the path to success. Keep at it now, girls, and you will achieve full and plenteous success. *(Applause.)*[20]

At a later meeting, it was reported that the proprietors of *Flake's Bulletin* of Galveston, Texas, wished to have the Women's Typographical

Union send a woman compositor, but at a rate of pay below that paid to men. President Augusta Lewis vigorously rejected the offer, and she was supported by both Anthony and the assembled membership.[21]

Shortly after the women typesetters had organized their own union, Local No. 6's representatives returned, this time with a formal offer of assistance. "Knowing that your interests are identical with our own," Local No. 6 proposed to the women that it would "hire a hall for your meetings, furnish you with books, stationery, etc., and assume all other expenses which it may be necessary for you to incur in getting your association into working order, and to continue to do so until your Union shall be in a condition to support itself."

John Clark, secretary of Local No. 6, described the procedure by which the Women's Typographical Union could apply for a charter as a local of the National Typographical Union. The women typesetters voted to accept the union's offer of support. Although none of their remarks about the union's sudden concern for their welfare have been recorded, Anthony did hail Local No. 6's offer of aid as evidence that the union was ready to treat women workers as the equals of men and therefore as a stunning victory in the battle for equality.[22]

It was not until the spring of 1869 that the Women's Typographical Union was admitted as an all-woman local of the National Typographical Union, and by that time Anthony was not so enthusiastic over the development. On the contrary, her relationships with both the union of women typesetters she had helped found and Local No. 6 had become extremely bitter.

In January, 1869, Local No. 6 called a strike in the book and job printing sections of the printing industry to raise typesetting rates to the union rate for newspapers. Since women printers were a major working force in book and job printing, Local No. 6 counted on the support of the Women's Typographical Union when it decided to call the strike. Its confidence was justified. The Women's Typographical Union cooperated wholeheartedly with Local No. 6. Augusta Lewis reported that she found the women typesetters in the city determined not to repeat their experiences during the *World* strike of the previous year; they did not want to be hired during a strike only to be fired at its conclusion.[23]

The strike was settled in less than eight weeks, and three months later the Women's Typographical Union was admitted into the National Typographical Union. When the delegates assembled for their 1869 convention, they were presented with a document from the Women's Typographical Union explaining that the status of the large number of women typographers was "a detriment to the trade, and disastrous to the best interests of all printers." The women's labor had been used during strikes to defeat the organized male workers, and necessity compelled them "to work at a price at which they cannot earn a living and which tends to undermine your wages." When the employers' goal had been accomplished, the women were set adrift. Convinced that "the interests of labor, whether that labor be done by male or female, are identical, and should receive the same protection and the same pay," the woman compositors had formed their own union, inspired by "the assistance, exertions and praiseworthy example" of the New York Typographical Union. They now appealed to the national union to recognize their organization and seat their delegates at the convention.

The appeal was accompanied by a set of resolutions already adopted by Local No. 6 and recommending the recognition of the women's union. In addition, it was endorsed by the president of the national union, who stated in his report to the convention that the recognition of woman labor was one of the most important problems before the delegates. Referring to the assistance Local No. 6 had received from the women typesetters during its recent strike, he declared that the existence of local unions often depended on the attitude they adopted toward the women in the trade.

The delegates, impressed, voted unanimously to accept the credentials of the delegates from the Women's Typographical Union of New York. In addition, they revised the national union's constitution to permit the chartering of women's locals in other cities—on condition that the women work at union rates and have the support of a majority of male union members.

The antistrikebreaking activity of the Women's Typographical Union had played a major role in advancing their entrance into the national union. But it had the very opposite effect on relations between Susan B. Anthony and the printers' unions. To Anthony, the strike of Local No. 6 presented an opportunity to train women typesetters, and so, while it was in progress, she urged the employing printers to assist the Working Women's Association financially "to establish a training school for girls in the art of typesetting at once" and assured them that if they responded, she would soon give them competent women compositors.[24]

Gray and Green (publishers of the *Revolution*) responded by establishing a two-week training program for women typesetters. By the end of March, fifteen graduates were ready and another thirty-eight women were being trained. Actually, the training program did not produce very competent typesetters, but the employers were confident that they could be used to compel the union to settle the strike on the employers' terms. Even at that, however, the union was able, with the assistance of the Women's Typographical Union, to force the employers to yield. But two concrete results did flow from the scab-training program. One was that even though the Gray and Green program was discontinued after the strike, it did provide the firm with women typesetters, so that Anthony could now claim that women were employed in printing the *Revolution*.[25]

The other was that it set the stage for the challenge from Local No. 6 to Anthony's credentials as a delegate to the 1869 National Labor Union convention.

Local No. 6 condemned Anthony's petition to the employing printers as "an infamous measure." The Women's Typographical Union did not say anything for the record, but its warm support of Local No. 6 speaks for itself. It is not difficult to imagine what the members must have thought when they learned that their president, Augusta Lewis, had been fired from the Gray and Green shop because of her union affiliation and activities. When she appealed to Anthony, she was told that it was not Anthony who employed the typesetters, and that she had no control over the employment policies of the firm that did her printing.[26]

Although Anthony was able technically to use this answer in responding to the charge at the 1869 NLU congress, it was a lame defense. Some of the delegates who later supported her in the battle over her credentials were angered by her conduct in the printers' strike. The *Workingman's Advocate,* whose editor was a leader in the fight to seat Anthony at the NLU congress, expressed itself as "very much angered to see our good friend, Miss Susan B. Anthony, take the path she did," while Lewis Hine, corresponding secretary of the National Labor Union, asked her to reconsider her stand and acknowledge her error. Both Cameron and Hine pointed out to Anthony that her petition to the employers violated the basic trade union concept of labor solidarity during a strike. None of this, however, made any impression on Anthony. She insisted that her sole motive in appealing to the employing printers had been "to open the way for a thorough drill to the hundreds of poor girls, to enable these women to earn wages with men everywhere," and she could not understand why Local No. 6 considered her actions antagonistic to the union.[27]

The collapse of the suffragists' alliance with the women typesetters was part of a general conflict emerging between middle-class and wage-earning women in the Working Women's Association. The breakdown in relations between the Women's Typographical Union and the *Revolution*'s editors was a fatal blow to the association, already severely weakened by the contradictions between its rich and poor members.[28]

At first the formation of the Women's Typographical Union appeared to coincide with and advance the general strategy of the Working Women's Association. "Out of the present Association will be formed effective unions in every branch of industry," Stanton exulted in the *Revolution.* "As the gods help those who help themselves, we call on all working women to rouse up from the lethargy of despair and make one combined determined effort to secure for themselves an equal chance with men in the whole world of work." They could achieve this, she said, through producers' cooperatives or through unions, or both.[29]

A meeting to launch the organizing drive among workingwomen in other trades was held at the Working Women's Home, a benevolent institution set up by philanthropists, which provided room and board for workingwomen at reasonable rates. At the meeting, woman after woman got up and recounted her wages, hours, and working conditions, which were all duly published in the *Revolution*. As the recital of grievances continued, there was increasing agitation among the women. At one point, Lewis Hine, representing the NLU, sought to channel this discontent into organization, pleading:

> The importance of laboring unions must be plain to you all. It is the only means of lifting you from this misery. Get together and form associations and establish scales of prices. . . . These meetings will also be a means of making sanitary inquiries after your bodily health. I don't see how it is possible for any girl after obtaining her majority to live ten years at this kind of work exhibited tonight. You are here for a year or so and then you are gone forever.

Anthony concluded the meeting with a familiar plea for suffrage: "Get the ballot, and then if you strike, the men of the Trade Unions will sustain you with money and assistance." (Anthony never ceased predicting that woman suffrage would win women's strikes.)[30]

The content of the meeting so alarmed the philanthropic backers of the Working Women's Home that they denied any further use of the facility to the Working Women's Association. But Anthony needed no additional meetings. Without consulting any needleworkers, she unilaterally announced in the *Revolution* the formation of the Sewing Machine Operators' Union, affiliated to the Working Women's Association. Nothing came of it, since the *Revolution*'s editors were able to do little for sewing women besides publicizing their miserable wages and deplorable conditions, and these facts were already familiar through repeated public meetings and articles in the commercial press. With or without the ballot, the "men of the Trade Unions" were not prepared to sustain the sewing women if they organized and struck, for the women posed no threat to any unions and the male unionists had no material interest in coming to their aid. It was to take another half century before male unionists in the needle trades were ready to act to organize women as the cigarmakers and printers had already done, and when they were ready it was for much the same reason.

The sewing women also lacked the resources to operate producers' cooperatives, which was the other solution proposed by Stanton and Anthony. When even powerful unions like the molders were finding producers' cooperatives impossible to operate successfully in the face of competition from private industry,[31] it was hardly to be expected that they would lift the sewing women out of their misery.

"Whether it is worse for women to strike as men do for higher wages may be a question, but they have at least the same right." So began an article in the *Revolution* of April 22, 1969, which bore the heading, "Jennie Collins and the Dover Strike." A Lowell mill worker in the 1840s, Collins had gone on to do volunteer work in Boston's military hospitals during the Civil War while trying to earn a living as a seamstress. She soon became known as the champion of the cause of workingwomen; she taught free evening history classes for women workers in Boston and included in the curriculum the history of the Female Labor Reform Associations in the cotton mills of the 1840s.

In 1869 eight hundred mill workers at the Cocheco mills in Dover, New Hampshire, walked out over a wage cut of 12 percent. Jennie Collins presided at meetings of factory women held throughout New England in support of the strikers. She worked hard to organize a boycott against all Cocheco mill products. "We working women will wear fig-leaf dresses before we will patronize the Cocheco Company," she declared at meetings in behalf of the strikers.

The *Revolution*'s editors rallied to Collins' aid. It reported her speeches, publicized the boycott, and raised funds for the strikers. The strike was lost, but the contact established between Collins and the *Revolution*'s editors during the struggle led to her opening a center in Boston modeled after the Working Women's Association in New York. Like the New York Association's training school for female compositors, the Boston center was financed by employers, and, as might be expected, had no connection with trade unionism for workingwomen.*[32]

The New York Working Women's Association was itself moving away from unionism, shifting instead to fact-finding investigations of conditions in various industries, "to place these facts before the public, in order that they may fully comprehend the dire necessities" of the workingwomen of New York. The association did provide a good deal of detailed information on the wages and conditions of women in a variety of trades as well as on the interconnection between the economic, social, and political exploitation of women. But often the conclusions of such reports were merely rhetorical appeals both to employers to be more generous and to the workingwomen to be more industrious. In any case, the emphasis on investigatory efforts not only turned the Working Women's Association away from the organization of workingwomen into unions and cooperatives but also tended to involve professional, middle-class women; workingwomen were the object of their efforts but had no voice in their activities. Not only middle-class women were thus drawn into the association, but some wealthy women as well. In fact,

*For evidence of a more militant note struck by Boston workingwomen, see Rosalyn Baxandall, Linda Gordon, and Susan Reverby, "Boston Working Women Protest, 1869," *Signs* 1 (Spring 1976): 803–8.

Stanton believed that the best hope for workingwomen might be to get "women of wealth, education and leisure" to join in studying the conditions under which their working-class sisters labored and lived so that their influence could be utilized for humanitarian appeals to employers to change their ways. The Working Women's Association soon became a center, not so much for the unskilled wage-earning women who formed the bulk of the female labor force as for professional women, free-lance authors and journalists, and businesswomen, many of them attracted more by the suffrage outlook of Stanton and Anthony than by the economic problems of workingwomen. Anthony herself conceded that "ladies—not work women—are beginning to look eagerly towards the movement," and predicted, with a great deal of pleasure, that a flood of such women would soon inundate the association.[33]

As the middle-class women took over, the Working Women's Association became less comfortable for poor workingwomen. The association changed its meeting place from the Cooper Institute to the Women's Bureau, the uptown mansion where the *Revolution* was put together, which was both geographically and psychologically far removed from poor workingwomen. Dues were raised from 10 cents to 25 cents a week, despite protests that needlewomen could not afford such an increase. Anthony's support of both changes indicated that, despite speeches and editorials in the *Revolution* affirming her devotion to the women of the working class, she was closer to the middle class than to the working class.[34]

By the spring of 1869 the regular membership of the Working Women's Association was entirely middle-class. Most of them opposed trade unions on the ground that they intensified conflict by advancing an "unwarranted" and "pernicious" distinction between manual and intellectual labor. "In this country," said one association leader, "we are all workers, and it does not come with any grace for any class to find fault with another because the work is different."[35] By the time Anthony attended the 1869 convention of the National Labor Union as a delegate from the association, it had been transformed into an antiunion organization. Had this information been available to the NLU congress, it is likely that even the original vote on seating Anthony would not have been in her favor.

The Working Women's Association did not last long after the 1869 NLU congress. Anthony lost control of it to Sarah Norton, a middle-class novelist and lecturer, and under Norton's leadership the organization became even more middle-class in its outlook. The last recorded act of the association before its formal dissolution in November, 1869, was to drop the descriptive word "Working" from its title.[36]

In June, 1870, the *Revolution* finally succumbed to financial difficulties despite Anthony's frantic efforts to keep it alive.[37] But before it disappeared, about fifty women met in the women's Bureau and formed the National Woman Suffrage Association. Many of the founders were the same middle-class women who had dominated the Working Women's Association during its last period. Now, together with Stanton and Anthony, these feminists were looking for a new constituency to advance the suffrage cause, and they were not to be diverted by such "side issues" as labor reform and other social questions affecting workingwomen. The National Woman Suffrage Association would devote itself exclusively to female enfranchisement unconnected with any other social movement.[38]

The disappearance of the Working Women's Association was no great loss to workingwomen. When Kate Mullaney visited the association in the summer of 1869, she was amazed at what she found: "She had understood that they were an association of working women, and that was the reason she had come among them . . . but as she looked around upon them, they were not the working women she had been accustomed to see. She had to work all day in the shop and did not think, judging from their appearances, that they did."[39]

Mullaney had come to visit the association as part of a campaign to raise funds for the striking Troy Collar Laundry Union. In the spring of 1869, the collar ironers demanded a raise of ½, 1½, and 2 cents per dozen pieces, "according to the size of the article," and when they were refused, they went on strike. The starchers joined the walkout, which eventually included 430 workers. The entire community of Troy stood behind the union. Seven thousand citizens attended a mass meeting in support of the striking laundresses. Unions in printing, the building trades, iron work, shoemaking, and molding contributed sums ranging from $25 to $250. The molders, recalling how loyally the laundresses had stood behind them three years earlier, voted $50 a week for support and pledged "to continue the same for weeks to come rather than see such a brave set of wenches crushed under the iron heel of the laundry nabobs."[40]

To bring the struck manufacturers to terms, plans were announced for a cooperative laundry. Kate Mullaney was chosen president, and in that capacity, as well as as president of the Collar Laundry Union, she addressed appeals to the working people of the country and sympathizers urging them to buy stock at $5 a share. "The stock . . . is only an investment which will directly benefit working girls, not a charity," she wrote. "The interest will be regularly paid, and the stock bought in by the girls themselves as soon as possible." She assured prospective investors that "we are starting up with a good prospect of getting a quick sale for our goods as soon as we have got them ready for the market."[41]

The "good prospect" proved to be very good indeed. In December, 1869, the *Workingman's Advocate* announced that "the merchant prince of New York, A. T. Stewart" had agreed to take all the goods manufactured by the laundry girls' cooperative and place them immediately on the market. The labor paper, a leading advocate of producers' cooperatives, was confident that this would enable the laundry girls to overcome their chief obstacle—the dealers' fear that by handling the collars of the cooperative they would antagonize the struck manufacturers. Now the laundry girls' union was certain to succeed, for when the manufacturers saw that they could not destroy the cooperative, they would be willing to deal with the union on any terms it desired, thereby proving the *Advocate*'s thesis that producers' cooperatives could serve as a lever with which to pry better wages and working conditions from employers.[42]

But this was not to be. The struck employers advertised that they were putting a new paper collar on the market, and the sales of the laundresses' cooperative collars dropped precipitously. Meanwhile, the molders' union, weakened by the death of William H. Sylvis and by the failure of its own cooperative venture, had stopped contributing to the strikers. The laundry workers were forced to dissolve their cooperative. The fact is that nearly all the producers' cooperatives organized by trade unions in this period were doomed by a combination of market restrictions, mismanagement, lack of capital, and the oppositionof established and more heavily financed corporations. The Laundry Union and its Co-Operative Collar Company were no exceptions. As a condition of getting their jobs back, the laundresses were compelled to dissolve their union, and in February, 1870, the Troy Collar Laundry Union passed into history.[43] But, as we shall see, its spirit lived on, and the militant laundry girls of Troy were to write new labor history as part of the Knights of Labor.

Just as the Troy Collar Laundry Union was passing from the scene, another union of workingwomen was emerging that was also destined to make labor history. This was the Daughters of St. Crispin, the first national women's trade union in American history.

Beginning in 1862, a worker at the McKay stitcher took the place of the skilled shoe bottomer, turning out eighty pairs in the time it took a journeyman bottomer to seam one pair of shoes. The mechanization of other hand skills followed. By 1880 every operation except lasting and cutting uppers had been mechanized. In 1875, as contrasted with 1855, two thousand fewer Lynn workers—men and women alike—produced 7 million shoes! As the machine factory became common in the industry, it brought with it reduced wages, longer hours, speedup, and domination over workers' lives by arrogant foremen interested in adding to the corporations' profits.[44]

This development also sparked a collective effort to check the increasing power of the manufacturer. It had made itself felt during the great 1860 strike, and it was to emerge in the post–Civil War years in the organization of the Knights of St. Crispin. Formed originally in 1867, its lodges began to be organized rapidly in dozens of shoe towns, and soon the Knights grew into the nation's largest trade union. Whether its membership at its height was 100,000, as the Crispins boasted, or 50,000, as later historians assert, the fact remains that between one-third and one-half of all the men in American shoe manufacturing were members of the organization. Most of them were not, as historians have usually claimed, old-fashioned artisans who organized to resist the encroachment of machinery and green hands, but rather were factory workers who united to secure higher wages, shorter hours, and better working conditions and to reduce the power of the corporations over their lives.[45]

Male workers in Lynn's shoe industry established a local of the Knights of St. Crispin in 1868, and a sister organization, a local of the Daughters of St. Crispin, was organized shortly thereafter. This is hardly surprising, since sexual divisions in Lynn's labor force had been obliterated by the great 1860 strike. Men shoe workers knew from that experience that without the aid of the women in the factory work force, they could not even contemplate resisting corporate power.

The founding convention of the Daughters of St. Crispin as a national union was held on July 28, 1869, in Lynn. Thirty delegates were present, representing eleven local lodges—seven in Massachusetts and one each in Auburn (Maine), Rochester (New York), San Francisco, Chicago, and Philadelphia. Carrie Wilson and Abbie Jacques, both veterans of the great strike of 1860 in Lynn, were elected president and secretary, respectively.

The Daughters of St. Crispin remained centered in Massachusetts, but the order spread to nine states from Maine to California, and lodges were also established in Canada. The Lynn lodge, with 360 members, represented one-quarter of the local female work force in that city. The largest lodge was the one at Rochester, with 400 members. But in Lynn additional hundreds of women participated in another organization friendly to the Crispins, called the Working Women's Associates.[46]

Although the Daughters worked closely with the Knights of St. Crispin, they were not merely ladies' auxiliaries. Two officers of the Daughters were present as delegates to the 1870 convention of the National Labor Union. That year the Daughters of St. Crispin passed a resolution that demanded "the same rate of compensation for equal skill displayed, for the same hours of toil, as is paid other laborers in the same branches of business; and we regard a denial of this right by anyone as a usurpation and a fraud." They followed this bold assertion with an assurance: "We only desire to so elevate and improve our conditions as to better fit us for the discharge of those high social and moral duties which devolve upon every true woman."[47] This was hardly a statement that would have been published in the *Revolution* without critical editorial comment.

However, there was nothing demure about the Daughters when they went about fighting for their rights. They organized secretly, as did the Knights of St. Crispin (and indeed as did many labor unions of the period, which feared discharge and blacklisting if the membership became known before they were strong enough to resist). In Baltimore the shoe manufacturers learned through a spy who the women were who were building a lodge in their factories, and discharged every one of them, "at the same time offering to continue them at work upon their withdrawal from the Society." The Daughters unanimously rejected the ultimatum, and the Baltimore lodge of the Knights of St. Crispin voted to strike all the shoe factories until the Daughters were rehired and their union recognized. Two thousand Crispins—Knights and Daughters—jointly picketed the factories until the employers yielded. At the third convention of the Daughters of St. Crispin, held in May, 1871, in New York City, a delegation from the victorious Baltimore lodge was greeted with enthusiasm and songs as they joined twenty-nine other lodges at the gathering.[48]

Two months after the convention, the Daughters scored another victory. On August 29, 1871, several hundred Daughters in Lynn gathered together to combat new "encroachments on our rights." Their employers had proposed as a condition of employment that they stay at their jobs for a minimum of three months, depositing $5 from their first paycheck with the payroll office, which would be forfeited if they left before the time was up. Reminding the manufacturers of their resolve that "American Ladies Will Not Be Slaves," they rallied such support from the Knights and the Lynn community that the employers had to abandon the scheme.[49]

The Knights and Daughters of St. Crispin held joint celebrations on two annual occasions. The first was on Washington's Birthday, to commemorate the great strike of 1860. The other was the Fourth of July, which was hailed as a day in honor of the Sons and Daughters of Liberty, and one on which to fulfill the promise of the Declaration of Independence.[50]

The year 1871 marked the high point of the Crispins; the following year saw the beginning of a decline, which led eventually to the demise of both the Knights and Daughters. Early in 1872 the Daughters lost a strike in Stoneham, Massachusetts. Three hundred Daughters from three factories struck for higher wage rates. They held out for two weeks, but called off the strike when the companies threatened to bring in strikebreakers. The Daughters were rehired, but two of the union leaders were fired and blacklisted throughout the area.[51]

Encouraged by this result, the Lynn manufacturers revived their attempt to compel every woman shoe worker to sign a pledge that she would give two weeks' notice before leaving her position or else forfeit $5 of her pay. Now they added insult to injury by also attempting to cut wages. Nine hundred workers voted unanimously to denounce this "attempt at robbery and bondage," and their resolution merits quoting at length:

> Resolved, That we, the workingwomen of Lynn, known as Upper Fitters and Finishers of Boots and Shoes, do enter a most solemn protest against any reduction of wages, on any pretext whatever; and that we will not submit to any rules that do not equally affect our employers.
>
> Resolved, That we feel grateful to the shoemakers of Lynn for their interest and determination to stand by us in our time of need.
>
> Resolved, That we, the free women of Lynn, will submit to no rule or set of rules that tend to degrade or enslave us.
>
> Resolved. That we will accept no terms whatever, whether with regard to reduction of prices, notices to quit, or forfeiture of wages. That while we utterly ignore the spirit of selfishness and illiberality which promoted the late action of our would-be oppressors, we will not hesitate to resist, in a proper manner, the unjust encroachments upon our rights.
>
> Resolved, That a copy of these resolutions be given to every one of the committee, to be by them presented to each girl in every shop, and her signature thereon obtained; and should anyone of the employees of the shop be reduced in her wages, or ill-treated, we will desist from our work until she has obtained her rights.

The firm resolve of the women and the support promised by the Knights forced the manufacturers to back down a second time.[52] It also increased their determination to destroy both the Knights and Daughters of St. Crispin. Two years earlier, in 1870, the Knights had compelled the manufacturers to sign a wage agreement for the following year. The agreement was renewed a year later, but facing severe competition and determined to destroy the order, the manufacturers repudiated it in 1872. The Knights struck and were supported by the Daughters, who joined out of sympathy. But this time the manufacturers, well prepared in advance, withstood the strike, and eventually both the Knights and Daughters went down to defeat.[53]

The defeat wiped out the lodges of the Knights and Daughters of St. Crispin in Lynn and presaged the downfall of both national organizations. Those locals of the Knights and Daughters that were still alive in the opening months of 1873 succumbed to the panic and depression that got under way later that year. An attempt to reorganize the Daughters was made in 1876, but it had no significant impact.[54] However, as in the case of the union of laundry workers in Troy, the spirit of the Daughters of St. Crispin was to reassert itself magnificently in the Knights of Labor.

In the years immediately following the Civil War the labor movement gained strength throughout the country, in various trades and among people of various races and nationalities. Women workers were part of this great labor upsurge. They formed associations and unions and were among the most militant workers in this period. The NLU took a more advanced position on the question of female labor than had been taken up to that time in American history, and it made world labor history by reaffirming the right of women to equal pay for equal work. Finally, two national unions opened their membership to women workers in their respective trades.

Despite these obvious advances, the picture for women workers in 1872 was hardly encouraging. The first national union of women workers and the strong union of laundry workers both lay in shambles. Only two of the thirty-four national and international unions functioning during the period from 1866 to 1872—the printers and the cigarmakers—admitted women, in both cases with extreme reluctance. It is true that at the 1870 convention of the International Typographical Union,* Augusta Lewis had been elected to the position of corresponding secretary, and that at the 1872 convention a committee appointed to consider the question of women printers had reported, "The experiment of establishing separate unions for females has resulted unsatisfactorily ... chiefly because a difference has resulted from the two scales (men and women) of prices in force." It was therefore decided that the union should favor the principle that "there should be no difference in compensation paid to competent workers, based upon a difference of sex." To give this ruling force, it was also decided not to grant any more charters to "female unions," and a recommendation was made to all locals "to admit female printers to membership upon the same footing, in all respects, as males." The Typographical Union, as it was then called, boasted that it was the only national or international union that accorded women equal rights with male members.[55]

But did they? The truth is that female members of the International Typographical Union found that their membership only served to reduce their access to jobs—for they *would not* work as strikebreakers yet they *could not* work in union shops. Augusta Lewis put it clearly to the 1871 Typographical Convention:

> A year ago last January Typographical Union No. 6 passed a resolution admitting union girls in offices under control of No. 6. Since that time we have never obtained a situation that we could not have obtained had we never heard of a union. We refuse to take the men's situations when they are on strike, and when there is no strike if we ask for work in union offices we

---

*After the affiliation of Canadian locals, the National Typographical Union was renamed International Typographical Union in 1869.

are told by union foremen "that there are no conveniences for us." We are ostracized in many offices because we are members of the union; and although the principle is right, the disadvantages are so many that we cannot much longer hold together. . . . It is the general opinion of female compositors that they are more justly treated by what is termed "rat" foremen, printers and employers than they are by union men.[56]

Since women were not admitted into union apprenticeship programs, they were unable to raise their wages to the level of men printers. The ITU conceded that it had two types of members—first-class (male printers) and second-class (women printers)—when it revoked the constitutional provision that members of the Women's Typographical Union would not work below the scale of union men.

Despite Augusta Lewis's efforts, the Women's Typographical Union was unable to recruit new members because the men unionists simply refused to grant their sister typesetters the right to work in union shops and receive equal pay. By 1874 its membership had shrunk to twenty-eight. That year Augusta Lewis married Alexander Troup and the couple moved to New Haven, where Troup launched a newspaper and his wife left the labor scene. Four years later the Women's Typographical Union passed out of existence.[57]

By 1872 most of the women's labor organizations of the postwar era had disappeared. The National Labor Union had appointed Kate Mullaney to organize women into unions, but there is no evidence that any organizations were established as a result of her efforts. Moreover, despite the resolutions that the NLU had passed since 1868 in favor of equal pay for equal work, the principle was far from being acknowledged, much less practiced. The *New York Times,* in an editorial entitled "Equal Wages for Equal Work," expressed doubts that it would be in effect by the time of the bicentennial of American independence in 1976, to say nothing of the approaching centennial.[58]

The average earnings of working women who had no special trade was estimated by the *Times* to be "less than $4 a week," and every other study of the time confirmed it. "What kind of subsistence this pittance affords may be imagined in a city where the necessaries of life are higher than in any city of the world, where the meanest meal costs fiteen cents, the darkest cellar a dollar a week, where coal is rarely less than $6 a ton, in bulk, and clothing and all other necessaries are raised in proportion."[59]

A report from the Ladies' Christian Union of New York noted that "the wages of girls are one-third less than those of young men, and their expenses connected with clothing and health one-third greater." Nor, according to the New York *Daily Graphic,* was there much prospect that the women would be able to improve their conditions: "Women have not had any of the advantages of trade unions, nor are they likely to have them." The *Graphic* predicted that "the coming winter is certain to be a hard one with poor girls and working women."[60]

The "coming winter" referred to was the winter of the depression of 1873, one of the most devastating economic crises this country has ever experienced.

10

The Long Depression

In September, 1873, amid a wave of postwar speculation, the banking house of Jay Cooke & Company suffered losses that forced it to close its doors. This brought on a chain reaction of failures among smaller banks. Overnight, the entire credit structure of the nation collapsed. By the end of the year, five thousand businesses had fallen, and the country suffered the worst depression it had known to that time. For the next six years, unemployment rose and wages fell. Conservative calculations indicated that in the second half of 1874, one-fourth of New York City's population was without work—a total of almost 94,000 people. And still the number kept increasing. In 1877 the number of unemployed in the nation rose to well over a million—with a population less than one-third of what it is today. The Bureau of Labor Statistics of Pennsylvania estimated that the number of unemployed amounted to at least one-third of the working population, which was said to be 10 million.[1]

Many of the jobless drifted across America, with no means of support except occasional charity. The New York *World* of October 26, 1873, asserted: "As is generally the case, the females seem to suffer most. . . . The results of the retrenchment reach women in all phases of employment. Families that had two chambermaids are getting on with one, and those that had only one send away the nurse and give the chambermaid the care of the children. Shop girls are being dismissed from the stores in large numbers." At the beginning of November, the New York *Bulletin* reported gloomily,

> Women are being discharged in bands of ten, twenty, fifty, and in too many cases, one hundred. What is worse, there is no immediate prospect of their obtaining work very soon. Those having comfortable homes are, unfortunately in the minority. There are too many to whom their daily pay is a matter of life and death, and to whom it may, in wretched extremity, make all the difference between lives of honor and shame. The office of the Workingwomen's Protective Union is painfully crowded with women seeking employment, and every day increases the list of applicants—yet every day some

new avenue or source of employment is cut off. With no homes, no relatives to fall back upon, many girls and women know that it is only a question of a few days or hours when they will be turned out of their boarding or lodging houses—to a fate too painful to contemplate.[2]

A month later, the *New York Times* reported that the picture had gotten worse: "There never was a period at which working women were in more need of help than now. There are thousands of them out of employment while there are many more, perhaps, who earn a scanty livelihood working on half or quarter time." Those fortunate enough to retain their places had had their wages cut between 40 and 50 percent.

Just how many women were unemployed was difficult to determine. The superintendents of the Working Women's Protective Union estimated in mid-December, 1873, that at least ten thousand women in the city who had been working prior to the crisis were now unemployed. On the other hand, the New York *Mail* suggested the number was closer to fifty thousand. Still, as Herbert Gutman points out:

> What is important is that even those women who worked, worked under more severe conditions than their male co-workers; and that the actual living conditions which faced the average woman worker were worse than those which faced the male worker. The *World* did not exaggerate this crisis when it suggested that women workers faced the alternative of starvation or prostitution.[3]

Such conditions as these prompted the Federal Council of the International Workingmen's Association to issue a memorial to the mayor and the Common Council on November 26, 1873, pleading:

> No provision has been made for the unemployment or sustenance of the working women of this city. We therefore would respectfully recommend to your honorable body the formation of a bureau of labor of lady volunteers, and the utilizing of our idle armories for the manufacture of under and other clothing, to be sold at market rates, and the profits of said manufactured articles, after deducting the cost of goods, paid over to the working women. We hope and believe that the authorities . . . will find the ways and means to save one hundred thousand of our wives, mothers, and daughters from starvation, prostitution, and crime.[4]

Needless to say, no action was forthcoming on this suggestion. Throughout the nation, the press ran stories of the tragic impact of the depression on workingwomen. The columns of the *Chicago Tribune,* in particular, were filled with letters from workingwomen describing their plight. A seamstress, for example, wrote:

> The sewing machine has become a curse instead of a blessing to us. It used to be that all the tools I needed to sew could be had three for a cent. But today a sewing machine costs sixty-five or seventy-five dollars, representing the en-

tire wages of from eight to eighteen weeks. Week after week, in the face of a hundred needs, I must put aside the instalment of the machine which I was sold on "easy terms." If by sickness or loss of work, I miss a payment, the company's men come and carry off the machine, and refuse to return a cent of what I have paid. This has happened to several of my friends within the last two weeks.

Meanwhile, wages for the work we do with the machine have been steadily growing less until I can no longer earn a livelihood. Last week I worked making water-proof cloaks on my sewing machine. I made one in ten hours for which I received forty cents. Ten long and weary hours at 4 cents an hour! Six days' work, for ten hours a day, on a sewing machine, gives $2.40! After paying $1 for the rent of my room, only $1.40 is left for food, fuel and clothing, and that, too, after I had invested $75 in a machine![5]

A servant wrote:

I am a servant-girl, and even so always try and get a few minutes Sundays to read a little of your valuable paper, and see from time to time a few remarks from the ladies.* Will you please allow a servant to state a few facts? Some ladies are very anxious to practice economy these hard times, and the first step they take towards it is to reduce the servants' wages, say 50 cents per week. Now, I suppose in your eyes that is very little, but taken from our small income it is in our eyes a great deal. If you do not think I earn $4 hard enough, working from a quarter to six in the morning till 8 at night, and when any extra company is expected have to work very often till 11 and 12, and no extra pay, then you know little of what it means to be a servant-girl.

That same lady who wants me to work for $3.50 per week paid $100 the next day for a silk party-dress. She had two beautiful ones home, but one she wore to a wedding, and it was described in the papers, and if she wore it again every one would know it was the same one. The other she wore twice before, and she gets tired of wearing the same dress too often.[6]

The *New York Times* commented: "How these women continue to exist at all under the circumstances is a mystery."[7]

While the situation cried out for government intervention, the business community frowned on such interference. Unemployment, they announced reassuringly, was a by-product of the natural laws of trade. American workingmen and workingwomen, however, were not at all convinced that God had decreed that all who worked should starve, and they backed up their beliefs through unemployed demonstrations and strikes against wage cuts. Mass meetings of the unemployed, in which workingwomen also participated, took place in a number of cities under

*Between September 14, 1873, and February 7, 1874, the letter columns of the *Chicago Tribune* became involved in a public debate between "servant girls" and their middle-class mistresses over wages, hours, and working conditions. Most of the middle-class letter writers who debated this topic in the *Tribune* felt that servant girls were overpaid and underworked, lacked "proper character and habits," and under no circumstances ought to be considered as equals.

the leadership of the American sections of the International Workingmen's Association. In Chicago five thousand men and women attended a meeting sponsored by the International and the trade unions on December 21, 1873, and drew up a petition demanding jobs for all those willing and able to work, at eight hours a day and for adequate wages. They also called for the extension of food and money to the unemployed through a committee to be appointed by the workers.[8]

On the following day, twenty thousand unemployed men and women marched through the streets of Chicago to the City Hall, where they held the largest meeting Chicago had ever seen. A committee of men and women went to see the authorities and demanded "bread for the needy, clothing for the naked, and houses for the homeless." Several years earlier, more than a million dollars had been contributed to the Relief and Aid Society for the victims of the great Chicago fire. About $700,000 still remained in the fund, but George Pullman, Marshall Field, Rufus King, and other multimillionaires who were board members had invested the relief money in their own companies at bargain interest rates instead of using it for relief. The delegation demanded that the money be turned over to assist families who were in need and that its committee be allowed to participate in the selection of the families to receive assistance, since they knew better than any official who was really hungry.

A conference of the mayor of Chicago, a committee of the Common Council, the Relief and Aid Society, and representatives of the unemployed took place on December 26, 1873, but the society refused to call in its funds and turn them over to the city treasury. Thereupon, the committee representing the unemployed called another mass demonstration, a march on the Relief and Aid Society to appeal for relief. The society contrived a plan to thwart the demonstrators by ruling that only those who submitted to vaccination would obtain relief, apparently believing that the unemployed were too superstitious to comply. However, so many men and women appeared before the society's doctor that the police had to be called. Finally, the society gave up the struggle; during the first week of 1874, almost ten thousand families of unemployed workers were provided with some assistance. But the city of Chicago would neither use its funds nor borrow others to help the unemployed.[9]

In New York City a meeting of the unemployed at Cooper Institute on December 11, 1873, called by a joint committee representing the trade unions and sections of the International, was packed to the doors, while an overflow audience waited outside to hear its decisions on action to be taken in behalf of the unemployed. Inside, the thousands of men and women present adopted resolutions proclaiming that the meeting represented and spoke for "industrious, law-abiding citizens, who have paid all taxes and given support and allegiance to the government" but the time had come for the government to meet the needs of those who were starving through no fault of their own. And they warned that if it did not act within a reasonable time, they would supply themselves with proper food and shelter and send the bills to the city.

The meeting appointed a Committee of Safety to organize the unemployed to petition the city government for action, scheduling a demonstration for this purpose on January 13, 1874. Originally it was planned to terminate the parade in front of City Hall, but when this was forbidden, Tompkins Square was chosen. Public meetings and parades needed approval from both the Department of Parks and the Police Board. The Department of Parks granted the committee a permit to meet in Tompkins Square, but the Police Board not only turned down the proposed parade route, but also persuaded the Department of Parks to cancel the meeting permit in order to protect "public order and safety." However, the police neglected to inform the committee of this decision.

Men, women, and children marched to Tompkins Square expecting to hear Mayor Havemeyer present a program for the relief of the unemployed. When the demonstrators had filled the square, they were attacked by the police. One account went: "Police clubs rose and fell. Women and children ran screaming in all directions. Many of them were trampled underfoot in the stampede for the gates. In the street bystanders were ridden down and mercilessly clubbed by mounted officers."

Many women and children as well as men "were laid low," wrote an indignant reporter for the New York *Sun.* At a packed protest meeting at Cooper Union, John Swinton, editor of the *Sun,* denounced the police action as an outrage to "liberty, order, decency and human misery." However, a *New York Times* reporter found the scene "not unamusing," and labeled the men and women who were victims of the police brutality "foreigners and Communists . . . [since] Communism is not a weed of native growth."[10]

Those women who were employed were involved in fighting to beat back repeated wage cuts. The first strike against a wage cut was conducted in October, 1876, by the Female Umbrella and Parasol Makers Union, even though it had a membership of only two hundred workers out of twelve hundred in the trade in the city. Union members at Dawes & Fanning, a leading manufacturer, struck rather than accept the wage cut. At a meeting held on October 13, a spokesperson for the union declared:

> If the employers knew their working women were united and ready to assist one another in a struggle for right, they would not dare threaten a reduction of wages just at the approach of winter. A large body of umbrella workers—150 or more—were asked to work at starvation prices. It was a

cruel thing and demonstrated the necessity of maintaining the organization at all times.

But the employers were not impressed. "You will be glad to come back to work when you are starved out," one employer told a striker. It was an accurate prediction. On December 20, the *New York Times* reported that the parasol makers had submitted to wage cuts that had reduced the price paid on most parasols from 11 to 7 cents per unit, and the workers still had to buy their own thread.[11]

Despite this defeat, the union remained active throughout the winter, and late in January, 1874, it reported a membership of four hundred—twice as many as it had had when the strike was lost a month earlier. In March the union felt strong enough to demand a 25 percent increase in the price paid for each parasol. In one large shop the workers accepted a compromise offer of an increase of 10 percent. But elsewhere, they went down to defeat. When the *New York Times* listed all the unions in New York City in December, 1874, the Female Umbrella and Parasol Makers Union was not among them.[12]

The cap- and hatmakers of New York City were more successful in resisting wage cuts. Indeed, their strike (which lasted almost two months) was one of the most important of the early depression years. Although a cap- and hatmakers' union had been formed a few years before the depression, it had no control over either prices or its members. Cap- and hatmakers worked for prices set by their employers, and individual members made their own agreements. Wages, already low before the depression, were cut in half and even more soon after the crisis got under way. Waterproof caps, which formerly paid 40 to 75 cents a dozen, now paid 12 cents a dozen, while conductors' caps dropped from the predepression level of $1.75 a dozen to 75 cents, and linen hats, which formerly paid $1.25 a dozen, now paid only 37½ cents. Where formerly a skilled capmaker could earn $20 a week working ten hours a day, it was now impossible to make half that amount working twelve hours.

Male capmakers, mainly German, Jewish, or native-born, averaged $8 to $10 a week, and women workers, mostly Irish, averaged $5 or $6. Even these pittances required "work from morning till evening." Moreover, much work was "given out . . . to families where young girls, many of them under ten years of age, are kept sewing a dozen hours a day, gaining perhaps, for their week's labor, a dollar and a half."[13]

In mid-January, 1874, after first having reorganized and strengthened their union, the hat- and capmakers voted to take steps to achieve a 25 to 30 percent wage increase. On January 29 a major strike closed at least seventeen shops, as more than one thousand of the fifteen hundred cap- and hatmakers, four hundred of them women and girls, left their jobs. That night, seven hundred strikers—women as well as men—pledged not to return to work till this strike was finished. The vote "was carried without a dissident voice amid intense enthusiasm."[14]

The strikers banked heavily on the employers' need to fill orders for the spring and summer trade and, with stocks extremely low, expected an early capitulation from the bosses. On February 3 Wolff & Company accepted the new wage list, and seventy-five workers—sixty of them women—returned to work the following day. Two other companies accepted the union's terms. But three others, which employed 229 workers, reported that rather than submit to the union's wage demand they would have their orders filled by nonstriking workers in Boston, Philadelphia, and elsewhere. To meet this threat, the union sent a circular "To the Capmakers, Operators, and Blockers of Boston, Philadelphia and other cities," in which it explained the reasons for the strike and urged

> you gentlemen of the other cities to support to the utmost of your ability—not by sending us money, but by adopting the same resolutions that we have passed here, for the following reasons:—
>
> First—If the manufacturers in those cities get their work done cheaper by you, they will sell cheaper.
>
> Second—When, in consequence of this, the manufacturers here have to contend against opposition in other cities, and the dealers can get goods cheaper than in New York, it will draw our trade away. Although this latter contingency will hardly come to pass, we ask you to demand the same prices for your labor that we are doing here. We understand, as a matter of course, that your prices are not better than those we are getting ourselves.
>
> United, we stand; divided, we fall.
>
> Let us be a united people of brothers.[15]

Although women strikers were playing an active and militant role, tradition dictated that the union leaders omit any mention of "sisters." Even when they referred to the women strikers, they reported gleefully that the women had turned out "to a man." Employers were more sensitive, for they publicized the fact that the strikers' "brothers and sisters in Philadelphia, Chicago, and Boston all had work."[16]

While the capmakers held out for their wage demands, contributions supporting the strikers came from furriers, who sent $100; tailors, who sent $200; the International Workingmen's Association, which sent $13; and individuals, who contributed $500 in one single day, February 17. Working cap- and hatmakers in Philadelphia sent $125 as their response to the union's circular.[17]

By the end of February, all but two of the employers had agreed to the following demands of the union: (1) a ten-hour working day; (2) no discharge of any union member who had participated in the strike; (3)

no one who continued to work during the strike should be employed "without first becoming a member of the Central Union"; and (4) a wage increase of 25 to 30 percent over existing prices. The union called off the strike except for the recalcitrant employers. The cap- and hat-makers' strike was a remarkable success in view of the deepening economic crisis, and while the seasonal factor was important in the achievement of the victory, far more significant were the solidarity of the strikers in New York City—male and female—and the cooperation they received from men and women in the trade outside of New York.[18]

In November and December of 1874, strikes of factory girls broke out in the mills of Paterson, Passaic, and New Brunswick, New Jersey, against wage reductions. They were called off after several weeks because, as one reporter wrote, "many of the females say that in view of the prospects of a hard winter, it is better to work at reduced wages, than have no wages at all."[19]

The most militant strikes in the textile industry during the Long Depression took place in Fall River, Massachusetts. By the eve of the depression, Fall River had emerged as "Spindle City," outstripping both Lowell and Lawrence in the production of textiles. Between 1870 and 1872, the years of the "Great Expansion," most of the 1,390,830 spindles that were operating in Fall River a decade later were being put into place. Fall River specialized in the production of printed cloth, and by 1875 it was manufacturing nearly 57 percent of the national output. By this time, the five corporations in existence in 1860 had increased in number to twenty-two, and the number of textile workers had grown from 2,654 to about fifteen thousand. In 1875 more than 80 percent of the city's invested capital and more than 85 percent of the value of manufactured products were in the textile industry.[20]

In the fall of 1874 wages in the industry were reduced 10 percent. A few months later another cut followed. Whatever unions had existed in Fall River had been practically eliminated early in the depression, but after the first cut, a mass meeting was held of all mule spinners,* weavers, and card room operatives to decide what action to take. The mule spinners, who were skilled immigrants from England with union experience, led the resistance to the wage cuts. The spinners and weavers, all men, set up the Weavers' Protective Association to represent both groups of workers, and the card room operatives, all women, formed the Carders' Union. A delegation from the weavers' and carders' unions visited the manufacturers and presented their demand for rescinding the wage cut. The manufacturers rejected the demand and refused to discuss arbitration on the ground that it was "un-American."[21]

---

*Mule spinners worked on a "mule" (also called a "mulejenny"), a type of spinning machine that makes thread or yarn from fibers.

The card room women thereupon met separately, voted to strike whether or not the men did, and walked out of the mills. The men soon joined the strike, and by February, 1875, more than three thousand workers had stopped work. All the members—one thousand—of the Carders' Union were on strike, but the same was not true of the men. However, those workers who were not affected by the walkout were taxed to support those on strike. After a month of struggle, the employers agreed to rescind the cut on April 1, and the strike was called off.

The following summer the manufacturers again tried to cut wages by 10 percent. Again the workers called a strike, and by August nearly every mill in the city was closed down; the walkout had assumed the character of a general strike in the industry. This strike, which was called the "Great Vacation," lasted for eight weeks and ended in a defeat for the workers. When the strike entered its third week, the discouraged spinners and weavers met and decided to call it off. The Carders' Union went along. But when the mill workers discovered that the employers were now demanding more than the 10 percent cut, they continued to hold out. On September 27, 1875, the strikers marched to the City Hall, with the members of the Carders' Union in the front. They were greated by three companies of militia and a cordon of police, who prevented them from presenting their demands. For many years thereafter, September 27 was marked in Fall River by mass meetings to commemorate these textile strikers—spinners, weavers, and card room operatives.

Late in October, the workers returned to the mills, having accepted the wage cut and signed the "yellow-dog contracts"—or "ironclad oaths," as they were called at the time. All workers who had in any way helped lead the strike were blacklisted. This defeat wiped out both the weavers' and carders' unions. Before the Long Depression was over, the Fall River workers were forced to accept wage reductions of approximately 40 percent.[22]

It was soon after this crushing defeat that workingwomen were able to score a singular victory. Immediately after the Centennial of American Independence, the female salesclerks of the St. Louis department stores announced that the principle of the "pursuit of happiness" was meaningless to them if they had to continue standing on their feet from the time the stores opened in the morning until they closed at night. They cited statements by physicians that it was harmful to health and often fatal for a woman to have to stand constantly and continuously.*

---

*This was brought out in Azel Ames' *Sex in Industry*, published in Boston in 1875. Ames, a well-known gynecologist, especially emphasized the health perils of factory work, but pointed out that even sales work, an occupation many girls favored, had its share of occupational hazards. Long hours of standing impaired the generative organs of girls and young women, even to the extent of permanently injuring their reproductive capacity (pp. 114–24).

They asked their employers to provide each saleswoman with a comfortable high-backed chair, and to allow her to sit down when she was not actually attending to the wants of a customer.

When the demand was rejected, the saleswomen went on strike. They distributed leaflets to potential customers—which included statements by physicians concerning the damage to their health caused by long hours of standing—urging them not to enter the stores until their demands were met. The same point was made in a song written for the strikers by a sympathetic St. Louis socialist:

Oh, Let the Girls Sit Down
By J.R.S.

I tell that 'tis very wrong.
　It is cruel and not right,
To keep the girls upon their feet
　From morning until night.

Their systems have not strength enough
　Such great fatigue to bear—
Their faces will all freshness lose,
　Ere long and paleness wear.

　　Then, let the girls sit down, I pray;
　　Oh, let the girls sit down;
　　Don't keep them on their feet all day—
　　Oh, let the girls sit down.

　　　　　． ． ． ．

When there's no one to wait upon,
　No customer at hand,
I cannot see what earthly use
　There is to make them stand.

Why do you not at such times give
　(Oh, I don't heed your frown!)
The tired girls a little rest,
　By letting them sit down?

　　　Then, let the girls sit down, etc.

My neighbors and myself have met,
　And talked the matter o'er;
And we've resolved and firmly too,
　To patronize no more
Those barbarous establishments
　Not one of them in town—
That keep the girls upon their feet,
　And let them ne'er sit down.

　　　Then, let the girls sit down, etc.

Toward the end of August, 1876, the St. Louis stores accepted the strikers' demands, and the salesclerks went back to work and to the relative comfort of high-backed chairs.[23]

A year later St. Louis salesclerks were out on strike again. This time it was as part of the general strike that closed down the entire city, which, in turn, was part of the Great Labor Uprising of 1877.

In mid-July, 1877, with the nation prostrate after three and a half years of severe depression, a general railroad strike developed into a nationwide uprising of labor. On July 16, 1877, railroad workers at Martinsburg, West Virginia, reacting to an attempt of the Baltimore & Ohio Railroad to cut wages another 10 percent—the second such cut in eight months—refused to take a cattle train out that evening. Other trainmen refused to replace the strikers. A crowd gathered, and train crews uncoupled the engines and put them back in the roundhouse. As the militia was called out and violence broke out, the strike extended up the B&O line and spread rapidly to other lines. Other workers came to the support of the railroad strikers, and by the weekend, angry crowds of workers were attacking the railroads and fighting with militia in the cities of West Virginia, Pennsylvania, and Ohio. The local militia generally sided with the strikers, and, for the first time since Andrew Jackson's administration, federal troops were called in to suppress a strike.

Almost before the public was aware of what was happening, the strike had spread as far as Chicago, St. Louis, and Kansas City, and then on to San Francisco. Within a few days, 100,000 workers were on strike in the first nationwide labor upheaval in history. All the main railway lines were affected, and even the employees of some Canadian railroads joined the strike.

The railroad strikes served as a fuse, carrying the spark of rebellion to other workers who were suffering from wage cuts and to the unemployed multitudes in the cities. In St. Louis, the original strike on the railroads developed into such a systematically organized and complete shutdown of all industry that it became the first truly general strike in history.[24]

In every community, women were part of the so-called "mob." The reporter for the *Baltimore Sun* concluded his description of the outbreak in Martinsburg with an observation that was to appear frequently in other communities as the Great Strike developed: "The singular part of the disturbances is the very active part taken by the women, who are the wives or mothers of the firemen. They look famished and wild, and declare for starvation rather than have their people work for the reduced wages. Better to starve outright, they say, than to die by slow starvation."[25]

On the afternoon of July 19 a coal train was prepared to leave Martinsburg for Baltimore under the protection of the state militia and federal troops. The engineer and firemen were on hand to take out the first train to leave Martinsburg since the strike started when, according to a *Sun* reporter, "The wife and daughter of Engineer Bedford climbed to the foot board, and pleaded, tears in their eyes, that he would not go.... The women were heroines immediately, and were applauded by other wives and children who had gathered around the engine. Bedford turned to the officials, saying that he could not go."[26]

The role of the wives of the strikers on the Erie Railroad at Hornellsville, New York, also aroused considerable attention. While the strikers were willing to let mail cars leave, the company was determined to run all trains, and on the morning of July 22, a section composed of an engine, a mail car, a baggage car, and two passenger coaches started out of the yards for Tiptop Mountain, the only way for westbound trains to get out of Hornellsville. Thirty soldiers were detailed to guard the train. On the long flat stretch before the ascent of Tiptop Mountain—one of the steepest grades on the road—engineer Dave Cary threw open his throttle to build up speed and momentum. The train reached twenty, then twenty-five miles an hour. At the base of the mountain, Carey opened his sand pipe a bit for traction, and fireman Matt Dewey energetically shoveled coal into the furnace, as the train raced up the side of the hill. Then suddenly, its wheels began to slip. The strikers' wives had prepared buckets of soft soap, and they and the men had slathered it liberally all over the rails for a quarter of a mile up the hill.

As the train slipped backward, the strikers and their wives on the hillside cheered wildly and threw on more soap for good measure. When the train was forced to a halt, the strikers rushed on board, shoved their way past the halfhearted militiamen, disabled the brakes, and forced all the passengers to get out. With everybody out, the strikers detached the passenger cars and sent them thundering down the hill to the Erie freight yards. Engineer Cary was dispatched with the mail, and the troops and passengers were left to make their way through thickets and briars down the hillside to the Erie depot—accompanied by laughing strikers and their wives.[27]

But it was the role of women during the Great Strike in Chicago that received the greatest publicity. On July 26 a battle raged all day between strikers from the railroads and from many other trades and industries of Chicago and their sympathizers, on the one hand, and armed police, militiamen, and federal troops, on the other. The fighting was particularly fierce along Halsted and Twelfth Streets, near the viaduct at Sixteenth Street, and at the bridge near Archer Avenue. Thousands of working people milled and massed in the streets, taunting the troops and in some cases actually engaging them with guns, sticks, and stones. Despite gunfire and repeated charges, the crowds would not disperse, and the authorities continued to send reinforcements into the area. From mid-morning on, as news and rumors of the Halsted Street battle spread, working people from across the city began to mass there. Irrespective of language and nationality differences, they united against the police and troops. The newspapers took note of this development among the working people, "who ordinarily draw the line of nationality in making up their gangs."[28]

The papers also pointed out that sexual differences, too, were overcome in the heat of the struggle. "It is a noticeable fact to all who have taken more than a casual view of the crowd of 'strikers,'" the *Chicago Times* reported the next day, "that at least one-third of the gathering were women." The *Chicago Tribune,* in fact, charged that "the women had been exciting the men to action throughout the morning." "The women," the paper concluded, "are a great deal worse than the men."[29]

The *Chicago Inter-Ocean's* account of the role of women in the crowd action aroused nationwide attention and was reprinted in newspapers the country over. Headed "Women's Warfare: Bohemian Amazons Rival The Men In Deeds Of Violence," the account told of how, when groups of men in the crowd became "thoroughly demoralized," "hundreds of these Amazons" rushed to replace them.

Women with babes in arms joined the enraged female rioters. The streets were fluttering with calico of all shades and shapes. Hundreds were bareheaded, their disheveled locks streaming in the wind. Many were shoeless. Some were young, scarcely women in age, and not at all in appearances. Dresses were tucked up around the waist, revealing large underthings. Open busts were as common as a barber's chair. Brawny, sunburnt arms brandished clubs. Knotty hands held rocks and sticks and wooden blocks. Female yells, shrill as a curlew's cry, filled the air. The swarthy features of the Bohemian women were more horrible to look at in that scene than their men in the Halsted Street riots. The unsexed mob of female incendiaries rushed to the fence and yards of Goss & Phillips' Manufacturing Company. The consternation which this attack created extended to Twenty-second Street, at that hour very quiet. A crowd of men gathered on Fish Street to witness this curious repetition of the scenes of the Paris Commune. The fence surrounding the yard gave way, and was carried off by the petticoated plunderers in their unbridled rage. There was fear for a while that the Amazonian army would continue their depredations. Word was dispatched to the Himmon Street Station, and a force of officers under Lieutenant Vesey pushed down to the corner of the contest. The women hissed as they saw the blue coats march along. Some of the less valorous took to their heels. . . . Others stood their ground.

A shower of missiles greeted the boys as they came smiling along left front into line. One woman pitched a couple of blocks at the heads of the officers, and then moved on to attend to her family duties. The men were weak in the strength and forcefulness of their language compared to these female wretches. Profanity the most foul rolled easily off their tongues with horrid glibness. Expressions were made use of that brought the blood mantling to the cheek of the worst-hardened men in the crowds of spectators. It was awful.

The police finally drove them off with clubs and revolvers, but the women remained in the area, threatening any man who said he was "not in sympathy with the mob" and joining women of other nationalities in caring for the wounded. As fast as any man was injured, he was taken into some house in the vicinity, "and the women being in strong sympathy with and doing all in their power to aid the rioters, they would not say whether they had any wounded in the house or not." The *Chicago Inter-Ocean* viewed the large number of women involved in the crowd action, as well as their militancy, as "the most disgusting revelation that has yet deepened the already black record of riot and villainy which for nearly a week has disgraced the fair name of Chicago."[30]

In St. Louis, during the general strike, women marched with men in closing down the manufacturing establishments of the city. The city's press described the situation as the "St. Louis Commune," and the *Missouri Republican* declared that the role of the "working women of this city since the strike reached us is reminiscent of the most fanatical women during the French Revolution and the Paris Commune."[31]

In Galveston, black longshoremen joined the nationwide walkout and forced employers to sign agreements granting them $2 a day. As the male laborers were returning victoriously to their jobs, another strike broke out in Galveston, this time among "the washerwomen, all colored." The *Galveston Daily News* explained: "The colored women, emboldened by the liberties allowed their fathers, husbands, and brothers, and being of a jealous nature, determined to have a public hurrah of their own, and as the men had now gained two dollars a day for a day's labor, they would ask for $1.50 or $9 per week."[32] The black washerwomen went from laundry to laundry, urging the women at work to demand $9 a week and to join the strike if their employer rejected the new wage scale:

> So down Market Street they went, led by a portly colored lady. On the way many expressions as to their contentions were heard, such as "We will starve no longer." Success awaited them as many laundries, including those owned by the Chinese, granted their demands while at those which did not, the women were forced to leave and join the strikers.
>
> The women proceeded through Market to Eighteenth Street where they scattered after avowing they would meet again at 4 o'clock on the corner of Market and Eleventh Streets, and visit each place where women are hired, and if they receive less than $1.50 per day or $9.00 per week they would force them to quit.[33]

In city after city, the Great Strike was beaten back by police, militia, and federal troops. On August 5, 1877, it passed into history as President Rutherford B. Hayes wrote in his diary: "The strikers have been put down *by force*."[34] It had cost over one hundred workers' lives, but that was less than Lucy Stone, founder of the American Woman Suffrage Association, had called for. Stone had raged in the *Women's Journal:* "The insurrection must be suppressed, if it costs a hundred thousand lives and the destruction of every railroad in the country."[35]

A month after the Great Strike was crushed, there was another "great uprising," this time among the cigarmakers of New York City, and in this one, too, the role of women was significant. Thousands of Bohemian women cigarmakers had come to New York in 1871 and 1872 after the Prussian army invaded Austria and destroyed the cigar factories of Bohemia. By the time the disastrous depression got under way in 1873, more than half of the cigarmakers in New York were women. Most of them were employed as unskilled workers under the mold-and-filler system.

The cigar trade, as a luxury industry, was one of the hardest hit by the depression. The conditions of the workers in the trade sank. In 1869 the average wages of cigarmakers had been $12.35 a week, but by 1877 they were only $5 to $10, and that only if the work was steady. The employees had their wages further reduced by being paid in cigars instead of cash, so that they had to peddle the cigars in saloons at whatever price they could get. Working hours in the trade ranged from fifty-four to sixty a week.

Even though the Cigar Makers' International Union had been the first national union to admit women to membership in 1867, many locals were reluctant to permit the female mold workers to join their ranks. As a result, their strikes ended in defeat when women were used to break them. So serious was the problem that at the union's 1871 national convention, special action was taken to urge the local unions to encourage the organization of women. But once again the locals resisted, and at the 1872 convention President Edwin Johnson pointed out that the union, comprising but a small minority of the workers in the trade, was not in a position to combat the evils of the mold effectively. He therefore urged that the constitution be amended to deprive locals of the ability to bar female cigarmakers from membership. However, it was not until 1875 that this advice was taken. Several locals immediately disaffiliated from the international. The Cincinnati local refused either to abide by the decision or to disaffiliate, and the international union had to remove its charter before it could get the Cincinnati local to change its policy of absolute exclusion of women.[36]

The same conditions that had provoked the railroad workers to strike produced the "Great Uprising" of the cigarmakers of New York. In the winter of 1876–1877, wages were again reduced, thousands of workers were idle, and more and more work was being transferred from the factories and shops into the tenements, where whole families worked from early in the morning until late at night, seven days a week, for a pittance. Against this background, the cigar workers were stirred by the Great Strike of 1877. Samuel Gompers, president of the United Cigar Makers of New York (a coalition of English-speaking, German, and Bohemian cigarmakers), recalled that the willingness of the strikers throughout the country to fight back militantly against wage cuts and police and military brutality "brought us the message that human aspirations had not been killed or cowed."[37]

In September, 1877, the cigarmakers launched a strike against the tenement house system, for higher wages, and for recognition of the union. All the Bohemian women cigarmakers, as well as women of other nationalities, joined the strike. Workers in the tenement houses also joined the strikers' ranks. The cigar manufacturers, faced with empty shops, met and passed the following resolution:

> *Whereas,* No special skill being requisite to make cigars under the present method of manufacturing by the use of molds (people of ordinary intelligence being able to acquire sufficient knowledge of the same in two to four weeks), therefore be it
> *Resolved,* That we proceed at once to the instruction of such as are willing to learn, and it having been our experience that females more readily learn the trade than males, be it
> *Resolved,* That we give the former the preference, and endeavor thereby to open for them a new industry, both pleasant and remunerative.[38]

This sudden concern for women did not, however, extend to those who had formerly been employed by the cigar manufacturers and were now on strike for a decent livelihood. The police were called in to take care of these women. Siding openly with the manufacturers, they arrested large numbers of strikers without preferring charges against them and beat women as well as men on their way to jail. Charges of conspiracy and intimidation were lodged against women strikers who fought the scabs and the police. While they remained in jail—the union did not have the $100 bail demanded by the judge for each of the strikers—their sister and brother strikers picketed the manufacturers. The *Cigar Makers' Journal* of November, 1877, reported: "Striking men and women formed in line in front of Stratton & Storm's tenement cigar factory, where a scab was working, in order to show their contempt by spitting before the door of the traitor." The December issue carried this notice: "Mrs. Treish left her husband, a scab; the union is dearer to her than her family. Brave woman!"[39]

Bohemian women cigarmakers in Springfield, Detroit, and elsewhere sent financial contributions to the strikers in New York. The international union assessed all its employed members 10 percent of their wages, and the funds collected were sent to New York. A unique feature of the relief program was the operation by the union of a cigar factory, purchased by the strike committee to provide work for some of the strikers, to lighten the relief burden, to increase the funds for support of the strikers, and "to create consternation" in the employers' association. About 2,400 workers, equally divided between men and women strikers, were employed in the shop, and a percentage of their wages was deducted to pay for the factory.[40]

But the militancy and self-sacrifice of the strikers were not sufficient to overcome the organized resistance of the manufacturers, the cold and hunger, and the strikebreaking activities of the police. When the strike was finally broken early in 1878, the Manufacturers' Association publicly thanked the police commissioner. In January the workers began to go back to whatever shops they could and for whatever wages the manufacturers would offer. The strike was officially called off in February, more than four months after it began. The *Tobacco Leaf,* the employers' organ, gloated over the victory but acknowledged that the strike had been "the most formidable and skillfully managed labor revolt ever inaugurated in this country, and, among other things, proves that women can be as effective and powerful in such struggles as any men."[41]

Although the strike did not achieve its objective, it did reduce the number of cigars manufactured in the tenements and brought the issue of tenement house manufacturing to the attention of the public, thereby preparing the ground for the final struggle against the system. In addition, the "Great Uprising" of 1877, as it was called by the union, gained wide support among cigarmakers throughout the country and checked the relentless wage-cutting policy that had been pursued by the employers in every city for several years. It was a tremendous stimulus to organization and marked the beginning of a rapid increase in the membership of the Cigar Makers' International Union. Many of these new members were female. The contribution of the women cigarmakers during the "Great Uprising" helped both the organization of women and the overcoming of much of the resistance to their entrance into local unions as equal members.[42]

The depression had accentuated a serious problem faced by young workingwomen: adequate housing at a reasonable cost. By 1877 the situation was desperate, and rich philanthropists in a number of cities established homes for workingwomen so that they would "find shelter and employment until able to secure a permanent position." Boston's Home for Working Women, financed by rich women, and New York's Woman's Hotel, funded by A. T. Stewart, the merchant prince and department store magnate—both established around 1877—were two examples of these developments. The Young Women's Christian Association, founded in Boston in 1866, also tried to meet this problem, while the Women's Educational and Industrial Union, established in 1877 by

Boston's rich women, provided reading rooms, parlors, and inexpensive lunches for workingwomen, as well as some housing.

While some of these establishments met a real need, there was a tendency on the part of the sponsors to patronize the workingwomen, which the women resented. Especially resented were the strict rules of conduct imposed on those who resided at the homes. At a mass meeting in New York's Cooper Institute on June 1, 1878, hundreds of working-women gathered to vent their resentment at the operation of the Woman's Hotel. The chairperson introduced "A New Set of Rules" for the hotel, which exposed, through ridicule, the prevailing practices. Some of the "new" rules were:

> Application for admission must be made by letter, and be indorsed by 12 prominent women of New York. (Great laughter.)
> The service of the hotel will be exclusively performed by men. No women need apply. (Laughter.)
> Smoking, chewing, spitting, swearing, singing, talking above a whisper in the dining-rooms, parlors, or bedrooms, expressly forbidden. (Laughter.)
> Lounging on sofas, chairs, chair-tilting, placing feet on mantles or furniture of rooms especially forbidden. (Laughter.)
> Dominoes, cards, checkers, and dice prohibited in bedrooms. (Laughter.)
> No visiting from room to room allowed without special permission of the Board of Managers. (Laughter.)
> Dogs of every description expressly forbidden in parlors, dining-rooms and bedrooms. Horses also excluded. (Laughter.)
> Gentlemen are requested to provide themselves with a regulation full-dress before coming to the hotel.
> The management reserve the right to discharge the boarders at their option, with or without cause, should they deem it expedient at any future time to open the hotel as an orphan asylum, zoological garden, or museum. (Great laughter and applause.)
> A cheerful compliance with the above rules is requested. The boarders are also expected to pledge themselves to respect any additional rules the management or any employe may lay down for their benefit and that of the proprietors. (Laughter.)

In a more serious vein, the workingwomen adopted resolutions condemning the management of the hotel for discriminating against working-class females, criticized wealthy philanthropists who sought to dictate how workingwomen should live and conduct themselves, and denounced the "spirit of avarice and tyranny which denies to a working woman a flower pot, bird, sewing-machine, or permission to see father, brother, sister, or mother, on the pretense of exact order" as reflecting "that public estimate and legal enactment which classes women of the present day among minors, idiots, criminals, and Indians not taxed." The resolution recommended that the education of youth emphasize classes "in business probity and practical morals . . . so that instead of producing, as too often is the case, grasping merchants, dishonest lawyers, weak-minded legislators, and the like, all bent on exploiting working women, they shall graduate men proud in the consciousness of their rectitude and scorning to do such a mean thing." Finally, the resolutions took a slap at wealthy philanthropists who patronized working-class women by resolving "That equal privileges, equal changes and emoluments in the walks and employments of life, for men and women, equal justice in social estimate and administration of law, is what the world demands and values more than the patronizing of a spurious generosity. (Great applause!)"[43]

Business nationwide began to revive by the middle of 1878, and a year later industrial recovery was in full swing throughout most of the country. American workers had sustained terrible losses during the depression years. As a result of the struggles of organized workers, the length of the workday had been reduced from the fourteen and fifteen hours common in the early part of the century to an average of eleven on the eve of the Long Depression. In 1874, amid great jubilation, the ten-hour law had finally become a reality in Massachusetts. But as the depression deepened, the working hours for those employed lengthened, and even in the Bay State manufacturers freely violated the new ten-hour law. Meanwhile, wages declined sharply as a result of repeated reductions. By the end of the depression, wages had dropped back to the 1864 level, and it was estimated in 1883, five years after recovery got under way, that wages were lower than they had been in 1870.[44]

As far as the labor movement was concerned, the picture was equally bleak. While trade unionism did not entirely disappear, the majority of the unions lost most of their members. Unions of workingwomen fared even worse. By the end of the depression, the two statewide organizations for female workers (the Massachusetts Working Women's League and the Working Women's Labor Union for the State of New York) and all the independent women's unions of the 1860s and 1870s—female typesetters and parasol and umbrella makers in New York City, collar starchers in Troy, and shoemakers in Lynn and other cities—had disappeared. The shoemakers held out the longest. In 1875 and 1876, the Daughters of St. Crispin made their existence known in Lynn when they "turned out" against the bosses. But in 1878 the shoe manufacturers finally succeeded in forcing the Knights and Daughters of St. Crispin to sign the so-called ironclad oaths, agreeing to give up unionism as a condition of employment.[45]

As the depression grew to a close, a handful of workingwomen in Chicago tried to instill a spirit of unionism among their sisters. Led by Lizzie Swank and Elizabeth Rogers, they founded the Chicago Working

Women's Union in the late 1870s. Their aim was to convince other workingwomen that unified action could bring improvements in their appalling conditions. They sponsored lectures and forums in public halls on the value of trade unionism. More often, however, they met in private homes, where they could discuss each other's problems without fear of reprisals.

The founders of the Working Women's Union encountered great difficulty in convincing workingwomen to attend. Many looked on their employment as only temporary, expecting to marry. Others feared that trade unions were too "bold and common" for girls to join. Few young workingwomen seemed willing to give up their Sunday afternoons for either organizational meetings or discussions of the economic issues of the day.[46]

In 1881 the Working Women's Union collapsed. Undaunted, its leaders turned to an emerging labor movement that was beginning to organize workingwomen and established a woman's assembly of the Knights of Labor. At precisely the same time, two other groups of workingwomen were turning to the same organization: shoemakers and textile workers. During the 1880s the Daughters of St. Crispin were to prove, as part of the Knights of Labor, that they may have been defeated in 1878 but they had not been destroyed. In the years 1878–1880, under the leadership of the International Labor Union—an industrial union for unskilled factory workers organized by a combination of Marxian Socialists and Yankee eight-hour advocates—textile workers in Paterson and Passaic, New Jersey, Clinton and Cohoes, New York, and Fall River and other mill cities had conducted a series of militant strikes. The strike of 1880 in Cohoes, conducted mostly by Irish and French-Canadian women textile workers, ended in a complete victory for the more than five thousand workers who won a 10 percent wage increase and fifty minutes for dinner.[47]

The 1878–1879 strikes in Paterson and Fall River were among the greatest in American history up to that time. A third wage cut in less than a year convinced 550 unorganized workers in Paterson, mostly women and children, to quit the textile mills owned by Robert and Henry Adams. On June 20, 1878, announcing their determination to strike against the latest wage cut, the workers sent out a notice appealing "to their fellow workingmen and women throughout the United States to aid them in their struggle against starvation and poverty." All contributions to the strikers were requested to be forwarded to Miss Maggie Henry, treasurer of the strikers' committee. Since both Paterson papers (the *Guardian* and the *Press*) supported the company, all contributions would be acknowledged in the *Labor Standard,* published in New York City by J. P. McDonnell, one of the Marxists who had founded the International Labor Union.

McDonnell endorsed the strike wholeheartedly and described the mills in which the strikers worked as "penitentiaries" and their wages as "hunger rates." He appealed to labor to support the strike with financial aid:

Many of these strikers—the greater number perhaps—are brave, heroic women who will hold out till victory crowns their efforts, and who are determined to make organization their watch-word in the future. The heroism of these 550 is more sublime than that of the 300 who fought and died at Thermopylae. They stand in the pass fighting for the rights not of Paterson or of the weavers, but of the whole human family.

To their rescue workingmen and women of America. Success for the Paterson operatives means less poverty and more organization and power for our class.

McDonnell came to Paterson, organized the strikers into the International Labor Union, and helped them in their battle. He was one of the speakers at the great demonstration on July 20, a demonstration featured by a procession through Paterson that rivaled the great procession in Lynn during the shoemakers' strike of 1860. A contemporary description went in part:

The workers gathered early. The girls came forth in their prettiest dresses, their handsome faces covered with smiles. The men were at their post in due time, wearing upon their backs the best clothing that starvation prices allowed them to buy. Two hours before the time announced for the procession to move, the streets were thronged with crowds of spectators. At four o'clock the procession formed in Ellison Street. First came a brass band, then the male operatives of Adams' and other mills, then a fife and drum band. The ladies' procession followed. Transparencies bearing the following inscriptions were carried aloft in different parts of the procession:
"The laborer is worthy of his hire."
"We ask to live comfortably and educate our children."
"Without labor there can be no capital."
"Labor has rights that capital is bound to respect."
"Join the International Labor Union, a union which organizes all without regard to sex, color, nationality or race."
At 4:30 the mounted marshals gave the word to march and the bands played "The March of the Toilers." The procession then proceeded through Ellison Street to Mill, from Mill to Van Houton, Van Houton to Main, Main to Market, thence to the romantic grounds of the Passaic Falls. At least 8,000 toilers walked in the procession, while all Paterson seemed to line the sidewalks. The people on the sidewalks expressed their abhorence of Adams and their sympathy with oppressed labor by lusty cheers and waving of handkerchiefs. . . .
At the Falls there were at least 10,000 spectators. After several speeches by a number of speakers headed by Mr. J. P. McDonnell, the strikers sang "The March of the Toilers," all joining in the chorus:

> We'll fight, we'll fight, for justice and fair play,
> We'll fight, we'll fight, nor care what despots say,
> We'll make the cruel Adams' class stand back and clear the way.
> We'll give them a taste of our Union.*

This was only one of several demonstrations and processions held during the strike.

When the Adams brothers brought strikebreakers in from Fall River and other New England towns, the strikers and their supporters met the new workers at the rail depot and stopped them in the streets, urging them not to help the company. When they won the strikebreakers over, the strikers, with financial aid from the community, financed their trips home.

In March, 1879, the nine-month-old strike came to an end with a victory for the strikers. The company conceded defeat, rescinded the wage cut, and offered an increase in wages.[48]

In Fall River over five thousand men and women—spinners, weavers, and carders—struck for more than six months for a nine-hour day and for restoration of the 15 percent in wages they had lost during the depression. Unfortunately, a split developed when the spinners called off their strike in return for a restoration of part of their wage cut, while the weavers and the women carders stayed out and went down to defeat. But the industrial peace that followed did not last long. In 1883 the spinners, weavers, and carders united once more to rock Fall River with their strike demonstrations, this time under the leadership of the Knights of Labor.

As the 1880s opened, a labor paper reminded the employers that although the labor movement was exhausted, it was not destroyed, and that "the spirit of resistance to wrong, which is the spirit of Trade Unionism, will never die while labor can be wronged, either by individuals or by law." That "spirit of resistance to wrong" was to manifest itself in the next few years in the amazing growth of the Knights of Labor, the first mass organization of workingmen and workingwomen in American history, and, with the one exception of the Chinese, of workers of all races and ethnic groups.

---

*"The March of the Toilers," words set to the tune of "Marching Through Georgia," was the strike song and was sung repeatedly during the strike. For the full text of the song, see Philip S. Foner, *American Labor Songs of the Nineteenth Century* (Urbana, Ill., 1975), p. 134.

11

The Knights of Labor

In 1869 nine Philadelphia garment cutters, whose union had been shattered and its members blacklisted, formed a secret society, which they named the Noble Order of the Knights of Labor. Its founder, Uriah H. Stephens, became master workman, the title of the presiding officer. Stephens placed great emphasis on solidarity. Labor, he argued, had to be powerful and unified in order to cope with the strength of organized capital. Since all workers had common interests, they should logically belong to a common society and be united by bonds of "universal brotherhood." "I do not claim any power of prophecy," he is reported to have said, "but I can see ahead of me an organization that will cover the globe. It will include men and women of every craft, creed, and color; it will cover any race worth saving."[1]

But Stephens, though far in advance of many of the members of the early Knights, was so obsessed with the value of secrecy and with the sexist view that women could not keep secrets that, while he favored the inclusion of all male workers and mentioned women, he did not advocate opening membership to women. They were excluded from the Knights for more than a decade. Meanwhile, the Molly Maguire episode had the effect of discrediting secret organizations,* and the Catholic clergy would not countenance secret oaths. Faced with this opposition, Knights leaders moved to eliminate some secret parts of their ritual in

---

*The Molly Maguires was a secret society of Irish workers, named for a legendary Irish revolutionary, which operated in the mining regions of Pennsylvania, and was accused of plotting the assassination of mine superintendents and others whose policies they resented. Today many labor historians argue that there was no society in America calling itself the Molly Maguires; that the name was tagged to the Ancient Order of Hibernians by the coal operators and their allies in order to crush any organization in the mining industry, and that the Pinkerton agency hired to ferret out the so-called criminals actually committed many of the crimes. Ten miners, all Irish, were hanged as ring-leaders in the "conspiracy" after a biased trial.

On January 16, 1879, the government of Pennsylvania granted a pardon to Jack Kehoe, the miners' leader and one of the ten men executed.

1878. These efforts were consummated at the General Assembly meeting held in Detroit in September, 1881, where delegates voted to abolish oaths and other secret aspects by the beginning of the following year. Terence V. Powderly, who had replaced Stephens as master workman, predicted that making the Knights' names and objectives public would result in an increase in the order's membership.[2]

If nothing else, the new policy removed one obstacle to the admission of women. More important was the fact that the census of 1880 revealed that the population of the country had increased by 30 percent in the preceding decade, but the number of males over sixteen years of age employed in manufacturing had increased by less than 25 percent while that of females over fifteen had increased by 64 percent. The 2,647,000 women gainfully employed in 1880 constituted 15.2 percent of the nation's work force, and employers were still continuing to replace men with women at lower wages. By 1890 there were 4,005,500 gainfully employed women, making up 17.2 percent of the total labor force. This figure included almost 300,000 girls under fifteen years of age.

About a quarter of the 4 million women workers in 1890 were housekeepers, stewards, hostesses, or family servants. Women factory workers were distributed as follows:[3]

Clothing manufacture	389,231	Tobacco	10,868
Laundries and cleaning	109,280	Printing	9,322
Cotton textiles	92,394	Silk and rayon	9,211
Other textiles	42,420	Carpets and rugs	7,674
Shoes	21,007	Hats	6,357
Containers and boxes	14,126		

At its first national convention in 1878, the Knights delegates discussed the impact on men's wages of unskilled females working as machine operators. In an effort to protect the men, they included in the Knights' constitution the provision that one of the order's goals would be to secure "for both sexes equal pay for equal work," as the National Labor Union had done ten years earlier. But the Knights' constitution still made no provision for the admission of women.

At the 1879 convention Philip Van Patten, a socialist, introduced a resolution to permit women to become members and to organize local assemblies under the same conditions as men. After some quibbling over details, the resolution received the necessary two-thirds approval, but it was tabled until the next assembly. At the 1880 General Assembly, Powderly was authorized to convene a committee to prepare regulations and a ritual for the induction of women. He never convened the committee, explaining later that "a separate ritual will bespeak inequality, lead to confusion and is unnecessary." It actually *was* unnecessary, for early in 1881, when male shoe workers of Local Assembly 64 in Philadelphia refused to accept a wage cut, management turned to the unorganized female shoe workers and cut wages 30 to 60 percent. Under the leadership of Mary Stirling, the women struck. Local Knights organizer Harry Skeffington promptly inducted the strikers into the order. Garfield Assembly 1684, the first local composed exclusively of women, was chartered in September, 1881. Its members elected Stirling to the District Assembly, which sent her to the General Assembly that year.[4]

Once the doors were opened, the number of women's assemblies grew sharply. One other women's local was formed in 1881; 3 in 1882; 9 in 1883; 13 in 1884; 46 in 1885; and 121 in 1886. The organizational structure of the Knights of Labor provided for two types of local assemblies under the jurisdiction of the broader District Assembly, and women participated in both. When a small community did not contain sufficient workers in a given trade to form a separate local, it formed a mixed local, including all eligible Knights. Many of these mixed locals contained only women members. The Garfield Assembly was the first of these, but the idea caught on, so that by 1887, the majority of the female locals were of this type. In the large cities, organizers encouraged workers in specific trades to form separate trade assemblies. In New York, Chicago, Fall River, and other large centers, such trade assemblies included both men and women. Still, it was not automatic that assemblies should include both sexes. "L.A. 5426 which has hitherto been composed entirely of men requests permission to admit women," Charles Lichtman, a member of the General Executive Board, wrote to Powderly. "I have told them it needed dispensation from you and that to save them time I would request one from you. The address of the R[ecording] S[ecretary] is Will C. Bailey, Riverside, California. Will you please attend to this?" Powderly granted the dispensation, but in some cases, even this did not solve the problem. John A. Forsythe, the recording secretary of Assembly No. 2317 in Seymour, Indiana, complained to Powderly:

> Our Assembly is a "mixed" one of about 140 members, all men workers. Recently, new by-laws were adopted fixing the price of initiation for ladies, and eight good and true women, ladies in the best sense of the term and wives of honest workers, have been proposed and balloted in due form and each one has been rejected.
>
> The Assembly has good reason to believe that, in each instance, these black balls were cast by the same individuals. . . . The majority is powerless to repair the very great injury that has been done.
>
> The questions we, as true Knights, desire you to answer at your earliest convenience are:
>
> 1. What, if anything, can we do according to law in the matter?
> 2. Are men who, professing to be Knights, will skulk behind the ballot box, and in the way and with the weapon of a coward, assault good and true

women in the virtue dearest to the heart of every true wife, mother or daughter, her reputation and social standing, worthy to be recognized as Knights?

3. Must the very large majority of our Assembly, who recognize the true principles of Knighthood—the equality of woman—submit to the action of the very small minority in thus ruling her out of our circle?

The rejection of these women has aroused the most intense indignation and, for the good of the Order, we ask you, as our acknowledged and honored head, to point us, if possible, to some way out of the difficulty.

Powderly praised the Assembly's majority for upholding the "true principles of Knighthood," and granted dispensation to overrule the blackballs. The "eight good and true women" were initiated as members of Assembly No. 2317.[5]

Figures on the number of women members in the order vary. The highest estimate was made by M. B. E. Kelley in 1898. "One hundred and fifty, even two hundred thousand would probably be quite within bounds," Kelley wrote, but quickly added that this "must be pure guesswork." The most acceptable estimate is that in 1886, when the Knights' membership was at its highest point, there were about 50,000 women members, constituting 8 or 9 percent of the total membership.

Who were these female Knights? A breakdown of the occupations of the women assemblies in 1886 reveals that nineteen of the ninety-one assemblies listed were composed of shoe workers; seventeen of mill operatives; twelve of housekeepers; five each of sewers, tailoresses, and laundresses; four each of knitters, collar and shirt ironers, and dress- and cloakmakers; two each of hatters, weavers, and paper-box makers; and one each of bookbinders, carpetmakers, cigarmakers, farmers, feather curlers, gold cutters, lead pencil workers, and rubber workers. There was one assembly of Bohemian women in Chicago, and fifteen of black women whose occupations were housekeepers, farmers, chambermaids, and laundresses.* Clearly the Knights did not limit the order's membership to wage earners; a few women's assemblies had both middle-class and working-class women as members. An example is the Myrtle Assembly in Baltimore, a women's union to which middle-class women also belonged; however, workingwomen held all the offices.[6]

The first union of female government employees in Washington, D.C., joined the Knights of Labor in 1883, the same year that the Civil

---

*Assemblies of black domestics existed in Washington, D.C., Norfolk, Virginia, Wilmington, North Carolina, and Philadelphia. However, the Atlanta black washerwomen who formed an association in a black church in 1880 and a year later struck for a dollar per dozen pounds of wash, were not affiliated with the Knights of Labor. Three thousand washerwomen struck, but threats from landlords to raise the rent of all strikers and arrests by police broke the strike (David M. Katzman, *Seven Days A Week: Women and Domestic Service in Industrializing America*, New York, 1978, p. 196).

Service Act made a limited number of government posts in Washington subject to competitive examinations. For the first time, women were encouraged to compete directly with men for jobs in the federal government. The Pendleton Act, as the Civil Service Act was then known, represented a first step in the fight for equality for women in government employment, although the 1870 measure permitting department heads to pay women less than men for identical work was still in effect. When the first test under the Civil Service Act was administered in 1883, the highest score was achieved by Mary Frances Hoyt, a Vassar College alumna, who was appointed to a $900 clerkship on September 5. But she actually received only $600, while men already in the post were paid the higher amount. Secretary of the Interior Henry M. Teller found a simple solution to the problem—he refused to employ any women in the Department of the Interior.

In September, 1882, women clerks in a number of government departments formed the Women's National Labor League, with Charlotte Smith as president and Elizabeth S. Bryant as secretary. The League affiliated with the Knights of Labor in February, 1883, giving the Knights of Labor an assembly of female government employees in the nation's capital.[7]

Since shoe and textile workers were an important part of the female membership in the Knights, it is not surprising that the largest part of that membership was in Massachusetts. In the year and a half preceding 1887, no fewer than 13,200 Bay State women were admitted to the Knights, 80 percent of them in the shoe and textile industries. The largest center was Lynn, where the women shoemakers, former Daughters of St. Crispin, were affiliated as assemblies of the Daughters of Labor and the Ladies' Stitching Association. Women Knights were part of the ten thousand members of the labor movement in Lynn at a time when the total number of workingpeople in the city was not much more than fifteen thousand.[8]

Women garment workers made up another important element in the Knights, and in several cities they formed viable union organizations under the banner of the order. By 1886 women garment workers in Chicago had organized two local trade assemblies—Local No. 7170 for women cloakmakers and Local No. 7707 for tailoresses. Additional garment workers participated in trade assemblies supported by both men and women. Other local assemblies for female garment workers operated in New York City, Rochester, Toledo, Newark, Baltimore, and St. Louis.

The reason these women joined the Knights is illustrated by the case of Rebecca, a New York city workingwoman, who wrote a series of letters to the editor of *John Swinton's Paper* concerning her plight and that of her fellow employees. She worked at a sewing machine in a underclothing factory from eight until six for a salary of $5 a week. Rebecca ended her first letter with a plaintive question on behalf of herself and her sister in the factory: "*How* do we live on $5 a week with good girlish appetites for nice things, good girlish fondness for nice clothes and ornaments, and good girlish liking for dances, excursions, and holidays—how do we get along?"

Her next letter informed the editor that a reduction in business had caused a corresponding reduction in the work force at her place of employment from a peak of one hundred to thirty. Those who remained had to work ever more quickly. Still, she complained, the employer treated them like dogs and used terms like "liar," "hussy," and "lazy good-for-nothing" in shouting at them. Although he insisted that they start work punctually, he delayed ringing the bell in the evening in order to steal a few minutes from them. Rebecca concluded the letter with the news that she and her sister had been "laid off."

In her next letter Rebecca reported that she and her sister had obtained work as apronmakers. The girls now earned $3.60 a week each, working from six in the morning until ten at night. After a month's absence, Rebecca returned to her former job. Conditions had grown worse in the interim. Not only did the workroom now lack adequate heating, but the employer prohibited the girls from warming themselves in the hall room during the lunch period. They also received violent scoldings if they so much as looked up from their work.

Rebecca concluded her series of letters by stressing the need for organizing the workingwomen into trade unions in order to eliminate the injustice, capricious and insulting behavior, and repeated humiliations she had described and to introduce fair wages and decent conditions. The impulse for organization, she pointed out, must come from outside, since the girls lacked the time needed for effective organization and were resigned to a daily life of drudgery.

In the next issue of *John Swinton's Paper* a letter from a reader advised Rebecca to join the Knights of Labor and listed the address where she and her fellow workingwomen could become members of the order. Within two weeks, the girls in Rebecca's factory had all joined the Knights.[9]

While the Knights did not wage a consistent campaign to eliminate racism in the order's ranks, it did bring large numbers of black workers into the predominantly white labor movement for the first time. The constitution promulgated for all local assemblies in 1884 declared that the order made no distinction with respect to "nationality, sex, creed, or color." It has been estimated that of a total membership in 1886 exceeding 700,000, no fewer than 60,000 were black.

The Knights of Labor included both all-black assemblies and those of mixed black and white membership. Although segregated locals were predominant, especially in the South, even some locals below the Mason-Dixon line were mixed. The Knights began organizing in the South in 1878, assigning fifteen organizers to the area, and Negroes as well as whites were asked to join. The blacks either formed or joined locals of longshoremen, miners, iron- and steelworkers, and farm workers.[10]

A number of women's locals were organized in Atlanta, Richmond, Durham, Memphis, Raleigh, and Jacksonville, usually composed of domestic workers and seamstresses. Nearly all these locals were segregated, but there were a few integrated locals of female Knights in the South. Ida B. Wells, a black journalist and teacher, soon to become internationally famous as a crusader against lynching, wrote in the Memphis *Watchman* in 1887:

> I was fortunate enough to attend a meeting of the Knights of Labor.... I noticed that everyone who came was welcomed and every woman from black to white was seated with the courtesy usually extended to white ladies alone in this town. It was the first assembly of the sort in this town where color was not the criterion to recognition as ladies and gentlemen. Seeing this I could listen to their enunciation of the principle of truth and accept them with a better grace.[11]

By 1887 the order's black recruits came primarily from rural areas in the South, where black men and women formed assemblies together in an effort to escape the evils of tenant farming and sharecropping, low wages, low per capita income, high illiteracy, poor public services, lynching, the convict-labor system, and chain gangs. The Knights, whose program stressed land reform, increased education, and workers' cooperatives, held out the only hope to landless blacks in an agrarian society, barred from textile, tobacco, furniture, and other industries and oppressed and dominated by landlord-merchant power. Lack of capital generally prevented the successful operation of black Southern cooperatives, but black members of the Knights were able to establish a number of them. Usually the first floor of the union hall was the site of a cooperative store. The Knights, moreover, provided blacks with the mutual-benefit and social functions—picnics, banquets, socials, and the like—associated with the churches and fraternal societies in which black women had traditionally played an important role. Since the Knights appeared more willing than any other organization of the era to extend to blacks a measure of both acceptance and dignity, the blacks eagerly joined.[12]

Young black men in Chicago set up a tailoring establishment after their employer locked them out for attending a labor parade. By soliciting subscriptions, they raised the $400 needed to begin production. Nine months later they had produced $36,000 worth of garments. In Baltimore and New York, women operated cooperative shirt factories, while women in Waterford, New York, ran a collar-and-cuff factory. Black women in Richmond operated a cooperative laundry under the auspices of the Knights of Labor.

In spite of the hostility of its leadership to the strike as a weapon, the Knights of Labor attained its greatest membership as a result of the order's role during strikes.* The first major strike conducted by the Knights was that of the telegraphers against Western Union in 1883. It was also the first K. of L. strike in which men and women struck together. The telegraphers were defeated after a three-months walkout; many were refused reemployment and were blacklisted. "The Ostracized Female Operators," read the headline of a story in a New York paper early in September, 1883, reporting that a fund was being raised in behalf of the telegraphers who had gone out on strike against Western Union and who had been refused reemployment. "Aid is especially asked for the ostracized female operators, who have been persistently rejected when applying for their old positions. These ladies, however, have no desire to live in idleness, and ask those who sympathize with them to give them notice of any situations that can be obtained."[13]

Taking his cue from Western Union, a Philadelphia shoe manufacturer discharged the grievance committee and every officer of the Garfield Assembly in his shop. The male Knights in Philadelphia advised the members of the assembly not to resist, but the female Knights rejected their advice. They decided that unless they fought the issue through and established a precedent of opposing discrimination against union members, the organization of women workers would suffer. They therefore called the shop on strike, and after a bitter struggle, succeeded in reinstating every one of their members.[14]

In most cases, women shoe workers received more support from male Knights than those in Philadelphia. On April 25, 1885, shoe manufacturers Brennan & White in Williamsburgh (Brooklyn) discharged all women employees belonging to the Knights' shoemakers' union. When the male workers walked out in protest, scabs were hired, given loaded revolvers, and told to "shoot to kill" if necessary to protect themselves against strikers' violence. At the same time, Brennan & White had the women blacklisted in other Williamsburgh shoe factories and sought female convicts from the Kings County Prison as replacements.

When some convicts refused to work, the women strikers issued a

---

*The great growth of the Knights of Labor followed its victory over Jay Gould in the strike on the Southwestern railroad system, involving 10,000 miles of railroad and 4,500 workers. When Gould yielded on March 16, 1885, the spectacular triumph over one of the greatest capitalists of the day brought thousands of new workers into the ranks of the K. of L. Between July, 1885, and October, 1886, membership in the Knights of Labor jumped from 110,000 to over 700,000.

statement praising them and assuring the manufacturers that with the "power" of the union, they would triumph: "We will live to witness the day of our victory." And they did. A boycott declared by the New York Protective Association (controlled by District Assembly No. 49 of the Knights of Labor) and Brooklyn's Central Labor Union came to the aid of the strikers. Shoe laster John Flynn described how it worked in the local neighborhoods. Committees of men and women strikers "go right into our neighborhood, where we live and tell our mothers and sisters not to buy the company's shoes." Before long, Brennan & White reinstated all the strikers and signed an agreement with the union representing the women in their shop.[15]

A boycott also helped women hatters at Berg's hat factory in Orange, New Jersey, who were fired when they decided to form a local of the Knights in the spring of 1885. The boycott instituted by the Knights and other trade unionists caused Berg to back down.[16]

In 1881 a union of cloakmakers joined a newly organized group of dressmakers and proceeded to ally themselves with New York City's Knights. Although this particular organization was short-lived and excluded women in the trades, many of the same men launched a second effort in 1882, once again forming a local trade assembly of the Knights of Labor. When the order permitted women to join, they invited women to join them. Although none of these workers—men or women—had ever participated in a strike, they gathered in July, 1883, in Standard Hall to listen to speeches favoring a walkout, delivered in both German and English. The rallying cry for these Polish Jews, Germans, and Bohemians became "When men and women cannot earn enough to live they must strike." Women workers met separately upstairs and expressed their determination to stand together with the men.

More than 750 workers, about half of them women, agreed to go out on strike for a $2.50 daily wage rate and a ten-hour day. They also insisted that piece rates be reconstructed so that operators who were paid according to that system could earn $15 a week.

After women in the remaining shops still working joined the walkout, the manufacturers acceded to the workers' demands. By August, 1883, the successful strikers had returned to work. While the New York clothing workers' strike was not the first Knights of Labor strike to unite men and women—the telegraphers had already done this in their strike against Western Union—it was the first such strike to end in victory.[17]

Not all the women in the clothing trade were as militant as those in New York City. Lizzie Swank, organizer of an assembly of women garment workers in Chicago, was working in an unorganized factory whose owner first cut prices paid for piecework, then introduced a new rule that work would not be credited to an employee's book until it was returned from the buttonhole maker and presser. As a result, some workers had to go without any income for from two to four weeks, meanwhile falling behind in their rent and facing eviction from their boardinghouses. Swank suggested that they complain to the manufacturer. When each girl voiced her fear of approaching him individually, Swank suggested that they pass around a petition listing their complaints. She wrote the petition; 150 signatures were collected, and only four workers refused to sign. The signers agreed that if even one woman was fired, all the others would walk out. When the women presented the petition, the supervisor called them "silly hussies," and the manufacturer called them ingrates who did not appreciate the generous benefits he provided his workers. Then he singled out four, including Swank and her sister, the group's spokeswomen, and fired them. Not one of the other 146 girls who had signed the petition defended their discharged sisters or walked off the job, as they had agreed to do.[18]

However, on May 3, 1886, during the great eight-hour strikes in Chicago, Lizzie Swank led several hundred sewing women in a strike for the eight-hour day, and they closed down shop after shop along Sedgwick and Division streets. The *Chicago Tribune* of May 4, 1886 called them "Shouting Amazons," and reported: "Between 300 and 400 girls and women were affected with a malignant form of the eight-hour malady yesterday morning." One women told the *Tribune* reporter: "We'll never give in. Never, never, until we get our demands. We want eight hours with ten hours pay." The paper noted that when the march was over, the women signed up to join the Knights of Labor.

In 1882 men, women, and children employed by the Harmony Company Cotton mills in Cohoes, New York, struck against a wage cut—the fourth reduction in seven years. The majority of the strikers were Irish and French-Canadian women, and after six months, the company brought in Protestant Swedish families to replace the Catholic strikers. The strikers responded directly and vigorously, gathering at the mill entrances to "greet" the scabs with stones. The strike was crushed by a combination of police protection for the scabs and starvation. However, the strikers joined the Knights of Labor, and within a year the mill was compelled to rescind the fourth wage cut. The working-class community of Cohoes elected to the State Assembly one of the men who had worked with the women strikers in 1882 and was head of the K. of L. in the city.[19]

The 1884 strikes of women members of the Knights in the textile mills of Fall River and Worcester, in the hat factories of South Norwalk, Connecticut, and of tobacco workers in the Durham, North Carolina, plant of W. Duke Sons and Company were outstanding for the militancy and perseverance of the strikers. One of the most memorable strikes of the decade of militant strikes was conducted in 1885 by women Knights in the carpet-weaving industry. There were some men involved in the strike of three thousand carpet weavers employed by Alexander Smith's Sons in Yonkers, New York, but 90 percent of the strikers were young women. The strike began on February 20, 1885, when Smith refused to reinstate a 10 percent wage reduction (imposed the previous December), to pay wages already due, and to rehire at least twenty women who had been fired for membership in the Knights. The company's stringent factory discipline was another cause of the strike. In late March the strikers' executive committee issued a statement listing the principal demands, together with a long discussion of company fines for actions that the women considered harmless. The committee's complaints were quite specific:

> If a girl is caught looking out of a window her loom is stopped, and she is sent to the boss to explain, and very often she is docked for it. If a girl is discharged from one department she cannot get employment in any other without first begging of her former boss permission to go to work, and they are not allowed to talk to one another during working hours, *or at noon time,* under penalty of being discharged.... They are not allowed to eat dinner together; even two sisters working in two different departments are not allowed to eat their meals together in the factory.[20]

On the eve of the strike, only seven hundred of the women were members of the union, but immediately after the struggle began, all 2,500 women joined the Knights. Unable to hire enough replacements, the company closed down for a few weeks in April and May. When the mills reopened, few strikers accepted Smith's offer to rehire all but those who had begun the walkout three months earlier. The company did find between three and four hundred girls who would work, but the strikers fought to prevent them from entering the plants. The police attacked the pickets and seized three of the women strikers—Ellen Tracy, Lizzie Wilson, and Mary Carey—and charged them with "walking upon Nepperhan Avenue" near the struck mills. The women were haled into court in a police wagon and held for trial.

The arrest of the women strikers aroused tremendous indignation in Yonkers. At a mass protest meeting at Getty Square, resolutions were adopted denouncing "the action of the police as being despotic," and pledging "moral support" to the strikers. Fearing that no jury would convict the women, the court ruled that the strikers could be tried without a jury, but an appeal to the higher courts reversed this decision, and the trial was held before a jury.

As a mark of admiration for the brave conduct of the three young women Knights, and as a token of respect "for the whole striking sisterhood of Yonkers," the entire labor movement of New York City joined in a testimonial meeting sponsored by the powerful Central Labor Union and the Excelsior Labor Club. Delegates from every New York union were among the two thousand people of both sexes who packed the hall for the meeting. Seated on the platform were the honored guests—the three young women members of the K. of L. from Yonkers. Next to them was seated John Swinton, who had been designated to present them with medals in honor of their militancy and courage. The medals carried these words below the insignia of an American eagle:

IN HONOR
of the
ARREST OF A PICKET
in the
YONKERS STRIKE
May 18, 1885

As the Yonkers officials had feared, the jury quickly acquitted the young women.[21]

Meanwhile, the strikers used the boycott against the stores selling Smith's carpets. *John Swinton's Paper* reported (with tongue in cheek) that the women strikers sometimes used "a father or mother, sister, brother or lover to help them. They never say that a man or store is *boycotted*— that is 'un-American' and they don't believe in it—but some tradesmen could tell a wonderful tale and the quiet 'ostracism' (that's an odd word) will result in displacing 'capital' in Yonkers."[22]

Although the strike ended late in August, 1885, without the union's being recognized, the wage cut was rescinded, the fining system was completely revised, and several other grievances of the workers were remedied. The strikers' militancy brought increased respect for women workers both among employers and in the labor movement.[23]

Wives of members of the order and women Knights were also of great assistance to male Knights engaged in strikes and boycotts. They helped on the picket lines, gave scabs the "ditch-degree" and "water cure" (throwing strikebreakers into ditches and dousing them with dishpans of water), and in Cleveland's Rolling Mill strike, they threw "stones, pieces of slag, stone and cinder" at both the strikebreakers and the police who protected them.

"Women as Boycotters" was the title of an article dealing with the effectiveness of the boycott as used by the Knights. The writer noted that since women did all or most of the buying for the family, it was they who determined the success or failure of a boycott. He cited the case of grocers who refused to sell the bread of an antiunion baker, and pointed out that "it was the women Knights who visited his customers and successfully forced compliance with the boycott." The experience of the Knights in both the shoe and garment industries suggests to David Montgomery

that effective unionization of women operatives was likely to have a remarkably radicalizing impact on the organization. In Philadelphia, Toronto, Cincinnati, Beverly, and Lynn both the resistance of the manufacturers to unionism and the level of mutuality exhibited by the workers leapt upward noticeably when the women shoe workers organized along with the men.

Small wonder, then, that Powderly observed that women "are the best men in the Order."[24]

While women occupied positions of leadership in the Knights of Labor, it was in no way commensurate with their number in and contributions to the order. Powderly received frequent requests from women assemblies that they be allowed to induct men as assembly officers because of the women's lack of experience in leadership roles. "These requests were so numerous," James J. Kenneally notes, "that they were treated as routine, and a special form was designated for granting the required dispensation." But Powderly drew the line on the number of men who could function as such officials: "I will not grant dispensation to more than one male member to act as officer of a women's Assembly. Alfred Murray may act as M[aster] W[orkman] but that is all. The others can give as good advice to women officers out of office as in it and it will help the new Assembly much better than if they sat around and let the men do the work of running the Assembly."[25]

A number of assemblies responded sympathetically to women who aspired to leadership positions. Some women members held several posts. Mrs. Elizabeth C. Williams-Patterson was variously organizer for Local Assembly No. 2999 of San Francisco, state lecturer and organizer for the Knights of Labor of Illinois, editor of the *Labor Signal,* the K. of L. paper in Indianapolis, and state lecturer and organizer for the state of Indiana. She was praised as "an expounder and teacher of the principles of the Order," and, said a union circular, "Her enthusiasm and faith in the work are unsurpassed, and never fail to cause both women and men, yes, and children to consecrate themselves to the holy cause. Victor Hugo says 'the 19th century is the century for woman's work,' and no one can rouse women to the necessities of the hour like Sister Patterson."[26]

The highest post occupied by women in the Knights of Labor was that of master workman of a District Assembly. The first to do so was Mrs. Elizabeth Rodgers, who was chosen master workman of a Chicago women's assembly in 1881 and master workman of District No. 24 in the same city in 1886. She presided over the entire Knights' organization in the Chicago area outside of the stockyards, and her district encompassed fifty thousand men and women. In reporting the selection of "A Woman Master Workman," the *New York Times* observed that although Rodgers was only thirty-nine and the mother of eleven children, eight of whom were living, she had "yet managed to make a reputation as a labor reformer." She had served as supreme judge of District No. 24 and as a delegate to the Trades Assembly.

Leonora M. Barry, who headed a District Assembly of nearly a thousand women Knights in upstate New York, was also elected a master workman in 1886. Elizabeth Morgan was elected master workman of Local Assembly No. 1789 of Chicago in 1887, and Mrs. Mary Elizabeth Lease—the famous female orator who urged Kansas farmers to "raise less corn and more hell" was elected master workman of "one of the largest Local Assemblies in the State of Kansas"[27] in 1891.

Rodgers and Barry were among the sixteen women delegates (out of a total of 660) at the General Assembly of 1886, held in Richmond, Virginia. The other fourteen included one salesclerk, six shoe workers, five textile operatives, one dressmaker, and one ironer. Rodgers was listed as a housewife and Barry as a machine hand. Rodgers brought her youngest child, a two-week-old girl, to the convention. (The delegates presented a gold watch to the child and nominated Rodgers to the post of general treasurer, an honor she declined.) In an interview with Frances Willard, the temperance leader and herself a member of the order, Rodgers paid tribute to her husband, George, a leader of the Knights in Chicago, for making her role in the order possible. "My husband always believed that women should do anything they liked that was good and which they could do well," she said proudly. "But for him I would never have got on so well as a Master Workman. I was the first woman in Chicago to join the Knights. They offered us the chance, and I said to myself, 'There must be a first one, and so I'll go forward.'"[28]

The Richmond convention made history for working women. It was at this convention that the Knights of Labor became the first labor organization in America to establish a Department of Woman's Work. It appointed a woman as general investigator to head this department.

So many female assemblies had sprung up in towns and cities throughout the United States that by 1885 the General Assembly meeting in Hamilton, Ontario, authorized the creation of a Committee on Woman's Work. The committee, composed of Mary Hanaflin (a salesclerk) and Lizzie Shute and Mary Sterling (both shoe workers), undaunted by lack of experience, sent out a questionnaire to all local assemblies with women members asking how many members they had, what trades they represented, how many hours constituted a day's work, the average wage paid them, whether the laws concerning child labor were enforced, and if the local had representation in the district. The results were distressing. Ten hours, the committee found, constituted the average workday, and women workers earned an average of $5 per week, although the shoe trade paid more. Laws prohibiting child labor were rarely enforced, and when boys and girls were employed, the girls were "obliged to work more steadily and for less pay than the boys."

When Mary Hanaflin supplemented the report with an address to the assembled Knights in Richmond, she insisted that the first task confronting workingwomen was not to secure the franchise but rather to achieve decent working conditions, and that unionization was the key to this achievement. She proposed wide-ranging investigations to determine the most serious problem areas for workingwomen, to be followed by a strong campaign to publicize the appalling working conditions and additional measures to bring women into the organization.* It was in response to this report that the delegates established the Department of Woman's Work and created the office of general investigator. The object of the department was "to investigate the abuses to which the female sex is subjected by unscrupulous employers, and to agitate the principles which our Order teaches of equal pay for equal work, and of the abolition of child labor."[29]

The Knights appointed Leonora M. Barry, an enthusiastic Knight and outstanding orator, as general investigator. Born in Cork, Ireland, Barry had come to the United States as a young girl. Her family had settled in St. Lawrence County in upstate New York, where she married and had three children. Widowed at an early age, she went to work as a machine hand in an Amsterdam, New York, hosiery mill in order to support herself and her children. She had received *65 cents* for her first week's work. She joined the Knights in 1884 and by September, 1886, had risen to become master workman. The following month, she represented her district at the General Assembly in Richmond.[30]

Operating full-time and with her salary and expenses paid by the order, Barry set out immediately on her mission "to free from the remorseless grasp of tyranny and greed the thousands of underpaid women and girls in our large cities, who, suffering the pangs of hunger, cold and privation, ofttimes yield and fall into the yawning chasm of immorality." For the next three years she conducted an extensive correspondence and traveled throughout the country organizing, investigating, and lecturing. In 1888 she reported to the convention delegates that in one eleven-month period "there have come to the Woman's Department . . . 537 applications for my presence, 213 of which have been filled by actual service, and all others answered from the office. Communications requesting advice and information, 789, all of which have been answered by the faithful and efficient secretary, Mary A. O'Reilly."[31]

Barry delivered more than five hundred lectures and organized half

---

*Actually, some work of this kind was already being carried on in Chicago. As statistician of the women's assembly in that city, Lizzie Swank assumed the task of gathering facts on wages, sanitary conditions in workrooms, and hours of labor. Other members visited workshops and talked to both employers and workers in an effort to uncover abuses and then bring them to public attention. Although they were hampered in their efforts by employer opposition and by workers' fear to cooperate, Swank and her colleagues did bring to light the conditions in the Chicago garment industry. The majority of women earned between $1 and $10 a week for a ten to twelve-hour day.

a dozen new women's locals, in addition to increasing membership in the old ones and organizing scores of male workers as well. An account of one of her lectures in the *New London* (Conn.) *Telegraph* went:

> There was quite a large attendance in Lawrence Opera House last night to hear Mrs. L. M. Barry, general instructor of the Knights of Labor.... She is a pleasing and forcible speaker with a perfect knowledge of the demands of labor and how they best can be secured. She clearly illustrated the aims of the Knights of Labor and the advantages of forming assemblies, both male and female, and touched upon all phases of the various social and other elements that have a bearing upon the labor question, with some good advice regarding the guidance of political affections.[32]

A number of male Knights, however, resented Barry's work and refused to cooperate with her. She also aroused the opposition of several Catholic priests, one of whom, Father Peter C. McEnroe of Mahoney City, Pennsylvania, denounced her as "Lady Tramp" and called the order "a vulgar, immoral society" for encouraging women to act as organizers. Barry met the attack head on in a stinging letter to Father McEnroe in which she denounced his "slanderous attack" upon her "character and motives as representative of a grand and noble Order pledged to the support of humanity," and defended her right as "an Irishwoman, a Catholic and an honest woman" to serve the cause of her fellow workers.[33]

Despite his usual sensitivity to criticism by Catholic priests, Powderly defended Barry and encouraged her to extend her activity. He did advise her, however, not to spend any time lecturing to and organizing for men:

> The men in this Order have, in my estimation, acted selfishly in encroaching upon your time as they did. Devote every moment to the service of women for their affairs have been kept too long in the background and no one ever had the opportunity you have at hand to make the indignation heaped on defenceless woman a burning question in the near future. To do so you must waste no more time on men, except it be to secure their intercession in behalf of struggling women.[34]

Barry frequently combined her educational trips for the Knights with speaking engagements for women's suffrage and temperance groups. "When I found an opportunity of laying before other organizations of women, the cause of their less fortunate sisters and moulding a favorable sentiment, I felt I was doing that which is an actual necessity, as woman is often unconsciously woman's oppressor," she declared. Barry's speech before the National Woman's Suffrage Association "roused the convention more than that of any other person." Representing the Knights, she attempted to explain the order's goals to the middle-class delegates: "We are trying to teach the outside world that the working

woman has feelings, has sensitiveness, has her heart's longings and desires for the better things of life." Any industrial system or society that
prevented some women from participating in it must be abolished because it was false. It was upon the working class that the suffragists
should rely for their most consistent and effective allies. The Knights of
Labor, she said, "are educating our men to know what the ballot means,
not only for the working man, but for the working man's wife and
sister."* Still, it was not enough to battle for the suffrage and other legal
advances:

> Do not, I ask you, in the name of justice, in the name of humanity, do not
> forget to give your attention and some of your assistance to the root of all
> evil, the industrial and social system that is so oppressive, which has wrought
> the chain of circumstances in which so many have become entangled, and
> which has brought the once fondly-loved mother to the position of the twelve
> or fourteen-hour toiler of today. If you would protect the wives and mothers
> of the future from this terrible condition we find these in today, give them
> your assistance.[35]

Barry delivered three reports to annual gatherings of the Knights'
General Assembly—in 1887, 1888, and 1889. All three are of great importance in the history of workingwomen, but perhaps their outstanding
feature is the space devoted to the conditions of workingwomen in various cities throughout the United States.† She paid particular attention to
conditions in the garment industry, describing the women garment
workers as "huddled together in close, stifling back-rooms, where the
machine operatives furnish their own machines, and in most cases,

---

*Although the 1886 K. of L. General Assembly adopted the position of the Committee on
Woman's Work that "there is more important work for women to do before they are
prepared to vote in the affairs of the Nation," the order did endorse the demand for
woman suffrage, and leading Knights often spoke from the same platform as Susan B.
Anthony and Elizabeth Cady Stanton. Anthony was inducted into the order. (*Proceedings
of the K. of L. General Assembly,* 1886, p. 288; Terence V. Powderly, *The Path I Trod* [New
York, 1940], p. 389; Elizabeth S. Bryant to Powderly, 1 February 1883, Terence V.
Powderly Papers, Catholic University of America.) However the Knights refused to endorse the 1890 suffrage campaign in South Dakota, and the organization's stand helped
to defeat the proposal.

†In none of her reports to the General Assemblies did Barry deal with black women.
However, in a letter to Powderly from Montgomery, Alabama, on March 29, 1889, she
complained: "These southern people beat the D- - - - for internal wrangling and quarrels.
They are all ignorant, the best of them, narrow-minded and bigoted and stand in their
own light. It is a constant struggle for supremacy with them. Bro. Powderly, if it be in any
way possible for you to appoint a colored man for lecture it is a dire necessity that you
should do so as in some places the white K. of L. would not allow the Colored K. of L. to
come into the hall where I was giving a public lecture. Of course, you know how I fumed
inwardly at this violation of Knighthood laws, but what could I do? You can't force public
sentiment; it must be molded or won by degrees." (Terence V. Powderly Papers, Catholic
University of America.) Barry seems to have been unaware that the Knights' leadership
made no attempt to educate Southern white workers on the need to combat segregation
and the importance of racial equality.

thread ... for 5 cents a pair [of pants]. They are then turned over to the finisher who puts on the buttons, makes button-holes and puts on buckles for 5 cents a pair; 6 pairs is an average day's work."

Barry condemned the "contract sweating middlemen" (contractors who obtained cut goods from manufacturers and recruited workers to complete the garments at a rate lower than the one he received when he returned the finished garments), and blamed them for bringing ruin and misery to the workers. The contractor who employed five operatives made 30 cents per unit, or $1.50 a day, while each worker received only 30 cents per day. "Men's vests are contracted out at 10 cents each, the machine operative receiving 2½ cents and the finisher 2½ cents each, making 5 cents a vest for completion." Since twenty vests constituted a day's work, a contractor who employed five operatives reaped $1 a day for doing nothing, while his "victim has 50 cents for eleven and twelve hours of her life's energies."[36]

Barry described female employees in a Philadelphia corset factory who had to pay a 10-cent fine for eating, laughing, singing, or talking while on the job. When an employee in a Newark corset factory reported even one minute late, she was locked out and fined two hours' pay "for wasted time." A clothing manufacturer in Terre Haute, Indiana, demanded that his female operatives pay 25 cents a week for the steam required to operate their machinery and for the needles they used. He also insisted that employees, whose weekly pay ranged between $2 and $6, pay for necessary repairs to their machines. Even the experienced Barry was shocked to discover practices such as those prevailing in an Auburn, New York, establishment in which

> upon accepting a position, an employee was compelled to purchase a sewing machine from the proprietress who is an agent for the Sm- - Co. This must be paid for in weekly payments of 50 cents, if the operative makes $3.00. If at any time before the machine was paid for (through a reduction of the already meager wages) she was dismissed—as a consequence of the enforcement of some petty tyrannical rule, sickness, anger, or any other cause—she forfeited the machine and any money paid on it, and the machine was resold to the next applicant. She must also purchase the thread for doing the work, as the proprietress is the agent for the thread company. It takes 4 spools of thread at 50 cents a spool to do $5 worth of work and when $2 is paid for thread and 50 cents for the machine, the unfortunate vicitm has $2.50 wherewith to board, do the laundry, and care for herself generally, and it is only the experts who can make even this.

But even this blatant exploitation paled compared with what she found in a linen mill in Paterson, New Jersey. There, "the women stood on a stone floor with water from a revolving cylinder flying constantly against the breast. They had in the coldest weather to go home with underclothing dripping because they were allowed neither space nor a few moments of time in which to change their clothing."[37]

Barry compiled the first nationwide statistics on women's work and found that they earned from $2.50 to $3 for a work week of eighty-four hours.[38] The information she gathered was turned over to the newly established state bureaus of labor.* But unlike the labor bureaus, Barry did not content herself with merely accumulating statistics and describing working conditions.† She also emphasized the need to change those conditions through unionism. She soon discovered, however, that there were many obstacles to be overcome in organizing workingwomen. The three major ones were the opposition of employers, the opposition of male Knights, and the opposition of workingwomen. She had expected the first, but the last two came as a shock to her. On November 15, 1887, she wrote to Powderly:

> I have been racking my brain for months past to try and devise some means or method whereby I might create an interest in our Order among working women. I have found the one stumbling block to be what good will it do us? And as these minds seem to have been trained in such narrow grooves that it was impossible for them to see or understand the benefits accruing from organization without some present benefit, I have formulated a plan which, with your sanction, I propose to suggest and endeavor to make a success in every possible locality.

Barry's plan called for every local assembly having women members to appoint a committee of three, which would meet and found a "Workingwomen's Beneficial and Protective Association to be governed and conducted by the Order of the K. of L." The convention would set the fee for membership and monthly dues, and the sum to be paid per week in case of sickness or accident. The association would have a Protective Committee to which any member might come "with any grievance or wrong done them by an employer, such as defrauding of wages, unjust

---

*In 1869 Massachusetts created the first department to collect and correlate labor statistics, under the leadership of Carroll D. Wright (later the first U.S. Commissioner of Labor). By ten years later, six states had labor bureaus, which proceeded to gather a wealth of information about labor conditions, including those of workingwomen.

†Investigators for state labor bureaus refused to recommend any action to remedy the abuses they exposed. Some felt that their duty simply required them to present the material in raw form, together with the complaints of workingwomen, without any official recommendation whatever. Even Carroll D. Wright, while he sympathized with the women, maintained that "no suggestion might be made by which these girls' wages might be improved," since their pay depended on the natural laws of economics which neither legislative fiat nor trade unionism could repeal. Probably the only solution to the problems of workingwomen, Wright suggested, was through humanitarian appeals to employers, the opening of religious and social facilities for workingwomen, and the establishment of respectable boardinghouses for them.

fines, etc., said committee to investigate the matter and be empowered to procure the necessary legal advice and counsel to prevent it."

"What do you think of it?" Barry asked Powderly. Apparently she never found out, since after her letter was received, it was stamped "No Answer Required." In any case, Barry reached the conclusion that the existing locals were not doing enough to convince women that the Knights merited their support,[39] and she did not hesitate to make this point in her reports to the general assemblies. Insisting that women workers would remain degraded as long as "the selfishness of brothers in toil continues," Barry warned that

> within the jurisdiction of our District Assemblies starvation and sin are knocking at, aye, and have gained entrance at the doors of thousands of victims of underpaid labor. And the men who have pledged themselves to the "assistance of humanity" and the "abolition of poverty" are so engrossed in the pursuit of their own ambitious desires, that upon their ears the wail of woe falls unheeded, and the work of misery still goes on.

The longer she traveled, the more convinced she became that the K. of L. platform of "equal pay for equal work" was a mockery, and she challenged delegates to either erase the plank from the platform or turn their attention toward upholding it. She pleaded: "O brothers of the Knights of Labor, I implore you by your love for mothers, wives and daughters ... to uproot the corrupt system that is making slaves—not alone in poverty, but slaves to sin and shame—of those who by right of divine parentage we must call sisters."[40]

Barry did not absolve workingwomen themselves from responsibility for their continued exploitation. She discovered that many women workers dreaded having others learn that they worked in factories. "If there is one cause more than another that fastens the chains on Baltimore working-women," she reported, "it is their foolish pride, they deeming it a disgrace to have it known that they are engaged in honest toil." This unfortunate attitude enabled employers to pay inadequate wages and provide intolerable working conditions. Again, not only did employers refuse her permission to investigate their premises, but frequently cautious friends of workingwomen would warn them against discussing their conditions with her lest their employer retaliate. In addition to what she called "the habit of submission and acceptance without question of any terms offered them," many workingwomen were reluctant to participate in union activities because they expected to be married soon. "All this," Barry concluded, "is the result or effect of the environment and conditions surrounding women in the past and present, and can be removed only by constant agitation and education."[41]

Not all Barry's experiences were discouraging. In some cities she found enthusiastic, well-organized groups of women and others eager to join them. The women members of the Detroit assembly were "intelligent, earnest, and active; they are a power for good." The women's assembly in Minneapolis evidenced "the clear brain and honest heart of its members, although a great deal of work remained for the women of that mid-western city."[42]

Experiences like these caused Barry to maintain for two years her enthusiasm and optimism about the potential for the Woman's Department. She concluded her report to the 1888 General Assembly on this encouraging note: "Ten thousand organized women today look to the Woman's Department for counsel, advice and assistance. It is their hope, their guiding star."[43]

But by the time she attended the 1889 General Assembly, her optimism had faded. The Order's influence had declined sharply and there was little she could do to stem the tide. Her annual report for 1889 reflected both her disappointment and her sense of defeat.

First, Barry startled the delegates by confessing that she had always believed woman's place was in the home. "If it were possible," she said, "I wish that it were not necessary to women to learn any trade but that of domestic duties, as I believe it was intended that man should be the breadwinner." But since this was impossible under existing conditions, she believed "women should have every opportunity to become proficient in whatever vocation they choose to find themselves fitted for."* What really stunned the delegates, however, was Barry's request that they disband the Woman's Department. After a careful analysis of the obstacles she had had to confront in three years of investigating and organizing, Barry concluded that she had not achieved the results she had hoped for. She suggested that the organization terminate her position as investigator and eliminate her department: "There can be no separation or distinction of wage workers on account of sex and a separate department for the interests of women is a direct contradiction of this." She agreed to continue serving the order, but refused to "stand at the head of something that, owing to the failure of the women to organize more thoroughly, does not exist except in name."[44]

---

*Barry clung to this position through the remainder of her life. Interviewed by Marguerite Martyn for the *St. Louis Post-Dispatch* long after she had left the Knights of Labor, she was asked: "How do you reconcile your belief in woman suffrage with your disapproval of the modern tendency to desert the home?" "I do not admit that suffrage makes women desert their homes," she replied. "History of states where women vote proves they do not aspire to office. The few who do would express the ambition for public notice in some other direction if not in this." She went on to argue that what government needed "is the subtle touch which we cannot describe except to call it womanliness. . . . The home is the cradle in which the nation is rocked, reared and fostered." (Undated clipping in Leonora M. Barry Lake Folder, Sophia Smith Collection, Smith College Library.)

Barry's recommendation is especially puzzling in view of a letter to Powderly on October 4, 1888, in which she had written:

As to wishing the Woman's Department abolished, I never have nor ever will. First, because it is an absolute necessity as an encouragement to our working women, many of whom look to the department as their guiding star. Second, because I am prepared to show that it has done as much good for the Order as any other, and more than some other departments.

Still another reason was that it would deprive her secretary, Mary A. O'Reilly, of a livelihood on which she and her children depended. From other correspondence, it appears that a number of the top leaders of the Knights, especially John W. Hayes of the General Executive Board, were pressing for abolition of the Woman's Department and for Barry's removal. When Powderly failed to stand up for her, Barry told him frankly that she had become "disheartened and bitter." Evidently she was also discouraged by Powderly's insistence that she not speak to men, for she wrote: "I ask you to release me from the stricture of talking to women only as I can best reach them through men."[45] Just what she meant is not clear, but she was correct in noting the opposition to the Woman's Department and to the two women who ran it. As early as November 5, 1887, the *Labor Enquirer,* the K. of L. paper published in Chicago, sneered that "creating two fat jobs for the sisters will do little towards lifting the burdens from the workingwomen's shoulders. So far the effect of the Woman's Department has only been to increase the list of office-holders."

Despite all this, Barry's recommendation was not accepted; the Woman's Department continued, and Barry herself continued as "General Instructor and Director of Woman's Work," lecturing and investigating. Then, in November, 1889, Powderly informed her that "owing to the straitened circumstances in which the Order is placed," she had to stop traveling and would have to concentrate on activity in Philadelphia, "and work among the women of that city until such time as you have effected an organization among them." He added ominously: "What we most require at present is an organization; without it the bills of the Order cannot be paid, and until we have it no lecturing can be done at the expense of the Order."[46]

Barry followed his advice and continued organizing in the Philadelphia area until November, 1890, when she married Oliver R. Lake, a St. Louis printer and fellow Knight. In a letter to the 1890 General Assembly, signed L. M. Barry Lake, she urged the delegates to select her successor. She also wished the new investigator success in "women's struggle for justice, equity and complete emancipation from political and industrial bondage."[47]

An effort was made to continue the Woman's Department, and the office Barry vacated was offered to Alzina P. Stevens, the only woman delegate to the 1890 convention*—a far cry from the sixteen women delegates who had attended the 1886 Assembly. When she declined the post, the Woman's Department of the Knights of Labor was abolished.

On the surface, nothing much seemed to have been accomplished by Barry's four years of investigating, speaking, and organizing. But she had brought to public attention a full picture of the abysmal conditions of workingwomen and had collected a body of statistics and descriptions that were to prove useful in future struggles. While Barry herself never again worked actively for the labor movement,† Mary A. O'Reilly, the secretary of the Woman's Department, continued to work in the order for three more years. When Pennsylvania passed its first factory inspection law, she became deputy factory inspector, one of the first women to hold such a post, and continued in the position for six years.[48]

After 1886, when the Knights of Labor reached the pinnacle of its success, with its membership rolls reaching nearly 700,000, the order began a rapid decline. The tremendous employer counteroffensive that followed the Haymarket Affair‡ wiped out the order's substantial membership gains and left many locals in severe distress. Lockouts, blacklists, arrests, and imprisonment were used to drive workers out of the Knights.[49] But many workers were also driven out by the order's leadership, and among them were many of the most militant women Knights.

In the spring of 1886, the District Assembly in the area of Troy, New York, had eighty-eight local assemblies. The Joan of Arc Assembly, made up of "collar girls," had a membership of more than four thousand. Some were veterans of the Troy Collar Workers' Union of the 1860s, but the majority were newly recruited.[50]

Early in May, committees of the Joan of Arc Assembly met with representatives of the Collar Manufacturers' Association and asked for a

---

*Stevens was master workman of a women's assembly in Chicago and owner and editor of her own newspaper. She was later appointed assistant factory inspector for Illinois.

†Leonora M. Barry Lake continued to lecture after her retirement from the Knights of Labor, speaking at conventions of suffragists and for the Chautauqua circuit on a number os subjects. Asked if she had "some pet reform," she replied: "If any, it is on behalf of working women." (Interview in *St. Louis Post-Dispatch*, undated clipping in Leonora M. Barry Lake Folder, Sophia Smith Collection, Smith College Library.)

‡The Haymarket Affair resulted from the explosion of a dynamite bomb in the midst of a squadron of police attempting to disperse a peaceful labor meeting in Chicago, on May 4, 1886. Seven police were killed and some sixty were wounded. During a wave of hysteria, eight men, all anarchists and alleged anarchists, were arrested and placed on trial. Though no evidence proved their connection with the actual bomb-throwing, they were tried for their opinions only and condemned to death. Four were hanged on November 11, 1887, one committed suicide in prison (or was murdered by the prison guards), one was sentenced to 15 years imprisonment, and two had their sentence commuted to life imprisonment.

wage increase for the "collar girls," who had suffered a series of wage reductions, and for a new price list that would equalize wages throughout the city. The manufacturers rejected both demands and offered only the existing price schedule. At this point, 250 Joan of Arc laundresses employed by George P. Ide & Company went on strike to restore a wage cut put into effect the previous year. Immediately, thirty-one of the largest companies in Troy notified the Knights of Labor that they were going to institute their own price schedules regardless of the order. They also warned the "laundry employees of George P. Ide & Company who have struck for increased wages" to return to work on Monday morning, May 17: "And in case the said employees do not return to work on said date, however much we regret the necessity of so doing, we each and all agree to close the manufacturing department of our factories on Tuesday, May 18, at 6 p.m., and remain closed until all differences are adjusted."[51]

The lockout threatened over fifteen thousand people who either were employed in the Troy collar factories or worked in their homes on collars and shirts, as well as those who made boxes for the factories. "The grave importance of the situation is easily to be seen," the Troy *Northern Budget* commented. "A shut-down will throw out of employment thousands of the best class of working people in the city and vicinity." It added: "The striking girls express their determination to stay out until their demands are granted," and noted that the Knights of Labor of the entire district had promised full support, and had let the paper know that "the Knights of Labor are people who wear shirts and collars" and were well experienced in the art of boycotting. Since the plan was to start a cooperative factory if the laundry workers were locked out, there would be collars and shirts for the boycotters to purchase.[52]

On May 19, 1886, all the collar factories closed down. That same day the locked-out "collar girls" paraded through the streets of Troy carrying signs that charged the manufacturers with attempting "to beat back their workers to the condition of slaves."[53] A group of "collar girls" wrote a letter to the Troy *Northern Budget* in which they accused "outside agitators" of being responsible for the lockout. "We ask the striking laundry girls of Geo. P. Ide & Co. to be considerate and return to work," the "loyal" workers went on, "for judging by our own experience, their employers will deal justly with them." Once they had returned, the manufacturers would call off the lockout, and all could be working again under employers who would be, in the future as in the past, "kind and considerate, ready and willing to listen to any grievances that the girls wished to bring to them."[54]

The great majority of the "collar girls" indignantly repudiated the statement that they had been provoked by "outside agitators." They reminded the few who had defended the employers that "more men have been made wealthy in Troy by the shirt and collar business than by any other, and that in some instances they have become independently rich within five years, just from the income of this business." But the workers who were responsible for their wealth "still live in poverty" and were even "forced to accept wage reductions." When their sisters struck against this tyranny, the very men they had made rich threatened "to deprive all of their workers of their ability to earn their daily bread." Already they were sending agents to Albany to replace the locked-out girls. But they should understand that "the locked-out employees will never permit new help to work," that "Troy never has given protection to its manufacturers when there was trouble with the working women, and it will not do it now if the collar factories attempt to open with new girls."[55]

This warning had its effect. No attempt was made to introduce strikebreakers into the factories. The manufacturers relied instead on starving out the workers. But on June 12, a month after the lockout began, the Joan of Arc Assembly met in front of the Troy City Hall and adopted the following resolutions:

> Resolved, That we can never accept the schedule of prices offered us by the Combined Manufacturers' Association, for the reason that that schedule is the result of a persistent and long continued system of cutting down prices, until they have reached a point far below the real value of our services, and are actually insufficient for our necessary support, and
>
> That whenever our employers are ready to give us a fair price for our labor, we are ready to go back to work; also
>
> Resolved, That we return our sincere and hearty thanks to our brothers and sisters of the locals belonging to our district assembly who have so promptly and generously sent us money, which our committees are now using to supply the needs of hundreds of those who are deprived of work in consequence of this unjust and cruel lockout, and we duly appreciate the promise that this supply shall be continued until this lockout is at an end.[56]

Unfortunately, the promise had to be repudiated at the bidding of the Knights' top leadership. On June 21, John W. Hayes, leading member of the K. of L. General Executive Board, came to Troy and proposed an agreement under which the "collar girls" would return to work at existing wages while a committee continued to negotiate a new agreement. The manufacturers rejected even this proposal, insisting that they would never reopen their laundries until the strikers returned unconditionally. Without consulting the Joan of Arc Assembly or any of the striking women, Hayes replied: "Since you refuse to accept our proposition, we will accept yours, and thereby prove to the public that we have more interest in the welfare of the city than the combined capital of the Collar and Shirt Manufacturers' Association." To the laundry workers, Hayes issued the following notice: "You are hereby ordered to return to work tomorrow, Wednesday, June 24, at your respective places." And he sent notices to the entire District Assembly ordering locals to give no further assistance to the locked-out workers.[57]

On June 25, 1886, the "collar girls" returned to the laundry factories, but within two months the Joan of Arc Assembly had ceased to exist. Most of its members had left the Knights of Labor in disgust, and their action was widely publicized among other assemblies of women members of the order.[58]

Black women Knights, too, were driven out of the order by a combination of employers' terror and the policies of the Knights' leadership. In October–November, 1887, black male and female sugar workers in Louisiana, members of the Knights of Labor, struck for wages of $1.25 a day without board or $1 a day with board, and for wages to be paid every two weeks in money. They were arrested, evicted from their cabins, and shot down in cold blood by state militiamen and vigilantes hired by the sugar planters. With no assistance from the national leadership of the Knights of Labor, most of the strikers were forced to return to work on the old terms.[59] Some of them left the order, but other blacks remained steadfast members. However, the K. of L. leadership eventually drove them out, too. Frightened by the fact that the order in the South was fast becoming an all-black organization, they retreated from the stand moderately in favor of racial equality they had taken early in the Knights' history. By 1894 the retreat was in full swing.

The Knights announced that the only solution for the black problem was to raise federal funds to deport blacks to the Congo Basin, Liberia, "or some other parts of Africa," and Grand Master Workman James R. Sovereign, Powderly's successor, was instructed by the General Executive Board to mobilize support for an appropriation of funds to deport blacks.[60] Blacks were outraged. "Negroes have been residents of this country for two hundred and forty years and are as much American citizens as anybody," the Chicago Colored Women's Club announced. "If this country is too small for the Knights of Labor and the Negro, then let the Knights leave."[61] The Knights—or what remained of the order—stayed, but blacks left the organization in utter disgust. The once-great Knights of Labor, the only organization in American life that had challenged the patterns of discrimination and segregation up to that time, had joined all other institutions in relegating black Americans to an inferior status.[62]

By 1895 the membership of the Knights of Labor had plummeted to twenty thousand. Although it continued to exist thereafter, it ceased to be a viable labor organization after 1895.[63]

The Knights of Labor was the largest labor organization in nineteenth-century America. At its height, the order had twelve thousand locals distributed in every metropolis, in virtually every industrial center, large or small, and in hundreds of small towns and rural villages, mine patches, and country crossroads. Of all places in America with populations over one thousand in the decade from 1880 to 1890, half had at least one local assembly of the Knights of Labor, while many major urban centers had over a hundred. Locals varied in size from just over ten members to over a thousand. Assemblies were formed in a thousand distinct occupations, ranging from urban and rural day labor to factory and artisan labor. Membership composition was diverse, with hundreds of assemblies consisting entirely of women or blacks or members of individual ethnic groups.

After an early reluctance to accept women as members, the Knights opened the doors of the house of labor to more women than had any organization up to that time, and to more than many who succeeded the order. For black women, especially, it represented a milestone in labor history. Thousands of women found a sisterhood in the Knights, and through it they fought some of the most militant battles of the 1880s. Out of the Knights emerged a cadre of courageous and tireless female leaders—Leonora M. Barry, Lizzie Swank, Elizabeth Rodgers, Mary Hanaflin, Mary A. O'Reilly, Lizzie H. Shute, Mary Sterling, Bridget O'Keefe, and others—who worked valiantly to improve the lot of workingwomen.

It is difficult to estimate the effect of the Knights of Labor on the conditions of women workers. The New Jersey commissioner of labor declared in 1886: "Since the girls have joined the Knights of Labor here they make the same wages as the men."[64] But Leonora M. Barry's findings indicate that no other commissioner of labor could make the same statement.

The Knights did win the reputation as the first labor organization to place women on an equal footing with men. "In all our assemblies, local, district, state, trade, and general," Mary Hanaflin told a woman's convention, "woman has an equal voice, when a member, with her brother trade unionist." But here, too, there was another side to the story. In many assemblies, male Knights did not favor the organization of women and did not accord them "an equal voice." Eventually, the Knights denied black women any semblance of equality. Grand Master Workman Powderly seems to have been a consistent champion of the necessity and justice of organizing women workers and devoted a portion of the *Journal of United Labor,* the Knights' official organ, to news of women's activities and articles on workingwomen. But he was in advance of many Knights on this issue, and he constantly had to remind his fellow members of the order of their verbal commitment to equality of men and women.[65]

Not a few women Knights were passive and shied away from complaining about conditions of their employment and fighting to improve them. At the same time, many were militant and defied both convention and male supremacists in the order. While Lizzie Swank in Chicago often encountered passivity and a reluctance to stand up for their rights among women workers, another observer at a Chicago women's assembly reported that "timid young girls—girls who have been overworked from their cradles—stand up bravely and in steady tones, swayed by conviction and the wrongs heaped upon their comrades, talk nobly and beautifully of the hope of redress to be found in organization."[66]

The *Los Angeles Union* exaggerated when it said: "The Knights of Labor is the only organization we know which encourages the membership of ladies, demands for women exact equality, and insists on equal pay for equal work."[67] But while the Knights as a whole did not challenge the traditional ideas about woman's sphere, many assemblies did advocate "the true principle of Knighthood—the equality of women."*

For a brief period the Knights of Labor broke down sexual, ethnic, racial, trade, and skill barriers in an attempt to mobilize men and women, black and white, skilled and unskilled, in a union of all the toilers. While this brief period did not fundamentally change the status or conditions of workingwomen, it did bring forth a number of female labor leaders who were to carry their knowledge and experience with them into the next period in the history of organized labor and the woman worker.[68]

---

*The Ladies' Social Assembly of Olneyville, a mill town in Rhode Island, composed of female members of the Knights of Labor who had gained the reputation of being among "the hardest workers" for the Order, established "a most remarkable institution, a 'socialistic' day nursery in one of Olneyville's largest churches, for the women mill workers to leave their children in safe charge." (Paul Buhle, "The Knights of Labor in Rhode Island," *Radical History Review,* vol. XVII, Spring, 1978, p. 58.)

12

The American Federation of Labor, 1881–1894

THE DRAMATIC UPSURGE in labor organization in the mid-1880s was linked to the meteoric rise of the Knights of Labor, but it continued even after that organization's rapid descent into oblivion. In fact, even while the K. of L. was disintegrating, the new American Federation of Labor was experiencing a slow but steady growth. First organized as the Federation of Organized Trades' and Labor Unions of the United States and Canada, it was renamed and reorganized in 1886. By 1892 the thirteen original member unions had increased to forty.[1]

No women were present at the founding convention of the federation in 1881, but the debate over the new organization's name indicated the intent to include workingwomen. Originally it was proposed that the organization be called "The Federation of Organized Trades' Unions of the United States of America and Canada," and that it be composed of trade unions only. But one delegate, speaking for the majority, pointed out that the convention's purpose was to found an organization that would take into its folds "the whole labor element of this country," not just skilled workers, and not solely men. For that reason, he proposed the name "Federation of Organized Trades' and Labor Unions," with the skilled workers entering through the trade unions and the unskilled and semiskilled, of whom women formed a great percentage, coming in through the so-called labor unions. The proposal was adopted.[2]

At its 1882 convention the federation extended an invitation to all women's organization to join and assured them that they would be represented at future sessions "upon an equal footing with trade organizations of men."[3] The following year Mrs. Charlotte Smith, president of the Women's National Industrial League, was admitted as a delegate and addressed the convention.* She appealed to the delegates to advise, cooperate, and assist in the formation of women's unions, and pledged that women would stand by male unionists, making a concerted effort against their common foes. The convention responded by drafting "An Address to Working Girls and Women," urging them to organize and unite with the federation in establishing the principle that "equal amounts of work should bring the same prices whether performed by man or woman." A convention delegate supported the appeal with the assertion that treacherous employers who exploited female workers, especially seamstresses and factory operatives, could only be thwarted if the workingwomen of the land would "array themselves under the banner of united labor."[4] At the 1885 convention, the delegates repeated the appeal to the workingwomen of this country to protect themselves by organizing into unions of their respective trades or callings and authorized the legislative committee to assist women in organizing wherever the opportunity offered itself.[5]

But beyond recognizing the problems faced by women workers, adopting lofty pronouncements calling for them to join unions, and reasserting the principle of "equal pay for equal work," the AFL made little concrete progress for workingwomen during the 1880s. Moreover, Samuel Gompers, the first president of the AFL, and, with the exception of one year (1895), the head of the federation until his death in 1924, was frank enough to acknowledge that enforcement of "equal pay for equal work regardless of sex" would probably help men more than women, since many women workers had been hired precisely because they could be paid lower wages than men.[6] Only two national affiliates of the AFL—the Cigar Makers' Union and the Typographical Union—accepted women as members, and others actually passed resolutions prohibiting them from joining. Only one woman delegate appeared at any AFL convention prior to 1891, and women were conspicuously absent at meetings of affiliated local unions. Gompers was able to do little to help them because of the federation's policy of trade union autonomy and noninterference.[7]

In the main, women workers, being relatively unskilled, did not fit into the craft unions of the AFL, and to the degree that they were organized in the early federation, the tendency was to set up separate unions for women workers. Indeed, it was not uncommon for AFL

*Mrs. Smith, it will be recalled, had helped found the union of female government employees affiliated with the Knights of Labor, but it was quite common for unionists to hold dual affiliation with both the Knights and the federation during the latter organization's early years. Mrs. Smith appeared before the U.S. Senate Committee on Education and Labor in 1883, where she attacked the Western Union Company for its low wage scales for women and urged the women of the nation to donate funds for the striking Western Union women. (U.S. Senate Committee on Education and Labor, *Report Upon the Relations Between Capital and Labor* [Washington, D.C., 1884] 1: 442.)

organizers to form two unions in a shop or factory—one for women and one for men—and to arrange for negotiations with employers to be conducted by a joint committee representing both unions. The women workers frequently complained that they got the worst end in such an arrangement, since "the men think that the girls should not get as good work as the men and should not make half as much money as a man."[8] Very few women were willing to join such unions, and the plan was quickly abandoned.

Practically the entire history of the American Federation of Labor and women workers in the 1880s was written by one organization: the Ladies' Federal Labor Union No. 2703 in Chicago. Its founder and guiding spirit was Elizabeth Chambers Morgan, wife of Chicago's leading socialist, Thomas J. Morgan. Born in Birmingham, England, in 1850, she came from a family of ten children and parents who were factory operatives. Her formal education ended at the age of eleven, when she went to work in a factory. After marrying Morgan in 1868, she emigrated with her husband to Chicago. In September, 1874, she became a charter member of the Sovereigns of Industry, a society concerned mainly with establishing consumers' cooperatives for the distribution of the necessities of life among wage earners and "designed for the laboring classes, especially working men and women."[9] Women were active in the Sovereigns, and she became a secretary of the Chicago Assembly. The Sovereigns disappeared before the end of the decade, and Elizabeth Morgan continued her labor activity in the Knights of Labor. She was one of the first women admitted into the Knights and became, as we have noted, master workman of the Chicago Assembly. She was also one of the earliest Knights to leave the order, resigning in disgust in 1887 over the leadership's increasing conservatism. In June, 1888, she led a small group of Chicago women in organizing the Ladies' Federal Labor Union No. 2703. It was a mixed union, composed of typists, seamstresses, dressmakers, clerks, music teachers, candymakers, gum makers, and other female workers. The year it was organized, it received both a charter from the American Federation of Labor and state recognition as a legal corporation.[10]

Elizabeth Morgan quickly earned a high place among those women who have made distinguished contributions to the American labor movement. She was secretary of the Ladies' Federal Labor Union and its delegate to the Chicago Trade and Labor Assembly, a citywide association of trade unions. She did excellent work in recruiting members into the Ladies' Federal Labor Union and, through it, in organizing other workingwomen into unions.[11] Although her limited education required that she seek assistance in polishing her literary style, she wrote the recruiting leaflet "The Aims and Objects of Ladies' Federal Labor Union No. 2703," which began:

Without organization for self protection, with the many disadvantages of sex, and the helplessness of childhood, the female and child workers are the victims of every avaricious, unscrupulous and immoral employer. The Ladies' Federal Union has been organized to prevent to some extent, the moral, physical and mental degradation of women and children employed as wage workers in this city.

This it hoped to accomplish by "the organization of all women"; by investigating the complaints brought by women and children "against unjust and inhuman employers, and by every honorable means, attempt[ing] to remove the wrongs complained of"; by securing the enforcement of local and state laws that would tend to improve the conditions of employment of women and children, and agitating for the enactment of further legislation; by obtaining "the aid and co-operation of the great labor organizations of this city and country, and the active assistance of the many women's organizations"; by discussing the labor question for "intellectual improvement"; by assisting members in case of sickness or accident; and by "social enjoyment." All workingwomen were eligible for membership; the initiation fee was 25 cents, and dues were 5 cents a week. Sickness benefits were $3 a week. Morgan supplemented the leaflet with speeches outlining the advantages of unionism for workingwomen. One argument she raised was far in advance of her time: she pointed out that unions would make women "self-reliant" so they "need not marry worthless husbands for a home and the bare necessities of life."[12]

By February, 1892, the Ladies' Federal Labor Union had brought into being twenty-four women's organizations, including unions of bookbinders, shirtmakers and cloakmakers, watchmakers, and shoe workers. When ten women of one craft had been recruited into the federal union, they set up a union of their own, received a charter from the AFL, and began to organize other women in their trade. Nearly all these unions were organized by Mrs. Morgan, who, although so small in stature that she had "to climb on a chair to light a gas jet," was a woman with "a face every line of which betoken[ed] energy, shrewdness and determination."[13]

After 1891 Mrs. Morgan acquired "a national reputation."[14] In her monthly reports to the Chicago Trade and Labor Assembly, she called for the mandatory schooling of children under fourteen, the arrest of truants, the prohibition of child labor, the appointment of women to the school board, and the designation of factory inspectors. All her proposals were adopted by the assembly and forwarded to the state legislature.[15] In the late summer of 1888, the *Chicago Times* ran a series of articles entitled "City Slave Girls," depicting the misery of women employed in factories and workshops.[16] Stirred by this exposé, Mrs. Morgan persuaded the Ladies' Federal Labor Union to establish a com-

mittee to determine the authenticity of the articles and to seek the cooperation of the Trade and Labor Assembly and various women's groups
in combating these evils.[17]

After the investigation confirmed the accuracy of the *Chicago Times*
articles, the committee formed the Illinois Women's Alliance to protect
workingwomen and children. The alliance was composed of the Ladies'
Federal Labor Union and a number of women's groups with suffrage,
medical, literary, religious, and temperance interests. The coalition
aimed "to prevent the moral, mental, and physical degradation of
women and children as wage-workers" by enforcing the existing factory
ordinances and compulsory education laws and by seeking the enactment of such new laws as might be necessary. Morgan was a member of
the alliance's executive committee and also chairman of the Trade Assembly delegation to the alliance.[18]

The Women's Alliance compiled an impressive record of achievement. It thoroughly exposed the weakness of Illinois's Compulsory Education Act of 1883, under which children between the ages of eight and
fourteen were supposed to be in school for not less than twelve weeks
each year. Since the law had no effective enforcement provisions, it was
virtually useless, and the alliance found thousands of school-age children
roaming the streets and working in factories and stores. It obtained the
passage of an improved law in 1889, which required children to begin
school at age seven, extended the minimum time spent in school to
sixteen weeks a year, and, most important, provided for enforcement
through truant officers appointed by the school board, with fines for
violations. Thousands of Chicago's children were taken from the streets
and factories and placed in the schools. But the alliance soon discovered
that there was an insufficient number of public schools in the city to
educate them. "Children cannot be driven into schools which have no
existence," it pointed out. The alliance therefore led the mass campaign
that resulted in the construction of new schools.[19]

The organization also secured passage of a city ordinance empower-
ing the commissioner of health to appoint five women factory inspectors; it sponsored a clothing drive for school-age children from poverty-
stricken families; and, after a long struggle, it obtained the appointment
of an alliance member to the Board of Education. With Elizabeth
Morgan as chairperson, the alliance's Committee on Child Labor worked
for a comprehensive child labor law and succeeded in gaining both a
local ordinance and a general child labor law in the state legislature
prohibiting the employment of children under fourteen years of age.
Unfortunately, a combination of a lack of enforcement provisions and
exemption clauses rendered the laws practically worthless.[20] But the five
women factory inspectors appointed as a result of pressure by the Wom-
en's Alliance won international fame for their accomplishments. The

"No. 5" issue of the *Eight Hour Day,* a four-page flier published in Zurich on April 10, 1890, carried a report from "North America" proudly noting that "five women inspectors in Chicago have fulfilled their tasks during the past year," and went on: "They have succeeded in compelling the larger shopowners to provide seats for women clerks, as prescribed by law. Moreover the women inspectors have told the clerks that if they are fired for using the seats they should file a complaint with the city's Health Department." Evidently the women workers had feared a blacklist if they complained. But Chief Inspector Ruth Young had sent notices to all the shops warning against reprisals, and the *Eight Hour Day* reported that "the women have seats." "The work of the Women's Alliance," the flier concluded, had in this case paid off.

The victories scored by the Women's Alliance sponsored by the AFL Ladies' Federal Labor Union No. 2703, under the leadership of its dynamic secretary, Elizabeth Morgan, were evidence of what a coalition of trade union and middle-class women could accomplish. Similar coalitions were beginning to emerge in a number of other cities, generally composed of Working Girls' Clubs, Working Women's Improvement Associations, Working Women's Societies, Social Settlements, and Consumers' Leagues.

In 1884 a small group of young workingwomen in New York City banded together to form the Working Girls' Club, to gain cultural enrichment through talks on literary, religious, and moral questions. Grace M. Dodge, a young heiress, became a prime mover in the undertaking and helped set up Working Girls' Clubs in other cities. By 1885 there were branches in Brooklyn, Philadelphia, and Boston, all dedicated to providing young workingwomen with opportunities "for moral intercourse and the development of higher and nobler aims." Girls fourteen and older were eligible to join the clubs. Those over sixteen paid a 25-cent initiation fee and monthly dues of 25 cents, while girls in the fourteen-to-sixteen age group participated in Junior Clubs and paid lower dues. Once enrolled, a member could use the club's comfortably furnished rooms and its circulating library, piano, and writing supplies. She could also attend frequent lectures, "entertainments," and sewing and embroidery classes, and had the privilege of joining dressmaking, cooking, millinery, and school extension classes upon the payment of nominal fees. Through the efforts of Dodge and other wealthy benefactors, the New York members enjoyed the use of two summer houses on Long Island, for which they paid only $3 for weekly board.

The Working Girls' Clubs could not have survived without the financial support of middle-class philanthropists, and participation in the clubs' varied cultural, educational, and recreational activities did bring working girls and middle-class women together. But many young women who worked long hours in shops and factories could not find the spare time to participate in these social activities. Nor did the clubs do anything to improve the economic status or conditions of the girls so that they could find the time to participate. In the main, the rich women who formed these clubs and financed the boardinghouses for young women workers "were concerned primarily with imbuing their members with good work habits and genteel notions of femininity." The very names given to the clubs—"Endeavor Club," "Enterprise," and "Steadfast," for example—reflect their outlook. Moreover, a collection of essays by the members published by the Working Girls' Clubs, entitled *Thoughts of Busy Girls, Who Have Little Time for Study, Yet Find Much Time for Thinking,* offers still another insight into the movement's orientation. In the spirit of the *Lowell Offering,* the collection contained essays on such topics as "What Constitutes an Ideal Womanhood and How to Attain It," and "Purity and Modesty: Two Words of Value." The themes repeated throughout the essays were those of self-sacrifice, gentleness, and tenderness.[21]

The subject of trade unionism was neither discussed in the essays nor broached at the lectures and forums. The *American Hebrew,* a publication that was hostile to organized labor, hailed the formation in October, 1888, of the "Emma Lazarus Working Girls' Club" in the vestry room of the Shearith Israel synagogue on West Nineteenth Street in New York City. The club, named in honor of the Jewish poet whose poem is inscribed on the Statue of Liberty, aimed at seeking "the elevation of the Jewish working girls by their own efforts." But such "elevation" through unions was not to be discussed.[22]

The Chicago Working Women's Improvement Association, on the other hand, did make a serious effort to acquaint workingwomen with the benefits of trade union membership. Founded in 1887 by professional and wage-earning women, the association received advice and support from the social workers of Hull House, one of the pioneer settlement houses in the United States.[23]

The settlement house movement, which spread rapidly throughout the United States, was inspired by the establishment of Toynbee Hall in London in 1884. The idea was for men and women who had recently graduated from universities to set up a "settlement" in a slum, share the problems of the poor, and work with them to reform neighborhood conditions. By 1891 there were six such settlements in the United States, but by 1900 the number had grown to over a hundred, by 1905 to over two hundred, and to over four hundred by 1910.

Two of the oldest settlements were in Chicago: Hull House, established in 1889 by Jane Addams and Ellen Gates Starr, and Chicago Commons, founded in 1894 by Reverend Graham Taylor. Alice Hamilton, a pioneer in industrial medicine, remembered that "at Hull House we got into the labor movement as a matter of course without realizing how or when."[24] Labor unions met regularly at Hull House (as they did at Denison House and South End in Boston, and at University and Henry Street settlements in New York). The constitution of University Settlement pledged "to bring men and women of education into closer relations with the laboring classes for their mutual benefit," and the same principle was adopted by many, though by no means all, of the settlement houses. In addition to working for labor and social welfare legislation, many settlement house workers took an active part in strikes and helped organize unions, especially among working girls and women. While there was inevitably some patronizing of working-class women by the upper-and middle-class settlement workers, the relationship, in the main, was of benefit to the female workers.[25]

Jane Addams welcomed the formation of the Chicago Working Women's Improvement Association and encouraged the group to hold its meetings at Hull House. There they were joined by Florence Kelley, socialist daughter of Republican Congressman William D. Kelley of Pennsylvania. Miss Kelley had been educated at Cornell University and the University of Zurich. While in Europe, she had made contact with Friedrich Engels and continued to correspond with the cofounder of scientific socialism after her return to the United States. Kelley had joined the Knights of Labor, and after its decline, she became part of the Hull House settlement workers. That group helped Elizabeth Morgan in organizing unions among the workingwomen of Chicago.[26]

At about the same time, a group of well-to-do sympathizers in New York City, particularly Josephine Shaw Lowell and Louisa Perkins, was meeting with young workingwomen to discuss the problems of woman workers and the techniques needed to end the abuses they suffered. The principal working-class woman at the meetings was an Irish garment worker, Leonora O'Reilly. In 1881, at the age of eleven, Leonora was forced to leave school and go to work in a New York collar factory, earning $1 per dozen finished collars. In three years, when the rate had declined to 50 cents a dozen, O'Reilly joined the Knights of Labor and participated in her first strike.[27]

That same year she assembled a group of fellow collarmakers on New York's Lower East Side to discuss their grievances and explore possible remedies. In time she met Lillian Wald, Stanton Coit, and Felix Adler, who were soon to organize the settlement movement in New York. They helped O'Reilly put the group on a more solid foundation and participated in discussions on how to build unionism among the exploited workingwomen in New York City. The group was soon joined by shopwomen and factory operatives, among whom were Alice L. Woodbridge and Ida Van Etten. Woodbridge had been a stenographer and saleswoman but had been obliged to give up several lucrative positions because of improper advances by her employers. Van Etten, a former garment worker and a member of the Socialist Labor Party, had tried unsuccessfully to organize women into independent unions after she had "discovered" the sweatshop system during a visit to a tenement workshop on New York's Lower East Side:

> In every room were crowded together from six to ten men and women, four to five machines, with a cooking stove at white heat for the use of the pressers. Women with white pinched faces, unkempt hair, dressed in ragged, dirty, "unwomanly" rags, were working from sixteen to eighteen hours a day for a pittance from 50 to 75 cents. No word of mine can picture to you the horror of it—the dirt, the squalor, the food these people eat, the clothes they wear, the air they breathe, and more pitiful than all, their weary faces, out of which all hope and joy had long since been banished. All made up a scene that would linger in the mind, like Dore's pictures of Dante's inferno.[28]

Ida Van Etten joined the club of workingwomen and, together with O'Reilly, Woodbridge, and Mrs. Lowell, helped organize the Working Women's Society. Its objectives, according to a *New York Times* story were: "to found trades' organizations in trades where they at present do not exist, and to encourage and assist labor organizations to the end of increasing wages and shortening hours." In due time the society discovered that it could not remedy the deplorable working conditions of saleswomen and cashiers in department stores through unionism; the women were too young (most of them being between fourteen and twenty years of age), and with the decline of the Knights of Labor and the dominance of craft unionism in the American Federation of Labor, they lacked the skill to be accepted by any of the existing craft unions. As an alternative, it was decided to organize the shoppers in an effort to improve the conditions of these women workers. Out of this determination emerged the first Consumers' Leagues.[29]

Unlike the Working Girls' Clubs, the Working Women's Society believed that through unionization, workingwomen could increase their wages, shorten working hours, and end cruel and tyrannical treatment on the part of employers and their managers.[30] The problem was to transmit this understanding to the existing trade union apparatus and to convince it to organize workingwomen.

Early in 1891 Ida Van Etten undertook, on behalf of the Working Women's Society, to attempt to move the AFL in the direction of doing more for workingwomen. She prepared a circular urging the AFL to appoint a special organizer to bring the message of unionism to workingwomen and to appropriate the necessary funds for the campaign. She also asked President Gompers for permission to appear before the AFL Executive Council to press the need for the organizing campaign and to assure the trade unionists that the Working Women's Society would do its share in organizing and rallying public support for strikes by workingwomen.[31]

The pressure of the New York Working Women's Society helped produce results. Gompers invited two women to address the 1891 convention. Eva McDonald Valesh, an organizer for the Minnesota Farmers' Alliance and editor of a fortnightly paper published for the Trades Assemblies in the twin cities of Minneapolis and St. Paul, vividly described the evils encountered by the workingwomen of the nation and pointed up the crying need for organization among them. She told the delegates: "If men seriously expect higher wages or shorter hours, they must, for their own self-preservation, organize the women, making them valuable allies instead of a source of danger." She was followed by Ida Van Etten, representing the New York Working Women's Society, who stressed the need for the immediate appointment of women organizers to bring exploited workingwomen into the federation. She concluded:

> It can readily be seen that women workers either must become organized and receive not only equal pay for equal work, but also equal opportunities for working, or they will, by degrees, naturally form an inferior class in every trade in which they enter; a class more poorly paid, and who will, in consequence, work longer hours; who will receive less consideration from their employers, and who will be without means of redress, even in those grievances which are most degrading to their womanhood. In this condition they will be a constant menace to wages; they will be used, in case of strikes and lockouts, to supply the places of union men; and, in short, we shall witness the horrible spectacle of workers whose interests are identical being used against each other for the purpose of lowering the general condition of the class.
>
> The bitterness with which employers oppose the organization of women furnishes the best evidence of their present value in supplying them with ignorant, unthinking and consequently cheap laborers.

The speeches were greeted by loud applause, and the convention appointed Valesh and Van Etten to a three-member committee on women's work (with Valesh as chairperson and Van Etten as secretary), to consider the AFL's engaging a woman to "lecture to working women of the land" and encourage female membership in the federation. The committee recommended that the Executive Council appoint such a woman, to be called the national organizer for women, at a salary of $1,200 a year plus expenses, and make her a member of the council. The convention failed to take decisive action on the recommendation, but at least the door had been opened.[32]

Meanwhile, other forces were helping to bring more women into the AFL. Organizers for the federation began circulating copies of Ida Van Etten's pamphlet *The Condition of Women Workers Under the Present Indus-*

trial System, and issues of the Working Women's Society's periodical, *Far and Near,* "with a view of organizing the girls who toil in the shops and mills."[33] New federal labor unions of women workers came into being and were chartered by the AFL in Toledo, Ohio, Terre Haute, Indiana, and Emporia, Kansas. The Anchor Federal Labor Union No. 5568 of Emporia circulated the following resolutions adopted on the occasion of the death of Carrie Bowen, one of its founders:

> *Whereas,* From being compelled to work in an unhealthy place, thereby impairing her constitution so that when disease attacked her she could not successfully resist it, we have lost through death our beloved sister, Carrie Bowen, therefore be it
>
> *Resolved* by Anchor Federal Labor Union that though we shall miss her from our midst, we will not mourn, for we trust that God in his Love for his children has prepared better surroundings for her in the land beyond than the toiling masses enjoy in this,
>
> *Resolved,* that we call upon all working girls to follow her example in joining with organized labor, thereby assisting in doing away with a system of wage slavery that compels the common people, whom Christ loved so well, to work under surroundings detrimental to health and the cause of taking thousands off before their time.
>
> > A thousand factories taking lives
> > A thousand different ways
> > So that the Rich and Robbing class
> > May pass sweet pleasant days.[35]

The AFL also chartered directly unions of women workers in a specific industry. The most important of these was the union of collar and shirt workers in Troy, New York.

From 1886, when they had dissolved the Joan of Arc Assembly in disgust over having been sold out by the Knights of Labor leadership, until the beginning of 1891, the "collar girls" of Troy had been without a union. During these same years, reductions imposed by the United Shirt and Collar Company had brought wages down to an average of 50 cents a day. "Many of us," wrote Mary S. Evaline, spokeswoman for the "collar girls" at United, "have others dependent on our work, and this wholesale attack on our wages can only result in privation and want to those who are near and dear to us."[36]

On January 6, 1891, the collar, cuff, and shirt workers employed at the Lansingburgh factory of United struck. Within a few days the strike spread to other factories in Troy, and with five hundred girls on strike, a good section of the shirt and collar industry was tied up. The State Branch of the AFL, responding to an appeal from the strikers, sent several representatives into the area. The strikers then formed a union under the AFL and elected Mary Evaline, the twenty-three-year-old strike leader, president and Dora Sullivan vice-president.

The United Shirt and Collar Company was a powerful concern with sales of close to $1 million annually. When it refused to discuss a settlement with the strikers, the State Branch of the AFL issued a boycott against its products. The company promptly capitulated. A committee composed of the strike leaders and the state AFL drew up a new scale of wages for United. This scale served as a basis for other companies involved in the strike, and it was to serve similarly for all shirt and collar establishments in Albany and Glens Falls. The State Branch of the AFL resolved "to ask all members of labor organizations to withhold their patronage from such firms who fail to pay their employees such reasonable rates of wages as they may demand in accordance with the scale of prices accepted by the United Shirt and Collar Co."[37]

On February 1, 1891, the *Troy Northern Budget* announced the end of the strike, describing it as having "perhaps attracted more attention and sympathy for the strikers . . . than any fight which has occurred between capital and labor in this vicinity for many years. . . . The girls go to work under an increased schedule of prices and they have won a victory." On the same day, H. J. Ogden, AFL general organizer in Utica and first vice-president of the New York State Branch, wrote jubilantly to Gompers: "You have no doubt learned the result of the collar girls strike at Troy. It was a great victory for the girls and the Federation. . . . We expect to have seven thousand of them organized in the very near future under the banner of the Federation."[38]

To achieve this goal, the state branch engaged Mary Evaline as a special organizer with the power to establish local unions of collar and cuff workers. A few months later the national AFL commissioned Dora Sullivan as a "general organizer" for the workingwomen of Troy and vicinity. By November, 1891, there were six unions in the collar, cuff, and shirt industry of Troy, all affiliated with the AFL. Several unions in the industry, composed of female operatives, were also organized in the principal shirt manufacturing centers at Albany, Cohoes, Glens Falls, and Greenwich, New York.[39]

The year 1891 also witnessed affiliation with the AFL of a national union with a substantial membership of women—the United Garment Workers of America, the first national union in the men's clothing industry. The women's garment industry, on the other hand, had neither a national union in the 1890s nor a substantial number of women members in those local unions that did exist.* Most of the women's clothing industry in the 1890s was characterized by what came to be known as

---

*The term "garment industry" at this time covered several dozen needle trades, including not only men's and women's ready-made clothing, but also the millinery, men's hat and cap, neckwear, and corset industries. The term "garment worker" included both highly skilled craftsmen, such as cutters; semiskilled sewing machine operators; and unskilled manual workers, such as button seamstresses and thread trimmers.

"seasonal unionism"—that is, local unions that were formed during sudden, unpremeditated strikes when the season began and manufacturers introduced new styles. Eventually the opposing parties reached a temporary agreement. But enthusiasm for the union lasted only during this brief bargaining interval. After the agreement was reached, members lost interest until the following year.

Still, as the individual unions came and went and the strikes were won and lost, a body of experience was being accumulated. On October 9, 1888, the United Hebrew Trades was founded by the Jewish socialists in the garment trade to centralize and stabilize the trade union movement in order to deal effectively with the "sweating system" and other evils. Each of the "seasonal unions" usually included a women's branch; in the strikes that led to the season agreement, women were among the most militant strikers, and they were naturally included in the unions that emerged after the strikes were settled. The Jewish workingwomen also joined the unions established by the United Hebrew Trades. But the men who dominated these unions made only token efforts to organize women workers. Organizers in the women's clothing industry complained that Jewish women made poor union material because of their preoccupation with marriage. They cited examples of women who were good strikers but quit the union after the strike ended with a contract that included the women—conveniently ignoring the many men in the unions who did precisely the same thing. For their part, the young women garment workers, working at the tasks that required the least skill and experience, found that their path to the more skilled jobs was blocked by the men who dominated the unions. Small wonder, then, that they regarded the unions as having little value for them.[40]

In early April, 1891, forty-seven cutters and tailors from the five largest men's clothing manufacturing centers met in New York City and founded the United Garment Workers of America. The UGW immediately affiliated with the AFL. Although the convention delegates had united to form a new national union, they had chosen a leadership that hardly reflected the views of a great many of the clothing workers who were to be members of the union. This conflict was destined to cause controversy and discord that was to plague the UGW throughout its history. The union members back home were mainly immigrant workers, Jewish socialists, who demanded sweeping social and economic changes in society. But the delegates had chosen as their leaders conservative, American-born workers who supported a "pure and simple" trade unionism and rejected socialist demands for broad social changes.

Although the UGW was as thoroughly dominated by men as were the local unions in the women's clothing industry, it was more willing to open its doors to women workers. At its founding convention, the UGW determined to fight the contracting evil and the growing production of clothing in tenement sweatshops under intolerable, nonunion conditions by issuing a label for clothing to designate that it had been made by workers who received adequate wages and worked a limited number of hours per day in acceptable surroundings. In order to receive the label, a manufacturing establishment had first to recognize the UGW as a legitimate bargaining agent, and all employees in the shop had to be union members. Consequently, UGW organizers felt a greater pressure to recruit women workers than did organizers for the unions in the women's garment industry. Encouraged by the UGW to join, women entered the union in sizable numbers. On June 26, 1892, Charles F. Reichers, UGW national secretary, informed Gompers "that three-fifths of the United Garment Workers of America consist of women, two Locals No. 8 & 16 are entirely composed of young girls, and No. 18 of Newburgh, N.Y. which is mixed has about 400 women in good standing."[41]

Actually, while UGW organizers encouraged women to organize, men usually assumed the leadership positions in the newly formed locals. Often when union leaders demanded that manufacturers pay higher wages and shorten the hours of work, they requested such improvements only for the cutters and operators, skilled jobs held by men, and ignored the women buttonhole makers and finishers, who worked longer hours for lower wages.[42]

The organization of women in the United Garment Workers resulted more from the activity of women than from that of men organizers, and nearly all these women were working for the AFL rather than the UGW. Dora Sullivan's work as "general organizer" for the AFL was confined to the collar-and-shirt industry. Meanwhile, Gompers was receiving requests from women workers for a woman to be a general organizer for various other industries. The correspondents complained that male organizers often omitted women from the agreements drawn up with employers, and that even when they were interested in organizing women, they were often ineffective because they "used strong language" and were "guilty of drunkenness." Male organizers themselves conceded that they had trouble in reaching women workers after working hours:

> If a girl is living at home, it is not quite so awkward, but if she is in lodgings, I can't possibly ask to see her in her own room. If I talk to her at all, it will be out in the street, which is not pleasant, especially if it is snowing or freezing or blowing a gale. It is not under these conditions that a girl is likely to see the use of an organization or be attracted by its happier or more social side.[43]

Then in April, 1892, evidently acting on the recommendation of the three-member committee appointed by the 1891 AFL convention, Gompers appointed Mary E. Kenney as a general organizer for the federation, with no limitation on the trades in which she would do her organizing work. Born in 1864 to Irish immigrant parents, Kenney had dropped out of school after the fourth grade, when her father was killed in an accident on the job, and went to work in a bindery to help support her ailing mother. In 1887, for an average of sixty-five hours of labor a week, she received $2. Still she was fired when she demanded a raise, and she had to begin again in a new shop where conditions were even worse. As she recalled:

> Every woman in the bindery worked from Friday morning at 7 through the night till Saturday afternoon at 4. In spite of the strain, we all tried to work with good spirit, but many girls' heads began dropping on the table by midnight from sheer exhaustion. I held out till about 3:30 in the morning. Then I sat on the floor, leaned up against the wall and gave up for about 15 minutes.

Kenney rebelled against such treatment and almost singlehandedly began organizing her fellow workers. She had participated in a Chicago Working Girls' Club but found the members' preoccupation with social outings meaningless and went instead to the Ladies' Federal Labor Union No. 1703. With the assistance of Elizabeth Morgan, she organized the Chicago Bindery Workers' Union, one of the offshoots of the Ladies' Federal Union.

Inevitably she met Jane Addams, and, after an initial period of distrust, became convinced that the social settlement people at Hull House were also interested in the cause of the working class. She later recalled that it "was one of the greatest moments of my life when I discovered that there were really people outside of workers who cared." Through Jane Addams, Kenney met Henry Demarest Lloyd, a Midwest reformer, who in 1891 was working on *Wealth Against Commonwealth,* a classic exposé of monopoly, and Clarence Darrow, the pro-labor lawyer. With Lloyd's support and the encouragement of Hull House, Kenney began organizing the shirtwaist workers and assisting them in their strikes for improved working conditions and higher wages. She even burst into Marshall Field's office to protest the fact that workers at his factory received only $4.85 a week for a ten-hour day and in addition were required to pay for the ice in their water and to clean the factory's floors. When Field refused to correct these injustices, she threatened to publicize these wretched working conditions through the press. A few days later, the practice of requiring workers to pay for ice and sweep the factory floors was abolished.[44]

Gompers met Kenney in 1891 during a visit to Chicago and was impressed with her, and when he decided to appoint a woman general organizer for the AFL without restricting her scope, he asked whether Kenney would come to New York to help organize women workers in the East. Kenney headed for New York on May 26, 1892. All during that hot summer, she shuttled back and forth between New York City and Troy, where she tried to organize some of the unorganized "collar girls" and straighten out a serious dispute that had arisen between Dora Sullivan and her followers and the AFL Executive Council.

The conflict arose over the introduction of the McKay Starching Machine in the laundries of Miller, Hall & Hartwell in Troy. Sullivan and the union members working for the firm insisted that if the machine was to be used the company should guarantee against reducing either wages or the number of women employed. When it refused, the women went on strike and Sullivan asked the AFL Executive Council to boycott the firm's products. The Executive Council complied, but later charged Sullivan and her supporters with having ordered the strike and the boycott over the objection of most of the members of the union, a charge she heatedly denied and on which she was supported in an affidavit by a group of union members. Ordered by Gompers to attend a hearing on the issue in New York City, Sullivan refused on the ground that the union could not afford the cost. Kenney was unable to resolve the dispute. Eventually the strike was lost, and Gompers suspended the charter of the Collar, Cuff and Shirt Starchers' Union No. 5577.[45]

Kenney also shuttled between Massachusetts and New York, signing up and educating garment workers, bindery workers, women printers, shoemakers, carpet weavers, and textile operatives. On September 28, 1892, she wrote a report on her activities to Gompers:

I began work as organizer May 31st in New York City. June 2nd I called a meeting of undergarment workers. The meeting was a failure. June 21st I held a meeting of bindery girls, the following meeting we organized a union. Up to the time I left New York they were not in a position to take out a charter in the A. F. of L. I addressed three social clubs of working women in New York, July 29th. The Garment Workers held a meeting and formed a Union. August 2nd left New York for Troy. Held a large meeting in Troy in which a number of non-union girls joined after the meeting. August 16th held a mass-meeting of shirt makers and bindery girls in Albany. A large number of nonunion shirt makers joining the Union and promising at their next business meeting to take out a charter in the A. F. of L.

Thursday the 18th the bindery girls of Albany formed a Union. I left Troy August 26th for New York. The following week I worked in the office of the A. F. of L. addressing envelopes for Homestead.* August 27th I left New York for Boston. While here the first week I failed to call any meeting or address any owing to Labor Day. Sept. 7th I addressed a social club of working women. Sept. 16th the Custom Tailoresses Union. Sept. 23rd a

---

*The reference is to the historic Homestead strike of 1892 by the Amalgamated Association of Iron, Steel, and Tin Workers, called to oppose wage cuts instituted by the Carnegie Steel Company at its Homestead, Pennsylvania, plant.

mass-meeting of working women of various trades, tonight, Sept. 28th, the bindery girls hold a meeting to form a Union which I am sure of a Union. Thursday, Sept. 29th, I speak in Middleboro to shoe workers, Friday, Sept. 30th at Haverhill to shoe workers, Saturday, Oct. 1st, women carpet workers weavers. I have an engagement for Oct. 6th to address a mass-meeting of all the Club members together. Oct. 7th the Printers Union arranged a meeting for me to address the women of their trade. . . .

I have met and talked with several girls of different trades and callings and believe that the time is near when their trades will be organized, even if women are slow in so doing. The extreme hot weather has put the work back very much.[46]

Working with Leonora O'Reilly, Kenney helped organize Local No. 16 of the United Garment Workers. Kenney and O'Reilly found the new union members, most of them Jewish women, to be bright, effective speakers, interested in union activities.[47] These young women were now part of the national union as a result of the activities of two militant female organizers, not because of the UGW men, who had repeatedly refused their assistance.

In Boston, with the aid of John F. O'Sullivan, a leading union organizer (whom she later married), Kenney helped seventy-five Irish-American women who worked at the Plymouth Rock clothing factory form Women's Tailors' Union No. 37 of the UGW.[48] She also formed a federation of trade union women modeled after Chicago's Federal Ladies' Union No. 2703. From Boston Kenney wrote to Gompers on September 15: "I don't believe organization of women can be accomplished as readily as men. To me it seems slow, and if I had my choice of organizing either, I would take the men every time—it would make a better showing. I believe though much can be done for the women and I also do the best I can."[49]

While her "best" was good enough for Gompers, the other members of the AFL Executive Council were disappointed. When Gompers recommended on September 30 that Kenney's commission as general organizer be renewed, he was voted down. Chris Evans, United Mine Workers leader and AFL secretary, informed Gompers bluntly that the federation "is not in a condition financially to keep a woman organizer in the field without better hope of success than at present indicated." Kenney's efforts, he said, were "worthy of commendation, yet the fact remains that they have proved futile." John B. Lennon, of the Journeymen Tailors' Union, the AFL treasurer, suggested that Kenney be paid her salary until October 29 and "return fare to Chicago so as to give her time to secure employment."[50]

Kenney took her dismissal philosophically, but she warned Gompers that if the AFL was serious about organizing women, it had better appoint more rather than fewer female organizers: "I believe that the key to the situation in organization of women is that they need their leaders with them all the time." The advice was lost on Gompers. In his report to the 1892 AFL convention, he commended Kenney for her five months' organizing work, describing her activities as "missionary in nature," but failed to request either her reappointment or the appointment of another woman organizer.[51]

Back in Chicago, Kenney started a cooperative garment factory, helped financially by Lloyd, Darrow, and Jane Addams. She lived at Hull House, doing volunteer work for the Women's Cloak Makers' Union, distributing literature on the eight-hour day and beginning to pick up the work she had abandoned the previous May in the continuing campaign against the sweatshops.[52]

The sweatshop campaign had started in the summer of 1891. On August 20 Elizabeth Morgan wrote to Gompers: "The union cloak makers are having lots of trouble with the sweaters and the Trade Assembly put this work in the hands of committee Mr. M. H. Madden and myself. So we made a raid into 15 shops so far, and such things we see is a disgrace to the city and workmen. . . . The committee is not yet finished their visits to these sweaters shops."[53] Thus began what was to develop into one of the most important and influential reports in American labor history, which eventually called the attention of the entire nation to the evils of the sweating system.

Although the sweatshop had existed before the large Eastern European immigration at the end of the nineteenth century, it became more fully established in the garment industry as a result of the influx of the immigrants. "There are not many things an unskilled foreigner, knowing no English, can do," wrote Ray Stannard Baker at the turn of the century, "but almost any man or woman can sew." The sweaters, contractors paid by the large manufacturing companies to finish products begun in their factories, hired the cheapest nonunion labor possible (usually immigrant women and children) to do piecework, such as hand sewing, in their tenement dens. Since he was paid according to the number of finished products he returned to the manufacturer, the sweater literally "sweated" the work out of his employees by working them twelve to fifteen hours a day. Once they found that they were able to have work done at less cost outside the factories, the manufacturers stopped hiring piece workers entirely and cut the wages of their regular employees.

The immigrants had come to America in search of a better way of life. Instead, they found the sweatshop. "Nowhere in the world at any time, probably," Baker concluded, "were men and women worked as they were in the sweatshop—the lowest paid, most degrading employment. The sweatshop employer ground all the work he could from every man, woman and child under him."*[54]

By 1891 the sweating system, whose very existence was denied by the manufacturers, had become so entrenched in Chicago that it was both undermining the conditions of women workers and preventing their unionization. Early in August the wages of Chicago's female cloakmakers, members of the Ladies' Federal Labor Union, were cut by 40 percent. Morgan took the case of the cloakmakers' drastic cut to the Chicago Trades and Labor Assembly and argued that an intensive campaign against sweating was absolutely imperative. She called for an immediate investigation to expose the true conditions and disprove the manufacturers' repeated denials. The assembly responded by appointing a "Committee on Abuses" to investigate the sweatshop problem, made up of Elizabeth Morgan and M. H. Madden, also a member of the assembly. An officer of the city's Health Department, the city attorney, an official of the Cloak Makers' Union, and members of the local press (to whom advance notices had been sent) accompanied the committee on its fact-finding tour. As a result, Chicago newspapers began to run front-page stories denouncing the sweating system whose existence they had been dismissing for years.[55]

Elizabeth Morgan used the committee's visits to the tenement shops to fill a serious gap in the prior campaigns against the sweating system—the absence of reliable statistics. She began with the report of the Labor Assembly committee's visits to the sweatshops, *The New Slavery: Investigation into the Sweating System . . . as Applied to the Manufacture of Wearing Apparel,* and continued in speeches and testimony before a congressional committee. In the report, Morgan published previously unknown and unobtainable information on twenty-six sweating establishments, detailing the name and address of each sweater, his employer, the type of work, the sanitary conditions, the working space, the number of men, women, and children employed, and their hours and wages. She included the names of such highly respectable Chicago stores as Siegel & Cooper and Marshall Field's.

About a third of the report was devoted to vivid descriptions of the overcrowded dens of filth, vermin, and disease where women (nearly half the labor force) and children under fourteen years of age ("some . . . as young as 5 years") toiled from ten to fourteen hours a day. The conditions at specifically identified sweatshops were set forth in detail partly because Morgan was convinced that humanitarian argu-

---

*For a picture of sweatshops (native style and immigrant style), which reinforces the point that the post-1880 immigrants did not bring the sweatshop to the United States but found it here, see Leon Stein, *Out of the Sweatshop: The Struggle for Industrial Democracy* (New York, 1977).

ments in favor of closing the sweatshops would have little appeal "to a selfish public." But when "dainty ladies" of the middle and upper classes learned that they were being exposed to diphtheria, scarlet fever, and other contagious diseases spread by workers with "fevered hands, infected with the spatter of the consumptive," they would be more willing to join the campaign to close down these "pestilence-breeding sweat holes."

Morgan closed her pamphlet with a plea for enforcement of the city child labor and inspection ordinances, warning that if the laws were not enforced, Chicago citizens would be guilty of "murdering" a whole class of laborers who were "working in but ONE-TENTH of the space required by law . . . and one-fifteenth the space provided for criminals in our jails."[56]

On September 6, 1891, the Chicago Trades and Labor Assembly received Morgan's findings with "cries of indignation." A Chicago paper, *Rights of Labor,* printed it first in two issues.[57] Ten thousand copies later published by the assembly were snapped up, leaving "a number of people . . . begging for more."[58] Mrs. Morgan then used the Committee on Child Labor of the Illinois Women's Alliance to continue the investigation of sweatshops. During February and March, 1892, the committee exposed a number of new sweatshops.

In March, 1892, learning that Congress was preparing to investigate the sweating system, Morgan sent a copy of her Trade Assembly report to the special committee appointed to conduct the inquiry. The congressmen, impressed, decided to start their inquiry in Chicago and invited Morgan to be the first witness. Unfortunately, she was the only person to testify against the sweaters, while fifteen other witnesses, all "manufacturers and wholesale dealers in clothing," testified in their behalf. "I cannot understand this," Morgan wrote to Gompers. "Here the Tailors and Cloak Makers were present at the Trade Assembly Sunday and I ask them to be on hand Monday, when Labor has a good chance to use their force . . . and then . . . I alone a woman, have to do all their work. It is a disgrace to Labor Men of Chicago."[59] (Evidently, Elizabeth Morgan did not yet realize that the men who headed these unions were mainly concerned with the more skilled workers, who were male and, despite their public avowals to the contrary, were not too concerned about the plight of the women who made up a vast majority of the sweatshop workers.) In any case, the Chicago press concluded that Morgan was a "valuable witness," that her testimony "was listened to with a great deal of interest," that her use of statistics and specific examples and "intelligent and thoroughgoing statements" convinced the committee that Congress should "bring about a remedy for the evils complained of."[60]

" 'Abolish the sweating system' was the keynote of the mass-meeting which filled Central Music hall yesterday," began the lead article on the front page of the *Chicago News-Record* of February 20, 1893. It was to take a number of such meetings, together with tireless activity on the part of Elizabeth Morgan, Mary S. Kenney, and Florence Kelley, the strong support of trade unions and Hull House residents, and the cooperation of Illinois's great liberal governor John Peter Altgeld, before victory was won. But in June, 1893, the Illinois legislature passed the Factory and Workshop Inspection Act, or, as it became known, the Sweatshop Act. That pioneer law set sanitary standards for certain types of sweatshop manufacturing and regulated the labor of children and the working hours of women. Section 5 of the Act, for which Elizabeth Morgan fought hard and long, limited the employment of women in any factory or workshop to eight hours a day, six days a week.*[61]

All the while that she was investigating and exposing sweatshops and lobbying for antisweatshop legislation and for an eight-hour law for women, Elizabeth Morgan was also serving as secretary of the Federal Ladies' (now Women's) Union No. 2703, organizing unions of working-women in the Chicago area—watchmakers in Elgin, women shoe workers in Chicago, and various types of factory operatives—addressing strike meetings of these workers, and mobilizing relief for strikers.[62] The 1894 AFL convention gave Elizabeth Morgan a standing ovation in recognition of her strenuous efforts on behalf of workingwomen and children. She was the only female delegate at the convention and accepted the nomination for first vice-president, marking the first time a woman had run for high federation office. Although the incumbent, Peter J. McGuire, was one of the founders of the AFL and had been reelected to that post each year since 1890, Morgan received 226 votes against his 1,865 in a totally male-dominated convention. The convention paid her further tribute by endorsing her three basic proposals: state compulsory education laws to be instituted everywhere, and, if already on the statute books, to be fully enforced; an eight-hour law for women and children employed in manufacturing establishments to be enacted by all states; and abolition of the sweating system and tenement house manufacturing by state action.[63]

Morgan was pleased with the convention's action, but she would have been more pleased had there been more female delegates at the conven-

---

*The Illinois Manufacturers Association challenged the constitutionality of the eight-hour law for women in the courts. Elizabeth Morgan organized and chaired a public debate on "the justice, necessity, and legality" of the law, but on March 15, 1895, the Illinois Supreme Court found Section 5 of the Sweatshop Act unconstitutional. The unanimous opinion was the first court decision in the United States against the eight-hour law, and Earl Beckner notes that it "effectually closed the question of legislative restriction of the hours of employment of women for a number of years." (Mrs. T. J. Morgan to Gompers, 20 April 1894, *AFL Corr.;* Earl R. Beckner, *History of Labor Legislation in Illinois* [Chicago, 1929], p. 190.)

tion and had there been a woman general organizer functioning at the time the gathering met. She had been unhappy over the failure to extend Mary Kenney's organizing commission and had pleaded with Gompers for more female organizers.[64] But the AFL had remained without a woman general organizer until December, 1893, when Gompers commissioned Miss E. E. Pitt, a member of the Typographical Union in Boston. Pitt had done considerable work in her spare time organizing the women garment workers, and, at the request of the Boston AFL office, which urged that she be empowered to "extend her field of operations . . . among the women of other trades," Gompers commissioned her to begin "organizing women regardless of their trades or callings."[65]

In January, 1894, Gompers recommended to the AFL Executive Council that four additional women organizers be appointed, but he was quickly voted down. The Council gave four reasons for its negative stand. First, a financial one: "That on account of the present depression in trade that action on the appointment of four female organizers be deferred until a more propitious time." Then it was argued that it would not be possible to find qualified women to fill the four jobs. Again, the argument was raised that the money could be spent more effectively by hiring men as organizers. And finally, specific requests for organizing help were being received from unions composed entirely of men, these requests had to be filled and promised more than the vague suggestion that additional women organizers might be successful in organizing more women. On top of this, the council insisted that Pitt's work as organizer of women be cut short because of lack of funds, and she was allowed to carry on for only a few additional months. By the time the AFL convention met in 1894, the federation was once again without a woman general organizer.[66]

Even though the federation maintained a corps of "several hundred organizers" in the field, Gompers and his lieutenants took few additional concrete steps after 1892 to promote the organization of women.[67] The bulk of the AFL was made up of national trade unions that were basically craft in structure and were interested solely in the organization of skilled workers. They persistently ignored the resolutions adopted at federation conventions calling for the organization of women workers. In its issue of July 5, 1893, the *Coast Seamen's Journal*, official organ of the Sailors' Union of the Pacific, explained this indifference when it editorialized:

> Mentally and physically, women are incapable as a sex of achieving great things, but they are capable of being instrumental in making it impossible for men to be what nature intended them to be—the providers and protectors of women and children. The labor movement, which is the only movement that can possibly accomplish anything in the way of social reform, has the special responsibility of giving every man a chance to earn sufficient money to provide for a wife and family. Once that has been accomplished, the issue of women in industry and in the unions will soon cease to exist.

13

The American Federation of Labor, 1894–1900

ON MARCH 4, 1893, the National Cordage Company, which had declared a stock dividend of 100 percent only five months earlier, failed. A general break in the stock market followed, and soon the country was going through another severe economic crisis, bringing with it runs on the banks, thousands of business failures, and widespread unemployment. During 1893 more than sixteen thousand business firms went into bankruptcy; thousands of shops and factories shut down, while more thousands worked only part-time. By December, 1893, reports showed about 3 million people without any means of earning a livelihood. With at least three-fifths of the total labor force of 5 million unemployed, and with two to five times as many people dependent on them for existence, it is clear that by the end of 1893 a large percentage of the population was unable to procure the necessities of life. But when Emma Goldman advised a Union Square audience of unemployed men that "it was their sacred right" to take bread if they were starving, she was sentenced to a one-year term of imprisonment on Blackwell's Island in New York.[1]

As unemployment claimed from 50 to 75 percent of their members, many trade unions were barely able to survive. "There are probably not more than two national unions affiliated with the American Federation of Labor which have not had their resources greatly diminished and their efforts largely crippled by reason of trade struggles and the enormous number of members who have suffered through lack of employment," Gompers wrote in the fall of 1894.[2] The unions with women members were especially hard hit. Few cloakmakers' unions were able to survive the depression, and the United Garment Workers failed to hold a national convention between 1894 and 1897. Its membership rolls dwindled disastrously, and only those locals that had established substantial benefit funds were able to survive the hard times.[3]

The laundry workers' unions in Troy, New York, were shattered. When Wiliam Lippman, an AFL general organizer, visited Troy in April, 1895, he found the unions "falling to pieces" from widespread unemployment and "lack of funds," and saw little immediate prospect for the revival of unionism among the "collar girls."[4]

Yet it was during the depression winter of 1893–1894 that Mary Kenney went to Boston with the specific aim of organizing women workers into unions—and succeeded. While working as general organizer for the AFL in the summer of 1893, Kenney had made the acquaintance of Hannah Parker Kimball, a "wealthy lady feminist." On learning that Kenney had been removed as organizer, Kimball wrote to her from Paris urging her to settle in Boston and continue the work of organizing the women workers of that city:

> Your official recognition by the AFL will still be a great help, and even though the Federation does not see the value of putting more money into your important work, I cannot bear to think of the work among the women lagging for lack of money or enterprise among the men. I shall keep any aid that I was thinking of sending the Federation to assist your organizing work when you decide to come to Boston.[5]

In 1893, therefore, Kenney accompanied Hannah Parker Kimball to Boston and began organizing women workers there. She renewed her friendship with John F. O'Sullivan, the AFL organizer in Boston, and together they visited factories and shops to organize hundreds of women workers, support those already on strike, and help others to strike for better conditions and to resist wage reductions. On May 24, O'Sullivan wrote to Gompers:

> A strike took place among the silk workers of Newton Upper Falls, about 150 persons, 100 of whom are young girls.
> The girls have been receiving $5 per week of 58 hours, and were reduced to 40 hours and to $3.10 per week.
> They struck for the restoration of the 58 hours wage, claiming that it cost them $3 for board and that they could not properly clothe themselves on 10 cents per week.
> Mary Kenney and myself went down there last Wednesday and formed two unions, one for women and one for men, and had them appoint a committee to wait upon the firm along with Miss Kenney to see if the wages could not be restored.
> We found that there were 18 girls and 20 men at work in the mill and we waited upon them at the mill gate and invited them to come to the meeting which we called that evening.
> At this meeting, which was held in a basement because we could not get a hall, we talked with the people and succeeded in organizing them and there is every indication that the strikers will fight this thing out.
> They live in corporation houses and expect to be fired out as soon as the rent expires if they don't win before then.[6]

Two weeks later O'Sullivan informed Gompers that the strike had been won.[7] The *Boston Globe* credited Mary Kenney with having achieved what many thought was impossible—"organizing a new union of women workers and winning a strike and restoration of a wage reduction during the depths of a depression." What made the victory even more astounding, the *Globe* pointed out, was the fact that there were sixty thousand unemployed women in Boston.[8]

By November, 1894, Kenney and O'Sullivan had succeeded in establishing about forty unions of women workers.[9] By then, both were serving together on both the organizing committee of the Boston Central Labor Union and the legislative committee of the Massachusetts Federation of Labor. "There is considerable surmising about Mary and I," O'Sullivan wrote humorously to Gompers, "and the boys are pressing as are my friends in the AFL office. Some of the old maid union men are chewing over our being together on the committees as if it was an extraordinary thing. I keep them guessing, as usual, and Mary enjoys it."[10]

On November 28, 1894, Mary Kenney invited Gompers to visit Boston to speak for the "Industrial Education of Women," an organization she had founded in order to teach the newly organized women the methods of bargaining with employers. "I shall promise you the largest audience of women you have ever seen together," she wrote, "and working women at that."[11] After the meeting Gompers attended the marriage ceremony of John F. O'Sullivan and Mary Kenney in New York. Mary Kenney O'Sullivan continued her efforts to organize female wage earners and remained active in Boston's labor movement after she had become pregnant. She was greatly disappointed when in 1895 she was unable to participate in the strike of a local of women garment workers she had founded because of her confinement.[12]

The achievements of the Kenney-O'Sullivan team during the depression were truly unique. The depression had dealt a devastating blow to the Working Women's Clubs, as well as to many unions of women workers. As jobs grew scarce, the mutual benefit funds were emptied, members allowed their dues to lapse, and the vacation holiday houses fell into disrepair.[13] But the economic crisis of the 1890s brought the woman suffrage and labor movements closer together than at any time since the 1868 convention of the National Labor Union. The hardships they endured during the depression years stimulated women workers' interest in the ballot, while male unionists saw more clearly that an enfranchised working class of women would strengthen their demands for public works and other relief measures for the unemployed. At the same time, the plight of the unemployed workingwomen was brought more sharply to the attention of the suffragists.[14] Hamilton Wilcox informed Gompers that quite a number of women associated with his suffrage association had been shocked by the sight of "a hundred thousand struggling women having to starve and freeze through the dreadful winter."[15]

Helen Campbell, daughter of a prominent New York lawyer and banker, published *Prisoners of Poverty: Women Wage Earners, Their Trades and Lives* in 1887, and the *Woman's Journal* offered the book as a premium for obtaining subscriptions to the magazine, commending the volume for its bibliography on the "woman question in its social and industrial aspects."[16] In Massachusetts, where, since 1874, the labor of women and minors had been limited to sixty hours a week, woman suffragists joined with labor unions in campaigning for shorter hours for women and children, while the unions petitioned the legislature for municipal suffrage for women. Although the coalition did not succeed in persuading the legislature to pass a fifty-four-hour-week law for women and children against the opposition of the mill owners' lobby, it did finally get a compromise measure—the fifty-eight-hour week, and no night work.[17]

During the summer of 1894, the Massachusetts State Federation of Labor endorsed woman suffrage, while the New York State Federation of Labor gathered 140,000 signatures on its behalf for presentation to the state's Constitutional Convention. Trade unions throughout the state distributed copies of *The Value of the Workingwoman to the State,* a speech delivered by Harrietta A. Keyser, organizer for the New York City Woman Suffrage League's Constitutional Amendment Campaign, before the suffrage committee of the state Constitutional Convention. Keyser's pamphlet was put on sale at the *Woman's Journal* office in Boston and was distributed widely throughout the state by the Massachusetts Suffrage Association.[18]

By 1899, Susan B. Anthony could assure Gompers that since "you and the Labor Organizations of the country agree with us in our demand for a 16th Amendment, our movement can claim to have behind it the weight and influence of all the trade unions and labor organizations of the country."[19]

When prosperity began to return in 1897, there already existed an alliance between women of leisure and workingwomen to improve the lot of the woman worker and to bring about her enfranchisement. There were, to be sure, as Aileen S. Kraditor points out, distinct limits to the interest displayed by women of the leisure class in the problems and needs of workingwomen. However, one must not underestimate the impact of the depression of the 1890s on the consciousness of both middle-class women and the labor movement as far as woman suffrage and the working conditions of women were concerned.[20]

As the nation climbed out of the depression, the trade unions sought to rebuild their shattered membership rolls and regain the losses they had sustained during the economic crisis. In these struggles, the male workers were often supported by their wives. In no battle of that era were the wives of strikers more conspicuous than in the strike of the AFL woodworkers of Oshkosh, Wisconsin, for a wage increase and union recognition. The June 23, 1898, issue of the *Oshkosh Daily Northwestern* reported:

> The Morgan plant at the corner of Sixth and Oregon streets was closed this morning as a result of a riot and will remain closed for an indefinite period. . . .
>
> Long before six o'clock this morning, strikers and their wives commenced to gather around the plant of the Morgan company, and as the crowd grew in number, it became evident that they were following a preconcerted plan of action and that trouble would result.
>
> By the time the first non-union men arrived in the vicinity of the factory, on their way to work, the strikers were in the vicinity in the hundreds. Non-union men who had the temerity to attempt to make their way through the crowd were handled in rough style. . . .
>
> A dozen infuriated women, wives of the strikers, constituted the most disorderly element in the crowd. Urged on by the cheers of the men, the women, with pouches filled with eggs, sand and pepper, hanging in front of them, and with great clubs in their hands, three and four feet long, swung up and down the street, halting pedestrians and chasing every non-union man who appeared within a block of the mill.
>
> They hurled their clubs at those whom they could not catch, and for that matter took complete control of the thoroughfare. . . .
>
> Oregon street, from the south approach of the Light street bridge to the Morgan company's office at the corner of Sixth street, was patrolled by the women, while the strikers constituted a body guard.

The plant remained closed until August 3, when scabs were brought in under police protection. "Again Strikers Riot," read the headline in the *Daily Northwestern* of August 5, 1898. Nine women were arrested and jailed. The *Daily Northwestern* described them as a group

> of the toughest looking women eyes ever looked upon. . . . They were the leading lights of the female contingement and were themselves pictures of anarchy. Some had no stockings, but wore flapping slippers. Various colored handkerchiefs were tied over their heads and some carried umbrellas and stones hidden under their aprons. One had a long club concealed in a roll of paper.[21]

The following morning, a delegation of about forty women, wives of the strikers, poured into the mayor's office uninvited and demanded that he immediately release the women from jail and "either make the mill men raise wages or close down the factories." "The women," the *Daily Northwestern* reported, "insisted that they could not live on the wages their husbands had been getting, and said they were in debt and had little to eat."[22]

With the mills filling up with scabs deputized as policemen and carrying clubs, and with city police protecting them still further outside the gates, the strike began to wind down. On September 17 the strikers returned to work, and on the 20th the AFL union called off the strike. All that the strikers were promised was an increase in wages in a few weeks if business continued to improve.[23]

Another tactic utilized by wives of unionists to help their husbands' struggles was first used in Muncie, Indiana, early in 1899. Mrs. Sarah Crossfield explained in a letter to Gompers:

> We have just organized the Woman's Union Label League. This League is composed of the wives, mothers, and daughters of laboring men and working girls and was organized for the purpose of helping weak union men to stand up for their rights and to educate the workmen's wives in the labor movement. This is a woman's union, and our *main* object is to *agitate* for the union label.[24]

In the fall of 1899 Crossfield set out to organize branches of the Woman's Union Label League. In letters to local papers, she appealed:

> Justice and purity are written on the face of every union label, and I never look at one but that it suggests to me well-paid workmen with happy homes, and I can also fancy the presence of well-fed, well-clothed children, not toiling in factory and shop, but in the school-room, from which they emerge developed into bright, intelligent citizens, ready to fill our places as mothers and fathers when our life work is complete.
>
> Housewives are the purchasers of most all the necessaries of life. Therefore they must create a demand for, and protect, the union label.[25]

The League then renamed itself the "Women's International Union Label League of the World." The preamble to its constitution included the sweeping statement: "We, the women of the world, who are classed as belonging to the wage earning system, deem the time opportune for us to place ourselves in touch with the tidal wave of organization and band ourselves under one banner that shall say to the world at large: This part of humanity stands on its motto which is 'Elevation and Education for the Laborers of the World.'" The league's aim now was not merely to support the union label but "to promote the advancement and raising of wages of women who are engaged in manufacturing industries."[26] Locals were established in many Indiana towns and cities, and AFL organizers reported that branches had been organized in St. Louis; Bridgeton, New Jersey; Belleville, Illinois; and elsewhere.[27] Locals of the league were credited with helping to organize the Glass Packers Union of Bridgeton,[28] the street car unions in Indiana,[29] and various trades in Topeka, Kansas.[30]

The most famous member of the Label League was Kate Barnard, a young Catholic social worker from Oklahoma City, who had become convinced that the only way to eliminate poverty and achieve social justice was through the organization of labor and the use of union-made products. Barnard formed and became secretary of the Oklahoma chapter of the Women's International Union Label League in 1905, and two years later, she also founded Federal Union No. 12374 of the unskilled laborers in Oklahoma City, and was elected its representative to the Oklahoma City Trades and Labor Assembly. As a leader of the Label League and a member of both the Trades' Assembly and the Farmers' Union, Barnard became an important force in the labor-farmer-social reformer campaign to write a progressive state constitution for the territory of Oklahoma. The consitution included several provisions she especially fought for: prohibition of the use of convict-lease labor and the employment of children under fifteen years of age in hazardous occupations, and the establishment of compulsory education.[31]

The renewed interest in unionization that emerged with the return of prosperity was reflected among workingwomen as well as men. New organizations were formed and older ones were revived. Some were temporary associations, while others were longer-lasting. In the category of new and temporary unions were those formed by servant girls. In April, 1897, the American Servant Girls' Association was organized in Kansas City, Missouri, by Mary Hartropp, herself a servant girl. Within a few weeks it was reported to have thirty locals and a membership of five thousand, and was credited with being "the first organization effected and put on a working basis in America for the protection of servant girls." The objectives of the association were set forth in a pamphlet issued for use in recruiting new members, which stated that the union would seek

> To secure for the servant girl a better appreciation of her services on the part of the employer.
> To protect the servant girl against the infamous backlisting system adopted by mistresses generally.
> To secure for the servant girl a revised system of household duties and the payment of a fair remuneration for her services.
> To secure for servant girls the consent of all employers for a general half holiday each week, and for the privilege of enjoying freedom from bondage on the Sabbath day.
> To provide a means of concerted action whenever occasion requires such action.
> To furnish employment for the unemployed members, and to care for them when disabled.

The plan was eventually to develop a department that would furnish insurance to members against illness, injury, and death at comparatively low cost.[32]

Hartropp used an interesting method in organizing a local. Before visiting a city, she would send postcards to all servant girls whose names and addresses were listed in the city's directory, advising them of a meeting to be held on her arrival in the area. In Duluth, Minnesota, in response to such an advance notice, 175 girls employed in private houses, boardinghouses, and hotels met and, after listening to an address by Hartropp, formed the Duluth Division of the American Servant Girls' Association. Each member paid an initiation fee of 25 cents, half of which went to the National Lodge in Kansas City and the rest to the local. They also agreed to pay monthly dues of 12 cents.

Unfortunately, the organization soon passed out of existence. But three years later, in December, 1900, a second attempt was made to form a union of servant girls. This time the initiative came from a social reformer, Mrs. St. Justin Beale, of New York City. Although only twelve servant girls responded to her call for a meeting, and Herman Robinson, AFL organizer, declared that he could not see how a servant girls' union could fit into the federation, Mrs. Beale persisted. As a result, the Domestic Servants' Union was organized on December 12, 1900, with six members. The organization talked bravely of calling a "general strike" of servant girls in New York City, but it breathed its last before this could get beyond the talking stage.[33]

Then, on July 27, 1901, the Workingwomen of America, a union of servant girls, came into being in Chicago, and adopted a wage scale and a set of rules governing employment conditions. For cooks and housekeepers, the recommended wages were $5 to $7 a week; for general second girls (assistants), $4 to $5 a week; and for young and inexperienced girls, $3 to $4 a week. The five rules read:

> Rule 1. Work shall not begin before 5:30 o'clock, and shall cease when the evening's dishes are washed and put away. Two hours each afternoon and the entire evening at least twice a week, shall be allowed the domestic as her own.
> Rule 2. There shall be no opposition on the part of the mistress to club life on the part of the domestic. Entertainment of friends in limited numbers shall not be prohibited, provided the domestic furnishes her own refreshments.
> Rule 3. Gentlemen friends shall not be barred from the kitchen or back porch. Members of the family of the house shall not interrupt the conversation arising during said visits.
> Rule 4. Domestics shall be allowed such hours off on Mondays as will permit them to visit the bargain counters of the stores and enjoy on that day the same privileges enjoyed by the mistress and her daughters.
> Rule 5. All complaints shall be made to the business agent of the union. The question of wages shall be settled at the time of employment, and no reduction shall be allowed.[34]

With three hundred members at the time of its organization, the Workingwomen of America was not to be sneered at. "Householders who were at first inclined to make a jest of the union are now beginning to see that the matter is serious," wrote a reporter in Chicago. He revealed that while the union had made the names of its officers public, it had announced that it would not disclose their addresses until the membership reached one thousand. At that time, too, a move would be made to secure a charter from the American Federation of Labor.[35] That goal, however, was never reached, and like its predecessors, the Workingwomen of America disappeared from the scene.

This period did witness the formation of one national union with a large female membership that has lasted up to the present—the International Ladies' Garment Workers' Union. In some respects, the mere formation of such a union at the turn of the nineteenth century was something of a miracle. The very nature of the ladies' garment industry produced unique problems that seemed to make it impossible for a stable union to be created. In an age of trusts and monopolies, large factories and mass production, the making of ladies' garments was scattered in small units and among countless contractors' shops operating in isolation. Fierce competition not only kept the industry unstable but led to extreme labor exploitation. On top of this, such unionism as did exist was seasonal in nature and was weakened even more by ideological disputes between socialists and anarchists.

In the late 1890s the unions in this industry included women waistmakers, wrapper makers, and reefer (children's wear) makers. Their existence was the result of both technological innovations and the women's determination to organize. The electric sewing machine, introduced in the mid-1890s, required less strength and skill to operate than the foot-powered model it replaced and therefore enabled unskilled women to obtain jobs formerly held by men. At the same time, machines for edge pressing, collars and padding, and felling also came into use, and these, too, enabled women to obtain jobs that had previously required special skills. Women quickly moved into new branches of the women's garment industry, producing shirtwaists, wrappers, underwear, and children's clothing in factories.[36]

The women held meetings in settlement houses, where they formed local unions, mapped out demands, and organized strikes. But they were no more successful in overcoming "seasonal unionism" than the men cloakmakers had been.[37] In 1898 members of various cloakmakers' unions began calling for the formation of a national union. As in the past, the call proved futile, and in 1899, when the usual seasonal strikes broke out, the manufacturers, armed with injunctions, successfully resisted the workers' demands for higher wages. Thus, when, in March, 1900, the United Brotherhood of Cloak Makers' Union No. 1 of New York and Vicinity issued a call for a national union to enable the workers to resist injunctions and promulgate a national label, the response was positive. Encouraged, the Brotherhood invited all workers employed in the manufacture of ladies' cloaks, suits, and shirts to attend a convention on June 3, 1900, in New York City, the center of whatever strength and leadership existed among the ladies' garment workers.

On that date, delegates representing seven locals in five cities (New York, Brooklyn, Newark, Philadelphia. and Baltimore), with a combined membership of two thousand, met in New York's Labor Lyceum to elect national officers. On June 23, the AFL issued a charter to the new union—the International Ladies' Garment Workers' Union (ILGWU). A week later, the first session of the General Executive Board met in Philadelphia.[38]

Although the founders and leaders of the ILGWU were socialists and rejected the AFL's "pure and simple unionism" with its opposition to political activism, they were essentially conservative. The leaders discouraged strikes and relied instead on popularizing the union label and on the boycott. Unlike most AFL unions, the ILGWU could not simply ignore women workers, for they controlled shirtwaist and underwear manufacturing and dominated the ladies' garment industry in an overall sense. However, the new union shared the AFL view that men should occupy all positions of leadership in labor organizations. Like the typical AFL leaders, they had little confidence in the ability of women to sustain a strong, viable organization and were convinced that women's preoccupation with marriage made them apathetic unionists.[39] As we shall see, it took a struggle to make a dent in these sexist attitudes.

The year 1900 also saw the formation of a national union of laundry workers affiliated with the AFL. As the nation's economic revival got underway, the laundries were characterized by a work week of more than sixty hours, low wages, and a sweatshop environment. Conditions such as these inspired laundry workers to strike for improvements,* but they invariably failed. A group of men laundry workers in Troy, New York, then decided to form the United Laundry Workers of Troy, which the AFL chartered as a federal labor union in 1898. Within the next two years, the United Laundry Workers set about forming other locals with the aim of becoming a national union. The platform of the ULW had three objectives: (1) to organize a national trade union; (2) to secure a "universally equal and just rate of prices, without strikes"; and (3) to maintain a death benefit for all members by assessment. This last seemed to be the chief objective, since it was spelled out in detail, and laundry workers were warned: "Remember, death may accidentally overtake you—so unite with us." Even a living wage and better conditions, which unionization of the laundry workers would bring "without a strike," would

---

*Nearly all these laundry strikes were for higher wages and a reduction in the terribly long working hours, but in 1896 New York laundresses conducted a sit-down strike—probably the first such strike in American labor history—in support of the strike called by the United Garment Workers. Despite this assistance, the UGW lost.

have as their chief benefit the means of enabling a member to "provide your family in an easy way, with the means of a decent burial."[40]

Perhaps this ghoulish emphasis in the organizing literature helps to explain Gompers' reluctance to grant the United Laundry Workers a charter as an international union. On July 15, 1900, Charles E. Nordeck, ULW secretary, complained to the AFL president that if he was not willing to charter the union "as an International Trade Union," they would have to look elsewhere: "For while we have time and money on hand it should be put to use now, and not left until we are dead, for we are looking for present benefits."[41] Eventually Gompers did issue an appeal to laundry workers' unions, inviting them to send delegates to a convention to be held in Troy on November 12, 1901, "for the purpose of forming an International Union of Laundry Workers."[42]

What emerged from the convention, however, was not an international union confined to laundry workers. Herman Robinson, the AFL organizer who worked with the founders, asked Gompers whether a charter had been granted to the shirt- and waistmakers. If not, the laundry workers would claim jurisdiction over all branches of the trade, including shirt and waist workers. Gompers replied that no charter had been granted, and the delegates to the Troy convention then organized the Shirt, Waist, and Laundry Workers International Union. On November 19, 1900, the AFL issued it a charter under that name, including jurisdiction over the making and laundering of shirts and collars.

Robinson was delighted. "Seventy-five percent of shirts manufactured are made in Troy and Vicinity," he informed Gompers, "and it will be the means of organizing the entire craft in all its branches under one head." He was confident that the new international was "in a position to build up a large organization in the course of time." He exulted: "Just think, about 15,000 to 18,000 people are employed in this craft in Troy and Vicinity, many of them girls who are ready to be organized. The delegates have elected a good set of several officers who can do the job—their general president John J. Manning of Troy is a very conservative fellow." He then went on to list all the other officers, each one of them male.[43] It never occurred to Robinson that this might not be the best way to organize "girls who are ready to be organized."

The new international union immediately set out to convince the female laundry workers that "every good can only come through a hearty cooperation between employer and employee without resort to strikes."[44] But it made little headway. and the original membership of two thousand remained at that level for a number of years.

Another ineffectual union affiliated with the AFL in an industry employing large numbers of women was the National Union of Textile Workers (NUTW). What made this union historically significant was the fact that even though it had little membership in the North, it became the vehicle through which the AFL hoped to organize Southern textile workers.

On April 14, 1896, L. H. McCateer, AFL general organizer in South Carolina and Georgia, sent an alarming letter to Gompers warning him that every textile mill in the North would close down unless the AFL quickly organized the workers in the Southern mills. To make his point clear, he enclosed a clipping from a South Carolina paper that carried the gleeful headline: "Give Up the Fight. New England Mills Find They Can't Compete With the South." The story that followed went in part:

> New England cotton mills are giving up the fight against competition in Georgia and the Carolinas and will soon cease to manufacture coarse cloths. The Lawrence Manufacturing Company of Lowell, Mass., one of the biggest plants in that section, stopped making cloth entirely. This is only the first of a series. Other New England mills will very soon have to shut down. Treasurer Baker of the Lawrence Company says that this is a crisis that has been pending for three years. He says that the low wages paid for Southern mill labor is the cause of the trouble here. The cost of labor there is 30 per cent lower than it is here. Consequently the Southern manufacturers have an advantage over those of the North of from ½ to 2 cents per pound.[45]

Shortly after sending this letter, McCateer helped to organize a union of textile workers in Columbus, Georgia, and led them in a strike against a wage cut. The strike was lost, but he informed Gompers that the union was still alive and could serve as a jumping-off point for organizing the cotton mills of the South. "Would it not be possible for the AFL to send some experienced organizers here to continue the work I have been doing?" he appealed. And he went on:

> I have been boycotted and ordered out of mill yards and I can no longer reach these slaves of the mills. Rather they are worse than slaves for when one dies there is three more to take his or her place. Children 6 and 7 years old taking the place of grown people at 10 and 15 cents per day and no law to prevent them poor children from being so treated. Again I must warn you that all of the mills in the North will have either to shut down or move South and work 14 and 15 hours per day.[46]

In December, 1896, Gompers responded by sending two special organizers "to endeavor to organize the textile workers of the South."[47] The chief organizer, Robert Howard, spent ten days in Georgia. He found some unions of textile workers in existence in Columbus and helped strengthen them. By the time he left that city, he reported, there were six textile unions there. He organized textile unions in Atlanta and in Augusta and expressed the belief that both would soon affiliate with the AFL. His report concluded:

> I am very much encouraged with the work done, and found it just as easy to organize the Southern textile operatives as it was to organize the textile

operatives of New England. I believe the seed we have sown will bear fruit in the near future and instead of women and children toiling from 66 to 79 hours weekly as they are now doing in the South, that through organization and persistent agitation they will be able to reduce the hours of labor to a level to those of the New England operatives who toil from 58 to 60 hours per week only.[48]

If Howard was right, the Southern textile operatives had very little to look forward to. This says something about a labor leader who believed that the Southern woman should hail the opportunity to work "only" fifty-eight to sixty hours a week.

Will H. Winn, the AFL's leading organizer in the South, agreed with Howard that the organizing trip was "sowing the seed," but he was far less confident about the time it would take for it to bear fruit.[49] One of the problems involved in organizing the Southern textile mills was racism, and it was already making itself felt. In the summer of 1896, workers in a mill in Rome, Georgia, had struck against the replacement of a white worker by a black and succeeded in having the white reinstated. Another strike occurred the next year in Atlanta to protest the employment of two Negro women spinners, who were to work alongside white women. The white women immediately quit, and the men "walked out in obedience to the orders of the Textile Workers' Union, and in sympathy with the striking female operatives." Fourteen hundred workers were out. The strike lasted for only a day. The company offered to discharge the blacks if the workers would extend their own hours without extra pay, as they readily agreed to do.[50]

The textile workers' flagrant act of racism, coupled with their agreement to worsened conditions, received no rebuke from Winn. Like all the AFL organizers in the South at this time, he was himself a racist and opposed the unionization of black workers. In his view, blacks did not possess "those peculiarities of temperament such as patriotism, sympathy, sacrifice, etc. and which alone made an organization of the character and complexity of the modern trade union possible." Instead of wasting its time and money in vain attempts to organize Negro workers, Winn proposed that the AFL support the colonization of blacks in Liberia or Cuba.[51] Under these circumstances, it is hardly surprising that Winn did nothing to convince the white textile workers of the Fulton Bag & Cotton Mill that it was necessary to unite with the blacks in order to present a common front against the employers rather than surrender their conditions to keep the plant lily-white.

On March 30, 1891, the National Union of Textile Workers was chartered by the AFL and given the mission of organizing the textile industry of New England. But by 1898 the union was so weak financially and had so few Northern members that the newly affiliated Southern locals were in the majority, and Prince W. Greene of Alabama was elected president to serve from 1898 to 1900. Typically, the General Executive Council and the organizers were all male. But then the NUTW never had shown any interest in organizing the women in the industry. H. S. Mills, general secretary and treasurer of the union, advised all local unions to organize only those who could afford "high dues," an obvious warning against bothering with the lowest-paid workers in the New England mills, who were, of course, the women operatives. In a circular sent from Lawrence, Massachusetts, he wrote: "'High Dues is the key to the success of the trade unions, and too much stress cannot be laid upon the necessity of all our local unions adopting such a system at all times."[52]

The most important strike in the Southern textile industry up to this time began on November 21, 1898, against all the mills in Augusta. The Augusta unions were independent locals but were affiliated with the Augusta Federation of Trades. The workers walked out to protest a wage reduction of from 25 to 40 percent, with "women who were making the smallest wages, cut the most." The employers countered with a lockout.[53]

It soon became evident that the Augusta strike and lockout were the key to unionizing the Southern textile industry. Indeed, at the 1898 AFL convention, Gompers cited the strike as proof that "a better [opportunity] for organizing American textile workers of the South prevails than at any time heretofore." He revealed that he had ordered the National Union of Textile Workers of America to enroll the strikers as members of the AFL and had wired Prince W. Greene and Will H. Winn to do everything possible to help them.[54]

The Augusta strikers were not impressed. "The strikers claim that the National Union of Textile Workers is impotent; that it is in no condition to render assistance, which is desperately needed," Winn wrote to Gompers, and he added: "The NUTW is a dead organization, if indeed it ever lived."[55] John T. Pugh, president of the Augusta Central body of textile workers, endorsed Winn's position and sent a pathetic appeal to Gompers for direct AFL assistance to the strikers.[56] But the AFL sent no assistance, and Prince W. Greene had to report sadly to Gompers that "having exhausted all resources, the strikers are dribbling back into the mills in squads." In the end, strikebreakers, evictions of workers from the company houses, and starvation defeated the Augusta strike. The strike leaders were not only refused work but blacklisted as well throughout the industry in the South.[57]

Following the Augusta defeat, Greene tried to revive textile organization throughout the South, but he had to confess to Gompers, "I am afraid it will be impossible to do much as I am simply financially not able to form textile unions. It will certainly never do for workers to know the financial condition of the National Union of Textile Workers of

America."[58] In 1901 the National Union of Textile Workers of America
went out of existence.

From the summer of 1894, when E. E. Pitt was dismissed for lack of
funds, until 1898, the AFL was without a single woman general organizer. In 1898 Eva MacDonald Valesh of Minnesota was appointed
organizer.[59] But she was also made assistant editor of the *American
Federationist* and devoted most of her time to that journal. The only other
woman commissioned by the AFL was Irene M. Ashby, who, before
coming to the United States from England, had been associated with the
Workers' Union, founded by Tom Mann.* She was sent to Alabama by
the federation to investigate child labor conditions and to agitate for
passage of regulatory legislation by the state legislature, then in session.
She visited scores of cotton mills in Alabama, studying labor conditions
and making what Elizabeth H. Davidson calls "probably the first extensive investigation of child labor in the cotton mills of Alabama or any of
the Southern states."[60]

Ashby also held meetings with members of WCTU groups and other
women's clubs, and with educators, clergymen, and physicians, to gain
support for legislation directed against child labor. She drew up two bills
and agitated for their passage by the state legislature. One of these bills
would have prevented the employment of children under twelve in mills
and factories, and the other would compel children between the ages of
six and twelve to attend school for a specified number of weeks each
year. In a letter to Gompers from Huntsville, Alabama, on December 17,
1900, Ashby wrote: "The deeper I go in my investigations the more I am
convinced that a Child Labour Bill will be of very little service without a
Compulsory Education Bill. If we can get a Compulsory Education Bill
through and some limitation of hours and possibly an age limit (12) for
entering the mills, a great deal will have been accomplished."[61]

On January 3, 1901, Gompers ordered Ashby to finish her work and
cease functioning for the AFL. This order came in response to a letter
from Ashby dated December 26, 1900, in which she reported:

An extraordinary suspicion has greeted me in several quarters. I am suspected of acting in the interest of several Northern mill owners and corporations who are jealous of the Southern development. I am assured on good
authority that money has been collected with a view to stirring up trouble in
the trade. Do you know anything of this and can you assure me on your

---

*Ashby, a college graduate, had organized the women who worked for Sir Thomas Lipton
to protest against their conditions of employment. This brought her to the attention of
Tom Mann, and she was invited to join the Workers' Union. (Irene M. Ashby-Macfayden,
"The Last Stronghold of Infant Mill Slavery," *Social Service* 4 [1901]: 202.)

sacred word of honour that I am not being used as the tool of any such design?[62]

Gompers, furious, retorted:

I do not think it necessary to give you any such assurance. I am not accustomed to give anyone such assurance, and yours is the first instance of anyone, acting in the interests of labor, on behalf of the American Federation of Labor, who has even harbored such a suspicion much less given expression to it. It were best that you drop the work immediately and return.[63]

While Gompers had good reason for his anger, it is worth noting that both in the *American Federationist* and at AFL conventions he (and other AFL leaders) had called upon the New England textile employers to help correct the disparity between the North and the South and to begin by supporting the campaign against child labor.[64] Ashby continued to work for the AFL in the South after her return from a trip to England to get married. Gompers, moreover, published her articles exposing child labor conditions in the *American Federationist* and arranged for her to lecture before Northern organizations.[65]

In July, 1900, several hundred women workers in Cincinnati, employed in a large variety of trades and callings, sent a petition to the AFL national office complaining: "We have some time ago, made application to join the Trades Unions, but could never get the members to meet us, having always the same excuse. We feel satisfied that they are trying to keep us out of the unions." The Cincinnati Central Labor Council had called for "the enforcement of a living wage for the man—the natural protector of the woman," but said nothing about the fact that the "natural protector of woman" did not permit the women workers of the city to join his unions. Nor did it act when members of the waitresses' union complained of the "practice of head waiters and others in authority over them (members of the male waiters' union) of using profane and vulgar language and utterly ignoring all respect due their sex."[66]

The experience of the women of Cincinnati was being duplicated by women workers in other parts of the country. While only a small number of unions affiliated with the AFL during this period actually forbade the admission of women,* most of the craft unions achieved the same purpose without resorting to specific constitutional clauses barring women. They did this through the system of long apprenticeship requirements, the high fees charged for admission, and special examinations that women were required to pass. Some unions admitted only those women employed in certain branches—usually not the best-paid sectors of the

---

*Among these were the Barbers, Engravers, Switchmen, and Molders, which prescribed that only men were eligible for membership. The Molders even imposed a penalty of a fine or expulsion on any member who so much as dared to give instructions to female workers in any branch of the trade.

trade. Describing an engraving plant he had visited in Bridgeton, New Jersey, an AFL organizer reported in March, 1900, that about six hundred of the one thousand workers employed there were women who were permitted by the union to work only in the lowest paid positions, where they received "about $2.50 a week." In the engraving departments, he explained, "there are about 50 girls employed but they are not allowed to do the better class of work. The engravers' union . . . will not take them in their organization."[67]

It was bad enough that many AFL unions kept women out by constitutional bars, by openly declared policy, or by simply refusing to organize them. What made matters even worse was their refusal to sanction the granting of a special charter for a women's local to be affiliated directly to the national AFL.

In 1900 a group of women workers in the shoe industry in Illinois appealed to the AFL's Boot & Shoe Workers' Union for permission to become members. Informed of the dues, they protested that they could not pay such a high sum on the meager wages they earned. They appealed to the AFL national office to urge the Boot & Shoe Workers' Union to reduce the dues. The request was forwarded, but Horace M. Eaton, secretary-treasurer of the union, bluntly informed the AFL secretary-treasurer, Frank Morrison, that the union was not interested in recruiting members "on the bargain counter plan." Morrison, in turn, told the women there was nothing the AFL could do to compel the union to alter its stand.

The women thereupon organized a local union and asked the AFL national office to grant them a charter. The Boot & Shoe Workers' Union protested vigorously, and the AFL national office turned down the request.[68] This was a pathetic termination of a relationship between men and women in the shoe industry that earlier in the century had produced a great demonstration of unity of men and women in the Lynn strike of 1860, the solidarity of the Knights and Daughters of St. Crispin of the 1870s, and the organization in the Knights of Labor of the 1880s.

Fortunately, there were some exceptions to this antifeminist attitude. When Mary MacDowell helped establish Local No. 183 of the Amalgamated Meat Cutters and Butcher Workmen of North America—the first women's union in the meat-packing industry—she won the support of Michael Donnelly, the Amalgamated's president, who addressed meetings of the local.[69]

More typical, however, was the case of the National Brotherhood of Electrical Workers (later named the International Brotherhood in 1897, when Canadian members joined). Originally organized to recruit only wiremen and linemen, it did not even concern itself with the question of admitting female workers. But that question did arise in many locals as the union's jurisdiction was extended to the electrical manufacturing establishments. Since the constitution did not expressly prohibit women from joining, a few were admitted to membership as early as 1892. This so offended the male supremacists in the union that at the convention the following year the constitution was amended to read that only male electrical workers were eligible for membership. But women were entering the industry in increasing numbers, and it became clear even to the die-hard elements that the Brotherhood could not exercise effective control unless women were included. The result was that in 1895 the all-male provision was repealed, and female workers, if not actually invited to become members, "were at least not offered the insult of refusal."[70]

However, many locals simply refused to go beyond that point. In fact, so little was done to organize women by some of the key locals that J. F. Kelly, the national secretary, asked Gompers to urge the locals in the General Electric plants of Schenectady and Lynn to organize females working for GE. In identical letters, Gompers reminded these officials that

> the electrical workers is quite an industry in your city and there are a large number of female electrical workers. These girls thus far have been unorganized and are suffering a great many adverse conditions which could be mitigated and improved if they were brought into the union. Of course I know the conditions which surround you but the thought has occurred to me that you might be successful in organizing these girls into a union and have them attached to the National Brotherhood of Electrical Workers.[71]

This correspondence did produce some results at the GE plant in Schenectady, but progress was impeded by a provision in the International's constitution that any women engaged in the manufacture or operation of electrical apparatus could only belong to a sublocal under the supervision of the men's local in the city. In the event that male and female members had to be organized into the same local, no female would be eligible for the presidency.[72]

Although under the charter of the International Brotherhood of Electrical Workers telephone operators as well as linemen were eligible to join, before 1912 little effort was made to organize them. Discussions at IBEW conventions emphasized that women telephone operators were simply not worth bothering with. They were accused of not being interested in unionism or of coming to the union only when they were in trouble and dropping out just as soon as the trouble was over. In the main, the women telephone operators were described as being more loyal to the companies than to the union and the principles of labor solidarity.[73]

Yet in one city where women telephone operators and linemen worked effectively together in the IBEW, the facts of life gave the lie to these prejudices. That city was San Antonio, where the IBEW had organized electrical workers, telephone operators, and linemen. Early in November, 1900, both the electrical workers and the telephone workers presented demands to the electric light and traction companies and the Southwest Bell Telephone Company for an eight-hour day and time and a half for overtime. Telephone operators and linemen also added demands for an increase in their wage schedules, with the former asking for a schedule that could reach the maximum level of $30 a month after one year of service.

The electric light and traction companies capitulated without a struggle. But the telephone company refused to reduce the operators' and linemen's work day from twelve to eight hours or to increase their wages. However, in an effort to split the male linemen and the female operators, Southwest Bell offered the women an increase of $5 a month and a reduction in hours from twelve to nine—provided that they left the union. The response was immediate: "We would rather starve than desert our brothers in their struggle for what they are entitled to." Instead, linemen and operators walked out together.[74]

Within two weeks, the striking girls were replaced by experienced male operators imported from Galveston. Union linemen were brought in from Chicago, but they refused to work when they learned that they were to be used as strikebreakers. They reported to union headquarters rather than to the Bell office.

The strike lasted for almost two months, and women operators and male linemen picketed together every day without any respite. "A perfect system of pickets is being maintained by the men and women strikers," reported the San Antonio *Daily Express*. "On a vacant lot opposite the telephone exchange there has been pitched a tent with camping outfit for the purpose of watching the other side's movements, both night and day." The local community supported the strikers to the end. The Business Men's Club voted unanimously that "the demands of the telephone girls and linemen are just and in our opinion should be granted."

"Not a few of the telephone subscribers," wrote a local reporter, "refused absolutely to talk over the phones. Generally speaking, they were in sympathy with the strikers and backed up any demand made by them. Many business men would allow no one to use the phones. At a number of places the bells were muffled with anything from a wad of chewing gum to a Turkish bath towel. In some instances people went so far as to entirely remove the telephones. At one of the downtown residences a phone was hung on a peach tree and there received jeers from passers by." The San Antonio Trades Council not only fully endorsed the strike but called upon its affiliated members to "withdraw their patronage from all who use their telephones during the continuance of the strike."[75] During the strike, twelve hundred of the eighteen hundred telephone subscribers requested removal of their phones, while the fire chief posted notices in all fire stations that read: "It is positively forbidden for anyone to use the telephones in this house for any purpose other than that which is absolutely necessary for the direct operation of the fire department."

But Southwestern Bell was determined to destroy the union that had so effectively united men and women. "I would rather spend $100,000 to win this strike for the effect it would have in other cities," the vice-president of Southwestern Bell told a reporter for the *San Antonio Express*. Nonunion employees continued to be brought into the city, and in a battle between the union men and the scabs, shots were fired and a policeman guarding the scabs was killed. In its appeal "To the People of San Antonio," the union deplored the fatal shooting, but blamed it on "the refusal of the Southwestern Telegraph & Telephone Company to furnish its employees humane treatment and pay them living wages." In the end, despite citywide support, the workers were unable to defeat the huge corporation. By the middle of January, 1901, the Bell Exchange was functioning normally with nonunion operators and linemen.[76]

The solidarity of the men and women telephone operators in San Antonio did not seem to have made much of an impression on the IBEW. "The lady operators," a contemporary paper reported, "are not members of the Electrical Workers' Union save in Texas. The plan of admitting them to membership is an experiment and was first put into effect in Texas. Mr. H. P. Trip, a member of the National Executive Board of the Electrical Workers' Union, did not know whether they would be taken into the union in other states or not." They were not, for the IBEW continued to view female telephone operators as an element hostile to unionism with whom it was impossible to build permanent unions.[77]

The same indifference to women's efforts to organize was reflected in the leadership of the United Garment Workers. Mary Maloney was a charter member of Local No. 50 of the UGW, located in Newburgh, New York, and held the office of president since its founding in June, 1897.* But this made little difference to the UGW leadership elsewhere. Local No. 16 in New York City, a small union of women shirtmakers, with Leonora O'Reilly as its guiding spirit, sought unsuccessfully to interest the UGW's leadership in helping it to grow. In June, 1897, O'Reilly wrote hopefully in her journal: "The Local 16 met. Meeting was not as

---

*Maloney was also sixth vice-president of the Workingmen's Federation of the State of New York and represented her union in the Newburgh Central Labor Union, of which she was financial secretary. On March 18, 1899, the *Toiler*, official journal of the Workingmen's Federation of the State of New York, declared: "In honoring Miss Maloney with a seat on the Executive Council, the Federation has honored itself."

large as it ought to be. The men sent word that, as yet, they were too busy with contractors to spare a minute to strengthen the organization of either men or women, but this week will end the strike and then the regular business of organization will begin."[78]

But "the regular business of organization" never included Local No. 16. When O'Reilly spoke to the official organizer of the UGW, he informed her that he could organize twenty-five men's shops a day, "while the women laugh at him or refuse point blank to attend [meetings]," and that even though he conceded the importance of educating and organizing women, he was not going to waste time attempting to do it. The most he was prepared to do was to permit the women to organize themselves, and when a group of Brooklyn female garment workers asked Local No. 16 for help in organizing, the organizer promised only "to send the address of the Executive Board of Brooklyn so that we may learn just what is needed." In short, O'Reilly and other members of Local No. 16 could organize women if they desired to do so, but were told not to expect any real financial or organizational assistance from the New York UGW leadership.[79]

In desperation, Local No. 16 filed a formal protest at a UGW convention in the late 1890s in the form of a resolution that read:

> Whereas, the female garment workers have not been given the necessary cooperation by the other tailor unions of the United Garment Workers of America in order to improve their condition; therefore
>
> Resolved, That it is the sense of this convention that in all recognized union shops all female employees be obliged to be good-standing members of their respective unions.
>
> Further resolved, That the incoming General Executive Board be instructed to devote special efforts in organizing the women workers of the trade.

The resolution had little effect. Without financial and organizational assistance, Local No. 16 failed.[80]

Thus, in general, the AFL was content to pass resolutions urging the organization of women workers, and even urged "those international and national organizations that do not admit women workers to membership to give early consideration for such admission." But nothing was done to give these resolutions force and meaning. The few women's unions that existed at the beginning of the twentieth century were, in most cases, organized by the women workers themselves, sometimes with the help of a settlement house.

14

The Turn of the Century

IN 1901 the government published the *Report of the Industrial Commission on the Relations and Conditions of Capital and Labor Employed in Manufactures (including testimony taken up to November, 1900)*. It contained a vivid picture both of conditions of workingwomen at the turn of the century and of the hostility of many male unionists toward the employment of women in trades and industry. Many of those who testified subscribed to the sentiment that "under a rational system," women would be "practically eliminated from the wage question," and her place would be that of "queen of a little house—no matter how humble—where there are children rolling on the floor." Veteran labor leader and AFL spokesman George E. McNeill summed up this view in commenting on the "effects of employment of women on male employment":

> I believe that woman is not qualified for the condition of wage labor. The mental and physical make-up of woman is in revolt against wage service. She is competing with the man who is her father and husband, or who is to become her husband. Wherever she goes she is reducing his wages, and wherever a large number of women are employed in any occupation there the point will be reached where woman gets as much as man by making man's wages as low as woman's.

Anyone reading such testimony had to feel that the witnesses were living in a dream world. Even as they were testifying, the Industrial Commission was finding that "the wives—mothers of the family—go into the factory and work for a living," and that many families, those of Italian street laborers, of Polish and Slovak coal miners. of native-born American railroad workers, of Jewish clothing workers, and of all types of black workers, managed to survive only because wives and daughters were able to find work in the garment, textile, tobacco, and canning industries, or by cleaning, cooking, and ironing for others.[1]

If fully employed, a male worker might expect to work at least 312 days a year (assuming a holiday for Christmas). But in most cases the earnings of such a worker were not sufficient to support a single man, much less his family. To work fewer days, as most workers did,* meant a reduction in income. It was actually easier for a married man to survive in America at the opening of the twentieth century than for a single man, since a wife and daughters could supplement the family income by housing and feeding boarders.† The added earnings of a wife and/or children who worked outside the home could keep the male worker fed and sheltered during periods of unemployment, sickness, or injury. Although male unionists complained incessantly that women competed with their husbands and fathers for jobs, the fact was that for the average working-class family, their labor was an economic necessity. So essential was it for women to work that immigrant communities would take root and persist only in areas where sources of female employment were available.[2]

Most women worked not for "pin money" with which to purchase luxuries but rather to keep themselves and their families alive. In 1890, when the government began keeping detailed records, 3.7 million women of working age had jobs. That number did not include the millions of wives and daughters performing arduous farm chores in then-rural America. Still, the number was small, representing only 18 percent of all working-age families. By 1900, however, 5,319,397 women—one in every five—were in the labor force,‡ and of 303 occupations listed in the 1900 Census, women were represented in 296. Included were

---

*The problem of partial or irregular employment even in periods of prosperity and of constant unemployment in years of depression is a theme that runs through the letters of many immigrants to their relatives in the old country. See, for example, William I. Thomas and Florian Znaniecke, *The Polish Peasant in Europe and America* (Boston, 1918), vols. 1 and 2.

†Bessie (Mrs. John) Van Vorst, with her sister-in-law, Marie, left a comfortable upper-class life and, disguising herself as a workingwoman, went to work in a mill in Perry, New York. She discovered that almost every family took in six or more factory employees as boarders, charging $2.75 a week for board, lodging, heat, and light. (Mrs. John Van Vorst and Marie Van Vorst, *The Woman Who Toils* [New York, 1903], pp. 67–68.) With her sister, Mrs. Van Vorst set out to "discover and adopt their [workingwomen's] point of view, put ourselves in their surroundings, assume their burdens, unite with them in their daily effort . . . to give a faithful picture of things as they exist, both in and out of the factory, and to suggest remedies that occurred to me as practical. My desire is to act as a mouthpiece for the woman laborer." She transformed herself, with shabby clothing, "into a working girl of the ordinary type," and took on the name of Esther Kelley (ibid., pp. 4, 5, 11).

‡The percentage varied with different nationality groups. In 1900, of the 1,943,137 Irishwomen of working age 600,900 or 32.6 percent, were gainfully employed. "This meant," notes Mary Susan Hewitt, "that although first and second generation Irish made up only about 6.9 percent of the total United States population at that time, slightly less than one out of every seven women workers was a first or second generation Irish woman." She also points out that "slightly more than one out of every three Irish working women in 1900 was a factory worker." (Mary Susan Hewitt, "Irish Women in the United States, 1870–1914, A Case Study: Factory Workers" [Master's thesis, University of the Pacific, 1975], pp. 55–60, 60.)

503,000 women office workers of all kinds—an increase of 2,700 percent in thirty years—while stenographers and typists showed an increase from 4.5 percent in 1870 to 40 percent in 1900. During the same thirty-year period, women telegraph and telephone operators had increased from 4.3 percent to 29.3 percent. In 1870 there were only 350 women engaged in telegraphy—the telephone was not introduced by Alexander Graham Bell until 1876—but by 1900 there were 21,980 women working as telegraph and telephone operators. The number of women salesclerks had grown from only 10,000 in 1870 to 175,000 in 1900. And half a million women taught school at the turn of the century.

The rise of the corporation during the last decades of the nineteenth century, along with developments in banking, insurance, and public utilities, created a more complex business operation requiring a large increase in correspondence, record keeping, and office work in general. This expansion, in turn, created a demand for an expanded clerical labor force. Women public school and high school graduates constituted a labor pool qualified for jobs that demanded literacy. And as opportunities for teaching became more limited, with men increasingly entering the field, these women were available for clerical jobs. As Margery Davies puts it: "The expansion of enterprises in the 1880s and 1890s created a large demand for clerical labor; the large pool of educated female labor constituted the supply."[3]

Thus, new jobs were opening up for women in addition to the jobs they traditionally filled—as seamstresses, cotton mill operators, laundresses, domestics, and teachers. Most women workers, however, still found their opportunities for employment limited to occupations regarded as undesirable by males. Jobs that were viewed as a natural extension of household activity, such as sewing garments and manufacturing textiles, still employed most of the female workers. Even in such industries as shoe manufacturing and food processing and canning, and in heavy industries such as foundries and tin-plate mills, they held "women's jobs," which for the most part were unskilled and offered little chance to learn a trade or move up the job or pay ladder.

The typical female industrial worker in early twentieth-century America was young and single. Many began work at age sixteen or seventeen and remained in the work force for an average of six or seven years. Marriage always ended their labor outside the home, at least for a while; not a few of them found it necessary to return to the factory or shop in order to keep the family alive.

By the turn of the century, more than 350,000 women were gainfully employed in New York City alone, the majority of them in service occupations. Nearly 150,000 were personal servants and domestic workers. Tens of thousands labored as retail clerks, waitresses, or laundresses. But 132,535 women worked in the city's manufacturing establishments.

Indeed, New York employed more female industrial workers than any other American city. The heaviest concentration of female industrial workers was in the needle trades. Approximately 65,000 women were engaged in the manufacture of clothing: 15,000 in the men's garment industry and over 50,000 in the women's ready-made clothing trades.[4]

The typical female worker in New York City was young, single, and an immigrant and lived with her family and contributed her wages to it. Women who did not live at home faced special problems. In *The Long Day: The Story of a New York Working Girl,* Dorothy Richardson told of a young schoolteacher, forced to live in a cheap boardinghouse. Paid only $2.50 a week, after she had paid a dollar for her room she had only $1.50 with which to buy food, pay carfare, keep herself clothed, and have a social life. In order to survive, she began to starve herself: "Bread and butter and black coffee for breakfast, and potato-soup and bread and butter for supper, with plain bread and butter done up in a piece of paper and carried with me for luncheon—this was my daily menu for the weeks that followed, varied on two occasions by the purchase of a half-pint of New Orleans molasses."

At last she obtained a job paying $3.50 a week in a paper-box factory. The noise and confusion, the foul smell of glue, and the agony of blistered hands were unendurable. At the Pearl Laundry, where she worked as a "shaker," the long day was an "unspeakable agony." The heat emanating from the engine room directly beneath the work area, together with the humidity of the steam-filled room, forced the employees to strip off half their clothes before noon. During the afternoon, the girls suffered not only from "aching backs and arms and legs, but feet parboiled to a blister on the burning floors." And all this for $3.50 per week, which was raised to $4 when she became a skilled hand!*[5]

Marie Van Vorst, who worked in Lynn, Massachusetts, making shoes, wrote that she already felt tired by ten o'clock in the morning, and that by 3:30, her fingers had "grown wooden with fatigue, [and the] gluepot and folding-line, board, hammer and awl had grown indistinct. It was hard to continue. The air stifled. Odors conspired together. Oil, leather, glue (oh, that to-heaven-smelling glue!), tobacco smoke, humanity."[6] Her sister-in-law, Mrs. John Van Vorst, worked at a box-and-label factory in Chicago, where she earned $3 a week for a working day that lasted from seven until six during the week and until one-thirty on Saturday. She described the environment as one in which "a fine rain of bronze dust sifts itself into the hair and clothing of the girls at our end of

---

*Because her book emphasized the sexual degradation of workingwomen in the factories and shops and charged that many were made immoral by their surroundings and recruited for prostitution, Dorothy Richardson was sharply attacked by Leonore O'Reilly, who charged that the work was not the story of a workingwoman but of a reporter in search of sensational copy. The book provoked considerable controversy.

the room," and where "the sweet, stifling smell of printer's ink and cheap paper" permeated the room.[7]

At the pickle factory in Pittsburgh where she worked, she made $4.20 a week, and spent $3 of this for board alone. Her main fear was that she would not be strong enough to keep her job:

> My hands are stiff, my thumbs almost blistered. . . . Cases are emptied and refilled; bottles are labeled, stamped and rolled away . . . and still there are more cases, more jars, more bottles. Oh! the monotony of it . . .! Now and then someone cuts a finger or runs a splinter under the flesh . . . and still the work goes on. Once I pause an instant, my head dazed and weary, my ears strained to bursting with the deafening noise. Quickly a voice whispers in my ear: "You'd better not stand there doin' nothin.' If she catches you she'll give it to you."

Finally, after the "long day," she could report: "I have stood ten hours; I have fitted 1,300 corks; I have hauled and loaded 4,000 jars of pickles. My pay is seventy cents." On Saturdays the women had to spend four hours on hands and knees scrubbing the tables and stands and "every inch of the factory floor." The men, however, "only use hoses on the floor" and rubbed them down with "long-handled brooms and rubber mops"; they were not required to get down on their hands and knees. They were also furnished a hot lunch for 10 cents, while the women had to bring their own sandwiches. She learned, too, that the lowest-paid man earned more than the highest-paid woman.[8]

After her stint as a shoeworker in Lynn, Marie Van Vorst took a job at Excelsior, the largest cotton mill in the world, in Columbia, South Carolina. Wearing "simple work garb," she obtained a job as a spooler under the assumed name of Belle Ballard. Since room and board at the town's seedy hotel cost $2.25 a week—more than her week's wages—she set out to rent a room in the mill village surrounding the factory. After searching all over town, she finally found a boardinghouse in which she had to share a bed with a sick woman whose daughter also slept in the tiny garret room. Her lunch as a boarder consisted of "a little salt pork (on a tin saucepan) and on another dish a pile of grease-swimming spinach." But there was little time to eat it, since it took a half hour out of the forty-five minutes allowed for lunch to get to the boardinghouse and back. Supper consisted of "one plate (in the middle of the table) . . . piled high with fish-bones, skin and flesh all together in one odorous mass. Salt pork graces another platter and hominy another."[9]

Her day began at four-thirty in the morning, when the Excelsior whistle shrieked every settler awake." By half-past five, she had breakfasted and left her boardinghouse for the mill. Inside the mill, the women and children wore "felt hats pulled down well over the eyes," to protect their hair from "the flying pieces of cotton": "The cotton . . . thistledownlike, flies without cessation through the air—spins off from the spools; it rises and floats, falling on the garment and in the hair, entering the nostrils and throat and lungs . . . the expectoration, the coughing and the throat-clearing is constant."[10] She quickly discovered that pneumonia, consumption, and other lung diseases "are the constant, never-absent scourge of the mill village."[11]

Her work as a spooler required her to run machines that wound the yarn from one rapidly turning spool onto another to make a continuous thread for the looms. The room she worked in was the quietest in the mill, but the work was "hard on the left arm and the side." She learned that heart trouble was an occupational disease of the older spoolers. As a result, most of the spoolers were children and young girls—some of them "tiny, tiny children" who "had to stand on a box to reach." They made 40 cents a day—$2.40 a week. Other children were spinners, even weavers, while many swept the cotton-strewn floors.

She saw children who had not yet been assigned work for the day sleeping against the bales of cotton. During the brief lunch period, some of the children would fall asleep "between mouthfuls of food, and so lie asleep with food in their mouths until the overseer rouses them to their task again. Here and there totters a little child just learning to walk; it runs and crawls the length of the mill."

Most of the children returned home about 8 P.M.—or later if the mill was working overtime: "They are usually beyond speech. They fall asleep at the tables, on the stairs; they are carried to bed and there laid down as they are, unwashed, undressed; and the intimate bundles of rags so lie until the mill summons them with its imperious cry before sunrise, while they are still in a stupid sleep." Their mothers, too, could think only of sleep—and no wonder:

> They rise at four; at a quarter before six they are at work. The day in winter is not born when they start their tasks; the night has fallen long before they cease; in summer they are worked long into their evenings. They tell me that they are too tired to eat; that all they want to do is to turn their aching bones on to their miserable mattresses and sleep until they are cried and shrieked awake by the mill summons.[12]

Health hazards to which cotton mill workers, North and South, were exposed included dust from the cotton itself, heat, long periods of standing, plus a good deal of stooping, the monotony of the work, excessive noise, and the vibration of the machinery. Crystal Eastman attributed the widespread accidents to "the speed and intensity of the work, the heat and noise of the place, and the weariness of the workers." The condition of the toilets in the mills contributed to the generally unsanitary environment. As a government investigation pointed out:

> The water closets in many mills have poor fixtures, which are in many cases broken, and receiving no attention they remain in a disgusting condi-

tion. . . . Some mill officials complain that their attempts to keep the water closets sanitary . . . receive little or no cooperation from the employees. It is evident, on the other hand, that in many cases the conditions found can exist only as a result of the neglect of ordinary care on the part of those responsible.

In twenty-two Massachusetts cotton mills, none had a dressing room for women, and only two had a women's washroom.[13]

The overwhelming desire for sleep after the long day was the common experience of nearly all workingwomen at the turn of the century. One of them testified: "Many a time I've been so tired that I hadn't the courage to take my clothes off. I've thrown myself on the bed and slept like dead until I got so cold and cramped that at two or three in the morning I'd rouse up and undress and crawl into bed—only to crawl out again at half past five." This was from a saleswoman in San Francisco. In New York City, saleswomen testifying before the Reinhard Committee of the state legislature told of employers who required them to work long hours, in many cases from 8 A.M. to 9 P.M., six days a week, plus two to four hours on Sundays. Frances Donovan, another upper-class woman who donned working-class clothes to learn what it was like to be a wage-earning woman, became a saleswoman. She wrote:

Never in my life had I been so conscious of my feet. . . . During that first week I would have been willing to increase their size fourfold if it could have lessened the dull, feverish throb with its agonizing persistence.

Next to the feet, was the pain in the small of my back. . . . There is no doubt that there is both a physical and mental strain in department store work.[14]

Saleswomen stood for twelve or more hours a day and sometimes fainted from exhaustion. As we have noted, before 1900 some states had passed laws mandating that seats in stores be provided for saleswomen, but these were rarely enforced. In Maryland, for example, an investigation disclosed that the leading store in Baltimore had installed only two seats for eighty-five saleswomen. One of them said, "If we sat down, we'd get the grand bounce."[15]

Saleswomen complained that the owners supplied only a few ancient toilets for hundreds of women. One group even had to send out a public appeal: "For God's sake, help us! We have had no water in the water closet for over a week."[16] One Baltimore store had only one toilet room for all its women customers and its 282 women employees in both its six-story annex and its four-story main building. A saleswoman could not get back to her counter in the allotted five minutes, particularly since there was usually a line at the toilet room. What with having to get a pass to use the toilet and to explain the delays—and to a man, at that—most girls simply refrained from using the toilets at all. Small wonder that many said they had developed kidney ailments.[17]

Women toiled long hours both day and night. Indeed, night work was a common practice among women. Many women worked night shifts in book binderies and laundries, as well as in candy, paper-box, and garment factories. Work usually started after supper and lasted into the early hours of the morning, or even until dawn. Many women with homes and children to care for slept only four hours a day. Investigators described these women as "worn looking" and "pale, with drawn white faces and stooping gait."[18] One investigator wrote:

> Standing outside the door of a factory where twine is manufactured, we watched the women come out. Pale, narrow-chested, from head to foot, they were covered with fibrous dust. . . . They were types of factory workers— pale, haggard feeders of machines—like those described in the days of a century past in England. The fibre . . . must rest heavily in the lungs of women who bend over rushing, whirring machines ten hours a day without fresh air and exercise.

The same writer also told of girls in the binding industry who worked thirteen hours a day, seventy-eight hours a week, and were discharged if they refused unpaid overtime.[19]

Mrs. Florence Kelley, at one time a factory inspector in Illinois, observed:

> In Chicago, the laundries maintain hours which are regularly irregular, Monday being a short day and Friday and Saturday having neither beginning nor ending except as work is completed. It is no rare thing for girls to faint at their work. Girls have been removed from the laundry to the hospital suffering exhaustion after working sixteen, eighteen, and even twenty hours in heat and dampness in ill-ventilated laundries.[20]

The Illinois Supreme Court had invalidated the eight-hour law for women workers, and in New Jersey and Michigan, the legislatures or courts had so weakened women's hour laws as to render them inoperative. At the turn of the century, twenty-six states, four territories, and the District of Columbia had no restrictions at all on working hours for women. Many states that did have laws restricting hours of work enforced them only perfunctorily. Connecticut, Maine, Rhode Island, and New Hampshire, moreover, still permitted employees to make "voluntary" contracts for overtime work, or allowed managers to extend the regular workday if they operated a shorter shift at the end of the week. In any case, since most statutes did not stipulate posted times of opening and closing, a woman would have to sue for her rights, probably at the cost of her job.[21]

In one area of labor legislation affecting women workers, there was some improvement. The danger of spread of contagion through sweatshop-manufactured clothing, emphasized in all of the investigations of the sweating system, played a large part in legislation aimed at curtailing the sweatshop system of production. Concerned citizens joined forces with labor leaders and social reformers to fight for such legislation, and the middle-class public, fearing that the contagions of the ghetto would spread to their own comfortable homes, pressured legislators not only to pass the laws but also to tighten loopholes in them after they were enacted. In 1899 the Illinois legislature passed a revised law designed to drive out small contractors and to encourage the establishment of factories that inspectors could supervise more effectively. Once passed, this law had a favorable impact. An 1897 New York law, passed after investigation by a committee of the state legislature and revised in 1899, severely restricted and regulated sweatshop production. By 1900 both official and unofficial observers noted a decline in tenement house manufacture and some improvement in working conditions among garment workers.[22]

Women's wages, the Industrial Commission reported in 1900, were "in many cases . . . less than the actual cost of the necessities of life."[23] In New York City, Leonore O'Reilly pointed out, "the wages of 40,000 women . . . are so low that they must eke out an existence by charity or starve or worse."[24] Noting that women workers in New York's garment industry earned 30 cents a day in 1900, Frederick Lewis Allen observed in 1952: "Try translating that into terms of today: even after you have multiplied it by three . . . you arrive at the noble sum of 90 cents a day, which is $5.40 a week, which is $280.00 for a full working year!"[25] As late as 1910 women were working in Chicago's cigar factories from 5 A.M. until 6 P.M. for $2.40 a week, averaging 40 cents a day.[26]

In 1905 the average weekly wage of women in all industries was $5.25, from which most paid at least $2.25 for board and lodging if single, and with which many women tried to support families. But many worked for less. Of 473 women workers interviewed, 28 percent earned less than $300 yearly, 53 percent between $300 and $500, and only 7 percent $600 or more. The position of these workers was best expressed by a woman who earned $6 a week: "I didn't live. I simply existed. I couldn't live what you would call living. I certainly had to deprive myself of lots of things I should have had. It took me months and months to save up money to buy a dress or a suit or a pair of shoes. . . . I had the hardest struggle I ever had in my life."[27]

Employers continued to discriminate against women by paying them less than men for the same work. In 1897 Commissioner of Labor Carroll D. Wright cited 781 instances of men and women engaged in the same occupations and performing their duties with equal efficiency. In only 57 of these cases did the women receive equal pay with the men, while in 595 cases their pay was appreciably less. A report drawn up in 1899 showed that in twenty-three industries where men and women did the same work, men's wages were 150 to 300 percent higher than women's wages. The clothing industry paid women 68.5 percent of the salary given to men employees doing the same work: the hourly rate for women aged sixteen and over was 14.8 cents, while that for men was 21.6 cents. In the packing plants, if a man received $1.75 a day for a certain job, a woman would receive $1.25 for performing the same task. After an exhaustive study of the subject, the Commission on Industrial Relations concluded: "It seems to be unanimously admitted that, barring a few exceptional cases, the wages paid to women are lower than the wages paid to men for similar work."[28]

An illustration of discrimination against women workers in a new and developing industry is provided by the case of women workers at the Westinghouse Electric & Manufacturing Company. Women began entering the electrical industry by the turn of the century, and at Westinghouse, about 650 of the plant's 10,000 workers were women in 1902. From the beginning, women were second-class citizens as far as work was concerned. The company manufactured coils, armatures, transformers, and motors. "Girls' work" consisted of building armatures and winding coils, and "men's work" included the actual assembling of transformers and armatures.

The only reason for sex segregation at Westinghouse was that it enabled the company to pay women workers exactly *half* the wages male workers received. This could not be explained on the theory that the "girls' work" was "light work." Young women were employed in coil winding, which was a very strenuous job. "The power action is so strong," wrote an investigator, "that the operator sways back and forward and is often forced to exert considerable physical strength to keep the tape in place." Years later the National Industrial Conference Board, seeking an explanation for women's low wages in the electrical industry, came up with the answer that "certain occupations came to be regarded as women's work at a time when the principle of equal wages was seldom accepted."[29] In other words, as soon as Westinghouse was able to label certain types of jobs "girls' work," no matter how heavy they were, the wages paid could be set at half those paid to men.

Although pay scales and working conditions varied widely, women in shops and factories that were unionized received markedly higher wages and enjoyed more sanitary working conditions than their unorganized sisters. A United Garment Workers member who worked in a Brooklyn shirt factory reported getting up at five-thirty each morning, eating a piece of bread and some fruit, and drinking a cup of coffee before leaving for the factory at 6 A.M. Work began at seven, and "the machines go like mad all day, because the faster you work the more money you get. . . . I am getting so good at the work that within the year I will be making $7 a week, and then I can save at least $3.50 a week." She paid 25 cents a month union dues, and felt that union membership definitely benefited her.[30]

Compare this with the conditions facing workers in a shop were the men were unionized and the women were not, a common feature of the era. Rose Cohen recalled such a situation in a cloak shop in the late 1890s in her autobiography, *Out of the Shadow:*

> I had no idea what a union meant or what all this trouble was about. But I learned a little the next day. When I came in a little after six in the morning, I found only the three girls who were at my table. Not a man except the boss was in the shop. The men came in about five minutes to seven and then stood or sat at the presser's table talking and joking quietly. The boss stood at his table brushing coats furiously. Every minute or so he glanced at the clock and his face looked black with anger.
>
> At the first stroke of seven the presser blew a whistle and every man went to his place. At a minute of twelve the presser again blew the whistle and the men went out to their noon meal. Those who remained in the shop ate without hurry and read their newspapers. The boss kept his eye on us girls. We began last, ate hurriedly, and sat down to work at once. Betsy looked at the men reading their newspapers and grumbled in a whisper. "This is what it means to belong to a union. You get a time to straighten out your bones. . . ."
>
> The men returned a little before one and sat waiting for the stroke of the clock and the presser's whistle. At seven in the evening when the presser blew his whistle the men rose almost with one movement, put away their work and turned out the lights over their tables and machines. We girls watched them go enviously and the boss turned his back toward the door.[31]

Then there is the following report on conditions in a Rome, New York, mill at about the same time:

> The plant employs about five hundred workers, most of whom are women. The work is mostly piece-work. A finisher receives five cents per dozen for finishing sheets, and twelve and one-quarter cents for drawers; for putting patches in bicycle knickerbockers, eight cents per pair. Some earn as little as two dollars per week. The hours are 7 a.m. to 12 noon and 12:30 to 6 p.m., stopping on Saturdays at 5 p.m., thus making sixty-one and a half hours per week. Every alternate window is left open for ventilation, but no toilets are provided. It is not a union factory—the subject is hardly thought of.[32]

Evidence presented before the Industrial Commission proved conclusively that unions benefited workers, but there was also evidence that very few women were actually unionized. Of the 350,000 women employed in New York City at the turn of the century, fewer than 10,000 belonged to unions. Nearly all of them were in the garment, cigar, or printing unions. No unions at all existed in many of the occupations that employed large numbers of women—laundries, hotels and restaurants, retail stores, and paper-box factories, among others.[33]

If white women suffered from low wages and other evils as a result of their unorganized status, the lot of black women workers was far worse. They had a double burden to bear: discrimination as women and as blacks. They were excluded from employment and from unions by both sex and color.[34]

By the opening of the twentieth century, the AFL was in full retreat from the position it had taken up to 1895—that of insisting that unions desiring to enter or to remain in affiliation must eliminate the color clause from their constitutions. By 1900 about a dozen AFL unions barred Negroes by specific provisions. Some had constitutional clauses specifying that only "white-born" applicants were eligible; others removed the constitutional ban, but not its practice, by transferring the restriction to the rituals (the initiation ceremonies). Each member was bound by the ritual to propose only whites for membership.

The absence of specific clauses barring black members in a union's constitution or rituals did not mean that it admitted blacks. Even some unions whose constitutions proclaimed the principle of equality of all workers still kept blacks out by tacit agreement. Others achieved the same objective by such practices as demanding high initiation fees, which black workers could not pay; requiring special licenses, which blacks could not obtain; requiring applicants for membership to pass a technical examination, which blacks invariably failed, and prohibiting blacks from becoming apprentices. The last device was especially important, for by refusing to open their apprenticeship programs to young blacks, many AFL affiliates kept black workers from acquiring the necessary training to qualify as skilled workers.[35]

While racist practices effectively limited the black membership of the AFL and made the Railroad Brotherhoods totally white, they virtually guaranteed that no black women would become union members. Some AFL unions that did permit women to belong specified that all members had to be of the "white race." Most of the black membership in the AFL in 1900 was concentrated in one union—the United Mine Workers of America—and there were no black women miners. The rest of the black union membership was made up of skilled mechanics and artisans, mainly in the South, who belonged to Jim Crow unions of their trades.[36] But hardly any black women worked in skilled occupations, the main areas that were being organized by the AFL craft unions. Black spokeswoman Fannie Barrier Williams may have exaggerated the opportunities available for white women in her 1903 publication *The Problem of Employment for Negro Women,* but her main point was only too valid:

> For reasons too well understood to be repeated, ours is a narrow sphere.
> While the kinds and grades of occupation open to all women of white com-

plexion are almost beyond enumeration, those open to our women are few in number and mostly menial in quality. The girl who is white and capable is in demand in a thousand places. The capable Negro girl is usually not in demand. This is one of the stubborn facts of today.

Another "stubborn fact" was that black women had no problem in obtaining employment as domestics. "Girls of other nationalities," Williams pointed out, "do not seem to compete with colored women as domestics."[37] Indeed, as David Katzman points out, blacks, barred from nearly every kind of work, formed in the South "a permanent servant caste." A black woman entering domestic service in her early teens could expect to remain in the work for life. Marriage promised no release, for the job market for her husband was even tighter than it was for her.[38]

Mary White Ovington, a white New York social worker who became one of the founders of the National Association for the Advancement of Colored People, made the same point in her study of the black woman: "She gets the job the white girl does not want."[39] Ovington demonstrated that black women were confined to domestic and personal services and were not able "in any numbers" to obtain work in a factory.[40] The "Women at Work" volume of the Federal Census of 1900 substantiated this conclusion by revealing that 90 percent of the black women in New York were engaged in personal and domestic service and that in New York City's leading industry for women—dressmaking—only 813 black women were employed out of a total of 37,514 women in the trade.[41]

In his 1899 study The Philadelphia Negro, W. E. B. Du Bois summed up the situation in the "City of Brotherly Love" in a single sentence: "A Negro woman has but three careers open to her in this city: domestic service, sewing, or married life."[42] Du Bois found that one out of every ten black domestic workers had some high school education and was qualified to hold a more skilled job—but could find none. The Christian Recorder, the organ of the African Methodist Episcopal Church, conducted a study of Philadelphia's department stores in 1900 and found that not a single black woman, no matter how educated she was, was employed as a salesperson in any of the stores.[43]

Meager as were the wages of women workers in general, those of black women were far lower. Du Bois found that black women's earnings in Philadelphia ranged from $2 to $4.06 weekly. Cooks and laundresses averaged $4 a week. A black laundress earned a total of $180 a year, broken down as follows: October–March, $5 to $6 a week, and April–September, $1.50 to $2 a week.[44]

Just as women workers in general received from one-half to one-quarter less pay than men for equal work,[45] so black women averaged one-third to one-half less pay than white women for equal work. This differential between white and black women workers prevailed in every occupation. Indeed, in many occupations, black women never knew what they would receive for their work. In the words of one black woman:

"You never know what you are going to get; you just take what they give and go."[46]

Mary White Ovington pointed out that a higher percentage of blacks were poverty-stricken than any other group in the city. While many of the other working-class groups were poor, "the greatest majority of Negroes of New York live in poverty" and were mired in unskilled, menial occupations. Sixty-two percent of the men were in domestic and personal services, and those employed in large stores or factories "do the work of porter or general utility man, not the better tasks." Often the black man could not find any work at all, and the burden of family support fell on the woman. It was not surprising, Ovington noted, that the 1900 Federal Census revealed more than seven times as many black married women engaged in gainful occupations as their white counterparts.[47]

Ovington found, too, that the black faced a double exploitation. Not only did blacks, like the poor in general, live in slum tenements, but they paid more and got less for their money than other tenants. Restricted by racism to a narrow area in which they had to live, they were forced to pay whatever the landlord wished to charge. For the same reason, blacks in New York paid higher prices for inferior food than did white workers. Thus, while all of New York's immigrant working-class population faced poverty and abuse, the black faced all this and more. And the black woman had to endure most of all, for she was excluded from all the trade unions and deprived of the opportunity to move out of her place on the lowest rung of the economic ladder.[48]

At the turn of the century the vast majority of black women still lived in the South. They were concentrated in agricultural and domestic jobs, in laundries, and in tobacco factories, where they were confined to the hardest and lowest-paying division, that of tobacco stripping. Where black women did work in mills, it was not at the machines but at the heavy labor jobs or as janitors. As we have seen, there were instances in which white women, poisoned by racism, struck to keep black women from being hired to work at machines in the textile mills.

In 1902 a black woman in Alabama told what it meant to be black and a woman in the South:

> Many colored women who wash, iron, scrub, cook or sew all the week to help pay the rent for their miserable hovels and help fill the many small mouths, would deny themselves some of the necessaries of life if they could take their little children and teething babes on the cars to the parks of a Sunday afternoon and sit under the trees, enjoy the cool breezes and breathe God's pure air for only two or three hours; but this is denied them. Some of the parks have signs, "No Negroes allowed on these grounds except as servants." Pitiful, pitiful customs and laws that make war on women and babes! There is no wonder that we die; the wonder is that we persist in living.[49]

15

The Socialist Party and
Socialist Women

As THE NUMBER of women working outside the home was reaching the 5 million mark, in 1900, an organization was coming into existence that proclaimed itself the champion of all workers, women as well as men. This was the Socialist Party of America, formed in Indianapolis in July, 1901, by delegates representing all socialist groups in the country except the followers of Daniel De Leon, leader of the Socialist Labor Party.

There were eight women delegates at the founding convention of the Socialist Party of America. The platform of the new party contained a clause demanding "equal civil and political rights for men and women." But there was no discussion either of women's activities within the party or of the need to create special propaganda for reaching women. It was taken for granted that the end of capitalism and the ushering in of a new society of socialism would solve the problems of both men and women.[1]

Sally M. Miller notes that women made up almost 10 percent of the membership of the Socialist Party in these early years, were present at national conventions, constituting from 6 to 10 percent of the accredited delgates, and participated in the party "with a level of involvement that surpassed that of women in the 'major' American parties." But she is quick to add that while the party accepted women as members in good standing, it "failed to recognize women as the other half of the working class with a distinct role to play in the class struggle.... Disinterest marked the party posture, at best."[2]

The truth is that at the time of the founding of the Socialist Party, the American Socialist movement had not as yet developed any significant theoretical position on the "woman question." In the main, it drew its ideological guidance from the writings of Marx and Engels, which it expounded principally in discussions about the family, and from the

German Marxist August Bebel. In the *Communist Manifesto,* Marx and Engels had argued that communism would eliminate the structure of the bourgeois family, "do away with the status of women as mere instruments of production," and establish a new order in which women would be valued for more than their reproductive capacities.[3] In *The Origin of the Family, Private Property and the State* (1884), Engels expanded on the Marxist belief that as the private property system evolved, women were enslaved and stripped of their social power. On the basis of the findings of Johan Jakob Bachofen and Lewis Henry Morgan, he argued that men and women had been equal until private property changed relationships within the group, replaced promiscuity with monogamy, and produced a situation in which the mother of a child belonged sexually exclusively to the father ("the woman became the slave of his lust and a mere instrument for the production of children").[4]

Engels emphasized that the mass of women were victims not only of capitalist oppression but also of the family structure. He maintained that in order to regain their social status, women had to reenter social production. But under capitalism the effect of participation in industry for proletarian women was not liberating but disastrous. In *The Condition of the Working Class in England,* Engels blamed capitalism for destroying family life and its values. The solution was socialism: "The first premise for the emancipation of women is the re-introduction of the entire female sex into public industry."[5]

This is not the place to examine the various critiques that have been published of the treatment of the family by Marx and Engels, other than to say that the tendency has been to appreciate some aspects of their contributions while also pointing to what are regarded as their failings.* But when the Socialist Party was founded, these writings by Marx and Engels were accepted as gospel. Nevertheless, August Bebel's *Woman and Socialism* probably had a greater influence among American radicals of the period than any other work dealing with the "woman question."

While Bebel accepted the viewpoint of the origin of the family expressed by Engels, he devoted more space to the place of women in a socialist society. He emphasized that the goal of socialism was "to remove all barriers that make one human being dependent on another, which includes the dependence of one sex upon the other." Socialism, he said, would remove such practices as pay differentials and the lack of protection for women in industry. Moreover, through the institution of public laundries and kitchens, socialism would free women from bondage to the home.

*For a critique of Marx and Engels on the family, see Sheila Rowthbam, *Women, Resistance, and Revolution* (New York, 1972), chap. 3. A critique of Engels' *Origin of the Family* by Ann J. Lane appears in *Liberating Women's History: Theoretical and Critical Essays,* edited by Bernice A. Carroll (Urbana, Ill., 1976).

However, Bebel was quick to emphasize that while socialism was the ultimate solution, men and women must not simply wait for the new social order. Gains through unionization, wage increases, reduction in working hours, and health protection would help build women's economic independence, although full independence would have to wait until the means of production were socially owned.[6] Women's fight for freedom, in Bebel's view, rested on a fundamental justice:

> Woman has the same right as man to develop her abilities and to employ them fully. She is a human being as well as man and should have the freedom of disposing of her own body and mind and be her own master. The chance of having been born a woman, must not affect her human rights. To exclude a woman from equal rights because she has been born a woman... is as unfair as to make rights and privileges depend upon religious or political opinions.... Such views are unworthy of a free human being.[7]

Many European socialists were horrified by the abominable conditions for women and children in the era of rapid industrial expansion. They saw children left to raise themselves while their parents worked. Furthermore, the influx of women, who normally received lower wages than men for the same work, presented a clear and immediate threat to the workers' movement. Rather than favoring the integration of women into industry, these socialists sought to protect women from the brutality of the factory and to confine them to the home.

It was Clara Zetkin who, more than any other European socialist, clarified the conflicting and confusing issue of what position the movement should take with respect to workingwomen. In her 1889 pamphlet, *The Question of Women Workers and Women at the Present Time,* the German socialist argued that "women must remain in industry despite all narrow-minded cater-wauling; in fact, the circle of their industrial activity must become broader and more secure daily." Against those who objected that female labor should be abolished because it was harmful to women, Zetkin replied that the expulsion of women from industry was a "reactionary proposal which would result in their relegation to their previous position of powerlessness and that the destructive effects of labor on women would be overcome only through its socialization, i.e., through socialist revolution."[8]

Zetkin's approach to the issue of women in industry became the position of most European socialists, and was adopted by the influential Social Democratic Party of Germany. But most American Socialists knew of her, if at all, only as the founder, in 1908, of International Women's Day. Her clarification of the socialist position on women workers, not yet translated from the German, was practically unknown to English-language party members.* It is not surprising, therefore, that the very

---

*Articles by Clara Zetkin did appear occasionally in *Socialist Woman,* founded in 1907 (see, for example, Clara Zetkin, "The Third Social-Democratic Woman's Conference in Aus-

same issues that had caused confusion and dissension among European socialists with respect to the woman question should have the same effect on the American scene. For one thing, American Socialists could not agree on whether the introduction of female labor into the factories and shops was a positive development or not. Some thought it was and opposed restricting women to the role of homemakers. Others advanced the woman's-sphere-is-in-the-home argument. "If a married woman takes proper care of her family and loved ones," argued one socialist, "and sheds her gentle and motherly influence over and around them, she will have so much to do that she will not have time to look for fields of vain glory to conquer." In any case, even those socialists who denied any desire to confine women to the home insisted that once the need to supplement their husbands' earnings was eliminated, "ninety-nine women out of every hundred would choose the lot of wife and mother."[9]

There were, however, other socialists who saw the movement of women outside the home as having revolutionary implications—who felt that by earning their own income, women would become independent of men, and therefore emancipated. Still others argued that enlarging women's role to include industrial work would bring with it an expansion of their consciousness to encompass the entire social sphere of life.[10]

Despite the increasing numbers of women working outside the home, the majority of American women were still doing housework. Many Socialists therefore believed that the party's attention to the woman question should be directed toward organizing and recruiting housewives. Although their analysis of the housewife's role is quite relevant today and is "in fact very similar to recent theoretical contributions by present-day Socialist feminists,"[11] its effect was to divert attention away from the women working outside the home.

As long as the male Socialist Party member did not consider his wife an equal, he could not be expected to concern himself very much about women workers, to fight for their inclusion in his union, or to struggle for equal pay for equal work. The Socialist man, Mary Garbatt complained,

> does not seem to recognize that the work the housewife does cooking, washing, sewing, mending, nursing and caring for the children is in any sense commensurate with the work he does for wages. If he tried it for a week, I am sure he would change his mind. . . . He would come to realize that she is an economic factor in the home as truly as he himself and because of her service entitled to an equal and joint right in the money he earns on the outside, and an equal voice in everything that concerns the home.[12]

---

tria," *Socialist Woman* 2 [August 1908]: 7). American women, moreover, did establish some contacts with Clara Zetkin through the headquarters of the *Gleichheit,* which she edited in Germany, and which functioned as a kind of international bureau for socialist women after 1907.

But it was not only the home that was involved. The *Worker,* the Socialist weekly published in New York City, pointed out that too many men in the party, "good Socialists in most respects . . . look with disapprobation or with more irritating contempt on any participation by women in the affairs of our movement." The reason for this attitude, according to the *Worker,* was that they saw women as inferior to men in their organizational ability, uninterested in improving their position, and "dominated by strictly personal preferences and narrow views." The *Worker* itself regarded every one of these charges as true, and contended that "most thoughtful women will admit [their] truth." Still, it felt that women should not be discouraged from attempting to make their contribution to the movement.[13] The paper failed to explain how women could be expected to overcome the male superiority views of the so-called "good" Socialists.

Discussions of problems of workingwomen in the Socialist press during the early years of the twentieth century tended to revolve around the suffrage issue. There was good reason for this. Because of the emphasis in the Socialist Party on the achievement of socialism through the conquest of political power, the ballot was considered all-important. The recruitment of women would add little to the party's strength in electoral contests unless they were enfranchised. While a few Socialists predicted that working women, once enfranchised, would vote conservatively, the majority viewed them as natural allies in the struggle for socialism. But working-class women also needed the ballot as an additional weapon to be used in self-defense against employers. Once they had the ballot, workingwomen would be able to put pressure on legislators to draft measures regulating women's employment, assuring women of equal pay for equal work, and enforcing the existing regulations. Thus, the need for the ballot was even more crucial for working-class women than for middle-class women,[14] and the Socialist Party continually prodded the women's suffrage movement to show more concern about the suffrage needs of women from the working class. The Socialists reminded the suffragists that their movement had had little success. After some gains in the Western states in the 1890s, the suffrage movement had entered into what it itself called "the doldrums," losing the few referendums that were held on the question of women's enfranchisement. Only by paying special attention to the needs of workingwomen, the Socialists maintained, could the women's movement for suffrage make further headway. While it is true that efforts to convert workingwomen went back to the 1870s, and that the National American Woman Suffrage Association had been passing resolutions since at least 1893 urging women to join the suffrage associations, this concern, the Socialists charged, was nothing more than a formality. Despite their desperate need for the right to vote, working-class women were still almost totally unrepresented at suffrage conventions.[15]

In short, the Socialists' argument went, suffrage would take care of the special needs of workingwomen under capitalism and hasten the day when socialism would arrive, bringing with it the solution to the problems of all women—especially workingwomen. This last theme appeared frequently in Socialist pamphlets and journals. In his pamphlet, *What to Do and How to Do It, or Socialism vs. Capitalism,* the black minister George Washington Woodbey attempted to convert his mother to socialism. In the course of their dialogue, he had his mother say, "Like all other women, I want to know where we are to come in." Her son assured her that it was in the interests of "the women, more than the men, if possible, to be Socialists because they suffer more from capitalism than anyone else." For one thing, the Socialist platform demanded "the absolute equality of the sexes before the law, and the repeal of all laws that in any way discriminate against women." Then again, under socialism, each woman would have her own independent income, like each man, and would become "an equal shareholder in the industries of the nation." Under such liberating conditions, a woman would have no need "to sell herself through a so-called marriage to someone she did not love in order to get a living," and, for the first time in history, she could marry only for love. Under capitalism, Woodbey continued, the workingman was a slave, "and his wife . . . the slave of a slave." Socialism, he declared, would liberate both, but since it would give women political equality and economic freedom, it would actually do more for women than for men.[16]

But neither Woodbey nor most Socialist journals and other publications had any program for the immediate problems faced by workingwomen. The Los Angeles *Common Sense,* a Socialist weekly, reported the formation of the Anti-Women Stenographers' Society, organized by women in Columbus, Ohio, exclusively to influence parents not to permit their daughters to accept positions as stenographers. The weekly enumerated the hazards of the trade. First, in the previous ten years, 6,263 divorce cases had been filed by wives naming their husbands' stenographers as corespondents. In 595 of these cases, sufficient proof was produced to persuade the courts to grant the decree of divorce. During the same decade, 796 employers had been defendants in breach-of-promise suits instituted by their stenographers, and it was proved in court that the employer had first "caused the disgrace of the plaintiffs under the promise of marriage." The society also charged that such a position rendered a woman unfit for the duties of a wife, and that not one in twenty women stenographers was considered suitable by men as a wife. Finally, it argued that women stenographers worked for salaries ranging from $5 to $12 per week, whereas young men had been paid from $75 to $125 per month for performing the same work.

Having outlined the reasons that led to the formation of the Anti-Women Stenographers' Society, *Common Sense* proceeded to deal with the problem from a "Socialist" viewpoint. First it noted that the conditions described were to be expected: "Here is one sample of the temptations and pitfalls that confront every working girl, only one illustration of the treacherous and perfidious methods employed by the capitalistic masters to degrade and lower the social and physical condition of their wage slaves." Next came the prescription for dealing with the problem:

> Under Socialism, stenographers and all other working girls will be afforded an opportunity of earning a good and honorable living under the protecting wings of the government, where these greedy monsters of passion will no longer be permitted to carry on their nefarious practices. Of course, the employer of wage slaves does not want Socialism; certainly not; but every woman who is a wage earner and every mother who has daughters working away from home should never cease to promote the cause of Socialism; no, not for one minute, for therein lies the emancipation of all womankind, and there, only.[17]

Not a word about unionizing the workingwomen, establishing equal pay for equal work, or using the collective strength of the women workers, aided by male unionists, to keep employers from molesting or otherwise abusing the women who worked for them.

However, there were socialist women who did not want to wait for the arrival of the new society and who felt that suffrage alone was not enough to liberate women under capitalism. They believed that the unions that excluded women from membership and apprenticeship should be condemned and a fight waged to open their ranks and the trades they controlled to women. They felt, too, that unions, especially those with large Socialist memberships, should involve women in every phase of their activities—including union leadership. While conceding that because of his greater strength and experience, a man was more able "to compete with the labor question than woman," one of these Socialist women asked: "But is our inferior strength and lack of experience a just cause to let men have their way in everything?" And she answered firmly:

> I say NO! How do they know anything concerning women's work, unless the women themselves present their views? Should we be like the comic pictures would have us, a creature afraid of a mouse and clinging to man for protection? If woman's influence is good in the house, why should it not have the power of goodness in our trade unions? If some of us should be content in the four walls of our home, then what about our sisters who do not have the means of securing the necessary walls? The divine injunction says, "By the sweat of thy brow shalt thou eat bread." If our unprotected sisters sit idly by in their "four walls," and let our male comrades handle their problems, I am afraid their supply of bread will be very meager.[18]

Women in the Socialist Party came up against a number of major obstacles in raising and fighting for these broader issues. One was the fixed view that the Socialist Party should concern itself with political matters, leaving "economic" questions, including the composition of their membership, to the trade unions. Another was the determination of Socialist trade union leaders not to antagonize the AFL leadership while they were "slowly but surely" being converted to socialism. To raise such issues as organizing the unorganized, especially unskilled women and blacks, and the need for the federation to abandon its rigid craft unionism and adopt industrial unionism in order to achieve this, would cause unnecessary conflict and thus delay the conversion of the AFL leaders to socialism.[19]

But what of those union leaders who were already Socialists, such as those in the International Ladies' Garment Workers' Union? All the contradictions in the Socialist Party's approach to the woman question came to the surface in the ILGWU. On the one hand, there is no doubt that the formation of the Socialist Party gave the newly formed ILGWU a much-needed stimulus. The dissensions among the various factions within the Socialist camp receded temporarily, and union officials were able to concentrate their energies on organizing. By 1902 fifty-one locals had affiliated with the international, and its membership had reached 8,865. Union leaders waged a jurisdictional battle with the United Shirt and Waist Workers' Union and won the right to organize ladies' shirtwaist makers.[20]

The international paid $5 to any organizer who founded a local, a practice that encouraged organizers to recruit women who held jobs in the newer branches of the industry. (The organizers received the same financial reward for a women's local as for an all-male branch.) But the organizers were all men, and the result was that women, while representing a majority in the industry, represented only a minority in the leadership of the union. In 1903 union records showed 5,527 male members and 3,338 female members, a ratio that did not at all correspond to that of males and females in the industry. In Chicago, for example, three thousand women worked at manufacturing women's clothing, but only five hundred of them belonged to the union.[21]

The first time women were mentioned explicitly in ILGWU convention proceedings was in 1902, when Carrie Chapman Catt, representing the National Woman Suffrage League, addressed the delegates and explained why, according to the suffragists, women worked for lower wages than men. As recorded in the proceedings, she declared "that so long as the woman worker was debarred from the right of the ballot, so long would necessity compel her to labor at a lower wage rate than man, and that it was nothing but common justice to permit the woman who, under present conditions, was with man equally interested in legislation the right of the ballot." Catt introduced a resolution to the convention that developed this theme. It read: "Recognizing that the inferior legal and political status of women compels them to underbid men in the labor market, therefore the ILGWU in convention assembled, advocate the extension of the political franchise to women on the same terms as men."[22]

The resolution passed without a single dissenting vote. Not one delegate reminded Catt that the unionization of female workers was an important factor in the achievement of higher wages for them. In fact, the only reference to the organization of women workers at the 1902 convention was in a resolution calling upon members to "make sure that none but union buttonhole makers work in shops under their [the ILGWU locals'] control, and that as soon as there are a sufficient number of buttonhole makers in Local 94 who work mostly on cloaks and other ladies' garments, a local will be organized under the jurisdiction of the ILGWU."[23] Since buttonhole making was a female trade, this at least was a step in the direction of expressing concern for organizing women workers. But it was also evident that the union was not going to take the initiative in organizing, and that the female buttonhole makers would have to organize themselves before the ILGWU would accept them as members. To be sure, the young ILGWU was a weak organization, but it could hardly expect to grow stronger if it was going to depend on the women to organize themselves and then deign to permit them to become union members. It would appear that the union leadership was more interested in staking out jurisdictional claims than in organizing.[24]

At the 1903 convention the issue of organizing women workers did come directly before the delegates, and a resolution was passed calling for additional recruiting of females into the trade. But no steps were taken to add any women organizers to the staff. Joseph Barondess, who had risen from a cloakmaker, earning only $5 a week in 1888, to leadership of the ILGWU, stood firm against women organizers. A Socialist himself—he had conducted an unsuccessful campaign as a Socialist Party candidate for Congress—he echoed the familiar argument that women's preoccupation with finding husbands made them poor organizers and even weakened their effectiveness as union members. After all, the argument went, did not many women in the garment shops express their wish for a husband by singing:

> "Day the same as night, night the same as day,
> And all I do is sew and sew and sew.
> May God help me and my love come soon
> That I may leave this work and go."

How could one expect such women to make good union organizers?[25]

Meanwhile, Local No. 39 in Boston, which comprised two hundred women members and whose officers were all women, had achieved a reputation as a stronger union than the local of men and had succeeded in winning recognition and substantial wage increases from its employers. But the Socialist leadership of the ILGWU continued to argue that women made poor organizers and even poorer union leaders. It is therefore not surprising that when New York's waistmakers, who had demonstrated their militancy in strikes demanding recognition from their employers, joined the ILGWU in a body in 1903, men were designated to head the local.[26]

Only two women delegates appeared at the 1903 ILGWU convention, and they received insignificant appointments to the Boycott Committee. But they were privileged to hear rousing speeches by Joseph Barondess on the need to support the Socialist Party and its ultimate goal of a socialist society, and they heard the delegates enthusiastically endorse resolutions favoring socialism.[27]

It was hardly to be expected that the United Garment Workers, with its conservative leadership, would bring women into positions of responsibility. (There were, of course, a few exceptions, such as Mary Maloney, president of Local No. 50 in Newburgh, New York.) The UGW rarely sanctioned strikes but instead used the union label as an organizing tactic. An employer could use the label if he agreed to employ only union workers, maintain sanitary standards in his shop, and comply with labor legislation and "regular hours and wages in accordance with union standards maintained in the locality."[28] Because many employers found it to their advantage to use the UGW label, they "unionized" their employees. In reality, many of these locals were company unions.

Most of the women who joined the UGW, therefore, did so under pressure from employers who were eager to display the union label. While the UGW officials were happy to recruit women in this way, they made sure that the union's leadership remained in the hands of men. Until 1899 women convention delegates had served only in general capacities and had held no national offices. A woman served on the union's Executive Board for the 1899–1900 term, but in 1901 all board members were men. In 1903 eight thousand members, or nearly one-third, of the union's total membership of twenty-five thousand, were women. The UGW boasted the largest number of women members among the AFL affiliates.[29] Nevertheless, women had little voice in making policy for this union.

There was one bright spot for women unionists in the garment industry: the Cloth Hat and Cap Makers. Both men and women took part in the union's activities, and both served on the union's Executive Board. The capmakers' union, like the ILGWU, was Socialist-dominated, but it did not adhere to the view held by too many male Socialists that women made poor union organizers and officials.

One of the board members was an outstanding union organizer—

Rose Schneiderman. She had been born in Russian Poland in 1891 and had come to America as a child of nine. After working for three years as a saleswoman, Schneiderman took a job in a cap factory, where she made linings, for a salary of $6 a week. A stay with a Socialist family in Montreal had converted her to both socialism and a recognition of the need for union organization. The women in her factory were unorganized, although the men belonged to the union. Increasing speedups and wage cuts convinced Schneiderman of the need for organization. As she recalled later: "It began to dawn on me that we girls needed an organization. The men had organized already and had gained some advantages, but the bosses lost nothing, as they took it out on us."[30]

Schneiderman organized the twelve women in her shop, and, along with some of these women, approached Maurice Mikol, the Socialist president of the Cloth and Cap Makers Union, who informed them that a union charter required that twenty-five women from a number of factories must express their willingness to join. At the factory closing hour, Schneiderman and her friends waited at the factory doors and approached the women as they left for home. Within days, they had the charter for Local No. 23, and the members elected Schneiderman as secretary and delegate to the Central Labor Union. In 1903 Schneiderman—all four feet, six inches of her—attended the capmakers' convention as a delegate, and although her mother wailed that nobody would marry a girl who spent so much time at union meetings, she was on her way to becoming one of New York City's leading women unionists and Socialist activists.

The most prominent and effective Socialist woman union organizer was, by her own account, seventy-one years old when the Socialist Party of America was formed. The legendary Mary Harris "Mother" Jones was born in Cork, Ireland, on May 1, 1830. She was the daughter of an "Irish agitator" and construction worker, Richard Harris, and came to America at the age of five. Harris' employment as a laborer with railroad construction crews took the family to Toronto, where Mary attended parochial and public schools, studying elementary education and dressmaking. In 1861 she accepted a teaching position in Memphis and married George Jones, "a staunch member of the Iron Moulders' Union" and organizer for the Knights of Labor in the Southern and Southwestern coalfields. In his extensive travels for the Knights, Jones was accompanied by his wife and their four children.

In 1867 a yellow fever epidemic swept western Tennessee and struck the Jones's Memphis home. All four children and their father died.[31] To earn a living, Jones began a dressmaking business in Chicago. After the fire of 1871 she moved her shop to a building adjacent to the office of the Knights of Labor. By day she worked "for the aristocrats of Chicago," among whom she had ample opportunity to observe luxury and extravagance, while from her shop window she saw "the poor, shivering wretches, jobless and hungry."[32] At night, she attended the rallies of the Knights of Labor.

Jones witnessed the great labor uprising of 1877, which began with the strike of the railroad workers of the Baltimore & Ohio. She took part in her first coal strike in 1882 in Hocking Valley, Ohio. But it was her immersion in the struggles of the United Mine Workers of America, then a rising, vigorous, rapidly growing union, that made a labor leader of her. Until she was nearly one hundred years old, Mother Jones was where the danger was greatest—crossing militia lines, spending weeks in damp prisons, incurring the wrath of governors, presidents, and coal operators—as she helped organize the United Mine Workers with the only tools she felt she needed: "convictions and a voice." She led the miners in strikes in Virginia in 1891; in the anthracite region in 1900 and 1902; in Paint Creek and Cabin Creek, West Virginia, in 1912-1913; in Ludlow, Colorado, in 1913–1914; and in Kansas in 1921, among others. She organized women to shame scabbing men into joining the union. She fought as hard against corrupt union leaders as she did against operators when she felt they were blocking progress.

In 1891, when she began her work as a UMW organizer, the fourteen-hour day was not uncommon, and the company owned everything—the miner's shacks, the stores, and the churches. The company even thought it owned the miners, but Mother Jones thought otherwise. Again and again, she would get a hurried call from some harassed local official: "For God's sake, come over to my area." It might be Roaring Branch or Hazleton, Pennsylvania, or Fairmont, West Virginia, or somewhere in Colorado, where the miners were desperate after a long struggle and ready to go back to work. Wherever it was, she would go, and with flaming words and rich wit, she would bolster the lagging courage and help carry on the struggle against starvation, company gunmen, and every other aspect of the company's power.

In her first efforts for the UMW, a mine superintendent in the Dietz fields of Virginia threatened to kill her, but she defied him. She likewise defied company harassment in 1900, and again in 1902, when 150,000 UMW anthracite miners went on strike in Pennsylvania. The future of the young union was at stake, and every UMW family knew it. When the much-hated Coal and Iron Police were brought in by the coal operators, the mining families retaliated by organizing a boycott. No member of a striking family would have anything to do with any strikebreaker or scab supporter. Any store that traded with strikebreakers would not have the business of the strikers.

At the height of the boycott, 1,100 young women walked out of the Wilkes-Barre Lace Mill, demanding that the mill owners fire five women whose fathers or brothers were scabbing in the mines. During the same strike, a group of striking miners' wives in Mount Pleasant, Pennsylvania, discovered that a company agent was bringing in strikebreakers from Virginia. They caught the man and tore out most of his beard. Soon after, the man quit his job with the coal company.

It was during this strike that Mother Jones developed the tactic that later became her trademark. In Arnot, Pennsylvania, she organized the men and women to take the union pledge. The wives rose before the men, with babes in their arms, and pledged themselves to see that no one went to work. The company tried to bring in scabs, but Mother Jones persuaded the men to stay at home with the children while the women attended to the scabs. She organized an army of housekeepers who dressed themselves in a wild assortment of rags, let their hair fly loose, and marched up the hill to the mine entrance, banging on their pot and pans. The scabs and mules were scared off by the group, after which the women conducted a "'round-the-clock" patrol of the mines. Jones also convinced the wives of the local farmers to support the strike and the local Swedish colony not to scab. Her work was described to the then UMW president, John Mitchell, as "Mother Jones raising hell up in the mountains with a bunch of wild women."

Together with the women of Shamokin, Pennsylvania, Mother Jones "mopped up Coaldale" during the 1900 strike. The women of Coaldale not only organized the entire camp but also helped to organize the mining town of Lattimer by going to the steps of the miners' shacks and shouting, "No work today!" They sang patriotic songs to drown out the voices of the scabs. Mother Jones told of an old Irishwoman who had two sons who were scabs: "The women threw one of them over the fence to his mother, who thought he was dead. She ran into the house for a bottle of holy water and shook it over Mike. 'Oh, for God's sake, come back to life,' she hollered. 'Come back and join the union.' He opened his eyes and saw our women standing around him. 'Shure, I'll go to hell before I'll scab again.'"

In these and other strike incidents, Mother Jones was able to utilize the element of surprise by having the miners' wives step out of their traditional roles as housewives. They were thus able to cause the company gunmen and strikebreakers to panic by surprising and confusing them.

In 1902 President Mitchell sent Jones to West Virginia. Immediately the frightened coal operators met her with court injunctions prohibiting her from addressing the miners. She was arrested in a rented lot in Clarksburg for violating the court order. She urged her mining audience not to abandon the struggle, declaring: "Goodbye, boys, I'm under arrest. I may have to go to jail. I may not see you for a long time. Keep up the fight! Don't surrender."[33]

In July, 1902, Jones appeared before the City Central Labor Council of Cincinnati to ask the delegates' support for the striking miners. In the process, she promoted the cause of workingwomen, saying:

> On Thursday I go to jail, but I am not afraid of their jails. I go for a principle. There are no convictions except for cowardice when a principle is to be upheld.... You pay Senators, Governors, legislators, and then beg on your knees for them to pass a bill in labor's protection. You will never solve the problem until you let in the women. No nation is greater than its women.... Women are fighters.[34]

Jones was found guilty of contempt of court for violating the injunction, but her sentencing was deferred. She immediately returned to union work—organizing, using her sharp wit and tongue to rouse workingmen and workingwomen, and boldly confronting mine owners, as well as treacherous or indifferent public figures and labor officials who stood in the way of militant struggle. She broke with John Mitchell after the UMW president joined with Gompers and other AFL leaders in the National Civic Federation and sat down to banquets with such antiunion capitalists as August Belmont, John D. Rockefeller, and J. P. Morgan. "Poor John," Mother Jones said of Mitchell's presence at such banquets, "he couldn't stand feasting with the rich. He is no good to his own people any longer." To demonstrate her opposition to Mitchell's policies, Jones resigned as a UMW organizer and did not return until 1911.

By 1902 Mother Jones was nationally renowned in both the labor and socialist movements. In 1894 she had helped J. A. Wayland establish the Socialist weekly, *Appeal to Reason,* and four years later she was a founding member, along with Eugene V. Debs, of the Social Democratic Party. She joined the Socialist Party of America as soon as it was founded, and in 1902 she campaigned for a Socialist mayoral candidate in Brockton, Massachusetts, and lectured throughout that state and New York under Socialist auspices.[35]

In 1900 the *International Socialist Review* reported that Mother Jones was "forming a union of domestic servants" in Scranton, Pennsylvania, while organizing the miners and rallying their wives and daughters in their support.[36] Until 1903 Jones built a great reputation for mobilizing these women to parade, protest, and picket on behalf of their men on strike. But that year she led a different parade, the famous "March of the Mill Children," marching helpless, mutilated children before the public to expose the injustice of child labor.

On May 23, 1903, a hundred thousand textile workers left their jobs at six hundred mills in the Philadelphia area. Over sixteen thousand of the strikers were children, many of them under twelve years of age. Although the state law prohibited the employment of children under twelve, in Pennsylvania, as in other Northern states, only the parents' oath was required to certify a child's age. Poor families perjured themselves in order to keep starvation away from their door. The strikers demanded a reduction in the work week from sixty to fifty-five hours, even if this meant a decrease in wages, which at the time of the strike ranged from $2 a week for children to $13 a week for adults.[37]

Although the Philadelphia local of the Socialist Party was critical of the strikers for being willing to decrease their wages in order to obtain a shorter work week, it rallied to their support. Caroline H. Pemberton, a member of a distinguished Philadelphia family and state secretary of the Socialist Party, published articles in the local press defending the strikers' struggle and calling for aid. To the strikers, she appealed: "Textile workers! Be brave in your fight and open-eyed! There is no virtue and no heroism in passive submission to grinding poverty; to conditions that keep your children in the mills instead of in schools." Pemberton urged "comrades everywhere . . . to assist in this great work."*[38]

Mother Jones arrived in mid-June in response to the appeal. She observed that every day little children, some not more than ten years old, came into union headquarters with missing fingers, and she tried to get newspaper publicity about the plight of these children. When newspaper men advised her that they could not carry the stories because the mill owners held stock in their papers, she replied: "Well, I've got stock in these little children and I'll arrange a little publicity." On June 17 she began with a rally in front of Philadelphia's City Hall: "I put the little boys with their fingers off and hands crushed and maimed on a platform. I held up their mutilated hands and showed them to the crowd and made the statement that Philadelphia's mansions were built on the broken bones, the quivering hearts and drooping heads of these little children."[39]

Although the rally was reported throughout the East, it brought no response from either the mill owners or public officials. So, drawing inspiration from a tour of the Liberty Bell, Mother Jones decided with the consent of the textile union leaders, to go on a tour with the children in order to dramatize the evils of child labor.

Jones knew she faced an uphill battle. Most Americans not only tolerated child labor but looked upon it with favor. They accepted the fact that poor children had to work and felt that, within reason, work was good for all youngsters. After all, work removed boys and girls from the

---

*Until recently Caroline H. Pemberton has been totally neglected. She deserves to be known not only for the fact that she became a Socialist after being brought up in an upper-class family but even more so because she was the leading Socialist in the early years of the party to stand for equality of black Americans. She was critical of the party for its failure to advocate such equality. For a study of Pemberton and especially of her views on the Negro question, see Philip S. Foner, "Caroline Hollingsworth Pemberton: Philadelphia Socialist Champion of Black Equality," *Pennsylvania History* 43 (July 1976): 227–52.

unwholesome influence of the streets and was a cure for juvenile delinquency and female promiscuity, as well as the first rung on the ladder to success. As a result, during the late nineteenth and early twentieth century, young children frequently toiled long hours under brutalizing and unhealthy conditions, six and even seven days a week, particularly in the cotton textile mills, mines, and glass factories of the nation's largest cities. The textile industry was the country's largest user of child labor, employing eighty thousand children, most of them little girls.[40]

Jones planned to march the mill children and their adult sympathizers to President Theodore Roosevelt's summer home at Oyster Bay on Long Island, some 125 miles away, and thus win the president's support for the child strikers. On July 7, 1903, the march got under way. John Spargo, a Socialist intellectual who was studying child labor and had aided the strikers, addressed the marchers and the crowd that had gathered to see them off, crying out: "Child slavery's awful curse eats at the vitals of the nation. But nowhere to a more alarming extent than in the city of Philadelphia. The great textile industries rest upon the enslavement of children and women. Not even in the South are conditions worse than here." Then Mother Jones—attired in her familiar black bonnett, full skirt, and immaculate shirtwaist, trimmed with ruffles at the neck and wrists—gave the signal to depart. About three hundred men, women, and children were led by three children dressed as Revolutionary soldiers, representing the Spirit of '76. The children carried only knapsacks and banners with the slogans, "We Only Ask for Justice," "55 Hours or Nothing," "More Schools, Less Hospitals," "We Want to Go to School," "We Want Time to Play," "Prosperity, Where Is Our Share?"[41]

"Mother Jones' Crusaders," or "Mother Jones' Industrial Army" (names variously bestowed on the marchers by the press)* marched into Bristol, Pennsylvania, a mill town, and after being halted by the police, were allowed to parade through the streets. They were watched by not only the "local textile workers but by the better people as well."[42] After a speech by Mother Jones denouncing child labor, the group moved on to Morrisville, Pennsylvania, across the river from Trenton, where it spent the first night. That evening Jones spoke before the Plumbers' Union in Trenton and collected donations to aid the strikers in Philadelphia and to help defray the expenses of the march.[43]

Mother Jones addressed five thousand people in Trenton in the presence of city dignitaries, headed, in the absence of the mayor, by the president of the Select Council. She told the audience: "Women have learned that their children are taken away from them and put to work

*The name "Industrial Army" was taken from Coxey's Army of the unemployed in 1894, of which Mother Jones was a member.

when they should be in school. What is the use of bringing a lot of children into the world to make more money for plutocrats, while their little lives are being ground out in the mill and workshop?"[44]

On July 11 the group moved on to Princeton, where Mother Jones spoke opposite the university campus. When she was requested by a professor to speak to his class, she brought before the undergraduates a stooped, ten-year-old boy, and said: "Here's a text book on economics. He gets three dollars a week and his sister, who is fourteen, gets six dollars. They work in a carpet factory ten hours a day, while the children of the rich are getting their higher education."[45]

The first week on the road ended in New Brunswick, New Jersey. A reporter who interviewed the group wrote that even though they were tired, they were going to continue, for they were "marching for a 'principle,' and are determined to reach New York and make a demonstration." Before they left New Brunswick, they were met by delegates from the Central Labor Union, who contributed to the strike fund.[46]

On July 14, in Rahway, New Jersey, the entire city government, along with the judiciary, the ministry, and organized labor, was on hand to greet the army. Mother Jones addressed a crowd of two thousand and promised to continue traveling around the country until an aroused public ended child labor.[47] In Elizabeth, delegates from fifty-six unions, representing more than a hundred thousand workers, attended a dinner in honor of Mother Jones tendered by the Allied Trades Council of Union County. The first toast was: "Mother Jones. May Her Crusade Be Successful." The local reporter observed that "it was a union banquet throughout. Everything served, including the beverages, was either union made, grown or sold, and the speeches and toasts were of the same brand. But beside the royal union welcome there was generous aid, money being collected to help the army, and funds were promised for the strikers in Philadelphia."[48]

It was from Elizabeth that Jones sent the first of three letters to President Roosevelt. She reminded him that he was the "father" of the nation, yet it was possible that he knew nothing of "the crime of child slavery." The thousands of textile strikers, she wrote, were asking for a reduction from sixty to fifty-five hours of work a week, when in reality forty-eight hours were more than "sufficient." Had Congress passed an eight-hour law, she said, the Philadelphia strike could have been averted. Jones then read Roosevelt a lecture on the hardships of the mill children, with a gibe at his repeated claims about widespread prosperity:

> These little children, raked by cruel toil beneath the iron wheels of greed, are starving in this country which you have declared is in the height of prosperity—slaughtered, ten hours a day, every day in the week, every week in the month, every month in the year, that our manufacturing aristocracy may live to exploit more slaves as the years roll by.

The president was urged to convey his sentiments "towards suffering childhood" in a letter addressed to "Mother Jones' Crusaders."[49]

On June 20 Mother Jones made a side trip to attend the annual picnic of the New York City Social Democratic Party. To the cheers of four thousand listeners, she vowed that she would be in New York City within a few days "with my children from the textile works." She promised, too, "to complete the journey to Oyster Bay with my army to see the president." She would find out, she declared, whether the newspapers were correct in predicting that Roosevelt would not see her—indeed, "if he is the president of the capitalists only, or whether he is the president of the workingmen, too." If the former were true, Jones predicted, "he will be wiped out in the next election."[50]

Jones picked up the threat to defeat Roosevelt at a meeting of several thousand Paterson unionists. At the end of a stirring indictment of child labor, she asked: "Will you vote next time for an aristocratic president, who will not listen to the wail of suffering childhood? . . . Pledge yourselves; pledge yourselves," she cried. Almost every one of the unionists took the pledge not to vote for Roosevelt if he were to deny an audience to Jones' children. "Never since the beginning of the 'crusade,'" wrote a reporter, "has 'Mother' Jones had such a reception. Men thronged the stage, fighting to shake her hand, while some of the foreigners kissed her fingers."[51]

Amid rumors that Secret Service agents were trying to dissuade her from visiting the president, Jones prepared to enter New York City. First, she sent a committee to the chief of police to obtain permission for a march up Fourth Avenue to Madison Square Garden, where she hoped to hold a rally. When permission was denied because the marchers were not city residents, Mother Jones went to Mayor Seth Low and challenged the city's right to deny the marchers access to the streets, when the city had entertained Prince Henry of Germany ("a piece of rotten royalty") and other foreign dignitaries, who added nothing to the nation's well-being. "Well, Mr. Mayor," Jones summed up her tirade, "there are the little citizens of the nation and they also produce its wealth. Aren't we entitled to enter your city?" Low agreed, and the crusaders marched from the Socialist Party headquarters preceded by a band "provided by the Socialists" to an outdoor rally.[52]

Since Madison Square Garden had been preempted by the Henry George "single-taxers," Mother Jones spoke on July 24 to about fifteen hundred people at the corner of Fourth Avenue and Twenty-fourth Street. In the course of her speech denouncing child labor, Jones brought to the podium "a little fellow of twelve, whose job it was to sit all day on a high stool, handing in the right thread to another worker." He worked eleven hours a day for $3 a week.[53]

On July 29, after a day's entertainment at Coney Island, Jones, two men, and three children went to Oyster Bay to ask President Roosevelt to meet with a delegation of the child marchers. The Secret Service would not allow them through the gates, but finally they met with the president's secretary, who told Jones that Roosevelt had no authority to act on matters relating to child labor. He suggested that Mother Jones submit her views to the president in writing.

Jones sent two letters to Roosevelt. In the first she asked only for an audience at a time convenient to the president. In the final communication, she explained:

> I have been moved to this crusade, Mr. President, because of actual experience in the mills. I have seen little children without the first rudiments of education and no prospect of acquiring any. I have seen other children with hands, fingers and other parts of their bodies mutilated because of their childish ignorance of machinery.* I feel that no nation can be truly great while such conditions exist without attempted remedy.

Jones asked that federal laws be passed "governing this evil," and begged the president to see "three boys who have walked a hundred miles, serving as living proof of what I say."[54]

The only reply was a letter from Roosevelt's secretary indirectly expressing the president's "heartiest sympathy" with every effort to prevent child labor in the factories. Addressing meetings of unionists and Socialists in New York City, Mother Jones expressed her bitterness at the treatment the mill children had received from the president of the United States. With this, the crusading army, or what was left of it by this time, disbanded and headed back by train for Pennsylvania.[55]

John Lopez, the reporter from the Philadelphia *North American* who accompanied the march and covered it from beginning to end, wrote an interesting confession. He acknowledged that he had started out as if on a lark, and his first dispatches reflected his view that the whole affair was rather ludicrous. But as the march proceeded, he began to see the serious side of the movement, and his reports reflected this changing attitude. From tolerant amusement, his writings expressed more and more admiration and respect for Mother Jones. By the time the march was only half over, he acknowledged that he could now understand why Mother Jones was viewed as the "Jeanne d'Arc of workers in their indus-

---

*Mother Jones was referring to the fact that she had worked in the cotton mills of Alabama in 1894. "I wanted to see for myself," she wrote later, "if the gruesome stories of little children working in the mills were true." She found it to be even worse than she had heard. Sometimes, she recalled, she had an urge to flee "the most heart-rending spectacle in all life," and go to the coal fields, "where the labor fight is at least fought by grown men." She reported seeing the machinery-tending children's "helpless limbs torn off, and then when they are disabled and of no more use to their master, thrown out to die" (Mary Field Parton, *The Autobiography of Mother Jones* [Chicago, 1925], pp. 117–19; Mother Mary Jones, "Civilization in Southern Mills," *International Socialist Review*, March 1901, pp. 540–41).

trial warfare." He could understand, too, why she was called "mother by all the laboring class": "It is because she fights their fights with a mother's love, sacrifices herself for them, complains of no hardship, and will lead them in a losing fight." He was absolutely certain that the "March of the Mill Children" was such a "losing fight." "It can gain nothing," he concluded.[56]

Lopez was wrong. It is true that Mother Jones' army did not help the strikers win, for on August 17, the starved-out textile workers returned to the mills, defeated. Nor did the march bring about any federal legislation outlawing child labor. But the crusade had attracted crowds all along the way and had brought the abuses of child labor dramatically before the public; it was probably instrumental in the passage of child labor legislation in Pennsylvania, which, in Mother Jones' proud words, "sent thousands of children home from the mills, and kept thousands of others from entering the factory until they were fourteen years of age." Dale Fetherling, Jones' biographer, claims further that the march also had an effect on child labor legislation in other states, especially New York and New Jersey.[57]

Although some Socialist men resented the prominence Mother Jones had achieved during the march, most of them admired and respected her tireless activity and her bold denunciation of child labor. In a number of communities, the Socialist Party opened its facilities to the marchers and sponsored meetings, parades, and demonstrations in their behalf. The Philadelphia *North American* reporter, hardly a Socialist himself, was impressed by the fact that "Socialists will travel distances to listen to Mother Jones speak, and after the meeting, deem it a great honor to be able to shake her hand."[58] Traditional sex prejudice in Socialist circles gave way, at least as far as Mother Jones was concerned.

16

Birth of the National Women's Trade Union League

I~N~ *Century of Struggle: The Woman's Rights Movement in the United States,* Eleanor Flexner notes: "The Years between 1903 and the entry of the United States into the first World War in 1917 saw the growth of the first unions composed largely of women. These unions remain a stable part of the American labor movement down to the present time."[1] Although the Women's National Union Label League and women's auxiliaries of men's unions were active in 1903, it was a new organization—the National Women's Trade Union League, founded by middle-class reformers and working-class women in that year—that became the first national body dedicated to organizing women workers.

During the 1880s and 1890s an increasing number of middle-class women turned their attention toward those of their sex who worked in factories, shops, and tenements. Since the Civil War, when the Workingwomen's Protective Union was established by New York *Sun* editor Moses Beach and financed by philanthropists to aid New York seamstresses, there had been rich and professional people who sought to help women workers. Although they were all too often visionary, impractical, condescending, and paternalistic, these reform advocates did represent a break from most pre-war middle-class reformers, especially among women, who ignored the hardships of female workers and considered their life style unladylike. To be sure, even many of the postwar reformers believed that women's normal occupation was in the home, that their employment, especially of wives, violated natural law, and, further, that the children of such women would be unfit citizens and workers. Even some of the reformers who were most outspoken in advancing the rights and dignity of labor remained convinced that women should not work outside the home.

290

Nevertheless, most of the reformers ultimately came to the realization that the women were working to support themselves or their families, and not, as many employers maintained, for "pin money." This, in turn, led to a recognition of the need to help them change the miserable conditions under which they worked.[2]

During the 1890s, there was an increase in the number of middle-class women, frequently college-educated, who came to this conclusion, who demonstrated a real concern for workingwomen, and who directed their energies to assisting them. The various reformers arrived at varying answers in seeking effective means for helping workingwomen. Some believed that if the female laborer became better educated and worked hard, she could win her employer's appreciation and, with it, higher wages. Others felt that employers could be persuaded to improve working conditions through appeals to their wives. Still others lobbied for remedial legislation, while some set up programs and organizations that encouraged self-sufficiency and independence. Another group established residence in working-class neighborhoods and assisted trade union organizers in their work. Some even temporarily abandoned their professional lives in order to experience the life of workingwomen. They then exposed the terrible conditions they discovered, in the hope of convincing others that these conditions could and should be changed. Another group believed that consumers could be persuaded to boycott firms that refused to provide minimum standards of decency for their workers. Then there was the controversy between those who believed that the answer lay in women's trade unions and those who felt that such trade unions were impractical because the work was too temporary and the labor supply too great and women could or could not organize effectively. The answer, this group felt, lay in legislation limiting working hours and establishing minimum wages.

Some of the activities of the 1890s were transitory and represented nothing more than titillation for bored women with nothing else to do. Some reformers abandoned their efforts during the mid-decade depression, just when the need was greatest. But most continued their activities, and not a few came to view social work as a chance to do something really useful.

Regardless of their motivations or the length of their activity, most of the middle-class reformers agreed on two main points: first, that individual women could not be blamed for their poverty or immorality—the fault lay with society, not with individuals; and secondly, that these evils could be eradicated by harmonious accommodation between working-women and their employers, without conflict or any fundamental change in society, such as the overthrow of capitalism and the establishment of socialism. For all their avowed interest in improving workingwomen's lives, the middle-class women who participated in these various efforts never actively cooperated with wage-earning women when they chose to use economic weapons like the strike to win advances.[3]

To be sure, Socialist men and women who were associated with upper- and middle-class social reformers in these activities neither shared their naive beliefs nor rejected labor's economic weapon. But they did not insist on the acceptance of their views as a condition of the collaboration. In fact, some Socialists were convinced that even with their rejection of class conflict and sweeping social goals, the social reformers were able to accomplish more for workingwomen than the Socialists themselves. Writing to Frederick Engels from Hull House on May 27, 1893, Florence Kelley emphasized the importance of the work being done by the settlement houses "among the wage earners." While conceding that Socialists, too, were "active," she noted that they were "practically unorganized and very few at best." She herself continued to advance Socialist ideas through articles, pamphlets, reports, and papers, but she found that she could accomplish more for workingwomen through her work in Hull House than in the Socialist movement.[4]

Kelley went on to organize branches of the Consumers' League in Chicago, along with her other important work. In 1898 she represented the Chicago office at the national convention of the Consumers' League, and in 1899 she was chosen its first executive officer. She became the driving force behind the National Consumers' League and by 1903 had helped to set up fifty-three units and three college societies in eighteen states. By that time forty-seven factories in eleven states were utilizing the Consumers' League's label, attesting to the fact that these employers' labor standards met league stipulations.[5] In some cities, the league was also able to reach agreements with the larger department stores that they would stay open late for only two weeks before Christmas. Elsewhere they lobbied for state laws prohibiting the work of girls under sixteen years of age after nine o'clock at night.

Yet the relationship between the Consumers' League and the trade unions was anything but friendly. The unions feared that the league's award of its label to nonunion firms made organization even more difficult. At the 1903 AFL convention, Gompers criticized the league as an organization of well-intentioned young ladies who issued the label when they found working conditions sanitary but who ignored wages and hours.[6] Florence Kelley herself eventually came to recognize the limitations of the Consumers' League's "white lists" (which served as a method for screening and recommending products and stores for shoppers) and sought out new means for aiding workingwomen.[7]

Meanwhile, two groups that had participated in the settlement house movement were becoming more and more convinced that the trade union was the most promising vehicle for improving the economic status of workingwomen. These groups comprised middle-class advocates of social justice who had seen at first hand the need for labor organization and workingwomen who were themselves active in unions.[8]

As Gertrude Barnum, an upper-class activist in the Women's Trade Union League, explained:

> I myself have graduated from the Settlement into the trade union. As I became more familiar with the conditions around me, I began to feel that while the Settlement was undoubtedly doing a great deal to make the lives of working people less grim and hard, the work was not fundamental. It introduced into their lives books and flowers and music, and it gave them a place to meet and see their friends or leave their babies when they went out to work, but it did not raise their wages or shorten their hours. It began to dawn on me, therefore, that it would be more practical to turn our energies toward raising wages and shortening hours.[9]

Nevertheless, only a minority of the settlement house workers concerned themselves with helping women form trade unions. Those who did had become discouraged by the slow approach of social reform organizations and by the elitism of traditional charity work. A major problem lay in winning the cooperation of male unionists in recruiting workingwomen into existing unions. The average male trade unionist regarded the middle-class social worker as more concerned with gathering statistics than with improving the workers' lot. It was not to be easy to convince such men that the social reformers were sincerely interested in improving the economic status of workingwomen through trade unionism, especially since the hostility to the middle-class women often served as an excuse for the male unionists to do nothing themselves to organize women.

During the 1890s settlement houses became regular features in large cities. A number of settlement houses were hostile to trade unions and refused to support the labor movement, but this was not true of the large social settlements. Labor unions met regularly at Chicago's Hull House, at Denison House and South End House in Boston, and at University and Henry Street Settlements in New York. Many union locals of women were founded at Hull House, Denison House, and the Henry Street Settlement, and while settlement house workers generally tended to favor the peaceful resolution of labor disputes, all three settlement houses supported the strikes of the women workers they had helped to organize and, in general, endorsed strikes that they felt were justified.

Eventually the settlement workers won the support and cooperation of young, militant workingwomen in the effort to organize unions of women workers. In fact, most of the women's unions that existed at the beginning of the twentieth century had been organized by these militant women workers, often with the help of a social settlement.[10]

In 1901, after lengthy hearings, the Industrial Commission issued a report linking prostitution to low wages and demanding equal pay for equal work. The commission pointed out that evidence presented before it indicated that unions had helped to improve the welfare of working-women, and it placed the burden of implementing its recommendation on the existing trade unions.[11] But the American Federation of Labor, the major body uniting these unions, had already amply demonstrated that it was not prepared to fulfill this function. Except for adopting routine convention resolutions sympathetic to women, the AFL practically ignored the needs of 5 million female workers.

Both groups in the settlement houses—the social reformers and the workingwomen—realized that most existing trade unions, because of their emphasis on organizing only skilled workers, failed to reach the women who needed their assistance most. Even the garment industry unions, which included more women than most other unions, accepted the disparity in wages between men and women and did little to encourage women to assume leadership positions. Nearly all unions—Socialist and non-Socialist alike—were handicapped by the belief that women's sojourn in the world of work was temporary; that their real goal was marriage; and that they were too passive and too inarticulate to contribute a high degree of commitment to unionism. With these premises, these union leaders reasoned that it would be a waste of the union's time and money to attempt to organize them.

The settlement house groups knew that while there were elements of truth in this analysis, it was not the whole truth. The most recent decades had demonstrated that many female workers were receptive to unionization, and the militancy of the women in strikes proved that they could teach male unionists a thing or two about struggle. Certainly, the militancy of the women garment workers disproved many of the myths surrounding workingwomen.

In 1902 the militancy of the women in the garment shops found its way into the streets of the working-class neighborhoods. In mid-May, Jewish women, most of them housewives on New York's East Side, but also including a sprinkling of women in the garment trades, formed the "Ladies Anti-Beef Trust Association" to protest the rapidly rising price of kosher meat and the betrayal of a boycott of wholesale distributors by the Jewish retail butchers. (After the wholesalers had yielded and reduced prices, the retail butchers refused to pass the lowered prices on to the consumers.) The outraged women boycotted the retail butchers, battered those butcher shops that remained open, threw meat into the streets, poured kerosene on it, and prevented nonboycotters from buying meat. "Eat no meat while the Trust is taking meat from the bones of your children and women," read a Yiddish circular decorated with a skull and crossbones.[12]

Dozens of women were beaten by the police, arrested, fined, or jailed. Rebecca Ablowitz, one of the women boycotters, engaged in the following exchange with the magistrate:

> Why do you riot?
> Your Honor, we know our wounds. We see how thin our children are and that our husbands haven't strength to work. . . .
> But you aren't allowed to riot in the street.
> We don't riot. But if all we did was to weep at home, nobody would notice it; so we have to do something to help ourselves.[13]

Like the women who struck the garment shops, the women who boycotted Jewish butchers were denounced by the commercial press. The New York *World* described them as "a pack of wolves," and the *New York Times* devoted its lead editorial on May 24, 1902, to them:

> The class of people . . . who are engaged in this matter have many elements of a dangerous class. They are very ignorant. . . . They do not understand the duties or the rights of Americans. They have no inbred or acquired respect for law and order as the basis of the life of the society into which they have come. . . . Resistance to authority does not seem to them necessarily wrong, only risky, and if it ceases to be risky, the restraint it can have on their passions is very small; practically it disappears. . . . The instant they take the law into their own hands, the instant they begin the destruction of property, and assail peaceable citizens and the police, they should be handled in a way that they can understand and cannot forget. . . . Let the blow fall instantly and effectually. . . .
> These rioters were plainly desperate. They meant to defy the police and were ready for severe treatment. They did not get treatment nearly severe enough, and they are therefore far more dangerous than they were before.

But to the workers at New York's Henry Street Settlement and University Settlement, these women were upholding the best in the American tradition of protest against greed, and had demonstrated by their militancy that lower-class women were neither passive nor inarticulate. One of these settlement workers was William English Walling, the son of a prominent doctor, grandson of a Kentucky millionaire. At Hull House Walling had become increasingly interested in trade unionism, eventually, he was to become a prominent member of the Socialist Party. For the time being, he decided that he could make his best contribution to social reform through the settlement.

In 1902 Walling became a resident at University Settlement. His interest in the plight of poor women was heightened by his personal observation of the activities of the "Ladies Anti-Beef Trust Association," whose angry demonstrations took place just outside the settlement. More than ever convinced that workingwomen could organize effectively and fight for decent conditions, and having read accounts of the British Women's Trade Union League, which had been organized in 1874 and had had considerable success in organizing women workers—or so it was reported in the United States—he decided to study its work at first hand. In 1903, with the support of Lillian Wald and Florence Kelley of the Henry Street Settlement, Walling went to England to learn more about the League.[14]

As Allen F. Davis notes, the organization of the Women's Trade Union League is "an interesting example of the cross-fertilization of reform ideas between the United States and Great Britain."[15] The impetus for the formation of the British Women's Trade Union League came from two temporarily successful American women's trade unions: the New York Parasol and Umbrella Makers' Union and the Women's Typographical Union. Emma Ann Paterson, an Englishwoman who was active in the suffrage movement and became honorary secretary of her local Workingmen's Club and Institute, had been impressed, while traveling in the United States in 1873, by these two unions of women in New York. She returned to England "fired with the idea of urging her countrywomen to form trade unions,"* and, together with other interested women, formed the British Women's Protective and Provident League in 1874. She remained its honorary secretary until 1886, when she was succeeded by Clementine Black.[16]

"The Women's Trade Union Provident League is a society of people who give time or work or money to try and establish trade unions among women," Clementine Black wrote in the *Women's Union Journal* of 1888. "That is, and always has been, its first and main object."[17] But up to this point, the league had not accomplished very much in pursuit of its objective. To be sure, it had helped to form societies of women workers, such as female typists, in the late 1870s, but most of them had been short-lived and were at no time part of the established trade union movement of the day.[18] Meanwhile, the number of women workers in British industry had multiplied, as did the exploitation to which they were subjected. According to the 1881 Census, almost one-third of the total labor force in England between the ages of twenty and sixty-five were women. They formed the majority in the textile trades, and, including girls under twenty years of age, there were more than 1,750,000 females employed in various industries, with another 2 million in domestic and other services. Their earnings were roughly 50 percent of the male rate.[19]

On July 5, 1888, despite their fear of dismissal and the lack of funds, sixty-two East End women matchmakers struck. Within two weeks, with

---

*Although a pioneer in the field of organizing female workers, Paterson was adamantly opposed to special legislation for their protection. Indeed, when a Home Office Enquiry in 1873 "recommended a reduction of women's hours from 60 to 54 and a bill to this effect came before Parliament, the opposition of the 'feminists' led by Paterson killed it" (Harold Goldman, *Emma Paterson* [London, 1974], p. 73).

the assistance of the Women's Trade Union Provident League, which collected £400 for the strike fund and sent down a corps of organizers to help form a union and hold it together, and aided further by the arbitration of the London Trades Council, these female strikers won major concessions. Fines and deductions were abolished, wages were raised, and, most important of all, these unskilled female workers formed the Matchmakers' Union. It remained "the largest union composed entirely of women and girls in England" for many years, with a membership of 800, of whom 650 regularly kept up their weekly contributions. In their history of British trade unionism, the Webbs wrote that the celebrated "match-girls' strike" of 1888 "turned a new leaf in Trade Union annals. Hitherto success had been in almost exact proportion to the workers' strength."[20]

This was followed by the great 1889 strike of gas workers in London. During this strike, Eleanor Marx-Aveling (daughter of Karl Marx) formed the first women's branch of the National Union of Gas Workers and General Labourers. The Executive Council of the Gasworkers formally admitted the Silvertown Women's Branch and its secretary, Mrs. Marx-Aveling, into the union. In May 1890, when the first Annual Conference of the National Union of Gasworkers and General Labourers took place, the union already had some forty thousand members in eighty-nine branches, including two composed entirely of women. Eleanor Marx-Aveling was elected a member of the fifteen-member Executive Board by acclamation. On a motion from the floor, moved by both a male delegate and a woman representative, a resolution was adopted that the union should include in its demands, wherever possible, that women should receive the same wages for doing the same work as men.[21]

As these developments were occurring, Clementine Black wrote to the editor of the London *Times* on behalf of the Women's Protective and Provident League, pointing out that

> under whatever system workpeople are employed, the want of a proper trade organization among them inevitably tends to the existence of conditions of employment in every respect unjust and repressive. It is, the League submits, largely to a development of its work in the formation of women's unions that the public must look for a removal of these industrial conditions, which are not only a disgrace to our civilization, but are fraught with elements in the highest degree dangerous to the peace and well-being of society.[22]

The success of the strikes of women workers and their incorporation into the existing unions had its impact on the league's name. In 1874, "fearing that storms of opposition would be aroused if the words 'Trades Union' were introduced,"[23] the league's founders had adopted what they hoped would be an inoffensive title—the Women's Protective and Provident League. Since then, however, trade unionism had become one of the facts of public life, especially with the emergence of the "new unionism," which organized the unskilled. The strikes of 1888 and 1889—first of the match workers, then of the dockers and the gas workers—hastened this development. In September, 1888, the league's name was changed to the Women's Trade Union Provident League. And in December, 1890, the league changed its name again to the Women's Trade Union League, which it remained until its fusion into the larger trade union movement in 1919.[24]

Three decades after Emma Paterson had founded the British league, William English Walling visited England to study its operations. Early in 1903 he met members of the British Women's Trade Union League and other trade union leaders and learned how the organization encouraged women to join existing men's unions. He was especially impressed by the fact that the British league united both upper-class and working-class women in a common effort to organize women into their own unions and integrate them into established men's locals. Walling became convinced that a similar organization could improve conditions for American workingwomen, and he carried the idea back to the United States.[25]

Filled with enthusiasm, Walling went to Boston in November, 1903, to attend the annual AFL convention. Walling explained his plan to form an American Women's Trade Union League to the recently widowed Mary Kenney O'Sullivan, and she enthusiastically agreed to help him. The two—one a wealthy reformer and the other a working-class labor leader (both settlement house residents)—worked out the tentative plan for the new organization designed specifically to help workingwomen enter unions. They arranged for a meeting in Faneuil Hall and invited AFL Executive Council members and convention delegates whose trades included large numbers of women.[26]

The meeting, held on November 14, included several AFL delegates and a number of Boston settlement workers. The group selected Walling, O'Sullivan, and Nellie B. Barker, of the Women's Label League, to draft a constitution. In addition, O'Sullivan and Walling agreed to visit Boston settlement houses to explain their program and gather support. Walling had insisted that the new league must have the support of the American Federation of Labor, and he and O'Sullivan conferred with Gompers during the AFL convention. "When they submitted to me a proposal, I gave it my hearty approval and participated in the necessary conferences," Gompers wrote later in his autobiography. Actually, the statement was an exaggeration on both counts. He gave the proposal only passive support and appointed Max Morris of the AFL Executive Council to attend the conference.

On November 17, 1903, four leading Boston settlement house workers—Vida Scudder, Helena S. Dudley, Robert Woods, and Philip

Davis—together with a number of union officials, including Max Morris, met with Walling and O'Sullivan. After some discussion, the participants decided that before the proposed organization could undertake a recruiting drive in a particular industry, it must first contact the national union possessing jurisdiction over these women. They also adopted a resolution requiring that the proposed Women's Trade Union League should, wherever possible, affiliate with the central labor body in a given locality. Finally, they decided to request that the AFL employ a full-time woman organizer.[27]

Two days later a third meeting was convened. This time Harry White, president of the United Garment Workers, Michael Donnelly, president of the Amalgamated Meat Cutters & Butcher Workmen, and John F. O'Brien, president of the Clerks International Protective Union, met with other members of the trade unions and the settlement workers—among them, Mary Morton Kehew of the Women's Educational and Industrial Union, Emily Balch and Helena S. Dudley of Denison House, and Philip Davis of Civic Service House. With the exception of Nellie Parker, an AFL delegate from a Boston women's union, all of the labor delegates were men. By contrast, nearly all the participants from the Boston settlement houses and reform groups were women.[28]

Before this meeting adjourned, the new organization had a name— the Women's National Trade Union League (changed in 1907 to the National Women's Trade Union League)—a set of officers, and a constitution. To lend prestige to the new organization, the unionists and reformers suggested that several nationally known figures be asked to serve as officers. Mary Morton Kehew, a wealthy Bostonian long known in social reform circles and the former president of the General Federation of Women's Clubs, was selected as the league's first president and Mary Kenney O'Sullivan as secretary. Jane Addams agreed to serve as the league's vice-president. Mary McDowell, a University of Chicago settlement resident, was asked to fill a position on the Executive Board, in recognition of her work in organizing women in the meat-packing industry. Also elected to the Executive Board were Lillian Wald, who, during the 1890s, had worked to organize small women's unions of New York City garment finishers and buttonhole makers; Leonora O'Reilly, New York settlement worker and United Garment Worker organizer; Mary Freitas, a textile worker from Lowell, Massachusetts; and Ellen Lindstrom, a long-time Chicago unionist and former walking delegate for the Special Order Clothing Workers and the United Garment Workers.* There were two settlement workers and three trade unionists, one of whom was also a settlement worker, on the Executive Board.[29]

The constitution of the new organization stated that its object "shall

---

*A walking delegate was a trade unionist who was sent to labor areas or groups to encourage organization of workers.

be to assist in the organization of women workers into trade unions."
(Shortly thereafter. there was added, "and thereby to help secure conditions necessary for healthful and efficient work and to obtain a just
return for such work.") Anyone was eligible to be a member upon declaring "himself or herself willing to assist those trade unions already existing, which have women members, and to aid in the formation of new
unions of women wage workers." Nonunion members (called "allies"
because of the antilabor connotation of the term "nonunionist") were
eligible not only to join the league but to hold any office. However, the
constitution stipulated that membership on the Executive Board was to
be divided as follows: "The majority . . . shall be women who are, or have
been, trade unionists in good standing, the minority of those well known
to be earnest sympathizers and workers for the cause of trade
unionism."[30]

The ally was described as one who "must have patience, lofty faith
and unalterable humility. It is the girls who must ever be the movement,
but the ally can help immensely. She has often time, money, and the
touch with the outside world." This was Walling's definition and reflected his concern that the new organization would be dominated by
upper-class allies. This concern was already evident in the provision that
workingwomen were to hold the majority of Executive Board positions.
It was also reflected in Walling's warning to Leonora O'Reilly that the
upper-class allies must rid themselves of any trace of the "Lady with
something to give her sisters." They were, he advised, to step aside and
make way for working-class members in the leadership of the organization. He urged that they learn about trade unionism, labor organizing,
and working conditions from the women who had firsthand experience
in such matters. Finally, unlike the charity organizers and even many
settlement house workers of the period, the allies were advised to let
their working-class colleagues define their own goals and avoid the
temptation to impose upon them a middle-class culture or life style, or to
use the league as an instrument for social control.[31]

Walling was also concerned about relations with the AFL. The founders of the new organization considered asking for a formal endorsement from the federation but decided to delay until "the League should
have accomplished some definite work."[32] However, the desire for ties
with the AFL was reflected in the provision that an annual conference
would be held jointly with the federation's convention.

The newly formed group was encouraged by the fact that Gompers
had permitted O'Sullivan to announce the league's formation from the
podium of the AFL convention, although they noted that the federation
president was somewhat less enthusiastic in his introduction of O'Sullivan than he was in introducing Martha Moore Avery for an attack on
socialism. While he remained silent after O'Sullivan's remarks, he pre-

sented Avery with a small bouquet, which he ostentatiously fastened to her dress.

The scarcity of women delegates at the convention was another cause for the league's lack of enthusiasm for immediate affiliation. There were only five women among the 496 AFL members present, and while they succeeded in getting the convention to adopt resolutions calling for special efforts to organize women, for the appointment of at least one female organizer, and for endorsement of woman suffrage, as the women knew all too well, as far as female workers were concerned, in the AFL there was a great difference between resolutions and action. A final damper on the enthusiasm of the league's founders came when Gompers did not view the organization's formation as sufficiently newsworthy to merit mention in the *American Federationist* of December, 1903, even though the issue was full of convention news.

Still, it was with a good deal of optimism that the league's charter members returned to their own cities to set up local branches. After all, the organization had been born in a moment of ebullience, at the very height of gains in union members during the period from 1897 to 1904.* Branches were rapidly formed in New York, Boston, and Chicago. In each case, the birth took place in a settlement house—in New York at University Settlement, in Chicago at Hull House, and in Boston at Denison House. In each case, too, the settlement workers sought to enlist the support of labor leaders. It took considerable work on the part of Leonora O'Reilly to overcome the hostility of the Central Labor Union toward the New York League and win even token cooperation. In Boston and Chicago the union leaders were more receptive. John Fitzpatrick, president of the Chicago Federation of Labor, not only endorsed the League, but praised it for not being afraid to blaze new trails.[33]

When the Women's Trade Union League held its first annual meeting in October, 1904, league members were even more optimistic than they had been in March. They enthusiastically agreed to work for the eight-hour day and for a limitation on the work week to fifty-eight hours; to achieve legislation preventing the hiring of workers with false promises; and to help displaced workers find new jobs. Several promising possibilities emerged from a wide-ranging discussion of techniques that might be used to further the league's goals. Members reaffirmed their determination to cooperate with existing trade unions in organizing women and to attempt to organize workers in trades that were not

---

*Between 1897 and 1901 the total membership of American trade unions more than doubled, rising from 447,000 to 1,124,000. But this was only the beginning. From 1900 to 1904, union membership more than doubled, rising from 868,500 to 2,072,270, with the AFL tripling its membership from 548,300 to 1,676,200 (Philip S. Foner, *History of the Labor Movement*, New York, 1964 3:27).

yet unionized. They agreed, too, to appear before women's clubs whenever the opportunity arose, to explain the aims of their new organization. Finally, they planned the establishment of a bureau of information that would offer members ready access to statistics and data on investigations of factory conditions.[34]

While its membership was still small and while concrete accomplishments still lay in the future, the new Women's Trade Union League had survived the first difficult year of its existence and approached its second with optimism.

17

The League Begins Its Work

THE ECONOMIC REVERSALS of 1904 soon dissipated the widespread optimism that had accompanied the formation of the National Women's Trade Union League in the fall of 1903. The league's initial successes had been stimulated in large measure by the unprecedented gains in union membership during the preceding years. With the rise in unemployment and the general financial dislocation in 1904, competition for existing jobs intensified, and there was a corresponding increase in the hostility of male workers toward women workers. At the same time, employers seized upon the economic recession as an opportunity to destroy the burgeoning union movement. All over the country, they banded together in associations specifically designed to crush the unions through lockouts, blacklists, ironclad oaths (pledge not to join a union), blatant abrogation of existing union contracts, injunctions, speedups, wage cuts, and an increase in the hours of work.[1]

The new National Women's Trade Union League and its affiliated local organizations faced the additional difficulty of attempting to clarify both their objectives and the means of achieving them. The female unionists and upper-middle-class reformers, who had founded the league to stimulate organization among workingwomen and to integrate them into the mainstream of the American labor movement, had assumed that their objectives would entail a dual campaign: education of workingwomen to the importance of unionization, and education of male unionists to the need to change their negative attitudes toward women workers. But at its first Executive Board meeting, the national league agreed that its most useful contribution would probably lie in providing general education and investigating factory conditions. Jane Addams and William English Walling volunteered to work on publications and union propaganda, and Emily Greene Balch, a Wellesley College professor, with a typical professorial approach, agreed to work on bibliographies on labor topics.[2]

This lack of clarity over objectives continued. At its meeting in October, 1904, the national board recommended that the league work for "the adoption of progressive industrial legislation and uniformity in factory laws throughout the United States"; arrange for speakers before women's clubs; establish a bureau of information; and further the compilation of statistics on women in the labor movement. Although the board suggested that the league should also help in the formation of labor unions for women, its main emphasis was on what today would be called public relations as opposed to the difficult work of organizing.[3]

The league's first national convention in 1907 adopted a six-point platform: "equal pay for equal work; full citizenship for women; the organization of all workers into trade unions; the eight-hour day; a minimum wage scale; and all the principles embodied in the economic program of the American Federation of Labor." But the following year the United States Supreme Court decision affirming the constitutionality of Oregon's law limiting the workday for women to ten hours (*Muller* v. *Oregon*, 1908) encouraged league members to agitate for protective legislation at the expense of organizational activities. In fact, Florence Kelley, of the National Consumers' League, who had been an advocate of women's unions, reacted to the court decision (the brief for which she had helped prepare) by abandoning her earlier union position and calling upon the WTUL to join her in campaigning for protective legislation as the remedy for female exploitation.

The league did not go that far in these early years; the Executive Board actually placed its main emphasis on the organization of women workers into trade unions. But others in the organization continued to argue that the major purposes of the league were education, the investigation of industrial conditions, and the securing of legislation.

These objectives were not contradictory, and both might have been carried on simultaneously but for the fact that the league suffered from inadequate finances. Walling had initially hoped that the trade unions would help defray the league's expenses, but he and the other league founders were disappointed in this respect. The labor movement never gave the league substantial financial assistance. Because of financial exigencies, no national convention was held in 1906, and the same reason limited the number of representatives at the 1907 convention to eight, most of whom were also delegates to the AFL convention.[4]

In 1905 the center of power in the league shifted from New York to Chicago, when Ellen M. Henrotin, a wealthy Chicago woman, was chosen national president, a post she held until 1907. Among other officers elected was Margaret Dreier of Brooklyn, another upper-class reformer. In 1903, while participating in a reform mayoralty candidate's campaign, Dreier discovered the world of New York's young immigrant women. Thereafter, her life was never the same. Disreputable employment agencies were sending agents to greet incoming ships at Castle

Garden and to coax unsuspecting young women into prostitution. Shocked by these practices, Dreier joined a determined group in lobbying for a state law to regulate these agencies. Soon after the state legislature passed the regulatory bill, Leonora O'Reilly asked Dreier to help in organizing a New York branch of the new Women's Trade Union League, and Dreier threw herself into the affairs of the fledgling organization. Although she had no prior experience in labor organization and little knowledge of the labor movement, Dreier became convinced that trade unionism was the proper vehicle to help self-supporting women help themselves. In the 1905 capmakers' strike, she took on the job of publicizing the strikers' cause to direct public opinion against the manufacturers' effort to destroy the union. Her work helped the union win an advantageous contract with the manufacturers. When the New York League's first president, Margaret Daly, found that her duties as a United Garment Workers organizer left her little time for sustained league activity, the members chose Margaret Dreier as president.

In 1905 Dreier met Raymond Robins of Chicago, who had come to Brooklyn to preach on the "social gospel." Robins, who had acquired a fortune in mining, was a social reformer dedicated to the causes of labor, religion, and progressive government. In Margaret Dreier he found a kindred soul, and in less than three months they were married. The newlyweds moved to Chicago, where they took up permanent residence in a cold-water tenement in a dilapidated settlement house in the city's worst slum. The league's national headquarters had moved to Chicago, and Margaret Dreier Robins became its moving spirit. Members rewarded her enthusiasm and dedication by electing her president of the national league, and she served in that capacity from 1907 to 1922.[5]

In January, 1905, Gertrude Barnum, a member of a wealthy Chicago family and a Hull House resident, was appointed full-time national executive secretary and national organizer of the league. Helen Marot, a Philadelphia Quaker and Socialist, joined the league in 1906 and became secretary after Barnum resigned. The wives of a number of leading New York reformers also worked with the organization, including Mrs. Walter Weyl, Mary Beard, Mrs. John Dewey, and Eleanor Roosevelt. Of all the branches, only the one in St. Louis, organized in 1908, appears to have failed to win a dedicated group of middle-class allies to the league.[6]

Soon after her appointment as national organizer, Gertrude Barnum found herself deeply involved in the struggle of the collar starchers' union in Troy, New York. The union was affiliated with the AFL's Shirt, Waist and Laundry Workers' International Union, whose status was set forth in a 1904 letter from its president, Walter Charriere, to Gompers. "It is a fact," he wrote, "that we have during our existence since our founding in December, 1901, had as members possibly 20 per cent of the people who are eligible to membership in our organization. Today we have about 7 per cent. That fact should give us cause for consideration." Charriere blamed the union's decline on "lack of interest in the trade union movement" among the workers. As soon as a woman organizer had built a solid following among the laundresses, he charged, she was lost to the union "due to the fact of her entering the matrimonial state." In addition, he cited the existence of a "very strong Laundrymen's Association," determined to maintain the open shop. He also accurately attributed the organization's poor state to the disgust female members felt at the hostility displayed toward them by AFL organizations, an attitude that caused "many to drop out of the union." As he explained to Gompers:

> A major handicap to our already exceedingly difficult task of organizing our craft throughout the country arises from the fact that in many localities the Central Labor bodies, dominated by unions composed almost exclusively of men, refuse to recognize our locals and the women delegates duly elected by them. We feel that no results can be accomplished unless this is satisfactorily adjusted, as the female members of our craft are naturally timid about joining the labor movement, and with the evidence now apparent that the unions of men in the Central bodies are hostile to them and unwilling to support them, they are even more timid. This condition does not have a tendency to increase their desire to become active in the labor movement. On the contrary, it is causing many of our members to think of leaving organized labor. Hence our appeal to you to take this up at your earliest convenience.[7]

It is not clear whether Gompers did anything in response to this appeal, but when the collar starchers in Troy struck, they did win the support of the local central labor union. The strike was precipitated when Cluett, Peabody & Co., the largest of the laundry factories in Troy, introduced a new starching machine. Other factories, all members of the Employers' Association, followed suit. The female starchers insisted that the new machine did nothing to lighten their work but did give the manufacturers an excuse to reduce their piece rates. A protest to Cluett, Peabody & Co. was ignored, but when several hundred starchers refused to accept a reduction of wages following the introduction of the machines, they were locked out. When the employers sent goods to the other factories of the Employers' Association and starchers in these factories refused to handle the collars, the strike developed into a citywide walkout of laundry girls. Within a week after the lockout, on March 5, 1905, not a single laundry in Troy connected with the Employers' Association was in operation.

The girls then proceeded to list other grievances that they insisted had to be remedied, in addition to the removal of the starching machines. They demanded an end to the practice of docking pay for what the companies called "poor work," actually caused by the use of "cheap starch," and the elimination of excessive fines for what was called "carelessness" by the company—"for every collar dropped on the floor the girl must starch five dozen collars for nothing." And they demanded union recognition.[8]

Gertrude Barnum, the National Women's Trade Union League's new organizer, and Rheta Childe Dorr, a league member, traveled to Troy to assist the strikers. New York league members helped to raise strike funds, in part by selling special editions of the *New York Tribune* dealing with the strike. The league also prevailed on Samuel Gompers to issue a public statement urging labor to support and cooperate with the strikers. By May nearly $18,000 had been sent to the strikers.[9]

But the association refused to budge. "Manufacturers have their Association, but insist on dealing with 'individual girls,' " Gertrude Barnum wrote bitterly to Margaret Dreier Robins on September 20, 1905, and she proceeded to make what was probably the first statement by a league member justifying violence: "No wonder labor uses its fists—it's about all the weapon we allow them—the law, public opinion, arbitration are all hard and slow to get."[10]

At the time this was written, twelve thousand strikers had been out for seven months, and the *Literary Digest,* in an article headed "How Women Can Conduct a Strike," called it "in many respects the most remarkable strike ever witnessed in this country." While there had been other large strikes, and even some that were longer, "few have such a record of length without serious defection from the ranks of the strikers. No other strike has been like it, however, for the 12,000 strikers are women, and the entire conduct of the strike is a revelation of what women can mean to the labor world."[11] An on-the-spot observer agreed, noting particularly

> the amazing determination shown by those women who have stood together as few working men and no other working women have stood together for such a length of time. In the history of labor in the United States, there is no record of a strike enduring for a similar period without serious defections from the ranks or any internal dissension among the strikers. The women are quietly, doggedly, courageously determined to fight to the last ditch.[12]

The uprising ultimately failed when hunger forced the workers to return to work, defeated.[13] But it did provide the league with an argument with which to answer skeptical male unionists who asked women members, "What good are the women when trouble comes?" The league noted that "the best reply . . . is an account of the strike in Troy."[14]

The Troy strike clearly demonstrated that the league could not maintain its emphasis on investigation. Even before the Troy uprising, the New York League had been turning away from investigating working conditions and toward active involvement in strikes. In January, 1904, after a 10 percent piece-rate cut, 120 young children employed at a large

Broadway box factory—many of them under twelve years of age—walked off the job. The league leaders entered the strike when the young strikers were arrested and brought to court on a charge of violently resisting the scabs who tried to break their picket lines. League leaders helped the strikers form a small union of paper box makers and raise the demands for higher wages and shorter hours. They also assisted the strikers financially and aroused public opinion in favor of the miserably exploited children. But the manufacturers, confident that they could easily replace the unskilled children, refused to recognize the small union, and the strike ended with the 10 percent rate cut that had precipitated the walkout still in effect.[15]

Undaunted by the strike's disappointing outcome,[16] and bolstered by the militancy and solidarity of the Troy strikers, the New York league began agitating for the organization of the city's laundry workers, still among the most oppressed of women wage earners. In a bulletin on laundry work, the league asked:

> How would you like to iron a shirt a minute? Think of standing at a mangle just above the washroom with the hot steam pouring up through the floor for 10, 12, 14, and sometimes 17 hours a day! Sometimes the floors are made of cement and then it seems as though one were standing on hot coals, and the workers are dripping with perspiration. Perhaps you have complained about the chemicals used in the washing of your clothes, which cause them to wear out quickly, but what do you suppose is the effect of these chemicals upon the workers? They are . . . breathing air laden with particles of soda, ammonia, and other chemicals![17]

But the league's early work with laundresses met with failure. Its laundry committee disbanded early in 1906, explaining that its efforts had been untimely—the workers themselves had never been "conscious of a common cause." The Executive Board concluded that the women were "under too high pressure and too timid to accept action."[18]

Nevertheless, at about the same time, the similarly exploited laundry women of San Francisco were successful. In some respects, conditions were even worse in the San Francisco laundries, for the girls "lived in," with each laundry providing board and lodging for its employees. And what board and lodging!

> The dormitories were wretched places, with four beds in each small room. The food was poor and scanty, and even though the girls worked until midnight or after, no food was allowed after the evening meal at 6 o'clock. Half an hour only was allowed for lunch. Early in the morning, the women were routed out in no gentle manner and by 6 o'clock the unwholesome breakfast was over, and every one hard at work.[19]

Those who "lived in" earned no more than $8.10 in cash wages each month, in addition to their room and board. Those who lived at home could expect from $17.50 to $25 a month. Both groups worked unbearably long hours under intolerable conditions. An investigation by the California State Labor Commission, prompted by letters of complaint to the newspapers, found violations of the law that forbade work after 10 P.M., with women on the job until two in the morning. As a result, a new law was passed forbidding work after seven at night.

Experience had already demonstrated that laws dealing with shorter hours, in particular, were never enforced unless the workers were sufficiently well organized to compel their enforcement. Three hundred San Francisco laundresses applied to the international union for a charter. Although the men in the laundries urged the international not to permit women to belong to their union, the parent organization, starved for membership, insisted that the women be admitted. Since the women who led the organizing drive knew full well that the laundry workers were too intimidated by their employers to join the union openly, they conducted the campaign in secrecy. Not until the union was strong enough did it announce its demands: elimination of the boardinghouse system, shorter hours, wages of $6 to $10 a week, nine holidays a year, time and a half for overtime, and a regular lunch period. The employers, caught by surprise, capitulated. Thus, at precisely the same time that the New York league was admitting defeat in its campaign to unionize the laundresses and blaming it on the women's timidity and lack of consciousness, San Francisco laundry women were forming a strong union that won gains for the workers (including the nine-hour day in 1905). It even survived the San Francisco earthquake and fire of 1906, which destroyed the union headquarters and two-thirds of the city's laundries.

A year later eleven hundred San Francisco laundry women from fourteen laundries went on strike for an eight-hour day. After eleven weeks they accepted a compromise settlement under which the fifty-one-hour week was to be reduced gradually until the eight-hour day was instituted by April, 1910. There was to be no work before seven in the morning, and all work after 5 P.M. was to be paid for at overtime rates of time and a half, except on Monday, when laundries worked until six. Year after year, the laundry union won additional gains. By 1912 it had brought wages up by 30 percent, installed safety measures in the plants, and organized all the city's steam laundries.[20]

All this was achieved without the assistance of the Women's Trade Union League. Clearly, the young league had much to learn about the techniques and strategies of unionizing women in low-wage, unskilled industries. Events were making it essential that the league act quickly to solve this problem. Workingwomen planning a strike or actually out on strike began increasingly to turn to the local leagues for advice and assistance, since they considered many labor unions as either indifferent or hostile to them. The leagues were eager to help and dispatched committees of organizers and upper-class "allies" to work with the women. They placed one major condition on the offer of assistance: the women had to pledge allegiance to the American Federation of Labor.[21]

Problems soon arose. Some allies displayed a condescending attitude toward the workingwomen, who complained bitterly. A San Francisco workingwoman league member explained, "Working women and women like that cannot mix, and the only thing to do is separate and try to be as pleasant as we can and let the outsiders think we are harmonious."[22]

Leonora O'Reilly was infuriated by the allies' praise for and the league's endorsement of Dorothy Richardson's 1905 book *The Long Day*. It will be remembered that Richardson was a teacher who had spent some time as a member of the working class, and that the book recounted her bitter experiences during this sojourn. While the book treated workingwomen sympathetically and included a plea for serious and systematic efforts to improve working conditions, Richardson contended that heredity as well as environment produced the average workingwoman's apathetic nature. O'Reilly viewed the book as an insult to workingwomen that "lacked even a scrap of sympathy or understanding of them." Charging betrayal, she resigned from the league and demanded that her name be removed from every committee. Gertrude Barnum finally succeeded in winning O'Reilly back, and conceded that she "had resigned from an overdose of allies."[23]

It was clear that what the leagues really needed was an "overdose" of bona fide union women. Fortunately, a number in each city did join the league and helped to win support for the organization among workingwomen. The first to become a dedicated WTUL member was Rose Schneiderman. As we have seen, as a direct result of her efforts, a women's local of the United Cloth Hat and Cap Makers Union was chartered in January, 1903, and Schneiderman served as its secretary and representative to the Central Labor Union of New York. The following year, Schneiderman, then only twenty-two, was elected to the union's General Executive Board, the first woman to hold such a position in the capmakers' union. In 1905, while leading a thirteen-week strike against the open shop, she was assisted by the New York WTUL, and through this contact she met the Dreier sisters, Margaret and Mary, who became her lifelong friends. With her suspicions of upper-class allies dissolved, Schneiderman joined the league, and in 1906, a few months after her initiation, the New York league elected her vice-president. The league members knew that they had acquired an invaluable asset. Not only had she already proved herself to be a successful organizer, but she was familiar with New York's East Side in ways that upper-class allies could never be. At the time, too, she was the only league member who spoke Yiddish.

In 1908 Dr. Samuel Johnson, the head of a well-known preparatory school, heard Schneiderman give an address on workingwomen, and he promptly offered her the opportunity of attending his school on a scholarship. One of the allies, an anonymous benefactress, provided a special fund to compensate her for her lost factory wages and thus enabled her to work as a special East Side organizer and attend classes concurrently.[24]

Melinda Scott was another bona fide union woman who joined the New York league early in its existence. Scott was an English-born hat trimmer who had come to the United States when she was sixteen and had helped organize, in Newark, New Jersey, a small hat trimmers' union, of which she became president. Scott's union admitted only women to membership and maintained a self-sustaining treasury. Although it was affiliated with the AFL Hat Trimmers' Union, the local insisted upon its autonomy. It formulated its own policies with respect to dues, grievances, and strikes.[25]

Margaret Daly served as the New York league's first president, but she found that her duties as leader of the UGW Overalls Makers Local No. 92 did not allow enough time for league activities. League members voted to pay Daly $3 a week so that she could continue to help them organize garment workers. Perhaps Daly's most important contribution to the league was the fact that she introduced league members to Clara Silver. Silver, a workingwoman, agreed to take on the task of organizing the buttonhole makers, who had been ignored by the UGW and forced to endure inadequate wages and unbearable conditions. With league assistance, Silver organized these young women—Italian and Jewish immigrants and English-speaking Americans alike—and brought the new Buttonhole Workers Union, of which she was president, into both the UGW and the league.[26]

In Boston, Mary Kenney O'Sullivan continued to participate in league affairs, but when her job as trade union reporter for the *Boston Globe* demanded more of her time, she urged the Boston league to enlist the services of a dynamic garment worker, Josephine Casey. Casey's forceful and aggressive personality won the confidence and allegiance of women workers, but the allies found her difficult to work with.[27]

The Chicago league recruited a considerable number of allies, but far fewer workingwomen and women unionists. Those who did become league members, however were important figures on the labor scene: Ellen Lindstrom, Catherine Goggin, Margaret Haley, and Agnes Nestor. Lindstrom, who had been walking delegate for the Special Order Clothing Workers and the UGW, became an enthusaistic member. Concerning Goggin and Haley, who were respectively president and business manager of the Chicago Federation of Teachers, *Public Opinion* wrote:

Under the executive skill of Catherine Goggin and the astute generalship of Margaret Haley, the erstwhile meek and reserved teachers have revolutionized the school-board affairs in Chicago, and introduced the unique spectacle of an educational body working hand in hand for a common purpose with the hod-carrier and the coal-teamster. More money, less work, shorter hours. To get these things, the teachers have stormed the city hall; they have pleaded their cause in the circuit courts; and when they failed to get justice in Cook County, they went to Springfield for it, and what is more to the point, got it.[28]

Agnes Nestor first went on strike in 1898, when she was not yet fifteen. The cutters at the Eisendrath glove factory in Chicago (all men) had been organized for more than a year when the banders and "glove closers" (all women)* walked out for one day in revolt against a new piecework system. "We began to chant," Nestor recalls in her autobiography, "'We are not going to pay rent for our machines!' We repeated it again and again." Few of the "kid glove girls," the aristocrats of the factory, joined their picket lines. When one of them passed the line on her way to work, she was ducked in a water trough. Nestor was accused as the striker who had done the ducking and even of having pushed a policeman into the trough as well. She contended that the charge was quite incongruous, in view of the fact that she was "small for my age and frail-looking at the time."[29] Her frailty, however, did not prevent her from leading the glove operators to victory and heading the local that was established by the victorious strikers—a glovemakers' union separate from the large cutters' union. Nestor represented her local at the Glove Makers' National Convention in 1902, and at the 1903 convention she delivered an impressive speech in which she analyzed a complex jurisdictional dispute. She soon won fame as a keen negotiator for the union. "Got a mind like a trip-hammer," a Chicago lawyer told a reporter. "Miss Nestor (in bargaining sessions) has all the details of the glove business down pat, so far as they affected the employees, and her job was to drive a bargain with the employers and get these details fixed just a little better for her people the next year. And she did it."[30]

Despite her responsibilities as local president and representative to the Chicago Federation of Labor, Nestor found time for league activities. She maintained a hectic speaking schedule, appearing frequently before various women's groups. At the 1905 and 1906 conventions of the Illinois State Federations of Women's Clubs, she spoke of her experiences as a glove worker and trade unionist and of workingwomen's

*After the gloves were cut, they went to the silker, who did the fancy stitching on the backs; then to the closer, who sewed in the thumbs and joined the pieces to the palms to form the backs; then they went to operators each of whom did a small part of the banding.

need for support in their legislative fight for an eight-hour day.[31] Illinois had enacted an eight-hour day, with a forty-eight-hour week, for women in 1893, but the statute was nullified by the Supreme Court on the ground that it violated "freedom of contract." In 1908, when the Supreme Court upheld Oregon's ten-hour law for women, the Women's Trade Union League and the Chicago Federation decided to try again in Illinois. Under Nestor's leadership they set up an "EXHIBIT TO DYNAMITE SWEATSHOPS," demonstrating the need for legislation regarding working hours. The league, the glove operators, the waitresses, and other women's groups succeeded in getting an eight-hour bill introduced. Nestor fought the violent opposition from the employers, lobbying in committee after committee, only to find that after long months of work, the law that was finally passed called for ten hours a day, seventy hours a week!*[32]

With the assistance of Michael Donnelly of the Amalgamated Meat Cutters and Butcher Workmen, Mary McDowell, president of the Illinois WTUL, had established the first women's union in the Chicago stockyards. Women's Local 183 of the Amalgamated was chartered in March, 1902, and by the spring of 1904, it had grown to a membership of over a thousand. The local was one of the first workingwomen's organizations in this country to initiate black women as members. Hannah O'Day, one of the founders, had gone to meetings of the men's union in the trade at which a black man presented white candidates for membership, and the incident hit her as a "sort of revelation." One night she was a doorkeeper at the meeting of Local 183 when a young black woman applied for admittance. Mary McDowell, who was present, noted that O'Day did not automatically turn the black applicant away:

> It was a dramatic occasion on that evening, when an Irish girl at the door called out—"A colored sister asks for admission. What shall I do with her?" And the answer came from the Irish young woman in the chair—"Admit her, of course, and let all of you give her a hearty welcome!" And as a tall, dignified, but frightened colored girl walked up the aisle between a crowd of girls, Irish, German, American, Polish, Bohemian, some well-dressed, others with a shawl or handkerchief for the head, one felt that there was here a law stronger than that of Roberts Rules of Order.[33]

Since Local No. 183 was affiliated with the Women's Trade Union League, the "frightened colored girl" who was initiated was probably the league's first black member.

---

*The eight-hour bill failed to pass by twenty-six votes, and it took from 1909 to 1937 to gain those votes. When the eight-hour law was finally won, the women sang:

"Twenty-seven years years we labored
Just to get twenty-six votes."

One of the first activities of the Chicago WTUL was to take up the cause of a group of striking corset workers in Aurora, Illinois. In 1905 the owner of the Kobo Corset Company locked out his women workers. The Chicago WTUL sent out letters to every women's club in Illinois, describing the shocking conditions under which these women worked for 25 cents a day, explaining their strike demands, and asking the club women to boycott the company's products until the strike was settled. League members traveled to Aurora to encourage the corset workers to unionize and raised money for the strikers as well. Kobo's attorney threatened the league with a suit because of the boycott letters. So much publicity ensued that the company dropped its threat. The boycott helped bring the strike to a successful conclusion, as a result of which the wages of the corset women were raised to $3 a week. The union then affiliated with the Chicago league.[34]

Both the Chicago and the national WTUL found a valuable ally in John Fitzpatrick, president of the Chicago Federation of Labor, who was instrumental in establishing a Woman's Department in the *Union Labor Advocate*, the federation's official journal.[35] The columns were edited by Ann Nichols, secretary of the Illinois WTUL, until 1908, when she went abroad to study the conditions of European workingwomen. She was succeeded by Alice Henry, who was editor until January, 1911, when the league launched its own journal, *Life and Labor*. She also edited the new periodical for four years.

Henry, an Australian reform journalist born into a radical family, studied workers' movements and the problems of handicapped children in Australia and England. She came to the United States and lectured on handicapped children in a number of cities before settling down in Chicago in 1906 to help Jane Addams campaign for municipal suffrage for women. Her meeting with NWTUL President Margaret Dreier Robins led to her appointment as office secretary of the Illinois branch, the beginning of a long relationship with the league, and a career of service on behalf of American women that ended only with her return to Australia in 1933.[36]

The May, 1908, issue of the *Union Labor Advocate*, the first issue with Henry as editor of the Woman's Department, opened with a poem that began:

> However the battle be ended,
>   Whoever sings victory's song,
> The question will not be settled,
>   If victory sides with wrong.
> The masters may win the battle,
>   And bind slavery's chains more tight,
> But no question is ever settled
>   Until it is settled right.

Then followed brief articles on the establishment of a circulating library by the Women's Trade Union League and of a Women's Trade Union League Chorus. A longer article on "The Living Wage," by Margaret Dreier Robins, emphasized that while the ballot in the hands of women would prove to be important, "the greatest immediate opportunity and one within her reach is organization. The strongest force today helping wage-earning women obtain just remuneration, normal working hours and conditions which make healthful living and efficient work possible, is the trades union organization." Annie Fitzgerald, listed as "General Organizer, American Federation of Labor," stressed the same point, but went on to assure male unionists that "women can be organized. Will you men do your share in the necessary work? Speaking for the women, I can say, we will do our share, if given proper encouragement. Send me any information that will assist me in the work of organizing women especially and I will try and do the rest."

The Woman's Department for that issue closed with several pages devoted specifically to the Women's Trade Union League, which included the national league's constitution and reported various activities of the Chicago league and unions associated with it. Six pages were devoted to the Report of the Immigration Committee of the Women's Trade Union League of Chicago, which had been formed the previous July to cooperate with the Women's Municipal League of New York City and the Council of Jewish Women "in meeting the needs of the immigrant women and girls who come to America via Ellis Island." The Immigration Committee set itself four goals: (1) to study the social and economic aspects of the immigration problem, "with special reference to women"; (2) to find work for the young immigrant woman under good conditions, "and to secure for her the necessary protection";(3) to protect both the housekeeper and the houseworker from "their common dangers"; and (4) "to bring the immigrant woman into sympathetic understanding and relationship with American ideals and standards." This last aim was not spelled out specifically.

In citing what had been accomplished toward these goals, the committee observed that "friendly relations" had been established with young immigrant women; a department of "Friendly Visiting" had been created to help the immigrant woman find "fair employment and good living conditions"; a subcommittee had been set up to prepare a list of reputable and reliable employment offices or agencies; employment had been found for several young immigrant women as domestics or in business houses; and a clearinghouse had been established "to bring friends together who have not been able to find one another."

Ordinarily, the "Woman's Department" of the *Union Labor Advocate*, like the Women's Trade Union League itself, shied away from tackling problems of the marriage relationship and tended to uphold traditional views of society. But in one issue, it reprinted an article by Charlotte Perkins Gilman, a major critic of the traditional marital relationship,* who contended in this piece that housework was a form of economic production contributing much to the financial support of husbands, and recommended that it be investigated by Congress. She concluded by warning: "Wives today realize that the situation of their work in the home is more intolerable than the possible consequences of their wage-earning."[37]

The Chicago league was also commended by the Chicago Federation of Labor for its assistance in a strike by the telephone women in 1906 to compel the Chicago Telephone Company to rescind the practice of requiring them to enter the building by the rear, forcing them to pass through a muddy alley and endure the taunts and indecent propositions of men at three saloon entrances.[38] But its most publicized activity was its sponsorship, with Jane Addams and others, of the Chicago Industrial Exhibit in March, 1907. The purpose of the display was to "reveal the hard and material side of life which goes on in factories and workshops, to epitomize the labor which clothes and feeds the modern world." Statistics displayed at the exhibit showed that women were earning an average of $7.25 a week, many as little as $3. The *Chicago Tribune* dismissed the evidence presented at the exhibit with the comment that a bright young women earning such a small sum had only herself to blame, since she could easily earn more if she applied herself. The league replied that the *Tribune* was implying that the women could do this by applying themselves to a life of vice.[39]

Afternoon teas and dances—"sociables," as league members called them—English classes for both Yiddish and Italian-speaking women, Labor Day parades and picnics, union label campaigns, folk dancing, outings, library rooms, and a workingwomen's chorus, all were brought into existence by the various leagues to attract workingwomen.[40] However, it was the need to organize women into trade unions that had given rise to the league, and social and cultural activities were no substitute for organizing. The New York league was the first to realize the dangers of

*In her most famous work, *Women and Economics: A Study of the Economic Relation between Men and Women as a Factor in Social Evolution,* Gilman contended that marriage had become an economic relationship established by law and sanctioned by religion. Society, she maintained, had conditioned women to believe that it was to their economic advantage to secure a mate, so that "the personal profit of women bears too close a relation to their power to win and hold the other sex." Sexual functions therefore became economic functions, for women degenerated into house servants, seeking the support of a husband in the inferior relationship of marriage. To achieve equality, Gilman insisted, women must obtain economic independence, and to maintain it required fundamental change in home and family relationships. She therefore advocated that the duties of housekeeping, cleaning, and maintaining central kitchens and child-care centers be performed by specialists, for only as women think, feel, live, and work outside the home do they become humanly developed and civilized.

concentrating too much time and energy on these social and cultural activities and was also the one that helped more workingwomen in struggles than any other branch during the early years of the WTUL. The New York league assisted strikes of hat trimmers, embroidery workers, textile workers, bakery and confectionery workers, white-goods workers, straw hat makers, laundry workers, paper box workers, and shirtwaist workers. Most of these strikes failed to materialize into established unions, but a few did, such as those of the shirtwaist workers and the white-goods workers, who made women's underwear and lingerie.[41] As early as 1905 the New York league helped Local No. 12—a waistmakers' local—conduct a shop-by-shop organizing campaign and several shop strikes. Herman Grossman, the ILGWU's president, and John Dyche, its executive secretary, joined the league in 1906. Dyche was a member of the Executive Board throughout 1906 and 1907, although he seldom attended meetings.[42]

The most critical problem facing the national and local leagues during these early years was their relationship with the American Federation of Labor. At first it seemed that the cordial relations established with the Chicago Federation of Labor might be extended. In his speech before the "First National Conference on Women in Industry," sponsored by the National League in 1905, Gompers commended the WTUL for broadening the work of unions and enlisting the cooperation of sympathetic men and women. The overflow audience applauded when he declared that "no intelligent man here will deny the right of women to work," but some must have felt some cynicism when he assured them that the trade unions had worked "to the full limit of their ability and power" to organize women and achieve equal pay for men and women. Still, he was applauded when he assured the league that it would "receive the cooperation of the American Federation of Labor in your cause, as a matter of right and fraternity."[43]

Encouraged by Gompers' platitudes, the WTUL linked its fate with that of the American Federation of Labor and made it clear that it would adhere scrupulously to AFL policies and principles. Indeed, a good deal of the league's time during these early years was spent in trying to appease AFL leaders in the hope that this would bring tangible results for the organization. To a limited extent, the policy did pay off. Gompers continued to encourage the league publicly and promised the federation's support, "not as a mere compliment, not from a mere desire to please . . . but as a matter of right and fraternity." He was pleased that the league's leaders sought his advice on difficult decisions and he even magnanimously allowed the league to print "Endorsed by the American Federation of Labor" on its letterhead. In a burst of enthusiasm over such concessions, the league, in its new constitution of 1907, redefined its objectives as assisting "in organizing women into trade unions . . . such unions to be affiliated, where practicable, with the American Federation of Labor."[44]

But the league soon learned that Gompers usually ignored the organization and opposed many of its suggestions. He agreed that delegates from the league could attend national AFL conventions and assured the organization that they would be "courteously welcomed"—but they could not be seated as delegates. "I am sure that I but repeat the views of many active men in the trade union movement," he wrote to Gertrude Barnum, "when I say to you that they believe that this idea of fraternal delegates with either voice or vote may go too far in upsetting the American Federation of Labor as a constituent representative body, voicing the sentiments and reaching the conclusions desired by the membership, which they are destined to affect." Thus, indirectly, Gompers was making it clear that he did not trust the league because it had too many members who were not from trade unions.[45]

Gompers was pleased when the league did his bidding, but angry when its leaders acted against his wishes. Although league delegates could not be anything but observers at AFL conventions, he was furious when the league did not schedule its conference at the same time that the AFL convention would be meeting in Pittsburgh in November, 1905. Although he invited league members to deliver addresses at several national conventions, he remained adamantly opposed to the league's repeated urgings that the AFL hire women organizers, thereby effectively demonstrating that the interests of the AFL leadership in the early twentieth century did not include women workers.[46] Finally, when the AFL Executive Council at last agreed to name a woman organizer in 1908, Gompers rejected the WTUL candidate and instead selected Annie Fitzgerald, president of the International Trade Union Label League, an enthusiastic supporter and promoter of the union label in Chicago but no friend of the league. Appointed "for the purpose of organizing wherever possible all women who work in gainful occupations," Fitzgerald took her work seriously, appealing to the male members of the AFL for assistance. But before she could get started, her commission was revoked. Despite repeated requests by the league for a new woman organizer, the AFL remained without one until the period of World War I. Fitzgerald's remarkably brief tenure in office was the only concession made by the AFL leadership to the rising demands for women organizers.[47]

In June, 1908, a request to AFL headquarters that Annie Fitzgerald be sent to New York to help the league in that city organize women received the curt reply that since Fitzgerald was no longer an organizer, the request had been forwarded to Herman Robinson, its New York organizer. Robinson, assuming that the league's failure to consult him in the first place was a personal slur, bitterly condemned the league leadership. The fact is that league members had grown increasingly disturbed by the inadequacy of the AFL's support for women who were organizing or on strike. Even Melinda Scott, a staunch AFL supporter, had told Leonora O'Reilly that "the AFL is a bag of wind."[48]

Still, the league was caught in a bind. AFL policies and practices weakened its own efforts to unionize workingwomen, for the league had to contend with the fact that the AFL's craft union orientation rejected women as unskilled, that AFL discriminatory policies toward immigrants from southern and eastern Europe rejected women as immigrants, and that male chauvinism in the AFL's ranks rejected women as women. Indeed, the AFL's policy of craft unionism alone automatically excluded most women workers, for the great majority were unskilled manual laborers or semiskilled machine operators and could not be readily organized along craft lines.[49]

League leaders could not hope to challenge the powerful union leaders, so they adopted a policy of appeasement, attempting diplomatically to coax union officials to include women in their programs. The delicate problem posed for the league by the AFL's position on union dues is a typical case in point. Dues of $4 to $7 a week were impossibly high for many workingwomen. Yet league leaders, fearful of antagonizing AFL union leaders by challenging the federation's dues standards, simply expected women to pay whatever dues and initiation fees an AFL affiliate required. Moreover, in deference to the AFL, the New York league denied affiliation to the Progressive Rolled Cigarette Makers, a small independent women's union that had been forced to organize separately because the AFL International Cigar Makers charged such high dues and initiation fees as to exclude these women, in effect. After Gompers condemned the Rolled Cigarette Makers as a dual union, the league denied its request for affiliation.[50]

If work with the AFL's top leadership was difficult and unrewarding, that with the male-dominated leadership of international unions, local labor unions, and city central labor bodies was even more so. Only a few national trade unions during this period actually forbade the admission of women. Among these were the Barbers, the Watchcase Engravers, the Switchmen, and the Molders. The last-named union resolved in 1907 to seek "the restriction of the further employment of women labor in union core rooms and foundries, and eventually the elimination of such labor in all foundries." A penalty of a $50 fine or expulsion was levied on any member who dared to give instruction to female laborers in any branch of the trade.

But constitutional clauses barring women were only the most overt method used to achieve this end. Some unions admitted women employed in certain branches but not in others; usually the women were excluded from the main branches of the trade. (The Upholsterers, for

example, admitted women when they were employed as seamstresses.)
Practically none of the AFL unions opened new employment opportunities to women, and by restricting their apprenticeship programs to
men, they confined women to the unskilled jobs. "It is an evil combination," one woman protested to Gompers. "Lack of skill keeps many of us
from entering unions of skilled craftsmen, and rigid apprenticeship
regulations prevent us from becoming apprentices to the trade and
thereby rising to the rank of skilled workers."[51]

The AFL did point out to the league that many of the international
unions did not openly discriminate against women, and that some had
even passed regulations reducing fees and dues for women and had
adopted resolutions in favor of apprenticeship training for women and
equal pay for equal work. But it ignored the fact that the demand for
equal pay for equal work was often used as a device to eliminate women
from the trade, since experience had shown that when employers were
required to pay women the same wages as men, they simply stopped
employing women. The federation leaders also failed to mention the
huge gap between the policies of the national unions and the practices of
their locals. Actually, the local unions had final control in carrying out
policy, and many of them simply disregarded the declarations of their
international union, denying admission to women applicants, refusing to
permit the granting of a special charter for a women's local, and reject-
ing female applicants holding transfer cards. In 1902 the national secretary of the Amalgamated Meat Cutters & Butcher Workmen called
upon the local unions to organize all women in the industry, correctly
pointing out: "It is useless . . . to attempt to stem the tide of female workers. It now rests with us to bring them into our organization . . . to see
that they are affiliated with us . . . and that we extend to them the protection which thorough organization affords . . . is a duty which we cannot
shirk without grave danger to ourselves." But when the women in a
sausagemakers' department formed a union in 1903, the local not only
refused to grant them a charter but demanded, as part of their agreement with the employers, "Abolition of Women Labor in the Sausage
Department."[52]

Moreover, the AFL refused to act against internationals that had
constitutional clauses barring women or discriminated against women in
their locals, on the ground that each international union was autono-
mous and could not be disciplined. Again and again, league organizers
helped to unionize women workers only to find the international union
involved unwilling to grant the group a charter on a variety of grounds:
because they were insufficiently skilled or "because the men's union
would not allow it" or because "the International is not ready to organize
the women" or even, in the case of a union of female tobacco workers,
"because women had no colour discrimination."[53] In anger and disgust,

league leaders appealed to the AFL Executive Council either to take action to compel the international unions to accept the women or to charter them directly to the federation in separate federal labor unions. Some male unionists supported this appeal. In October, 1904, the president of District No. 5 of the United Mine Workers wrote to Gompers:

> Several groups of the working women of the Pittsburgh area requested me to give them information on how they could get organized. I contacted various unions of the whole trades involved after which the women themselves approached them. I have learned that these women were told that there was no room for them in the unions they approached. Most of the women are so discouraged that they are ready to abandon the plan to organize, and I wonder if there is not some way that they could be attached to the American Federation of Labor.[54]

But such appeals always came up against the autonomy doctrine, and league leaders were coldly informed that "the American Federation of Labor had no authority to touch the question, either through its Executive Council or in conventions—that so long as the Internationals claimed jurisdiction, the AFL could never compel them to accept women as members nor issue federal charters to women whom the International refused to organize." In one instance, the league asked whether the AFL could not say to the International Typographical Union: "If you will not organize the [women] copyholders or accept them into your organization, you must relinquish the jurisdiction." The answer was still "No!"[55]

In 1907 members of United Garment Workers Local No. 23 in Chicago discovered that Robert Noren, UGW leader in that city, had issued labels to shops that employed nonunion finishers and did not maintain even the minimum union standards. Noren had also pocketed union dues and refused to call meetings at which members could raise these issues. The Chicago leagues, at the union women's request, investigated the situation and found appalling unsanitary conditions, prevalent use of child labor, and home finishing by shops that had been given the union label—in short, the very conditions the label was supposed to eliminate.

At about the same time, the New York league discovered that a similar situation existed in that city, where UGW's Local No. 102, a small union of female buttonhole makers in the men's garment industry that the WTUL had helped to launch, was finding it difficult to recruit new members because shops employing unorganized buttonhole workers were using the UGW union label. Here, too, as in Chicago, the shops with the label operated under abominable conditions.[56]

In both cities the UGW women and the leagues brought the issue to the attention of the UGW's national leadership, urging it to investigate the complaints and, if they proved accurate, to remove the union label immediately from the offending shops and correct the other grievances. The UGW leadership did not even respond to the requests, and in Chicago, Noren took reprisals against the women who had complained by outlawing their local, declaring it out of business, tearing its charter from the wall, demanding its books, and publicly organizing a new local union. With the aid of the Chicago league, the desperate women outlined their problem to AFL Secretary Frank Morrison and appealed to him to investigate the entire controversy. Morrison's curt reply summed up the problem facing workingwomen and the leagues: "I desire to say that an appeal of this character should not be taken to the American Federation, but to the next convention of the United Garment Workers of America." Morrison then read the complaining women a lecture: "Autonomy means that it [the trade union] has the right to carry on its business in such a way as its members shall dictate without interference by the American Federation of Labor.... It should be the duty of every local union to comply with the instructions of their officers."[57]

Finally, members of Local No. 232 turned to the Chicago Federation of Labor for help. The Federation's Executive Board met on October 6, 1909, and agreed to hear the case. An exhaustive study by a special committee determined that Noren had indeed sold union labels to nonunion shops and had worked relentlessly to destroy Local No. 232. The federation's final report supported Local No. 232 and urged the UGW to act in a proper trade union spirit to adjust their grievances. Moreover, the Executive Board condemned numerous UGW practices, especially its label policy. Finally, the Board urged the women of Local No. 232 "not to be intimidated or browbeaten into submission, but to stand for what they believe to be right, square and honest."[58]

Despite the Chicago Federation of Labor's unequivocal stand, Robert Noren's position was upheld by the UGW General Executive Board, while Local No. 232 remained outside the UGW. To the AFL Leadership, there had never been an issue, and the situation had not changed one iota.[59]

From its inception, the WTUL's primary objective was to encourage women to form unions or to join existing locals and then to affiliate to the appropriate AFL national union. But AFL principles and practices repeatedly frustrated the organization's efforts to achieve that objective. In one respect, women suffered more from these principles and practices than even black men. Although the AFL agreed, as a "solution" to racial discrimination by its affiliates, to charter black workers excluded from all-white unions—thereby giving its blessing to Jim Crow trade unionism—it refused to accord even this possibility to women. The result, the leagues were often compelled to report sadly, was that the women they had helped to organize were forced to abandon the union "and as a group, are lost to organized labor."[60]

The following experience is an example of the attitude of some women workers toward AFL central labor unions. On May 30, 1905, thirty Polish women employed in the spool room of the Chicopee Manufacturing Company in Chicopee, Massachusetts, went out on what was called "a small strike." The women refused to accept a speedup in their work and a reduction of 2 cents a box on the warp they picked, explaining that "they consider their present wages small enough." "The most skilled," they told a reporter, "Get only $4 a week by hard work."[61] When the AFL Central Labor Council in nearby Springfield advised the strikers to return to work while it arbitrated the dispute with the company, the women refused. They informed the press that the council had always been hostile to the workingwomen of Chicopee and could not now be trusted to defend them adequately. "The strikers refuse to allow the men from the Council to negotiate for them, and will only arbitrate the strike directly with a committee from their own number," wrote a rather astonished reporter for the *Springfield Republican*.[62] The strikers' committee negotiated with the aid of a "Polish girl interpreter," while their sisters picketed the plant. Unable to break the strike, the company made what the local paper called "the liberal proposition that the girls choose a committee of their own from among fair-minded citizens, those in Chicopee preferred, and leave the matter to be settled by them." The paper added somewhat sadly: "The girls indignantly refused this, and, in fact, will not arbitrate, except with a committee from their own members."[63]

The strikers' persistence paid off. "Strikers Back at Work," read the report from Chicopee in the *Springfield Republican* of June 15, 1905. The women who had resisted Central Labor Union mediation and conducted their own negotiations through their own interpreter had won all their demands.

The New York league probably had the Chicopee experience in mind, as well as its own disappointing experiences with male-dominated international unions and the AFL hierarchy, when it pointed out in its 1907–1908 report: "While the Women's Trade Union League has been working for the organization of women into trade unions, it has recognized that the direct work of organization will be done by the women themselves and that its own work is largely educational."[64]

A year later, in 1909, a revolution began in the garment trades that was to prove the validity of this estimate. However, the role of the Women's Trade Union League in this series of the most famous women's struggles in American labor history was destined to be far more than just "educational."

18

The Waistmakers' Revolt

On November 24, 1909, eighteen thousand waistmakers in Manhattan and Brooklyn walked out of nearly five hundred shops. By the end of the day, more than twenty thousand workers were on strike.

The women working in New York City's dress and waistmaking shops astonished the nation by staging this dramatic strike. This great uprising served as a catalyst for workers in other branches of the industry. And it spearheaded the drive that turned the shells of unions into mass organizations, thereby laying the foundation for stable and lasting organizations in the women's and men's clothing industries and for the widespread unionization of women workers.

The manufacture of shirtwaists was a comparatively new branch of the garment trade. It had developed rapidly after 1900, especially in New York and Philadelphia, and by 1909 there were about six hundred waist and dress shops in New York City, employing from 35,000 to 40,000 workers. About 80 percent of them were young women between the ages of sixteen and twenty-five, most of them unmarried, two-thirds of them Jewish, with a couple of thousand Italians and a few hundred blacks. Men accounted only for about 20 percent of the workers, but they occupied the high-paying jobs that demanded special skill and experience.[1]

While dress- and waistmakers experienced the typical economic inequities that were prevalent throughout the industry, working conditions in this segment of the industry were better than those in other branches. Since most of the shops had been set up comparatively recently, they were more sanitary than those in the rest of the industry. Most work rooms contained windows that provided adequate lighting. Wages, too, were generally higher than those in other branches of the trade. However, they varied both from shop to shop and within shops, depending on skill and on the prevailing system of work. Despite the fact that by the end of 1909 the industry was prosperous, wage rates had fallen steadily since the 1908 depression. Thus, early in 1908 a woman machine operator on waists could earn as much as $12 or $13 a week at piece rates, whereas late in 1909 she was lucky to make $9 or $10. In addition, some workers received their wages directly from inside subcontractors who negotiated individually with the manufacturer.* This system inevitably created inequities in the pay scale. Some women received only $3 or $4 per week, while others, who worked directly for the manufacturer, received as much as $15 or $20 per week. As in other branches, wages fluctuated because of the seasonal nature of the industry. The workers' annual income was cut considerably by enforced idleness for three months of the year. One contemporary study declared that the average weekly wage for the industry was $9, but seasonal layoffs brought the average down to only $5—and this was for fifty-six to fifty-nine hours' work each week, with only the usual rate for overtime.[2]

The inside subcontractors exploited the very young women through an oppressive system of apprenticeship. Workers were subjected to strict discipline: subcontractors and examiners levied fines for lateness and for sewing errors. "In the shops we don't have names," declared one waistmaker, "we have numbers." Manufacturers charged for needles and thread—often as much as $1.50 a week—as well as for electric power, for the chairs the workers sat on, and for the lockers in the shops, all at a substantial profit. They fined their employees for being a few minutes late or for accidentally spoiling a piece of cloth. A ticket system prevailed, under which a worker, after completing a task or piece, would receive a tag, which was turned in at the end of a period as the basis for calculating her wages. Workers complained that the manufacturers deliberately made the tags very small, in the hope that some of the workers would lose them. This is exactly what often happened, and as a result the worker received pay for only part of her output.

Because the industry operated on a piecework basis, the employer or his agent could easily show favoritism to "cooperative" workers by giving them larger bundles of work. To top it all off, the entire system was characterized by tyrannical bosses, nagging, pettiness, espionage, favoritism, rudeness, and discourtesy.[3]

Local No. 25 of the ILGWU had jurisdiction over the waistmakers. Founded in 1906 by seven young women and six men, the local had failed to attract many members. Just four weeks before the strike, union

---

*Subcontracting was a variation of the traditional contracting system in the garment trades. Like the contractor, the subcontractor contracted with a manufacturer to complete a specified amount of work for an agreed-upon price. Like the contractor, too, he supervised a team of workers in completing the bundles of garments. Unlike the contractor, however, the subcontractor did not own a shop but worked in the manufacturers' large inside establishments. Subcontractors, not manufacturers, were responsible for paying their workers, and when manufacturers lowered rates, the subcontractors passed the decrease on to their teams of workers.

officers noted that the membership had barely reached eight hundred workers, described as irregular and unenthusiastic. Few of them had any knowledge of union organization. To be sure, Women's Trade Union Leaguers, especially East Side organizer Rose Schneiderman, had helped small groups of dressmakers learn the principles and practices of unionism and had convinced a group to affiliate with Local No. 25 in 1908. However, men controlled the union, holding all the officers and eight of the fifteen positions on the Executive Board.[4]

Nevertheless, unrest had been building steadily and visibly for at least a year before the uprising. Throughout late 1908 and 1909 walkouts became increasingly frequent in the large waist factories in the Washington Square area. Confrontations between manufacturers and workers over wage and piece-rate cuts, subcontracting, and the practice of charging workers for electricity, needles, and other materials became increasingly sharp.

In late July, 1909, the two hundred employees of the Rosen Brothers ladies' waist shop walked out on strike in protest against inadequate pay scales. During the strike, thugs assaulted pickets, and the police, obviously acting at the employers' request, arrested women who shouted "scab" at strikebreakers. However, the strikers' perseverance brought results, for on August 26, Rosen Brothers capitulated. The victorious strikers gained full union recognition and a 20 percent wage increase.[5]

Early in September, one hundred and fifty young women walked out of the Leiserson factory, accusing their employer of paying starvation wages. The strike spread to the Triangle Waist Company (which was to become nationally infamous in 1911 because of the tragic fire on its premises). After Triangle's owners learned that a few of their employees had joined the union, they promptly locked out the entire shop of five hundred workers and advertised for replacements. The infuriated employees literally besieged Local No. 25's headquarters and signed up en masse with the union.[6]

Although some magistrates conceded that New York State law sanctioned the right to picket, they countenanced arrests and beatings of the strikers, many of them teenagers. Every day, scores of pickets were fined or sentenced to the workhouse. On the other hand, the magistrates discharged entire contingents of thugs arrested for assaulting young strikers, in spite of their criminal records.[7]

Despite the militancy of the strikers, it was clear that shop-by-shop strikes would not work and that only by tying up the entire trade during the busy season could the workers gain their demands. On October 21, 1909, a general meeting of union members declared for a general strike in the trade, demanding an immediate 10 percent increase in wages and recognition of the union by the employers.[8]

Meanwhile the striking women of Local No. 25 received new moral and material support. The United Hebrew Trades, the central organization of Jewish unionists in the city, began a fund-raising appeal among trade unionists and succeeded in obtaining pledges from the working shirtwaist employees to give 10 cents each on behalf of the strikers. The Women's Trade Union League of New York City, which had been helping the strikers from the outset of the walkouts, now established a corps of forty-eight volunteers, generally women from the upper middle classes, who accompanied pickets in order to prevent their unwarranted arrests. They were attacked by the police on the picket line along with the strikers, and some were even arrested. But when the police learned that they were dealing with socially prominent women, they changed their tactics. Mary Dreier, the league's president, was arrested by accident and quickly released when her identity was discovered in court. The arresting officer apologized humbly, asking, "Why didn't you tell me you was a rich lady? I'd never have arrested you in the world." Such obvious bias in favor of the rich was widely publicized by the WTUL and was contrasted with police outrages committed against the strikers, thereby arousing public sympathy for the girls. The police, in turn, grew resentful of the league's support of the strike and kept asking why educated women insisted on involving themselves with lower-class workingwomen strikers.[9]

During the weeks of the shop strikes, about two thousand workers joined the union, and hundreds crowded the cramped union office daily with talk of a general strike. Now the union, too, began to consider calling a general strike. Because the New York WTUL had been active in assisting the workers in the Triangle, Leiserson, and Rosen strikes, and because any large undertaking would require the league's financial assistance, the union shared its deliberations with that organization. The two organizations met on November 22 to discuss the question of an industry-wide walkout, as well as to protest actions of the struck companies and the police. Among the speakers scheduled to address the rank-and-file workers were Samuel Gompers, Mary Dreier, Meyer London, and Ernest Bohm, secretary of the New York City Central Federated Union.[10]

On the night of the meeting Cooper Union auditorium was packed with an overflow crowd of shirtwaist workers. For over two hours, as the tension in the auditorium mounted, the workers listened to one speaker after another urging caution and moderate action. Gompers reminded the audience that he always looked upon strikes as the method of last resort. He cautioned the workers against acting too hastily, adding, however: "If you cannot get the manufacturers to give you what you want, then strike. And when you strike, let the manufacturers know that you are on strike." Wild applause followed this remark, but there was still no action for a general strike.

Finally, after hearing one moderate voice after another, a young workingwoman leaped to her feet and asked for the floor. The workers in the audience recognized her as one of the most militant rank-and-filers—Clara Lemlich from Leiserson's, where the workers had already been on strike for eleven weeks. They knew, too, that she had just returned from the hospital after having been brutally beaten on the picket line. Barely five feet tall and not more than twenty years old, she spoke in impassioned Yiddish—the native tongue of the majority of the shirtwaist workers—and proceeded to berate the cautious speakers who had held the platform during the evening. She concluded: "I have listened to all the speakers, and I have no further patience for talk. I am one who feels and suffers from the things pictured. I move we go on a general strike!"

Instantly, the crowd was on its feet—adult women, men, and teenagers—cheering, stamping, crying approval. Chairman Feigenbaum called for a vote. Three thousand voices shouted their unanimous approval, waving hats, handkerchiefs, and other objects.

"Do you mean faith?" cried the chairman. "Will you take the old Hebrew oath?"

Three thousand right arms shot up, and three thousand voices repeated the oath: "If I turn traitor to the cause I now pledge, may this hand wither from the arm I now raise."

Meanwhile, messengers carried the news of the meeting to the other halls where the waistmakers had gathered. There the strike vote was ratified just as enthusiastically,[11] and thus began the famous labor struggle that has become known as the "Uprising of Twenty Thousand,"* "women's most significant struggle for unionism in the nation's history."[12]

Both Local No. 25 and the WTUL were stunned by the waistmakers' response to the general strike call. At most, they had expected four or five thousand Jewish workers to strike.[13] Instead, on the first day, eighteen to twenty thousand shirtwaist workers came out in response to the strike call. Women by the thousands stormed the small union office on Clinton Street to enroll in Local No. 25. Soon, nearly thirty thousand operators, cutters, pressers, and finishers were on strike. Although

*Estimates of the number of strikers range from the New York State Department of Labor Bureau of Mediation and Arbitration figure of fifteen thousand to Local No. 25's estimate of forty thousand. The estimate of thirty thousand is based on Helen Marot's calculation based on WTUL records. (Helen Marot, "A Woman's Strike: An Appreciation of the Shirtwaist Makers of New York," *Proceedings of the Academy of Political Science, City of New York* 1 [1910]: 122. The report on the strike in the *Annual Report of the Women's Trade Union League of New York, 1909–1910,* is entitled "The League and the Strike of the Thirty Thousand" [New York, 1910], p. 11.)

four-fifths of the female strikers were Jewish, several thousand Italian and nonimmigrant women participated as well.*

Many small waist manufacturers, unable to stand even a short interruption during the busy season, were soon parading to union headquarters to sign agreements with the union. These agreements included a provision for a union shop; a fifty-two-hour week; limitation of overtime work; equal division of work among union members; and a price list of changing styles to be fixed by conference between employer, employee, and union representatives. In addition, the employers promised to employ only contractors who used union labor; to furnish machines, needles, thread, and other supplies; and to allow a weekly check of their payroll by union officials. Any party violating the agreement would have to pay a $300 penalty. By the time the strike was hardly four days old, almost half of the original twenty thousand strikers had won improved conditions, including union contracts, and had returned to work.[14]

Because many employers made quick settlements, Local No. 25 and the WTUL were optimistic that the strike would be short and spectacularly successful. But the employers who settled at once were those who could not afford a protracted work stoppage. The larger firms that dominated the industry were determined to fight it out to the bitter end. They formed the Association of Waist and Dress Manufacturers of New York and, on November 27, declared open war against the union, recruiting strikebreakers and vowing to hold out against a settlement. A member of the association warned that a trade agreement with the union was not "worth the paper it was written upon" and urged employers who had signed such agreements to repudiate them. It warned that only manufacturers who opposed unionism would be eligible for membership in the employers' organization. "We insist upon the open shop," the president declared, "and from that stand we will not budge."[15]

Thus, very early, the strike settled down to a protracted campaign of siege warfare against the larger firms. It required a good deal of spirit and devotion to unionism to maintain this siege. The winter of 1909–1910 was exceptionally cold and snowy in New York City. Many a frostbitten young picket was taken directly to the hospital or clinic. In addition, the ILGWU, then only nine years old, was not yet firmly established and had a scanty treasury, so that regular strike benefits were few and far between and the strikers were hard put to meet their rent and grocery bills. Most of the original $60,000 strike fund and the funds

*Helen Marot calculated that the overwhelming majority of the strikers were Russian-Jewish women. She broke down the ethnic backgrounds of the strikers as follows: 20,000 to 21,000 Russian-Jewish women, 6,000 Jewish men (cutters and pressers), 2,000 Italian women, and approximately 1,000 native-born American women (ibid.).

collected during the strike had to be used to pay the fines of women convicted by biased magistrates.[16]

The members of the association tried to break the strike by exploiting Jewish and Italian antagonisms and sought to drive a wedge between the girls by keeping black workers on the job, importing professional strikebreakers, and arranging with out-of-town plants, particularly in Philadelphia, to supply them with goods. But they depended primarily on brute force, arrests, and convictions. By December 22, 1909, over seven hundred pickets had been arrested; nineteen were sentenced to the workhouse on Blackwell's Island on charges of disorderly conduct and vagrancy, and the rest were fined. At Blackwell's Island, the young girls were thrown into cells with prostitutes, sex perverts, and criminals.[17]

A magistrate summed up the prevailing attitude of the courts in these words: "You have no right to picket. . . . Every time you go down there you will get what is coming to you and I shall not interfere." Regardless of the evidence, or lack of it, the girls were usually convicted. When prosecutors failed to substantiate their charge that Nennie Bloom had assaulted a forelady, Magistrate Joseph Corrigan fined her $10 for disorderly conduct and stated that if more strikers appeared before him, he would send them to the workhouse. Another magistrate declared bluntly that while "the higher courts have held that strikers had the right to employ pickets and call names," he personally would forbid the right to picket. Still another magistrate told a group of bruised and bleeding girls: "You are on strike against God and nature, whose prime law is that man shall earn his bread in the sweat of his brow." Members of the WTUL cabled this remark to George Bernard Shaw, who replied: "Delightful. Medieval America is always in the most intimate personal confidence of the Almighty."[18]

The cruel treatment of the female strikers failed to dampen their spirit. "There never was anything like it," one union official declared in amazement. "An equal number of men never would hold together under what these girls are enduring."[19] It was precisely because women, who were not expected to take either their jobs or unionism seriously, were such militant strikers that the press expressed such amazement and devoted so much space to the waistmakers' uprising. The New York Women's Trade Union League, in its role as liaison between the strikers and the public, capitalized on the fact that the majority of the strikers were women. Members circulated detailed reports of police attacks on peaceful pickets, kept a careful tally of arrests, and described the callousness of police magistrates who sentenced young women to several weeks of hard labor for offenses as minor as yelling "scab" at strikebreakers. The league volunteered legal services in police courts, provided witnesses for arrested strikers, cross-examined those who testified, raised $29,000 in bail, and acted as a complainant at police headquarters. On December 6 the league established a strike headquarters, encouraging women who had been arrested to come in and report their experiences in detail. From these reports they drew up rules for pickets designed to minimize the chances of arrest. League members distributed copies of the "rules" to all strikers.[20]

League members also organized workingwomen's marches and rallies. On December 3 a group of ten thousand striking waistmakers, carrying banners that read "Peaceful Picketing is the Right of Every Woman," marched four abreast to City Hall to protest to Mayor McClellan against the abuse they had received at the hands of his "cossacks." Three league women—Ida Rauh, Mary Dreier, and Helen Marot—along with a representative group of strikers, handed the petition to the mayor and described to him their own experiences and those of other workingwomen at the hands of "New York's finest." The mayor assured the committee that he would take up the matter with the police commissioner.[21]

Strike headquarters were at the league office, where the WTUL provided an information bureau, coordinated all activities, dispatched lecturers, defended pickets, revitalized the practically defunct Local No. 25, and helped lift the morale of the young demonstrators. WTUL members and strikers edited and sold a special issue of the *New York Call* and the *New York Journal,* in which appeals for contributions were interspersed with a dramatic history of the strike. League members spoke to civic groups and church organizations, with invariably enthusiastic results. After Rose Schneiderman delivered a short speech at the Manhattan Congregationalist Church, its members passed a resolution supporting the strikers and urging the public "to find out who are these mean manufacturers . . . that are grinding down the girls." Even the Consumers' League departed from its customary practice and gave public support to the waistmakers—the first such action since 1905, when it had supported the strike of the laundry starchers in Troy.[22]

Accompanied by a sixteen-year-old waistmaker who had spent thirty days in jail for picketing, Rose Schneiderman raised money lecturing in colleges and at parlor meetings in Massachusetts with the president of the Boston WTUL. The league's Vassar graduates took Schneiderman and Pauline Newman, a young waistmaker who had joined the league during the strike, to Poughkeepsie to speak to the college community. Under the league's auspices, young strikers spoke about their working conditions at clubs and women's colleges. At one widely publicized luncheon at the Colony Club, one young woman after another told of her experiences as trimmer, tucker, operator, or finisher. "I can trim the neatest waist in town," one young striker told the club women, "but I get only $6.50. . . . I support our family." Such testimony brought over

$20,000 in contributions from clubwomen and college students. In addition, as a result of the league publicity, dozens of students from Vassar, Bryn Mawr, Barnard, and Wellesley served as volunteer pickets.[23]

Anne Morgan, J. P. Morgan's niece, was one of the women who was deeply stirred by the description of the working and living conditions of the waistmakers. Although she had never before shown any interest in labor disputes or in the trade union movement, she appeared on the waistmaker's picket line soon after the strike began. She explained her interest in the strike to the *New York Times:*

> We can see from the general trade conditions how difficult it must be for these girls to get along. Of course, the consumer must be protected, but when you hear of a woman who presses forty dozen skirts for eight dollars a week, something must be wrong. And fifty-two hours a week seems little enough to ask. These conditions are terrible, and the girls must be helped to organize and to keep up their organizations, and if public opinion is on their side they will be able to do it.

The New York league immediately made Anne Morgan a temporary member of its Executive Board.[24]

Another new upper-class board member was Alva Belmont, widow of Oliver P. Belmont. A few days after the strike began, she appeared on a waistmakers' picket line and announced her support for the strikers. "It was my interest in women, in women everywhere and of every class, that drew my attention and sympathies first to the striking shirtwaist girls," she explained to the press. "Women the world over need protection and it is only through the united efforts of women that they will get it."[25] As president of the Political Equality League, one of the city's newer and more active suffrage organizations, Belmont repeatedly linked the suffrage cause and the strike. At a highly publicized appearance at Jefferson Market Courthouse, she made this clear:

> I have arrived at the conclusion that we would all be better off if we visited the night court more frequently. Conditions in the mismanaged social life of New York City are nowhere else so forcefully brought out. . . .
> There will be a different order of things when we have women judges on the bench. Let me assure you, too, that the time is not far away when we will have women judges. During those six hours I spent in that police court I saw enough to convince me and all who were with me beyond the smallest doubt of the absolute necessity for woman suffrage . . . and the direct influence of women over judges, jury and policemen.[26]

Alva Belmont arranged weekly suffragist motorcades in which rich suffrage supporters drove striking shirtwaist makers through the neighborhoods of the Lower East Side to publicize the struggle. In addition, she hired the Hippodrome for a huge "women's rally" and invited leading suffragists and trade unionists to speak. An audience of eight thousand, including suffragists, trade unionists, Socialists, and even anarchists, applauded wildly as Reverend John Howard Melish of Brooklyn; Rose Pastor Stokes, Socialist organizer and lecturer; and Dr. Anna Howard Shaw, Methodist preacher and president of the National American Woman Suffrage Association, pleaded for justice for the shirtwaist strikers.* Leonora O'Reilly, with tears streaming down her face, delivered a heartrending account of a young garment worker's life of toil and despair. Several young strikers narrated their experiences at the hands of the police, the magistrates, and the employers' hired thugs.[27]

On December 20 the strike spread to Philadelphia. Leaders of Local No. 25 had known for some time that New York manufacturers were sending materials to Philadelphia for completion. ILGWU officials visited Philadelphia in November and early December determined to halt the manufacture of goods destined for New York. However, the Philadelphia strike grew, basically, out of the same deplorable conditions that existed in New York. The conditions of the fifteen thousand waistmakers in Philadelphia were summed up in an interview with an eighteen-year-old waistmaker, who told a reporter for the *Public Ledger* that she had gone into the shops seven years earlier, then only eleven years old. When there was plenty of work, she could sometimes earn as much as $9 a week, but in the summer she could not average more than $3, and some weeks she made so little that she could barely pay her carfare. Then there were the petty exactions: 2 cents a week to pay for an outing sponsored by the proprietor every summer; 25 cents for a key to the closet; needles sold at four times what they cost; and the tyranny of some of the forewomen, who kept the girls at their machines all day long in the summertime, even when there was no work and they earned nothing. Excuses of illness made no difference: "She would keep you in if you were most dead."[28]

While only 3,500 of these workers belonged to the union, officials believed that the nonunion workers would join the walkout if they called a strike. And so, demanding union recognition, a nine-hour day, a fifty-hour week, and uniform wage scales, the Philadelphia dress and waistmakers walked out in a general strike.[29]

The Philadelphia strike followed much the same course as that in New York: the waistmakers faced "gorillas" and police brutality, and the magistrates of Philadelphia were eager to sentence pickets to the county prison. The Central Labor Union endorsed the strike, and many trade

*The National American Woman Suffrage Association itself, however, refused to endorse the shirtwaist strike. A few days before the Hippodrome rally, the organization issued a statement stressing that it "neither stands for labor organization nor against it." Dr. Shaw, the statement continued, would speak as an individual at the Hippodrome meeting, and not as the association's president (*New York Times,* Dec. 3, 1909).

unions supported it. Throughout their fight, moreover, the striking workers were given support by leading society women and progressive-minded college women.[30]

WTUL leaders Margaret Dreier Robins and Agnes Nestor hurried from Chicago to Philadelphia and opened an office in the heart of the factory district, where pickets could report and strikers could receive sandwiches and coffee. The youth and enthusiasm of the strikers amazed league members. Day in and day out, despite attacks by the "gorillas" and arrests by the police, they were on the picket lines. On January 14, 1910, when a severe snowstorm hit the city, "the pickets proved faithful to their duty."

Society and college women, some in caps and gowns, mingled with the waistmakers on picket lines, and as in New York the police, in rounding up pickets, arrested a number of the upper-class women. Among them was Martha Gruening, a graduate student at Bryn Mawr College, who patrolled the street carrying a placard demanding justice for union girls. Charged with inciting to riot, she explained to the magistrate that she visited the factory daily to determine whether the police were arresting workers unjustly. He exploded: "It is women of your class, not the actual strikers, who have stirred up all this strife. Had you and your kind kept out of this, it would have been over long ago." She was sent to prison with three shirtwaist strikers.[31] The Philadelphia newspapers strongly condemned Mayor John Rayburn's administration for its lack of courtesy to the upper-class women. But the police continued to arrest and arraign young Philadelphia society women. In one case, a prosecutor angrily charged a woman with perjury for overstating the property she put up for bail.[32]

On January 12, 1910, the Philadelphia *Public Ledger,* under the headline "Women of Social Distinction Give Aid to Strikers," noted that this marked a turning point in Philadelphia's labor history, since "this large and influential class heretofore have not shown concern in labor movements of any sort." The actions of Bryn Mawr students as pickets provoked the comment from an officer of the college that "our girls do not do that sort of thing, you know." But the growing list of arrested Bryn Mawr girls contradicted her denial.[33]

On January 13, the Pennsylvania Women's Suffrage Association endorsed a strike for the first time in its history by calling upon the manufacturers to recognize the shirtwaist workers' union. After the resolution was unanimously adopted, college students went through the audience attired in caps and gowns and passed collection baskets. Several hundred dollars was turned over to the strikers.[34]

These were not the only unusual features of the strike in Philadelphia. On January 15 the *Public Ledger* reported "an entirely new propaganda adopted by the striking girls." Instead of shouting at the girls still at work to join their ranks, thereby guaranteeing their arrest, the pickets offered them cards on which the following was printed: "You are doing little more than starving to death on the dollar-a-day wages that you are getting. Why not starve outside? Outside we have fresh air and starvation is not so deadly. Inside, if you don't starve to death, you will die of tuberculosis. Come on, get a little fresh air."

"It is wonderful to note the effect of the mixture of humor and philosophy," reported the *Public Ledger*. "Last night several workers saw the cards and prompted further by the meagerness of their purses, asked to be taken to the union headquarters." Among those who signed up and joined the picket lines were blacks and Italians.[35]

When Local No. 15's leaders disclosed that they would be willing to settle without achieving union recognition, they created an uproar among the strikers. The girls insisted on including the union shop in the settlement, and Agnes Nestor supported their stand. "This sounds like a trick to get you back," she told the pickets. "Don't go into this thing blindly. We have plenty of money and can afford to wait." The *Public Ledger* called this "bravado," pointing out that "the treasury of the union is admittedly empty," but conceded that the Philadelphia "girl strikers still support the demand for the union shop enthusiastically.[36]

With their production almost completely halted by the Philadelphia strike, the New York Manufacturers' Association was more inclined to seek a settlement. On December 23, employers and union officials agreed on a compromise. The employers conceded to the demands of the workers for shorter hours, higher wages, and prompt consideration of an entire list of grievances, but they refused to recognize the union or establish the closed or union shop. The work week would be reduced to fifty-two hours; there was to be no discrimination against union members; needles, thread, and appliances were to be supplied free by the employers, as far as practicable; equal work was to be given during the slow seasons; four paid holidays annually were to be granted; all shops were to establish wage committees; and all strikers were to be reemployed and no others hired until this was accomplished. The Manufacturers' Association agreed that it would give consideration to any communications from any source concerning violations of the agreement and that it would welcome conferences about any differences that could not be settled between the individual shop and its employees. But the president of the association said that the manufacturers insisted on an open shop and "from that stand we will not budge."[37]

On December 27, the negotiated settlement was submitted to a vote of all union members. Since many of the women working in nonassociation, independent shops had earlier gained full union recognition, it was hardly to be expected that the strikers in the association shops would settle for less. Addressing the strikers, Morris Hillquit, Socialist Party leader, reminded them that the crux of their demands was union recognition: "Collectively the waistmakers are strong, individually they are helpless and defenseless. If the employers were today to concede all the demands of the strikers, but be allowed to destroy or even the weaken the union, they could and would restore the old condition of servitude in their shops, within a very few weeks or months." It came as no surprise, therefore, that the strikers overwhelmingly disapproved of the proposed settlement.[38]

After the rejection, the strike dragged on. While the enthusiasm of the strikers continued at a high pitch, funds ran low, and many of the pickets were obliged to depend on the WTUL soup kitchen for their meals. Meanwhile, the arrests continued and so did the fines, which ate up what little remained of the strike fund. Illness kept many of the strikers confined to their beds, while those who still picketed continued to shiver without winter clothing. League members also continued to picket. Their fur hats and coats stood out in sharp contrast to the clothing of the waistmakers, but they too suffered during the terrible winter. Vassar graduate Violet Pike, for example, reported daily for either picket or court duty. "Her hands deep in her pockets, her beaver hat a bit to the side and an angelic smile on her red lips," she was described as truly the "bravest of the brave, day in and day out shivering from cold and at times drenched to the skin."[39]

The climax of the New York strike occurred on January 2, 1910, at Carnegie Hall. Originally, several members of the Political Equality Association, led by Anna Shaw and Alva Belmont, had proposed a sympathy strike of all women workers in the city. But when this did not materialize, the Carnegie Hall mass rally was organized.[40] The audience sat spellbound as speaker after speaker heaped accusations and recriminations upon the heads of New York's public officials. The sponsors had sold box seats to liberal clubs and organizations and netted a substantial amount for the strike fund. On the stage, in the front row, sat twenty strikers who had served sentences in the workhouse. The 350 young women who had been arrested by the police and fined by the magistrates filled the rest of the stage. Each girl wore a printed sash stating how the court had dealt with her, such as "Workhouse Prisoner" or "Arrested."

The high point of the evening came when Leonora O'Reilly introduced Rose Perr. No taller than the average ten-year-old girl, with her hair in a long braid, Perr stood before the enormous gathering and told, in simple words, the alarming story of her arrest. The police had taken her to court as a witness because she had asked a police captain to arrest a "gorilla" who had slapped her companion. At the courthouse, she was suddenly accused of having assaulted a scab. Without any evidence, the magistrate thereupon sentenced her to five days in the workhouse before she even had an opportunity to testify.

Hillquit praised the strikers for forming a powerful union practically overnight and fighting a gallant battle to maintain it. He declared that the strike had demonstrated how women permeated industry life and proved how absurd it was for any man to say that woman's place was in the home: "Let him remember the thirty thousand women strikers of one single industry in one city and let him remember that in the factories these women are treated with even less consideration than men." These women, he continued, had shown that they could fight for their rights with heroism. "Be of good cheer, your victory will be glorious," he closed to thunderous applause. At the conclusion of his speech, the audience unanimously adopted a resolution condemning "the conduct of the police in this case as an indefensible abuse of power" and denouncing the court actions against the strikers as examples of "a prejudiced and vindictive mind": "The office of Magistrate has been perverted into an instrument of persecution and oppression."[41]

Following the Carnegie Hall meeting, the State Bureau of Mediation attempted to resolve the remaining questions in dispute between the union and the association. While Local No. 25 was willing to discuss the open or closed shop, the manufacturers' association refused. Likewise, on January 11, the association rejected the union's proposal, transmitted through the State Mediation Commissioner, for arbitration hearings by the commission, which would include consideration of the closed shop.[42]

And so the strike dragged on through January and into February. As strike benefits dwindled, hunger and privation became urgent problems. Then, too, the rich women's commitment to the strikers began to waver after the strikers rejected the settlement offered by the association. The strikers were not disturbed when the *New York Times* reversed its earlier cautious endorsement of the union shop and justified its change on the ground that the proposed settlement met all the strikers' other demands. But when some settlement workers and many of the upper-class women voiced their disapproval of the strikers' decision, this did affect the morale of the women on the picket lines.[43]

Meanwhile, underlying conflicts began to surface between the Socialists in the strikers' ranks and the rich women supporters of the strike. Even before the January 2 meeting at Carnegie Hall, a contingent of strikers visited Alva Belmont's home asking for a discussion with her about her real purpose in supporting the strike. Belmont refused to see the strikers and asked the girls to submit their questions to her secretary. They handed her two provocative questions: "(1) Are you interested in strikers because they are possible suffragists or because they are workers in trouble? (2) Do you believe the interests of the employers and workers are identical or could ever be identical?"

The secretary, after delivering the questions, promptly returned to announce that Belmont was too busy to answer. When the strikers asked for a future meeting, the' secretary responded with a curt "No."[44] Still, most Socialists among the strikers felt that although the interview indicated that Belmont harbored insincere motives, it was necessary to smooth over the differences between the opposing groups in order to present a united front before the press and the association.[45]

To make matters worse, the Socialists believed that non-Socialist negotiators were trying to sabotage the negotiations and force the workers into worthless contracts. They were especially bitter over the role played by Eva McDonald Valesh, who, acting in a semiofficial capacity as AFL organizer, involved herself in many of the negotiating sessions. "It makes me wild to see that woman [Valesh] in our midst," Theresa Malkiel wrote in her diary of the strike. "And I'm almost sure that we aren't going to succeed until we make an effort to shake these serpents."[46]

By the beginning of February, with the strikers' resources nearing depletion, and with the society women showing a growing coolness toward the struggle, the end was inevitable. The union was compelled to sign agreements with many of the larger shops without either recognition of the union or endorsement of the union shop. It was on this basis that the Triangle Waist Company settled with the strikers in the first week of February.

By the second week of February almost the entire trade had resumed operation, and those few strikers whose stubborn employers refused to sign straggled back to their shops without a contract. On February 15 officials of Local No. 25 declared the general strike at an end. The great uprising of the shirtwaist makers, which had begun with such fanfare, ended unceremoniously without any rejoicing.[47]

On February 6 the Philadelphia strike was settled through arbitration between Local No. 15 and the Philadelphia Manufacturers' Association. Under the terms of the settlement, each side nominated two members to a Board of Arbitration, and these four chose a fifth impartial member. In the settlement the employers were not permitted to make any charges for straps, needles, or any other part of the machines, unless they were willfully broken by the operator, and the hours of labor were reduced to fifty-two and a half per week. But both wages and the issue of the union shop remained to be arbitrated. The disappointed strikers, who had hoped for more, returned to their shops. But Agnes Nestor, before returning to Chicago, urged the waistmakers to "build up the union so that when the time comes to make another agreement, you will be in a position to get better terms."[48]

Nestor was either too polite or too cautious to add that the settlement was probably the best the Philadelphia women strikers could gain in view of the fact that, in addition to the opposition they faced from their employers and the police, they also had to overcome the lukewarm attitude of the male-dominated union leadership, the lack of enthusiasm of many of the male workers, and a similar lack of enthusiasm on the

LOWELL OFFERING

December, 1845.

" *Is Saul also among the prophets?* "

A REPOSITORY
OF ORIGINAL ARTICLES, WRITTEN BY
"FACTORY GIRLS."

LOWELL: MISSES CURTIS & FARLEY.
BOSTON: JORDAN & WILEY, 121
Washington street.
1845.

Entered according to Act of Congress, in the year 1845, in the Clerk's Office of the District Court
of the District of Massachusetts.

Title page from the "Lowell Offering." *The Bettman Archive.*

When the binders joined the striking Lynn shoemakers in their fight for higher wages, they decided to mark the day with a great procession. Here, marching dauntlessly through the snow, are the strikers, carrying signs such as "American Ladies Will Not Be Slaves. Give us a Fair Compensation and We Labour Cheerefully." *Library of Congress.*

This woodcut, showing women working in a New York cigar factory sweatshop, was done around the time of the Great Uprising of 1877, when Samuel Gompers rallied the workers to strike for higher wages and for recognition of the union. *The Bettman Archive.*

An early employment agency for women workers: applicants are interviewed in the Working Women's Protective Union, 1879. *The Bettman Archive.*

Women delegates to the 1886 Knights of Labor Convention. *Library of Congress.*

In a New York sweatshop, an owner browbeats a seamstress. *Library of Congress*.

A young girl dreams of picnics in the country, while her fellow workers petition the boss for half day Saturdays. *The Bettman Archive.*

New York's Labor Day Parade in 1909 brought out this bus filled with members of the Women's Auxiliary Typographical Union. *The Bettman Archive.*

Striking shirtwaist workers show the determination that enabled them to sustain the beatings, arrests, and imprisonment that characterized the waistmakers' strike in 1909 and still emerge victorious in their struggle. *Library of Congress.*

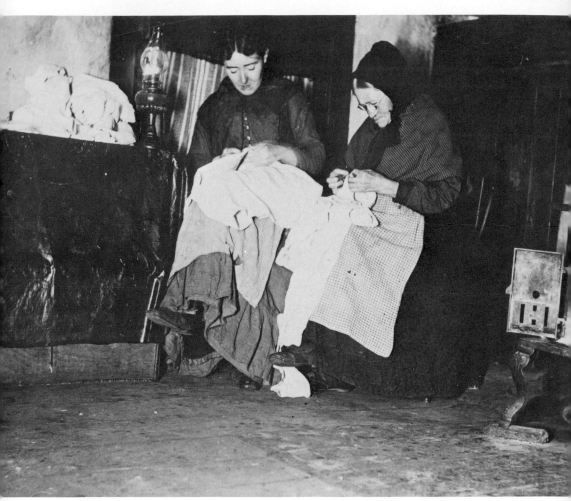

This photograph of a tenement sweatshop was taken by Lewis Hine, one of the most committed documentary photographers. *Library of Congress.*

part of most of the male unions in the city. Not only did male cutters and markers in the shirtwaist shops not go on strike until four days after the walkout by the women began: they also returned to work three days before the women settled. The men believed that it was impossible to win the strike, but the women refused to relinquish their goals and finally settled with great reluctance on the basis of the negotiated terms. While a number of male unions in Philadelphia endorsed the strike, they gave it little more than verbal support. Only the Jewish cigarmakers' union and the United Hebrew Trades offered any concrete financial assistance to the striking union. Small wonder, then, that the shirtwaist workers were compelled to look to upper-class women for support.[49]

When the strikes in both New York and Philadelphia were over, the ILGWU was able to point with justifiable pride to definite gains made by the strikers. Women who had worked sixty or more hours a week before the strike in New York now had a guaranteed work week of fifty-two hours (fifty-two and a half hours in those Philadelphia shops that had settled with the union), and in New York they were to be paid time and a half for overtime work. Workers no longer had to pay for power and materials, and other petty impositions had also been eliminated. Most important, nearly twenty thousand had joined Local No. 25 and ten thousand had become members of Local No. 15 during the strike.[50]

But the strike settlement had obvious limitations, and the waistmakers' contracts were weak. Because many manufacturers had to make individual settlements with the union, and because each shop determined its own piece-rate scale, neither conditions nor grievance procedures were standardized. As Hillquit had predicted, the failure to win a union shop opened the door to attempts by employers to restore previous conditions. Within months, waistmakers were coming to the WTUL to report violations, and shop strikes were becoming increasingly common. Unfortunately, a number of union leaders, instead of blaming this on the weaknesses in the settlement, attributed it instead to "the main illness of our Jewish organization—strike fever."[51]

Some controversy developed over the role played by black women during the struggle. On January 20, 1910, in an editorial entitled "The Waistmakers' Strike," the New York *Age*, a black weekly, boasted that it had recruited "colored girls as ironers with the firms whose employees are now on strike." After reporting that it had been asked to reject strikebreaking advertisements, and instead, to "help induce these colored girls to join the union, and that we dissuade other colored girls from taking the places of those now on strike," it went on to assert: "We have refused these requests both on general and specific grounds."

What were these grounds? The *Age* maintained that before the strike, "Negro girls were not asked to join the union." This, it declared, was tantamount "practically to an exclusion from the union and the workshop." Moreover, it was safe to assume from past experience that prior to their walkout, the waistmakers would have demanded the immediate discharge of any black girls hired by the employers. Finally, the *Age* claimed, it had asked the "philanthropic sponsor" of the strikers—presumably the New York Women's Trade Union League—for assurances that "the unions would admit Negro girls in the future without discrimination as to employment, should they refrain from taking the positions now open." Since it had received no such assurance, the *Age* asked its readers if it could "in sense and justice advise competent Negro girls, being idle and until now denied employment, to turn down this opportunity?" And it asked: "Why should Negro working girls pull white working girls' chestnuts out of the fire?"

According to the *Age,* the waistmakers' strike brought into the "clearest light the issue of the Negro and the union." Trade unions and trade unions alone, it declared, were responsible for aligning the black on the side of the capitalists, and it was to be hoped that they would learn the lesson from the waistmakers' strike that "the Negro will continue to be the pivot upon which future strikes will turn so long as labor will ignore his right to work and thwart his ambition to advance in the mechanical world. The friends and leaders of labor should consider the Negro in days of prosperity as well as in those of adversity."

It is undeniable that the *Age* raised a pertinent issue; indeed, blacks had registered similar complaints against AFL unions and the Railroad Brotherhoods for a number of years. But the controversy arose over the application of this issue to the waistmakers' strike. Margaret Dreier Robins, national president of the WTUL, immediately wrote to the *Survey* insisting that the union did have black members—*one* in New York and *two* in Philadelphia—and that in the latter city "two of the most devoted pickets are colored girls, for they have not only been able to persuade the girls of their own race and color to stand by their sisters, but have also been most successful in persuading the white girls to stand by them." A black woman in New York who had joined the strike early in the battle was not only welcomed, wrote Robins, but "she is now chairman of her shop committee, elected by white girls to that office."*[52]

---

*Evidently even the national WTUL caught the irony of answering the charge with evidence about *one* black member in New York and *two* in Philadelphia, for at the poststrike meeting of the National Executive Board, the organization passed a resolution pledging to do something about organizing black women. The entry in the minutes read:

"The question of the increasing practice of bringing in Negro workers as strike breakers and underbidders was discussed, and it was felt that action must be taken to organize the colored women workers, both for their own protection and for the protection of the white workers. In this discussion, the help given by the National to strikes in New York and Philadelphia, preventing several hundred colored girls being used as strikebreakers was referred to with great appreciation. It was moved and seconded that this Executive Board offer its services to the National Association for the Protection of Colored Women stating the very great desire of the League to cooperate with them in their efforts to protect the colored women workers through organization. Unanimously carried" (Minutes of the Executive Board Meeting of the NWTUL, May 21, 1910, NWTUL Papers, Library of Congress).

Elizabeth Dutcher, an officer of the New York WTUL, charged publicly that the *Age* had distorted the waistmakers' union's policy toward blacks. In a letter published in the *Horizon,* founded and edited by W. E. B. Du Bois, she wrote:

> In New York, colored girls are not only members of the union, but they have been prominent in the union. One colored girl has been secretary of her shop organization all through the strike and has been very frequently at the union headquarters doing responsible work. The editor should also know that meetings were held during the strike at the Fleet Street Methodist Memorial Church (colored) in Brooklyn and St. Marks Methodist Church in Manhattan and that in both, members of the Ladies Waist Makers Union said definitely and publicly that colored girls were not only eligible but welcome to membership.

The *Horizon* expressed its pleasure at the opportunity to publish Dutcher's letter and urged all black Americans to read and study it carefully, especially "those persons and editors who, some unwittingly, are assisting in the present insidious effort to make our people Ishmaelites in the world of labor, or as someone has put it, to make us 'Cossacks' of America."[53]

If there was controversy about the role of blacks, there was none concerning that of Italian women during the strike. Both contemporary and later accounts agree that young Italian women "not only refused to come out of the shops but also took the place of Jewish strikers." Despite the fact that they made up at least one-fourth of the labor force in the waist industry, only two thousand of the strikers were Italians. According to the league, most of the Italians who struck did not remain out until a settlement was reached but went back to work early. However, it should be added that the ILGWU had no Italian-speaking organizer and had to depend on English to inform Italian strikers of developments, and that the Italian and Jewish women strikers, divided as they were by the barrier of language, met separately—a situation that was hardly conducive to the maintenance of solidarity among the Italians.[54]

Whatever the reasons, the union's failure to bring and keep out most of the Italian workers was clearly a factor in the waistmakers' inability to win a complete victory. There was also the contention that the failure of Local No. 25's leaders to anticipate the strike and prepare adequate funds for it seriously hampered the struggle from its beginning right up to the final settlement. Finally, the point is also made that the waistmakers did not enjoy the full support of either the international or the labor movement as a whole because a large percentage of the strikers were women, while the union officials were men. A great strike of unorganized immigrant women "was hardly calculated to win the support of the American Federation of Labor."[55] Although Pauline Newman and Rose Schneiderman traveled throughout New York State appealing for assistance from local labor unions, they only raised $600 through this method.[56]

In view of all these handicaps, it could be argued that without the yeoman service provided by the Women's Trade Union League, with the support of middle-class and upper-class women, the waistmakers would not even have gained a limited victory. "Not the least memorable feature of the New York waistmakers' strike," the *Literary Digest* observed even before the strike was over, "has been the evidence it affords of woman's humanity to woman." The weekly endorsed the following comment of the *Brooklyn Standard Union:* "The earnestness with which many prominent women have joined hands with the girls is in marked contrast with the aloofness of men of wealth when there is a strike in which only men are involved. *There is reason to believe that if a complete victory is won the rich women who enlisted in the cause made it possible*" [emphasis added].[57]

Apart from the fact that "a complete victory" was not won, the statement contained elements of both fact and distortion. It is true that league members did appeal to upper-class women in the language of sisterhood, stressing the need for these women to demonstrate their solidarity with the strikers by coming down to the factory district and inspecting conditions there for themselves. More important, they insisted that the women should join their sisters on the picket lines and help the strike effort by boycotting nonunion waists. As the special strike edition of the *New York Call,* edited by league members, put it: "Now is the time for women in New York, Philadelphia, and in fact everywhere where American shirtwaists are worn, to rise in their might and demonstrate that with them bargain-hunting can be subordinated to principle and that they have said goodbye to the products of the sweatshop. . . . Friends, let us stop talking about sisterhood, and MAKE SISTERHOOD A FACT!"[58]

To a remarkable extent, the strike did just that. "Women [of the upper class]," wrote Helen Marot, "who came to act as witnesses of arrests around the factories ended by picketing side by side with the strikers."[59] Mary Durham, a league official, wrote to Agnes Nestor in February, 1910: "Isn't it good to see this sisterhood of women at last really demonstrated in the active interest of women of wealth and leisure? Good to see them take up some of the crying needs of their sister women who are out in the world of work struggling for a living."[60]

And yet there is no justification for the conclusion drawn by the *Literary Digest,* the *Brooklyn Standard Union,* and several other contemporary observers (along with some later historians) that it was the "rich women" who made victory for the shirtwaist workers "possible." It was the female garment workers themselves—their militancy and endurance in manning the picket lines in frigid weather and in sustaining beatings, arrests, and imprisonment—and not the supportive activities of what

Rose Schneiderman called the "Mink Brigade" that made victory possible. The press even exaggerated the effect of the financial contributions of the upper-class women, through the league. Since the strike cost $100,000, it is clear that the league's contributions, which totaled $20,000, could not have financed it. Indeed, in its report dealing with the strike, the WTUL pointed out: "It is untrue to state, as has been stated, that the League financed and led the strike. The strike was organized and led by the Union."[61]

As we shall see, the exhibition of sisterhood that had united upper- and working-class women during the strike proved to be both exceptional and short-lived. But the Women's Trade Union League continued and was strengthened by the strike. Despite all the controversy provoked by its activities, they did help to attract workingwomen to the organization. The strike also brought to the fore a number of able and intelligent workingwomen who became active participants in both the ILGWU and the WTUL. Clara Lemlich, famous for her Cooper Union speech, Pauline Newman, and Mollie Schepps, an American-born dressmaker, joined the league during the strike and soon became members of its Executive Board. The composition of the league's organizing committees reflected the increased proportion of workers in the organization. In the years before 1909, most of the WTUL's standing trade committees were headed by allies; by 1910, all of them were led by workingwomen. Moreover, the league's major organizers in the years following the strike included Rose Schneiderman, Pauline Newman, Melinda Scott, Rose Sashon (another young waistmaker who joined the league during the strike), and Mollie Schepps. All of them were workingwomen.[62]

In truth, the shirtwaist strike appeared to have heralded the New York league's real initiation into the labor movement. During most of the strike, Local No. 25—in contrast to the attitude of the ILGWU officials—had treated the league as an equal partner and had solicited its assistance and advice in formulating strategy and settlements. In recognition of the league's service and as a guarantee of future cooperation, the union elected Rose Schneiderman to its Executive Board. Nor was this new acceptance limited to the waistmakers' union. When Leonora O'Reilly attended the New York State Federation of Labor convention in the summer of 1910, she noted that the delegates greeted her warmly and were very much interested in the league's work. In addition, the president of the Workingmen's Federation of the State of New York publicly praised the work of the league, and the president of the Boston Central Labor Union expressed the hope that it would be able to become a full-fledged member of the AFL. Even the *American Federationist* noted the league's existence and editorially applauded its achievements, while Gompers himself actually had friendly words for the league members and stated that the strike had demonstrated the practicality of unionism among women workers and "the capacity of those misused toilers to suffer, fight, and dare that justice might be done."[63]

Despite the strike's less-than-successful settlement, it marked a turning point in the history of the union movement among women workers, as well as in the union movement of the garment industry. The strike was both the largest and bitterest strike of women in the history of American labor struggles up to that time. During the eight weeks of preliminary skirmishing and the thirteen weeks of the general strike, the strikers had clearly demonstrated that workers who were regarded by leading officials of the AFL (and even by some of the ILGWU) as impossible to organize could be united in effective economic action. In this struggle, very young women, most of them recent immigrants, working primarily at an unskilled trade, were able to gain important concessions from their employers. Without either preparation or finances, the women had walked the picket lines through the rain and snow, remaining "solid" in spite of beatings, arrests, fines, and jailings. They had laid the foundation for future gains. Their conditions and struggles had gained the attention of middle-class and well-to-do individuals in New York, and their strike marked the first time these individuals were actively involved in championing the cause of the working masses. The strike pointed up for many New Yorkers the inadequacies of both their police department and the city's judicial system. It awakened many in the city to a new awareness of the problems facing workers in general and workingwomen in particular. "The great moral significance of the shirtwaist makers' strike," Morris Hillquit noted, "is that it helped awaken our dormant social conscience. The people of this city began to realize that society owes some duties to the toiling masses."[64]

Finally, the three months of picketing created a solidarity among the women workers and fostered a new awareness of what unity could achieve on the economic front. The strikers had gained the understanding that together they were a powerful force. As one woman phrased it: "This is not just a strike for self. Only by standing together can we get better conditions for all."[65]

Almost a quarter of a century later, an ILGWU veteran recalled that in the opening years of the century, "the waist and dress shops were the vilest and foulest industrial sores of New York and other big cities." And he went on: "Then came 1909. Then came the most heroic labor struggle in the history of the great city. Then came the beginnings of a strong and permanent organization in the needle trades. Then came the beginnings of decency in a vilely sweated industry."[66] These were true words. The impact of the women's strike in the waistmaking industry was a tremendous inspiration to the workers in the other branches of the industry and paved the way for the major advances in unionizing other garment workers. In years to come, thousands of workers would sing "The Uprising of the Twenty Thousand," the song dedicated to the waistmakers of 1909:

> In the black of the winter of nineteen nine,
> When we froze and bled on the picket line,
> We showed the world that women could fight
> And we rose and won with women's might.

Chorus:

> Hail! the waistmakers of nineteen nine,
> Making their stand on the picket line,
> Breaking the power of those who reign,
> Pointing the way, smashing the chain.

> And we gave new courage to the men
> Who carried on in nineteen ten
> And shoulder to shoulder we'll win through,
> Led by the ILGWU.[67]

19

Repercussions of the Garment Workers' Uprising

BARELY FIVE MONTHS after the shirtwaist makers had returned to work, another and more extensive general strike paralyzed the ladies' garment trade. In July, 1910, some sixty thousand workers employed in the cloak-and-suit branch of the industry left their workbenches en masse and marched to the picket lines.

In 1910 in New York City cloaks, suits, and shirts were manufactured in about fifteen hundred shops employing approximately sixty thousand workers, of whom about forty thousand were Jewish and ten to twenty thousand were Italian. After 1890, partly because legislation outlawing "homework" had virtually ended sweatshops, many small shops had sprung up. The newer clothing factories used lighter, better, and more specialized machinery run by steam or electricity. But even in these more modern factories, working conditions remained poor. Little provision had been made for adequate sanitary facilities; workers were still forced to buy their own sewing machines and to pay for repairs, oil, and thread; and inside subcontracting, which prevailed in most of the shops, created a chain of bosses whose common interest was in keeping wages down. In 1910 the average wage for operators was $15 to $18 a week, and for pressers, $14. Men worked for nine to nine and a half hours a day during the slack season and fourteen to sixteen hours a day when the shops were busy. In short, the cloakmaker's life, like that of the shirtwaist maker, was a bitter struggle for existence. This was especially true for the female workers, who held 10 percent of the jobs in this branch of the industry. They played a minor role in cloakmaking, working primarily as "helpers" in the finishing departments, and earned the woefully inadequate wage of $3 to $4 a week.[1]

Unlike the waistmakers' strike, which had been spontaneous and haphazard, the cloakmakers' strike in the summer of 1910 was carefully planned. Unlike Local No. 25's leaders, the cloakmakers' officers had anticipated the strike, had prepared adequate funds, and enjoyed the full support of the international union. Strike agitation had begun in August, 1908, and by the spring of 1909, about two thousand members had been recruited by the New York Joint Board of Cloak and Shirt Makers Unions. With the strike of the waistmakers, the movement for a general strike in the cloak and suit trade was ignited, and membership in the Joint Board soared. In July, 1910, a secret ballot on the general strike issue showed 18,777 for striking and 615 against, and a committee decided on the following set of demands: union recognition, the forty-eight-hour week, double pay for overtime work, and the abolition of subcontracting.[2]

When the strike call was issued on July 7, about sixty thousand cloakmakers, six thousand of them women, walked off their jobs. On this occasion the Italians, who constituted about a third of the labor force in the industry and who had been involved in all stages of planning and executing the strike, joined the Jewish workers.[3]

The cloakmakers began at once to negotiate with the smaller employers, who could not afford a long-drawn-out conflict and who rushed to arrange satisfactory agreements. But the larger manufacturers refused to yield to the demand for union recognition and the closed shop. A number of these larger cloak manufacturers thereupon formed the Cloak, Suit and Shirt Manufacturers' Protective Association and pledged not to bargain with the Cloakmakers' Union.[4]

Like the shirtwaist makers before them, the cloakmakers soon had to contend with the association's special policemen and thugs, in addition to the New York City police. All three groups joined forces in escorting strikebreakers into the struck shops. As in the shirtwaist makers' strike, too, magistrates regularly fined or sentenced pickets to the workhouse, while the police generally protected the thugs who were terrorizing the strikers. Moreover, the association obtained a limited temporary injunction restraining the union from coercing any worker into leaving his job through the use of "force, threat, fraud or intimidation." The strikers defied the injunction by mass picketing in the face of violence by the police and the special guards hired by the employers.[5]

Even though women workers made up a small minority of the strike force, they quickly assumed important positions in the strike organization. For example, Dora Landburg, who had grown up in the cloakmaking trade, enthusiastically directed the strike headquarters, coordinated the picketing, and dispatched aid to arrested strikers who requested bail.[6] In contrast to the shirtwaist strike, the WTUL played only a peripheral role in the cloakmakers' revolt, mainly because women constituted only a small percentage of the strikers. But John Dyche, the ILG-

WU's national secretary-treasurer, having learned something from the previous strike, requested help from the league and named Helen Marot and Leonora O'Reilly to the cloakmakers' strike committee. Every few days Marot visited the headquarters of the settlement committee, where the national officers sat in session. The union leaders appointed Marot and Rose Schneiderman to negotiate a settlement with those manufacturers who employed female alteration hands. League members formed a committee that raised money to distribute 209,000 quarts of milk to strikers' children.[7]

After mediation efforts by the State Bureau of Arbitration had failed (the association refused to enter into negotiations until the union agreed to abandon its demand for recognition and the closed shop),[8] A. Lincoln Filene, the Boston department store owner and a leading member of the Boston branch of the National Civic Federation, contacted Louis D. Brandeis and asked him to go to New York to help arrange a settlement of the strike. As counsel for the Boston cloak and suit manufacturers' association, Brandeis had helped to break a four-month general strike there in 1907 by obtaining injunctions against the union leaders.[9] Now he appeared in New York as a friend of labor but an enemy of the closed shop, one of the union's main demands. Under Brandeis' clever and persuasive maneuvering, Dyche and the majority of the strike committee agreed to eliminate the closed shop from the list of the union's basic demands. But the more radical of the union's executive officers, as well as the majority of the rank and file, declined to accept arbitration without some consideration of the closed-shop issue. In fact, the active personal intervention of Samuel Gompers was needed before indignant union leaders and members would agree to enter into a conference with the employers on July 28.[10]

The conference quickly came to an understanding on the specific grievances of the cloakmakers, but it could make no headway on the closed-shop issue. At this stage Brandeis put forward the formula of the "preferential union shop," which would bind an employer to give preference in hiring to any available union member while still permitting him to hire nonunion members and retain scabs. Brandeis did not invent the preferential union shop; the plan had been promulgated as a union demand in the 1892 strike of the AFL teamsters, scalemen, and packers in New Orleans.[11] Where the AFL was weak and fighting against an open-shop drive, it put forward the preferential union shop as a step toward the closed shop. By 1910, however, when the closed shop had been won in many contracts, acceptance of the preferential union shop represented a retreat.

Gompers, however, urged the union to accept the plan.[12] But with the *Jewish Daily Forward* denouncing the preferential shop as a "scab shop with honey," and with the *New York Call* urging the strikers to stick to their guns, Brandeis' maneuverings failed. The mass of the workers rejected his proposal, and on August 3 the union concluded all joint conferences and renounced all offers of peace and arbitration, declaring: "The rank and file of our organization demand the closed shop. There can be no compromise on that score and if we were to accept any compromise, the rank and file would not abide by our decision."[13]

So vigorously did the strikers oppose any retreat on the closed-shop issue that members of the strike committee who favored the preferential shop were actually threatened with violence.[14] But when the strike leadership, bowing to the determined opposition of the rank and file, rejected the agreement proposed by the association, Justice John W. Goff of the New York Supreme Court made the injunction against the strikers permanent. Goff labeled the strike a common-law civil conspiracy to obtain the closed shop and thereby to deprive nonunion men and women of the opportunity to work and drive them out of the industry. The police were authorized to disperse all pickets, peaceful or otherwise.[15] "For the first time in the history of labor disputes in the state," observes Graham Adams, Jr., "an injunction not only permanently restrained men from peaceful picketing but also forbade them to interfere in any way at all with those who wished to work."[16]

Even Julius Henry Cohen, the attorney for the manufacturers, described the injunction as "the strongest one ever handed down by an American court against trade unionism," and the New York *Evening Post,* which seldom favored the cause of labor in any strike, commented: "One need not be a sympathizer with trade-union policy as it reveals itself today in order to see that the latest injunction, if generally upheld, would seriously cripple such defensive powers as legitimately belong to organized labor."[17] Speaking for the AFL, Gompers called the decision another example of the "tyranny of the autocratic methods of concentrated capital and greed." The New York City Central Federated Union, in conjunction with the Socialist Party, organized a huge demonstration against this "judicial tyranny."[18]

Meanwhile, negotiations were continuing, and on September 2, the manufacturers presented a new proposal for a settlement with additional concessions. The strike committee, supported by only two hundred hastily assembled shop chairmen and with a minimum of debate, ratified the first collective bargaining agreement in the industry. No public announcement was made of the agreement, nor were any public assemblies held before the ratification.[19]

After nine weeks of bitter struggle, the "Protocol of Peace," as the agreement was called, won for the workers a fifty-hour week, bonus pay for overtime, ten legal holidays, free electric power installation for machines, no homework, weekly pay in cash rather than checks, limitations on overtime, a joint board of sanitary control to help clean up filthy shops, a committee for grievances and compulsory arbitration,* with no strike or lockout permitted before arbitration, and price settlements to be made in each shop by negotiation. As a concession, the manufacturers agreed to exert preference only between one union man and another: nonunion labor could be hired only when union help was unobtainable. The agreement also compelled employers to declare their belief in the union and in the ideal that all "who desire its benefits should share its burdens."[20] The settlement had tremendously important implications for unskilled women workers, since the agreement covered the wages and conditions of every worker in the trade, from skilled tailors to finishers.[21]

Despite these important gains, however, the settlement was a disappointment to many strikers, largely because it institutionalized the preferential union shop. Furthermore, unlike the usual collective bargaining agreement, the protocol had no time limit; it could be terminated by either side at will. Many rank-and-file workers also disapproved of the no-strike clause and the provision for compulsory arbitration.[22] Responding to this criticism, the union's official journal declared: "It is far better to strike for, and win recognition of our union, than an increase in wages, or decrease of hours, without the powerful organization needed to maintain the conditions once created. With such an organization, the possibilities of the future are unlimited."[23]

But events were soon to demonstrate that the union relied exclusively on the machinery of the Protocol and the good will of the employers to establish permanent industrial peace and failed to build a strong organization in order to enforce it. As a result, the employers were able to violate freely the terms of the Protocol.

The revolt in the garment trades next shifted to Chicago, where, on September 22, 1910, a small group of courageous women ignited the spark that led forty thousand unorganized clothing workers to strike. The uprising began when a few women employed in shop No. 5 of Hart, Schaffner & Marx, the largest clothing factory in the city, walked off the job when their piece rate was arbitrarily cut from 4 cents to 3¼ cents a pair. One of these girls was Bessie Abramowitz, an immigrant from Grodno, in White Russia, who had already been blacklisted in Chicago's clothing shops because of her militancy and was working at Hart, Schaffner & Marx under an assumed name. Under the leadership of Abramowitz and Annie Shapiro, twelve young women petitioned for a

---

*Minor grievances were to be submitted to a Committee of Grievances while important disputes were to be turned over to a permanent Board of Arbitration, whose decision was to be "final and conclusive."

return to the old rate. When this appeal was rejected, they struck and sought help from the United Garment Workers, which had a small, male-dominated local of clothing cutters within the Hart, Schaffner & Marx plant. The elite local had no interest in organizing young immigrant women, so the young strikers started to picket by themselves. At first they received little support from other workers in the plant, and it took three weeks of steady, day-by-day picketing by these fourteen determined strikers to convince the other workers that this was a serious effort to redress long-standing grievances of all workers. By the fourth week, other workers in the plant had begun to join the original fourteen women, and by mid-October almost eight thousand Hart, Schaffner & Marx workers had walked out. The walkout gradually spread to other manufacturing houses until the entire industry was paralyzed.[24]

With the United Garment Workers indifferent to their struggle, the strikers appealed to the Chicago Women's Trade Union League and the Chicago Federation of Labor for assistance. Both organizations responded instantly. However, the WTUL's National Executive Board had just established a policy requiring that any union requesting league assistance had to include two league members on its strike committee. Pressured by the strikers, the UGW leadership agreed to this stipulation.[25] Thereupon, the Chicago WTUL threw itself wholeheartedly into the strike. Members formed eleven separate committees to handle picketing, publicity, speakers, benefit meetings, public events, and relief. They established headquarters in the same building that housed the Chicago Federation of Labor offices.[26]

On November 2 the league held a formal breakfast and invited women strikers to attend and spell out their grievances. The strikers told of the low wages, the long hours, the inequities of the piecework system, and the unjust fines for damaged merchandise. They reported that the price of piecework had declined steadily. One young woman reported that she and her fellow workers received 12 cents for making a coat, including the pockets: "One week we would have to stitch single, and then the next week maybe we would have to stitch them narrow and then another week they would have to be wider. Of course, the change would make it take a longer time but they paid us the same." Other girls protested against the costly system of fines. At Hart, Schaffner & Marx, they reported, "any worker who damaged a pair of pants was made to buy them at the regular wholesale prices." If the canvas strips accidentally fell to the floor, the foremen fined the canvas makers 5 cents. Still others complained of the long workday. Some women complained about the petty tyrannies practiced by their foremen, who distributed work inequitably and used abusive and insulting language. A children's jacket maker explained that her foreman insisted that she carry a bundle of

350 pairs of sleeves to another room. Although she told him it was too heavy for her to lift from the floor, he insisted. When she lifted the bundle, she injured her back and was unable to work for several weeks.[27]

One of the original strikers explained why she and her colleagues had walked out:

> We started to work at seven-thirty and worked until six with three-quarters of an hour for lunch. Our wages were seven cents for a pair of pants, or one dollar for fourteen pairs. For that we made four pockets and one watch pocket, but they were always changing the style of the stitching and until we got the swing of the new style, we would lose time and money and we felt sore about it. One day the foreman told us the wages were cut to six cents a pair of pants and the new style had two watch pockets. We would not stand for that, so we got up and left.[28]

As in the New York strikes, the employers hired detectives and thugs and received the full support of the police. In fact, Chicago's police, long notorious for their brutality toward strikers, were even more barbarous than those in New York. By December, two of the strikers had been gunned down and killed by police bullets and many more had been injured by club-swinging members of the force. Arrests of strikers occurred daily, and members of the league's picket committee patrolled the streets in order to serve as witnesses for strikers arrested without cause. League members also joined the strikers' picket lines and reviewed the "Rules for Pickets" with the strikers each day.[29]

"Come, I want to introduce you to some of the girl strikers." So began an article in the *Chicago Daily Socialist* of November 21, 1910. The reporter, who had been invited to meet the strikers, continued:

> I met the girls. And such girls! One of them occupied the platform in front and her young strong voice rang out clear as a bell, penetrating every nook and corner of the great hall.
>
> Cheer after cheer went up from the three thousand strikers assembled there, as she urged the necessity of solidarity and the closed shop.
>
> These girls were the leaders of the strike and as pretty and sweet-voiced as any young women one could possibly meet anywhere. . . .
>
> They moved about among their men comrades gracefully, free and unaffected. Here was the perfect comradeship that had grown out of the sharing of work and struggles for better conditions.
>
> The men did not assume that chivalrous attitude of the gentleman, which oftentimes is but the thin coating of contempt, but consulted and advised with them as with those of their own sex.
>
> In fact, they appeared to consult the girls quite as often as the girls did them.

After forty thousand garment workers, ten thousand of them women, had walked off the job, the strikers received a crippling blow

from their own union. Thomas Rickert, president of the United Garment Workers, was a conservative, old-line labor leader, interested in
developing the union along craft lines. He was skeptical of the value of
unskilled immigrants to the union and eager to come to terms with the
employers. In November he announced an agreement with Hart,
Schaffner & Marx, but it came short of what the strikers wanted and was
unanimously rejected. Then league members and officials of the
Chicago Federation of Labor learned that the UGW District No. 6's
treasury was empty and that the union officers' offer to assist the strikers
lacked any substance. In fact, the union had issued worthless vouchers
for relief to over ten thousand people. Officials of the Chicago Federation of Labor, league leaders, and UGW officers then managed to raise
$700 and proceeded to distribute $3 for each $5 voucher to the angry
strikers.[30]

The strike revealed an extraordinary determination on the part of
the strikers not to yield, in spite of cold, hunger, and the brutality of the
thugs and police. A woman striker recalled that as she and her fellow
workers were negotiating with their employer to call a halt to the strike,
they heard a terrific noise: "We all rushed to the windows, and there we
[saw] the police beating strikers—clubbing them on our account, and
when we saw that we went out."[31]

On November 18 the Joint Conference Board, composed of strike
leaders and representatives of the Chicago Federation of Labor, the
WTUL, and the UGW, opened four commissary stores to distribute food
to the strikers—four loaves of bread, one-half pound of coffee, one
pound of beans, and two pounds of ham per family weekly. After
Thanksgiving, herring and codfish replaced the meat allotment. To
provide for these commissaries, which fed eleven thousand families each
week, the league raised close to $70,000.[32]

On November 5 Rickert reached an agreement with Hart, Schaffner
& Marx for arbitration of all issues without union recognition. Once
again the workers rejected the proposal, and this time they made their
hatred of the national officials so clear that Rickert had to leave the hall
by a back door. Thousands of striking cutters, trimmers, and spongers
resolved to "repudiate the action of . . . Thomas A. Rickert in signing any
agreement without presenting the same for approval." Despite mounting violence against them (the final count was 374 strikers arrested and
two killed), on December 8 the workers again rejected an agreement that
would have sent them back to work without union recognition. It took
another five weeks of hunger, cold, and violence before the workers of
Hart, Schaffner & Marx, on January 14, 1911, reluctantly agreed to go
back to work and refer all issues to an arbitration committee. But the
other thirty thousand strikers maintained their ranks solidly until, on

February 3, Rickert and his lieutenants, without consulting the strikers, the WTUL, or the officials of the Chicago Federation of Labor, declared the strike over.

Workers returned to their jobs without any agreement and with no method of adjusting the grievances that had driven them to strike. Those who had been the most militant of the pickets were not allowed to return to their former jobs. The twenty-five-year-old Sidney Hillman, Frank Rosenblum, Bessie Abramowitz (who later became Mrs. Hillman), and Sam Levin had risen to leadership among the workers during the strike, and they recorded that the great majority of the strikers "were forced to return to their old miserable conditions, through the back door; and happy were those who were taken back. Many . . . were victimized for months afterwards." Members of the WTUL and the Chicago Federation of Labor who had worked tirelessly for a just settlement felt as betrayed as the strikers themselves.[33]

Only the Hart, Schaffner & Marx workers operated under a contract as a result of the strike. This contract, drawn up by Clarence Darrow, the famous labor lawyer, who had volunteered his services in defense of the strikers, and company attorney Carl Meyer, is historically regarded as the first major victory in the annals of men's clothing workers' unionism. It established a minimum wage for various departments in the factory, a fifty-four-hour week, and time and a half for overtime. It also presaged future occupational safety and health measures by insisting that "all tailor shops be properly ventilated" and that "no sweeping of a character to raise dust in any of the shops be done during working hours." The agreement provided for overtime pay for extra work and initiated a permanent Board of Arbitration, composed of Darrow and Meyer, to hear and rule on future worker grievances.[34]

Despite its disheartening conclusion for most of the strikers, the Chicago strike brought new stature and vitality to efforts to organize garment workers. The Chicago workers learned to distrust the national leadership of the United Garment Workers, but they (and the leaders and members of the Chicago Federation of Labor) learned to appreciate and respect the contributions of the Women's Trade Union League. Indeed, the Chicago WTUL emerged from the struggle as "an essential element in the city's labor scene,"[35] while Margaret Robins' contributions to the negotiating commissions and the remarkable organizational skills and energy displayed by league members in operating the commissaries won wide acclaim throughout the nation. The strike also brought a new woman labor leader to the front. Following the strike, the league named Bessie Abramowitz organizer for the UGW and agreed to pay her salary.[36]

The Cleveland garment strike of 1911 followed the pattern that had emerged in New York and Chicago. Strikers—men and women alike—

held out for ten long weeks to end low pay, unsanitary working conditions, inside subcontracting, and long and irregular hours. The strike began in June, when 4,000 men and 1,600 women walked off the job, demanding a fifty-hour week, abolition of charges for supplies and electricity, elimination of subcontracting, union recognition, and a permanent joint wage committee composed of worker representatives, outside arbitrators, and employers, for the purpose of establishing a uniform wage scale. As in New York and Chicago, union recognition became a crucial factor. Middle-class women again lent invaluable support, while WTUL organizers rushed to the scene to offer assistance.[37]

As in earlier strikes, too, the police came to the manufacturers' aid. But in Cleveland they were even more brutal than elsewhere. The *Cleveland Plain Dealer* described an attack of the police on the girl strikers: "They [the mounted police] galloped headlong at the crowd when they first appeared and the hundreds who blocked the street fled in terror. They swung their clubs when they reached the crowd and forced their way through, driving scores before them down the streets. Some girls who ran from them were chased for blocks." At one of the factories, forty-five women were arrested at one time. They promptly held a meeting in the prison and adopted resolutions condemning the police. As one observer noted: "Girls who maintain this fighting spirit in police cells are not going to be easily beaten." Pauline Newman, who had been sent to Cleveland by the ILGWU to help the strikers, reported that "the spirit manifested by the girl workers in Cleveland" was an "inspiration" to the entire labor movement.[38]

As in other strikes in the garment trade, young women assumed positions of leadership. Florence Shalor, a young Italian woman who supported her family with her job, served as secretary for the Italian strikers. Rebecca Saul, spokeswoman for the Jewish women strikers, ran strike headquarters every day from 5 A.M. to 10 or 11 P.M., coordinating the pickets and arranging for speakers to visit shop meetings. When Pauline Newman arrived in Cleveland, she was met at the train by fifty young women, who assured her that they were prepared to hold out in spite of increasing police violence and arrests. Secretary-Treasurer Dyche called on Margaret Robins for aid, and the WTUL leader visited the city to appeal to Cleveland's club women for their support of the strike. In addition, she organized a successful strikers' parade and a number of citizens meetings. Josephine Casey, another WTUL leader, also hurried to Cleveland to aid the strikers, while Gertrude Barnum toured the Midwest under ILGWU auspices, encouraging consumers and retailers to boycott Cleveland-made garments.[39]

Unfortunately, the strike failed. As it dragged on into October, the International's funds fell dangerously low, and the Cleveland manufacturers found New York and Chicago shops to fill their orders. In desperation, the ILGWU turned to the AFL Executive Council for assistance, pleading:

> For fourteen weeks the strikers have maintained their ranks unbroken. The strike has already cost over a quarter of a million dollars, almost all of which has been contributed by members and locals of the International Ladies' Garment Workers' Union. The Cleveland strikers are ready to keep up the fight until the principle of collective bargaining is recognized by the employers. Be prompt with your aid lest the employers starve us into submission.

But the AFL Executive Council remained deaf to the appeal. "And so," writes Elizabeth McCreesh, "despite the strikers' heroism and valuable support from sympathizers and union officials, organized manufacturers succeeded in halting the union movement among Cleveland's garment workers."[40]

Milwaukee's garment workers were more successful in their strike, for good reason. Of all the garment workers' strikes of the period, only the one in Milwaukee was not accompanied by police violence against pickets and unjustified arrests and imprisonment, largely because of the election of Emil Seidel, a Socialist, as mayor on the eve of the strike, which broke out late in November, 1910. The police chief, a holdover from the previous administration, ordered the customary police brutality toward the pickets, whereupon Mayor Seidel addressed an official letter to him:

> Complaints have been made here that disemployed citizens have recently been subjected to abusive epithets and rough handling by policemen. Whatever may be the basis of these complaints, I want it understood that no man on the police force has the right to interfere with a citizen who is not violating the law. I expect you, as Chief of Police, to make clear to the members of your department that as long as a citizen is within his legal rights, he should not be manhandled or insulted. Officers tolerating such tactics and patrolmen practicing them will be accountable. Hoping that reports referred to will, on investigation, prove to be exaggerated.

Apparently the police got the message. Deprived of their usual allies, the manufacturers settled on December 9 on the basis of a fifty-four hour week, time and a half for overtime, double pay for holidays, an open door to the employers (over the heads of foremen) for complaints of ill treatment, and the appointment of a committee representing workers and employers to discuss a new wage scale and the issue of union recognition.[41]

Most of the women workers who spearheaded the strike in the garment industries of New York, Chicago, Cleveland, and Milwaukee were of immigrant background. However, nonimmigrant women in the industry also demonstrated the willingness to fight for their rights and for unionism. All the women corset workers of Kalamazoo, Michigan, who struck in 1912 were born in the United States, and in this community of 35,000 inhabitants, fully half of the citizens belonged to families supported by one or more factory workers. After a spontaneous strike in 1911 to protest wage reductions, the strike leaders formed Local No. 82 of the ILGWU. Then in February, 1912, officials of the Kalamazoo Corset Company refused to renegotiate a contract with the union and discharged a number of women employees, accusing them of "disloyalty." Six hundred angry women workers declared a strike, demanding reinstatement of their discharged colleagues, a wage increase, and a reduction of the weekly work hours.[42]

Once the strike was under way, the women added new charges against their employers. They complained that the foremen awarded the more desirable jobs to those women who acquiesced to their sexual advances and neglected to collect charges from their favorites. Many girls signed affidavits describing unsanitary conditions, inadequate toilet facilities, and filthy communal drinking cups. Others testified to their supervisors' obsession with achieving sexual relations with the women workers: "The management of that concern is run by superintendents, some of them diseased and filthy, whose minds are occupied more with carnal pleasure than with the business of the firm."*[43]

Josephine Casey, Pauline Newman, and Gertrude Barnum of the ILGWU and Leonora O'Reilly of the WTUL came to Kalamazoo to assist the strikers. Shortly after Casey's arrival in the Michigan community, the police arrested and imprisoned her for leading pickets in the following prayer:

> Oh, God, Our Father, Who are generous . . . Our employer who has plenty has denied our request. He has misused the law to help him crush us. . . . Thou Who didst save Noah and his family, may it please Thee to save the girls now on strike from the wicked city of Sodom. Oh, help us to get a living wage. . . . Grant that we may win the strike . . . so that we may not need to cry often, "Lord deliver us from temptation."

Casey remained in jail for thirty-seven days and provided a model of heroism for women strikers of the period.[44]

The ILGWU called for a boycott of Kalamazoo goods, and organizers, WTUL members, and strikers traveled through neighboring states

---

*Similar charges were leveled against manufacturers and managers during the strike of women button makers in Muscatine, Iowa, which began on February 25, 1911, and lasted fifteen months. The strikers, members of Button Workers' Protective Union 12845, insisted that managers used their power to force sexual relations upon the women button makers. One manager, for example, maintained a "resting room" where women who gave "in to his devilish demands were reciprocated with a steady job. Those who did not comply with his wishes received discharge notices" (Pauline M. Newman, "The Strike of the Buttonworkers of Muscatine," *Progressive Woman*, April 1911, p. 12).

to publicize the union's case against the company. The prolonged strike and the boycott proved fatal to the corset company, which closed its doors permanently.[45] But the strike of Kalamazoo, like those of Cleveland and Chicago, brought new women workers to the fore as organizers and strike leaders, and they were to use the valuable experience they had gained in the struggles that lay ahead.

What of the waistmakers who had initiated the great revolts in the garment trade? In the last months of 1910 the waistmakers' shop agreements were nearing expiration, and it was clear that Local No. 25 was too weak to renew the agreements without considerable outside assistance. Consequently, the local asked for help from the representatives of the New York WTUL, the *Jewish Daily Forward,* the Central Federated Union, and the United Hebrew Trades. After studying the situation, the league persuaded the union to hire a new business manager "to systematize the organization of the union"; when the union agreed, the WTUL chose the manager and paid his salary.[46] However useful the assistance of the league was, it was hardly an ideal relationship when an outside organization could choose a union's leader and pay his salary.

Even with the outside assistance, Local No. 25 was too weak to hold its own. During the shirtwaist strike, 350 manufacturers had signed agreements with the union. A year later, many of these small contractors had either gone out of business or moved to new locations. Of the two hundred shops that remained, the union was able to renew agreements with 164. The large inside Manufacturers' Association shops remained totally unorganized.[47]

One of the largest firms that had resisted the union was the Triangle Shirtwaist Company, located near Washington Square. This was one of the factories about which the New York fire commissioner, in testifying before the State Factory Investigating Commission, had said: "I think that a great many of the fire escapes in buildings today are only put up to be called a fire escape. They are absolutely inadequate and absolutely useless."[48]

How inadequate and useless they were became a matter of history on Saturday, March 25, 1911. Sometime after 4:30 P.M. on that day, a crowd began to gather in front of the Asch Building, on the corner of Washington Place and Greene Street. The crowd had come together because there had been a muffled explosion, "like a big puff." At first, only small wisps of smoke could be seen coming out of an eighth-floor window. "But within a few moments," wrote New York *World* reporter James Cooper, who happened to be at the scene, "the entire eighth floor was spouting little jets of flame from the windows as if the floor was surrounded by a row of incandescent lights."

Suddenly something that looked like a bale of dark dress goods was hurled from an eighth-story window. "Somebody's in there, all right," exclaimed a spectator. "He's trying to save the best cloth." Cooper's account continued: "Then another seeming bundle of cloth came hurtling through the same window, but this time a breeze tossed open the cloth and from the crowd of five hundred persons came a cry of horror. The breeze disclosed the form of a girl shooting down to instant death."

So began the catastrophic Triangle fire. The company occupied the three upper stories of a ten-story building that was supposedly "fireproof," but it had only a single fire escape that ended five feet from the ground. The fire escape quickly collapsed. "As the fire-crazed vicitms were thrown by the collapse of the fire escape," noted the New York *Herald,* "several struck on the sharp-tipped palings. The body of one woman was found with several iron spikes driven entirely through it."

The many corpses found after the fire still bending over their sewing machines attested to the speed with which the blaze took its toll. Many victims did not even have time to leave their workbenches before the flames reached them. Most of the dead had expired within the first ten to fifteen minutes of the fire.

Other women, crazed with fear and pain, their hair and dresses aflame, made the terrible decision to jump. "They didn't want to jump," said one of the survivors. "They were afraid. They were saying their prayers first, and putting rags over their eyes so they could not see. They said it was better to be smashed than burned.... They wanted to be identified." Fifty-eight women who could not bring themselves to jump crawled into a cloakroom on the ninth floor, where they were later found burned to death, their faces raised toward a small window.

Before it was over, the Triangle fire had snuffed out the lives of 145 women, mostly immigrants. Many were the sole support of families either in America or in Europe. The Women's Trade Union League and the Shirtwaist Makers' Union, which handled the relief activities, estimated that the contributions of the slain workers to their households came to $45,000 a year.

All the conditions in the loft that made the tragedy inevitable—floors littered with flammable materials; narrow staircases in drafty, vertical wells; doors at the landings that opened inward if they opened at all (and one did not); the absence of sprinklers—had been called to the attention of the owners and employers many times, but nothing had been done about them. On the contrary, a Fire Department suggestion for the use of sprinklers had been rejected by a property owners' association on the ground that the cost amounted to "confiscation."

"I can show you 150 loft buildings far worse than this one," Fire Marshal William Beers told a New York *Evening Post* reporter after the fire. Of 1,463 factories in New York's garment industry, practically all had hall doors that opened inward instead of outward, as the law required; five hundred had only one fire escape, sixty had halls less than three feet wide, and fourteen had no fire escapes at all.

On Sunday, April 2, 1911, a memorial and protest meeting was held at the Metropolitan Opera House, under the auspices of the Women's Trade Union League. Workingpeople from the Lower East Side packed the galleries, while the orchestra, boxes, and balconies were filled with wealthy reformers. As Rose Schneiderman, instantly identified as the leader of the Triangle Shirtwaist strikers the year before, rose to speak, the galleries demanded that she be heard. Choking back tears, she began:

> I would be a traitor to those poor burned bodies if I were to talk good fellowship. We have tried you good people of the public and we have found you wanting. . . . The old inquisition had its rack and its thumb screw and its instruments of torture with iron teeth. We know what these things are today: the iron teeth are our necessities, the thumb screws are the high-powered and swift machinery close to which we must work, and the rack is here in the firetrap structures that will destroy us the minute they catch fire. . . . We have tried you citizens! We are trying you now and you have a couple of dollars for the sorrowing mothers . . . by the way of a charity gift. But every time the workers come out in the only way they know how to protest against conditions which are unbearable, the strong hand of the law is allowed to press down heavily upon us. . . . I can't talk fellowship to you who are gathered here. Too much blood has been spilled. I know from experience it is up to the working people to save themselves and the only way is through a strong working class movement.[49]

Sobered by Schneiderman's words, the meeting took the first steps that were to lead eventually to the formation of the New York Factory Investigation Commission, whose work will be discussed below.

On April 5, 1911, eighty thousand workingmen and -women marched up Fifth Avenue for four hours in a drenching rain, amid silent crowds numbering over a quarter of a million people, to attend the funeral of the victims. The faces of the marchers expressed better than any speeches their hatred of a system that showed more concern for improved machinery than for improved working conditions. But their anger reached a truly explosive stage months later when they learned that Isaac Harris and Max Blanck,, owners of the Triangle Company, tried for manslaughter in the first or second degree, had been found "not guilty." "It is one of those disheartening failures of justice which are all too common in this country," even the conservative New York *Tribune* conceded. The *New York Call* put it differently: "Capital can commit no crime when it is in pursuit of profits."[50]

Enraged by the callousness of the employers and their indifference to the safety and other needs of the workers, the waistmakers insisted on a second general strike. The leaders of local No. 25 were forced to accede to their demand. But the Women's Trade Union League disapproved of the plan. At the 1911 National Women's Trade Union League convention, Margaret Dreier Robins made the organization's position clear. The New York League was convinced, she said, that without "effective leadership," capable of "instructing the rank and file in the principles of trade unionsim and the best methods of getting practical results," a general strike would bring "untold suffering." Local No. 25's leadership, according to the league, was anything but "effective." Apart from the fact that they lacked "business sense or executive ability" and had no way of fighting the employers except with words when what was needed was "business methods," the men who managed Local No. 25—like those who led all ILGWU locals in the women's trades—still thought very little of women's ability to participate in trade union activities. Over 80 percent of the waistmakers' union's rank and file were female, yet men controlled the leadership and few women held positions of any responsibility within the organization. "Local 25's leaders regarded women as ignorant," notes Nancy Shrom Dye, "and had no interest in educating them to be serious trade unionists."[51]

When Local No. 25 called a second general strike in October, 1911, the league refused to endorse it and gave the strikers only minimal aid. In other words, the league had moved full circle from a position of cooperating with unions on the basis of the unions' policies to one of seeking to *determine* those policies, and, if its advice was not heeded, remaining aloof from the struggle or giving it only token support. The WTUL launched a concerted shop-by-shop campaign, concentrating its efforts on the American-born skilled workers in the uptown branch of the waist industry, After considerable effort, league organizer Melinda Scott managed to establish a small union of ladies' tailors, which later became ILGWU Local No. 38.[52]

In the spring and summer of 1912 the pessimism among league members over the future of immigrant women in the garment trades was dissolved by a tremendous struggle in which these very women were involved. Women fur workers had a major role in achieving a "great and remarkable victory" in this strike, in which the league itself played only a small part.[53]

In 1912 there were ten thousand workers in New York's fur manufacturing shops. About seven thousand of them were Jewish, most of them recent immigrants from eastern Europe. The remainder were Germans, Greeks, Italians, French-Canadians, English, Bohemians, Slovaks, and other nationalities. About three thousand were women, mainly finishers.[54] In April, 1904, the International Association of Fur Workers of the United States and Canada was organized, but the union's failure to organize the Jewish furriers led to its collapse and the surrender of its charter to the AFL early in 1911. At that point, the United Hebrew Trades initiated an organizing drive, and by the spring of 1912 three thousand of the ten thousand workers in the industry had been organized into three locals, which affiliated with the AFL. With its enlarged membership and with $3,000 in its treasury, the union felt prepared for a major struggle with the employers.[55]

The need for changes in the working conditions in the fur trade made the union confident that there would be a positive response to its call. The poverty-ridden life of immigrant workers in New York City was nowhere better illustrated than in the case of the fur workers. The cutters, the aristocrats of the trade, earned about $12 a week. Operators averaged only about $6, and finishers, all women, only $5. Most fur workers worked fifty-six to sixty hours a week, and some even longer, in filthy, disease-breeding sweatshops, usually located in ancient, broken-down wooden tenements or in basements. In one or two small rooms, without even a pretense of ventilation, about twenty fur workers would labor. Stairs, hallways, rooms, and closets were packed with dust-saturated fur pieces and cuttings. Stench and dust blanketed everything. Hair, dust, and poisonous dyes ate at the workers' eyes, noses, skin, and lungs as they toiled at the bench or machine.

In 1911 a New York State commission conducted an investigation of sanitary conditions in fur shops. A special panel of doctors examined the workers. Two out of every ten fur workers had tuberculosis, and another two had asthma. The fingers of many workers were rotted by dyes. The skin on their hands had turned black. The commission reported that eight out of every ten fur workers were suffering from occupational diseases.[56] Little wonder, then, that the newly formed union was confident that there would be an enthusiastic response to its strike call.

The union began its preparations for a general strike in the spring of 1912, quietly framing a set of demands, including union recognition, the closed shop, a nine-hour day (the fifty-four-hour week), paid holidays, the abolition of homework and subcontracting, and a union scale of wages. On June 14, 1912, union members were balloted on the strike issue; the final tabulation showed an overwhelming favorable majority—2,135 for a general strike and only 364 against. Two days later the union sent its demands to the manufacturers. On June 19 the two employers' associations—the Associated Fur Manufacturers and the Mutual Fur Protective Association (the latter comprising about three hundred employers)—rejected the union's demands. The fur manufacturers were resolved to oppose union recognition and the closed shop, and the MFPA determined "not to enter into any contract, agreement or secret understanding that shall or may conflict with the principle of the open shop."[57]

On June 20 the strike call was distributed in the fur market. As was the custom in all garment strikes of the period, the strike bulletin was printed in red and was known as the *Red Special.* Calling on the fur workers to "Arise to Battle," the *Red Special* declared: "Victory is positive. . . . The general strike starts today (June 20th) at 10 a.m. No one shall remain at work. Leave your shops as one man." Seven thousand fur workers in forty shops responded to the union's call. On the second day, 8,500 workers—three-quarters of them Jewish and two thousand of them women—were out from five hundred shops. By the end of the first week, the strike was general in fact as well as in name. Only members of the German Furriers' Union remained at work until the fifth week, at which time they, too, joined the strike. With 9,000 workers out, the trade was completely paralyzed.[58]

With the entire trade at a standstill, the union leaders expected a brief, triumphant struggle, but it soon became evident that the fur workers were in for a long and bitter battle. Although some small employers settled with the union during the first three weeks of the strike, the two employers' associations were determined to fight to the end, convinced that they could win by starving out the workers. The manufacturers simply closed their shops for three weeks, announcing that on July 8 the shops would open for all workers to return under the old conditions.

There was some justification for the employers' confidence. After the first three weeks of the strike, the union's financial resources were approaching the vanishing point, and many of the strikers were faced with starvation and eviction. But the women pickets marched around the buildings that housed the fur shops, carrying signs in Yiddish and English that read: "Masters! Starvation is your weapon. We are used to starving. We will fight on 'til victory!"[59]

As July 8 approached, the eyes of all New York were on the furriers. Would their ranks break? Nine thousand strikers gave the answer that morning as they walked the picket lines. Every shop remained empty. The strikers had won the first test.

Nine times during the next ten weeks, the employers repeated their announcement that the shops would reopen. Each time, the strikers kept the shops closed by their militant demonstrations.

As in all of the garment strikes, except the one in Milwaukee, the fur employers unleashed gangsters against the workers, and the police protected the strikebreakers by clubbing and arresting the pickets. More than 800 strikers were arrested, including 250 women; 54 strikers, 40 of them women, received workhouse sentences; and 215, over 60 of whom were women, suffered serious injuries at the hands of the thugs. But the furriers remained steadfast. The union was compelled to issue an appeal to all sympathetic groups for funds. An aid committee was elected by the United Hebrew Trades, with Rose Blank, a member of the Women's Trade Union League and its delegate to the UHT, as chairperson.[60]

Over $20,000 was raised through the *Jewish Daily Forward.* The

Cloakmakers' Union, which had received contributions from the fur workers during its own great strike, contributed $20,000, and the capmakers, $1,500. Special strike issues of the *Forward* and the *New York Call,* tag day collections, house-to-house canvassing, picnics, and theater benefits netted additional funds.* Lodges of fraternal organizations contributed $1,000. Other AFL unions raised another $1,000. But not one cent of the $60,000 raised and spent by the union in the course of the strike came from the national AFL. When Morris Shamroth, a member of the strike committee, went to the AFL Executive Council in Washington seeking financial assistance, Gompers sent him back with the message: "Tell the strikers to let the world know they are hungry and keep up the fight."[61]

The chairperson of the two thousand women strikers was Russianborn Esther Polansky. She was so militant in helping to organize the union that she was selected a member of the strike arrangements committee and then as head of the women strikers. As chairperson, she won additional fame by her own example, "because she herself never stopped considering when it was necessary to take down a shop or go up to a place where scabs worked. She never stopped before any danger. This the workers appreciated so much that not only did she win their admiration but also their willingness to sacrifice if she ordered them to do so."[62]

Toward the end of August, when the strike had been on for the better part of two months, negotiations finally got under way between the union and employer representatives. On August 22, at a specially arranged meeting of the strikers, the terms of a proposed settlement were read and explained. The strikers were granted nearly all their demands, including union recognition; only the closed shop and the demand for a half day on Saturday throughout the year were omitted from the proposed agreement. The work week was to include a half day on Saturday during the first eight months of the year, but a full day on Saturday for the remaining four months.

Socialist Meyer London, the strikers' legal adviser, was cheered when he urged them to stick to their demands. So, too, was Samuel Gompers, who said: "Since you have rebelled, which is a sign that you no longer want to stand for it, stay out and keep up your fight until your employers yield to your demands." The strikers overlooked the callous advice he had given them when they appealed for financial assistance. They then affirmed by unanimous vote that they would not return to their jobs unless the employers granted them the half-holiday on Saturday all year round, instead of simply for the first eight months.

Two weeks later, in the thirteenth week of the strike, victory was won.

---

*Tag days were days on which contributions were solicited, with each donor being given a tag to wear.

On September 8 the manufacturers acceded to the strikers' demand for the Saturday half holiday. "The Fighting Furriers" also obtained a forty-nine-hour week; overtime work only during the busy season, at time and a half; ten paid holidays; the banning of homework; wages to be paid weekly and in cash; a permanent Board of Arbitration and a Joint Board of Sanitary Control; a standing conference committee to settle all disputes, with five from each side and with an eleventh and deciding member to be named jointly by both sides—*and union recognition.* The agreement was to last for two years.[63]

"The power of unity and solidarity triumphed over the power of money, the power of police attacks and hunger and want," declared the *Jewish Daily Forward* in hailing the victory. It was a historic agreement, the best thus far achieved in the revolt of the garment workers and the first collective agreement in an industry in which there was not yet even a national union, for the AFL charter to the International Fur Workers of the United States and Canada was not to be issued until July 1, 1913.[64]

During the opening weeks of 1913, the New York garment workers in both the men's and women's branches were participating in tremendous labor uprisings. At one time more than 150,000 workers in the trade were on strike—men's tailors, white-goods workers, kimono and wrapper makers, and shirtwaist makers. "The local needle industries," exclaimed the *New York Call* in some astonishment on January 13, 1913, "have been practically paralyzed by one of the most gigantic and general uprisings which Greater New York has ever witnessed."

That same day one of the greatest parades in the history of the city occurred, as thousands upon thousands—estimates varied from 25,000 to 80,000—of strikers in the men's and boys' garment industry marched in Manhattan and Brooklyn to protest the brutality of police and hired thugs and to demonstrate their solidarity. The line of march in the Manhattan parade extended for more than thirty blocks and included strikers from about eight hundred workshops and factories. "One of the remarkable features of the parade," noted the *New York Times,* "was the number of nationalities represented. Workers from fifteen countries were pointed out, and they all marched shoulder to shoulder, seemingly on the best of terms." It then went on to add: "Fully a third of the marchers were women. Some of these were girls ranging in age from 16 to 20 years." But there were also "older women, whose bent backs told of years spent over sewing machines."

On the reviewing stand in Union Square were the speakers, and reporters noted that there was considerable anticipation expressed about the speech to be made by Rose Pastor Stokes, a Jewish workingwoman from the Cleveland ghetto who had married a millionaire but continued to devote her life to improving the conditions of the laboring class and furthering the cause of the Socialist Party.* In her speech Stokes encouraged the strikers to persevere in their demands and to swear not to return to work until the union had been recognized. The time had come, she said, when the employers "must recognize the rights of labor, whether they wanted to or not."[65]

The action of the men's tailors was the only garment strike in which men constituted the majority of the strikers, but its course was to have great importance for the future of women workers in the industry. As was the case in Chicago, these workers remained unorganized because of the indifference of the United Garment Workers leadership to the needs of the Jewish and Italian immigrant workers. When the UGW leaders at last realized that these workers, inspired by the struggles of the waistmakers, cloakmakers, and furriers, were ready to fight, they perceived that they had to give at least token support and indicated a willingness to go along. On November 15, 1912, after a series of organizational meetings, the New York District Council of the union issued a call for "a general strike of the entire clothing industry of Greater New York," and predicted that out of it "a mighty tailors' union will be built up."[66]

The tailors voted 35,786 for and only 2,322 against the general strike, to begin on December 30. By the end of the first week, it was conceded that more than 100,000 workers were on strike in the largest of all the struggles in the garment trades that had begun with the shirtwaist strike in 1909. Of the 100,000 strikers, fully one-third were women, the majority of them Jewish or Italian, with Poles, Russians, Lithuanians, Greeks, Germans, Czechs, and other nationalities making up the rest.†

On January 6, 1913, the union announced the beginning of mass picketing, headed by a picketing committee of ten thousand strikers, to secure a general 20 percent wage increase, a forty-eight-hour week,

*Stokes was born Rose Harriet Wieslander on July 18, 1879, in Augusto, Russian Poland. She took the name "Pastor" from her stepfather. In the autumn of 1890, Rose settled with her family in Cleveland. She worked wrapping cigars, in a shirtwaist factory, and selling ladies' bonnets in a department store. A letter she wrote to the *New York Jewish Daily News* in July, 1901, on conditions of factory workers led to her being offered a job as assistant to the editor of that paper's English section. In July, 1903, the *News* assigned her to interview James Graham Phelps Stokes, a wealthy resident of the University Settlement House. They fell in love and were married on her 26th birthday, in 1905. At her request, the word "obey" was omitted from the marriage ceremony. In July, 1906, the couple formally joined the Socialist Party.

†The militancy of the Italians aroused admiration in the Jewish press. "The vitality of the Italian workers," reported the *Jewish Daily Forward* on January 6, 1913, "was wonderful, their energy is simply incredible, their devotion exceeds everything." On January 11, the *Forward* urged Jewish workers not to "fall behind their Italian brothers" in militancy, and then quickly added "sisters," observing that Italian women were among the most militant of the strikers.

union recognition, extra pay for overtime, electric power for machines, abolition of tenement house work, and improved sanitary conditions in the shops. The significance of the last demand is indicated by the fact that Frances Perkins, executive secretary of the Committee of Safety (and in 1933 selected to be the first woman Secretary of Labor), described the workshops and factories of the clothing industry as "fire and death traps." She added, "The lessons of the Triangle fire have not been learned by the employers."[67]

The workers did not have sufficient funds to provide sustenance for themselves and their families during New York's bitter winter. They faced daily the savagery of strikebreakers, thugs, and police. One report read: "Blood flowed freely, skulls were cracked, ribs were broken, eyes blackened, teeth knocked out and many persons were otherwise wounded in a brutal assault on the garment strikers and pickets, not by the hired thugs and gangsters, but by the Cossacks, who comprise a part of the New York City police force." As in past strikes, the judiciary did what it could for the manufacturers, and when the strikers defied state Supreme Court injunctions outlawing peaceful picketing, hundreds of them were arrested.[68]

The strikers' militancy, combined with mounting support from the public and from the labor and socialist movements, forced individual firms to settle. On January 21 the Clothing Contractors' Association, speaking for itself and for the United Merchants' and Manufacturers' Association, agreed to enter into a conference with the UGW for the purpose of devising a means of settling the strike. At this point UGW President Thomas Rickert stepped into the situation and, as he had previously done in Chicago, disregarded both the strike leadership and the workers and accepted an agreement to end the strike. The strike leaders, bitter over this sellout, rejected the settlement. On the last day of February, the three largest associations of clothing manufacturers submitted a proposal for settling the strike, and Rickert again ignored both the strike committee and the strikers and promptly accepted the offer. Under this latest proposal, the workers were to return to their jobs immediately, pending an impartial investigation into the issue of reducing hours; the tailors were to obtain a general wage increase of $1 per week, with a proportional raise for pieceworkers; sanitary conditions would be somewhat improved; subcontracting would be abolished; and there was to be no discrimination in the reemployment of the strikers. Even though there was not a word about union recognition in any form, the UGW officially proclaimed the walkout at an end.[69]

With their struggle already weakened, the strikers were set back still further when the *Jewish Daily Forward* suddenly reversed itself, lined up with Rickert, and urged the strikers to accept the settlement and return to their jobs. Then, on March 7, Mayor Gaynor, acting with Rickert's express approval, ordered the police to disperse all remaining pickets. The strike faltered, and, on March 11, it ended. While the persistence and militancy of the workers produced a better agreement than either of the proposals accepted by Rickert—the workweek was reduced to fifty-three hours up to January, 1914, and to fifty-two hours thereafter for all but cutters, who were to enjoy a fifty-hour week to January, 1914, and not more than forty-eight hours thereafter, along with a small wage increase—it was the only one of the garment strikes in which the final settlement did not contain at least some form of union recognition.[70]

However, the strike did encourage a number of workers in the trade to organize, and the underhanded, strikebreaking tactics of the UGW officials were to have important repercussions. Three days after the strike ended, Isaac A. Hourwich wrote in the *New Review*, a left-wing Socialist monthly: "The work of building up a permanent organization of the tailors must now begin. If they are to profit by the lesson of this strike, they must rid themselves of boss rule (by Rickert and his henchmen)—if need be, by cutting loose from the national organization."[71] As a matter of fact the strike paved the way for 1914 rupture in the UGW and the resulting formation of the Amalgamated Clothing Workers of America, bringing with it a brighter future for all workers in the men's clothing trade, including women workers.

Meanwhile, the ladies' garment industry was the scene of a series of militant revolts, including a walkout by the white-goods workers—teenagers who worked in the worst garment shops at the most tedious tasks and who were described by one WTUL observer as "the youngest, the most ignorant, the poorest and most unskilled group of women workers who ever went on strike in this country."[72] Most of these young women earned a meager $20 a month for attaching ribbons to corset covers. On this wage, they barely survived. Sadie Aronovitch paid $3 a month for a sheet and the right to half a bed. Twenty-five cents a day went for food: coffee and a roll for breakfast, a sandwich for lunch, and a dinner served in a basement café. This left her $9 for clothing, amusements, and supplemental payments to her family.

Adding to the tribulations of their dreadful living standard were the daily abuses at the factory. An irate girl complained: "The foreman insults the girls and says hard bad words to them if they don't save the pins. Fines, fines, fines all the time. Ten cents if you lose a screw. You must make a hundred yards of ticking to pay for the screw and then you have nothing to eat. In my place five girls get $10 a week. All the others get between four and five."[73]

A group of two hundred workers had been organized into White Goods Workers' Union, Local No. 62, several years earlier by league members, but the union had failed to grow. However, the league was still involved with the small union through Rose Schneiderman, in her capacity as East Side organizer. Throughout 1911 and 1912, Schneiderman, Samuel Ellstein, whom the ILGWU had appointed as part-time manager of Local No. 62, and Samuel Shore of Philadelphia, who replaced him, asked the ILGWU and the New York WTUL Strike Council to fund a full-time organizer and support a general strike. The international office, faced with similar requests from small unions in the other women's trades, and unwilling to risk large sums of money on these trades while it was preoccupied with the struggle to maintain the cloakmakers' Protocol, refused.[74] The league, on the other hand, paid Rose Schneiderman to devote herself exclusively to the organization of the white-goods trade; however, the Strike Council was reluctant to support a move for a general strike, despite Schneiderman's argument that only a general strike could bring about widespread organization and give the union the members and the treasury it needed to enforce union wages and conditions. She also stressed that the women in the union, impressed by the general strikes in the waist and cloak trades and frightened by the Triangle fire, were agitating for a general strike.[75]

But the Strike Council remained adamant. Schneiderman was told that shop-by-shop organizing, while not as spectacular as a general strike, would produce better results in the long run. Women who joined the union could be thoroughly instructed in trade union principles and could learn to participate in union affairs. As Helen Marot put it, "The business of the League . . . is to bring women into places of responsibility in the organization of their trade." In a general strike, she maintained, men would dominate the situation and the "women would have no place and power and probably mostly no voice."[76]

The members of the league gradually relented in their opposition to a general strike, and finally the Strike Council pledged it modest financial support. Late in 1912 the international, too, authorized a general strike in the white-goods industry. On January 6, 1913, approximately seven thousand white-goods workers—nearly half the workers in the trade—answered the strike call. They asked for a 20 percent increase in wages; a flat fifty-four-hour week; abolition of child labor, of the fining system, and of subcontracting; recognition of the union; and a closed shop.[77]

On the eve of the strike, Shore, Schneiderman, and union leaders Lena Gasson, Florence Zuckerman, Mollie Lifschitz, and Mary Goff spent the night in a vigil in the ramshackle building that served as union headquarters, while WTUL members readied the designated meeting halls and prepared to organize the pickets under Schneiderman's supervision. By noon of the day of the strike, strikers had jammed the halls and eagerly paid the $1 initiation fee to join the union.[78]

Once on the picket lines, the strikers encountered the usual indignities and brutalities. The police carried out their usual indiscriminate arrests, and the employers' thugs beat up the young pickets. When WTUL members who accompanied strikers on picket duty issued public protests, the bosses adopted a new tactic. Into the battle came the gangsters' "molls." They filled their pocketbooks with stones, and when a skirmish began, they swung their loaded bags against the pickets' heads. They also carried concealed scissors, and at an opportune moment they would cut the strikers' long braided hair. In addition, they dogged the strikers' steps, keeping up a steady barrage of obscenities and urging them to join their ranks, with promises of easy money and good times.[79]

But the picket lines held fast, and as the fifteen-year-old girls walked the lines, they sang the "Song of the White Goods Workers" to buoy their spirits:

> At last all New York's White Goods toilers,
>   Just dropped the life of Slavery,
> And went to join the "Golden Soil"
>   Of the Union's Bravery.
>
> Now we're all doing our duties,
>   The spell of slavery to break,
> And the Boss's wife shall pawn the rubies
>   To get herself a Union Cake.
>
> We're getting beaten by policemen,
>   With their heavy clubs of hickory,
> But we'll fight as hard as we can
>   To win "Strong Union Victory."[80]

These plucky teenagers did not hesitate to tell their persecutors that they would fight back, and fight back they did. When one boss ordered a scab to hit a young picketer, the striking girl shrugged off the blow. "[I] gave the boss such a smash with my umbrella that it flew into two pieces. He was so surprised he fell down.... I was arrested, but I was so little and he so big and fat, the Judge said "Go on home," and he let me off. And from that day he [the boss] found out he was fighting with someone who wasn't afraid."[81]

The brutalities they faced taught the strikers many lessons. One picket told interviewers that when she had lived in Russia, she believed Americans had liberty, "but now I know the workers must fight for liberty in this country, too. It's the same fight everywhere. In Russia it is the Czar. In America it is the boss and the boss's money. Money is God in America."[82] The strike experience also awakened a great union spirit in the girls. One declared: "I think the union is like a mother and father and its children. I'd give my whole life for the union." Another said: "You know if we had to go back [to work] without the union I would die. My heart and soul is just with the union. I makes you feel so big instead of like a piece of dirt in the world." Still another confessed: "I eat two meals a day and wear my clothes until they fall off me, but I wouldn't be a scab."[83]

As in the great uprising of 1909–1910, prominent society women took up the strikers' cause—although not this time in association with the WTUL—marching on the picket lines, holding benefit functions, assisting in police court, posting bond, and generally focusing public attention on the strikers' plight and their bravery. These women developed an enormous admiration for the white-goods workers' courage and determination. Theodore Roosevelt paid a whirlwind visit to the strike scene and announced his shock over the working conditions and the treatment the "future mothers of America" had received during the strike. Fola LaFollette, daughter of the Progressive Senator from Wisconsin, picketed with the strikers, along with students from Barnard and Wellesley. Victor Berger, the Socialist congressman from Milwaukee, called for a federal investigation into clothing industry conditions. And New York City Mayor William Gaynor warned employers against the use of strong-arm methods. After league members and their striking colleagues had brought twenty-five cases of false arrest before Police Commissioner William Baker, Baker changed a number of officers and reprimanded others for their treatment of the young strikers.[84]

Although the union put the league in charge of strike publicity, the WTUL did not make the same concerted effort for the white-goods strikers as it had in the shirtwaist strike. The league contributed only $1,000 to the union's strike fund and raised only $6,000 in contributions. Also in contrast to its behavior during the waistmakers' strike, the league kept itself aloof from the union's leaders. The WTUL had come to view these leaders as almost as great enemies of the women strikers as the bosses were. "Before we are members of a union, we let our employers decide just what we are worth," Helen Marot declared. "No trading of bosses will solve our problems. The purpose of a strike is to get rid of bosses."[85]

The tendency of the league members to view the struggle as one that would lead only to a change of masters undoubtedly had an effect on the nature of the final settlement. The agreement specified improvements in working conditions: hours were reduced from sixty a week to fifty-two; charges for power and materials were abolished; subcontracting was ended in the association shops; there were pay increases for both salaried workers and pieceworkers, extra pay for overtime, and four annual legal holidays with pay. In addition, the contract established a wage floor: no worker was to work for less than $5 a week. While the manufacturers refused to agree to a closed shop, they did consent to negotiate with shop chairpersons whenever a disagreement occurred. The workers had hoped for a closed shop, and at one point during the six-week strike the workers had voted to continue the struggle until such an agreement could be reached. However, the association members would only accept the preferential union shop, in which union members would be given preference in hiring. While many girls raised violent objections to the settlement, claiming that it should have at least included a protocol agreement, the majority eventually voted, at an emotion-filled mass meeting, to accept the contract.[86]

The ten-member Executive Board of Local 62, elected directly after the strike settlement, included nine women. While Samuel Shore continued as manager, Mollie Lifschitz also stayed on as financial secretary, and at the request of the IGLWU officials, Rose Schneiderman served on the Grievance Board that was established by the settlement.[87]

The women of the Wrapper, Kimono, and House Dress Workers' Union, Local No. 41, walked out on January 8, 1913, and a week later, the leaders of Dress and Waistmakers' Union, Local 25, issued a call for their second general strike. The waistmakers' walkout, involving 25,000 waist- and dressmakers, ended three days later, on January 18, with the acceptance of a protocol for the industry that provided for new wage scales, a fifty-hour week, improved sanitary conditions, union recognition, and the establishment of arbitration boards to deal with workers' grievances.[88] The strike of the Wrapper, Kimono, and House Dress Workers' Union lasted longer. Amid desperate personal sacrifices, the women strikers refused to accept any agreement that did not provide for union recognition. On February 13, 1913, the manufacturers' association, feeling the pressure of public support for the strikers, signed a "Protocol of Peace" with Local No. 41.[89]

Two weeks later, the upsurge in the garment trade spread to Boston, where women workers in the children's dressmaking industry walked out, along with Boston's dress- and waistmakers. With the assistance of Boston's Women's Trade Union League, both strikes were won. On March 15, 1913, representatives of the manufacturers' association signed a protocol agreement with Local No. 49, the Boston dressmakers' union, and the ILGWU. In addition to the usual protocol terms, this accord included provisions for a $5 minimum wage, the establishment of a wage scale board to investigate costs and wages, and the employment of experts to decide on equitable wages.[90]

By the middle of March, 1913, every branch of the ladies' garment industry in the most important center of that industry—New York City—had contractual relations with the ILGWU that were based more or less on the cloakmakers' protocol of 1910, and similar agreements were being signed in Boston and other centers. By year's end, these trade agreements covered 90 percent of the international's membership in an industry in which women virtually monopolized the jobs. The wave of strikes that women had waged in the various branches of the women's garment industry had won thousands of new members for the union, and by 1913 the ILGWU ranked as the third-largest AFL affiliate, boasting ninety thousand members and the second largest enrollment of women. In fact, women constituted over 50 percent of the International's membership. Moreover, women were becoming active in the union leadership as well. Women strike veterans were traveling around the country as organizers, helping other women strikers, and awakening union consciousness in otherwise apathetic regions. Other militant women unionists accepted office in their locals, attended national conventions, assumed numerous speaking and publishing duties, led demonstrations, and sat on arbitration boards.

At the 1913 convention of the National Women's Trade Union League, Rose Schneiderman triumphantly reiterated the gains that workers in the women's clothing industry had made over the years since the uprising of the waistmakers. She pointed out that in September, 1909, just a few months before the shirtwaist strike, approximately 3,000 women belonged to unions in the garment trades. A year later, 16,716 women were enrolled as members. By September, 1913, New York State trade union records listed 63,872 women as members of New York City unions in the needle trades. Moreover, at least 60,000 women had gained a nine-hour day and a half holiday on Saturday. They earned at least 20 percent more than they had in the years before the general strikes, and they had established reasonably stable unions to which they could turn for assistance.[91]

20

New Unionism in the Garment Industry

THE ERA of the general strike in the garment trade came to an end with the 1913 uprising of the white-goods workers. When the members of the Women's Trade Union League of New York looked back over the period from late 1909 to early 1913, they were able to see definite, impressive gains. More New York City workingwomen belonged to unions than ever before, and tens of thousands of them were covered by written agreements.

To many league members, however, this was not enough. Despite the increasing role played by the sixty thousand women members in trades that had been virtually unorganized only three years earlier, the unions to which they belonged were still dominated by men, and as long as such domination continued, these WTUL members felt, the women would remain "powerless in their unions just as they were powerless in their shops."[1]

During 1914 the longstanding discontent among rank-and-file workers with the leadership of the garment industry unions triggered a general upheaval that left the International Ladies' Garment Workers' Union with new national officers and the United Garment Workers rent asunder. Union women, although just recently organized, stood in the forefront of these developments, expressing their grievances, demanding internal reforms and a greater role in the functioning of the unions, and participating actively in the events that ultimately provided them with a greater share in the organizations they had helped to create.

It did not take long for workers in the women's garment trade to realize that union leaders who relied only on the machinery of the protocol and the good will of the employers to establish permanent industrial peace were not likely to build strong organizations. As early as February, 1912, workers in the trade complained openly that the pro-

374

tocol, by forbidding the use of the strike, had tied their hands and had paralyzed union action in their behalf. But ILGWU leader John Dyche opposed the demands of the rank and file for greater control over working conditions, and when strikes were called against protocol violations, he broke them by sending in union members to replace those who refused to return to work. Dyche was proud of maintaining "a spirit of cooperation between the Union and the Association," but the rank and file regarded this "cooperation" as valueless in the face of continued employer violations of the protocol.[2]

While support for Dyche's ouster from office was increasing among all garment workers, women members were especially angered by the fact that under his administration men continued to dominate the official positions of leadership within the ILGWU. By 1914 women constituted over 50 percent of the international's membership, but there were only eighteen women delegates at the biennial convention that year. Nine of these represented White Goods Workers' Union, Local No. 62. Local No. 25, the waistmakers' local, already the largest women's local in the nation, sent nine male delegates and three women to the convention. With a few exceptions, men held all union offices and Executive Board positions and staffed the protocol, grievance, and arbitration machinery as well. And the great majority of the international's organizers were men.[3]

Women garment workers did not just sit by in the face of this situation. Pauline Newman, who had taken on important duties on the Joint Sanitary Board staff, insisted that the ILGWU could not grow unless women assumed additional leadership tasks. She argued that "girls are apt to have more confidence in a woman than in a man" and that the failure of the union's leadership to understand this elementary truth was seriously limiting its influence. In August, 1914, Constance Denmark, editor of the women's section of the *Ladies' Garment Worker,* expressed it even more strongly when she complained: "It is certainly not normal if thousands of girls, many of them possessing active minds and intelligence, should have to be thrown upon the leadership of a comparatively small number of men. What is worse, the girls are numerically the backbone of the union."[4]

The mounting anger of the operation of the protocol and the increasing resentment of women members combined to present a serious challenge to the supremacy of the leaders who controlled the ILGWU. In June, 1914, the delegates to the union's convention swept Dyche and his cronies out of office and replaced them with a radical slate of officers, headed by Benjamin Schlesinger as president. Women garment workers hailed the convention's action and looked forward hopefully to a leadership that would encourage the presence of more women in executive positions and as delegates to the 1916 convention.[5]

A few weeks later the leaders of the United Garment Workers of

America faced a similar challenge. For several years, two factions within the UGW had vied for power. Lager and Rickert, the UGW's top leaders, were enthusiastic advocates of Samuel Gompers' "pure and simple unionism." They ran the union on business principles and carried this concept so far that they made a private business of selling the union label, even to firms that operated with nonunion workers and ran their shops and factories as they pleased. Frowning upon strikes and depending on the union label for their bargaining strength, the UGW leaders placed their main reliance on workers who lived in small communities and worked in large factories manufacturing overalls. A large section of their supporters were women born in the United States, and Margaret Daly was the link between the conservative union leadership and these women, visiting each local annually to negotiate a new label contract.

The other faction of the UGW was made up of tailors and operators who worked in the large urban shops. A great majority of these workers were of immigrant origin, most frequently Yiddish-speaking eastern Europeans. The nonimmigrant women in the small communities felt they had little in common with these workers in the urban centers, and the UGW leadership took advantage of this alienation by directing repeated sneering remarks at the non-English-speaking tailors in the big cities. They even encouraged the women in several UGW urban locals to complain to the WTUL about the "fact that the Yiddish-speaking men were practically crowding out the women, who did not understand Yiddish." UGW officers made few attempts to organize the other urban centers, and when the tailors in the big cities struck, the leaders refused to acknowledge their strikes as legitimate. Then, when the workers refused to abandon the struggle, the UGW leaders invariably sabotaged the strike by arranging secret settlements.

The tailors in the UGW called for a new unionism that combined industrial unionism, class-consciousness, and socialism. While they wanted to change the entire structure of society, they also understood the need to fight for such immediate demands as higher wages, shorter hours, and better working conditions. They bitterly resented the corrupt, class-collaborationist policies of the national and local officials, and were enraged by the irresponsible use of the label by these officials and by their intimate relationship with the manufacturers. Above all, they resented the fact that a minority of the membership—the overall makers—were being used by the autocratic leaders as a means of maintaining their domination of the union.[6]

In 1914 thirteen New York locals in the coatmaking trade formed the United Brotherhood of Tailors. The New York tailors and related workers in Chicago, Baltimore, and Rochester now represented a clear majority of the total UGW membership, sufficient to control the approaching biennial convention and wrest the leadership from the conservative leaders. But Rickert and Lager were determined to remain in power regardless of the will of the majority of the membership. They therefore scheduled the convention to be held in Nashville, a site far removed from any of the large urban centers and a city administered by officials sympathetic to the UGW leaders. A few weeks before the convention, the union's auditor announced that a number of locals in New York and Chicago had fallen into financial arrears and were therefore ineligible to send delegates to the convention.[7]

However, the New York tailors had a full delegation of 107 of the 350 delegates present when the convention opened and distributed a leaflet appealing for their right to be seated. It concluded with a firm plea for unity: "Let us unite in order to fight our common enemy, *capitalism,* instead of picking suicidal quarrels among ourselves."[8] Rickert, however, brushed aside this and other attempts to compromise the differences between the two groups. He surreptitiously circulated a rumor that the New Yorkers were planning to subvert the union and turn it into an instrument of the Jewish people. Not a single delegate from New York was recognized and seated.[9]

The excluded delegates moved to the balcony to witness the proceedings, while others on the floor challenged the conservative leaders. Two women led the battle on both sides. Bessie Abramowitz, an authorized delegate from Chicago, worked tirelessly whipping up support for the excluded delegates. She shared the platform with fellow Chicagoans Frank Rosenblum and A. D. Marempietri as they addressed the convention and fought for the reinstatement of the 107 suspended delegates. Margaret Daly, a member of the union's Executive Board, lobbied for the conservative leadership. She spoke to the women delegates and sought to dispel any sympathy they might have for the suspended delegates, who, she said, were anarchists and Jews determined to disrupt the union. Daly called a special meeting of women delegates at which she pictured the dissidents in the union as dangerous to the United States as well as to the UGW, instructing the women to vote against the New Yorkers in the interests of their nation, their families, and their union.[10]

The convention finally split apart when the tailors from New York, Chicago, Baltimore, and Rochester—authorized and unauthorized delegates alike—left the convention hall and regrouped at their hotel. In the meetings that followed the rupture, the bolters declared themselves the properly convened union's legislative body and elected new international officers. Bessie Abramowitz proposed Sidney Hillman, then serving in New York as clerk for the Cloak and Suit Protocol, as president. Once the convention had designated Hillman, Abramowitz pleaded with him to leave his New York job and accept the presidency. She wired him: "Understand that personal pledges must cease when sister organization at stake. To become a martyr, I urge you to accept the office." Hillman eventually did accept.[11]

At the AFL convention in November, 1914, delegates appeared from both factions of the United Garment Workers, each claiming to represent the union. Ignoring the fact that the anti-Rickert forces represented the great majority of the men's clothing workers, the AFL's Credentials Committee seated Rickert and his followers on the ground that they were the regularly and officially elected delegates of the union. Gompers promptly sent a circular to all locals of the United Garment Workers informing them that Rickert was the only president of the union, and that the organization he headed was the sole bona fide union of men's clothing workers affiliated with the AFL.[12] Ellen Gates Starr commented angrily:

> The hand which should have been the strongest and readiest to aid those brave and oppressed people who had rejected the existing leadership of the United Garment Workers was the one which shut off from them the most powerful sources of aid. . . . And why? Because a spirited body of people, unable to rid themselves, otherwise, of corrupt officials, had dared to secede in overwhelming majority and form a new and clean organization under honest and able leadership.[13]

The "new and clean" organization was formed at a special convention held by the insurgents in New York from December 26 to 28, 1914. Having lost in court the right to use the old union's name, the insurgents called themselves the "Amalgamated Clothing Workers of America," with Sidney Hillman of Chicago as president and Joseph Schlossberg of New York as general secretary. The union then represented forty thousand workers in the United States and Canada.[14]

The ideology of the new union, born in militant struggle against the clothing employers and the bureaucrats of the UGW, was set forth clearly in the preamble to its constitution. Noting the "constant and unceasing struggle" between those who owned the means of production and the class that had "nothing but its labor power," the union was characterized as "a natural weapon of offense and defense in the hands of the working class." Craft unions, it claimed, were outdated; only industrial unionism was able to meet the needs of all workers in the twentieth century. The preamble called for the eventual organization of the working class, both economically and politically, and looked forward to the time when working-class organization would "put the organized working class in actual control of the system of production and the working class will then be ready to take possession of it."[15]

The preamble, with its socialist ideology, intensified the hostility of the AFL leaders toward the new union of clothing workers, and they set about to attempt to destroy it in its infancy.[16] On the other hand, the creation of a new garment union dedicated to progressive principles offered a ray of hope to those who believed that women deserved to play a more prominent role in the union movement.

It did not take long to demonstrate that this hope was justified. During the first trying months of the new union's existence, three dynamic women assumed significant positions. In Chicago, Bessie Abramowitz, who was instrumental in the founding of the Amalgamated Clothing Workers, continued as an important adviser and confidante of the union's leaders. At the first national convention of the new union in December, 1914, she was chosen secretary-treasurer of District Council No. 6. She also served on the Board of Arbitration, which dealt with grievances between the union and Hart, Schaffner & Marx. In addition, Abramowitz lobbied and campaigned for passage of an eight-hour law for the women of Illinois.[17]

In Rochester, New York, Selma Goldblatt worked tirelessly for the new union. As recording secretary of UGW Local No. 235, she had attended the Nashville convention, joined the secessionists, and continued in her office after her local had aligned itself with the new union. She was a leading organizer for the Amalgamated and one of its most capable administrators.[18]

One of the most remarkable women in the new union was Dorothy Jacobs, the dynamic president of Baltimore's Buttonhole Makers Union, Local No. 170. She was born in 1894 in Latvia and had moved with her family to Baltimore at age thirteen. She took a job as a hand buttonhole sewer on men's coats. She worked ten hours a day and earned $2 a week. She soon began to agitate among her fellow workers, insisting that they join her in forming a union. Before she was fourteen, she had been labeled a troublemaker and fired from several jobs. Late in 1908 the women in her shop organized a union, which affiliated with the UGW as Local 170. Jacobs, then aged fourteen, was its first president. In 1912 she led the hand buttonholers in a successful strike, and by 1914 not only were all of Baltimore's women hand buttonhole makers organized, but they decided to unionize the male machine buttonholers as well. They formed committees to visit the homes of the unorganized men, whom they found totally ignorant of union principles and hostile to women organizers. After months of work, led and organized by Dorothy Jacobs, they succeeded in organizing the men in the larger factories so that 65 percent of the machine buttonholers belonged to the union.[19]

When the UGW split, Jacobs led her local into the ranks of the Amalgamated. She represented Local No. 170 at the first Amalgamated convention, where she introduced a resolution on behalf of the buttonhole makers' union of Baltimore, calling for the assignment of a woman organizer to that city.

The convention passed the resolution, but, as was too often the case with unions of that era, the Amalgamated did nothing to implement it. However, Jacobs did not stop agitating for greater attention to the organization of women. Soon after the convention, she was elected to represent her local on the Amalgamated's Baltimore Joint Board. From this position, she spoke out frequently on the importance of taking special measures to encourage women to join and participate in the union. She became the most outspoken champion of women's rights within the garment unions.

During 1915 and 1916 the Amalgamated Clothing Workers struggled for its life against the unrelenting opposition of both the manufacturers and the AFL. When the United Hebrew Trades in New York City, reflecting the general sentiment of Jewish labor, recognized locals of the Amalgamated, that organization was singled out as a major target in the AFL's campaign against the new union. In March, 1915, the Central Federated Union of New York and Vicinity—the AFL central labor council—suspended the United Hebrew Trades from membership and ordered every international union with locals represented in the UHT to instruct the locals to withdraw their delegates. But the UHT refused to retreat, declaring that it did not intend to "give up on a question of thousands of workmen who are struggling against a parasitic clique."[20] Its attitude infuriated Gompers. At a UHT meeting on May 10 he warned the organization to expel the Amalgamated's delegates or face the wrath of the AFL, which had already determined that the United Garment Workers must be upheld.[21]

The anti-UHT campaign reached its climax at the 1915 AFL convention, when the Executive Council reported that the UHT, in harboring the Amalgamated locals, was "injurious to the solidarity or progress of the trade union movement of New York City" and directed Gompers to have all AFL-affiliated unions resign from the United Hebrew Trades. Rather than see the UHT destroyed by the AFL because of its support for the new garment workers' union, the Amalgamated's New York Joint Board decided to remove its locals from membership in the Jewish organization.*[22]

But the war against the Amalgamated by the AFL and its affiliates continued. Each year, at AFL national conventions from 1916 through 1918, the ILGWU regularly introduced resolutions intended to restore peace in the men's clothing industry through recognition of the Amalgamated as the actual representative of the largest number of clothing workers in the trade. But on each occasion, the AFL Executive Council rejected the proposal.[23] After 1917 the Amalgamated did not attend another AFL convention until 1933, when it was finally accepted within the federation's fold.†

*Although the Amalgamated and the UHT severed all official connections, they continued to maintain working arrangements.

†At its 1916 convention the AFL awarded jurisdiction in the millinery industry to the United Hatters of North America and ordered the United Cloth, Hat and Cap Makers' Union, which had organized the millinery trade, to surrender these workers. Following

Even while they were battling against the AFL leadership, the members of the Amalgamated were busy extending the union into unorganized segments of the industry. In early 1915 the Amalgamated wrested control of the New York unions from the UGW. It also gained a strong position in Baltimore and Boston and initiated drives in Philadelphia, Cincinnati, Cleveland, and St. Louis.[24]

In 1915 the Amalgamated leaders decided to stage an all-out campaign in Chicago, where a strong manufacturers' association had devised an extremely effective program of blacklisting. Only a quarter of Chicago's forty thousand men's clothing workers belonged to the Amalgamated, nearly all of them workers at Hart, Schaffner & Marx. The organizing campaign during the spring and summer was highlighted by mass meetings, a giant May Day parade, and agitational speeches in several foreign languages. In mid-September union leaders presented a list of nine demands to the Chicago manufacturers. Instead of responding to the union's demands, the employers called on the Chicago police to provide additional protection for their factories.[25]

By September 29 between 20,000 and 25,000 men and women had walked out on strike. Strike leaders divided the strike area into four districts, each with its own headquarters, meeting hall, relief committee, and designated leader. Bessie Abramowitz headed one of the four districts and was called in to assist the others. The police responded in classic Chicago style—escorting strikebreakers through the picket lines by brute force. Riding through the picket lines on horseback, they arrested the strikers, men and women, at the slightest provocation, jamming fifteen to twenty of them into patrol wagons designed to hold less than ten. By the end of day, many women bore bruises delivered by the officers' clubs.[26]

As the press publicized the attacks on the picket lines and the arrests of female strikers, society women, settlement house workers, and other concerned citizens came to the aid of the beleaguered strikers. They joined the picket lines, marched in union parades, distributed circulars, raised money for the strikers, and campaigned to bring about arbitration. When a number of these upper- and middle-class citizens were arrested, newspaper protests and demands for an investigation of police

the Amalgamated's lead, the Cap Makers' Union refused to bow before the ultimatum. Then when the 1917 AFL convention ordered the Cap Makers' Union to comply with the federation's decision or stand suspended, the union walked out of the federation. It operated outside the fold of the AFL until 1934, when the Cap Makers and the United Hatters merged. Before the Cap Makers had organized the millinery workers, who were mainly young immigrant women, the United Hatters, whose membership was restricted to males, showed no interest in organizing the milliners (Donald N. Robinson, *Spotlight on a Union: The Story of the United Hatters, Cap and Millinery Workers' Union* [New York, 1948], pp. 200–204; *The Headgear Worker* 2 [February 1917]: 9–12; ibid. 3 [January–February 1918]: 83–84, 110).

brutality mounted. The mayor refused to order such an investigation, but members of the City Council launched their own examination of working and sanitary conditions in the city's sweatshops and clothing factories. A number of women workers appeared at the hearings to testify to the oppressive treatment that had caused the strike.[27]

But nothing could persuade the manufacturers to arbitrate. As the strike dragged on into October and November, the labor agitator Mother Jones, then in her eighties but with her energy and zeal undiminished by her incarceration and labors in a long series of miners' strikes,* rushed to the scene to add her voice to the calls for arbitration. Again the manufacturers held firm, and in a dramatic gesture, Mother Jones called on Secretary of Labor William B. Wilson, a former United Mine Workers leader, to enter the strike. "Send at once to investigate clothing strike," she wired. "It is fierce, girls getting 8 cents an hour as slaves. Signed Mother." Secretary Wilson replied that he had an observer on the scene but did not feel it was wise to interfere while the City Council committee was conducting its investigation. Mother Jones led a parade of women strikers and sympathizers through the streets of Chicago, hoping to dramatize the strikers' cause and bring additional pressure on the manufacturers. As usual, she came under attack from the conservative press as an "outside agitator" who was stirring up the peaceful, law-abiding clothing workers of Chicago. But the strikers appreciated Jones's assistance, since their allegiance to the AFL prevented both the Chicago Federation of Labor and the Women's Trade Union League from offering any concrete aid.[28]

By early December, the strike appeared to be lost. Strikers had begun to abandon the picket line and drift back to work. Even though a number of the women strikers urged continuation of the struggle, offering to do double duty on the picket lines to take the places of those who had left, Hillman and his strike leaders decided to end the strike. Only after the strike appeared doomed did Samuel Gompers speak out, voicing his hope that the strikers would achieve victory.[29]

---

*As a result of her break with John Mitchell, United Mine Workers president, whom she came to regard as a collaborator with the mine owners, Jones' efforts were directed for a number of years toward nonminers. When Mitchell resigned as UMW president in 1908, Jones renewed her efforts on behalf of the miners by organizing in Greensburg, Pennsylvania, where the wives of strikers were arrested when they patrolled the coal mines and harassed scabs in compliance with her instructions. Unable to pay a $30 fine, they were sentenced to thirty days. At Jones' suggestion, they brought their children to jail with them and sang to them all night, which so disturbed the sheriff and his neighbors that they were released after five days.

Jones' Pennsylvania activities were quickly eclipsed by her fearless endeavors in West Virginia and Colorado. After months of assisting the miners of Paint and Cabin Creek in West Virginia when they were fired and evicted from their homes in April, 1912, Jones was arrested with three miners while leading a protest group to the governor. When she was sentenced to twenty years' imprisonment, the uproar of protest from American workers forced the governor of West Virginia to order her release.

In early 1916, Amalgamated members launched strikes in a number of cities, including Boston, Philadelphia, and Baltimore. Everywhere, young women were among the leading activists in the strikes, and in Baltimore they practically ran the walkout in the three leading men's clothing establishments. The union had called the strike in order to gain control of that city's men's clothing market and to drive out the UGW, with its pro-employer policies. Once again, the police brutally arrested hundreds of young women, many of whom remained in jail for some time because they were unable to raise the money for the excessive bail. Once out of jail, they were back on the picket lines.[30]

The women of Baltimore's Hand Buttonhole Workers' Union had maintained a strong organization for years, successfully resisting repeated efforts by the manufacturers to weaken their union and cut wages. Following the local's somewhat limited success in organizing the male machine buttonholers, the women went on to organize women in other branches of the men's clothing industry. In one of the largest factories, the young women unionists gave up their lunch hours to visit different floors of the factory, spreading the message of unionism to their unorganized sisters.[31]

As in Baltimore, in the strikes in Boston, Philadelphia, and soon afterwards in St. Louis and Chicago, both the press and the Amalgamated organizers noted the devotion and spirit displayed by the female pickets. Clearly, women were demonstrating again and again their enthusiastic and constructive participation in union activities. But old stereotypes die hard, and the male leaders of the Amalgamated Clothing Workers were still unwilling to recruit women members actively. Amalgamated women organizers worked tirelessly among women workers, but they received little cooperation from male organizers. Dorothy Jacobs, president of the Hand Buttonhole Workers' Union and most active in the organizing effort, complained to Hillman: "It seems that the men are not awakened as yet to the importance of organizing the women and lose sight of the fact that women are the majority in the industry."[32]

Jacobs, Bessie Abramowitz, and Selma Goldblatt launched a campaign to compel the men to recognize that the union could not survive without the full cooperation of the women. They insisted that the Amalgamated undertake a campaign to recruit women, and, once they were enrolled, to sustain their interest. At the 1916 biennial convention, the demands began to pay off. This time, when the Baltimore delegation requested a woman organizer, the convention concurred. Then New York's Italian delegation, headed by the Bellanca brothers, demanded a special women's department, and Dorothy Jacobs supported the proposal with an eloquent appeal for greater emphasis on organizing women. Then four women delegates introduced a resolution pointing out that as the number of women workers in the clothing industry increased, the future of unionism in the industry demanded that women become a part of the organized labor movement. The women delegates asked the convention to instruct the new General Executive Board to make a special effort to organize women workers, to assign a special organizer, and to issue special literature for women.[33]

When the convention adopted this wide-ranging resolution, the women members of the Amalgamated believed that a new day had dawned for them. But they soon discovered that most men in the union continued to oppose any increase in the role of women in the organization. Dorothy Jacobs was elected to a position on the General Executive Board, but the opposition she encountered, sometimes taking the form of open and outright hostility, did not disappear even after she took her seat.[34] It was not until October, 1916, months after the convention, that the board did anything to implement the convention's instructions about women workers. It called on local unions to organize women's clubs and other organizations designed to promote the organization of women in the industry and to educate those already organized, and it notified local union officials that it planned to send a woman organizer out on tour periodically. In addition, it suggested that the locals enlist the aid of women belonging to organizations friendly to labor in arranging meetings, lectures, and entertainments for women. In order to sustain the interest of women members, the board directed the locals to conduct frequent meetings of an educational nature.[35] This was the most far-reaching position yet adopted by any international union to deal with the organization and retention of women workers.

Fortunately, in a number of important cities, the stand taken by the General Executive Board did not remain confined to paper. In Baltimore the chairwomen of the individual shops decided that they needed a special "girls' local" where women could discuss their special problems and new women members could be familiarized with the union's special activities. Women who joined the "girls' local" would retain their membership in the original shop local. In early December, 1916, the women working in Baltimore's Sonneborn factory elected the chairperson of Local No. 170 to represent them on the union's Trade Board—the first woman to hold this important position.[36]

In Chicago, Amalgamated women organized the Girls' Civic and Educational Club, which met weekly at Hull House. Members planned their meetings with specific training needs in mind. They presented lessons and drills in parliamentary law and procedure in order to prepare themselves for participation in union meetings. Other programs included discussions of specific social problems and lectures on industrial and personal hygiene.[37]

Thus, by 1917, the women of the Amalgamated Clothing Workers of

America, by dint of their tremendous contributions during organizing campaigns and strikes and by their incessant demands, had persuaded the male union leadership that unless they abandoned the unionism-as-usual approach to women workers, the Amalgamated would never succeed in its bitter struggles against the employers and the AFL. The Amalgamated's convention had yielded to the pressure of the women workers and had adopted a broad program designed to encourage women to join the union and to take an active and meaningful part in its affairs. Thereupon the women of the Amalgamated, with the support of the union's General Executive Board, had begun to apply this historic resolution where it counted—among the women workers themselves, organized and unorganized alike.[38]

During the years between 1915 and 1917 the women of the International Ladies Garment Workers' Union also began to assume a more important role within the union. Early in 1915 President Benjamin Schlesinger appointed Rose Schneiderman a full-time ILGWU organizer. Sent to Chicago, she offered invaluable assistance in the first successful strike of that city's women garment workers. A number of women glovemakers employed at the nonunion Herzog company walked out on strike and presented their grievances and a list of demands to their employer. Herzog refused to negotiate; instead, he called on the police to provide protection for strikebreakers. Police in patrol wagons promptly arrested both strikers and their friends and sympathizers. But the police brutality against the tiny group of strikers so enraged the women who had remained at work—and who also had complained of the low $6 and $7 weekly wages for a sixty-hour week—that soon all seven hundred workers were out on strike. ILGWU Local No. 59 offered Fannia Cohn to help the strikers; the Chicago Joint Board of the ILGWU, the International Glove Workers' Union, and the WTUL all contributed both members to the Strike Committee and aid to the strikers. On August 22, 1915, Herzog accepted the workers' demands, recognized the union, and agreed to the establishment of a price commission. The workers won a fifty-hour week, a half holiday on Saturday, a wage increase, and the abandonment of both fines and charges for materials. The teenage strikers were jubilant, and the ranks of Local No. 59 swelled to nearly one thousand members.

The success of the Herzog workers encouraged a group of women in the kimono and white-goods branches of the industry to carry through a successful strike. They organized the Chicago White Goods Workers' Union, and two years later,the waistmakers and the white-goods workers merged to form Local No. 100.[39]

National headquarters now called Schneiderman to Philadelphia, where she worked with Pauline Newman to build a new organization among the shirtwaist makers from the nucleus that remained from the drive of 1909–1910.*

By the time Schneiderman arrived, Newman had already accomplished a small miracle. She had come to Philadelphia in 1910, when only one shirtwaist factory was organized, and left the city several years later with not only the shirtwaist industry well unionized but with thousands of other workingwomen organized as well. One of her greatest triumphs was the service she held in the Labor Lyceum in 1911, at which three thousand Philadelphia workingwomen met in sorrow and anger to memorialize the women who had died in the Triangle Shirtwaist fire in New York City.

In June, 1911, Newman began to enter the garment factories of Philadelphia, where she argued with foremen who were cutting piecework rates and told the women they could not get higher wages unless they joined the union. In this way she was "able to convert most of the employees in the shop to union membership." Those garment workers who had joined the union and gained a higher wage scale brought other women workers to the meetings that Newman called in the office of the Women's Trade Union League.

Newman's achievements were especially remarkable in view of the fact that she received little cooperation from the male union leaders. In fact, they discouraged women from visiting the WTUL office. Frequently an AFL male organizer would "totally ignore the girls when they came in and continue to smoke his cigar behind his newspaper or would talk to them in an insulting way so they would leave the headquarters." When Melinda Scott, who was organizing for the WTUL, approached the Philadelphia AFL Central Labor Committee to discuss a plan to establish a chapter in Philadelphia and use the organization as a base for organizing women workers, "the men refused to allow her to speak."

Still, the ILGWU national headquarters was more sympathetic, and with the aid of Rose Schneiderman, Newman continued the work of

---

*Pauline Newman was hired as an organizer for the Philadelphia chapter of the Women's Trade Union League in 1910. She was a Lithuanian Jew who had come to New York as a child and worked in the garment factories from the time she was twelve years old. She became an ardent Socialist, for, as she later explained in an interview:

> You see around you the poverty and misery and you know from your own experience the conditions you work and live under, and *if you have any brains at all*, it doesn't take long for you to realize that this is the place where you belong, that the Party offers some hope, some change, and you want to be part of it in making the change. You become active, you learn how to speak in public and you learn how to lead more or less, and you learn to value people who know more than you do. . . . That's how my own career began. As soon as I was old enough, I joined the SP and traveled for the SP, not only in our own state but in many other states, and in between jobs that's what I did until I became officially an organizer for the ILGWU, and even then I used to be 'loaned' to the SP on occasions. . . . I think we all had the same vision, that we, the society, the people, all people, would have a chance to live in decency. We had a vision that justice and freedom and everything else we deserved would be there under socialism [Pauline Newman, interview in Columbia University Oral History Collection, Socialist Movement Project, vol. 8, pp. 7–8].

organizing the shirtwaist makers. They were later joined by the newly appointed national WTUL organizer, Mary Anders, and new locals were established. In February, 1916, after a brief strike characterized by the all too familiar clashes between strikers and the police, the union and the manufacturers agreed to a settlement.[40]

By 1916 the ILGWU had eight women organizers in the field. President Schlesinger summoned Schneiderman to New York for a long-term assignment to help the city's petticoat workers organize. Mabel Craig had unionized northern New Jersey's waistmakers in a year-long campaign during late 1915 and early 1916. Pauline Newman, in addition to her work in Philadelphia, had traveled to upstate New York and Worcester, Massachusetts, organizing corset makers. Fannia Cohn had become a full-time organizer in Chicago, working to amalgamate the city's locals into a single, unified body. Juliet Stuart Poyntz visited Philadelphia to assist the American Branch of Local No. 15, while another young woman worked with the immigrant women in that local.[41]

The year 1916 also witnessed a bitter lockout and strike of New York cloakmakers, which led to the scrapping of the Protocol of Peace. While there were other grievances, such as the practice by employers of ridding their shops of the most militant trade unionists, the interpretation of the preferential union shop was the key issue in the dispute. When the employers' association refused to submit the issue to arbitration and unilaterally broke the conciliation agreement, the union proclaimed a general strike in the New York cloak trade on May 3, in order to prevent association employers from subcontracting their work to independent shops. Some sixty thousand union members furnished their union's reply to the employers' lockout.[42]

The struggle of 1916 lasted for fourteen weeks and was notable for the outstanding solidarity of the strikers, assisted financially by the United Hebrew Trades, the Amalgamated Clothing Workers, the Workmen's Circle, the Furriers' Union, the Cloth Hat and Cap Makers' Union, the Central Federated Union, the AFL Executive Council, the Citizens' Committee for the Locked-out Cloak and Suit Makers, and the Women's Trade Union League. The league raised over $30,000, which it spent on services to the strikers and their families. The ILGWU spent more than $627,000 on the walkout, much of it raised by sympathetic unions and organizations.[43] In the face of the workers' militancy, the union labor solidarity, and the public support, including even that of newspapers traditionally hostile to organized labor, the manufacturers were compelled to agree to negotiate with the union officials. Pressure brought by Mayor John Purroy Mitchel and President Woodrow Wilson, who authorized the secretary of labor and commerce to intervene, helped to force the manufacturers to agree to negotiate a settlement with the union.[44]

The collective agreement of August 4, 1916, which ended the lockout and strike, also ended the protocol in the cloak trade. By its terms, the manufacturers were granted the absolute right to "hire and fire," while the workers were free to strike if they could not peacefully obtain redress from their employers. The new agreement, which had a two-year limit, also gave the workers increased wages, reduced hours, union recognition, and preference in employment.[45]

Thus, the era of the protocol in the ladies' garment industry of New York City came to an end. The workers had regained the right to strike and the ability to place reliance on their organization rather than on outside boards. The so-called harmony of interests of labor and capital had proved to be an illusion. The 1916 convention of the ILGWU proclaimed that the union was "capable of taking care of the workers' interests without the benevolent protection of the employers."[46]

The 1916 convention also established a permanent Educational Committee, charged in part with the development of programs to instruct women workers in the benefits of unionism, to train new leaders, and to broaden the intellectual horizons of young women workers. The convention empowered the committee to plan with the representatives of other AFL unions for the establishment of a workers' college where union members could train for leadership positions. The committee selected Juliet Stuart Poyntz as Educational Director and Fannia Cohn as its secretary.[47]

Even while the ILGWU was adopting broad social programs to involve its female membership, even while militant women garment workers were entering the union as organizers, contract negotiators, and educational directors, and even while women's ideas were beginning to reshape the union, men continued to dominate the official leadership positions. By 1917 women constituted over 50 percent of the international's claimed 82,000 members, but only one woman, Fannia Cohn, sat on the international's General Executive Board for the 1916–1918 term.[48]

Although it was smaller than either the ILGWU or the Amalgamated, the International Fur Workers' Union also underwent considerable growth during the years 1914 to 1916. In part this was because the union organized more shops in which women constituted a majority of the workers. The muff workers of New York City—young women who were employed in typical sweatshops located in attics, cellars, and basements—were organized. After a series of strikes, all the shops employing these women were forced to sign agreements that included a forty-nine-hour week, ten paid holidays, a union shop,* and a wage increase of $2 a week.[49]

---

*A union shop and a closed shop are almost the same thing, but not quite. A closed shop requires all workers to be union members of the union and the union shop requires all

In Chicago, St. Paul, Montreal, and Toronto, women operators and finishers were organized and chartered in separate locals. Their agreements with employers established the union shop, seven paid legal holidays, time and a half for overtime, and a reduction in the working hours. In Toronto, the local of women workers, none of whom had ever before belonged to a union, proved to be so militant that they forced the employers to grant the fur workers a forty-four-hour week, two and a half times the regular rate for holiday work, and a wage increase of 25 percent.[50]

The greatest victory of the fur workers was the organization of the largest fur dressing and dyeing plant in the industry—A. Hollander & Sons in Newark, New Jersey. More than seven hundred workers were employed in this shop, two hundred of them women. The wages were low, averaging $6 to $10 a week for men, while the women workers, often hired to replace the men, worked for even less. An atmosphere of fear pervaded the plant, with instant discharge for any worker who dared to complain or even talk of a union.

Yet April 6, 1915, the entire plant walked out. From the beginning, it was a bitter struggle. Hollander refused even to discuss union recognition, and on this issue the workers were adamant. From the very outset the firm imported scabs and hired gangsters to smash the picket lines. The police did their part by arresting workers who fought back against the thugs. On April 16 Morris Rubin and Abraham Novick, two of the most militant strikers, were shot and killed in cold blood by gunmen. The mourning strikers vowed not to return to the plant until the strike was won. They kept their oath. The contract, which ran until December 1, 1917, provided for an increase of $3 a week for skilled workers, $2 for unskilled workers, and $1.50 for apprentices. The work week was cut to fifty hours, with a half day on Saturday. Overtime was paid at time and a half, the union was recognized, and any new workers hired had to join the union after two weeks.

The ending of the strike was celebrated by a parade through the streets of Newark. The victorious strikers marched behind brass bands and flags, proudly carrying aloft a huge banner that read: "THROUGH STRUGGLE TO VICTORY. WE RETURN TO WORK AS UNION MEN AND WOMEN."[51]

By 1916 the International Fur Workers' Union had chartered twenty-seven locals and had greatly increased its membership. Agreements with significant gains had been signed in almost every organized fur center. Women fur workers had been in the lead in these achievements, and the first issue of the union's journal, the *Fur Worker,* on November 2, 1916, paid special tribute to these women, declaring: "In the great strike of 1912 and in the organizing efforts in New York,

---

workers to be union members or agree to join a union within a specified time after being hired.

Chicago, St. Paul, Toronto, Montreal, and Newark, victories gained by our union would simply have been impossible but for the militancy, heroism, and self-sacrifice of the women furriers." But even more so than in the ILGWU, women fur workers, who by now made up an important part of the membership, played little role in the union's leadership. Not one woman sat on the International Fur Workers' Union's General Executive Board during the years 1913 to 1917.[52]

The ILGWU, the Amalgamated Clothing Workers, and the International Fur Workers' Union symbolized the new unionism in the garment industry. All three had been founded by trade unionists from the Socialist Party, and all three proclaimed in their constitutions that their aim was to organize workers industrially into a class-conscious organization and to create a form of society in which workers would receive the full value of their product. The new unionism encouraged a sense of solidarity that was absent in the craft-oriented unions. It challenged the principles of business unionism, which continued to dominate the AFL craft unions and, instead, held aloft a spirit of idealism.

The new unions raised no barriers to the enrollment of women members, and they offered a variety of educational, cultural, and social programs for workingwomen, which were unheard of in the old-line unions. Women members saw their wages increase and their hours of work lessen. But in another respect the organizations that came to epitomize the new unionism were like the old-line craft unions: male-dominated. Women were permitted to exercise a greater role and influence on the lower levels than in the established craft unions, but men still monopolized all union offices, and male chauvinism expressed itself in a variety of other ways. When women were appointed organizers, the male leaders often made their lives miserable by being unwilling to trust them in critical situations. Often when these women were about to enter into a strike, leaders of the international would send in men to manage the battle, thus making clear this lack of confidence in the ability of the women to do the job effectively. Protests, even threats of resignation, from the women organizers fell on deaf ears.[53]

Rose Schneiderman was so furious at the tendency of President Schlesinger and other ILGWU leaders to deprive her of command in a crucial situation that she often turned in her resignation, only to withdraw it in the interest of the women workers she was seeking to organize.[54] Finally, she could stand it no longer. In a letter of December 1, 1916, in which she spoke for many women organizers in both the old and new unionism—including those who held on despite the rebuffs from male leaders—she sent in her resignation:

Dear Sir and Brother:—

   I herewith tender to you my resignation as Organizer of the International Union.

My abrupt severance of relations with the International, if it requires any explanation, is I judge very logical in the light of the attitude taken towards my work by the powers that be.... For the last few months I have found myself working in an atmosphere of distrust which, to say the least, is not conducive to putting forth one's best efforts.[55]

She returned to the women's movement.

21

The Wobblies and the Woman Worker

THE HEADLINE in the *Cincinnati Post* of January 9, 1905, fairly shrieked: "To SUPPLANT THE AFL, INTERNATIONAL LABOR ORGANIZATION LAUNCHED ALONG SOCIALISTIC AND INDUSTRIAL LINES." The story that followed described a "secret conference" held in Chicago for the purpose of launching a trade union movement that would consist of "one great industrial union, embracing all industries, founded upon the class struggle, and conducted in harmony with the recognition of the irrepressible conflict between the capitalist class and the working class."

The organization whose imminent birth was heralded on the *Post*'s front page was the Industrial Workers of the World (IWW). It came into being in 1905 because many progressive-minded elements in the labor and socialist movements were convinced that industrial unionism was superior to craft unionism in the struggle against the highly integrated organizations of employers; that it was impossible to convert the conservative American Federation of Labor into an organization that could achieve real benefits for the majority of workingmen and -women; and that existing industrially organized and radical organizations were ineffective in building a movement that would organize and unite the entire working class. In the eyes of these elements, there was a clear need for a new organization of labor that "would correspond to modern industrial conditions and through which they [the working people] might finally secure complete emancipation from wage slavery for all workers."[1]

The *Industrial Union Manifesto*, drawn up at the Chicago Conference of Industrial Unionists on January 2, 1905, stated the ideology of the new organization:

Universal economic evils afflicting the working class can be eradicated only by a universal working class movement.... A movement to fulfill these conditions must consist of one great industrial union embracing all industries—providing for craft autonomy locally, industrial autonomy internationally, and working class unity generally.

It must be founded on the class struggle, and its general administration must be conducted in harmony with the recognition of the irrepressible conflict between the capitalist and the working class.

It should be established as the economic organization of the working class without affiliation with any political party.

All workers who agreed with these principles were invited to meet in Chicago on June 27, 1905, "for the purpose of forming an organization of the working class along the lines worked out in the Manifesto."[2] An executive committee was appointed to help promote the meeting.

Although Mother Jones was one of the signers of the *Manifesto,* the executive committee was all-male. However, the founding convention of the IWW had twelve female delegates, including Mother Jones, Lucy Parsons (the widow of the Haymarket martyr), Emma F. Langdon of Denver Typographical Union No. 49, and Luella Twining, delegate of Federal Union No. 252 of the American Labor Union,[3] an industrial union movement active mainly in the West and one of the immediate predecessors of the IWW.[4] On Mother Jones' nomination, Langdon was appointed assistant secretary of the conference, and Twining served as presiding officer during the closing-day speeches. Parsons, who was named to the committee in charge of seeing that the minutes of the convention were printed, was the only one of the twelve who addressed the convention at some length. She spoke on June 29 and declared:

> I have taken the floor because no other woman has responded, and I feel that it would not be out of place for me to say in my poor way a few words about this movement.
>
> We, the women of this country, have no ballot, even if we wished to use it, and the only way that we can be represented is to take a man to represent us. You men have made such a mess of it in representing us that we have not much confidence in asking you; and I for one feel very backward in asking the men to represent me. We have no ballot, but we have our labor....
>
> We are the slaves of slaves. We are exploited more ruthlessly than men. Wherever wages are to be reduced, the capitalist class uses women to reduce them, and if there is anything that you men should do in the future, it is to organize the women.

Although Parsons mentioned the ballot, she made it clear as she continued that she opposed political action and saw the solution for labor solely through economic action.

> I believe that if every man and every woman who works, or who toils in the mines, the mills, the workshops, the fields, the factories, and the farms in our broad America should decide in their minds that they shall have that which of right belongs to them, and that no idler shall live upon their toil,

and when your new organization, your economic organization, shall declare as man to man and woman to woman, as brothers and sisters, that you are determined that you will possess these things, then there is no army that is large enough to overcome you, for you yourselves constitute the army.

Later in the convention Parsons spoke again, advocating revolutionary strikes such as were being waged that year by the Russian workers, who had already initiated the first Russian revolution by a general strike. "You men and women," Lucy Parsons told the delegates, "should be imbued with the spirit that is now displayed in far-off Russia and far-off Siberia, where we thought the spark of manhood and womanhood had been crushed out of them. Let us take example from them." Parsons also made a rousing speech at the convention's conclusion, urging the delegates to move on to the industrial areas of the nation, organizing the entire working class along the lines of industrial unionism, and to pay special attention to the long-neglected and especially exploited workingwomen.[5]

In comparison with the AFL, the IWW convention represented some important advances for women. It was not until 1907 that a woman (Agnes Nestor of the International Glove Workers' Union) presided over an AFL convention.[6] And the IWW motto, "An Injury to One Is the Concern of All" (a modification of the Knights of Labor slogan, "An Injury to One Is an Injury to All"), and the emphasis in the constitution barring exclusion of the unskilled—a very large section of the American working class—held out a real promise for workingwomen. In a statement that was to be restated and reprinted throughout the IWW's history, the Literature and Press Committee reported "to all working people" that "in this industrial union there is room for and no bar against any worker on account of race, sex, creed, or color, and an earnest invitation is extended to every worker to enroll him or herself a member of this union."[7]

In content this statement differs little from some of the AFL's utterances. The IWW, however, backed up its statement with concrete action. Initiation fees and dues were kept very low in order to make membership more readily available to the masses of low-paid, unskilled workers. During the debate, it was made clear that the delegates had the underpaid female workers very much in mind when they adopted this policy. One delegate argued for low initiation fees and dues by stating that they were necessary because "it is the women . . . that are the lowest paid," and noted that "there are women who are working for $3.60 a week—grown women!"[8]

The second convention lowered dues for women members even further, while maintaining the existing rates for men. While it could be argued that this was demeaning to the female sex, Paul Brissenden, one of the earliest historians of the IWW, was closer to the truth when he called the action evidence that the IWW favored feminine participation and was determined not to discriminate against women workers as the AFL and other labor organizations had done.[9]

At this same convention a heated debate took place over the appropriate term to be used in addressing general union meetings. The phrase "fellow worker" was finally agreed upon, as it "may be considered of the neuter gender, and applied to the masculine or feminine, as you chose, and . . . the committee deems that so far as the male members of the organization are concerned, they will never be lacking at any time in courtesy toward a lady."[10]

By setting forth their attitude toward workingwomen early, the founders of the new industrial union movement cleared the way for women to play an active role in it. Lillian Forberg, who had been a delegate to the first convention, was a member of Chicago's General Advisory Board as well as of the local Executive Board, and was cited for her activity as agitator and organizer among Chicago's textile workers. The IWW also cited a Mrs. Orr as being an extremely able secretary of Chicago Local No. 85.[11]

In 1909 the General Executive Board voted Ester Niemien "voluntary organizer's credentials" and assured that her expenses would be paid. The Portland IWW branch reported: "We have placed a lady organizer on the list (Miss Nina Wood) and believe she is going to do very effective work."[12] And in 1909, too, Elizabeth Gurley Flynn, the "rebel girl" of Joe Hill's song and the outstanding woman in the history of the IWW,* became a member of the General Executive Board, a position no woman has ever occupied in the AFL, or its successor organization, the AFL–CIO.[13] Thus, early in its history, the IWW employed women as organizers and union officials and soon accorded them representation in the highest body of the organization.

Elizabeth Gurley Flynn, born in 1890, was named after the family doctor, Elizabeth Kent. Annie Gurley Flynn, Elizabeth's mother, was an advocate of equal rights for women, and it was considered somewhat scandalous that she had her four children delivered and cared for by women physicians. She had been a member of the Knights of Labor in Concord, New Hampshire, before her marriage and continued to work as a tailoress after her marriage, helping to support the family. Tom Flynn, Elizabeth's father, was an Irish rebel who, although he was a competent engineer, was so absorbed in socialist pursuits that he kept losing jobs. As Elizabeth grew up, she met Irish revolutionists, feminists, socialists, and anarchists. One of her teachers, she wrote, instructed her

---

*Joe Hill, whose full name was Joseph Hillstrom, was an immigrant from Sweden and the most famous of the IWW songwriters. He wrote "The Rebel Girl" and dedicated it to Elizabeth Gurley Flynn while he was in a Utah prison awaiting execution on a murder charge. Joe Hill was executed in 1915.

so thoroughly in the Bill of Rights that "I have been defending it ever since."

Elizabeth won a gold medal in her grammar school debating society for urging that women should have the vote. By the age of fifteen she was insisting in public speeches that full freedom for women was impossible under capitalism and that the government should undertake financial support for all children, so that women could bear them without becoming dependent on men. Her maiden public speech, delivered on January 31, 1906, at the Harlem Socialist Club, was entitled "What Socialism Will Do for Women." Flynn discussed how socialism would bring about the abolition of prostitution, the economic independence of women, the social care of children, and the right of all women to an education, to participate in government, and to enter the arts, sciences, and professions.[14]

Flynn was arrested for the first time at sixteen, along with her father, for blocking traffic and speaking without a permit. At the trial her lawyer proclaimed her the "coming Socialist woman orator of America." Pardoned, she immediately returned to the soapbox.

Elizabeth Gurley Flynn joined the IWW in 1906 as a member of the mixed Local No. 179 in New York City. As a woman and a minor, she was exempt from the otherwise strictly enforced requirement that membership was for wage laborers only. Her first strike experience was during the summer of 1907 with the Bridgeport (Connecticut) Tube Mill workers. In that year, George B. McClellan, mayor of New York City, had boasted in describing his constituency: "There are Russian Socialists and Jewish Socialists and German Socialists. But, thank God! there are no Irish Socialists!" Thereupon James Connolly,* Tom Flynn, his daughters, Elizabeth and Kathie, and others formed the Irish Socialist Federation. Annie Gurley Flynn sewed a large green and white banner with the Irish slogan "Fag an Bealach" (Clear the Way) in a field of harps and shamrocks. In Connolly's view, the federation was formed not out of national sentiment but in estimation of the needs of a socialist movement growing in a cosmopolitan environment.[15]

Fifteen-year-old Kathie Flynn became secretary of the Irish Socialist Federation, and Elizabeth left New York to barnstorm the country for the IWW. The *Industrial Union Bulletin* wrote about a speech she delivered in Duluth, Minnesota, in November, 1907: "Elizabeth Gurley Flynn is nothing if not in earnest. Socialist fervor seems to emanate from her expressive eyes, and even from her red dress. She is a girl with a 'mission', with a big 'M.'" The Los Angeles *Times*, under the heading, "Most

---

*James Connolly, who was later martyred during the Easter uprising in 1916 in Ireland, was then living in New York, publishing the *Harp* to publicize the struggle for Irish freedom and organizing on the docks for the IWW. It was through Connolly that Elizabeth Gurley Flynn learned of the work of the IWW.

Bloodthirsty of Agitators are the She-Dogs of Anarchy," wrote of her speech in that city:

> E. G. Flynn is said to be only 17, but her power of speech has won her spellbound audiences all over the eastern cities and now the same thing is operating in the west. Never has she advised violence. But the teachings of the young girl are so intensely radical, and her demand for action so vehement that she is assured of a royal welcome from any audience of extremists.[16]

Gurley, as she was called, soon discovered that IWW members took seriously the admonition that all male members "will never be lacking at any time in courtesy toward a lady." She said she felt as safe among them "as in God's pocket."[17]

The Wobblies, as IWW members were known, were constantly seeking to convince women to join Flynn and carry the message of industrial unionism to the exploited workers. IWW publications carried frequent advertisements for "men and women to actually work in the industries and there organize the slaves."[18] In the main, the Wobblies dismissed the argument that women workers were impossible to organize, attributing their distrust for unionism entirely to their bad experience with the AFL. One IWW woman organizer blamed lack of agitation for the failure to organize women sufficiently. She not only called upon the IWW male organizers to make a special effort to recruit women, but also urged women to "organize themselves with our brothers into one great wage earners' army in the industrial field."[19]

In contrast to almost every other labor organization so far in American history, the IWW made an active effort to organize the Chinese, Japanese, and Mexican workers. In a leaflet entitled *To Colored Workingmen and Women* the IWW pointed out: "If you are a wage worker, you are welcome in the IWW halls, no matter what your color. By this you may see that the IWW is not a white man's union, not a black man's union, not a red or yellow man's union, but a working man's union. All the working class in one big union." Even in the deepest South, the IWW raised the banner of "No Race, No Creed, No Color" and united black and white workers in a common struggle on the basis of complete equality—without once establishing a Jim Crow local in the process.[20]

Wobbly writers pointed to the particular degradation of women, with their rock-bottom wage scales, and emphasized that this required "a special effort to organize the women workers." They also noted the restrictionist policies of the AFL, pointing out that each craft union "has its own means of limiting membership, by apprenticeship systems, initiation fees, closed books, and age, color, and even sex restrictions." To be sure, in time of strikes, the AFL unions did not "fail to appeal to the women for support—though when these women appeal for admittance on the same basis as men, they are told 'nothing doing.'" Thus, when the

AFL Drivers' Union of Stockton, California, went on strike, the laundry women refused to handle any scab work, and the AFL union won its demands. But later, when the girls struck for an eight-hour day and higher wages, "the men who belonged to the Drivers' Union all stayed on the job, scabbing on the girls, whose wages were $5.75 per week, scarcely enough to exist on." One had but to contrast this with the IWW policy and practice, the Wobbly writers said, to see the tremendous difference.[21]

The IWW repeatedly emphasized that women were in industrial life to stay: "They cannot be driven back to the home. . . . They are part of the army of labor." There was only one thing to be done: "Organize them with the men, just as they work with the men." In the IWW's concept, women were not personally responsible for any damaging effect their presence might have on wages and working conditions. Even more than men, they were victims of capitalist exploitation, "slaves" in the industrial system, and their exploited condition made their unionization even more vital. The IWW conceded that there were special problems in organizing women workers, but it rejected the old craft union cry that "women won't organize and strike" as merely an excuse for doing nothing or for barring women from the labor movement. The answer was "to encourage them wherever possible by granting them equal opportunities, duties, and privileges, even to the holding of executive office."

Male workers were urged: "Don't fight against woman labor; women find it necessary to work. They do not work because they enjoy making some corporation 'rich beyond the dreams of avarice!' They work because they have got to make a living." The advice continued: "Do not blame the women; blame the system. And do not be content with that! Educate, agitate, and organize for the purpose of improving conditions and changing the system."[22]

Yet the Wobblies also contradicted themselves on the question of women workers. If healthy men were jobless while women and children worked, the boss, not the women, should be blamed for the situation; but the solution was to organize the men and put the women where they belong, in the home.[23] But what about the assertion that women were in industry to stay? This statement, they said, meant only that young, unmarried women would always enter industry, providing a substantial, if shifting, element in the labor force. Of course they should be organized, for "the factory girl of today is the helpful and encouraging wife of the union man of tomorrow." The case of the married woman was entirely different. While it might be justifiable, even desirable, for the young, unattached female to enter the labor market, the Wobblies viewed with horror the thought of woman "leaving her home and children unprotected and uncared for during the working hours." (They did not appear to have considered any solution in the form of day care centers for children.) It was important, then, that they be eliminated from the work force.[24]

This was too much for one female member, who, signing herself "A Woman Toiler," wrote to the IWW press:

> Fellow Worker Man Toiler: You say you want us girls to keep out of the factory and mill so you can get more pay, then you can marry some of us and give us a decent home. Now, that is just what we are trying to escape; being obliged to marry you for a home. And aren't you a little inconsistent? You tell us to get into the IWW, an organization for wage workers only. We haven't heard of any Household Drudge's Union, not even in the IWW. Going from the factory back into the home means only a change in the form of servitude, a change for the worse for the woman. The best thing that ever happened to woman was when she was compelled to leave the narrow limits of the home and enter into the industrial life of the world. This is the only road to our freedom, and to BE FREE there is not anything to be desired more than that. . . . So we will stay in the factory, mill, or store and organize with you in the IWW for ownership of the industries, so we can provide ourselves with decent homes, then if we marry you, it will be because we love you so well we can't get along without you, and not to give you a chance to pay our bills, like we do now.[25]

Wherever possible, wives who were not directly involved in industry were organized into women's auxiliaries. Their existence appears to go back as far as 1906, when the *Industrial Worker* announced the formation of a women's labor auxiliary union in Muskogee, Oklahoma, and praised the work of the auxiliary for its efforts in defense of Moyer, Haywood, and Pettibone.* In addition, IWW agitators, in spite of considerable male opposition, especially among the newer immigrants, encouraged strikers' wives to attend strike meetings and to march on the picket lines. Thus involved, the women would be less inclined to call for a return to work.[26]

But the IWW never resolved the question of whether or not the wives of workers were eligible for membership. In 1908 a San Francisco housewife asked: "(1) Is a married woman of the working class a chattel slave or a wage slave? (2) Has she the right to belong to a mixed local of the IWW?"

She asked these questions, she continued, "because objection has been raised by some members of the Denver local to the effect that a married woman, a housekeeper, has no right to belong to a workingman's organization." Some Wobblies, she complained, even asserted

---

*The Moyer, Haywood, Pettibone case, one of the worst frameups in American history, flowed from the arrest of the three men, all active in both the Western Federation of Miners and the IWW, on a charge of murder of Frank Steunenberg, former governor of Idaho, on December 30, 1905. They were acquitted.

that these women "have no grievance against the capitalist class, therefore we have no place in the union. Our grievance is against our husbands, if we are dissatisfied with our condition." With this, the writer disagreed vehemently:

> I believe the married woman of the working class is no parasite or exploiter. She is a social producer. In order to sustain herself, she has to sell her labor power, either in the factory, directly to the capitalist, or at home, indirectly, by serving the wage slave, her husband, thus keeping him in working condition through cooking, washing, and general housekeeping.
>
> For being a mother and a housekeeper are two different functions. One is her maternal, and the other is her industrial function in society. I believe the wage slave's wife has got a right to belong to a mixed local. I think it should be encouraging for working men to see women enter their ranks and, shoulder to shoulder, fight for economic freedom.
>
> Civilization denies us the right of expressing our political opinion at the ballot box. Will the economic organization, the IWW our only hope, exclude us and deny us the right to record our discontent against the capitalist system?

The editor replied that he could see no reason why a married woman could not belong to a mixed local, but he had no idea what would become of the housewives when the mixed local developed enough members in the various industries to divide into industrial unions: "It is a matter to which the next convention will give attention."[27] The next convention, however, ignored the issue.

In some IWW circles, wives were regarded as the "ball and chain." In the West, IWW literature proclaimed that the migratory worker, usually a young, unmarried male, was "the finest specimen of American manhood . . . the leaven of the revolutionary labor movement," around whom would be built a militant nucleus for revolutionary industrial unionism. "The nomadic worker of the west embodies the very spirit of the IWW," a writer rhapsodized in *Solidarity*. "Unlike the factory slave of the Atlantic seaboard and the central states, he is most emphatically not 'afraid of his job'. No wife and family cumber him. The worker of the east, oppressed by the fear of want for wife and babies, dare not venture much."

This contradictory attitude toward wives and children convinced some observers that there were two IWWs—one in the West and one in the East. To some extent, this was true. The average Western member of the IWW was younger than his Eastern counterpart. He was likely to be unmarried, or at least without binding family ties. The Western members were born in the United States, for the most part, while the Eastern members were mostly foreign-born. Those Westerners who were of foreign birth were likely to have preserved old-country ties and characteristics. The Westerners were mainly men, while women were an important element among the semiskilled and unskilled factory workers of the East.[28]

But the similarities were greater than the differences, and the attitude expressed about wives and children in IWW literature more frequently emphasized the importance of their role in helping to build the industrial union movement than the "ball and chain" concept. As a matter of fact, the same paper might contain both notions in consecutive issues. Thus, the *Industrial Worker,* which frequently extolled the migratory worker because he was free of family ties, also carried articles stressing the point that the low wages and wandering life style migrant workers had to endure robbed them of a normal family life: "The workers as a class are homeless. Part of the men are forced into a migratory life, going from place to place in search of work and are 'hoboes'; while the women, those who should be the wives of the hoboes are slaving in the mills or are in the [red light] district."[29]

The plight of the prostitute was a favorite theme of the IWW press. A "girl out of work" summed up the Wobbly theory on this social problem: "I'm out upon the town, because my fact'ry has shut down. In times like this, in this here land, it seems there ain't no real demand for girls except in this one trade." Unmarried women were on the street because they did not earn enough and because men did not make enough money to put them into the home as wives. *Solidarity,* the IWW's official organ on the East Coast, proclaimed that "Poverty is the Principal Cause, Direct and Indirect, of Prostitution." It concluded with a plea for unionization: "Our sisters and daughters have to sell their bodies in order to live— why? Because you and your likes didn't organize so you could make enough to place the woman where she belongs—in the home."[30]

"Employment Agencies Promote White Slave Traffic," headlined the *Industrial Worker,* as it angrily pointed out that even girls seeking honest work ran the risk of falling into vice through procurers posing as employment agencies. Charitable institutions, like the YWCA, also came under fire for making it possible for some women to survive on inadequate wages and thereby depressing pay scales for the rest. Then there were what the Wobblies termed "Sex-Subsidized Industries," which encouraged prostitution by paying men too little to support wives. Some turned to prostitutes, and women who could have been workers' wives were forced into prostitution to support themselves. "It is plain every industry is receiving a subsidy from either repression of sexual desires or their expression for commercial purposes."[31] The editor of the *Industrial Worker* came up with an intriguing and rather original suggestion: "For women I would indeed set a minimum wage. Roughly it would be this: go on the street and inquire the maximum earnings of the white slaves, then say to the boss: 'If this is the worth of a woman's body in iniquity, you must pay it for the use of that body in your shop.'"[32]

In all the considerable IWW literature relating to marriage and the family, there is little criticism of the traditional institution of marriage. Occasionally, the Wobbly press printed attacks on monogamous marriage, usually in the form of reprints from socialist journals, like George Bernard Shaw's "The Marriage Mart," but IWW papers rarely criticized marriage themselves or offered alternatives to it. It would appear that the IWW's image of a worker's utopia included a family in which the male worker was so well paid that he could return at night to the embrace of his wife and children and a well-cared-for home. Even the farm migrant received literature depicting him as wooing and winning the farmer's daughter and building a respectable family life—all through the power of industrial unionism.[33]

Viewing large families as providing "more slaves for the boss," the IWW endorsed birth control within marriage and condemned the attacks on the planned parenthood movement. "Ignorance and large families go hand in hand," the *Industrial Worker* explained. "Many women are 'stuffed' with the 'dope' that it is God's will to have all the children possible. If God wants them, he should have sense enough to tell them where to find employment and where to decently live."[34] It discussed and praised the labor organizations in Sweden, which disseminated birth control information among the workers, and it gave continuous support to the efforts of Margaret Sanger, the birth control pioneer, who was both a Socialist and an active supporter of the IWW in several key strikes.*[35] Gurley Flynn tells of an incident in the Paterson strike that illustrates the IWW attitude and the reaction of workingwomen and the wives of workers:

> We had a women's meeting, too, in Paterson at which Haywood, Tresca, and I spoke.... Tresca made some remarks about shorter hours, people being less tired, having more time to spend together and jokingly he said: "More babies." The audience of tired working wives did not cheer this suggestion. "No, Carlo," interrupted Haywood, "we believe in birth control... fewer babies well cared for." The women started to laugh and applaud.[36]

The attitude of major Wobbly figures toward marriage is revealing. Most IWW leaders led at least outwardly respectable lives. "Big Bill" Haywood was married, and although he and his wife, Nevada Jane, were estranged after 1903, Haywood provided materially for her until her death in 1920. Although he had a succession of love affairs, he managed

---

*IWW leaders, however, did not agree with Margaret Sanger as she became more and more fixed in her idea that birth control information was the key to all social problems. Flynn argued with her that while her work was very important, economic exploitation and not large families was the fundamental cause of poverty. But Sanger did not agree. (See Noel B. Gerson, *The Crusader* [New York, 1971], pp. 187–88.) However, for an IWW view closer to the Sanger position, see "Birth Control Economics," *Solidarity,* July 29, 1916.

to keep them from both his enemies and the public. During the last month of his life, Haywood legally married the Russian woman who had been his companion during his final years in the Soviet Union.[37]

Vincent St. John was also married, as was Ralph Chaplin, apparently very happily.[38] Joe Hill, according to his own testimony, died "for a woman's honor." He refused to reveal the name of the married woman he cited as his alibi the night of the robbery and murder for which he was convicted. He insisted that he had received his wound in a dispute with her husband, and that concern for her reputation kept him from disclosing her name.[39] Whatever one may think of Hill's judgment, it was in keeping with his great interest in enrolling women in the industrial union movement and his hope to "establish a kind of social good fellowship between the male and female workers." His songs frequently referred to the need to organize women workers "in the OBU (One Big Union)," as in the case of "What We Want":

> We want all the workers in the world to organize
> Into one great big union grand. . . .
> We want the sailor and the tailor and the lumberjacks.
> And all the cooks and laundry girls,
> We want the guy who dives for pearls,
> The pretty maid that's making curls. . . .
> We want the tinner and the skinner and the chambermaid. . . .
> And all the factory girls and clerks,
> Yes, we want everyone that works,
> In one union grand.[40]

In January, 1908, during a speaking tour, Elizabeth Gurley Flynn met and fell in love with Jack Archibald Jones, a Wobbly organizer from Bovey, Minnesota. Their married life was brief and hectic: two years and three months, and most of that time they saw little of each other. Flynn was busy organizing and was arrested several times while agitating for free speech in Missoula, Montana, and Spokane. Jones, too, was in jail during part of the marriage.

The couple had two children. The first was born prematurely and died within a few hours—probably as a result of the harsh conditions Flynn had to endure while pregnant in a Spokane jail. When she became pregnant again, Jones demanded that she settle down to domesticity. This might have been a reasonable enough demand to make of a wife at that time, but it came with poor grace from a husband who had not shown enough marital concern previously to visit his wife in jail or to attend her two trials during this period. At any rate, by the time the second child was born, Flynn had had enough of Jones and the couple separated permanently. She later explained that continuing the marriage to Jones would have restricted her ambitions: "I wanted to speak and write, to travel, to meet people, to see places, to organize for the IWW. I saw no reason why I, as a woman, should give up my work for his. I knew by now I could make more of a contribution to the labor movement than he could. . . . But it wasn't easy in 1910."

However, it was made easier by her mother's assistance, for Annie raised Elizabeth's son while she resumed her speaking career. Although she did not remain on close terms with Jones, who pursued an eccentric political career, she was a character witness for him when his second wife died in an accident during their honeymoon. "He never killed *me*," Flynn told questioners, "and he had plenty of provocation!"

The real love of Elizabeth Gurley Flynn's life was Carlo Tresca, whom she met when they worked together during the 1912 Lawrence strike. Tresca was a prominent anarchist and editor of the newspapers *Il Proletario* and *Il Martello*. "He was then a tall, slender, handsome man in his mid-thirties and I was deeply in love with him," Flynn recalled. They lived together for thirteen tempestuous years, although Flynn and Jones were not officially divorced until 1920. "This," she wrote, "was according to our code at that time—not to remain with someone you did not love, but to honestly and openly avow a real attachment."[41]

A relentless "jawsmith" (as IWW speakers and organizers were called), a tireless fund raiser, and a frequent contributor to the IWW and Socialist press, Elizabeth Gurley Flynn, a Wobbly paper concluded, "was indefatigable as a worker for the cause" throughout her long and remarkably useful life.[42]

Charming, eloquent, and beautiful, Flynn was loved by workers wherever she went. The Lawrence strikers were moved to sing in 1912:

> In the old picket line, in the old picket line,
> We'll put Mr. Lowe* in overalls
> And swear off drinking wine,
> Then Gurley Flynn will be the boss,
> Oh, gee, won't this be fine
> The strikers will wear diamonds in the good
>   old picket line.[43]

Flynn tried to change some of the Wobbly attitudes and practices toward women, but she did accept their basic tenet that the problems of women could not be separated from those of the working class. She also shared the IWW's hostility toward socially prominent women becoming involved in strikes of working-class women. "So far as the Mrs. Belmonts and Miss Morgans from their high pedestal mix in labor battles and respectabilize them, so far do they weaken the revolutionary fibre of the workers."[44] Flynn emphasized that " 'The queen of the parlor' has no

---

*Arthur Lowe was manager of the Lancaster Mills Corporation and one of its largest stockholders.

interest in common with 'the maid of the kitchen,' the wife of the department store owner shows no sisterly concern for the 17-year-old girl who finds prostitution the only door to avoid becoming a $5-a-week clerk."[45] She did not formally oppose the woman suffrage movement and insisted that women had every right to vote. She even had praise for the militancy of Socialist women in the struggle for the vote.* But like the IWW as a whole, Flynn considered the vote largely irrelevant and of little importance to working-class women. The "vote will not free women," she insisted, advising them to "find their power at the point of production where they work." She considered the woman suffrage movement dominated by "rich faddists," and complained that working-class women were "made the tail of a suffrage kite in the hands of women of the very class driving the girls to lives of misery and shame."[46] Charles Ashleigh justified IWW opposition to woman suffrage by the curious argument that even though middle-class women were not the equals of men of their class, working-class women were. Therefore, they already had what middle-class women hoped to achieve by the vote:

> The woman wage-worker and the wife of the wage-worker are the victims of industrial exploitation, not of suffrage inequality. They are robbed in the mill, factory or shop, where they, or their breadwinners, work. The woman worker lives by the same method as the male worker; by the sale of her labor-power to the boss. She is robbed, as the male worker is robbed, by the master appropriating the large portion of the product of her labor. She is robbed WHERE the male worker is robbed; on the INDUSTRIAL FIELD. She should fight for better conditions WHERE the most enlightened of the male workers, in ever-increasing numbers, are fighting: on the INDUSTRIAL FIELD.
>
> The woman wage-worker is not concerned in a sex war; she is concerned in a CLASS WAR. The boss enslaves men, women and children in the same way: by the exploitation of their labor power. On the industrial field, the woman worker has the same power as the man: she has the power of WITHDRAWING HER LABOR-POWER FROM INDUSTRY.[47]

There is no evidence that any Wobbly theoretician bothered to ask workingwomen if they needed the vote to end their subordinate position in society or if they felt they enjoyed the same economic power as male workers. They certainly did not receive equal pay for equal work or share opportunities to rise into the better-paying jobs. In short, it was a vast oversimplification to say that women workers had the same eco-

---

*Most Wobblies especially admired the militant tactics and spirit of women suffragists in England who went to jail for their principles and refused an offer of pardon if it compromised their struggle. "They were just like the IWW boys," exulted *Solidarity*, (Dec. 2, 9, 1911). In 1916, the *Industrial Worker* declared that American suffragists were using direct-action tactics in their fight for the ballot, and wondered why "if the women are to use direct action, they do not use it to get for themselves something of value" (July 15, 1916).

nomic power as men to redress their grievances, and to conclude that they therefore did not need any political power.

Flynn did not accept the argument that under IWW leadership women were equal to men inside the class struggle. On the contrary, she emphasized that the IWW should become more sensitive to women's needs, make demands based on these needs, recruit more women into the organization, and eradicate the male chauvinism that prevented women from active participation. On this past point, she was quite specific. "I know a local," she wrote, "where members forbid their wives speaking to an IWW woman, 'because they'd get queer ideas'! I heard a member forbid his wife, who had worked nine hours in a mill, from coming to a meeting, 'because she'd do better to clean the house'! When I suggested an able woman as secretary of a local, several men said, 'Oh, that's a man's job! She couldn't throw a drunk out!'" Or she would describe the problem she faced when she gave lectures about birth control:

> I am besieged by women for information on this subject, and this opens up another avenue of assault upon the system, yet whenever the subject is selected by a local it is always amazing how few IWW workers bring their women folk to the meeting. It is time they realized that the IWW stands for a larger program than more wages and shorter hours, and the industrial freedom we all aspire to will be the foundation upon which a different world for men and women will be reached.

Even among revolutionists in the IWW, she heard the charge that women were "backward," "impossible to organize," "over-emotional, prone to take advantage of their sex, eager to marry and then submerged in a family, are intensely selfish for 'me and mine,' lack a sense of solidarity, are slaves to style and disinclined to serious and continuous study. . . ."

> Nearly every charge could be made against some men and does not apply to all women; yet it unfortunately fits many women for obvious reasons. It is well to remember that we are dealing with the sex that have been denied all social rights since early primitive times, segregated to domestic life up to a comparatively recent date, and denied access to institutions of learning up to a half a century ago. Religion, home and child-bearing were their prescribed spheres. Marriage was their career and to be an old maid a lifelong disgrace. Their right to life depended on their sex attraction and the hideous inroads upon the moral integrity of women, produced by economic dependence, are deep and subtle. Loveless marriages, household drudgery, acceptance of loathsome familiarities, unwelcome child-bearing, were and are far more general than admitted by moralists, and have marred the mind, body, and spirit of women.

She therefore insisted that the IWW must "adapt our propaganda to the special needs of women" and that special kinds of organization suited to the conditions of women's lives had to be developed if the IWW were to have lasting success in organizing women workers. Unfortunately, "some of our male members are prone to underestimate this vital need and assert that the principles of the IWW are alike for all, which we grant with certain reservations." IWW literature had to be translated for foreigners, simplified for illiterates, and published with technical phrases for various industrial groups. The Western locals called for a paper written in the style "peculiar to their district." Similarly, IWW literature and organizing tactics had to be specially directed toward women, "based on their mental attitudes adapted to their environment and the problems it creates."[48] Nothing, however, came of this suggestion, or from a proposal by Frank Little in 1916 that "a special literature be created for women workers, that space for articles concerning female workers be provided in our papers, and that a league for women, with lecturers, be formed to carry on a special agitation for the benefit of women."*[49]

In December, 1914, Joe Hill wrote that in the West, the IWW had "created a kind of one-legged, freakish animal of a union" because of its predominantly male membership. He recommended that the IWW's female organizers be used "*exclusively* for building up of a strong organization among the female workers."[50] Although *Solidarity* featured this letter and endorsed the suggestion, little was done to put it into effect.[51] When female organizers, acting more or less on their own, did organize women workers, they were not enthusiastically welcomed by the Western Wobblies and even had to combat male chauvinism among IWW leaders, in addition to the opposition of employers.

The experience of Jane Street, a radical Colorado domestic worker, founder and secretary of Denver's Domestic Workers' Industrial Union, IWW, Local No. 113, illustrates this last point. She was determined to build a union of revolutionary housemaids who "don't believe in mistresses or servants. They would do away with caste altogether. They believe in removing the degradation from domestic service by teaching their employers to look upon the hands that feed them and wash for them, and scrub for them with respect or fear and humility."[52] By March 19, 1916, after three months of intensive organizing, she had succeeded in

*This was not the first time such a proposal had been put to the IWW. The August 3, 1907, issue of the *Industrial Union Bulletin* contained an article by Sophie Beldner that said, "Women are a little behind, and a greater amount of energy is needed to call them to action." She proposed that "a literature fund be established in one of the industrial centers where there are enough active women to take the initiative to carry out this plan." In the meantime, IWW women would contribute articles to the *Bulletin* "bearing on the question of industrial unionism and working class emancipation," and the best articles would be published "in leaflet form with the sanction of the general administration of the IWW. That, in my opinion, would be the only means by which we could reach the women in factory and at home, and make out of them a powerful factor in the onward march of the working class."

gathering enough maids to hold a secret mass meeting, where they spoke of their grievances and formulated the demands they would work for in the future: $12 a week, no work on Sundays, shorter hours, and better treatment.

Domestic servants, an isolated and diverse group, could not use the traditional strike techniques. To meet their particular needs, Street developed a new organizing technique, which she outlined in a letter to Mrs. Elmer F. Buse, a "fellow worker" who was planning to organize domestics in Tulsa. (Buse never received the letter, since it was intercepted by the Post Office before it reached its destination and was forwarded to the Justice Department during the government's campaign to prosecute the IWW out of existence.)[53] Street wrote:

> My method was very tedious. I worked at housework for three months, collecting names all the while. When I was off a job I rented a room and put an ad in the paper for a housemaid. Sometimes I used a box number and sometimes I used my address. The ad was worded something like this, "Wanted, Housemaid for private family, $30, eight hours daily."
>
> I would write them letters afterwards and have them call and see me. If they came direct, I would usually have another ad in the same paper, advertising for a situation and using my telephone number. I would have enough answers to supply the applicants. Sometimes I would engage myself to as many as 25 jobs in one day, promising to call the next day to everyone that phoned. I would collect the information secured in this way. If any girl wanted any of the jobs, she could go out and say they called her up the day before.
>
> I secured 300 names in this way. I had never mentioned the IWW to any of them, for I expected them to be prejudiced, which did not prove the case. I picked out 100 of the most promising of the names and sent them invitations to attend a meeting. There were about thirty-five who came. Thirteen of the thirty-five signed the application for a charter. Thirteen out of three hundred in three months time! So don't get discouraged.

At the end of a year, Street had succeeded in personally interviewing about 1,500 or 2,000 women, "telling them about the IWW and making them more rebellious, and placing probably over 1,000 in jobs." However, only 155 had signed up with the IWW, "only about 83 of whom we can actually call members." Since a great many women left town or simply drifted away, it was impossible to develop a larger, more permanent membership. Nevertheless, the *Denver Post* published cartoons depicting Wobbly maids as demanding and obtaining better conditions from recalcitrant employers.

The secret of the domestic union's strength lay not in the number of its members but in the operation of its employment office. The new union planned to build a card file of all the jobs for domestic workers in Denver and to make this information available to anyone looking for domestic work. By acting as its own employment bureau it would drive the "sharks"—employment agencies that thrived on exploiting workers—out of business. It would also make it impossible for recalcitrant employers to get help unless they met the union's demands. And it would start a union boardinghouse that would serve as an organizing center, where women could stay and leave their baggage while they looked for work. Jane Street told each maid: "You have one great advantage over your mistress. She must have you in her house. She won't wash her own dishes. You can get your rights by working on the individual woman."[54] She explained further to her Tulsa "fellow worker":

> If a girl decides to shorten hours on the job by refusing to work afternoons, or refuses to attend the furnace or to use the vacuum, etc., as a rule her employer does not fire her until she secures another girl. She calls up an employment shark and asks for a girl. With the union office in operation, no girl arrives, the shark's business having been crippled. The employer advertises in the paper. We catch her ad and send our girl who refuses to do the same thing as the other girl. If you have a union of only four girls and you can get them consecutively on the same job, you soon have job control. The nerve-wracked, lazy society woman is not hard to conquer.[55]

The union initially met with great success. Its list of jobs grew from three hundred in March to two thousand in May and six thousand in November.[56] When someone advertised for a maid in the paper, dozens of "union maids" would answer and demand the same wages until the prospective mistress was convinced that that was the going rate. The union even had its own song, "The Maids' Defiance":

> We've answered all your door bells and we've washed your dirty kids,
> For lo, these many years we've done as we were bid,
> But we're going to fight for freedom and for our rights we'll stand.
> And we're going to stick together in one big Union band.

> *Chorus:*
>   It's a long day for housemaid Mary, it's a long day's hard toil
>   It's a burden too hard to carry, so our mistress' schemes we'll foil.
>   For we're out for a shorter day this summer
>   Or we'll fix old Denver town.

> 2.
> We've washed your dirty linen and we've cooked your daily foods;
> We've eaten in your kitchens, and we've stood your ugly moods.
> But now we've joined the Union and are organized to stay,
> The cooks and maids and chauffeurs, in one grand array.

> (*Repeat Chorus*):[57]

And in case words were not enough to bring the mistresses to terms, there was always the threat of sabotage—a favorite IWW weapon, although more often discussed in theory than utilized in practice. "It is almost uncanny the way dishes slip out of that girl's hands," wrote a "Union maid" in an article entitled "Housemaids' Union Plots Revenge." "Picture father putting on his favorite soft shirt to find that the new laundress 'sabotaged' it by using plenty of starch."[58]

So, Jane Street explained, with only a "handful of girls," the Denver Domestic Workers' Industrial Union had "got results. We actually have POWER to do things. We have raised wages, shortened hours, bettered conditions in hundreds of places.* This is not merely a statement. It is a fact that is registered not only in black and white on the cards in our files in the office, but in the flesh and blood of the girls on the job."[59]

As the union grew stronger, it met ever-increasing opposition, and its enemies united to destroy it. These included the rich women of Denver, the YWCA, and, of course, the employment sharks whose business the union had crippled.[60] After intimidation of members had failed to weaken the union, the antiunion coalition hit upon a device that was more effective. They knew that one of the union's great sources of power was its card file of information on employers, which enabled it to function as an employment agency. On November 11, 1916, *Solidarity* carried the following devastating report under the heading, "Denver Housemaids' List Stolen":

> The robbery occurred in the early morning when Secretary Jane Street had stepped out of the office for a few minutes to go to the washroom on the floor above. Fellow Worker Street had been sleeping in the headquarters at night with a "gatt" under her pillow and a section of gas pipe within each reach guarding against just such an occurrence. She locked the door when leaving and upon her return found the list gone with the exception of a few cards scattered over the floor that the thief had apparently been in too great haste to pick up.

The loss of the card file was a serious setback, but the union did not go under. However, Street herself was charging male Wobblies in Denver with having done the union "more harm than any other enemy, the women of Capital Hall, the employment sharks and the YWCA combined. They have cut us off from donations from outside locals, slandered this local and myself and from one end of the country to the other, tried to disrupt us from within by going among the girls and stirring up trouble." The final blow was their refusal to grant the domestic workers' union a charter and then persuading national IWW headquarters not to charter the local. Moreover, whenever Street assisted domestic workers from other cities in forming locals, the same opposition developed

---

*David M. Katzman, however, believes that this success "had but a limited effect on the Denver servant market," even though Street's employment bureau was a unique feature. (*Seven Days A Week: Women and Domestic Service in Industrializing Services,* New York, 1978, p. 235.)

among male Wobblies. Sadly, but still hopefully, Street concluded her letter to the Tulsa "fellow worker":

> I am so sorry to tell you of these things—you who are so full of hope and faith and spirit for the revolution. I have tried to keep out of this letter the bitterness that surges up in me. But when one looks upon the slavery on all sides that enchains the workers—these women workers sentenced to hard labor and solitary confinment on their prison jobs in the homes of the rich— and these very men who forget their IWW principles in their opposition to us—when we look about us, we soon see that the Method of Emancipation that we advocate is greater than any or all of us and that the great principles and ideals that we stand for can completely overshadow the frailties of human nature.
>
> Stick to your domestic workers' union, fellow worker, stick to it with all the persistence and ardor that there is in you. Every day some sign of success will thrill your blood and urge you on! Keep on with the work.... Your success will spur on the girls here.
>
> Yours for industrial freedom. Yours for a speedy abolition of domestic slavery.[61]

Despite the theft of the card file and the problems with IWW male chauvinists, the union was growing stronger every day and had moved into new offices. The movement was also spreading outside Denver. By June, 1916, domestic workers in Salt Lake City had organized, followed by Duluth, Chicago, Cleveland, and Seattle.[62] But all these unions of domestic workers vanished when the entire Industrial Workers of the World came under brutal oppression at the hands of the federal government, which utilized the Espionage Act during World War I to destroy an organization employers were eager to see eliminated. The attack on the IWW was especially repressive in the West, and the maids' union in that area went under along with many other IWW organizations.[63]

Not all Western Wobblies were as hostile to women workers and their needs as those in Denver. The special exploitation of women migrant workers in California agriculture was a catalytic agent in the IWW's extensive efforts to organize these workers. In the great Wheatland Hops field strike in August, 1913, along with the demands for higher wages and other improvements, the IWW emphasized that men be assigned to help women with heavy sacks and that separate toilets be installed for women.[64]

Still, there is ample evidence that in quite a few respects, IWW ideology with respect to women workers differed little from that of the AFL. Like the federation, the One Big Union accepted the traditional and idealized conceptions of woman's role as mother and wife. Like the AFL members, too, not a few Wobblies looked down on and/or resented efforts by women workers to deal with their special needs and problems. Moreover, while the IWW preached that women were entitled to "equal opportunities, duties and privileges even to the holding of executive office," few women ever achieved positions in the Wobbly high command.

Flynn did recognize the weaknesses of the IWW in dealing with the special needs and problems of women workers and did try on a few occasions to push the Wobblies in the direction of meeting those needs. But she ran into the inevitable contradiction in the IWW's view that both sexes were equal in the class struggle, and this view weakened her efforts to achieve a special approach to women workers. In "The IWW Call to Women," published in 1915, Flynn put it this way:

> To us, society moves in grooves of class, not sex. Sex distinctions affect us insignificantly.... It is to those women who are wage earners, or wives of workers, that the IWW appeals. We see no basis in fact for feminist mutual interest, no evidence of natural "sex conflict," nor any possibility—nor present desirability—of solidarity between women alone. The success of our program will benefit workers, regardless of sex, and injure all who, without effort, draw profits for a livelihood.... The sisterhood of women, like the brotherhood of man, is a hollow sham to labor. Behind all its smug hypocrisy and sickly sentimentality loom the sinister outlines of the class war.[65]

Flynn failed to realize that unless class solidarity was accompanied by the eradication of male-supremacist tendencies in every aspect of the movement, the women workers might find that the IWW, despite its proclamations and resolutions, was not much different from the traditional labor organizations as far as they were concerned.

Yet the fact remains that in many important respects, the IWW approach to and treatment of the woman worker differed radically from that of the AFL. Unlike most other labor organizations of its time, and even many today, the IWW was not content merely to lament the status of working-class women in industrial society but set out to organize the women, who formed a substantial proportion of the unskilled workers and factory operatives. As we shall see below, their participation and militant activity could and did make the difference between success and failure in strikes.

22

Rebel Women and the Free-Speech Fights

IWW WOMEN ACTIVISTS made their major contributions during the militant strikes conducted by the Wobblies and as organizers and "jawsmiths" between strike activities. A number of women were also active in the organization's great free-speech fights, which occupied a great deal of its time and energy, especially in the West, during the years before 1912.

The IWW usually described the free-speech fight as "the struggle for the use of the streets for free speech and the right to organize." Protection of the right to speak on the streets was essential for the IWW, because this was the method the Wobblies relied on to gather new recruits among the homeless, itinerant workers who poured into the Western cities by the thousands every winter. The Wobblies could distribute quantities of literature, newspapers, leaflets, and pamphlets at street corner meetings, all carrying the message of industrial unionism to the unorganized. Street speaking was important for still another reason. In a strike, the workers' side was either completely suppressed or distorted by the commercial press. The most effective way for the Wobblies to get their story to the public was by means of their open-air meetings. Being colorful speakers, the Wobblies usually attracted large audiences, and they not only aroused sympathy for the strikers but, through the sale of literature and collections helped build a much-needed strike fund as well.

For the IWW the issue was clear: the right to speak meant the right to organize, and the Wobblies rallied their strength across the continent to break down attempts by city officials, acting for the lumber, agricultural, and mining interests, and other employers, to crush the organizing drives and destroy the movement by passing ordinances suppressing the IWW's right to speak out on the streets.

The Wobblies worked out a pattern of fighting that enabled them to make spectacular use of their scattered membership. They would respond to attempts to halt their agitation by calling on all IWW members in the vicinity, and even from far-off distances, to come to the city involved, speak on the streets, and be arrested. In this way, the Wobblies hoped to fill the jails beyond their capacity and harass the law enforcement officials so that they would cease the campaign against the union agitators. Thus, the free-speech fighters invited arrests, cheerfully allowed themselves to be marched off by the police, and crowded eagerly into the jails, bull pens, old schoolhouses, abandoned hospitals, or any other available buildings that were pressed into use after the jails were filled, supremely confident that, as one of their songs put it:

> There is one thing I can tell you
> And it makes the bosses sore,
> As fast as they can pinch us,
> We can always get some more.[1]

From the very beginning of a free-speech fight, the police were always inordinately vicious. Yet as the battle continued—for days, weeks, and sometimes for months—their brutality grew even worse. In addition, private individuals, organized as vigilante committees, worked hand in hand with the police, and together they committed unspeakable cruelties upon the Wobblies and their sympathizers—women as well as men, for the free-speech fights were not strictly a male domain, although the men were numerically preponderant.[2]

It was in a skirmish with the authorities of Missoula, Montana, in the summer of 1909 that the Wobblies first established their pattern of free-speech fighting involving both men and women. Missoula was an industrial town of some importance, but more significantly, it was the gateway to many lumber camps and mining towns, and migratory workers moved regularly in and out of the town. With the aim of organizing these transient workers, Vincent St. John sent Elizabeth Gurley Flynn and her husband, Jack Jones, to Missoula. They opened an IWW hall in the basement of the leading theater and began recruiting the migratory workers at street corner meetings. The migrants responded eagerly to Flynn's vigorous attacks on the employment agencies that were fleecing the workers by collecting fees in advance and then sending them to nonexistent jobs or to jobs from which they were fired after their first wages, out of which they had to pay a fee. The employment agencies, in league with the employers, with whom they shared the fees, pressured the City Council to pass an ordinance making street speaking illegal. The handful of IWW leaders in town—five or six altogether—decided to defy the ordinance as unconstitutional. Four of the six were promptly arrested and sentenced to fifteen days each in the county jail.

The two remaining IWW leaders sent out a call for assistance, and a steady stream of Wobblies flocked into the embattled city, "by freight cars—on top, inside and below." The jail was soon filled, and the cellar under the firehouse was transformed into an additional jail. A number of Wobblies were badly beaten. The cost of feeding the prisoners soared, and so did the complaints of the taxpayers. Soon the townspeople began to call for an end to the arrests and trials. The authorities finally gave up. All the cases were dropped. "We returned to our peaceful pursuit of agitating and organizing the IWW," wrote Flynn.[3]

In Spokane the pattern begun in Missoula was fully developed. Agitating against the fraudulent employment agencies, the IWW was in the process of building the biggest local in the organization in Spokane. The authorities, pressured by the employers and sharks, passed an ordinance in October, 1908, prohibiting "the holding of public meetings on any of the streets, sidewalks or alleys within the fire limits" after January 1, 1909. The IWW violated the ordinance without provoking any arrests until the evening of November 2, 1909, when James P. Thompson, local organizer for the IWW, took the platform at a street corner meeting. A policeman yanked him down, arrested him on a disorderly conduct charge, and hauled him off to jail. Other Wobblies swarmed up to take his place on the stand. One hundred and fifty, including three women, were arrested and jailed for defying the ordinance. One of them was Edith Frenette, a member of the IWW's advisory board, whose earlier experience in a Missoula jail had not deterred her from joining the Spokane free-speech fight. She was arrested for leading a group in singing the IWW song "The Red Flag," charged with acting in a disorderly manner and conducting herself as a "lewd woman." Detained for two days under appalling conditions, she was released in a "weak and starving condition" after local Socialists put up her bond.[4]

Agnes Thecla Fair, an Alaskan woman who was arrested on charges of criminal conspiracy while street speaking on November 17, fared even worse. Here is her own description of what happened to her—accompanied by the request that she be pardoned for the "language used to get at facts, as I never heard anything so vile:*

> They put me in a cell with a fallen woman and left. They were gone but a few minutes when two officers returned and (although the other woman was not to go until Monday, she told me), they told her to get ready in two minutes and get out.
> When she was gone they put me in a dark cell, and about ten big burly brutes came in and began to question me about our union. I was so scared I could not talk. One said, "We'll make her talk." Another said. "She'll talk before we get through with her."

---

*The account, published in the *Workingmen's Paper,* of Seattle, almost resulted in its being banned from the mails.

Another said," F--k her and she'll talk." Just then one started to unbutton my waist, and I went into spasms which I never recovered from until evening.

I was hardly over the first when they brought in a man disguised as a woman and put him in a cot next to me. I thought it was a drunken woman until the officers went out. Then I felt a large hand creeping over me. It's too horrible to put on paper. I jumped out into an enclosure, screaming frantically and frothing at the mouth. Had not two of our girls been arrested and brought in just then I do not think I would ever come to.

Even then they showed no disposition to treat me as a human. I never slept or ate the three days I was in there. The third day I was so weak when the doctor called and they would not let me out then only the doctor said (a "trusty" told me): "She cannot stand it another hour, and her death will mean the end." Then they hurried in and carried me out near a window.[5]

Discharged on doctor's orders in a state of nervous collapse, Fair returned to the free-speech fight once she had recovered her health. Moreover, despite the barbarities visited upon their sex by the Spokane authorities, women continued to pour into that city. They came in response to an appeal from Beulah H. Hyde of Seattle calling for "women recruits." (Hyde herself left for Spokane "with whatever women" she could gather together so as to "help out as much as possible.")[6] This was followed by "A Call to Action," signed by a group of women who had spent two weeks in Spokane, "the newest province of Russia," which urged: "Every woman who possibly can, who believes in free speech and the ultimate emancipation of the wage-workers, should so arrange her affairs as to be on hand in Spokane.... Remember, if you are a wage-worker that this is your fight. We must fill their jails and raise their taxes until they are glad to surrender."[7]

On November 16, the press reported the arrival on the scene of "Elizabeth Gurley Flynn [who] addressed a meeting in the Municipal Courtroom and after roasting the newspapers, police judges and city authorities, took up a collection of $25." Since she was pregnant, the Wobblies decided that Flynn should not speak on the forbidden streets but only in IWW halls, clubs, and organizations willing to give her a hearing to raise defense funds. But her condition did not concern the police. Indeed, when a young attorney suggested that she be given special consideration, he was brusquely told off. "Hell, no!" a local official declared. "You just don't understand. She's the one we are after. She makes all the trouble. She puts fight in the men, gets them the publicity they enjoy."

On November 30 the police arrested a group of IWW leaders, Flynn among them, and threw them in jail. Flynn attracted a good deal of attention by chaining herself, suffragist style, to a lamppost to delay her removal. The Wobbly press flashed the news of her imprisonment in flaming headlines and issued circulars announcing that "Elizabeth Gurley Flynn, a girl organizer only 19 years old, soon to become a mother, was arrested, charged with criminal conspiracy, confined in jail with prostitutes and insulted by an officer of the law." The latter reference was to Flynn's charge that an officer had approached her in her cell and attempted to take liberties with her. Compare the report of William Z. Foster, then a correspondent for the *Workingman's Paper* in Seattle, who was jailed during the free-speech fight just for covering the event.* Foster described educational meetings held by the IWW prisoners at which rules and regulations were adopted, one of which forbade

> IWW members from shouting to the women prisoners who were confined within calling distance. This latter regulation was adopted in consideration of any woman prisoners who might be insulted by some of the doubtful remarks continually bandied between the men and women prisoners. Needless to say, these rules and regulations were scrupulously obeyed by the IWW members, as well as by many of the other prisoners, who fell under the magic spirit of the well known IWW discipline.[8]

On March 5, 1910, after twelve hundred had already been arrested, with fresh delegations arriving daily, the city officials surrendered and made peace with the IWW. Four days later, the City Council repealed the prohibitive ordinance, and the Wobblies were permitted to use the streets for their meetings.[9]

> Out there in San Diego
> Where the western breakers beat,
> They're jailing men and women
> For speaking in the street.[10]

So went a song about the San Diego free-speech fight, the most bitterly fought battle for free speech waged by the IWW. It began early in 1912 and continued for more than half a year. On February 8, 1912, the day on which the city ordinance barring street speaking went into effect, thirty-eight men and three women were arrested for violating the ban. One of the three women was Laura Payne Emerson, who became one of the most prominent figures in the fight. She was a member of San Diego's IWW Local No. 13 and had been cited frequently in the Wobbly press for her activities as an organizer in the drive to recruit American

---

*After the Spokane free-speech fight, Foster joined the IWW, but he left the Wobblies following a trip to Europe, where he became convinced that the correct strategy to follow was "boring-from-within" the AFL. He led the packinghouse strike of 1918 and the historic steel strike of 1919. Although he was a syndicalist after he left the IWW, he became a leader of the Communist Party when he abandoned his anti–political-action views. A leading theorist on trade union tactics and strategy, Foster headed the Trade Union Educational League and the Trade Union Unity League. He was the Communist Party's candidate for president in 1924, 1928, and 1932.

and Mexican workers employed at the San Diego Consolidated Gas and Electric Co. When the free-speech agitations broke out, Emerson became a prime target for police repression. She was addressing a protest meeting in front of the city jail on March 10, demanding better treatment for the free-speech prisoners. The police called in the fire department to halt the speaker and disperse the crowd of five thousand people by spraying them with a three-inch stream of water. An eyewitness reported for the Oakland *World:*

> For a full hour, hundreds packed themselves in a solid mass around Mrs. [Laura Payne] Emerson as she stood upon the speaker's stand. Bending themselves to the torrent that poured upon them they held their ground until swept from their feet by the irrepressible flood. An old grey-haired woman was knocked down by the direct force of the stream from the hose. . . . A mother was deluged with a babe in her arms. . . . An awe-struck American patriot wrapped himself in the flag to test its efficiency against police outrage, but he was knocked down and jailed and fined $300 for insulting the national emblem.[11]

Clubbed by the police, arrested and charged with conspiracy, Emerson bravely carried on the fight while Wobblies continued to be clubbed and arrested. But there was little that could be done to prevent the wholesale violation of their civil rights. "They have the courts, the jails and funds." Emerson complained. It was not until 1914 that the right of the IWW to hold street meetings was established. In 1915 Emma Goldman, who had been prevented from delivering a lecture on Ibsen's *An Enemy of the People* at the height of the free-speech fight, returned to San Diego and finally delivered the lecture.[12]

In the industrial form of organization espoused by the IWW, the aim was to organize an entire plant in a town and then move on to unionize the rest of the industry. The organization first put this principle into effect in the textile industry, where women formed a large percentage of the workers. By March, 1907, the IWW had a thousand members in Local No. 152, Silk Workers' Industrial Union of Paterson, New Jersey, and boasted that "we have a splendid opportunity to organize the entire silk industry."[13] Still, the local believed that unusual methods were necessary, and on June 29, 1907, it asked to be allowed to form an auxiliary in which women could be organized at a lower dues rate. (This was before dues for women were reduced by the second IWW convention.) Once the organization was strong enough to force a wage increase for all the silk workers of Paterson, these women could be absorbed into the main body of the union. The militancy of the women members thus recruited was frequently commended in the *Industrial Union Bulletin,* as in the following tribute:

It is very encouraging to see the splendid stand taken by the girls and women in these [silk] mills. They grasp the situation and perform their part in a very practical and creditable manner; and it must be said further, to their credit, that when anything is suggested that savors of exploitation of the union by officers or committeemen in the pure and simple fashion, the women point out its tendency and oppose it with an insight and honesty that is fine to see.[14]

The IWW felt sufficiently strong in the textile industry to issue an official call in the name of its General Executive Board for the "First Convention of Textile Workers," to be held on May 1, 1908, in Paterson. In the call (printed in English, French, German, and Italian) the claim was made that "over 5,000 textile workers have already been organized into the Industrial Workers of the World." The twenty-two delegates representing seven textile unions in Paterson and Hudson County (New Jersey), Providence and Woonsocket (Rhode Island), and Lawrence, New Bedford, and Lowell (Massachusetts), and a delegate from the United Brotherhood of Tailors, set up the National Industrial Union of Textile Workers, which was to function as a subdivision of the "Department of Textile and Clothing Industries" and was to be composed of wage workers of all branches of labor employed in the production of textile fabrics.[15]

One of the earliest IWW strikes in which women played an active role began in Skowhegan, Maine, on January 21, 1907, when 225 employees of the Marston Worsted Mills left their jobs. Trouble had been brewing at the plant since the discharge of one of the sewers, Mamie Gilodeau, a militant French-Canadian member of Pioneer Local No. 379, IWW. The local had demanded a 10 percent wage increase at the beginning of the year but had settled for a 5 percent increase and the promise of an additional 5 percent in July if the season was profitable. It appeared that management was out to rid the plant of active union members and rescind the wage increase. Hence, when the company notified twenty-six weavers, all members of the IWW, that there was no longer any work for them, the entire work force, the majority of them women operatives, struck.[16]

Within a week, Samuel J. French, IWW organizer, arrived from New York to assist the strikers. A letter was sent to the company demanding the reinstatement of all those employed at the mill on January 7; abolition of the fining system in the finishing room; discharge of the overseer of the finishing room, who was accused by the women of offensive sexual advances; the settlement of minor grievances; and recognition of a committee of employees to aid in the adjustment of grievances. The response of management was blunt: "There is nothing in your requests that the mill can grant." Upon receiving this reply, the strikers unanimously resolved: "That this note be stored in the archives of Local 379 for the benefit of some future historian of Skowhegan labor troubles."[17] Along with it, they might have stored the comment by the *Somerset Reporter* that the strikers were made up of "a coterie of individuals who have come to us from other manufacturing centers in none of which they have had anything but temporary residence."[18] Since the majority of the strikers were long-time residents of Skowhegan, it is obvious that the *Reporter* knew little about the town's working class.

With the plant completely shut down, the company should have been forced to settle early in the strike. But on February 7 the Somerset *Reporter* published a notice, at the request of the company, which management believed would force the strikers to surrender. It was a letter addressed to the employees of the Marston Worsted Mill by John Golden and Albert Hibbert, president and secretary-treasurer, respectively, of the AFL's United Textile Workers. The letter warned the strikers of "the so-called Industrialists" who "had no standing whatsoever as far as the recognized trade union movement is concerned, as exemplified by the American Federation of Labor," and whose only policy was to pull workers out on strike "on the most flimsy pretext, knowing full well at the time they have not a dollar practically speaking to assist the people they have forced out on the street." The UTW officials advised the strikers "to return to work before it is too late, and if they desire to belong to a union, to organize one that will have a legitimate affiliation with the recognized trade union movement of the country." But should the strikers "fail to take advantage of this advice," the UTW would not hesitate to "supply the firm" with workers to replace those out on strike. They would not be "scabs," but "union men and women, who, while standing out for their own rights, will not lose sight of the fact that other people have rights also that must command respect and consideration at their hands."

The *Somerset Reporter* described the letter as "self-explanatory." Indeed it was! The officials of the UTW were publicly offering to help the company break a strike in which every worker employed at the plant was involved—a strike called by the workers themselves without the knowledge of the IWW's national office, which had sent in an organizer to assist the strikers only after the workers had walked out. Management's hope that this letter would break the strike soon disappeared. Picketing continued throughout the bitter winter, with the thermometer ranging from zero to 44 degrees below. In the fact of the strikers' determined stand, the company found it impossible to take advantage of Golden's offer to fill the plant with "union scabs,"[19]

On April 23 the strikers won a complete victory. The terms of the settlement, as reported in the press, were: reinstatement of all workers discharged without discrimination; abolition of the fining system in both the finishing and weaving rooms; a day's pay for all work, instead of piecework; and recognition of a shop committee to be elected by the local, which was to meet with the company every two weeks to settle grievances, including the complaints stemming from the conduct of the overseers toward the girls. In July the second 5 percent increase in wages was granted by the company.

One of the earliest and certainly the most unusual of all strikes involving women associated with the IWW occurred in April, 1907, in New Orleans. A large number of prostitutes in the city were inspired by Wobbly activity in the area to walk out of the brothels and demand better conditions. The madams in several houses had attempted to double the rent of the "cribs" the girls used for entertaining. The girls, after a discussion of how things were done by the Wobblies. organized, elected officers, and "picketed the offending employers." In keeping with its principle of calling on all male members to show solidarity with their rebellious sisters, the IWW reacted by boycotting the struck houses. The strikers won their battle.[20]

The ladies were happy to reciprocate. At a later date, the *Voice of the People,* the IWW organ in the deep South, reported, "Girlies Boycott Yellow-legs." The paper noted that "the girls in the red light refuse to prostitute their bodies for the scab herders," the militia sent to suppress the strikers in Butte. Covington Hall, editor of the *Voice,* inquired: "I would like to know what charges they will or can bring against the girls?"[21]

Sexual activity of a different type was a factor in the bitterly fought IWW strike in McKees Rocks, Pennsylvania, against the Pressed Steel Car Company. The company, a U.S. Steel subsidiary located six miles from Pittsburgh, fabricated steel railway cars on an assembly-line basis, employing mainly foreign-born workers. In 1909 there were sixteen different nationalities represented among the five thousand workers employed at the plants—American, German, Hungarian, Ruthenian, Slovak, Croatian, Polish, Turkish, Lithuanian, Russian, Greek, Italian, Armenian, Rumanian, Bulgarian, and Swiss. The largest group were the Hungarians—or the "Hunkies," as they were derisively called by the corporation owners, the foreman, the press, and the leaders of the AFL craft unions—who also viewed them as "the least intelligent, the least independent, the least Americanized workers, and the most content to be driven like slaves."[22] The company forced the workers to labor at a feverish pace under a pooling system; it held them responsible for mistakes made by another gang or by company foremen, which reduced their weekly earnings; and it even refused to post the rates of pay, so that the workers had no way of knowing what was due them. All this was based on the theory that a working force composed largely of recent arrivals in the country, who were without money or friends and were unable to speak the language of the country or of many of the other workers in the plants, was in a helpless condition—so helpless, in fact, that company agents made it a practice to demand that wives and daughters of the workers submit to them sexually if they wished to prevent their male relatives from being peremptorily discharged.[23] Reverend Father A. F. Toner, pastor of St. Mary's Roman Catholic Church in McKees Rocks, made an on-the-spot investigation of the plants and issued the following angry statement:

> Men are persecuted, robbed and slaughtered, and their wives are abused in a manner worse than death—all to obtain or retain positions that barely keep starvation from the door. It is a pit of infamy where men are driven lower than the degradation of slaves and compelled to sacrifice their wives and daughters to the villainous foremen and little bosses to be allowed to work. It is a disgrace to a civilized country. A man is given less consideration than a dog, and dead bodies are simply kicked aside while the men are literally driven to their death.

To this, as to all other exposures of evils in the plants, President Frank N. Hoffstot of the Pressed Steel Car Company had but one reply: "If a man is dissatisfied, it is his privilege to quit."[24]

They did. On July 14, 1909, all the workers in the plant, except five hundred in the wooden works and a small group of union electricians, stopped work. Five thousand men were out, "without organization, without knowing how many would strike, without funds."[25] Three of the leaders of the strike were Wobblies, and the IWW local in nearby New Castle entered the strike officially in mid-August, helping the strikers to establish a twenty-four-hour picket system, a signal-and-watch system to notify them of any attempts to introduce strikebreakers, and committees of pickets to stop every streetcar entering the town and every ferry boat entering the area, compel the passengers to account for themselves, and take off anyone who might be a strikebreaker. Working with the Wobblies among the strikers, the IWW local organized speakers for each of the sixteen nationalities among the workers to address mass meetings, arranged by nationality, at which emphasis was placed on the importance of uniting all workers along industrial lines, which would eliminate craft, language, and nationality barriers. Women of the IWW's New Castle local operated the sttikers' relief station and worked with the women relatives of the strikers to assist in picketing and in resisting efforts to break the strike by brute force.[26]

Even before the IWW officially entered the strike, the women relatives of the strikers had demonstrated their determination to fight the company and its allies. By the morning of July 15, three hundred deputy sheriffs, armed with rifles and aided by two hundred state constables, including sixty-two mounted troopers—the hated "Cossacks"—surrounded the plant at McKees Rocks. Rioting started when fifty mounted constables tried to evict the families of the strikers from company houses. (Since the workers had no leases on the dwellings they were forced to rent from the company, they could be evicted by the company at any time.) The wives of the strikers fought back, threatening to burn the company houses, and shouting to their husbands: "Kill the Cossacks! Crush them! Stamp them out! If you are afraid, go home to the children and leave the work to us!" The mounted troops charged the strikers and their wives, riding them down. The workers and the women replied with rocks and missiles, whereupon the troopers fired volleys into the crowd, first of blank cartridges, and then of real bullets. Nearly one hundred men and women were injured. Twenty-five were arrested and charged with inciting to riot. But the evictions were stopped! As one reporter wrote: "The strikers and their wives have announced that any attempt to oust their families from their houses in the company row will be fought to a finish and more violence is sure to follow if this is attempted."[27]

Eventually, sufficient deputy sheriffs and state police were brought in to evict the strikers' families, but the evicted families were as determined to continue the struggle as those who still lived at home; indeed, the children of all the strikers agreed not to attend school until victory was achieved. Wives fought alongside their husbands to prevent scabs from entering the factory. Armed with household utensils—pokers, brooms, and rolling pins—the women were an awesome force.[28]

In September a settlement was reached that incorporated nearly all the strikers' demands. In addition to achieving an immediate 5 percent increase in wages, which was to be followed by an additional 10 percent within sixty days, the discharge of all strikebreakers and the rehiring of all strikers, a Saturday half holiday, and the abolition of Sunday work except where absolutely necessary, the strikers also won the elimination of many practices that they had grown to despise. They obtained the company's pledge that any foreman or agent found guilty of demanding sexual favors from workers' wives or daughters as a condition of continued employment would be immediately discharged.[29]

The strikers had left their jobs unorganized; they returned six and a half weeks later as members of an industrial union—the Car Builders' Industrial Union, a branch of the IWW. In a statement to the workers of America in their hour of triumph, the strikers urged them to "disseminate and spread the message of industrial solidarity among those who will draw their object lessons from the McKees strike."[30]

Early in 1910 the "spirit of McKees Rocks" spread to East Hammond, Indiana, and workers employed at the Standard Steel Car Company, another subsidiary of U.S. Steel, organized Car Builders' Union No. 302, IWW. On January 16, after futile efforts to achieve a settlement of grievances similar to those that had provoked the strike at McKees

Rocks, the workers of all departments quit, with the exception of the AFL electricians and machinists, who operated under contracts with the management. "But forcible persuasion prompted the machinists and electricians to quit also," the IWW reported. On January 17 the plant was completely shut down and fifteen hundred strikers were picketing to make sure that no scabs got through.[31]

The company refused to negotiate and rushed to operate with strikebreakers. When the police attempted to escort the scabs into the plant, the strikers and their wives fought back and stopped the first invasion. The company retaliated by ordering the strikers and their families evicted from the company houses, and when the workers and their wives resisted, many of them were clubbed and arrested. But those still on picket duty saw to it that the strikebreakers did not get through. "The plant is practically tied up," wailed the Lake County *Times* on January 19. The following day it announced gloomily: "The plant will remain closed for an indefinite period." And it was all due to the fact that "the foreigners, hundreds of them, are as sheep led to slaughter, in the hands of IWW strike leaders imported from McKees Rocks."[32]

On January 24 the wives of the strikers organized an antiscab battalion. The following day the battalion helped the strikers fight the police to a standstill and prevented the strikebreakers from getting into the plant. "Women Get Into Standard Steel Car Strike Trouble and Commit Mayhem," shouted the headline in the *Lake County Times*. A reporter for the *Indianapolis Star* wrote:

> Armed with brooms, clubs, stove pokers, rolling pins and other kitchen utensils, hundreds of women from the foreign settlement surrounding the Standard Steel Works today joined the ranks of their striking husbands as pickets and brought about the worst clash that the authorities have yet encountered since the strike began. The women stood with the husbands against the weight of the policemen who tried to open a way to the gate for the workmen going to work. . . .
>
> A number of the special police were targets for the broom-handles and irons, one of them being severely injured with a long poker that an Amazon had measured across his back.
>
> The women held a mass meeting this afternoon and promised to do picket duty again tomorrow morning.

The *Lake County Times* contained a further detail:

> A woman, whom officer Borchet was attempting to subdue, bit him on the arm and had it not been for the heavy coat he wore, she would have injured him severely. Emil Helwig, a special officer, deputized to serve during the strike, was struck over the back with a broomstick by a woman and when he tried to subdue her she bit his wrist and the flesh is badly lacerated.

One woman was shot by the police and twelve were arrested. But that same evening, the company sent the mayor and a representative of the

Hammond Businessmen's Association to the union headquarters to ascertain the terms of settlement. Several days of negotiation followed before the company capitulated and accepted practically all the strikers' demands. On February 4, 1910, the fifteen hundred strikers returned to work, and the labor press heralded the news, "Strike at Hammond Car Shops Won."[33]

The pattern of valiant contributions by strikers' wives in achieving victory, established at McKees Rocks and Hammond, was to be repeated in other IWW strikes. The 1912 Merryville, Louisiana, strike of IWW timbermen was characterized by both racial solidarity and the valor of the "women fellow workers." When the strikers were deported by thugs, their wives and daughters carried on the main job of picketing. Later, in a timber strike in Tacoma, the strikers received a strong boost from their wives. The women "went to the woods [and] cut five hundred switches, which they declared they would lay on the backs of men who go to work in the sawmills tomorrow."

The textile strikes of 1912 and 1913 in Lawrence, Massachusetts, Little Falls, New York, and Paterson, New Jersey, were the most publicized and vital of all IWW strikes of this era. In each of them, women workers constituted a majority or near majority of the strikers and played decisive roles in what were tremendous labor struggles. The Lawrence strike. however, is so important in labor history, and the role of women in the strike so crucial. that it merits a chapter to itself.

23

The Lawrence Strike

THE CHARACTER of the working population in Lawrence's textile mills had undergone a distinct change in the nearly seven decades between the founding of the city in 1845 and the great strike of 1912. Until the 1880s, the dominant elements in the textile factories were native Americans, English, Irish, Scottish, and French-Canadians, and many of them were skilled workers. With the technological advances of the 1880s, the skilled personnel were rapidly displaced, and Italians, Greeks, Portuguese, Russians, Poles, Lithuanians, Syrians, and Armenians took their places. By 1912 the newcomers had become the predominant groups in the textile mills of Lawrence. Within a one-mile radius of the mill district, twenty-five different nationalities lived, speaking half a hundred different languages. The largest ethnic group in the city was Italian.[1]

The U.S. Bureau of Labor Statistics made a study of the weekly payroll reports from seven mills in Lawrence about seven weeks before the strike. It covered 21,922 workers (excluding overseers and clerks)—about two-thirds of the total number in the mills on the eve of the strike. The average rate per hour of 16,578 operatives, skilled and unskilled, in the four woolen and worsted mills was 16 cents, and the average amount earned for the week under study was $8.75. These wages included premiums or bonuses! But 59.8 percent of the operatives in the woolen mills earned less than 15 cents an hour, and 14 percent of those in the cotton mills made less than 12 cents. Almost one-third—33.2 percent—of both woolen and cotton operatives received less than $7 a week. The study reports were based on earnings during a week when the mills were running full-time. But none of the mills worked full-time throughout the year. Although the Bureau of Labor Statistics declared that it could not ascertain the amount of unemployment, it conceded that there was a serious curtailment of earnings due to lost time, and concluded that the

426

$8.75 and $8.78 average wages for the week under study were far too high for an annual average.[2]

The Lawrence textile industry was a "family industry"—but this pleasant-sounding phrase had a deadly meaning for the workers. To keep the family alive, husbands, wives, and children worked in the mills. Even if the wife stayed at home to care for her young children, she was compelled to contribute to the family's income, by taking care of a neighbor's children for money, by doing another family's washing for a fee, or by taking in boarders or lodgers. Lodgers or boarders were an economic necessity for the majority of the immigrant households. They usually paid $3 or $3.50 per month for lodging and the use of the kitchen stove.

The prevalence of boarders and lodgers certainly destroyed any possibility of privacy, and, even though it eased the financial burden of the family, in many cases making survival posible, it also increased the burden of work for the woman of the house. She was often responsible for the cooking and laundry for the additional household members—sometimes in addition to working in the mills. Of 123 Italian families studied, 77 had boarders or lodgers, and in 34 of these 77 households, the wife of the head of the household also worked in the mills.[3]

The labor law of Massachusetts, passed as recently as 1909, stated that no child under fourteen years of age, and no child under sixteen who was unable to read and write "legibly simple sentences in the English language," should be employed in any factory, workshop, or mercantile establishment.[4] But as far as Lawrence was concerned, the law might never have been passed. On the eve of the strike in 1912, half the children in Lawrence between the ages of fourteen and eighteen were employed in the mills, and 11.5 percent of the textile workers were boys and girls under eighteen. If the earnings of the women were pitifully small, those of the children were even lower. Testimony before a congressional committee revealed that the youngsters earned $7 and $5, or even less, per week when the mills were running full time![5]

According to the U.S. Bureau of Labor, the average work week in the Lawrence mills was fifty-six hours. But 21.6 percent of the workers worked more than fifty-six hours, and none of the workers was paid more than the regular scale for overtime.[6] While the demand for a shorter work week was not an important issue in the strike—a fact that is hardly surprising, since with hourly rates as low as they were, the workers needed a longer week, not a shorter one, to earn enough to stay alive—one of the strikers' demands was for double pay for all overtime work.

Various complaints were voiced by workers appearing as witnesses at congressional hearings. Chief among their grievances were the premium, or bonus, system, a speedup plan designed to obtain the highest possible production from each worker;* the practice of holding back a week's wages on all new workers, thus imposing a heavy burden on them during the first two weeks of employment; and docking workers, especially children, one hour's pay for coming in five or ten minutes late, and if the lateness was repeated three times, firing them. Workers also complained that the tap water supplied by the mills was usually so warm, because of numerous steampipes, that they were forced to buy cold drinking water at a weekly charge of 10 cents in order to quench their thirst. And all witnesses expressed severe indignation at the tyrannical attitude of the foremen in their dealings with the workers. The overseers insisted that the women workers have sex with them as a condition of holding their jobs, swore at the men, women, and children indiscriminately, insulted the foreign-born workers, calling them "ignorant Dagoes and Hunkies," and in general treated them as if they were "dumb cattle."[7]

Lawrence had two dubious distinctions. It was one of the most congested cities in the nation, with 33,700 people dwelling in less than one-thirteenth of the city's area—the slum where nearly all the mill workers lived. And the infant mortality rate was one of the highest of all the industrial cities of the nation. In 1910, of the 1,524 deaths in Lawrence, 711, or 46.6 percent, were of children under six years old. Indeed, in that year, the death total in Lawrence was exceeded, according to the U.S. Census Bureau, by only six cities out of the forty selected. (Of the six, three others—Lowell, Fall River, and New Bedford—were also textile centers.) "A considerable number of boys and girls die within the first two or three years after beginning work," a medical examiner studying health conditions in the Lawrence mills wrote. "Thirty-six out of every hundred of all men and women who work in the mill die before or by the time they are 25 years of age."[8]

Foul tenements, poor diet, and lack of warm clothing were important factors in the high number of deaths. "Ironically enough," notes one student of conditions in Lawrence, "in the greatest woolen center in the country the producers of suits could not afford the price, which was prohibitive to them, nor could the women who made the cotton dresses pay $3.00 for them. . . . As for overcoats, they were out of the question,

---

*The premium system provided for a bonus to the worker whose output exceeded some fixed standard or for regular attendance. In the latter case, any worker who had not missed more than one day during a four-week period received a premium. But a worker could produce extra cloth for three weeks and then fall sick during the fourth and last week of the bonus period and he or she would lose the premium. If a machine broke down, a not uncommon occurrence, the record of regular production would be marred, and the premium for the entire four-week period would go by the board. (*See* Hearings on Strike at Lawrence, Mass., 62nd Congress, 1st Session, *House Document No. 671*, Washington, D.C., 1912, pp. 114–16.)

and to the spectator, it appeared that most of the workers of Lawrence wore sweaters beneath their suits or dresses."[9]

These, then, were the conditions that led to the great upheaval of the New England and other textile workers in 1912-1913—for conditions were no better in the other mill centers. But the spark that set off the explosion was the cut in wages for all workers following the passage of the fifty-four-hour law for women and for children under eighteen years of age. The law, adopted by the state legislature in 1911 as a result of pressure from organized labor in Massachusetts, was scheduled to go into effect on January 1, 1912. But the companies refused to pay the same wages for the shorter week as for the previous fifty-six-hour week, and since they applied the new law to all workers—male and female—it meant a reduction in pay for the workers. The corporations scoffed at the idea that the workers—separated into numerous crafts and twenty-five nationalities, speaking at least forty-five different languages, with fewer than 2,500 union members among the 30,000 mill workers, and even these divided between the United Textile Workers of America, AFL, and Local No. 20, IWW—could even consider a general strike, much less stage one.[10]

The Italian, Polish, and Lithuanian workers met on January 10 and 11 and voted to strike if their pay envelopes on January 12 showed any reduction. On the next afternoon, when it was clear that the mill owners had cut the wages, the general walkout began at the Everett Cotton Mill. The weavers, nearly all of them Polish women, stopped their looms. Officials attempted to explain the reduction in pay, but the women replied, "Not enough money," and left the mill. When the Italian workers in the Washington Mill opened their pay envelopes, they found that their weekly earnings had been reduced by an amount equivalent to two hours' work, or, as the workers put it, by "four loaves of bread."

The wages of these men and women were already at the starvation point. Suddenly, all the years of suffering from lack of food, miserable housing, inadequate clothing, poor health, and the tyranny of the foremen came to a head and erupted in an outburst of rage against the machines, the symbols of the bosses' repression. The workers ran from room to room, stopping the motors, cutting the belts, tearing the cloth, breaking the electric lights, and dragging the other operatives from the looms. Within half an hour, the work at the mill came to a standstill.

With the Washington Mill silenced, the unorganized strikers, many of them women, closed down mill after mill, waving American and Italian flags and shouting, "Better to starve fighting than to starve working"—which was soon to become the battle cry of the general strike. Repulsed by the police at several mills, they finally halted their attacks. But by Saturday night, January 13, an estimated twenty thousand textile workers had left their machines. By Monday night, January 15, Lawr-

ence was an armed camp. Police and militia guarded the mills throughout the night.[11] The Battle of Lawrence, one of the epic struggles between capital and labor in American history, was on!

Since the AFL United Textile Workers would have nothing to do
with the unskilled, immigrant workers in Lawrence, the strikers called
on the IWW for help, and "the IWW came on feet of lightning."[12]
Joseph J. Ettor, accompanied by Arturo Giovannitti, editor of *Il Proletario* and secretary of the Italian Socialist Federation, came immediately, and on January 13, under Ettor's leadership, the spontaneous
outburst quickly gave way to a methodical strike organization rarely
paralleled in the annals of the American labor movement. On January
15, pickets turned out en masse before each of the mills. This was the
beginning of a daily practice that continued until the end of the strike.
Never before had there been picketing on the scale employed in Lawrence. Indeed, it was the picket line that made the Lawrence strike a
milestone in the history of American labor struggles. Every striker took
his or her place on the picket lines, including those who, at first, joined
the walkout reluctantly.[13] To get around the prohibition by city authorities against gathering in front of the mills, the strike committee,
representing each of the different nationalities, developed the ingenious
strategy of the moving picket line. Day after day, for twenty-four hours a
day, long lines of pickets moved in an endless chain around the mill
district to discourage strikebreakers. Each picket wore a white ribbon or
card that said, "Don't Be a Scab." No one could get through the lines
without being accosted. What is more, the chain did not violate the law
because the strikers did not mass in front of the mills.[14]

The McKees Rocks and Hammond strikes had already demonstrated
the militancy of foreign-born women, and the Lawrence strike fully
corroborated it. The women strikers themselves and the wives of male
strikers trod the frozen streets alongside the men and often occupied the
front ranks in demonstrations and parades. Expectant mothers and
women with babes in their arms marched with the others, carrying signs
reading: "We Want Bread and Roses, Too." This slogan inspired one of
the great songs of the Lawrence strike, which has since come to symbolize women workers and their struggles:

> As we come marching, marching
>   In the beauty of the day
> A million darkened kitchens,
>   A thousand mill lofts gray,
> Are touched with all the radiance
>   That a sudden sun discloses
> For the people hear us singing:
>   "Bread and Roses! Bread and Roses!"

As we come marching, marching,
  We battle too for men
For they are women's children,
  And we mother them again.
Our lives shall not be sweated
  From birth until life closes.
Hearts starve as well as bodies;
  Give us bread but give us roses!

As we come marching, marching,
  Unnumbered women dead
Go crying through our singing
  Their ancient cry for bread.
Small art and love and beauty
  Their drudging spirits knew
Yes, it is bread we fight for—
  But we fight for roses, too.

As we come marching, marching,
  We bring the greater days.
The rising of the women
  Means the rising of the race.
No more the drudge and idler—
  Ten that toil where one reposes,
But a sharing of life's glories:
  Bread and Roses, Bread and Roses![15]

As the brutality of the police intensified, the women strikers and the workers' wives volunteered to lead the picket lines in an attempt to discourage police attacks. But chivalry in Lawrence did not extend to strikes of the mill women, who were often terribly beaten and then arrested. In fact, more women than men appear to have been arrested for intimidating scabs while picketing. Even when they had enough money with them, they refused to pay their fines and chose rather to go to jail. As soon as they were released from jail, they were back on the picket lines. "The women pickets were very active today and very few scabs entered the mills," read a fairly typical report from Lawrence. Most reporters agreed that the women proved themselves fiercer and more courageous than the men.[16]

On Monday evening, January 29, Anna LaPizza, a thirty-four-year-old Italian woman, was on her way to visit friends and passed through a gathering of about a thousand strikers. She was shot through the heart and killed. Even though nineteen witnesses testified that they had seen a soldier murder LaPizza, Ettor and Giovannitti were arrested, indicted for murder. imprisoned, and removed from the strike leadership.[17]

William D. ("Big Bill") Haywood, with Elizabeth Gurley Flynn, took over the leadership.

Impressed by the "active and efficient" women strikers, Haywood told how "the women caught a policeman in the middle of the bridge and stripped off all his uniform, pants and all. They were about to throw him into the icy river, when other policemen rushed in and saved him from the chilly ducking."[18] The police, Judge Mahoney of the Police Court, and the other authorities of Lawrence also testified to the activity and efficiency of the women strikers. On February 28, while considering the case of Mary Yuganis, who had been arrested for violating a city ordinance by obstructing a sidewalk, Judge Mahoney warned that while it was hard for the police to arrest women and children, disorder had to be prevented and the arrests would continue. He went on to charge that it was all a "game," and that the men strikers were simply putting the women in the front ranks in order to hamper the police from preventing disorders. One woman delegate to the strike committee protested, saying: "I want to say to the press that the women strikers are not being egged on by anyone or forced to go upon the picket line, as Judge Mahoney has said, but that we go there because that is but duty. We are not listening to anyone skulking in the background, as the judge has stated, and if we did, we would have gone into the mills long ago."[19] But the Lawrence authorities refused to retract the charge. The district attorney declared in court that the strike committee was made up of cowards who sent their women onto the picket line. He considered this grossly unfair, since "one policeman can handle ten men, while it takes ten policemen to handle one woman." The AFL, too, accused the IWW of putting women on the front line, to which Flynn responded: "The IWW has been accused of putting the women in the front. The truth is, the IWW does not keep them in the back and they go to the front."[20]

As the police became more brutal, women strikers responded with spontaneous street demonstrations. Fred Beal, then a young striker, describes one occasion:

> One day, after the militia was called, thousands of us strikers marched to Union Street again. In the front ranks, a girl carried a large American flag. When we arrived at the junction of Canal and Union Streets, we were met by a formidable line of militia boys, with rifles and attached bayonets. They would not let us proceed.
>
> An officer on horseback gave orders: "Port Arms! Disperse the crowd!"
>
> Whereupon the militia, boys between the ages seventeen to twenty, guns leveled waist-high, moved toward the crowd. Their bayonets glistened in the sunlight. On and on they moved. The strikers in front could not move because of the pressing of the crowd behind them. It looked as if the murder of Anna LaPizza would be multiplied many times. And then the girl with the American flag stepped forward. With a quick motion, she wrapped the Stars

and Stripes around her body and defied the militia to make a hole in Old Glory.

The officer on horseback permitted us to proceed and there was no further trouble.[21]

In the course of the strike, and with Wobbly encouragement, leaders began to develop from the rank and file, especially among the women. Three women were elected to the Strike Committee—Rosa Cardello, Josephine Liss, and Annie Welzenbach. Welzenbach, a highly skilled worker, did invisible reweaving, repairing tiny holes in the cloth. Her husband was also a skilled worker and, as Lawrence workers went, the family was relatively well off. But Annie had started to work at the age of fourteen and knew well what the conditions were for the mass of the workers. She told a reporter: "I have been getting madder and madder for years at the way they talked to these poor Italians and Lithuanians." Completely dedicated to the strike, she led the parade down Essex Street day after day and was elected to the ten-member negotiating committee. She was instrumental in winning the support of the skilled workers for the strike. She also showed her concern for the unskilled workers when, in a conversation with President Wood of the American Woolen Company in Boston, she told him not to consider her needs and those of the other skilled workers as much as the needs of the poorly paid women. She then delivered a lecture to him on the slavery imposed by the premium system and described how poorly the people of Lawrence ate.[22]

Many young mill women traveled to other towns to try to raise funds for the strike. Meanwhile, on the picket line, their sisters were beating back every attempt of the companies to break the strike by introducing scabs. "Man Intimidated by Women Pickets," "Woman Fined $20 for Assaulting an Officer," "Jeannie Radsiarlowitz Convicted of Intimidating Man," "Annie Rogers Arrested for Molesting Soldiers," "Annie Welzenbach and Her Two Sisters Routed from Bed and Dragged Down to Police Headquarters for Intimidation"—these were typical headlines in the *Lawrence Evening Tribune* during the strike. Even the *Tribune,* which ordinarily maligned the strikers, was moved to protest when the Lawrence police were issued orders to strike women on the arms and breasts and men on the head.[23]

The IWW understood that the women were the key to winning the strike, and special efforts were made to help them with their problems. Special women's meetings were held, at which Flynn spoke about the unique oppression facing women workers and the obstacles facing the wives of workingmen, particularly immigrants:

The women worked in the mills for lower pay and in addition had all the housework and care of the children. The old-world attitude of man as the "lord and master" was strong. At the end of the day's work—or, now, of strike duty—the man went home and sat at ease while his wife did all the work preparing the meal, cleaning the house, etc. There was considerable opposition to women going to meetings and marching on the picket line. We resolutely set out to combat these notions. The women wanted to picket. They were strikers as well as wives and were valiant fighters. We knew that to leave them at home alone, isolated from the strike activity, a prey to worry, affected by the complaints of tradespeople, landlords, priests and ministers, was dangerous to the strike.... We did not attack their religious ideas in any way but we said boldly that priests and ministers should stick to their religion and not interfere in a workers' struggle for better conditions, unless they wanted to help. We pointed out that if the workers had more money, they would spend it in Lawrence—even put more money in the church collections. The women laughed and told it to the priests and ministers the next Sunday.[24]

Women were able to vote on all strike decisions. Rosa Cardello, Josephine Liss, Carrie Hanson, and Mary Bateman were cited for their "bravery and practical helpfulness."[25] But it was Elizabeth Gurley Flynn who came to symbolize the leadership that women could exercise. Labor reporter Mary Heaton Vorse wrote:

When Elizabeth Gurley Flynn spoke, the excitement of the crowd became a visible thing. She stood there, young, with her Irish blue eyes, her face magnolia white and her cloud of black hair, the picture of a youthful revolutionary girl leader. She stirred them, lifted them up in her appeal for solidarity. Then at the end of the meeting, they sang. It was as though a spurt of flame had gone through the audience; something stirring and powerful, a feeling which has made the liberation of people possible, something beautiful and strong had swept through the people and welded them together, singing.[26]

Vorse called Flynn "the spirit of the strike," and recalled later:

There was ceaseless work for her that winter. Speaking, sitting with the strike committee, going to visit the prisoners in jail and endlessly raising money. Speaking, speaking, speaking, taking trains only to run back to the town that was ramparted by prison-like mills before which soldiers with fixed bayonets paced all day long.... Every strike meeting was memorable—the morning meetings, in a building quite a way from the center of things, owned by someone sympathetic to the strikers, the only place they were permitted to assemble. The soup kitchen was out here and here groceries were also distributed and the striking women came from far and near. They would wait around for a word with Gurley or Big Bill. In the midst of this excitment Elizabeth moved, calm and tranquil. For off the platform she was a very quiet person. It was as though she reserved her tremendous energy for speaking.[27]

"Speaking, speaking, speaking." Flynn had to employ a new method of speaking to the men and women of forty-five different nationalities. While the IWW organizers had interpreters, they had no way of knowing whether the interpreters were telling the strikers to stay out or go back to work. Haywood thereupon decided that the organizers would have to speak English in a way that could be understood by the strikers. "Now listen here," he told Flynn, "you speak to these workers . . . in the same kind of English that their children who are in primary school would speak to them and they would understand that." "Well," she recalled later, "that's not easy—to speak to them in primary school English. Well, we learned how to do it. The only trouble is with me it kind of stuck."[28]

Flynn was also responsible for fund raising and for support work outside of Lawrence. Flynn and Haywood organized special schools for children during the strike to offset the instructions they were getting in school, which was "directed at driving a wedge between the school children and the striking parents. . . . Some teachers called the strikers lazy, said they should go back to work or 'back where they came from.'" We attempted to counteract all this at our children's meetings," Flynn noted. "The parents were pathetically grateful to us as their children began to show real respect for them and their struggles."[29]

Flynn also took charge of what came to be called the "Lawrence Children's Crusade," probably the most publicized episode connected with the strike. From the beginning of the battle, the Italians had considered sending their children to the homes of Italian Socialist Federation members in other cities. Both French and Italian unions had used this tactic many times in strikes in Europe, but it had rarely been employed in the United States. The majority of the strikers voted to support the Italian workers' proposal for the exodus. Flynn arranged for the transportation; she placed children from four to fourteen years of age in suitable homes provided by Socialist women in New York and other cities but turned down "publicity seekers," such as the wealthy Mrs. O. H. P. Belmont, for not "having the interests of the strikers at heart."[30]

The exodus of the children eased the relief burden while it also attracted enormous sympathy for the strikers' cause. The pitiful, emaciated condition of the children as they paraded, inadequately clothed, in the bitter winter weather down New York's Fifth Avenue stamped Lawrence as a city of starvation wages and aroused great resentment against the mill owners.[31] Nevertheless, the antilabor press attacked the Children's Crusade as an inhuman practice and as a threat against the sanctity of the home. "It must be stopped," the *Boston American,* a Hearst paper, demanded in an editorial.

The mill owners, disturbed by the unfavorable publicity created by the crusade, determined to put an end to further departures.[32] A statement issued by the chief of police proclaimed: "There will be no more children leaving Lawrence until we are satisfied that the police cannot stop their going."[33] As the children were assembling at the Lawrence railroad station on February 24, the police sought to block them from boarding the cars that would carry them to Philadelphia. A member of the Philadelphia Women's Committee testified under oath that policemen "closed in on us with their clubs, beating right and left with no thought of the children who then were in desperate danger of being trampled to death. The mothers and the children were thus hurled in a mass and bodily dragged to a military truck and even clubbed, irrespective of the cries of the panic-stricken mothers and children."[34] Fifteen children and eight adults, including pregnant mothers, were arrested, clubbed, thrust into patrol wagons, and taken to the police station.[35]

As the nation's press headlined the news of the police brutality, a wave of protests swept the nation and even carried over to Europe. Petitions poured into Congress demanding an investigation of the Lawrence strike. Socialist Congressman Victor R. Berger urged quick action on a resolution he had previously introduced calling for an investigation of the strike. A congressional investigation was undertaken, along with one by the U.S. Commissioner of Labor.[36]

On the same day that the children were beaten and arrested at the railway station, the women strikers launched their first major independent offensive in the streets. Part of the plan probably was to draw police and troops away from the railway station. The offensive was organized the day before by a pregnant Italian woman at a meeting where Haywood was to speak. "Big Bill" lifted her onto a table and she spoke in broken English:

> Men, woman: I come to speak to you. I been speaking to others. Just now tomorrow morning all women come see me half past four at Syrian Church. Tonight no sleep. You meet me at half past four, no sleep tonight.
>
> You all come with me. We go tell folks no go to work. Men all stay home, all men and boys stay home. Just now all woman and girl come with me. Soldier he hurt man. Soldier he no hurt woman. He no hurt me. Me got big belly. She too [pointing to one of her friends], she got big belly too. Soldier no hurt me. Soldier he got mother.

A scene of incredible enthusiasm swept the fifteen hundred strikers who heard her, many of them in tears. "Big Bill" had to leave the hall without making his speech; the Italian woman had said everything that had to be said.[37]

Unfortunately, her optimism proved to be unfounded. The troops attacked the women demonstrators, beating and arresting them. The speaker herself miscarried. Congressional investigators looked into the tragedy, and Mrs. William Howard Taft, wife of the president of the United States, was reported to have rushed from the room in distress when the beating of the pregnant women was described. Chief of Police Sullivan gave a casual, matter-of-fact explanation of what had happened:

There were times when we had difficulty in keeping these women from getting in the patrol wagon to be arrested; they were martyrs, heroines; they wanted to be held up, they wanted to be brought to the police station and charged with an assault and interfering with people; lots of them had money in their pockets, but they would not pay fines and would not accept bail; they wanted to be sent to jail. Now, on that Monday morning, a great many people were arrested—that is, these women, for assaulting workers were going to the mills—and they were brought to the police station and locked up.[38]

And that was that! But the strikers presented their point of view in a letter to the governor of Massachusetts, in which they explained:

Since the federal investigation is on, women thought they were secure in walking on the streets and that their constitutional rights were guaranteed. Peaceful women went to a meeting on March first, on a Friday. Returning home, about 15 of them were suddenly surrounded by 50 or more Metropolitan police officers. There had been no provocation, no shouting even or any noise. These women were assaulted and clubbed, and an officer in blue, leaning out of a window of city hall, urged them on in their fiendish, savage attacks. Breaking into two divisions, they would not allow the women to escape.... Not until one of the women, Bertha F. Carosse, 151 Elm Street, was beaten into insensibility did the thugs in uniform desist. The beaten woman was carried unconscious to a hospital and pregnant with new life; this was blown into eternity by the fiendish beating and was born dead, murdered in a mother's womb by the clubs of hired murder of the law that you have so recklessly overridden and abridged.... We will remember, we will never forget and never forgive.[39]

The strikers remained united behind their strike committee. After eight weeks without a break in the strikers' ranks, the mill owners began to negotiate with the strike committee. First they offered a 5 percent increase in wages; then 7 percent; then 7½. All were rejected. On March 12 the negotiating committee came back from their meeting with an offer of 25 percent increases for the lowest-paid workers, with a decreasing of increases for higher-paid workers. The premium system was not abolished, but all workers would now get time and a quarter for overtime work, and the companies promised no discrimination against strikers.

On March 14 twenty thousand strikers voted unanimously to accept the offer and go back to work. They vowed to keep their organization intact and concluded, as always, by singing the "Internationale": "The earth shall rise on new foundations. We have been naught, we shall be all!"

The settlement was a great victory for the Lawrence workers and for the IWW. By the end of the strike, more than ten thousand Lawrence textile workers were members of the IWW, fully 60 percent of them women. More than 90 percent of these new members were Italians, Portuguese, Poles, Lithuanians, Syrians, French, and Belgians. Most of them had been in the United States for less than three years, and nearly all had been considered "unorganizable" because they were women and immigrants from southern and eastern Europe.[40]

In an article entitled "The Women of Lawrence," the *Industrial Worker* gave the chief credit for the unprecedented victory to the bravery and enthusiasm of the women strikers and the strikers' wives.[41] It was a fully merited tribute. On many occasions, these women had taken over the picket lines, refusing to shrink before police troop brutality. They had prepared the food in the soup kitchens and had organized the Children's Crusade to provide adequate care for the children, while also making it easier for themselves to attend to their strike duties. They had fought together with the men, but they had often made their own decisions.

The IWW understood very well that the strike could not be won without the full participation of the women, and the Wobblies paid special attention to the women's needs. It was a correct decision. The special women's meetings organized by Flynn and Haywood enabled them to stand up to their husbands and other male coworkers who disapproved of their participation. During the entire strike, women were considered to be equal to men, and as workers, they served on all committees, picketed actively, initiated tactics, and not only did everything the men strikers did but also performed some duties that men were not prepared to do. It was their own idea that women strikers should not furnish bail or pay fines but stay in jail instead.[42]

The women used the skills they had developed in their roles as wives and mothers to help sustain the strike. They made food available through the soup kitchens. They sacrificed being with their children so that they could participate more actively in the struggle. As one reporter wrote after witnessing the beating of women and children at the Lawrence station: "I saw something of the weeping mothers and knew what a sacrifice some of them had made upon the altar of the general cause. It was what they gave to aid the struggle."[43]

The Lawrence strike gave these women a new sense of power. They were able to vote as equals with men in all strike decisions. They assumed positions of authority and leadership by participating in all committees and speaking and picketing in public. They led the picket lines and faced arrest and jail, even after the police used force and violence against them. The determination and militancy of the women strikers were decisive in the final victory.

In the end, the success of the Lawrence strike was achieved as a result of the solidarity of the workers against an enormous campaign on the part of the mill owners, the city, and the state to defeat the strikers. In the process, the workers gained a new sense of unity. As Mary Heaton Vorse put it:

> Young girls had executive positions. Men and women . . . have developed a larger social consciousness. . . . Almost every day for weeks people of every

one of these nations have gone to their crowded meetings and listened to the speakers and have discussed these questions afterward, and in the morning the women have resumed their duty on the picket lines and the working together for what they believed was the common good.[44]

The women of Lawrence disproved many of the assumptions about the role women could play in the labor movement. For one thing, the majority of the immigrant women working in Lawrence were not "temporary" participants in the labor force but workers whose wages were an integral part of the family income. For another, women, in particular, proved during the strike that they were capable of assuming leadership and acting in new roles in addition to the ones traditionally assigned to them.

Unfortunately, however, the gains for the workers of Lawrence were short-lived. After the trial and acquittal of Ettor and Giovannitti, which was accompanied by a good deal of mass agitation and a one-day political strike, the main IWW organizers left town. The mill owners then initiated a two-year campaign of retaliation and union-busting that had three prongs: "God and Country" (a campaign designed to split those born in the United States from the foreign-born workers), massive blacklisting of activists, and a forced depression in the textile industry. The American Woolen Company, the largest in Lawrence, announced that it was moving south because it could not pay such high wages. By January, 1915, there were fifteen thousand workers walking the streets of Lawrence looking for work as the local depression became a national disaster.

The employers' offensive was mainly responsible for the loss in IWW membership in Lawrence. Still, it cannot be denied that the IWW's policies contributed to accelerating this decline. Because it was primarily interested in unionizing during strikes, it failed to build a strong permanent union, and it left the workers without strong leadership. These weaknesses resulted in precisely the same outcome in Little Falls, New York, where, as we shall see, there was no powerful employers' offensive after the strike victory but where the IWW membership also declined disastrously after a great upsurge.[45]

24

Little Falls, Paterson, and Other Struggles

THE OUTCOME of the Lawrence strike was more than a local victory. That struggle was the forerunner of a wave of industrial conflicts that swept through Massachusetts and other sections of New England and flowed over into upstate New York. In 1912 all Massachusetts was ablaze with strikes. The textile industry was the one most deeply affected (28.3 percent of all strikes and 66.6 percent of all strikers were in that industry, and of these, 58 percent were women).[1] Aside from Lawrence, important textile struggles took place in Lowell, New Bedford, and Fall River. Other strikes were prevented only when an alarmed textile industry decided voluntarily to grant wage increases and other concessions to the workers. By April 1 about 275,000 textile workers in New England had received wage increases as an indirect result of the Lawrence strike. In Manchester, England, the *Textile Manufacturer* commented in awe: "The increase in wages in the cotton and woolen mills in the five New England states that came into effect at the end of March was one of the most remarkable episodes in the history of the textile industries in the United States."[2]

The year 1913 opened with another IWW victory in the textile industry—this time in Little Falls, New York, a major center for knit goods and underwear.

In the decade from 1900 to 1910, the population of Little Falls, described as "The Lowell of New York State," increased by almost two thousand, almost all of them immigrants from southern or eastern Europe. The New York State Labor Department reported in 1913:

> Today the mass of all mill operatives in this city, and especially the unskilled and semi-skilled workers, are no longer American-born, nor even English, German or Irish. Slowly at first, then more rapidly, came the Slovak, the

Pole, the Italian, the Ruthenian, the Lithuanian, the Crainer, and in smaller numbers representatives of other European nations . . . replacing and crowding out their English, German, or Irish predecessors.[3]

The immigrants came to Little Falls to share in the city's considerable industrial development, but they received little of the prosperity that their labor created for the owners of the factories. The weekly wages of nearly half of the eight hundred male day workers amounted to $9 or less. Only one-quarter earned in excess of $12 a week. Almost half of the nine hundred female workers earned weekly wages of $7.50 or less. Only one-fifth earned $6 or more. Male boarders paid $4.75 per week for lodging, meals, and laundry, while female boarders paid approximately $4.25 for food and lodging alone.[4] The wages paid to textile workers were actually lower than these statistics indicate, since the data include the wages of superintendents, foremen, machinists, and other skilled workers.

Wages were low because management kept unions out. In 1912 there were only twelve unions in all of Little Falls, covering a mere 6 percent of the total labor force. The only workers in the textile industry covered by union representation were seventy-five jack spinners, and they made up 23 percent of the union membership in Little Falls.* They received day rates of $2.60 for a sixty-hour week.[5]

In his annual message to the New York state legislature in January, 1912, Governor John A. Dix called for a reduction in the hours worked by women and children. The legislature reacted by passing a fifty-four-hour law. In addition, it stipulated that women could not be employed for more than ten hours in any one day, nor before 6 A.M. or after 9 P.M.[6]

While New York's law addressed itself to certain areas of exploitation, it completely avoided the issue of wages, thereby creating the same kind of situation that had only recently precipitated the textile strike in Lawrence. When the Phoenix and Gilbert Knitting Mills in Little Falls responded to the law by slashing wages to compensate for the reduced hours of work, the workers spontaneously and peacefully began walking out—first eighty workers from the Phoenix Mill, and then, a week later, seventy-six employees of the Gilbert Mill.[7]

In response to a call from the strikers, two IWW organizers came from Rochester to provide whatever assistance might be needed. With each passing day, more workers joined the strikers, until fifteen hundred were out. Virtually all the strikers were immigrants who had arrived in Little Falls within the previous few years, mostly from Italy, Poland, Hungary, or Austria. Most still spoke only in their native tongues. Perhaps 70 percent were women. While the strikers declared angrily that

---

*Jack Spinners ran a machine that twisted the strand of cotton as it left the carding machine.

their wages were inadequate to support themselves and their families, the *Little Falls Journal and Courier* took a different view of the matter. "The question of whether the wages paid were starvation or not, did not, and cannot enter into the merits of the case," it argued. "The employer fixed the wages that he was willing to pay, and the men and women were at liberty to accept the employment or not."[8]

Socialists from across the state and Wobblies from across the country flocked into the community to help in organizing and directing the strike against entrenched local interests and an oppressive police force. Picketing, parading, and open-air meetings were not allowed, and it was dangerous even for a small group of strikers to gather in any one spot on the streets.[9]

From October 9, 1912, until January 4, 1913, the strikers and their supporters held out against inclement weather and the entrenched local interests, backed by a brutal police force. Mass arrests were the order of the day; on October 15, Major George R. Lunn of Schenectady, a Socialist, was arrested while addressing the strikers. His wife was arrested when she attempted to read aloud an editorial protesting the police action. Other Socialists were arrested for reading from the Constitution and the Bible.[10]

Although the Schenectady Socialists were helpful to the strikers, it was Wobblies like George Lehney of Chicago, Benjamin Legere of Bridgeport, and Fillipo Bocchini, an Italian anarchist, who did the real work of organizing the strikers and inculcating them with the doctrine of solidarity. None of these men had had much experience in this type of struggle, but the IWW was so deeply involved in a whole series of strikes after Lawrence that it had to send whoever was available to assist the workers in Little Falls. Legere had aspirations of becoming a playwright and actor as well as a labor leader, but the Lawrence strike had diverted him from the theater for the time being. Although he did not play a prominent part there, he did learn something about the IWW strategy for organizing unskilled immigrant workers, many of them women, and when he was called upon by IWW General Secretary Vincent St. John to take charge of the Wobbly strike headquarters in Little Falls, he moved there.[11]

Following the advice of the Wobblies, the strikers established a committee of twenty-four members drawn from each plant and every nationality involved. On October 22 the strike committee issued a proclamation calling on all textile workers to join in a general strike of the mills. "Strike! Don't Be a Scab! This Is a Fight for Bread! Don't Line Up on the Side of the Boss!" The proclamation continued: "Your bosses have taken advantage of a new 54-hour law to cut down still further the starvation wages of hundreds of your brothers and sisters in the mills.

You will suffer by this reduction. The fight is on. We must all unite to win." Later that afternoon, the committee placed three basic demands before the mill management: sixty hours' pay for fifty-four hours' work; an additional 10 percent increase in wages; and no discrimination against any workers for participation in the strike.[12]

The strike committee proceeded to appoint other specialized committees that were given the responsibility for raising strike funds, distributing relief to strikers, and providing for the legal defense of any member arrested. "Whatever may be the purposes and methods of the IWW," the *Utica Daily Press* remarked, "it apparently is teaching the strikers some of the fundamental principles of democracy. That is, they are taught to manage their own affairs and in their meetings, they make motions and argue their line of action with much more understanding than was the rule at first." What made this all the more remarkable, the paper noted, was the fact that all the strikers were newly arrived immigrants, the vast majority of them women—"both of which groups are traditionally viewed as incapable of managing their own affairs."[13]

On October 23 the strikers gathered for a sunrise meeting, signaled by a group of strikers who marched through the streets beating drums. After receiving instructions, the parade set out for the mills, led by a drummer and others carrying various national flags. Reaching the mill gates, columns of marchers, with the women strikers in front, walked back and forth urging workers not to cross the lines and yelling "scab" at those who ignored the appeals.[14]

The following day the strikers voted to affiliate with the IWW, and two days later, Local No. 801—the National Industrial Union of Textile Workers of Little Falls—was chartered. On October 27 the strikers put on an impressive show of strength with a parade and mass meeting of over a thousand men, women, and children, led by Benjamin Legere and a contingent of little girls carrying American flags. The marchers waved placards bearing such legends as "Help Our Fathers and Mothers Win This Strike—Don't Scab" and "We Are Not Fighting Flags or Religion—We Are Fighting Bosses for Bread." The paraders filed peacefully into the City Theater to the playing of the "Marseillaise."[15]

On October 30 a policeman beat a female striker, and when the others on the picket line took steps to defend her, the entire police contingent attacked the strikers, rounded up the IWW organizers, speakers, and committeemen, and arrested and jailed them. Slovak Hall, the strike headquarters, was raided, and anyone found in the hall was likewise arrested. Twenty people—two women and eighteen men, members of five different nationalities—were charged with the commission of the "crime" of rioting. Legere, nine Italians, including Fillipo Bocchini, and a Polish woman striker had to stand trial on additional charges of assault in the first degree, the penalty for which was as high as ten years in the penitentiary. They were alleged to be the attackers of two policemen injured in a clash between the police and the strikers.[16]

But the arrest of the strike leaders only served to strengthen the strikers' determination to continue until victory. Although "Big Bill" Haywood arrived to help, he was too tired and ill to be of much assistance. (He was already suffering from the diabetes that was to kill him ten years later.) Rather, it was an inexperienced IWW organizer, Matilda Rabinowitz. together with the women strikers and women sympathizers, who played the leading role in strike activities.

Rabinowitz, a middle-class Russian-Jewish girl from Bridgeport, Connecticut, and a close friend of the imprisoned Ben Legere, had worked in a corset factory, assisted in wage surveys in Massachusetts and Connecticut, and devoted whatever time she could spare to help the Lawrence strikers and to mobilize support for Ettor and Giovannitti during their trial. She was preparing to enter college when she heard of Legere's jailing. She wired Vincent St. John for confirmation of the fact and received a telegram in reply: "Go to Little Falls. Name national office as authority." She abandoned her college plans and took a train for Little Falls the next morning. She wrote later:

> I had never been in a strike. My short and unsuccessful effort to interest corset workers in a union was hardly even a beginning in the art of labor organization. To be sure, I knew both first-hand and in the contacts with scores of women workers interviewed in the surveys in Mass. and Conn. what the conditions were and how justified any strike would be. I had also read socialist and labor literature and formed ideas. But to be cast suddenly into the role of responsibility in a strike was rather frightening. Travelling all day from Bridgeport to New York, then on the N. Y. Central to Albany then on a branch line to Little Falls, I was both stimulated and oppressed.[17]

Arriving in Little Falls, she walked the streets, unwilling to ask directions from the wrong person, until she got to the working-class district and heard people speaking Slovenian. They took her to the strike headquarters, where she received a warm welcome. She lived with the strikers and learned how to organize strike activities. She came to respect and admire the men and women of so many nationalities working together as a solid force to end the miserable exploitation to which they were subjected in the mills. She recalled:

> Often of a morning the water was only a trickle and sometimes frozen. But we all made the picket line together. At six o'clock, stamping through snow, our breath steaming in zero temperature, we circled the mills and circled the mills—and often sang! Italian blended well with the Polish and Slavic revolutionary songs—there was hope and courage in them. . . .
> Appeals for funds to feed the strikers were rushed to unions, to Socialist Party locals, to individuals. The commissary was set up for distribution of

groceries to families and to feed single persons in its hall. Women strikers toiled long hours in the kitchen. As donations of clothing began to come in, a repair shop was set up adjoining the commissary. Women and men cleaned and repaired clothes and two Italian cobblers did wonders with worn shoes. It was a busy little world, struggling to survive. And yet what an example it was that men and women of different backgrounds, different languages could strive together against great odds in unbroken solidarity for three months, determined to wrest a little more life for themselves and their children.[18]

After the morning picket line, Rabinowitz would hold a daily meeting with the strike committee and get reports on fund-raising and strike developments. In the afternoon there was bookkeeping and correspondence, and then, at night, a meeting of all the strikers. Once a week, they held a social, with dancing and singing to the music of a fiddle or a harmonium. Twice a week, Matilda went to the county jail in Herkimer to visit Legere and Bocchini. Meanwhile, she had been using up all her savings, not thinking to ask for any salary. Then she began to get $18 a week as a national organizer—the same salary as Flynn.[19]

Rabinowitz received assistance from many IWW leaders who came through Little Falls, while others helped her by mail. Much valuable help came also from such notable women as Helen Keller. Foremost among the women activists was Helen Schloss. Schloss had trained as a nurse and settlement worker and had been a medical inspector for the New York City Department of Health. In 1912, she was hired by the Fortnightly Club, a charitable literary society composed of prominent Little Falls women, as a consumption inspector ("tuberculosis nurse"). The Fortnightly Club apparently neglected to look beyond her employment credentials into her labor and political activities, for her investigations into social conditions in New York had made a Socialist out of her, and thereafter she participated in the shirtwaist strike of women workers in New York City in 1909, demonstrating on several occasions on behalf of shopwomen.[20]

In Little Falls, Schloss attempted to improve the inhuman living conditions of the workers by publicly revealing both the conditions and those landlords responsible. "I saw at once that the right way to improve conditions was to go to the root of the evil," she explained. "I got the names of the owners and had notices sent to them telling of conditions of the tenements, what that condition meant, and asking them to better things." Her appeals were rejected by the local authorities on the ground that the people affected "are simply wops and ginnies. They don't count." Schloss responded bitterly: "They are more than 'wops' and 'ginnies' to me. They are human beings with hearts, souls, and thoughts just as you have, and I mean to fight and work for them." She resigned her position and led many of the strike's parades and demonstrations, taking the brunt of the wrath of the local officials. Not content with merely operating the strike soup kitchen and looking after the strikers' physical condition in her clinic, she traveled around the east, speaking on behalf of the strikers.

On several occasions she was physically assaulted by law enforcement officials, but she refused to be intimidated. Once, in an attempt to put her away indefinitely, the Little Falls police had three doctors examine her for insanity. She was able to secure her release on bail, and eventually her case was dismissed. "I hate the sight of Little Falls, but I mean to fight until I have cleaned those miserable tenements up," Schloss announced as she returned to work for the strikers.[21]

Most people probably know of Helen Keller as the deaf and blind girl who triumphed over her disabilities to become a noted author, educator, and source of inspiration to all humanity. Less well known, however, is Helen Keller the radical—member of the Socialist Party, defender of the IWW, and champion of the working class in its struggle against industrial exploitation. It was this Helen Keller who came to the aid of the Little Falls strikers.

From her home in Wrentham, Massachusetts, Keller wrote to the strikers in Little Falls. Describing them as "brave girls . . . starving so courageously to bring about the emancipation of the workers," she declared: "Their cause is my cause. If they are denied a living wage, I also am defamed. While they are industrial slaves, I cannot be free. . . . I cannot enjoy the good things of life which come to me if they are hindered and neglected." And she continued:

> Surely the things that the workers demand are not unreasonable. It cannot be unreasonable to demand the protection of women and little children and an honest wage for all who give their time and energy to industrial occupations. When indeed shall we learn that we are all related one to the other, that we are all members of one body? Until the spirit of love for our fellowmen, regardless of race, color or creed, shall fill the world, making real in our lives and our deeds the actuality of human brotherhood—until the great mass of the people shall be filled with the sense of responsibility for each other's welfare, social justice can never be attained.

Throughout November and into December, local officials subjected the strikers to constant harassment. The employers were also assisted by the efforts of the AFL organizer C. A. Miles to portray the IWW as a godless, anarchist organization. He repeatedly claimed that no industry could come up with a settlement satisfactory to the IWW and insisted that the Wobblies were turning immigrants into a "menace rather than a safeguard of society." Miles established a temporary organization of textile workers, which he claimed had an initial membership of fifty-two among the strikers. While the mill management refused to meet with any representative of the IWW, which spoke for over twelve hundred strikers, Mills was able to confer repeatedly with the owners. On December 2 he announced that a settlement had been reached.[22]

Still, the strikers persevered, indicating their determination to continue until victory was achieved by sending their children away. Socialists and sympathizers in Schenectady had offered to bring the children of strikers to that city and, having received the consent of the strikers, spent a month in making meticulous preparations for the exodus—inspecting the houses of prospective foster parents, securing the legal consent of parents, providing physical examinations for the children, and purchasing clothing for them.[23]

On the cold morning of December 17, eighteen children, the first group of a planned fifty, prepared to leave Little Falls. The strikers joined the children at strike headquarters for a march to the railroad station. From the time the parade assembled until the children actually departed, the police subjected the participants to a constant battery of harassment. As the entourage assembled, they ordered the strikers to remove all signs. When a little boy carrying the first sign failed to observe the order, a policeman tore the placard, which read "You can jail men and women, but you can't jail ideas," out of his hands. When they reached the railroad station, truant officers demanded that the strikers present legal documents authorizing the children's departure. Having already experienced similar outrages in Lawrence, strike leaders had prepared in advance for this contingency. As the train pulled out of the Little Falls station, the parents had to bid their children a silent farewell, for the police forbade any cheering.[24]

Although the strike leaders had learned from the Lawrence strike, the corporations and the police apparently had not. The actions taken against the parents had the same effect in arousing public sympathy for the strikers as had similar actions in Lawrence. On January 1, 1913, the new year was ushered in with a settlement offer from the mill operators, arranged by state mediators. At a ratification meeting of all the strikers, presided over by Matilda Rabinowitz, the proposed settlement was read to the strikers by interpreters in Italian, Slavic, and Polish. The strikers cheered as they learned that they had obtained a gain of from 5 to 18 percent in wages, and reinstatement of all workers, with no discrimination against individual strikers. "The terms on which the strikers agreed to go back to work are a substantial increase over what was paid previously," noted the *Utica Press*. On January 6 the victorious strikers returned to work. "Another victory scored for the One Big Union," IWW organizers wired from Little Falls.[25] The *Industrial Worker* declared proudly:

> For twelve long and worried weeks, a few hundred workers, the overwhelming majority women, divided into four nationalities and with all sorts of

differences in religion, customs, and habits of thought, held together and
emerged triumphant from a struggle in which every conceivable force was
brought to bear to defeat them. . . . Pass a home on the South Side now and
one will hear a women's voice singing "The Marseillaise" or "The Internationale" as she goes about her housework and small boys delight to give the
strikers' yell:

  "One for all and all for one.
  We'll stick together till the strike is done."[26]

When the National Union of Textile Workers met in convention
during January, 1913, delegate after delegate, many of them women,
recounted their exciting experiences during the previous months and
urged speedy mass action to release the fourteen strikers who had been
arrested during the Little Falls strike and were in the Herkimer jail.*
They pointed to the victories at Lawrence, Lowell, New Bedford, Little
Falls, and other textile centers as proof that the ideology and tactics of
the IWW represented the only hope for the textile workers of
America.[27]

Then came Paterson, however, and after that bitter struggle was
ended, the bright hopes of the IWW in the textile industry lay shattered.

The silk workers of Paterson, New Jersey, many of them women, and
most of them Italian or Jewish immigrants, rebelled against a long-
standing system of extreme exploitation. In general, the average silk
worker, with the exception of the dyer, was on the job ten hours a day, at
a wage that produced a yearly income of $580—the lowest-paid of any of
the twenty-five leading New Jersey industries.[28] Many of the mills were
firetraps. Sanitary conditions were abominable. Some factories were entirely unheated in winter, and the weavers had to work in overcoats.
Workers in the dyeing plants worked in steam-filled rooms all day,
where they were "unable to see the person they were working with."
Dampness, bad air, poor sanitation, and fatigue after long hours of
constant standing and stooping caused a high percentage of illness and
deaths among the silk workers.[29]

Several wage scales would be applied for the same work in the same
shop. One girl might receive a weekly wage of $1.42 after forty-two
hours of work, while another might receive a weekly wage of $1.85 after
thirty-two hours. Often very young workers, aged fourteen to seventeen,
received only half their weekly wage after fines were deducted. The
remainder was withheld until the end of the year, when it would be paid
out if the girl was still employed.[30]

In 1912 two strikes broke out to remedy these grievances and the

---

*Trials did not take place until March and May, 1913. Most were found "not guilty" or
fined, but Legere and Bocchino were convicted of assault and were not released from jail
until July, 1914.

introduction of the four-loom system, which meant the loss of jobs for many workers and sheer exhaustion with no increase in pay for those who remained employed. But by the fall of 1912 it became clear that nothing had been won. The silk workers were still thoroughly dissatisfied with their conditions, and they now knew that only a strong union could resolve their grievances over wages, working hours, and conditions and prevent the further installation of the four-loom system. They were ready to fight again, this time under the leadership of the men and women who had won fame at Lawrence.[31]

On January 27, 1913, eight hundred men and women—the entire working force of the Henry Doherty Silk Company—quit work because of the firing of four members of a committee that had carried the workers' protest over the resumption of the four-loom system. The walkout did not take place at the instigation or under the leadership of the IWW. (The event was not even mentioned in *Solidarity*.) But as soon as the Doherty workers struck, the hundred-member Local 152, IWW (which it will be recalled, had been in existence since 1907), decided to launch a campaign to win the allegiance of the strikers and involve the workers in the other mills. With pamphlets, meetings, pickets, and expressions of support, the IWW local threw its forces behind the strikers. "Do away with the four-loom system in Paterson," the IWW appealed. The slogan was music to the silk weavers' ears; they joined Local 152 and entrusted the leadership of the strike to the IWW.[32]

On March 3, 1913, the tie-up of the silk industry was complete. Upwards of 25,000 silk workers were out in what "Big Bill" Haywood called "the closest approach to a general strike that has yet taken place in American industry." Early in March the demand for the abolition of the four-loom system was supplemented by others, including recognition of the IWW, an eight-hour day, and a minimum wage of $12 a week. The manufacturers categorically rejected all the demands.[33]

Violence against workers had been a feature of all IWW free-speech fights and strikes, but the Paterson strike was one of the bloodiest confrontations in American labor history, as city authorities, police, mill owners' hired thugs, and local courts joined forces to break the strike. Mass arrests of strikers took place on an unprecedented scale. The right to peaceful picketing was simply suspended from the first day of the strike. It was also made illegal for the strikers to hold outdoor meetings in Paterson, so that they had to meet in the neighboring suburb of Haledon, whose mayor was a Socialist. On one occasion, 164 were sent to jail. Forty-one strikers were found guilty of unlawful assembly because they were doing picket duty around the Harding Mill. Judge Richard Kleinert sentenced thirty-one strikers to three months in the county jail at hard labor, and also admonished the strikers that if they did not like the laws, they were at liberty to leave the country. To facilitate their departure, he suspended sentence during good behavior. All the strikers thus addressed went right back to the picket line, and most of them ended up in jail. Seventeen-year-old Hannah Silverman, a young striker, was sent to the county jail three times during the strike and was on the picket line the following morning each time she was released. Haywood called her "the greatest little IWW woman in America." A close second must have been "Little" Carrie Torello, "one of the busiest of silk mill pickets," who, upon being arrested one morning, "indignantly told the policeman: 'I can't go to jail and leave my children.' She picked up five of her six little ones and put them in the patrol wagon, saying to one of the other strikers: 'If you see Freddie, tell him to come to jail.'"[34]

Well over half the strikers were women and children, and they supported the strike enthusiastically. When Elizabeth Gurley Flynn and three other Wobbly leaders were arrested for "unlawful assemblage" and "inciting to riot," the women strikers gathered outside the jail and sang the song about Flynn made famous during the Lawrence strike. They shouted that when they had won their struggle, "Gurley Flynn will be the boss."[35]

On March 13 the Paterson *Press* launched a campaign aimed at convincing the strikers that it was their patriotic duty to desert the IWW and return to work "under the American Flag and in the American Way." The mill owners set aside March 19 as "flag day," on which the city was to be decorated with American flags "as a protest against the 'foreign' and 'anarchistic' methods of the IWW." On that day the mill owners bedecked the city with flags and banners urging the workers to return to their jobs under the slogan: "We live under the flag; we fight for this flag; and we will work under this flag." The next day, the strikers hit back. Each striker wore an American flag on his or her chest and underneath it the message: "We wove the flag; we dyed the flag; we live under the flag; but we won't scab under the flag!"[36]

The wholesale sentencing of the strikers, their leaders, and their sympathizers to jail, and the general violation of fundamental democratic rights of free speech in Paterson aroused indignation throughout the country. But after fourteen long weeks of withstanding police clubbing, arrests, and jailings, and the efforts of the AFL to aid the employers and break the strike, the strikers needed more than indignant editorials in the press. The economic position of the workers and their families was desperate. Despite contributions from Socialists and Italian societies and by silk workers in districts not affected by the strike, the amounts raised had never been large. For most of the strike, the men, women, and children on the picket line lived on one not very filling meal each day. Now the treasury was empty, and unless it was replenished, the position of the strikers would be hopeless.[37] To raise money for the strike relief fund and, at the same time, tell the real story of the strike, which had been so distorted by the newspapers, it was decided to hold a dramatic "Pageant of the Paterson Strike" in New York City's Madison Square Garden, with all the parts to be played by the strikers themselves.[38]

On June 7, before a standing-room-only crowd of over fifteen thousand, more than twelve hundred striking workers from Paterson presented "America's First Labor Play," depicting the entire story of the strike—the brutality of the police against the mass picketing, the mothers jailed and torn from their babies as they picketed, and the women clubbed and abused. Songs composed by the strikers were sung in different languages. One of them went:

> Now friends and fellow workers,
> This strike we shall win!
>
> (*Chorus*):
>   This strike we shall win,
>   This strike we shall win!
>
> Let us all join in the chorus:
> Hurrah for Miss Flynn!
>
> (*Chorus*):
>   Hurrah for Miss Flynn,
>   Hurrah for Miss Flynn!
>
> Italian, French and German,
> Hungarian, Jew and Polish,
> Will make all together
> One nationality.[39]

The audience, deeply moved, demanded that the songs be sung again and again. But the strikers' vision of a swollen relief fund as a result of the pageant soon proved to be an illusion. On the night of the pageant, Haywood announced that there had been a $6,000 profit, but after expenses had been calculated, the pageant showed a deficit of $1,996. John Reed, who had first proposed the idea of a pageant, explained that it was impossible to make a profit from a single performance when it cost $690 to build a stage, $750 for scenes, and $1,000 for rental of the Garden, aside from the cost of transporting the huge cast to New York.* In any event, the financial failure of the pageant at a moment when the strikers had been led to expect thousands of dollars marked the beginning of the end of the strike.[40]

When the pageant failed to replenish the strike treasury, it became impossible to maintain the morale of the strikers. Less hardy workers

---

*A graduate of Harvard, class of 1910, Reed had come in contact with men with Socialist ideas in New York and went to observe the Paterson strike at first hand. He was arrested on April 18 in Paterson and jailed for four days for merely watching the strike. Upon his release from prison, Reed went back to Paterson again and again, and while working with the strikers, came up with the idea of the pageant (*New York Call*, Apr. 30, 1913).

began drifting back to their jobs, and by July 17, several plants were operating almost in full swing. The collapse came with a vegeance on July 18, when the general strike committee which had held out against shop-by-shop settlements, was compelled to give its approval to this method of settling the strike. Broken into three hundred separate groups, the strikers were forced to give up their demands and return, hoping to get some concessions from the employers. But the majority returned to work under the same conditions they had left four months before.

The strike was officially ended on August 1. Starved into submission, the strikers had been defeated in spite of their remarkable display of courage and solidarity for twenty-two weeks. Most of them had to go back to work unconditionally, so that as far as material results were concerned, the strike was a failure. The fifty-five-hour week was retained by the Paterson mills, and the four-loom system continued in operation. Finally, many mills refused to dismiss the scabs taken on during the strike, which meant no employment for the workers they had replaced.[41]

The IWW suffered a setback in Paterson from which it never completely recovered. Its prestige in the East, which had been at a high point following the victory at Lawrence, underwent a tremendous decline, and there was no longer talk about the IWW's infallibility in strikes. Then, in the same year—1913—the Wobblies suffered two additional strike defeats. In Akron, the "Rubber Capital" of the world, 150 tire builders at the Firestone Tire Company walked out on February 10, 1913, after a reduction of about 35 percent in the piecework price paid to the finishers in the automobile tire department. By February 12 over four thousand workers at Firestone, Goodyear, and Goodrich had left the factories, and half of them signed up with the IWW.[42]

Many of the strikers were women, earning about $5 to $12 per week at piece rates. The girls picketed and paraded through the streets of Akron with tin pans, taking up collections for the strike fund along the way. The Akron *Press* interviewed Annie Fetjko, an eighteen-year-old striker employed by Goodrich, who explained why she had joined the picket line:

> My average two weeks' pay is $8 or $9. I can't save anything and I haven't seen papa or mama or the little brothers and sisters since I came here. They only live in Pennsylvania, too, but I can't save enough to go and see them. The last day I worked I made 75 cents and lots of days I made less. . . . Friday, Charlie, one of the pickets, talked to me at noon. I decided I couldn't be much worse off so I laid down my tools and four other girls in that department followed me out.[43]

The number of strikers with little red ribbons on their coats, signifying that they had joined the IWW, grew rapidly. So, too, did the violence of the police and employers' gangsters against the strikers. Scores of strikers were clubbed, arrested, and jailed. The Citizens' Volunteer Police Association, a vigilante group composed of prominent business and professional men, were sworn in as deputy sheriffs and given license to operate freely against the strikers. Wherever and whenever the strikers gathered, the Citizens' Police Association broke up the gathering, often inflicting physical violence with their clubs.[44] By March 22 the strike was all but crushed by the reign of terror, and on March 31 it was officially terminated. The workers returned without a single change in their conditions, back to what the IWW sadly admitted was "a living hell, compared to which Dante's Inferno is but a flicker, to a speed-up system which drove men and women to an early grave." At the height of the strike, the IWW rubber local in Akron had a membership of 3,500. At the convention of the IWW held in Chicago in September, 1913, it reported a membership of approximately 150.[45]

The other defeat suffered by the IWW that year was among the Detroit auto workers. Although no women were involved in the strike, Matilda Rabinowitz was the leading IWW organizer. She originally came to Detroit to help organize the workers of the Ford Motor Company. "Russian Girl Leads Clash With Police" was the headline of a story in the *Detroit Press* of April 30, 1913, describing how "Miss Rabinowitz and a group of IWW men were arrested by the police and carted off to the police court as soon as they mounted the soapboxes and attempted to address a crowd of more than 3,000 employees of the Ford Plant." They were fined $5 each by a Highland Park judge on charges of obstructing traffic. Undaunted by the fine, Rabinowitz announced: "I am going to speak to the motor car workers of Detroit if I rot in jail for it." And after she was released, Rabinowitz and other Wobblies returned to the Ford plant and addressed the workers from a nearby vacant lot.[46]

The only strike of auto workers under IWW leadership, however, was that of the Studebaker workers. On July 20, 1913. Rabinowitz addressed a meeting of workers employed by Studebaker and was so eloquent that they voted to strike. She then helped them draw up demands calling for a weekly payday, eight hours' work with ten hours' pay, improved sanitary conditions, and no discrimination against strikers after the settlement. But the company refused to negotiate, and after a week, the strikers, blocked at every turn by the police, returned to the plant, defeated but, according to Rabinowitz, "more determined than ever to fight for bread and freedom, and intent on organizing the entire automobile industry." She was convinced that "the IWW has become firmly imbedded in the hearts and minds of those who, even for one week, fought under its banners," and that this would be reflected in future organizing campaigns.[47]

Rabinowitz herself did what she could to make this vision come true.

She moved ceaselessly about, organizing. ("There were never enough organizers and women organizers were still a novelty," she wrote later.)[48] Arrested and bailed out, she still persevered. After Akron and Detroit, her main work was in the South, for she was given the assignment of organizing textile workers in Greenville, South Carolina. It was the IWW's first attempt to break into the textile industry in the South, and Matilda Rabinowitz recalled speaking to workers who had migrated from their tiny farms in the mountains to the mill towns. One of the women told her:

> They came and told us how easy we'd have it in the mill. The young 'uns sho' be given an ejication in them there schools and make good money. We didn't have to be po' white trash no mo'. And pap he was right smart and told them agents how he'd sho' like to see they boys get up in the world. And I, too, was a-thinkin' how nice mebbe the girls 'ud look in city clothes. Our'n was a big brood—eight of 'em—and the oldest oney ten or so. Well, we come 'long to the mill and pap and me and Tommy we was took right in. Po' Tommy, he aint never been able to get nuff schoolin' to read proper. Purty soon me and pap and four young 'uns was duffin' and spoolin' and spinnin'. But they aint yet git ejicated, nor has they the fine clothes 'n all them things the agents were a-promisin'.

"What they got," Rabinowitz added, "was the enslavement of a quarter of a million of them in 800 southern textile mills, creating untold wealth for the privilege of living in company-owned houses, being compelled to buy in the company stores, the 'grab-all,' living and dying in starvation and being buried in the company cemetery."[49]

She found the workers in Greenville the most downtrodden, least-class-conscious workers she had ever met. Unable to obtain work in the mill as she had planned, she passed out leaflets and in this manner was able to meet the more advanced-thinking workers. She quickly discovered that they were ready to fight for a union, but she was amazed to learn that they knew nothing of the great struggles and gains of the textile and other workers in the North. They were astonished to hear from her that workers elsewhere dared to think of agitating for an eight-hour day and that there were places where child labor was prohibited. Rabinowitz began to hold small meetings, then larger ones. The workers began to find new pride, then hope. But it was still only the men who came.

> After supper, the man's tasks were over. But the women worked on. There were the dishes and clothes to be washed; there was mending and cleaning and a dozen other things to do—the interminable tasks of housekeeping unrelieved by any modern conveniences. No rest, no recreation, no social life did these women know. Mill slaves and the slaves of slave husbands, bringing into the world slave children.[50]

Finally, two women agreed to come.

> The first time that two women ventured to attend one of these meetings was something of a sensation. It took quite a bit of encouragement to bring these two into the union hall. But after them came others, until one day, when we held a meeting for women only, over fifty came to hear a discussion of questions of particular interest to them. At first they were rather embarrassed by the newness of their venture. But gradually their confidence grew and their constraint lessened as we talked over the familiar problems of job, home and children. . . . How hard it was to be wage-earner and mother. How difficult work was during pregnancy. How neglected the babies were when the mothers were forced to return to the mills too soon after childbirth. These women would have welcomed birth control.[51]

After six weeks in Greenville, Rabinowitz went back North, asking for help for the IWW local of one hundred members she had established—the first IWW local of textile workers in the South. But it seemed that no one from the IWW was able to join her in the South, and so she returned. This time, she found an antiunion campaign in full swing: "The newspaper took up the cry of 'invaders from the North' come to disturb the tranquility of the South. . . . Revival meetings in tents near the mills were calling on the mill workers to stay away from the union hall and come to Jesus. But the workers came to the nightly meetings. . . . The union was something real. They liked the Wobbly song of 'Pie in the Sky.'"[52]

The local grew stronger and the members began to make demands for wage increases and a shorter workweek. A strike was called in Greenville to win these demands, but it was lost. It was a terrible blow to Rabinowitz. She was convinced that "organizing textile workers was a long project and would mean often and again and again unremitting labor"[53]—and that the IWW did not have the capacity to do the job. The main problem, as she saw it, was too much emphasis on agitation rather than organization:

> Our perseverance is not commensurate with the magnitude of our task. The quick results obtained during strikes have made us impatient of subsequent uneventful union affairs. . . . The story is largely the same as told by members of different locals. Everyone remembers the eloquent speeches; the exciting demonstrations; the cheers and hurrahs; the enthusiasm and songs; but no knowledge, or very little of it, is found of carrying the message into the shop. There is almost no connection between the platform and the job; there is no affinity between revolutionary speeches and revolutionary action. The IWW, in most places, is viewed as a retreat from the harsh conditions of the shop, rather than as a means of changing these conditions. . . . We must learn how to organize. We must begin to build the new society, upon which our vision is riveted, around the job and the daily life of the workers.[54]

Rabinowitz's criticism was by no means the only one of its kind during this period.* For even where the Wobblies had been victorious, their influence disappeared when their leaders, instead of spending the necessary time, money, and energy consolidating the gains, went off proselytizing elsewhere. The result was that IWW locals fell into disarray. Lawrence is an outstanding example, although by no means the only one. Workers continued to join Local No. 20 (reorganized into fourteen different language branches) until September, 1912, when the IWW claimed sixteen thousand members, ten thousand in good standing. Following this peak, the union gradually lost strength until, by the summer of 1913, it was left with only seven hundred members.[55]

Since many of the original members right after the Lawrence strike were women, it was argued that the Lawrence local's record proved again that women made good strikers but poor union members. But women could hardly be expected to continue their commitment to the union when the national IWW leadership was interested only in waging strikes and not in building a strong, permanent union, and therefore left the workers without any leadership. Melvyn Dubofsky believes this explanation to be superficial and places the blame solely on the employers, arguing that they infiltrated the union with spies, carried on a strong antiunion campaign in the press, and forced militant workers to desert the organization,[56] but this contention does not explain the fact that the same disastrous decline that occurred in Lawrence after the spectacular IWW victory also took place in Little Falls. Moreover, as the IWW locals fell into disarray, conservative AFL union representation for the skilled workers replaced the once all-inclusive industrial unions of the IWW. Embittered by the disillusioning experience with IWW tactics and strategy, the textile workers never again rallied to its banner; never again were the Wobblies able to organize a major strike in a textile center. Their locals melted away, leaving the scattered remnants of the AFL United Textile Workers in sole possession of the field.[57]

Although the IWW had achieved spectacular successes in the textile industry, especially at Lawrence and Little Falls, where half the work force were women, few women organizers emerged from this drive, or from the work of the IWW in building a militant women's auxiliary in the mines and other male-dominated industries. The lack of women organizers limited the effectiveness of the IWW in conducting lasting organizing work among women. It is true that it was much more difficult

*Although she ceased to be an IWW organizer, Rabinowitz continued to write for the IWW and later was active in the Socialist Party in California. Over the years, she contributed poems and articles to the *Industrial Worker* and wrote a regular column, "From My Notebook." See chap. 20, "What's Wrong with the IWW?" in Philip S. Foner, *History of the Labor Movement in the United States, 4, The Industrial Workers of the World* (New York, 1965), pp. 467–72 for other criticisms of the IWW.

to be a national organizer for the IWW than, for example, for the Women's Trade Union League and AFL unions. IWW organizers had to travel constantly, making family life almost an impossibility; they faced the ever-present likelihood of arrest and imprisonment and the possibility of murder by vigilantes or armed thugs. They operated in more isolated communities, cut off from masses of women in a way that the WTUL and AFL women were not. More important, they were not able to overcome male chauvinism in the Wobbly ranks. For however sympathetic to the struggle of women IWW men claimed to be, they still tended to confine their acceptance of women as equals to periods of strikes. When the strike was over, there was no sustained struggle against male chauvinism or effort to tackle the special problems facing women workers. Suggestions from women strikers were treated with respect, but the same respect was not shown in the regular day-to-day work of the organization.

The IWW, however, proved more effectively than any other contemporary labor organization that the mass-production industries, in which many of the workers were both women and immigrants, could be organized, and that the method by which this could be achieved was industrial unionism. Together with the Jewish and Italian women in the great uprisings in the garment trades, the "rebel girls" of the IWW changed the entire history of women in the American labor movement. They fully merited the tribute paid to them by Joe Hill in his famous song dedicated to Elizabeth Gurley Flynn:

THE REBEL GIRL

There are women of many descriptions
    In this queer world, as everyone knows.
Some are living in beautiful mansions,
    And are wearing the finest of clothes.
There are blue blooded queens and princesses,
    Who have charms made of diamonds and pearl;
But the only and thoroughbred lady
    Is the Rebel Girl.

Chorus:
    That's the Rebel Girl, that's the Rebel Girl!
    To the working class she's a precious pearl.
    She brings courage, pride and joy
    To the fighting Rebel Boy.
    We've had girls before, but we need some more
    In the Industrial Workers of the World.
    For it's great to fight for freedom
    With a Rebel Girl.

Yes, her hands may be hardened from labor,
    And her dress may not be very fine;
But a heart in her bosom is beating
    That is true to her class and her kind.
And the grafters in terror are trembling
    When her spite and defiance she'll hurl;
For the only and thoroughbred lady
    Is the Rebel Girl.

Repeat Chorus:

25

Wages and Working Conditions

FROM 1911 TO 1915 the New York Factory Investigating Commission, created by the state legislature following the Triangle Shirtwaist Company fire, carried out the most extensive investigation of female employment in any state up to that time. The Commission's inquiries produced over fifteen thousand pages of data in thirteen volumes, covering nearly every trade in which women worked—from flower making to foundries, from boxmaking to baby clothes, and from pea packing to wig preparations. These studies revealed to the public the exploitation of women workers: their long hours, low pay, and arbitrary treatment and the unhealthful and unsanitary conditions under which they worked.

In a special report prepared for the legislature, Violet Pike, an FIC investigator, set forth the adverse physical and mental effects on women of long hours, continuous standing, and overcrowded conditions, among other situations injurious to their health. The Pike report announced forcefully:

> Modern industry has been developed chiefly by men for men. . . . Unlimited speed and unlimited production is the manufacturer's dream, but modern machine production is taking no account of the strain upon women workers of long hours of monotonous and nerve-racking tasks in destroying their health, and thus lowering the efficiency of future generations.[1]

The attention paid by the commission to women's wages stemmed in no small measure from the fear that underpaid women drifted readily into prostitution. In a letter to the *New York Times* Chairman Robert Wagner argued: "We realize that, as a result of not having a living wage, the girls are coming into prostitution, to the streets, to the courts, to the prisons of our city and of the state. How the vice problem is affected by the low wage is a matter that merits the most careful study."*[2] With funds appropriated by the legislature, the commission launched a comprehensive and extended study under the direction of Howard Woolstein, a noted economist and statistician. For a year and a half the commission's staff gathered and studied 100,000 wage schedules from companies throughout the state and interviewed two thousand typical workers about their wages and financial resources.† At the same time Dr. Frank H. Streightoff, an economist at DePauw University, conducted a cost-of-living study for the commission. On the basis of questionnaire responses from several thousand workers, labor leaders, employers, and social workers, Dr. Streightoff prepared typical budgets that included food, clothing, shelter, and "intellectual recreation and progress." He found that an *absolute minimum* would require a $9 weekly wage in New York City and $8.10 upstate. Women workers would require annual wages of $468 in New York City and $400 upstate, and such minimums included no provisions for savings or vacations.[3]

The figures tabulated by the commission presented a grim picture. Three-fourths of the women earned less than $9 per week, and twenty thousand of them less than $7.50. In sales work, the highest-paid of the trades, female help rarely got more than $8. In shirtmaking, the least remunerative occupation, more than half received less than $5.[4] In the paper box industry, weekly wages of $5 or less were common. More than half the female confectionery workers earned less than $6 weekly, and almost one-quarter showed actual earnings under $5. In order to earn 15 cents, a hand dipper of candies had to coat over seven hundred pieces

---

*The charge that low wages forced women into prostitution triggered other state investigations of women's wages and conditions. In the state of Washington, for example, the legislature appointed an Industrial Welfare Commission to conduct such an investigation shortly after a Seattle paper accused the city's mayor of paying some workers such low wages that they became prostitutes, and it declared firmly that poverty was "the parentage of prostitutes" (Joseph F. Tripp, "Toward an Efficient and Moral Society, Washington State's Minimum-Wage Law, 1913–1925," *Pacific Northwest Quarterly* 67 [July 1976], p. 98).

†Most women cooperated eagerly with the Factory Investigating Commission and had no hesitation about exposing conditions in the trade where they worked. An exception, however, was the case of the commission's investigation of women's employment in iron foundries, where the women balked. The study was undertaken at the behest of male labor unions that demanded the exclusion of women from the trade as a cheap labor competition, and even argued that "ladies" should not work with such people as themselves. But women foundry workers denied any ill effects of foundry work and bluntly told the commission that the male unionists were simply trying to take away their jobs and that the commission was conspiring to assist them in this endeavor. The commission recommended that the State Industrial Board require that foundry owners supply special rooms for women coremakers and prohibit women from making cores above a certain size and weight. It acknowledged that such restrictions would make it uneconomical for owners to employ women and would thus meet the demands of the male unionists, while seemingly providing for the welfare of the women coremakers (New York, Factory Investigating Commission, *Second Report*, 1913, vol. 3, pp. 143–45; vol. 1. pp. 261–63).

of candy with chocolate per hour. Nearly eight thousand of these workers received less than $6.50 during a busy week in the winter of 1914, and over four thousand got less than $5. And in button manufacturing, the actual weekly wages for more than half the women employees averaged less than $7. Both time workers and pieceworkers lost additional income when businesses shut down, dismissed their help, or cut wages because of business fluctuations. In the millinery trades, for example, half of the women workers received annual earnings of between $75 and $100, forcing them to hold more than one job.[5] "It is obvious," commission researchers concluded, "that a very large proportion of the workers. . . . receive less than is . . . considered sufficient to maintain persons independently. No woman can live properly on $5 or $6 or even $7 a week." Yet nearly half of those contacted received wages below $7!

The public learned what it meant for a woman to subsist on $6 a week. Young women complained that their meager wages permitted them to live only in "dingy, dirty and broken-down" quarters. One candymaker slept in the same bed with her landlady's children and helped with the housework (before and after a full day's factory labor) in order to reduce her rent. Many spoke of "just existing" and, when they bought a suit or a pair of shoes, of living on one meal a day and "sacrificing all recreation." On girl questioned "whether there is any difference selling yourself for $6 a week or $5 a night."

The Women's Trade Union League explained what this wage meant in specific terms:

What a $6.00 a Week Wage Means

The utter impossibility of living on a $6.00 a week wage is illustrated by the following schedule of expenditures:

WEEKLY EXPENDITURES

One half of a furnished room	$1.50
7 breakfasts, rolls and coffee, at 10 cents	.70
7 dinners at 20 cents	1.40
7 luncheons, coffee and sandwich, at 10 cents	.70
Carfare	.60
Clothes at $52 a year—weekly	1.00
TOTAL	$5.90

The remaining 10 cents to cover laundry, dentist, doctor, newspapers, church and recreation.

10 cents a week for 52 weeks makes $5.20.

But the girl works only 40 weeks.

She must live 52 weeks. How?[6]

Low wages constituted only part of the shocking disclosures. Leonora O'Reilly reported that the owners of hair-weaving shops left their workplaces in a deplorably filthy condition and allowed loose disinfectant powder, hair, and dirt to pile up on the floor for days before collecting it. Moreover, since there was no system of ventilation, the girls breathed foul air, often impregnated with poisonous chemical fumes. And the bosses did not supply washrooms or lunchrooms, so that employees could not clean themselves and had to eat their noon meal amid the toxic work materials.[7]

Pauline Goldmark, legislative secretary of the Consumers' League, revealed the outcome of a two-month probe of the sanitary facilities in three hundred business establishments on Manhattan's West Side, employing over two thousand women. At least two-thirds of the factories were in lamentably poor sanitary condition, one-third lacking adequate toilets and two-thirds lacking sufficient washing facilities. Where the employers provided dressing rooms, in many cases they allowed only the "white help," and of these, often only those who were not foreign-born, to use them.[8]

The commission's disclosure of the conditions under which women and children worked in the state cannery establishments rivaled the worst horror stories. In this unregulated industry, many cases were discovered in which women had contracted rheumatism from standing on wet floors, lost fingers to corn cutters, suffered heat prostration, or developed partial blindness after concentrated work inspecting or sorting peas and beans. Women in the canneries frequently worked as many as seventeen hours a day during the rush season, for as little as 10 cents an hour. It was common for women to work seventy hours a week continuously for many weeks. Before and after their grueling work in the cannery, most of these women had to do their own housekeeping— they cooked, made beds, washed, and took care of the children. One investigator testified that the noise of the machinery "was deafening" and that many of the women packers had permanently lost their hearing.[9] Another investigator, one of several women who took jobs in the packing sheds to obtain "inside" information on the labor situation, reported to the commission that she had received several immoral propositions. One of the foremen had told her: "You can't make enough money up here to pay your board, but I will give you a chance to make two or three dollars on the side any time."[10]

An investigation of women who worked at night in factories and took care of household duties during the day revealed that most of them chose night work because of the higher wages offered, although even with the higher night salary, the women received less than men day operatives with comparable skills. Few of the women who worked at night could maintain their health. Women night workers were also more prone to accidents than day shift operatives. In the case of one widow who worked at night to support herself and a large family: "When she

cut part of her finger off, she went to the office after the wound was
healed and asked them to pay for the loss. 'We only pay for the whole of
a finger being cut off,' they told her. The finger is always sore and hurts
her whenever the wounded end touches anything."[11]

The New York Factory Investigating Commission paid little attention to black women, reflecting the fact that black women were still
concentrated in agriculture and domestic service. The United States
Census of 1910 revealed that more than half of the almost 10 million
black people in the United States were women, and that just over 2
million of these 5 million were wage earners, grouped as follows:

```
Farm laborers ............................................967,837
Laundresses..............................................361,551
Cooks ...................................................205,929
Farmers ................................................. 79,309
Dressmakers ............................................. 38,148
School teachers.......................................... 22,441
Nurses .................................................. 17,874
Chambermaids ........................................... 14,071
Laundry operatives ...................................... 12,196
Housekeepers ........................................... 10,021
All other occupations ...................................284,594[12]
```

Since more than 70 percent of the black population in the United
States before World War I was rural, it is not surprising that the great
mass of black women should be found on the farm. (Actually, many of
the farms owned by black men were managed entirely by the women of
the family while the men worked in other occupations.) How much black
women detested domestic service is revealed in the following account by
an unnamed black woman living in Georgia, published in the *Independent,* a New York weekly, early in 1912 under the title "More Slavery at
the South":

> I frequently work from fourteen to sixteen hours a day. I am compelled
> by my contract, which is oral only, to sleep in the house. I am allowed to go
> home to my own children . . . only once in two weeks, every other Sunday
> afternoon—even then I'm not permitted to stay all night. I not only have to
> nurse a little white child, now eleven months old, but I have to act as play-
> mate or "handy-andy," not to say governess, to three other children in the
> home, the oldest of whom is only nine years of age. I wash and dress the baby
> two or three times each day; I give it its meals, mainly from a bottle; I have to
> put it to bed each night; and, in addition, I have to get up and attend to its
> every call between midnight and morning. . . . I am the slave, body and soul
> of this family. And what do I get for this work—this lifetime bondage? The
> pitiful sum of ten dollars a month! . . .
>   Of course, nothing is being done to increase our wages, and the way
> things are going at present, it would seem that nothing could be done to

cause an increase of wages. We have no labor unions or organizations of any kind that could demand for us a uniform scale of wages for cooks, washer-women, nurses, and the like. . . . So that, the truth is, we have to work for little or nothing or become vagrants! And that, of course, in this state would mean that we would be arrested, tried, and dispatched to the "State Farm," where we would surely have to work for nothing or be beaten with many stripes.[13]

Much as they disliked domestic service, the absence of other oppor-tunities forced black women into this work. In the major Northern cities, a network of employment agencies specialized in placing black women as domestics. These agencies recruited women in the South and paid their boat fare from Southern ports in return for their first month's wages in employment.[14]

"Generally, where anything worthwhile has been achieved, there is attached a story of bitter struggle against prejudice and its traditions," wrote Addie W. Hunter, organizer for the National Association of Colored Women, as she described the strong opposition to the entrance of black women into the skilled trades and professions.[15] A young black workingwoman spelled out what this meant:

I am a graduate of the Cambridge Latin and High School. I studied book-keeping and stenography at evening school after I had graduated. In 1912 I passed the Civil Service examination for the first time, and later tried for a position. I have been certified for almost every position in the clerical de-partments of Boston. From 1912 until 1915, I tried for positions, tried des-perately hard, and always I was refused. For three years I was forced to work in a factory for half the money I could get at the work for which I had been trained. And then, during all these years, I was forever chasing the will-o-the-wisp of the possible job. Again and again I would be certified. Again and again, as soon as I had a personal interview, I would be refused.

"Will you tell me the reason?" I would ask. The employer would shake his head. "The Civil Service law does not require us to tell," he would answer, in almost every case. But once in a while an exceptionally honest man would state his reason. It would always be because of my race; in every other particular I would have passed the requirement.

By complaining to the governor of Massachusetts she did finally obtain a position in a hospital under Civil Service. But then she discov-ered that she would be required to take all her meals in her office, since it was against the institution's policy for blacks and whites to eat together. When she insisted on taking her meals in the regular dining room, she was dismissed. Since, under the rules, no reason had to be given for dismissal of an employee during the six-month probationary period, she could not even get a statement as to the reason for her discharge. When she took her case to court, she lost. "This leaves me where I began," she wrote bitterly, "out of pocket, out of courage, without, at present, any defense in the law." All this turmoil had done her no good, but she did hope "it will make the way easier for other girls of my race." But she was not optimistic:

> For the way things stand at present, it is useless to have the requirements. Color—the reason nobody will give, the reason nobody is required to give, will always be in the way. Which, in other words, is the State standing back of a class of its children and saying: "No, you cannot enter here. You may study; you may pass the requirements, but that is as far as you may go."[16]

Acknowledging that department store saleswomen were underpaid, a Philadelphia study of 1913 noted, "The few colored women who find employment in them receive less than salespeople. The colored waitress receives a child's pay." Like black men, black women in Philadelphia were "denied the opportunity to earn an honest living in most of the big industries and commercial enterprises of the city." Indeed, the only such "enterprises" in which investigators found black women employed paid such low wages and were in such filthy surroundings that poor white women, who could find work elsewhere, refused to work there.[17]

Black waitresses in Philadelphia not only received "child's pay" but found themselves barred from jobs they had traditionally held. Abbott's Dairy Restaurant, in Philadelphia, had employed black waitresses exclusively until 1910. When customers began to object, the black women were relegated to counter work, where the pay and tips were lower and the work harder. When the black women walked out in protest, they were eased out of the restaurant entirely.[18]

At about the same time that the New York Factory Investigating Commission was conducting its investigation, an inquiry into working-women's conditions was being carried on in the state of Washington by the Industrial Welfare Commission, established by the state legislature. After speaking with several hundred employers and with more than two thousand workers, the commission concluded that workingwomen in Washington needed $10 a week to maintain a decent standard of living. Fewer than half of the women working in retail stores, telephone offices, and factories earned as much as this.[19]

"Tuberculosis," wrote Alice Hamilton, "is a disease of the working classes."[20] A Massachusetts investigation proved that in every age group, the mortality from tuberculosis was significantly higher among cotton mill operatives than among the remainder of the population. A study in Fall River, Massachusetts, covering the years from 1908 to 1912, disclosed that 70 percent of the deaths from tuberculosis were of operatives. In the hot, humid, and poorly ventilated mill rooms, in air loaded with cotton dust, the tubercle bacillus emitted by coughing and spitting found a hospitable environment and numerous new victims to infect. Unsanitary working conditions were compounded by fatigue, excessive exertion, insufficient rest as a result of long work shifts, poor nutrition, inadequate housing, and pressure on the family to send children into the mill to augment the family income. Married women. in particular, were affected, for their potential rest time was diminished by an average of 2.8 hours a day of housework upon completion of their shift in the mill. The tuberculosis death rate was 5.56 per thousand among the married women mill workers compared with 2.09 per thousand among the unmarried; among those not employed in the mills, the rate was 1.42 per thousand among the married women and 1.36 among the unmarried.[21]

Most of the findings of state investigations were confirmed by the United States Commission on Industrial Relations, which began in December, 1913, "to inquire into into the general conditions of labor in the principal industries of the United States . . . to discover the underlying causes of dissatisfaction in the industrial setting and report its conclusions thereon."[22] In its monumental study, the commission investigated the problems of workingwomen and devoted a number of public hearings to the issue. It also heard testimony from the wives of workingmen. One of its highlights was the May, 1914, hearings at which testimony was taken from the widows of two miners who had been killed by militiamen in the Colorado strike. Others testified that women frequently suffered insults and abuse from the militiamen and that restaurant waitresses were "so insulted by militiamen" that they refused to wait on them. The climax of the militia terror came at "Bloody Ludlow" on April 20, 1914, when the tent colonies, housing between nine hundred and twelve hundred men, women, and children who had been evicted from the company dwellings, were fired upon by rifles and machine guns. Hundreds of women and children ran from the tents to seek shelter in the hills and at ranch houses. However, scores of those who failed to escape hid in pits and cellars underneath the tents to protect themselves from the bullets. "During the firing of the tents," the commission reported, "the militiamen became an uncontrolled mob and looted the tents of everything that appealed to their fancy and cupidity." In one pit, eleven children and two women of the Ludlow strikers' colony were discovered suffocated or burned to death after the tents had been set on fire.[23]

The Commission on Industrial Relations even paid some attention to "a neglected factor of Industrial relations—the unpaid labor of wives." Mrs. Flora McDonald Thompson of Washington, D.C., was a leading champion of wages for wives. "It is a loss to the wealth of the nation," she argued before the commission, "to permit the sweating of wives in the home. . . . A living wage must be understood to mean a living wage for the man and his wife; it must provide not alone money enough to permit the man to do his best work, but also money enough to permit the wife to do her best work; the cause of labor demands wages sufficient to permit wives working in the home to have a fair shop." Thompson assailed the "absurdity" of fixing a minimum wage for women without taking into consideration the value of the domestic service they perform outside of their regular working hours.[24]

The commission reported that women were "exploited in industry, trade, domestic service, and agriculture, to an extent which threatens their health and welfare" and "menaces the wage and salary standards of men." They were also "subject to overwork, unreasonable hours, and personal abuse of various kinds."[25] For example, the commission presented a detailed picture of the wage rates and working conditions of telephone operators in seven "typical" cities, based on the findings of Nelle B. Curry, a field investigator. Madison, Wisconsin, started switchboard operators at 50 cents for a nine-hour day, with an hour off for lunch for beginners ($13 a month), which went up to $1.20 a day ($31.20 a month) for experienced workers. In Nashville, beginners worked for two weeks *without* pay, after which they earned $22.50 a month for a year and a half before being raised to $35 a month. Switchboard operators in other cities were paid slightly better—$20 to $40 a month in Kansas city, $7 to $10.50 a week in Salt Lake City, and $1.10 a day ($26.80 a month) to $1.80 a day ($46.80 a month) in Los Angeles. Chicago's scale started at 12 cents an hour ($26 a month), and rose to 20 cents an hour ($43.50 a month) after seven years of service. Since the average length of service in Chicago was two and a half years, most of the operators earned 16 cents an hour.

Curry prepared a minimum monthly budget for a telephone operator in 1915, which added up to $55. It broke down as follows:

Rent $12.00
Food (50¢ per day) $15.00
Carfare (10¢ per day) $2.50
Laundry (where she does part of it herself) $2.50
Clothes $13.00
Amusements and recreation $2.50
Incidentals (toilet articles, church gifts, etc.) 50
Newspapers and magazines $2.00
Emergency fund (insurance, sickness, medical attention, dentistry,
    unemployment) $5.00
                                                              $55.00

"It is doubtful," Curry observed, "if the amount in the foregoing suggested budget for room and board would allow the girl a room to herself in sanitary surroundings, with the proper bathing facilities, in such a place as would guarantee at least the most ordinary facilities for social intercourse such as receiving visitors, all of which I deem highly important in the enjoyment of a normal existence."

Supervisors, Curry reported, were constantly staked behind the operators to see to it that no one lagged: "It is a mistaken idea to suppose that, in the daily work of the operator, there are periods of relaxation which compensate for the high pressure hours." Relief periods were rigidly confined to, at best, fifteen minutes for each shift and were granted by the supervisors "not as a matter of right, but as a privilege." "The management expects you to be just a machine," a Los Angeles operator told Curry. Another said that being "poked in the back and told to hurry when you are working as fast as you can is not soothing to the nerves." Operators, still another explained, "are not allowed to speak one word to each other—not allowed to turn their heads—not even allowed to smile, nor to fold hands, nor cross feet, nor even to lean back in their chairs." Operators were literally pinioned for hours, "facing flickering lights, compelled to listen in meekness and humility to insults and complaints from irascible subscribers, plugging in and plugging out hundreds of calls with a thousand nervous muscular motions of the body, while a supervisor walked back and forth, urging alertness at the least sign of laxity or impatience. Secret monitors listened, recording all errors and deviations from the rules." Slow answers, "slow disconnects" (over ten seconds), or an "unanswered flash" were punished by requiring the offender to work certain undesirable hours for a given period. A Los Angeles operator, for example, was assigned a week's night work at the regular day rate of pay for a single "unanswered flash"! No wonder, then, that Curry reported: "There is possibly no woman in any industry whose remissness is more instantly checked by the incisive action of an overseer than the telephone operator. . . . :Hysterical attacks, where the operator, after reaching the limit of nervous endurance, throws up her hands, screams and faints at her work, are said to occur quite frequently during the busiest periods and most frequently during the summer days."

As a result, few women remained on the job for long. Curry reported that "a vast majority of the girls leave the service after about two years." This worked out very well for the telephone company, for few operators were able to reach the higher wage level paid for length of service. Since an operator could generally reach maximum efficiency in six months to a year, the company generally obtained maximum efficiency without having to pay maximum wages. "The company profits enormously by withholding the difference between the wages paid the girls and the amount which they actually earn on the basis of efficiency," Curry concluded.

The constant turnover made unionizing very difficult. A 1908 investigation into the telephone industry by the Department of Commerce and Labor found "practically no organization among telephone operators. . . . In the larger cities the attitude of the local managers is severely antagonistic to local organization among operators." Curry reported to the Industrial Commission that the 1908 finding had been "amply substantiated in my field investigations." She added:

> The officials of the telephone companies give many reasons why they think it is undesirable for their employees to organize, the principal one being that the telephone is a necessary public utility; that any interference with its functions would work great hardship upon the subscribing public; that the first duty of such a company is to the public; that strikes and other obstructive measures, which might follow the organization, could not be tolerated in such an industry, and finally, that clearly a labor organization composed of telephone girls would be an irresponsible body.[26]

The commission noted, however, that little had been done to organize the telephone operators because the International Brotherhood of Electrical Workers, which had jurisdiction over the industry, was primarily a union of linemen and cable splicers and considered the telephone "girls" flighty and likely dropouts from the union.[27]

The Commission on Industrial Relations insisted that the picture it had presented of telephone operators summed up fairly well the status of most workingwomen in American industrial life. What made the picture particularly grim was the fact that while not all corporations employing large numbers of women workers were as profitable as American Telephone and Telegraph, all of them gained enormous profits from the exploitation of these workers and, like AT&T, were well able "to afford the necessary improvements in working conditions."*[28]

---

*In its final report, the Industrial Commission identified the causes of industrial unrest as follows: workers did not receive a fair share of wealth; workers suffered too often from unemployment; most workers were convinced that they were denied justice; and, finally, workers resented the denial of their right to organize into unions (see Graham Adams, *Age of Industrial Violence, 1910–1915* [New York, 1966], pp. 216–17).

26

The League, the IWW, and the AFL

Long have we lived apart,
  Women alone;
Each with an empty heart,
  Women alone;
Now we begin to see
How to live safe and free,
No more on earth shall be
  Women alone.

Now we have learned the truth,
  Union is power;
Weak and strong, age and youth,
  Union is power;
On to the end we go,
Stronger our League must grow,
We can win justice so,
  Union is power.

For the right pay for us,
  We stand as one;
For the short day for us,
  We stand as one;
Loyal and brave and strong,
Helping the world along,
For end to every wrong,
  We stand as one!

YEAR AFTER YEAR, members of the Women's Trade Union League enthusiastically sang this song, written by Charlotte Perkins Gilman: but from the evidence disclosed by nationwide investigations, it was clear that despite over a decade of league activity, the gains of women workers were limited to those in the clothing industry, and even there, thousands of women still toiled at substandard wages under deplorable conditions. The conditions of women in most other industries remained much as they had been in 1903, when the league was founded. The same was largely true of union membership among women workers. The dramatic victories in the garment industry had obscured the fact that women's strikes in a number of trades between 1910 and 1913 had failed, and that in most industries union membership for women remained largely the same as it had been ten years earlier. In September, 1913, about 72,000 women belonged to New York City labor unions, over 63,000 of them in the garment and textile trades. Of the approximately 9,000 others, about 4,000 belonged to unions in the tobacco, printing, and bookbinding industries (a figure that had remained fairly stable since the start of the twentieth century); 3,000 women belonged to the musician's and theatrical unions; while the remaining women unionists were scattered in small, isolated organizations in the service occupations and marginal industries.

The national figures confirmed this gloomy picture. Among the slightly more than 8 million women gainfully employed in 1910, the facts about trade union membership were as follows: (1) of the 2,407 women employed in the liquor and beverage industries, from 20 to 30 percent were organized; (2) of the 333,000 employed in the clothing, printing, and bookbinding industries, from 10 to 15 percent were organized; (3) of the 145,870 employed in leather and in cigar and tobacco factories, from 5 to 10 percent were organized; (4) of the 415,000 employed in the lumber, furniture, and textile industries, from 1 to 5 percent were organized; and (5) of the remaining 7,180,000, less than 1 percent were organized. Apart from the increase in the percentage organized in the garment trades, the figures were much the same five years later, in 1915.[1]

Samuel Gompers attributed the small percentage of women unionists to the refusal of women workers to join men in a concerted drive to improve standards in the industries in which they were employed. "False standards, false pride, [and] misunderstandings," he declared, "have held many back from facing real conditions and facts and employing remedies" to improve their working conditions. Because women first began working for wages outside the home on a makeshift, temporary basis, Gompers continued, they never regarded their employment as a vital or permanent part of their lives and showed no interest in joining unions to improve their working conditions. They tolerated wretchedly unsanitary surroundings and endless hours of work in order to "help out" on a short-term basis. When employers discovered that women would work for lower wages, they eagerly hired them. For all the efforts of the trade unions to defeat these employers' programs, they had come up against a tradition of outright opposition or indifference to unionism on the part of women workers. Conditions such as those disclosed by the New York Factory Investigating Commission would continue as long as women workers continued to reject the remedies men had devised for their self-help. Rich women who offered their time and money to help workingwomen, he went on, could produce worthwhile results, but "permanent true betterment of the lives of the working women can be secured when these women achieve it by their own efforts."[2]

Women Trade Union League members must have bristled at Gompers' patronizing comment that rich women could help, particularly after their achievements during the great uprisings in the garment trade between 1909 and 1913. They were also shocked by the fact that even after the uprising of the militant garment women, Gompers still mouthed the time-worn stereotypes about workingwomen. The Factory Investigating Commission's own activities had exploded several of the myths to which Gompers still clung. Most women were not working for "pin money"; they depended on their wages to sustain their households. While it was true that for many young women matrimony presented the only escape from "ruthless" exploitation, a large number were forced to return to the labor market even after marriage merely to maintain a subsistence living.[3]

Not a few league members, in fact, were rapidly becoming infuriated by the AFL national leaders' attitude toward women and more and more convinced that the league's ability to meet the needs of workingwomen was being hampered by its ties with the federation. The Lawrence textile strike of 1912 played a particularly significant role in opening league members' eyes to the limitations of the AFL. It will be recalled that the IWW had taken over the leadership early in the strike after the AFL's United Textile Workers, led by John Golden, had demonstrated its unwillingness to organize unskilled immigrants. In fact, when Golden came to Lawrence at the request of the city officials "to assist in quelling the strike," he counseled the Women's Trade Union League to stay out of Lawrence. Nevertheless, as Sue Ainsley Clark, president of the Boston League, later recalled, the strike was a "magnificent uprising of oppressed, unskilled foreign workers. Our strike committee had many members who did not endorse IWW principles but were enthusiastic [about the] strikers."[4] Finally, in response to the Boston league's petitions, Golden allowed the branch to open a relief center in Lawrence to collect funds and distribute food and clothing. Meanwhile, the UTW was working to split the skilled workers off from the unskilled. Once Golden had achieved a settlement that the small number of strikers who were newly organized into UTW craft unions voted to accept, he ordered the

league to restrict its relief only to those workers who pledged to go back
to work. When workers who insisted on continuing to strike went to the
Boston league's relief station for assistance, they were told that they
could not receive help unless they agreed to return to work. In other
words, league members found themselves involved in a strikebreaking
operation, and some of them were appalled. Still, unwilling to antagonize the UTW–AFL leadership, the league withdrew from Lawrence
except for Mary Kenney O'Sullivan, the first woman hired by the AFL
and one of the original founders of the WTUL, who continued to aid the
IWW strikers. Later, the angry O'Sullivan publicly castigated Golden
and the UTW and criticized the league for its subservience. She pointed
out correctly that at Lawrence, the American Federation of Labor came
to be looked upon by the strikers as "almost as dangerous to their success
as the forces of the employers themselves." She not only unequivocally
condemned the actions of the UTW, but fully supported the IWW strike
committee:

> The sub-committee of the Lawrence strikers which conducted the negotia-
> tions that ended in a victory for all the textile workers of New England, is the
> most unselfish strike committee I have known. With two exceptions, its
> members are skilled workers in the Lawrence mills. It was at the suggestion
> of these skilled workers that the lowest paid, unskilled workers received the
> largest advance in wages and the highest paid skilled workers received the
> smallest.[5]

The league's actions in Lawrence also disgusted Elizabeth Glendower
Evans, a rich woman who was the financial mainstay of the Boston
league. She went up to Lawrence to see the strike committee in action
and realized that the WTUL relief station was "a travesty and a fake. It
simply filled me with despair for our League as a live thing at all, that
our secretary and Mrs. Conboy, vice-president and organizer, had been
there continuously for weeks and had muddled along as remote from
the real conditions, so it seems to me, as if they had been in Alaska." Mrs.
Evans thereupon resigned from the Boston WTUL, expressing the opinion that its affiliation with the AFL had doomed it to inconsequence:

> The AFL in Massachusetts and perhaps pretty generally is narrow and selfish
> and is losing its hold. Its strict craft organization is not adapted to the assimi-
> lation of the unskilled foreign races. Perhaps it has got to be smashed, or
> purged, or reorganized. Just at present, I don't see where a person in my
> position can lend a hand. And I don't see how a League linked strictly to the
> disintegrating AFL can become real.[6]

Although it was clear that this was an exaggeration, and that the AFL
was not "disintegrating," and although the Lawrence strike was settled
favorably, the strikebreaking role of the UTW leadership and the Bos-

ton league's acquiescence to it created a major controversy within the WTUL. The seriousness of the split was disclosed in an analysis Sue Ainsley Clark made for Margaret Dreier Robins:

> Certain members of the Boston League believe that its course was the only one open to it since it was affiliated with the AFL and aimed to propagate the principles of craft unionism endorsed by that organization.* Certain others believe that we might have cooperated with the strike committee from the first, as individuals, though they realize the restraints imposed by the AFL affiliation. Still others think that our part has been a disgraceful one in this great struggle. Others regard the success of the Lawrence strike, through IWW methods, as an object lesson by which the League—and the AFL—must profit in order to play a vital part in the rapidly moving evolution of the labor movement today.

Clark herself believed that many in power in the AFL had revealed themselves as "selfish, reactionary and remote from the struggle for bread and liberty of the unskilled workers." The danger to the AFL was the one "immemorially confronted by organizations in church and government when creed and consideration of safety obscure the original spirit and aim." The league must not become rigid, she maintained; "we must be free to aid in the struggle of the workers wherever and however we find the 'fight on.'" The crucial question now confronting the league could be summed up easily: "Are we, the Women's Trade Union League, to ally ourselves with the 'stand-patters' of the Labor Movement or are we to hold ourselves ready to aid the insurgents—those who are freely fighting the fight of the exploited, the oppressed, and the weak among the workers?"[7]

Important league leaders and many rank-and-file members struggled to find an answer to this question. A visit to Lawrence during the strike had persuaded Helen Marot that the league must now concentrate its energies on finding new ways to reach unskilled workers. She was convinced that "we have reached a crisis when the organization of the unskilled worker has become an all-important question of the labor movement." But how to achieve the organization of the unorganized, unskilled workers without breaking away from the AFL? Marot recommended that the league petition the national craft unions for financial contributions to help support the league in its work of organizing unskilled women.[8]

In Chicago, Mary E. McDowell, a league leader, had reached a similar conclusion. Emphasizing that the AFL had much to learn from Lawrence if it seriously wished to unionize women workers, she conducted

---

*In one sense, Clark's statement is not accurate: the WTUL never formally affiliated with the AFL.

an intensive campaign, shortly after the strike ended, to convince AFL leaders all over the country to apply the lessons of the struggle. To Homer D. Call, secretary-treasurer of the Amalgamated Meat Cutters & Butcher Workmen, McDowell wrote:

> I was east and have talked with several thoughtful and observant men and women who have been in Lawrence and have investigated the conditions before and during and after the strike. I am greatly impressed with what they told me. These people said to me that Haywood had a *method* of organizing the foreigners in a great industry where there was little skill and much specialization that was most wise and successful, and would have to be applied to such industries as Packing and Steel. . . . We dare not ignore the one fact that they [the IWW] have a *method* that will have to be used by the AFL or harm will come to the unions.

McDowell urged Call to try to persuade Gompers and other AFL leaders to begin organizing the mass-production industries, using the IWW's "method" of industrial unionism, employing militant organizers who spoke the languages of the foreign-born workers: "Mr. Gompers must not be afraid of even *socialists* if they are intelligent trade unionists and see the danger of letting the IWW get ahead." To another AFL leader, McDowell wrote:

> It will be a great waste of time and energy if the AFL misses the point that has been so terribly emphasized in Lawrence, Mass. . . . In such industries as steel, meat, textile, and harvesters, etc., Industrial Unionism of a constructive type is surely the need of this moment. The AFL will lose out unless it wakes up and adds to the IWW's clever method, that of permanent and constructive organization.[9]

When the league's Executive Board met in April, 1912, the events and lessons of Lawrence were the main subjects of discussion. Several members defended the IWW, saying that organization had handled the strike in a "splendid way," and questioned the value of the WTUL's alliance with a reactionary AFL. Since the organization of the vast majority of women workers could not be achieved through craft unionism, they maintained, why cling to an organization that would never abandon this outmoded method of unionization? This view, however, was vigorously challenged by Margaret Dreier Robins.

A year earlier, Robins had written angrily to Leonora O'Reilly that the AFL leaders' "arrogance & contempt of the working women" made her boil. She admitted that male chauvinism, "stand-pat" craft unionism, an unwillingness to organize any but the skilled craftsmen, and the conviction that the task of organizing female and foreign-born workers was virtually impossible were too deeply ingrained in AFL thinking to be eradicated.[10] Still, at the 1912 Executive Board meeting, Robins argued that the league must retain its close relationship with the AFL and even expressed displeasure at the fact that the Boston league had gone into Lawrence without consulting the national board.[11]

Robins put down the brief rebellion, and, on the basis that there was no alternative, the Executive Board reaffirmed its ties with the federation as being in the interests of female workers. In return, Gompers promised the league $150 monthly toward the cost of its organizational work among women. The AFL Executive Council rewarded the league for its loyalty by authorizing payment of this sum, which was used to organize glove workers. Agnes Nestor, secretary of the Glove Workers' Union, assumed the duties of national organizer.[12]

The funds, however, were too limited to permit much organizing, and Robins wrote to Gompers the following spring, reaffirming the league's loyalty to the AFL and asking for a continuation of federation assistance, by which the good relations between the two organizations would continue, "helping to create a mutual understanding so necessary to concerted action."[13] Although Marot and McDowell had insisted on the need for industrial unionism in organizing women workers, they and other league leaders adopted a scrupulously careful posture, believing that any rupture with the AFL would destroy the league's very reason for being. In the end, after much soul-searching, league leaders came to the conclusion that the league should concentrate on the organization of skilled, American-born women along traditional craft union lines.[14]

Furthermore, aware that Gompers was ardently antisocialist, and convinced that radical political and ideological affiliations could have only adverse effects on their organization's position within the AFL, league leaders requested members not to combine league work with Socialist Party activities. When Rose Schneiderman continued to include socialist principles in her league-sponsored speeches, members of the Executive Board suggested that she resign.[15]

In January, 1914, the AFL Executive Council approved the league's request for the continuation of its appropriation but instructed Gompers to keep a tighter control over its spending. Gompers promptly requested a personal interview with Robins, accompanied by Agnes Nestor and Alice Henry, and informed them of the Executive Council's requirement that the league prepare periodic reports explaining how they utilized the federation's donation. The league women accepted the decision, but privately they expressed their anger over this attempt to monitor their activities.[16]

The league leaders also privately conceded that there was little they could do to alter the humiliating situation they were now being forced to accept. But though the league sorely needed the AFL's financial subsidy, new branches in Denver, Los Angeles, and Philadelphia were joining the older ones in New York, Boston, St. Louis, Baltimore, and Kansas City.

Moreover, the league's School for Active Workers in the Labor Movement, which opened in Chicago in January, 1914, with one student, had developed a unique course of training for leadership in women's trade union organization. Three categories of students were to be accepted into the school: those whom the league asked to leave their trades to train as organizers; those sent by their own unions or central labor bodies to improve their effectiveness in working for the organization; and those who came on their own initiative and responsibility. After four months of academic work, there were eight months of field work, which included the theory and practice of organizing, attendance at meetings of unions and the AFL, conferences with men and women leaders, analysis of trade agreements, and instruction in suffrage and civic duties.*[17]

When the WTUL was founded, there was no such thing as a career as a women labor organizer. Women who organized unions did so because they felt they had a mission to help their exploited sisters. When Mary Kenney O'Sullivan made the decision to stop being a bookbinder and become an organizer, it was because "someone must go from shop to shop and find out who the workers were that were willing to work for better conditions. I must be that someone." She worked as an organizer for many years while supporting herself in her trade; out of a long life as an organizer, she was paid to do organizing work for only five months. Leonora O'Reilly did organizing for the United Garment Workers in the late 1890s for no pay. In 1908 she was enabled to become a full-time organizer by the gift of an annuity from Margaret Dreier Robins, but this was a personal gift.

The next generation of workingwomen activists began to find it possible to become paid organizers. They included Louisa Mittelstadt and Myrtle Whitehead of the Brewery Workers; Rose Schneiderman, Pauline Newman, and Fannia Cohn of the ILGWU; Josephine Casey of the Elevated Railway Clerks; Agnes Nestor of the Glove Workers; Melinda Scott of the Hat Trimmers; Elizabeth Mahoney of the Hotel and Restaurant Employees; Nellie Quick of the Bindery Workers; Mary Anderson, Emma Steghagen, Mary McEnery, and Mary Haney of the Boot and Shoe Workers; Hilda Svenson of the Commercial Telegraphers; and Alice Bean and Mabel Gillespie of the Bookkeepers, Stenographers and Accountants. Most of them moved up to paid full-

---

*The academic work included courses in English, public speaking, the study and analysis of judicial decisions affecting labor injunctions, boycotts, etc., economic history, the history of organized labor, elementary economics, and modern radicalism. Some of the courses were taken at the Chicago School of Civics and Philanthropy and the University of Chicago. The field work was under the supervision of Agnes Nestor or Mary Anderson. Later, an extensive correspondence program was begun, and similar training was sponsored by leagues in Philadelphia and Boston.

time organizing positions from rank-and-file work. But more and more of them were becoming paid organizers as a result of having graduated from the WTUL school and the experience they got as organizers-in-training.

The local leagues also trained women to be organizers and developed educational programs to assist in unionizing workingwomen. The New York league used its English-language classes to teach the principles of trade unionism. It published a reading primer, *New World Lessons for Old World People,* by Violet Pike, which contained lessons like:

> I go to work at eight o'clock.
> I work until six o'clock.
> I have only one-half hour for lunch.
> I work overtime in the busy season.
> I do not get extra pay for overtime work.
> I earn eight dollars a week in the busy season.
> I earn three or four dollars a week in the slow season.
> I have no work at all for three months.
> I pay for my needles and thread.
> I pay for my electric power.
> My trade is a bad trade.

In the series' next lesson, entitled "A Trade with a Union," the conditions are entirely different:

> I met a friend yesterday.
> She works at a good trade.
> She goes home at five o'clock.
> She goes home at twelve o'clock on Saturday.
> She has one hour for lunch every day.
> She earns twelve dollars a week.
> Sometimes she works overtime in the busy season.
> She gets extra pay for overtime.
> She belongs to the Union in her trade.[18]

Despite its pledge following the shirtwaist strike, the WTUL made little effort to organize black women workers or to campaign to lower the barriers against them in both industry and the trade unions. The reason is not difficult to discover. The league's association with and dependence on the blatantly racist AFL made such efforts practically impossible.[19]

The league's dependence on the AFL was heightened by the fact that it lacked a steady source of income and was therefore forced to solicit gifts and contributions from rich friends, men's unions, and the AFL. To compound these difficulties, a number of rich allies, including Mrs. Walter Weyl, who annually donated $1,000 to the New York League, experienced financial losses that precluded continuing their bequests. Even Margaret Robins found it necessary to reduce her support for the league's monthly periodical, *Life and Labor,* which ran at an annual defi-cit. An ominous foreboding of impending bankruptcy darkened the national secretary's report after Robins, who had financed the national league almost singlehandedly, also announced a cutback of her contribu-tions.[20]

While yielding to the AFL's conservatism temporarily eased the league's financial problems, relations between the two organizations de-teriorated as a result of conflicts over a number of issues, some of a transitory nature, others more fundamental.[21] A deep conflict surfaced as it became clear that the AFL and the league held diametrically oppos-ing views on the desirability of social legislation for women workers. This had not been an issue in the early years of the league's history, because the organization concentrated on unionization and even insisted that legislation would prove of little value if the women workers had no unions to enforce it.

But beginning in 1909 the league made the eight-hour day and a minimum wage for women key demands, and increasingly after 1913 it concentrated its time and energy on securing such legislation. On the issue of an eight-hour day, the league did not come into conflict with the AFL, for the federation continued to support special hours legislation for women. But the AFL and many of its affiliated unions were un-equivocally opposed to legislation establishing a minimum wage.

The concept of the minimum wage had spread rapidly in the English-speaking world. New Zealand and Australia, during the 1890s, were the first to enact minimum-wage statutes. Then in 1910 England adopted the Australian model. Traveling in Europe two years earlier, Florence Kelley had learned of the minimum-wage idea from Beatrice Webb, and, on her return to the United States, she got the National Consumers' League, which she headed, to publicize the new reform. Meanwhile, Mary Dewson in Massachusetts was aiding the cause by in-vestigating wage standards in that state, and the Factory Investigating Commission in New York was advancing it further with its own investi-gations and disclosures.[22]

But both the National Association of Manufacturers and the Ameri-can Federation of Labor refused to join the campaign for minimum-wage laws for women workers. To the NAM it was simply "fantastic and grotesque legislation," which was nothing less than "pure socialism."[23] The AFL, on the other hand, argued that "government paternalism" might discourage union organizing among women; that once women were guaranteed a minimum wage, men would demand the same, and all labor would then come within the grip of the state; and that any minimum wage would soon become the maximum for many workers. Gompers, the leading AFL opponent of such legislation, stressed that "attempts of the government to establish wages at which workmen may work, according to the teachings of history, will result in a long era of industrial slavery." Such laws, he predicted, would paralyze American labor and constitute an "infringement of personal liberty." He reminded the WTUL that the problems of men and women workers were identical: "Women work in industry side by side with men. Their relations to industry and their relations to employers contain no elements different from those of men's relations." Gompers and other AFL spokesmen were quick to point out to the league that they favored statutory limitations on women's working hours, for women needed special protection because they were weaker and more vulnerable than men. But they did not need a minimum-wage law, for "once the state is allowed to fix a minimum rate, the state would also take the right to compel men or women to work at that rate."[24]

It therefore came as a shock, as well as a source of considerable anger, to Gompers and other AFL leaders when they learned that, despite opposition from the AFL and a number of state federations of labor and leading international unions affiliated with the federation,* the National Women's Trade Union League and the local leagues had endorsed minimum-wage legislation—although not without a good deal of internal conflict—and had joined the National Consumers' League and the American Association for Labor Legislation in agitating for minimum-wage laws. Workingwomen, the league argued, deserved a "living wage," an income that would "allow a young woman to rent a small heated room and pay for sufficient nourishing food, purchase decent clothes, and have a little left over, not much, for candy and other pleasures." Such legislation, it maintained, would generate better living conditions, greater efficiency, and "a more prosperous buying public." And, the league argued, the humanizing touch of the minimum wage might well "make outright socialism undesirable and unnecessary."[25]

Along with that of the other organizations in the field, the league's activity was effective. Between 1913 and 1923 fourteen state legislatures wrote a specific minimum wage into law.† The league felt its contribution had helped considerably to justify its existence. It was therefore

---

*Not all AFL unions, however, opposed minimum-wage legislation for women. In New York and California, organized labor disapproved of the minimum-wage statutes, echoing the AFL argument that it was an expression of unwarranted government paternalism, but trade unionists in the state of Washington "worked hard and closely with reformist women's clubs to obtain a wage statute." Moreover, labor advocates of minimum-wage laws eventuallly persuaded both the Brooklyn Central Labor Union and the New York State Federation of Labor to campaign for the legislation.

†However, not all the laws were effective. Some legislatures wrote a specific minimum wage into the statute, but they did not provide for any administrative agency to enforce it. Massachusetts enacted the weakest statute. It established a commission, which was instructed to arrive at a wage that would not "threaten to interfere either with the general financial prosperity of the trade or with the 'reasonable profits' of an individual employer." Furthermore, it could only recommend the wage to employers, and they could

inevitable that, as the league's emphasis shifted from unionization to protective legislation, the battle for woman suffrage began to assume greater and greater importance in the WTUL's program. To be sure, the early leaders and members of the league had come to it already committed to the principles of woman suffrage; the first national convention in 1907 included "full citizenship" as one plank of its six-point platform, and in 1908 a Suffrage Department had been established within the league. Nevertheless, before 1909 the struggle for the vote was a peripheral issue, and many league members at first did not even see any connection between the fight for the ballot and the realities confronting workingwomen. Simply having the right to vote would not, after all, shorten working hours, raise wages, or provide decent, safe working conditions. And workingmen had had the vote for decades, yet the industrial conditions of vast numbers of male workers had not basically improved. To the degree that men had better conditions, shorter hours, and higher wages, they had achieved these things not because they could vote but because they had organized into effective trade unions. Since women were oppressed by the same industrial conditions that oppressed men, they, too, could only solve their problems the way men had. As one champion of placing priority on unionization put it to Leonora O'Reilly: "Woman suffrage is beginning at the other end. What the women need is *economic* emancipation, and, Sister, dear, how they need it! And they can't get it without organization."[26]

The antisuffrage forces in the WTUL were reinforced by the class bias of the early twentieth-century movement. While Susan B. Anthony continued to emphasize the need for establishing close links with the labor movement and workingmen, the rich matrons who now dominated the suffrage organizations made few attempts to appeal to women workers, and suffragist propaganda frequently included arguments that were bound to alienate many workingmen and -women. The suffragists had actually abandoned the traditional demand for suffrage as a universal democratic right and had begun to seek allies among middle- and upper-class men by arguing that granting the vote to women of these classes would offset the votes of the lower classes. There were exceptions to this attitude, especially in some of the highly industrialized states of the Northeast. In Connecticut, for example, Socialist and labor activist Ella Reeve Bloor was engaged by local suffragists to organize working-women into suffrage clubs. But the more common viewpoint of suf-

---

accept or reject it. If an employer refused to pay the recommended wage, the commission would add his name to a list of recalcitrants published in the state newspapers. Thus, Massachusetts, the most highly industrialized state with the largest number of employed women, made it easy for many employers to ignore the minimum wage (Dorothy W. Douglas, "American Minimum Wage Laws at Work," *American Economic Review* 9 [Spring 1919]: 701–38).

fragists of this era was expressed by the National American Woman
Suffrage Association, the major suffrage organization in the United
States, in a resolution of 1903 advocating educational qualifications that
would have had the effect of restricting the suffrage and would thus
have prevented many immigrants and other poor people from voting.
What is more, the NAWSA refused to endorse the labor movement.
Even during the high point of women's union activities—the 1909
waistmakers' strike—NAWSA issued a statement declaring that the association "neither stands for labor organization nor against it."[27]

And yet, it will be recalled that many prominent suffragists did support the strikers. These women became convinced that the success of
their movement depended on their ability to win the workers to their
cause. To promote suffrage among trade union members, Anna Howard Shaw, president of the NAWSA, hired the league's Rose Schneiderman to help in the 1912 Ohio suffrage campaign. Schneiderman was
delighted to accept the assignment, but she first told Shaw that she was
"a socialist and a trade unionist who looked upon the ballot as a tool in
the hands of working women with which, through legislation, they could
correct the terrible conditions existing in industry." Unfortunately,
Schneiderman was the only workingwoman used in the suffrage campaign, and she alone could not overcome the opposition of the Cincinnati and Dayton central labor unions, which refused to endorse women's
suffrage. Two years later, Margaret Dreier Robins wrote to Leonora
O'Reilly: "You know one of the biggest reasons for the defeat of suffrage
in Ohio was the inability of the suffragists to reach the mass of the
working men. Roschen, our Roschen, was practically the only trade
unionist they had."[28]

The league advanced the woman suffrage cause by working for it
actively within its own organization and in coalition with the NAWSA
groups. Moreover, the WTUL encouraged the formation of independent wage-earner suffrage leagues as a way of bringing female workers
into active involvement in the suffrage movement. It also devoted considerable energy to working with trade union men to gain their active
support for the suffrage cause. In fact, the league's chief organizers
began to devote their attention to full-time suffrage agitation. In New
York, Rose Schneiderman, Pauline Newman, Leonora O'Reilly, Mary
Dreier, Ida Rauh, and Mary Beard made numerous suffrage speeches.
The league also hired Margaret (Maggie) Hinchey, a laundry worker,
and Clara Lemlich, famous for her role in the 1909 waistmakers' strike,
as suffrage organizers. Most of the league activists worked with Mary
Beard in the Industrial Section of the Woman's Suffrage Party (the local
organization of the NAWSA). Early in 1912 Mary Beard wrote to Leonora
O'Reilly: "I sent Clara [Lemlich] to call upon our suffrage leaders in

several distinctly male labor unions to see what they had done toward getting hold of working women, whether they had any meeting rooms where we might hold a meeting and whether they could give us names of girls." Unfortunately, the women who ran the Industrial Section were not prepared for so radical a firebrand as Clara Lemlich, and it was not long before Beard was complaining to O'Reilly that "she can't swing the job."[29] And so she was discarded, even though she had proved herself capable of "swinging" a strike of thirty thousand women workers!

On July 12, 1913, the *New York Times* in a report of a meeting of suffragists on the Bowery, referred to

> the Billy Sunday of the suffragists—Maggie Hinchey, who represents working women. Maggie is big and sisterly and, above all, human in a good, strong way. When Maggie got up to speak, the Bowery succumbed to a man.
>
> "Brothers," began Maggie, rolling her r's with a good Irish brogue. As she went on her audience alternately wiped its tears and shook with laughter, and when she said at the close, "And now you know what you are going to do on Nov. 2 [on the referendum on woman suffrage], every hand went up to say yes, they would vote for the women. . . . The suffragists are canvassing the Bowery and are getting comparatively favorable results.*

The Woman's Suffrage Party sent Maggie Hinchey to Rochester, where she organized a delegation of six hundred workingwomen to call on President Woodrow Wilson in February, 1914, and ask him for the vote. While there, she also did some street-corner speaking: "I spoke outside of three factories at noon hour and when I got through the men took off their hats and said, 'Hurray, votes for women.'"

Still, like other working-class radicals of the WTUL, Hinchey found it difficult to work with the middle- and upper-class women of the suffrage movement. Too often, their paternalistic attitude, to say nothing of their contempt for workers, and especially immigrant workers, came to the fore. "I feel as if I have butted in where I was not wanted," Hinchey wrote to Leonora O'Reilly.[30]

For the sake of their working-class sisters, however, they carried on—speaking and emphasizing that while all women deserved the vote on the basis of equal justice, female workers needed it especially. Workingwomen needed the vote to develop confidence in themselves and to win the respect of both working-class men and employers, and as a tool that would give them some degree of control over their miserable working conditions. Without the vote, female workers faced tremendous handicaps in their efforts to get the legislation they needed. Rose Schneiderman emphasized this last argument at a mass meeting at

---

*It was not until 1917, however, that New York women got the vote.

Cooper Union organized by the New York Wage Earners' League for Suffrage in 1912:*

> I did some work last year for the 54-hour bill, and I can tell you how courteous our Senators and Assemblymen are when a disfranchised citizen tries to convince them of the necessity of shorter hours for working women. . . .
>
> During the hearing at Albany, our learned Senators listened to the opposition very carefully. . . . But when the Committee who spoke for the working women came to plead for the bill, there was only one Senator left in the room—he was the chairman—he couldn't very well get out. . . . Mind you, we were pleading for a shorter work week for working women. We had evidence to show that physical exhaustion leads to moral exhaustion, and the physical and moral exhaustion of women will lead to the deterioration of the human species. What did these men care? We were voteless working women—no matter what we felt or thought, we could not come back at them.[31]

Thus, in the view of the WTUL, suffrage now became the essential precondition for the unionization of workingwomen. Once they were able to vote, women would automatically gain the independence and confidence that male organizers often insisted they lacked. It would also help them in strikes. The NWTUL concluded a 1915 suffrage resolution with the observation that women were "heavily handicapped" during strikes because they lacked the vote. "Out of our experience in time of strikes," the resolution stated, "we have witnessed the close alliance of politics and police activity and police court justice."[32] In short, suffrage would abolish the sweatshop, raise women's wages, reduce their working hours, and help them unionize. "Behind suffrage," Leonora O'Reilly wrote to the Electrical Workers' Union, "is the demand for equal pay for equal work." Women workers would cease to be a threat to union men's wage scales once they gained the vote.[33]

The trend toward concentration on the battle for the vote intensified after the report of the United States Commission on Industrial Relations in 1915. The commission charged that the "labor problems of 6,000,000 women workers lie not merely in their relations with employers, but in their relations with men's unions." Given the hostility of most male unionists, the commission declared, it was not surprising that such relief as women workers had obtained from exploitation and abuse had come "through agitation and legislation." At the same time, however, "their disfranchisement" limited the extent of this solution. Therefore, the

*The Wage Earners' League was established in 1911, with WTUL encouragement, to persuade workingwomen to agitate for the ballot as an "industrial necessity." Both organizations shared the same headquarters in New York, with the WTUL providing financial support and leadership. Leonora O'Reilly served on the WTUL's suffrage committee and presided over the Wage Earners' League. O'Reilly helped to set up suffrage committees of workingwomen in Baltimore, Albany, Pittsburgh, New Jersey, Pennsylvania, and Delaware. (See collection of pamphlets on the Wage Earners' Leagues in Leonora O'Reilly Papers, Schlesinger Library, Radcliffe College.)

granting of equal political rights to women workers was "one of the means by which women in industry may obtain living wages."[34]

The criticism of men's unions and the emphasis on legislation and suffrage was, of course, hailed by most women's groups, including the Women's Trade Union League. But Gompers, while endorsing the commission's observation that women in industry menaced "the wage and salary standards of men," asserted heatedly that "workers are not bugs to be examined under the lenses of a microscope in a sociological slumming tour."[35]

Before public audiences, state legislatures, and congressional committees, league speakers argued that the right of suffrage was needed to improve women's working conditions. They also attacked the position of the National Association Opposed to Woman's Suffrage (a women's organization) that giving workingwomen the vote would increase the number of illiterate, uninformed, undesirable voters. Another women's organization opposed by the league was the Limited Suffrage Movement, which sought to enfranchise only English-speaking white women. Mary Kenney O'Sullivan claimed that women who endorsed these racist, antisuffragist arguments should be classed with scabs and strikebreakers as enemies of the people. A National Women's Trade Union League convention described these opponents of the suffrage as "women of leisure who, by accident of birth, have led sheltered and protected lives" and accused them of "selfishly obstructing the efforts of organized women to obtain full citizenship."[36]

In the years from 1915 to 1917 the Women's Trade Union League placed twenty organizers in the field. While they did do some unionization work, the main activity of these organizers was devoted to protective legislation and woman suffrage. Despite the AFL's continued support for suffrage as a means of improving the bargaining position of female workers—despite the publication of articles favoring woman suffrage in the *American Federationist*—despite convention resolutions in its favor and appeals to state legislatures for support, the AFL was still uneasy over the trend in the WTUL. In 1915 Gompers asked Leonora O'Reilly to write an article urging men to support proposed constitutional amendments for woman suffrage in four Eastern states, and he even outlined the text for her. But at the same time, he cautioned the league that it was traveling down a dangerous road by concentrating so heavily on legislation and suffrage. Working conditions, he declared at a league convention, were not sex problems but human ones, and "industrial freedom must be fought in the industrial field." Ballots could never replace the trade union, he cautioned, for votes could not solve industrial problems.[37]

By this time, however, WTUL leaders were not paying much attention to the AFL and its representatives; indeed, its advocacy of the ballot as the main means of improving women's working conditions came about precisely because of the disillusionment of these female leaders with the AFL. After a sharp encounter with male trade unionists at the New York State Federation of Labor convention in the summer of 1915, Leonora O'Reilly wrote to Mary Dreier Robins:

> Now, don't drop dead, but this is my last labor convention. Also my hands are off the Trade Union job in New York. I shall leave for the movement's good. My mind is made up. . . . Trade Unions are necessary. They must be worked for in season and out. Women must be organized better than men are organized. The powers that be in the labor movement of New York State do not and will not recognize an outside body's right to help with the work. Worse than that, they attribute their own shortcomings to the outside body's disinterestedness. They use its work to influence personal animosity or worse still they cover up their own crookedness. The crookedness will sooner become known to the rank and file when the outside body is not there as a scapegoat. By keeping in the struggle, we shall hinder more than help the rank and file from getting real light as to who it is that is playing foul in the game. . . .[38]

The truth is that the Women's Trade Union League was caught in a dilemma. The league had linked its fate with that of the AFL; it had acknowledged the superiority of industrial unionism over craft unionism in organizing the great mass of women workers but had turned its back on the IWW, the chief proponent of this type of unionism; for fear of antagonizing AFL leaders, it had refrained from playing any role in the "new unionism" that was emerging in the garment trades. When the AFL refused to abandon its traditional attitudes toward women workers and change its method of organizing to meet their needs, the league was left isolated. Just at this time, too, the IWW locals, established in militant struggles in the textile industry, fell apart, and the defeats of the Wobblies left the industrial union movement in the industrial East in a shambles. In this situation, it is hardly surprising that the Women's Trade Union League should look to the legislatures and courts for the protection and advancement of women workers.*

---

*In upholding the constitutionality of the fifty-four-hour law, the New York State Supreme Court held out considerable hope for the future. Justice Abel Blackmar delivered a strongly worded decision affirming the right of the state to enact laws for the general welfare of all people, notwithstanding the Constitutional guarantee of individual liberty (New York, *The Miscellaneous Reports of the State of New York*, 1913, vol. 79, pp. 140–49; *New York Times*, Jan. 11, 13, 1913).

27

On the Eve of World War I

"WE HAVE COME to the American Federation of Labor," declared Rose Schneiderman in 1915, "and said to them, 'Come and help us organize the American working girl' . . . but nothing was done."[1] Actually, something was started, but nothing came of it. At the AFL's 1913 convention, the time seemed propitious for at last inaugurating an aggressive movement to organize the great army of women in industrial life. For this purpose, the Executive Council was directed to levy "at whatever time it may see fit during the year 1914—an assessment of one cent . . . upon the membership of all affiliated unions, the money derived therefrom to be expended by direction of the Executive Council in whatever manner it may deem best and of the greatest advantage in the organization of the wage-earning women of our country."[2]

The financial records of the AFL indicate that the assessment was levied, but nothing was done with the funds collected. By the time the resolution was adopted, business failures were increasing, and by the end of 1913–1914, an economic crisis was in full swing. It was to increase in intensity after August, 1914, when the war broke out in Europe, severely disrupting American industry and causing food prices in the United States to skyrocket. The economic crisis reached its worst stage in the winter months of 1914–1915, when from 400,000 to 440,000 wage earners in New York City alone—18 percent of the 2,455,000 wage earners in the city—were unemployed, to say nothing of those workers who were kept on part-time. According to surveys, unemployment in other cities was pretty much in the same proportion as in New York. Maxwell Bertch has estimated that the total number of unemployed in the winter of 1914–1915 "reached as much as 4,000,000 and possibly higher." In addition, there were several million working only part-time.[3]

With the onset of this latest economic crisis and the rapid increase in unemployment, the usual cry of "Get the women out of the factories and shops!" began to be heard again in AFL circles. A group of embittered delegates to the 1914 convention of the AFL opposed any appropriation for organizing women and insisted that the employment of women and children was creating enforced idleness among men. They introduced a resolution declaring that "these conditions are destructive of the individual, the family, and our race," and resolving "that we do our utmost to restore individual, social, and racial health by restoring woman to the home." The convention did modify the resolution, but the original plan to organize women was shelved.[4]

Apart from seeking to eliminate women from industry, the AFL had no program for dealing with the problems of the unemployed. Indeed, even though the percentage of idleness among representative unions in New York had leaped from 17.5 percent in January, 1913, to 31 percent in January, 1914, and the percentage of unemployed among the organized workers in Massachusetts had increased from 11.3 to 16.6 percent during the same period, Gompers seemed blissfully unaware of the situation.[5]

It is to the credit of the IWW that it was the first organized group to recognize the existence of an unemployment problem, to call attention to the growing bread lines throughout the country and the increasing number of homeless men and women sleeping in doorways and cellars, and to point out that practically nothing was being done by federal, state, and local governments to relieve the suffering and distress of the unemployed.[6] IWW agitation among the unemployed started on the West Coast. Conditions in San Francisco were desperate. A large building on Market Street was converted into a shelter for the unemployed, and over two thousand men slept nightly in this vermin-infested place. Throughout the city, men, women, and children slept in "flops." An estimated 65,000 people were unemployed in San Francisco, and 10,000 a day were getting food on soup lines.[7]

On the night of January 20, 1914, a crowd of unemployed workers, led by the IWW, gathered in Jefferson Hall to hear Lucy Parsons, widow of the Haymarket martyr, Albert R. Parsons. The proprietor refused to let the crowd in, claiming that the hall rent had not been paid. Parsons led the crowd across the street and began speaking from the curb. She was immediately arrested and charged with inciting a riot, but not before the unemployed had voiced demands for work at $3 for an eight-hour day and had called upon Governor Hiram Johnson to convene a special session of the legislature to pass a right-to-work bill. But the Progressive governor denied that there was an unemployment problem and blamed the demonstration on a "few leaders who preach the tenets of the IWW, who neither wish to work themselves nor desire employment for others, and who preach an anarchistic doctrine at variance with organized Government."[8]

Under pressure from the IWW, the state government finally initiated a public works project. When the project supervisors refused to deal with the IWW's Unemployment Committee, ten thousand people marched to Union Square Plaza to protest. Unemployed women were in charge of the meeting, and Lucy Parsons, Ida Adler of the Cloak Makers, and Pearl Vogel of the Waitresses were the leading speakers.[9]

Lucy Parsons was also the principal speaker at Chicago's hunger demonstration of the unemployed on January 17, 1915. Above the speaker's platform was a banner with the word HUNGER on it, while other signs carried the slogans "We want WORK not Charity," "Why Starve in the Midst of Plenty?," and "Hunger Knows No Law." Parsons told the fifteen hundred men and women present that "as long as the capitalists can throw their cast-off rags and a few crumbs of bread at the working class in the name of 'charity,' just so long will they have an easy and cheap solution for the problem of unemployment." She then led the hunger marchers in a parade through Chicago's financial district. The police brutally attacked the marchers, and Parsons, five young women, and fifteen men were arrested.[10]

In New York, Portland, St. Louis, Sioux City, Des Moines, Detroit, Salt Lake City, Providence, and other cities, the IWW established Unemployed Leagues, which called upon the jobless to join with the IWW to "force the employers to cut down the daily working hours to 6, 5, or 4 or any number that may be necessary to make room for all our unemployed fellow workers to make a living." Most of the Unemployed Leagues were strictly IWW organizations, but in a number of communities, the Wobblies cooperated with other organizations. Moreover, as the crisis deepened, AFL unions and Socialist Party locals also became active. But it was the IWW that really succeeded in calling attention to the plight of the unemployed, that stimulated the unemployed to do something for themselves rather than resign themselves to starvation, and that forced the authorities to provide some relief for the men and women out of work. Henry Bruere, New York City municipal reformer, declared in the winter of 1914–1915 that "thanks to the activities of the IWW, the unemployed are no longer regarded as hoboes as they were last year."[11]

Although serious unemployment persisted until 1916, the depression began to lift by April, 1915, as European war orders caused mills and factories to rehire workers. Despite this change in the economic picture, Gompers was still insisting in 1915 that women be taken out of the factories to provide jobs for men and simultaneously end the long hours and low pay of women workers, which endangered the "perpetuity of our country."[12] But American industry, which was prospering by supplying goods to combatants abroad, was actually experiencing a shortage of labor to fill positions in the ironworks, steel mills, munitions plants, shipyards, mines, meat-packing plants. transportation companies, and many other industries that directly or indirectly played a role in supplying the war needs of the Allied Powers.

Previously, the immigrant masses had supplied American industry—largely concentrated in the North and Mideast—with a cheap, available labor supply. But the war drastically curtailed the flood of immigrants to this country* and, moreover, led to the departure of many already living here to serve the cause of their homelands. Great numbers of these individuals were workingmen.[13]

In the face of these developments, industrialists began to focus their attention on two still untapped sources of common labor. One was the Southern black. In the half century between emancipation and the First World War, few blacks had been able to secure work in the North outside of domestic and personal pursuits. Suddenly, however, the gates of Northern industry swung open to the black male worker, and he was presented, for the first time since the Civil War, with employment opportunities commensurate with those given white immigrants.[14]

The second source was women. Since 1910 the number of women employed in all general divisions of occupation, other than agriculture, forestry and animal husbandry, and domestic and personal service, had increased. But on the eve of the entrance of the United States into the First World War, women still constituted only one-fifth of the wage earners in the United States. If industry was to meet the demands from abroad, it was imperative that more women be drawn into the work force. Many employers had been reluctant to hire women if male help was available, unless they were bent on using female labor to lower wage standards. But now that Europe was at war and the United States appeared to be moving toward involvement, the demand arose that employers train women to replace the men who might be drafted.[15]

Many employers did not respond to any substantial degree. A study of the trend in Ohio, a major industrial state, is revealing. Both men's and women's employment began to increase in Ohio in 1915, but the increase was much more rapid for men. It was not until the middle of 1917, several months after the United States had entered the war, that

---

*The effect of the European conflict upon the influx of immigrants to the United States is clearly illustrated by the following table (U.S., Bureau of Immigration, *Annual Report of the Commissioner-General of Immigration* 1913–1919):

Year	Volume of Immigration
1913	1,197,892
1914	1,218,480
1915	326,700
1916	298,826
1917	295,403
1918	110,618

the rate of increase in women's employment almost equaled that of men.[16]

However, women workers began to enter the munitions industry in large numbers even before the United States became involved in the conflict. Up to the outbreak of the war in Europe, the American munitions industry was a small operation. With the demand from the combatants and with profits soaring, the industry expanded, and many industrial plants switched from turning out products primarily for peacetime use to producing munitions. As it became evident that women were especially suited to certain types of work in the munitions industry, they began to be employed in increasing numbers. "Many operations in the manufacture of munitions can not only be as well done by women as men, but are better done by female help," declared a speaker at a convention of the American Society of Mechanical Engineers and the National Machine Tool Builders' Association. "These operations are such as involve delicate work, requiring deftness and dexterity in the use of fingers." The *New York Times* was even more specific: "The filtering of the fine screw and the insertion of tiny springs in the assembling of parts of a shell made the sensitive touch perception and delicate handling of a woman's hands really needed." Florence Kelley, secretary of the National Consumers' League, charged that munitions manufacturers, eager to get women into the plants, threatened to discharge male workers "unless they induced their wives to work." "The manufacturers, of course, deny this charge," Kelley declared, "but we have found evidence of it on all sides. . . . The women, in order to conduct their homes, work at night."[17]

By January, 1917, four thousand women were already employed at a single plant in Bridgeport, Connecticut—the Remington Arms U.M.C. Company's plant—manufacturing cartridges to be shipped to the battlefields of Europe.[18]

Compared with women's rates in other industries, the rates of pay in munitions factories were high, but still far below those received by men in the same industry. The women worked long hours, often until as late as ten o'clock at night; while Connecticut's labor law forbade work for women after 10 P.M., it fixed no starting hour in the morning. Consequently, when the rush of war orders required continuous work in the munitions plants, the companies simply forced the women on the night shift to stop work from 10 P.M. until midnight and then set them to work again.[19]

These conditions produced what the U.S. Bureau of Labor Studies called the "munitions strikes." By a series of strikes in the spring of 1915, men and women munitions workers in Bridgeport converted that ten-hour center to the eight-hour day. From Bridgeport the eight-hour strikes spread through New England, as men and women munitions workers went out throughout Connecticut, Massachusetts, and Rhode Island. In the summer of 1915 the strikes swept across the whole Northeast, establishing the eight-hour day in plant after plant.[20]

In the spring of 1916, the strike wave spread to the complex of firms controlled by Westinghouse in the East Pittsburgh area. On April 21, 1916, more than two thousand men and women working on munitions at Westinghouse Electric in East Pittsburgh walked out on strike under the leadership of the American Industrial Union, which had been established in 1914 to organize "workers in all industries in Allegheny County and the Pittsburgh District, without regard to age, creed, race, sex, or craft."[21] By the afternoon, six thousand of the eighteen thousand workers in the plant complex were out, including three hundred women. Three major plants—Westinghouse Electric, Air Brake, and Union Switch & Signal, all controlled by Westinghouse—produced shrapnel shells and airplane engines.

The following morning, men and women pickets formed a human chain around the plant gates, and only a few workers crossed the picket line. A parade of six hundred strikers, led by a "dishpan drum corps," marched to the town's police station to demand the release of two arrested pickets. By evening, thirteen thousand workers, three thousand of them women, were on strike for higher wages and an eight-hour day.[22]

On the third day of the strike, the American Industrial Union held a mass meeting in Singer Hall, attended by two thousand workers. Anna Katherine Bell, a twenty-one-year-old Irishwoman and a three-year veteran at Westinghouse, spoke on behalf of the three thousand women strikers. A Pittsburgh paper gave some indication of the pressure she was under, from both the company and her family, in conducting her strike activity. "Anna Bell . . . of Braddock, leader of the 3,000 women strikers," it reported, "marched to the speakers' table, laid down a suitcase which she carried, and said she had lost her home, having been ordered out of it because she refused to return to work. She said she would not return to work until her followers won the strike."[23] She then went on to voice the strikers' demand for the eight-hour day at nine and a half hours' pay, plus a share in the company's wartime profits.

The words of the strikers' song went:

> Come on you rounders,
> We want you in the AIU.
> All we want is an 8-hour day
> With 9 and one-half hours' pay.
>
> Put a sign on your bonnet,
> With 8 hours on it

And we don't care what the bosses say.
When the strike is over
We will roam in clover
For we'll work 8 hours a day.

What are you? What are you?
We belong to the AIU.
What for? 8 hours![24]

By the fourth day of the strike, over eighteen thousand workers were out at both Westinghouse Electric and Westinghouse Machine. A parade of fifteen hundred strikers marched from East Pittsburgh to Wilderming to convince eighteen hundred shellmakers not to return to work. The East Pittsburgh strikers invaded the building, broke up the company's meeting, and spoke to the shellmakers. The parade homeward was led by a mysterious "Girl in the Paper Mask," who held a newspaper over her face. Some women were apparently afraid (either of the company or of their own families) to have their pictures appear in the newspapers.[25]

"While picketing the Air Brake plant," one account went, "Louisa Johnbusky, a 35-year-old, 195-pound female striker, pushed through the picket line waving a revolver and called workmen leaving the plant 'scabs.' Upon refusing to pay a $10 fine, she was jailed."[26] Almost spontaneously, new women took the lead when others were arrested. One Saturday, for example, Anna Bell was arrested after speaking at an open-air rally and charged with disorderly conduct. In another part of town, Anna Goldenberg was arrested for holding a mass meeting without a strike permit. But others took their places until they were bailed out, after which they spoke before a rally of four thousand workers from all four Westinghouse plants.[27]

Frightened by the militancy of the strikers and the growth of the AIU, the AFL's International Association of Machinists sent in sixteen organizers, including two women—Mary Schully and Mary Kules—and the two organizations cooperated in conducting the strike. They won the eight-hour day. On May 1 the IAM and AIU jointly called for a regionwide general strike.

On May 1, 1916, between two thousand and five thousand strikers marched through Braddock and Rankin, hoping to bring the steelworkers at Edgar Thomson and other mills of United States Steel out on strike. But United States Steel closed its mills and armed its private police and, in anticipation of a sympathy strike, granted its workers a 25 percent wage increase.[28]

When the strikers reached the Edgar Thomson mill—some newspapers reported that as many as twenty thousand of them surrounded the mill—they were met by a thousand company guards. Wave after wave of men and women stormed the mill, only to be beaten back and shot at by the company guards. "Four Girls Lead Frenzied Mob of Strikers in Fatal Charge Against the Company," screamed the headlines in the Pittsburgh papers. Three strikers were killed and at least three dozen wounded. Mrs. Mary Williams, the wife of a striker, was shot in the back, and Mrs. Anna Hitchih, a striker, was also wounded. The Pittsburgh papers blamed the foreign-born workers for the riot but emphasized: "Their women folk backed them up. When the men began to fall, the women rushed to the front and dragged the men away."[29]

Governor Martin Brumbaugh sent a thousand National Guardsmen to guarantee "labor peace," and, not surprisingly, the troops were quartered in the Westinghouse Electric plant. From then on, the company refused to negotiate with the strikers' mediation committee. President E. M. Herr ordered all the strikers back to work by May 9, threatening that workers would lose their jobs and pensions. Gradually, the strikers drifted back to the plants, and on May 16 the strike was officially ended.

Twenty-three strike leaders were arrested and charged with inciting to riot and accessory to murder. Four women leaders—Anna Bell, Anna Goldenberg, Bridget Kenny, and Patsy Delmar—were among those arrested. Eventually, all but one of the women were acquitted; Anna Goldenberg was found guilty of inciting to riot and spent a year in Blawnox, the Allegheny County workhouse.[30]

Although the 1916 strike was defeated, it marked another high point of women workers' militancy and of solidarity between men and women workers.* The "women strikes" in the garment trades of 1909–1910 in New York, Philadelphia, Cleveland, and Chicago had demonstrated that women were fully capable of labor organization. Other strikes had demonstrated their capacity to ignite and keep aflame the impulses of revolt in a largely male work force. Immigrant women had played leading roles in the celebrated struggles of Lawrence, Little Falls, and Paterson, which, like many other strikes of the period, culminating in the 1916 walkout at Westinghouse, had revealed an impressive level of cooperation between male and female workers.

The soaring cost of living brought to the surface new examples of women's militancy. After the outbreak of war in Europe in 1914, prices in the United States skyrocketed and continued to do so throughout the conflict. Within just two months—January and February, 1917—the price

---

*As the following report in the *Pittsburgh Post* of May 5, 1916, indicates, this militancy spread to other women workers in the city: "Officials of the McKinney Manufacturing Company... yesterday posted notices of a reward of $50 for the arrest and conviction of girl strikers who are alleged to have attacked girls leaving the plant Tuesday evening, and to have ducked one in a watering trough in Chartiers avenue. A strike was declared at the McKinney plant Tuesday morning and the girls employed in the plant walked out. Those who were attacked stayed at work."

of potatoes rose 100 percent; onions, 366 percent; cabbages, 212% percent and beans, 100 percent. "A dollar now is worth only 12 or 15 cents of its normal value as far as food-purchasing value is concerned," declared Meyer London, Socialist congressman from New York City's East Side at the end of February, 1917.[31]

Government orders to dilute wheat flour with cornmeal added fuel to the fire of discontent. Food riots flared. The lead story on the front page of the *New York Times* of February 21, 1917 began:

> Five thousand women on the East Side—some estimates ran as high as 10,000—fought like mad people to get into the Forward Hall, down on East Broadway last night, where a meeting had been called to protest against the high prices of food. The thousand that got into the hall fought for elbow room to shout denunciations of "capitalism" which they blamed for having so little to eat in the greatest, the richest city in the world. There were a few men in the shrieking, yelling crowd.

The meeting climaxed a day of tremendous demonstrations. A report in the *Literary Digest* went:

> Almost as if by premeditated signal, the women of various tenement districts of New York and Brooklyn began a campaign of riotous protest against the high price of food in the local markets. They upset the push-carts and barrows of the food-peddlers, and in some cases threw kerosene on the stock. They improvised boycotts and drove away intending purchasers. Hundreds of women of the East Side marched to the City Hall, shouting, "Give us food, Mr. Mayor!" "Our children are starving!" "Feed our children!" And later a mass-meeting adopted resolutions calling upon the Government for relief.[32]

The resolutions, in the form of an appeal to President Wilson, were drawn up by a women's committee of members of the ILGWU and housewives. They read:

> We, housewives of the city of New York, working women, mothers and wives of workmen, desire to call your attention, Mr. President, to the fact that in the midst of plenty, we and our families are facing starvation.
>
> The rise in the cost of living has been so great and uncalled for that even now we are compelled to deny ourselves and our children the necessities of life.
>
> We pay for our needs out of our wages and out of the wages of our husbands and the American standard of living cannot be maintained when potatoes are 7 cents a pound, bread 6 cents, cabbage 20 cents, onions 18 cents, and so forth.
>
> We call on you, Mr. President, in this crisis that we are facing to recommend to Congress or other authority measures for relief.[33]

In Philadelphia, on February 21, troops were called out to break up a march of the female relatives of the strikers at the Franklin Sugar Refining Company, who were out for higher wages in the face of rising prices.

"As they marched through the street," wrote a reporter, "the women cried that they were starving. The women were led to the refinery by Mrs. Florence Shadle, 32 years old, who carried a baby in her arms, as she shouted encouragement to her followers."[34] "Most of the women in the riot were of foreign birth," commented the *New York Times,* as though that excused calling out the troops. But women born in the United States joined them, and together they attacked provision stores and pushcart peddlers. On February 22 all food stores were barricaded and put under police guard, and martial law was declared in the Philadelphia food shopping district. One woman was killed and nine others wounded before the troops succeeded in breaking the women's occupation of the city's marketplace.[35]

On the West Coast, too, workingwomen were on the march, and in Seattle, they received a good deal of encouragement and assistance from the *Union Record,* official organ of the Central Labor Council. Unfortunately, that newspaper did not always take an enlightened attitude toward workingwomen. In 1909, for example, it showed its ignorance of the history of women workers in the United States when, in the course of urging enactment of an eight-hour law by the state legislature, it said:

> Twenty years ago, the mothers of the following generation were seldom employed in the stores and factories, wearing out their strength and losing the vitality which should be given in nourishing the unborn; they did not have to stand twelve or fourteen hours a day in a laundry feeding a machine which is continually calling for "more," "more"; they did not stand behind a counter trying to wear a smile and have a pleasant word for those who are "just looking around"; they did not have to chase from table to table all day long, taking orders from men in all conditions, drunk or sober, and then being insulted because the orders were not promptly forthcoming or were shy in some particular; they did not have to go into the canning factories and rub elbows with all classes of degenerates from foreign lands, especially the Jap and the Chinaman. No; our mothers and grandmothers had none of these things to contend with, and it was not necessary to make laws to grant them a few hours for rest and recreation. Not until the influx of the foreigner to our shores, with their old world traditions of women as beasts of burden, and the greed for gold ever dominant in the heart of men, was woman so degraded that it became necessary for her to seek employment to aid in the maintenance of the family.

The *Union Record* then voiced a typical AFL attitude: "Women at the mouth of the mine cheapened the miners' wages; women in all vocations of life have tended to bring down the wage received, and hence the lower the wage the more necessary it became for women to toil, for the burden became too heavy for the men." In short, woman was "the new Chinaman of the working class," threatening the wage standards of men by her presence.[36]

Later, however, the *Union Record* came to understand that nothing could be gained by calling for the exclusion of women from the trades and industries, as well as from the labor unions. On the contrary, it berated those AFL unions that excluded women. On December 16, 1916, it reprinted the following advertisement from the official organ of the Texas Federation of Labor:

> Refused a Union Shop Card on account of being a woman.
>
> I am union in principle, want to work as a union barber, and want to do work for union people, but am denied the privilege because—on account of my sex—I cannot get a Union Shop Card.
>
> All the work in my shop necessary to the installation of the fixtures was done by union labor. I respectfully solicit a share of your patronage, assuring you courteous treatment and first-class service.

After criticizing the publication of the Texas Federation for being willing to accept the advertisement (but unwilling to criticize the union for its exclusionary police toward women), the *Union Record* editorialized:

> Pressure of some kind ought to be brought to bear on an international which discriminates so narrowly and will not allow the various locals affiliated to receive efficient members into their union because of their sex. Women are in the industrial field to stay, and just as other exclusive large unions reasoned long ago—"It is better to have a strong force with us than to array them against us." If the women are not permitted to cooperate with the men of their craft, they will be compelled to operate against them.[37]

The *Union Record* did not leave it at that. It launched a campaign to convince Seattle's male workers that women worked because of necessity and that it would be a waste of time and energy to attempt to eliminate them from American industrial life. "Women Must Work Not by Choice but Compulsion" was the heading of a column that appeared regularly in the publication in 1916 and early in 1917. A typical entry went: "Thirty-five percent of the wives and mothers of working men are forced to work to keep the wolf from the door."[38] Another regular feature dealt with the contributions made by women to the labor movement.

One entry in the *Union Record* column was headed "Woman Surpasses Man as Militant Striker." The subhead read "Young Waitress Holds Record for Picketing Arrests." The story was about Madge Keith, a member of the Waitresses' Union of St. Louis, who established "the record for the heinous crime of picketing, for she was arrested 12 times in two weeks while doing picket duty in front of Robinson's Restaurant, being discharged each time. She has, altogether, been arrested 22 times for picketing the same restaurant, thereby causing great concern to the police of the city, who seem to be much afraid of the young waitress' picketing activities."[39] The *Union Record* pointed out that there were

"Miss Keiths" in their own city, for during the shingle weavers' strike,* it was the women who were the most active, militant pickets and the ones most often arrested: "The women have the men beat two to one doing picket duty. They succeed in getting the men out as fast as the scab herders bring them in."[40]

Prodded by the *Union Record,* Seattle's Central Labor Council established a female auxiliary called the "Union Card and Label League of Seattle," headed by Mrs. George T. McNamara, wife of the editor of the *Union Record.* Among its duties were "to secure equal pay for equal work regardless of sex, and political equality for women" and to assist in the unionizing of women workers. The league established a number of women's auxiliaries of Seattle unions and "assisted many unions in their strikes for better conditions and wages." It also popularized the union label, especially for unions with women members, and was credited with being "an effective factor in the settlement of many labor troubles."[41]

On June 10, 1916, a step was taken in Seattle for the establishment of the second citywide federation of women workers in American history.† Five organizations were represented at the founding conference: Carpenters' Auxiliary, Federal Labor Union, Seattle Union Card and Label League, United Garment Workers, and Waitresses' Local 240. A committee was appointed to call on every union in Seattle that had women in its ranks to inform the leadership about the purpose of the proposed federation and to secure representation from its ranks. The literature distributed by the committee explained that the new organization aimed

> to do for women of Seattle what the Central Labor Council of Seattle and Vicinity and the Washington State Federation of Labor have done for the men's organizations. Realizing that the spread of unionism among women must come from themselves, we have banded ourselves together for the purpose of strengthening the various organizations already in existence, organizing the unorganized women workers and the wives of union men who have not yet affiliated with the auxiliaries of the crafts of which their husbands are members. We propose also to take up civic and legislative work that pertains to the further advantage of union women.[42]

The response was gratifying, and in October, 1916, the Federation of Union Women and Auxiliaries was established. It was to be composed of delegates from any of the "trades union women's organizations, women's auxiliaries affiliated with trades unions, and the Seattle Union Card and Label League."

> The object of the organization shall be to increase the membership of all trades union organizations or trades union auxiliaries.

---

*Shingle weavers were mill workers who manned the saw cutting the lumber into shingles.
†See page 45 above for the first citywide federation.

To devise ways and means to organize the unorganized women workers into craft unions of their own, or to assist them to affiliate with those already established.

To promote the welfare of union women, financially or physically as the occasion may arise.[43]

One of the federation's first activities was to link up with the movement of women in the East for a national eight-hour day. At the Middle Atlantic States Eight-Hour Conference of the National Women's Trade Union League, held in December, 1916, resolutions demanding legislative action on an interstate basis to secure an eight-hour day provoked intense discussion. "Trades union women forgot their usual timidity and unaccustomedness to public expression," wrote an observer, "and argued the issue so warmly that the chairman had to resort to rigorous restrictions to keep the debate from extending beyond the hour marked for adjournment." Delegates were instructed to urge their organizations to introduce a bill for an eight-hour day into their respective state legislatures "so as to prevent interstate competition, and to urge the women not already organized to organize themselves into trade unions for the purpose of demanding an eight-hour day through collective bargaining as well as through legislation."[44]

The Seattle Federation of Union Women and Auxiliaries joined the crusade for the shorter working day, but it proposed that the ultimate objective should be a four-hour day. The proposal was picked up by Melinda Scott, president of the New York Women's Trade Union League, who recommended that "the league work to secure a reduction of the workday hours from ten to eight, then to six, and then to four hours. Working only four hours would give every one a chance for employment."[45]

Thus, on the eve of America's entrance into the First World War, women workers were involved in militant struggles and organizational activities—activities that foreshadowed the many battles women were to wage during the war years and in the postwar wave of industrial unrest.

Notes

Chapter 1: Colonial and Revolutionary America

1. EDWARD ARBER, ed., *Travels and Works of Captain John Smith* (Edinburgh, 1910), 1:360, 2:444; Alexander Brown, *Genesis of the United States* (Boston, 1891), 2:797.

2. ALMON W. LAUBER, *Indian Slavery in Colonial Times within the Present Limits of the United States* (New York, 1913), pp. 287–88.

3. NATHANIEL B. SHURTLEFF. ed., *Records of the Governor and Company of the Massachusetts Bay in New England* (Boston, 1853), 1:405.

4. BROWN, *Genesis*, 1:353; Gary P. Nash, *Red, White and Black: The Peoples of Early America* (Englewood Cliffs, N.J., 1974), pp. 56–57, 66–67.

5. KATHRYN ALLAMONG JACOB, "The Women of Baltimore Town: A Social History, 1729–1797" (Master's thesis, Georgetown University, 1975), p. 5.

6. CLAYTON COLMAN HALL, ed., *Narratives of Early Maryland, 1633–1684* (New York, 1910), p. 137.

7. RICHARD B. MORRIS, *Government and Labor in Early America* (New York, 1965), pp. 44–45.

8. PHILIP S. FONER, *Labor and the American Revolution* (Westport, Conn., 1976), pp. 7–8.

9. JACOB, "Women of Baltimore," p. 236.

10. Ibid., p. 241.

11. WINTHROP D. JORDAN, *White over Black: American Attitudes toward the Negro, 1550–1812* (Chapel Hill, N.C., 1968). p. 27; Jacob, "Women of Baltimore," p. 238.

12. PHILIP S. FONER, *History of Black Americans: From Africa to the Cotton Kingdom* (Westport, Conn., 1975), pp. 186–223.

13. Ibid., p. 220.

14. Ibid., pp. 220–22; Jacob, "Women of Baltimore," pp. 238–39.

15. FONER, *History of Black Americans*, p. 226.

16. J. HECTOR ST. JOHN CRÈVECOEUR, *Letters from an American Farmer* (New York, 1782), p. 132.

17. FONER, *History of Black Americans,* p. 220.

18. Ibid., pp. 224–35.

19. Ibid., pp. 249–50; Herbert Aptheker, *Documentary History of the Negro People of the United States* (New York, 1951), p. 12.

20. MARCUS W. JERNEGAN, *Laboring and Dependent Classes in Colonial America* (Chicago, 1931), pp. 48–56; R. Morris, *Government and Labor,* pp. 37, 47, 86–88.

21. MORRIS, *Government and Labor,* pp. 353–56; Dennis Clark, "Babes in Bondage: Indentured Irish Children in Philadelphia in the Nineteenth Century," *Pennsylvania Magazine of History and Biography* 101 (October 1977): 479.

22. *Maryland Gazette,* July 22, 1777.

23. JACOB, "Women of Baltimore," p. 239.

24. *Maryland Gazette,* Oct. 6, 1774.

25. LORENZO J. GREENE, "The New England Negro as Seen in Advertisements for Runaway Slaves," *Journal of Negro History* 29 (Spring 1944): 222–24; Donald D. Wax, "The Image of the Negro in the 'Maryland Gazette,' 1745–74," *Journalism Quarterly* 13 (Spring 1969): 113–15.

26. KENNETH SCOTT, "The Slave Insurrection in New York in 1712," *New York Historical Society Quarterly* 44 (Spring 1961): 133–49.

27. FONER, *Labor and the American Revolution,* pp. 9–10; Lawrence W. Towner, "A Good Master Well Served: A Social History of Servitude in Massachusetts, 1620–1750" (Ph.D. diss., Northwestern University, 1955), pp. 64–68; Lawrence W. Towner, "The Indentures of Boston's Poor Apprentices: 1734–1805," *Publications of the Colonial Society of Massachusetts* 43 (1956–1963): 417–34.

28. SAM BASS WARNER, JR., *The Private City* (Philadelphia, 1968), p. 246.

29. ALICE CLARK, *Working Life of Women in the Seventeenth Century* (1919; reprint ed., New York, 1968), pp. 299–300.

30. PAUL RYAN, *Womanhood in America* (New York, 1969), pp. 34–35; Ann D. Gordon and Mari Jo Buhle, "Sex and Class in Colonial and Nineteenth-Century America," in Bernice A. Carroll, ed., *Liberating Women's History: Theoretical and Critical Essays,* (Urbana, Ill., 1976), p. 279.

31. JAMES A. HENRETTA, *The Evolution of American Society, 1700–1815* (Lexington, Mass., 1973), pp. 105–6.

32. ELIZABETH BANCROFT SCHLESINGER, "Cotton Mather and His Children," *William and Mary Quarterly,* 3d ser. 10 (April 1953): 186 (italics in original); Mary Sumner Benson, *Women in Eighteenth Century America: A Study of Opinion and Social Usage* (New York, 1935), pp. 111–12.

33. ELIZABETH ANTHONY DEXTER, *Colonial Women of Affairs* (Boston, 1931), pp. 182–92.

34. FRANCES MAY MANGES, "Women Shopkeepers and Artisans in Colonial Philadelphia," (Ph.D. diss., University of Pennsylvania, 1958), pp. 97–98.

35. DEXTER, *Colonial Women of Affairs,* pp. 196–202; Jacob, "Women of Baltimore," pp. 286–87; W. Elliot Brownlee and Mary M. Brownlee, *Women*

in the American Economy: A Documentary History, 1675 to 1929 (New Haven and London, 1976), pp. 11–12.

36. JULIA CHERRY SPRUILL, *Women's Life and Work in the Southern Colonies* (1938; reprint ed., New York, 1972), p. 132; Jacob, "Women of Baltimore," p. 288.

37. JACOB, "Women of Baltimore," pp. 243–44; Debra Newman, "Black Women in the Era of the American Revolution in Pennsylvania," *Journal of Negro History* 61 (July 1976): 283–84.

38. ROBERT E. BROWN and B. Catherine Brown, *Virginia, 1705–1786: Democracy or Aristocracy?* (East Lansing, Mich., 1964), p. 55; Virginia Bever Platt, "The Working Women of Newport, Rhode Island," cited in Joan Hoff Wilson, "The Illusion of Change: Women and the American Revolution," in Alfred F. Young, ed., *The American Revolution: Explorations in the History of American Radicalism* (DeKalb, Ill., 1976), p. 434, *n.* 26.

39. ALICE EARLE, *Colonial Dames and Goodwives* (Boston, 1895), p. 48.

40. SAMUEL ELIOT MORRISON, *Builders of the Bay Colony* (Boston, 1930), pp. 116–19; Bella Squire, *The Woman Movement in America* (Chicago, 1911), pp. 34–35.

41. LINDA GRANT DE PAUW, "Land of the Unfree: Legal Limitations on Liberty in Pre-Revolutionary America," *Maryland Historical Magazine* 68 (Winter 1973): 360–61; Richard B. Morris, "Women's Rights in Early American Law," in David H. Flaherty, ed., *Essays in the History of Early American Law* (Chapel Hill, N.C.. 1969), pp. 419–24; Nancy F. Cott, "Divorce and the Changing Status of Women in Eighteenth-Century Massachusetts," *William and Mary Quarterly*, 3d ser. 33 (October 1976): 594–95; Jacob, "Women of Baltimore," p. 289.

42. Reprinted in Brown and Brown, *Virginia*, pp. 55–56.

43. DEXTER, *Colonial Women of Affairs*, pp. 233–34; Thomas J. Wertenbaker, *Torchbearer of the Revolution* (Princeton, N.J., 1940), pp. 8–14.

44. CURTIS NETTELS, "British Mercantilism and the Economic Development of the Thirteen Colonies," *Journal of Economic History* 12 (Spring 1952): 105–14; John C. Miller, *Origins of the American Revolution* (Boston, 1943), pp. 4–23; Foner, *Labor and the American Revolution*, pp. 28–32.

45. ALFRED F. YOUNG, "Some Thoughts on Mechanic Participation in the American Revolution" (Paper delivered at the Third Annual Conference on Early American History, Newberry Library, Chicago, November 1, 1974), p. 13.

46. FONER, *History of Black Americans*, pp. 292–94.

47. BENSON J. LOSSING, *Pictorial Field-Book of the Revolution* (New York, 1860), 1:482; R. J. Burker, "The Daughters of Liberty," *American Historical Register* 1 (1894): 29–36; *Boston Chronicle*, Sept. 28, 1769.

48. MILLER, *Origins of the American Revolution*, p. 344; *Ms.*, letter dated Boston, April 4, 1776, Miscellaneous Collection, Rhode Island Historical Society.

49. WILSON, "The Illusion of Change." p. 398.

50. *New York Journal*, Mar. 23, 1769.

51. BROADSIDE, Boston, 1770, portfolio 37, no. 2A, Library of Congress, Rare Book Room.

52. MILLER, *Origins of the American Revolution*, p. 271.

53. FONER, *Labor and the American Revolution*, pp. 186–87; Elizabeth Cometti, "Women in the American Revolution," *New England Quarterly* 20 (1947): 330.

54. *Boston Gazette*, Mar. 17, Apr. 21, 1777; *Independent Chronicle* (Boston), Apr. 24, 1777; Charles Francis Adams, ed., *Familiar Letters of John Adams and His Wife, Abigail Adams, During the Revolution* (New York, 1876), pp. 262, 263, 286–87.

55. FONER, *History of Black Americans*, pp. 328–40; June Sochen, *Her Story: A Woman's View of American History, 1600–1880* (New York, 1974), pp. 84–85.

56. For biographical information on Margaret Corbin and Margaret Hayes (Pitcher), see Elizabeth Ellet, *The Women of the Revolution* (New York, 1850), and Cometti, "Women in the American Revolution," pp. 329–46. For Deborah Sampson Gannett, see Herman Mann, *The Female Review: Life of Deborah Sampson, The Female Soldier of the American Revolution*, ed., John Adams Vinton (Boston, 1866), reprinted in 1916 as Extra Number 47 of the *Magazine of History with Notes and Queries;* Julia Ward Stickley, "The Records of Deborah Sampson Gannett, Woman Soldier of the Revolution," *Prologue* 4 (Winter 1972): 233–41.

57. *Independent Journal* (New York), Jan. 21, 1784; William Miller, "The Effects of the American Revolution on Indentured Servitude," *Pennsylvania History* 7 (1940): 134–36.

58. FONER, *History of Black Americans*, pp. 345–77; Ira Berlin, "The Revolution in Black Life," in Young, ed., *The American Revolution*, pp. 365–69.

59. ADAMS, *Familiar Letters of John Adams and His Wife, Abigail Adams*, pp. 149–50.

60. MORRIS, *Government and Labor in Early America*, p. 200; *Philadelphia Evening Post*, Feb. 27, 1779; Wilson, "The Illusion of Change," p. 395; Brownlee and Brownlee, *Women in the American Economy*, p. 12; Elizabeth Cometti, "The Labor Front during the Revolution," *West Georgia College Studies in the Social Sciences* 15 (June 1976): 80, 86.

61. *Mechanic* (Fall River), July 6, 1844; Philip S. Foner, *American Labor Songs of the Nineteenth Century* (Urbana, Ill., 1975), p. 62; Foner, *Labor and the American Revolution*, pp. 202–05.

62. *Mechanic* (Fall River), Aug. 3, 1844.

Chapter 2: In the Factories

1. VICTOR S. CLARK, *History of Manufactures in the United States* (New York, 1929), 1:379–80.

2. EDITH ABBOTT, "Harriet Martineau and the Employment of Women in 1836," *Journal of Political Economy* 14 (December 1906): 620–21.

3. W. R. BAGNALL, *Samuel Slater and the Early Development of the Cotton Manufac-*

ture in the United States (Middletown, Conn., 1890), p. 44; Caroline F. Ware, *The Early New England Cotton Manufacture* (Boston, 1931), p. 64.

4. *American State Papers,* Finance (Washington, D.C., 1858) 5:no.662; "Account of a Journey of Josiah Quincy in 1801," *Proceedings of the Massachusetts Historical Society,* ser. 2, 4 (1888): 124.

5. PETER J. COLEMAN, *The Transformation of Rhode Island, 1790–1860* (Providence, 1954), pp. 77–78; Bettina Eileen Berch, "Industrialization and Working Women in the Nineteenth Century: England, France, and the United States" (Ph.D. diss., University of Wisconsin, Madison, 1976), p. 236; Thomas Bender, *Toward an Urban Vision: Ideas and Institutions in Nineteenth Century America* (Lexington, Ky., 1975), p. 28.

6. KENNETH FRANK MAILLOUX, "The Boston Manufacturing Company of Waltham, Massachusetts, 1813–1848: The First Modern Factory in America," (Ph.D. diss., Boston University, 1957), pp. 1–8.

7. SAMUEL BATCHELDER, *Introduction and Early Progress of the Cotton Manufacture in the United States* (Boston, 1863), pp. 72–74; Jonathan Taylor Lincoln, "The Beginning of the Machine Age in New England: Documents Relating to the Introduction of the Power Loom," *Bulletin: Business History Society* 7 (June 1933): 6–20.

8. HENRY MILES, *Lowell as It Is and Was* (Lowell, 1845), pp. 128–30. The agent of Manchester Mill No. 1 (New Hampshire) informed the absentee capitalist owners that it was essential that they make certain that the factory women attended church regularly, and that "without reference to any feelings of philanthropy, self-interest in the preservation of our property would dictate a watchfulness on our part" (Manuscript. New Hampshire Historical Society, Concord, N.H.).

9. MAILLOUX, "Boston Manufacturing Company," pp. 60–65; Howard M. Gitelman, "The Waltham System and the Coming of the Irish," *Labor History* 8 (Fall 1967): 228–32.

10. VERA SHLAKMAN, "Economic History of a Factory Town: A Study of Chicopee, Massachusetts," *Smith College Studies in History* 20 (Northampton, Mass., 1935): 31, 37, 48.

11. HANNAH JOSEPHSON, *The Golden Threads: New England's Mill Girls and Magnates* (New York, 1949), p. 103.

12. THOMAS LOUIS DUBLIN, "Women at Work: The Transformation of Work and Community in Lowell, Massachusetts, 1826–1860," (Ph.D. diss., Columbia University, 1975), p. 37.

13. LUCY LARCOM, *A New England Girlhood* (Boston, 1890), p. 142.

14. EDITH ABBOTT, *Women in Industry* (New York, 1910), p. 122.

15. DUBLIN, "Women at Work," pp. 62, 90; Gitelman, "The Waltham System and the Coming of the Irish." *Labor History* 8 (Fall 1967): 231–32, 244–45; Mailloux, "Boston Manufacturing Company," pp. 66–69.

16. SETH LUTHER, *An Address to the Working-Men of New England . . .* (Boston, 1832), p. 17n.

17. HARRIET H. ROBINSON, *Loom and Spindle: Of Life among the Early Mill Girls* (New York, 1898), p. 30. *Working Man's Advocate,* Apr. 14, 1832.

18. Published in Helen Sumner, "History of Women in Industry in the United States," U.S., Congress, Senate, *Report on Condition of Women and Child Wage Earners in the United States, Senate Document No. 645*, 61st Cong., 2d sess. 1910–1913, p. 102.

19. LUTHER, *Address*, p. 36, app. G.

20. CARL GERSUNY, "'A Devil in Petticoats' and Just Cause: Patterns of Punishment in Two New England Textile Factories," *Business History Review* 50 (Summer 1976): 134, 136, 138.

21. BENDER, *Toward an Urban Vision*, p. 41; John F. Kasson, *Civilizing the Machine: Technology and Republican Values in America, 1776–1900* (New York, 1976), pp. 85–87.

22. SUMNER, "History of Women in Industry," p. 55; *Mechanics' Free Press*, Apr. 10, 1830.

23. JOHN R. COMMONS et al., eds., *A Documentary History of American Industrial Society* (Cleveland, 1910), 6:331–34.

24. Ibid., p. 101; Sumner, "History of Women in Industry," p. 75.

25. *Paterson Courier*, Aug. 12, 1835; Foner, *History of the Labor Movement*, 1:101.

26. SHLAKMAN, *Economic History of a Factory Town*, pp. 62–63.

27. GARY KULIK, "Pawtucket Village and the Strike of 1824: The Origins of Class Conflict in Rhode Island," *Radical History Review* 17 (Spring 1978): 14–16; *Manufacturers' and Farmers' Journal*, reprinted in *ibid.*, pp. 22–24; *Providence Patriot*, May 29, June 5, 1824; John R. Commons and Associates, *History of Labour in the United States* (New York, 1918), 1:156.

28. COMMONS et al., eds., *Documentary History of American Industrial Society*. 6:81–83; U.S., Bureau of Labor, *16th Annual Report, 1900*, p. 725.

29. New York *Evening Post*, July 29, Aug. 1, 5, 8, 1828; *Mechanics' Free Press*, Aug. 2, 1828; *Poulson's American Daily Advertiser*. Aug. 4, 1828; Foner, *History of the Labor Movement*, 1:105; Commons and Associates, *History of Labour*, 1:419.

30. Boston letter to the *Hartford Post*, reprinted in *New York Times*, Feb. 6, 1886. The article is incorrectly entitled "The First Strike."

31. FONER, *History of the Labor Movement*, 1:105; John B. Andrews and Helen Bliss, *History of Women in Trade Unions, 1825 to the Knights of Labor, Senate Document 645*, U.S., Congress, Senate, 61st Cong., 2d sess., 1911, 10:23–24 (hereafter cited as Andrews and Bliss, *Women in Trade Unions*).

32. *National Gazette*, Jan. 7, 1829, quoted in Andrews and Bliss, *Women in Trade Unions*, p. 23.

33. Boston Letter to *Hartford Post*, reprinted in *New York Times*, Feb. 6, 1886. Barbara Wertheimer asserts that the strikers did not win and that the leaders were discharged and blacklisted, but gives no source for the statement. (*We Were There: The Story of Working Women in America* [New York, 1977], pp. 67–68).

34. Boston Letter to the *Hartford Post*, reprinted in *New York Times*, Feb. 6, 1886. That same year, 1829, women in the factories of Ellicott Mills, Maryland, went on strike over both a reduction in pay and the practice of nailing the windows closed.

35. ALMOD H. DAVIS, *The Female Preacher, or Memoir of Salome Lincoln. Afterwards the Wife of Elder Junia S. Mowry* (Providence, 1843), pp. 49–52; reprinted in Gerda Lerner, ed., *The Female Experience: An American Documentary* (Indianapolis, 1977), pp. 275–77.

36. FONER, *History of the Labor Movement,* 1:100–115.

37. For biographical studies of Seth Luther, see Louis Hartz, "Seth Luther: The Story of a Working Class Rebel," *New England Quarterly* 13 (September 1940): 401–18; Carl Gersuny, "Seth Luther—The Road from Chepachet," *Rhode Island History* 33 (May 1974): 47–55. For Luther's influence, see Philip S. Foner, ed., *We, the Other People: Alternative Declarations of Independence by Labor Groups, Farmers, Women's Rights Advocates, Socialists, and Blacks, 1829–1975* (Urbana, Ill., 1976), pp. 9–12, 34.

38. LUTHER, *Address,* pp. 7–8, 23–25, 29–30.

39. EDWARD PESSEN, *Most Uncommon Jacksonians: The Radical Leaders of the Early Labor Movement* (Albany, N.Y., 1967), pp. 90–91.

40. KASSON, *Civilizing the Machine,* p. 93.

41. *Dover Gazette,* reprinted in *The Man* (New York), Mar. 8, 1934.

42. Ibid.

43. Ibid. and *Boston Transcript,* reprinted in ibid., Mar. 11, 1834.

44. For the full text of the new regulations, see Luther, *Address,* p. 36, app. G. They are summarized above, p. 22.

45. *Dover Gazette,* reprinted in *The Man,* Mar. 8, 1934.

46. Ibid.; Foner, *History of the Labor Movement,* 1:109; Ruth Delzell, *The Early History of Women Trade Unionists of America* (Chicago, Ill., 1919), pp. 82–83.

47. DUBLIN, "Women at Work," p. 112, citing Lawrence manufacturing records. See also Thomas Dublin, "Women, Work and Protest in the Early Lowell Mills: 'The Oppressing Hand of Avarice Would Enslave Us,'" *Labor History* 16 (Winter 1975): 107–8.

48. *Boston Evening Transcript,* Feb. 17, 18, 1834.

49. *Boston Evening Transcript,* Feb. 18, 1834; *The Man,* Feb. 22, 1834.

50. DUBLIN, "Women at Work," pp. 111–12.

51. Ibid., pp. 118–20; Dublin, "Women, Work and Protest," pp. 110–13.

52. PHILIP S. FONER, *American Labor Songs of the Nineteenth Century* (Urbana, Ill., 1975), p. 45.

53. *Boston Daily Times,* Oct. 6, 1836; Boston *Post,* Oct. 7, 1836; *National Laborer* (Philadelphia), Oct. 29, 1836.

54. DUBLIN, "Women at Work," p. 120, citing Tremont-Suffolk Mills record.

55. *Boston Evening Transcript,* Mar. 25, 1836.

56. FONER, *History of the Labor Movement,* 1:110.

57. ANDREWS AND BLISS, "Women in Trade Unions," pp. 32–34.

58. *Paterson Intelligencer,* July 6, 7, 12, 1835; Foner, *We, the Other People,* pp. 2–5.

59. *Paterson Courier,* Aug. 12, 1835; *Paterson Intelligencer,* Aug. 14, 1835; *Working Man's Advocate* (New York), Aug. 4, 11, 18, 1835.

60. *Working Man's Advocate,* Sept. 12, 1835.

61. *Paterson Intelligencer,* July 29, 1835; *Newark Daily Advertiser,* July 28–30, Aug. 10, 1835.

62. *Paterson Intelligencer,* Aug. 18, 1835; Luther, *Address,* pp. 42–46; Foner, *History of the Labor Movement,* 1:111.

Chapter 3: In the Trades

1. The only report of this strike was published in the *National Gazette* of Apr. 23, 1825, which did not indicate the outcome.

2. For a summary of the status of women in Jacksonian America, see Eleanor Flexner, *Century of Struggle* (Cambridge, Mass., 1959), chaps. 1–3.

3. BARBARA EHRENREICH AND DEEDRE ENGLISH, *Witches, Midwives & Nurses—A History of Women Healers* (Oyster Bay, N.Y., 1972); Gena Corea, *Women's Health Care* (New York, 1977), chaps. 3, 4.

4. GERDA LERNER, "The Lady and the Mill Girl: Changes in the Status of Women in the Age of Jackson," *American Studies Journal* 10 (Spring 1969): 2–3.

5. BARBARA WELTER, "The Cult of True Womanhood, 1820–1860," *American Quarterly* 18 (Summer 1966): 151–74; Barbara Welter, "Anti-Intellectualism and the American Woman: 1800–1860," *Mid-America* 48 (1966): 258–70; Carroll Smith Rosenberg, "The Hysterical Woman: Sex Roles and the Role Conflict in 19th Century America," *Social Research* 39 (Winter 1972): 655–56; Aileen S. Kraditor, *Up from the Pedestal: Selected Writings in the History of American Feminism* (Chicago, 1968), pp. 11–13.

6. LOUISE M. YOUNG, "Woman's Place in American Politics: The Historical Perspective," *Journal of Politics* 38 (August 1976): 295–335.

7. LINDA KERBER, "The Republican Mother: Women and the Enlightenment, An American Perspective," *American Quarterly* 28 (Summer 1976): 43–49.

8. T. S. ARTHUR, *The Lady at Home: or, Leaves from the Every-Day Book of an American Woman* (Philadelphia, 1847), pp. 177–78; Welter, "The Cult of True Womanhood," p. 163.

9. ANN DOUGLAS, *The Feminization of American Culture* (New York, 1977), chap. 1.

10. EGAL FELDMAN, "New York Men's Clothing Trade, 1800–1861" (Ph.D. diss., New York University, 1959), pp. 5–7, 35–37, 65–75; Helen Sumner, "History of Women in Industry in the United States," vol. 9 of U.S., Congress, Senate, *Report on Condition of Women and Child Wage Earners in the United States, Senate Document 645,* 61st Cong., 2d sess., 1910–1913, pp. 119–121.

11. SUMNER, "History of Women in Industry," p. 117.

12. MATTHEW CAREY, *Miscellaneous Pamphlets, No. 12,* quoted in ibid., pp. 127–28. Matthew Carey, *Appeal to the Wealthy of the Land,* quoted in Sumner, "History of Women in Industry," p. 132.

13. MATTHEW CAREY, *Select Excerpts*, quoted in Sumner, "History of Women in Industry," p. 132.

14. *Mechanics' Free Press*, Dec. 18, 1830.

15. CAREY, *Appeal to the Wealthy*, quoted in Sumner, "History of Women in Industry," pp. 131–32.

16. "A Working Woman," in *Working Man's Advocate* (Boston), reprinted in New York *Daily Sentinel*, Aug. 21, 1830.

17. "Report on Female Wages," Philadelphia, Mar. 25, 1829, cited in W. Elliot Brownlee and Mary M. Brownlee, *Women in the American Economy: A Documentary History, 1675 to 1929* (New Haven and London, 1976), p. 147.

18. CARROLL SMITH ROSENBERG, "Beauty, the Beast and the Militant Woman: A Case Study of Sex Roles and Social Stress in Jacksonian America," *American Quarterly* 23 (October 1971): 579.

19. New York *Daily Sentinel*, Aug. 28, 1830.

20. "M" in *ibid.*, Feb. 12, 1831.

21. Boston *Evening Transcript*, Feb. 22, 1831.

22. New York *Daily Sentinel*, Mar. 5, 1831.

23. *Ibid.*, June 12, 14, 16, 1831.

24. *Ibid.*, June 25, 1831.

25. *Ibid.*, July 22, 24, 26, 1831; *Working Man's Advocate*, Aug. 13, 1831.

26. New York *Daily Sentinel*, July 21, 1831.

27. Ibid., July 26, 1831.

28. *Baltimore Republican and Commercial Advertiser*, Sept. 14, 20, 30, Oct, 2, 3, 1833, cited in Andrews and Bliss, *Women in Trade Unions*, pp. 38–39.

29. *Baltimore Republican and Commercial Advertiser*, Sept. 14, 1835, cited in Andrews and Bliss, *Women in Trade Unions*, p. 39.

30. *Working Man's Advocate*, June 9, 17, 1835.

31. Ibid., June 23, 1835.

32. SUMNER, "History of Women in Industry," p. 125.

33. *Lynn Record*, Jan. 1, 1834; Andrews and Bliss, *Women in Trade Unions*, p. 41; Alan Dawley, *Class and Community: The Industrial Revolution in Lynn* (Cambridge, Mass., 1977), chap. 1.

34. SUMNER, "History of Women in Industry," p. 168.

35. ANDREWS AND BLISS, *Women in Trade Unions*, pp. 42–43.

36. *Lynn Record*, Jan. 8, 1834.

37. Ibid.

38. Ibid., Mar. 12, 1834; *The Man*, Mar. 12, 1834; *Boston Courier*, Mar. 11, 1834; Andrews and Bliss, *Women in Trade Unions*, p. 44.

39. *Pennsylvanian*. Mar. 25, 28, 1836.

40. *National Laborer*, Apr. 2, 1836.

41. *Pennsylvanian*, Apr. 1, 4, 1836; *National Laborer*, Apr. 16, 23, 30, June 6, 13, 1836.

42. *Baltimore Republican and Commercial Advertiser*, Sept. 14, 1833.

43. PHILIP S. FONER, ed., *The Democratic-Republican Societies. 1790–1800: A Documentary Sourcebook of Constitutions, Declarations, Addresses, Resolutions, and Toasts* (Westport, Conn., 1976), pp. 13, 104, 205, 220, 225, 227, 229, 230, 253, 309, 354, 392.

44. JOHN R. COMMONS and Associates, *History of Labour in the United States* (New York, 1918), 1:88–106; Foner, *History of the Labor Movement,* 1:60–68.

45. New York *Evening Post,* July 13, 1819.

46. *American Citizen* (New York), April 10, 1809. See also ibid., June 23, 1810.

47. *Mechanics' Free Press,* Apr. 2, 1831. See also issues of Apr. 9, 16, 23, 30, 1831.

48. See *Address to the People of Philadelpha in the Walnut Street Theatre on the Morning of the Fourth of July, Common Era 1829, and the Fifty-fourth Year of Independence by Frances Wright* (New York, 1829). For the events leading up to Wright's speech and its influence, *see* Philip S. Foner, ed., *We, the Other People: Alternative Declarations of Independence by Labor Groups, Farmers, Women's Rights Advocates, Socialists, and Blacks, 1829–1975* (Urbana, Ill.), pp. 3–6.

49. New York *Daily Sentinel,* Aug. 21, 1830.

50. *Working Man's Advocate,* Jan. 2, 1830. The proposal was made by Cornelius Camden Blatchly. David Harris calls Blatchly's essay, *Some Causes of Popular Poverty, Arising from the Enriching Nature of Interest, Investigated in Their Principles and Consequences* (published in 1817), "the first significant contribution to modern socialist theory in the United States," since Blatchly affirmed "both the right of those who work to receive the full product of their labor and the right of every person to his just share in the ownership of the common materials of the world which are in existence at the time he is born" (*Socialist Origins in the United States: American Forerunners of Marx, 1817–1832* [Assen, Holland, 1966], p. 10).

51. New York *Daily Sentinel,* Mar. 27, 1830: *Working Man's Advocate,* Apr. 12, 1834.

52. *National Laborer,* Apr. 16, 1836.

53. JOHN BORDEN, "The Association of Working People of New Castle, Delaware: The First Labor Party of Delaware" (Master's thesis, University of Delaware, 1927), pp. 54–55.

54. Ibid., p. 36; Foner, *History of the Labor Movement,* 1:126.

55. *Proceedings of the Government and Citizens of Philadelphia on the Reduction of the Hours of Labor, and Increase of Wages* (Boston, 1835), p. 9.

56. See, in this connection, Bettina Eileen Berch, "Industrialization and Working Women in the Nineteenth Century: England, France, and the United States" (Ph.D. diss., University of Wisconsin, Madison, 1976)," pp. 241–43.

57. *Mechanics' Free Press,* July 15, 1829.

58. Quoted in Berch, "Industrialization and Working Women," pp. 244–45.

59. "Report of the Committee on Female Labor to the National Trades' Union," *National Laborer,* Nov. 12, 1836, reprinted in John R. Commons, et al., eds., *A Documentary History of American Industrial Society* (Cleveland, 1910) 1: 291–93.

60. SETH LUTHER, *An Address on the Origin and Progress of Avarice, and Its Deleterious Effects on Human Happiness* (Boston, 1834), p. 3.

Chapter 4: The Battle for the Ten-Hour Day

1. SAMUEL REZNECK, "The Social History of an American Depression, 1837–1843," *American Historical Review* 40 (July 1935): 663–67; Foner, *History of the Labor Movement,* 1:167–68.

2. FONER, *American Labor Songs of the Nineteenth Century* (Urbana, Ill., 1975), p. 45.

3. NORMAN J. WARE, *The Industrial Worker, 1840–1860* (Boston and New York, 1924), p. 74.

4. *Voice of Industry,* July 3, 1845.

5. There is no biographical sketch of either Huldah J. Stone or Mehitabel Eastman in any biographical collections on American women, not even in the three-volume *Notable American Women,* ed. Edward T. James, Janet Wilson James, and Paul S. Boyer (Cambridge, Mass., 1971). There is a sketch of Sarah G. Bagley in vol. 1, but a more complete one may be found in Madeline B. Stern, *We the Women: Career Firsts of Nineteenth-Century America* (New York, 1963), pp. 84–94. Strangely, Stern lists Sarah Bagley as "America's First Woman Telegrapher" (which she was), but not as what she also was, America's first women labor leader. For biographical discussions of Huldah J. Stone, Mehitabel Eastman, and Sarah G. Bagley, see Philip S. Foner, *The Factory Girls: A Collection of Writings on Life and Struggles in the New England Factories of the 1840's by the Factory Girls Themselves, and The Story, in Their Own Words, of the First Trade Unions of Women Workers in the United States* (Urbana, Ill., 1977).

6. FONER, *History of the Labor Movement,* 1:193.

7. HARRIET H. ROBINSON, *Loom and Spindle: Of Life Among the Early Mill Girls* (New York, 1898), pp. 62–63.

8. RAY GINGER, "Labor in a Massachusetts Cotton Mill, 1853–1860," *Business History Review* 28 (March 1954): 67–91; Stephen Thernstrom, *Poverty and Progress* (Cambridge, Mass., 1964), pp. 126–31.

9. FONER, *American Labor Songs,* p. 66; Foner, *Factory Girls,* p. 25; Shlakman, "Economic History of a Factory Town: A study of Chicopee, Massachusetts," *Smith College Studies in History* 20 (Northampton, Mass., 1935): 135–36.

10. HANNAH JOSEPHSON, *The Golden Threads: New England's Mill Girls and Magnates* (New York, 1949), p. 281.

11. For the emergence of these magazines and excerpts from their contents, see Foner, *Factory Girls,* pp. 25–53. See also Bertha M. Stearns, "Early Factory Magazines in New England," *Journal of Economic and Business History* 2 (August 1930): 92–95.

12. WILLIAM SCORESBY, *American Factories and Their Female Operatives* (1845; reprint ed., New York, 1968), p. 88; *Old South Leaflets* 3, no. 151 (Boston, 1885); Charles Dickens, *American Notes* (New York, 1842), p. 77.

13. ORESTES S. BROWNSON, "The Laboring Classes," *Boston Quarterly Review* 3

(July 1840): 112–15; Ibid. (October 1840): 46; "A Factory Girl," *Lowell Offering* 1 (December 1840): 16–23; Foner, *Factory Girls*, pp. 27–28.

14. Published in *Working Man's Advocate,* Jan. 17, 1846.

15. ROBERT G. LAYER, "Wages, Earnings. and Output in Four Cotton Textile Companies in New England, 1825–1860" (Ph.D. diss., Harvard University, 1952), p. 176. A published summary of Layer's thesis is available as *Earnings of Cotton Mill Operatives, 1825–1914* (Cambridge, Mass., 1955).

16. *Lowell Offering* 3 (September 1840): 43, 284.

17. Ibid., 3 (October 1843): 56–57; Foner, *History of the Labor Movement.* p. 194; Lucy Larcom, *A New England Girlhood* (Boston, 1890), pp. 222–23; Gerda Lerner, "The Lady and the Mill Girl: Changes in the Status of Women in the Age of Jackson," *American Studies Journal* 10 (Spring 1969): 6–8.

18. WARE, *The Industrial Worker,* p. 121; *Voice of Industry,* July 3, 1845.

19. ALLAN MACDONALD, "Lowell: A Commercial Utopia," *New England Quarterly* 10 (March 1937): 44; *Awl* (Lynn), July 26, 1845; Foner, *History of the Labor Movement,* p. 198.

20. S.G.B., "Pleasures of Factory Life," *Lowell Offering* 1 (December 1840): 23–26; S.G.B., "Tales of Factory Life. No. 1," ibid., 3 (February 1842): 65–68; *Lowell Advertiser,* July 10, 1845; *Voice of Industry,* July 10, 1845.

21. *Voice of Industry,* July 17, 1845, Jan. 2, 1846; *Lowell Advertiser,* July 15, 26, 1845; Foner, *Factory Girls,* pp. 61–68.

22. FONER, *Factory Girls,* pp. 74–75; Stearns, "Early Factory Magazines," pp. 93–98.

23. *Voice of Industry,* May 8. 1846.

24. See "The Factory Girls Expose the 'Beauty of Factory Life,'" in Foner, *Factory Girls,* pp. 74–95, and "Operative" in ibid., p. 311.

25. *Factory Girls,* Jan. 15, 1845.

26. *Voice of Industry,* May 29, June 5, 10, 12, 1845; Andrews and Bliss, *Women in Trade Unions,* pp. 71–72.

27. *Voice of Industry,* Feb. 27, 1846. The constitution is also reproduced in Foner, *Factory Girls,* pp. 104–6.

28. *Voice of Industry,* Dec. 19, 26, 1845, Jan. 9, May 5, Nov. 13, 1846; *Young America,* Nov. 15, 1845.

29. *Voice of Industry,* Nov. 7, 1845.

30. Ibid., Sept. 5, 1845. See also *Working Man's Advocate,* Mar. 8, 1845.

31. FONER, *History of the Labor Movement,* 1:198; *Voice of Industry,* Nov. 7, 1845, Mar. 6, 13, 1845.

    For descriptions by Bagley, Stone, and Eastman of their speaking tours, see "Three Pioneer Woman Labor Leaders," in Foner, *Factory Girls,* pp. 159–211.

32. *Voice of Industry,* Jan. 9, 1846; "The Female Department of the *Voice of Industry,*" Foner, *Factory Girls,* pp. 42–56.

33. *Voice of Industry,* Feb. 20, 1846; "Factory Tracts No. 1," Boston Public Library, Rare Book Room; "The Factory Tracts," in Foner, *Factory Girls,* pp. 130–41.

34. *Voice of Industry,* Jan. 9, Apr. 17, Nov. 28, 1846.

35. Originally published in *Voice of Industry,* Nov. 7, 1845, and reprinted in "Factory Tracts No. 1," and in Foner, *Factory Girls,* pp. 138–40, and Foner, *American Labor Songs of the Nineteenth Century,* p. 59.

36. "Slavery, North and South," by a "Ten Hour Woman," in *Mechanic* (Fall River), Oct. 5. 1844, and *Manchester Operative,* reprinted in ibid., Nov. 2, 1844.

37. *Lowell Advertiser,* Feb. 10, 1845.

38. *Voice of Industry,* Sept. 25, 1845, Jan. 23, 1846. For these and other antislavery writings of the female operatives, see Foner, *Factory Girls,* pp. 275–79.

39. *Lowell Advertiser,* Feb. 10, 1845; *Voice of Industry,* Dec. 26, 1845.

40. FONER, *Factory Girls,* pp. 282–88.

41. ROBINSON, *Loom and Spindle,* p. 133. The article by "Ella" was entitled "Woman," and appeared in the *Lowell Offering* 2 (January 1841): 129–35; it is reprinted in Foner, *Factory Girls,* pp. 38–44.

42. *Lowell Offering* 2 (January 1841): 132–35; "Woman's Rights," in Foner, *Factory Girls,* pp. 293–323.

43. See *Lowell Offering,* December 1840, pp. 12–13; January 1841, pp. 125–29, and *Operatives' Magazine,* April 1841. pp. 12–14; March 1842, pp. 15–17.

44. *Factory Girls' Album,* Mar. 14, 1846, Feb. 15, 1847; *Voice of Industry,* Aug. 14, 1847; Foner *Factory Girls,* pp. 295–99.

45. *Factory Girls' Album,* Apr. 25, 1846; *Voice of Industry,* Apr. 2, 1847.

46. *Voice of Industry,* Jan. 22, 1847; Foner. *Factory Girls,* pp. 316–19.

47. See "Three Pioneer Women Labor Leaders," in Foner, *Factory Girls,* pp. 159–211.

48. *Voice of Industry,* July 13, 1847; Foner, *Factory Girls,* pp. 191–93.

49. *Voice of Industry,* July 13, Sept. 10, 1847; Foner, *Factory Girls,* pp. 192, 202.

50. *New Era of Industry,* Aug. 3, 1848.

51. For the ten-hour movement prior to 1840, see Foner, *History of the Labor Movement,* 1:102–3, 115–18, 130, 160, 163.

52. WARE, *The Industrial Worker,* pp. 129–30.

53. The arguments are presented in "The Demand for the Ten-Hour Day," Foner, *Factory Girls,* pp. 215–18.

54. *Voice of Industry,* Sept. 18, 1845; Foner, *Factory Girls,* pp. 180–81.

55. LAYER, "Wages, Earnings," pp. 496–503; *Voice of Industry,* Jan. 9, May 15, 1846.

56. JOHN R. COMMONS and ASSOCIATES, *History of Labour in the United States* (New York: 1918), 1:550–62; John R. Commons, et al., eds., *A Documentary History of American Industrial Society* (Cleveland, 1910), 8:23–25; Foner, *History of the Labor Movement,* 1:202.

57. For the petitions of 1842 and 1843 and the formation of the New England Workingmen's Association, see Foner, *History of the Labor Movement,* 1:202–7.

58. *Voice of Industry,* June 5, 1845. Bagley's speech is reprinted in Foner, *Factory Girls,* pp. 108–10.

59. *Voice of Industry,* Jan. 15, 1845; Massachusetts, House, *House of Representatives of the Commonwealth of Massachusetts During the Session of the General Court A.D. 1845,* no. 50 (Boston, 1845), pp. 1–5.

60. Massachusetts, House, General Court, *House Document no. 5,* 1845, pp. 1–6, 15–17. The full report is published in Foner, *Factory Girls,* pp. 236–42.

61. *Lowell Offering* 5 (April 1845): 96.

62. *Lowell Advertiser,* Sept. 2, 1845.

63. Ibid., Nov. 10, 1845; *Voice of Industry,* Nov. 28, 1845.

64. *Pittsburgh Journal* and *Pittsburgh Spirit of Liberty,* reprinted in *Young America,* Nov. 15, 1845.

65. New York *Tribune,* Oct. 31, 1845; *Young America,* Nov. 15, 1845; *Lowell Advertiser,* Dec. 13, 1845.

66. CHARLES E. PERSONS, *Labor Laws and Their Enforcement* (New York, 1911), p. 41; *Young America.* Dec. 27, 1846.

67. Massachusetts, Senate, General Court, *Senate Document No. 81,* 1846, pp. 19, 21.

68. *Voice of Industry,* Dec. 29, 1845; Apr. 10, Nov. 3, 1846; *Factory Girls' Album,* Sept. 2, 1846.

69. *Voice of Industry,* July 29, 1847.

70. *Manchester* (N.H.) *Democrat,* Aug. 22, 1847; Foner, *Factory Girls.* pp. 266–69.

71. FONER, *History of Labor Movement,* 1:211.

72. *Voice of Industry,* Oct. 30, 1847.

Chapter 5: A New Era Dawns

1. *Voice of Industry,* May 8, 1846.

2. THOMAS LOUIS DUBLIN, "Women at Work: The Transformation of Work and Community in Lowell, Massachusetts, 1826–1860" (Ph.D. diss. Columbia University, 1975), pp. 222–23.

3. PHILIP S. FONER, *The Factory Girls: A Collection of Writings on Life and Struggles in the New England Factories of the 1840's by the Factory Girls Themselves, and the Story in Their Own Words, of the First Trade Unions of Women Workers in the United States* (Urbana, Ill., 1977), pp. 325–26.

4. *Voice of Industry.* Jan. 8, 1847; Foner, *Factory Girls,* pp. 328–30.

5. *Voice of Industry,* Mar. 25, 1847; Foner, *Factory Girls,* pp. 331–35.

6. *Voice of Industry,* Apr. 18, 1848.

7. FONER, *History of the Labor Movement,* 1:205–7, 211–12.

8. *Pittsburgh Evening Post,* July 3–6, 17–23, Aug. 23–28, 1848; New York *Tribune,* Aug. 28–29, 1848.

9. *Western Pennsylvania Magazine of History and Biography* 5 (April 1922): 203–11; Andrews and Bliss, *Women in Trade Unions,* pp. 64–65.

10. FONER, *History of the Labor Movement,* 1:213; New York *Tribune,* Aug. 29, 1848; J. Lynn Barnard, *Factory Legislation in Pennsylvania: Its History and Administration* (Philadelphia, 1907), pp. 64–70.

11. *Pittsburgh Evening Post,* Sept. 1, 1848; Bertha M. Stearns, "Early Factory Magazines in New England," *Journal of Economic and Business History* 2 (August 1930): 102.

12. MARTHA HALLINGWORTH in *Voice of Industry,* Apr. 18, 1848.

13. H. E. BACK to Harriet H. Hanson, Lowell, 7 September 1846, in Harriet H. Robinson Manuscript Collection, Schlesinger Library, Radcliffe College, Cambridge, Mass., and reprinted in Foner, *Factory Girls,* pp. 333–35, and in Allis Rosenberg Wolfe, "Letters of a Lowell Mill Girl and Friends: 1845–1846," *Labor History* 17 (Winter 1976): 101–02.

14. *New England Offering,* April 1848, pp. 2–3; Foner, *Factory Girls,* pp. 336–37.

15. DUBLIN, "Women at Work," p. 218.

16. Ibid., p. 228.

17. Massachusetts, Bureau of Statistics of Labor, *Eleventh Annual Report (1880),* "Strikes in Massachusetts," pp. 9–14.

18. DUBLIN, "Women at Work," p. 228.

19. FONER, *History of the Labor Movement,* 1:216.

20. DUBLIN, "Women at Work," pp. 225–28.

21. New York *Tribune,* May 27, 1851; *New York Times,* Nov. 8, 1853.

22. ROBERT ERNST, *Immigrant Life in New York City, 1825–1936* (New York, 1949), pp. 48–52; Carl Degler, "Labor in the Economy and Politics of New York City: A Study of the Impact of Early Industrialism" (Ph.D. diss., Columbia University, 1957), pp. 135–38; William Burns, *Life in New York* (New York, 1851), pp. 26–35.

23. BARBARA WERTHEIMER, *We Were There: The Story of Working Women in America* (New York, 1977), p. 101.

24. New York *Tribune,* Nov. 14, 1850; New York *Citizen,* Feb. 25, Mar. 18, 1854; Philadelphia *Evening Bulletin,* Aug. 15, 1857.

25. FONER, *History of the Labor Movement,* 1:221–23.

26. Ibid., p. 222; John R. Commons and Associates, *History of Labour in the United States* (New York, 1918), 1:596.

27. *Cleveland Herald,* Aug. 19, 29, 1850.

28. Commons and Associates, *History of Labour,* p. 595.

29. New York *Tribune,* June 8. 1853; also quoted in Virginia Penny, *Think and Act* (Philadelphia, 1869), p. 84. See also Carol Groneman, "She Earns as a Child; She Pays as a Man: Women Workers in a Mid-Nineteenth-Century New York City Community," in Milton Cantor and Bruce Laurie, eds., *Class, Sex, and the Woman Worker,* (Westport, Conn., 1977), p. 130.

30. New York *Tribune,* June 8, 1853.

31. *Cincinnati Enquirer,* Jan. 30, 1852.

32. Ibid., Apr. 12, 1853.

33. Ibid., Apr. 26, 1853.

34. JAMES MATTHEWS MORRIS, "The Road to Trade Unionism: Organized Labor in Cincinnati to 1896" (Ph.D. diss., University of Cincinnati, 1969), p. 82.

35. Ibid., p. 83.

36. Philadelphia *Public Ledger,* Philadelphia *Evening Bulletin,* Feb. 15-16, 1850; New York *Tribune,* Feb. 23, 1850.

37. JOHN FERGUSON, "George Lippard and the Brotherhood of Man," *Pennsylvania Magazine of History and Biography* 94 (April 1954): 132-34.

38. *Philadelphia Tailoress Company* (Philadelphia, 1850), pp. 5-6. I am indebted to Professor Ron Benson of Millersville State College for kindly furnishing me with a copy of the pamphlet.

39. *A General Report of the Industrial Union, with a Statistical Account of the Operations of the Tailoress' Cooperative Store* (Philadelphia, 1853). Copy in Library Company of Philadelphia.

40. PHILIP S. FONER, *American Labor Songs of the Nineteenth Century* (Urbana, Ill., 1975), p. 76.

41. RUTH DELZELL, "Women and the Labor Movement." *Life and Labor* 6 (July 1916): 21.

42. ANDREWS AND BLISS, *Women in Trade Unions,* p. 83.

43. FONER, *History of the Labor Movement,* 1:234-35; Commons and Associates, *History of Labour,* pp. 550-51.

44. EDGARD BARCLAY CALE, *The Organization of Labor in Philadelphia, 1850-1870* (Philadelphia, 1940), p. 6.

45. Quoted in Andrews and Bliss, *Women in Trade Unions,* p. 60.

46. ALAN DAWLEY, *Class and Community: The Industrial Revolution in Lynn* (Cambridge, Mass., 1977), pp. 38-64.

47. *Newburyport Daily Herald,* Feb. 24, 1860; *Boston Advertiser,* Mar. 21, 1860; *Haverhill Gazette,* Feb. 24, 1860; *Lynn Weekly Reporter,* Apr. 7, 1860; New York *Herald,* Feb. 27, 1860; Massachusetts, Bureau of Statistics of Labor, *Eleventh Annual Report, 1880,* pp. 17-19; *Boston Traveller,* Feb. 25, 26, 1860.

48. *Lynn Weekly Reporter,* Jan. 21, 1860; Phillips Barry, "The Fall of the Pemberton Mill," *Bulletin of the Folksong of the North East* 3 (Fall 1931): 16-17.

49. *Boston Traveller,* Feb. 15, 1860; New York *Herald,* Feb. 26, 1860; *Lynn News,* Feb. 22, 1860.

50. *Boston Traveller,* Feb. 28, 1860; *Newburyport Daily Herald,* Feb. 29, 1860; *Lynn Weekly Reporter,* Mar. 3, 1860.

51. *Lynn Weekly Reporter,* Mar. 6, 1860; *New York Times,* Mar. 8, 1860.

52. *New York Times,* Mar. 8, 1860.

53. New York *Herald,* Feb. 27, Mar. 1, 1860.

54. *Newburyport Daily Herald,* Mar. 7, 1860; Foner, *History of the Labor Movement,* 1:243; *New York Times,* Mar. 7, 1860.

55. *Lynn News,* Mar. 7, 1860; *Lynn Weekly Reporter,* Mar. 10, 1860; *New York Times,* Mar. 7, 1860.

56. *Lynn Weekly Reporter,* Mar. 10, 1860.

57. Ibid., Mar. 12, 1860; *Lynn News,* Mar. 12, 1860.

58. *Lynn Weekly Reporter,* Mar. 24, 1860, Mar. 10, 17, 1860.

59. *Lynn News,* Mar. 21, 1860; *Lynn Weekly Reporter,* Mar. 10, 1860; *Boston Advertiser, Boston Courier, New York Times,* Mar. 8, 1860.

60. *Boston Bee,* Feb. 23, 1860; *Newburyport Daily Herald,* Feb. 29, 1860.

61. *Springfield Republican,* Mar. 2, 1860; *Newburyport Daily Herald,* Mar. 23, 1860; Dawley, *Class and Community,* p. 112.

62. *Lynn Weekly Reporter,* Apr. 7, 1860.

63. *Boston Courier,* Feb. 27, 28, 1860.

64. *Lynn News,* Mar. 7, 1860; John G. Nicolay and John Hay, eds., *Complete Works of Abraham Lincoln* (New York, 1905), 5:247-50; Foner, *History of the Labor Movement,* 1:292.

65. *Lynn Weekly Reporter,* Apr. 14, 21, 1860.

66. *American Workman,* Feb. 29, 1869.

Chapter 6: Black Women before the Civil War

1. For a useful introduction to the subject of slave women, see Gerda Lerner, ed., *Black Women in White America: A Documentary History* (New York, 1972), pp. 7-65.

2. JOSIAH HENSON, *Father Henson's Story of His Own Life,* (New York, 1962), pp. 12-13.

3. ROBERT S. STAROBIN. *Industrial Slavery in the Old South* (New York, 1970). pp. 64-72.

4. EUGENE D. GENOVESE, *Roll, Jordan, Roll: The World the Slaves Made* (New York, 1974), pp. 495, 497.

5. RICHARD WADE, *Slavery in the Cities* (Chicago, 1958), pp. 46-50.

6. HUGH P. WILLIAMSON, "The State against Celia, A Slave," *Midwest Journal* 8 (Spring-Fall 1956): 408-20.

7. ULRICH B. PHILLIPS, *American Negro Slavery* (New York, 1918), pp. 303-4; Ulrich B. Phillips, "Plantation and Frontier Documents," in John R. Commons, et al., eds. *A Documentary History of American Industrial Society* (Cleveland, 1910), 2:31; W. W. Siebert, *The Underground Railroad from Slavery to Freedom* (New York, 1899), pp. 28-29, 152.

8. ROBIN WINK, *The Negro in Canada* (New Haven, 1972), pp. 144-56.

9. WILLIAM STILL, *The Underground Railroad* (Philadelphia, 1872), pp. 608-10;

10. WILLIAM CRAFT, *Running a Thousand Miles for Freedom, or, The Escape of William and Ellen Craft from Slavery* (London, 1860).

11. PHILIP S. FONER, ed., *The Life and Writings of Frederick Douglass,* (New York, 1975), 5:391.

12. GILBERT H. BARNES AND DWIGHT L. DUMOND, eds., *Letters of Theodore Dwight Weld, Angelina Grimké Weld, and Sarah Grimké, 1822-1844* (New York, 1934), 1:234.

13. SARAH E. BRADFORD, *Scenes in the Life of Harriet Tubman* (Auburn, N.Y., 1869), pp. 10–33; Earl Conrad, Harriet Tubman (Washington, 1943), pp. 15–102; Mary T. Higgenson, ed., *Letters and Journals of Thomas Wentworth Higgenson, 1846–1906* (Boston, 1913), pp. 52–53.

14. SUSIE KING TAYLOR, *Reminiscences of My Life in Camp* (reprint ed., New York, 1968), p. 6.

15. *African Repository* 16 (November 1851): 146.

16. CARTER G. WOODSON AND LORENZO J. GREENE. *The Negro Wage Earner* (1930, reprint ed., New York, 1969), p. 213; Jean Collier Brown, "The Economic Status of Negro Women," *Southern Workman* 60 (October 1931): 430–31.

17. *Frederick Douglass' Paper,* June 17, 1852.

18. W. E. B. DU BOIS, *The Philadelphia Negro* (Philadelphia. 1899), p. 143; E. Franklin Frazier, *The Negro Family in the United States* (Chicago, 1969), p. 148; Philip S. Foner, *Organized Labor and the Black Worker, 1619–1973* (New York, 1974), pp. 5–6.

19. SHARON HARLEY, "Northern Black Female Workers: Jacksonian Era," in Sharon Harley and Rosalyn Terborg-Penn, eds., *The Afro-American Woman: Struggles and Images* (Port Washington, N.Y., 1978), p. 6.

20. ALAN DAWLEY, *Class and Community: The Industrial Revolution in Lynn* (Cambridge, Mass., 1977), pp. 128–29.

21. LEON F. LITWACK, *North of Slavery: The Negro in the Free States, 1790–1860* (Chicago, 1961), pp. 131–33.

22. PHILIP S. FONER, "The Battle to End Discrimination against Negroes on Philadelphia Street Cars: [Part I] Background and Beginning of the Battle," *Pennsylvania History* 40 [July 1973]: 261–92; ["Part II] The Victory," ibid. 40 (October 1973): 355–80.

23. FONER, *Organized Labor and the Black Worker,* p. 51.

24. BERT JAMES LOWENBERG AND RUTH BEGIN, eds., *Black Women in Nineteenth-Century American Life* (University Park. Pa., 1976), p. 189.

25. *Frederick Douglass' Paper,* Feb. 10, 1854; Philip S. Foner, ed., *Frederick Douglass on Women's Rights* (Westport, Conn., 1976), p. 18.

26. *Frederick Douglass' Monthly,* October 1859; Foner, *Frederick Douglass on Women's Rights,* p. 76.
    The reference to "no rights which white men are bound to respect" is to the language used by Chief Justice Roger B. Taney in the Dred Scott decision, March 6, 1857. In writing the majority decision rejecting Dred Scott's petition for freedom, Taney insisted that the Negro possessed "no rights which a white man is bound to respect."

Chapter 7: The Civil War

1. BARBARA WERTHEIMER, *We Were There: The Story of Working Women in America* (New York, 1977), p. 143.

2. CATHERINE V. SORAGHAN, "History of St. Louis, 1865–1876" (Master's thesis,

Washington University. 1936), pp. 2–4; U.S., Bureau of the Census, *Manufactures of the United States in 1860 Compiled from the Original Sections of the Eighth Census*, 1865; U.S., Bureau of the Census, *Manufactures of the United States in 1870, a Compendium of the Ninth Census*, 1872.

3. Ross K. Baker, "Entry of Women into Federal Job World—at a Price," *Smithsonian* 8 (July 1977): 83–85.

4. Virginia Penny, *Five Hundred Employments Adapted to Women* (Philadelphia, 1868), pp. 190–93, 301–11, 331–34; David Montgomery, *Beyond Equality: Labor and the Radical Republicans, 1862–1872* (New York, 1967), pp. 34–35.

5. "The Working Classes," *New York Times*, Mar. 17, 1869.

6. New York *Tribune*, Oct. 9, 14, 1863, Mar. 22, 1864; New York *Herald*, Nov. 14, 1863.

7. Philip S. Foner, *History of the Labor Movement in the United States* (New York, 1947), 1:338–40.

8. *Fincher's Trades' Review*, Nov. 21, 1863, Apr. 16, 1864.

9. Ibid., June 6, 1863.

10. *Boston Daily Evening Voice*, June 28, 1864.

11. *Fincher's Trades' Review*, Sept. 26, Dec. 26, 1863, Jan. 2, Apr. 30, 1864.

12. St. Louis *Daily Press*, Dec. 28, 1864, Feb. 26, Mar. 14, Sept. 6, 1865.

13. *Fincher's Trades' Review*, Apr. 8, 1865, *Boston Daily Evening Voice*, Apr. 8, 1865.

14. *Fincher's Trades' Review*, Mar. 11, 1865.

15. *Boston Daily Evening Voice*, Apr. 8, Nov. 28, May 30, 1865.

16. New York *Tribune*, Oct. 9, 14, 1863; New York *Herald*, Nov. 14, 16, 1863; *Fincher's Trades' Review*, Apr. 2, 1864; Agatha Young, *The Women and the Crisis* (New York, 1959), pp. 68–69.

17. *Fincher's Trades' Review*, Nov. 21, 1863; Foner, *History of the Labor Movement*, 1:343.

18. *Fincher's Trades' Review*, Nov. 21, 1863.

19. Ibid., Nov. 21, 28, 1863.

20. Ibid., June 25, 1864, Feb. 5, 1865.

21. Ibid., Feb. 5, 1865.

22. Ibid., June 10, 17, 24, 1865.

23. Ibid., Sept. 10, 1864, Apr. 29, 1865.

24. *Boston Daily Evening Voice*, Jan. 28, 1865; *Fincher's Trades' Review*, Feb. 4, 1865.

25. *Fincher's Trades' Review*, Feb. 4, 1865.

26. Ibid., Mar. 18, 1865.

27. *Boston Daily Evening Voice*, June 12, 1864; *Fincher's Trades' Review*, Aug. 13, 1864.

28. *Detroit Tribune*, Nov. 22, 1864; *Fincher's Trades' Review*, Dec. 3, 1864.

29. *Boston Daily Evening Voice*. Mar. 23, May 20, 1865.

30. Ibid., May 20, May 3, 1865.

31. PHILIP S. FONER, "The *Boston Daily Evening Voice:* A Labor Voice for Black Equality, 1864–1867," *Science & Society* 32 (Fall 1974): 238–39.

32. ALBON P. MAN, JR., "Labor Competition and the New York Draft Riots of 1863," *Journal of Negro History* 36 (October 1951): 380–88; Foner, *History of the Labor Movement,* 1:325–28.

33. *Christian Recorder,* Sept. 12, 1863.

34. *Fincher's Trades' Review,* Aug. 12, 1863; Philip S. Foner, "The Battle to End Discrimination Against Negroes on Philadelphia's Street Cars: [Part I] Background and Beginning of the Battle," *Pennsylvania History* 40 (July 1973): 278–79.

35. New York *Sun,* Nov. 5, 11, 13, Dec. 8, 9, 17, 1863.

36. Ibid., Nov. 21, Dec. 17, 1863.

37. Ibid., Feb. 18, 19, 20, 1864. Moses Beach's account of the origins of the union is in *Report of the Working Women's Protective Union, 1863–1894* (New York, 1894), p. 8.

38. Accounts of the Protective Union's activity include *New York Times,* Nov. 29, 1870, Apr. 26, 1875; New York *Tribune,* Dec. 9, 1879, Jan. 19, 1881, Nov. 10, 1885; U.S., Commission of Labor, *Fourth Annual Report, 1888,* p. 51; and the annual reports of the Working Women's Protective Union. A copy of the thirteenth annual report is in the Tamiment Library of New York University.

39. *Boston Daily Evening Voice,* May 20, 1865. See also issue of Mar. 2, 1867.

40. New York *Sun,* Aug. 15–17, 1867.

41. ANDREWS AND BLISS, *Women in Trade Unions,* pp. 54–59.

42. *Fincher's Trades' Review,* Dec. 2, 1864, Mar. 12, 1865; *Boston Daily Evening Voice,* April 15–16, 1865.

Chapter 8: The National Labor Union

1. *Boston Daily Evening Voice,* Jan. 12, 1865.

2. *New York Times,* June 16, 1865; New York *Herald,* July 14, 1865.

3. *Boston Daily Evening Voice,* Aug. 9, 1865, Dec. 18, 1866.

4. *Leslie's Magazine,* July 22, 1865.

5. *Boston Daily Evening Voice,* Nov. 8, 1865.

6. ANDREWS AND BLISS, *Women in Trade Unions,* pp. 106–7.

7. EDITH ABBOTT, *Women in Industry* (New York, 1910), p. 236; Horace Greeley and others, *The Great Industries of the United States* (Hartford, Conn., 1870), pp. 540–42.

8. Quoted in Ruth Delzell, "1866—Laundry Workers Union, Troy, N.Y.," *Life and Labor* 2 (November 1912): 333.

9. NANCY DUCATTE, "The Shirt and Collar Industry and Kate Mullaney," Troy, N.Y., undated paper, p. 3. Copy in library of Trade Union Women's Studies, Cornell University, 7 East 43rd Street, New York, N.Y.

10. *Boston Daily Evening Voice,* Apr. 2, 12, 1866; *Rochester Union and American,* May 16, 1866; *New York Times,* Dec. 26, 1866.

11. *Jackson* (Miss.) *Daily Clarion,* June 24, 1866. I am indebted to Ken Lawrence of the Deep South People's History Project, Tougaloo, Mississippi, for furnishing me with a copy of this issue of the *Daily Clarion.* A brief excerpt from the petition appears in Ken Lawrence, "Mississippi's First Labor Union," Tougaloo, Mississippi, Deep South People's History Project, Freedom Information Service, 974, mimeographed pamphlet.

12. "Resolutions of the International Industrial Assembly of North America," in John R. Commons, et al., eds., *A Documentary History of American Industrial Society* (Cleveland, 1910), 9:123.

13. *Fincher's Trades' Review,* Sept. 10, 1864.

14. JAMES C. SYLVIS, *The Life, Speeches, Labors and Essays of William H. Sylvis, Late President of the Iron-Moulders International Union and also of the National Labor Union* (Philadelphia, 1872), pp. 120, 217–22, 398–400; Jonathan Grossman, *William Sylvis, Pioneer of American Labor, A Study of the Labor Movement During the Civil War* (New York, 1945), pp. 98–99, 226–28, 229–32, 257–60; David Montgomery, *Beyond Equality: Labor and the Radical Republicans, 1862–1872* (New York, 1967), p. 234; Foner, *History of the Labor Movement,* 1:421–23.

15. "Resolutions of the Founding Convention of the National Labor Union," in Commons, et al., eds., *Documentary History of American Industrial Society,* 9: 135; Foner, *History of the Labor Movement,* 1:384–85; *The Address of the National Labor Congress to the Workingmen of the United States* (Chicago, 1867).

16. ABBOTT, *Women in Industry,* pp. 192–93; Andrews and Bliss, *Women in Trade Unions,* pp. 91–92; *Workingman's Advocate,* Apr. 12, 19, 1867.

17. *Workingman's Advocate,* Apr. 26, 1867.

18. ANDREWS AND BLISS, *Women in Trade Unions,* pp. 95–96.

19. *Workingman's Advocate,* Aug. 24, 31, 1867.

20. Admittedly this is a simplified presentation of one of the most complex issues in the history of the women's rights movement.

21. PHILIP S. FONER, ed., *Frederick Douglass on Women's Rights* (Westport, Conn., 1976). pp. 30, 151, 184.

22. KATHERINE ANTHONY, *Susan B. Anthony: Her Personal History and Her Era* (New York, 1954), p. 215.

23. *Revolution,* July 2, 1868.

24. Ibid., Sept. 21, 1868.

25. Ibid., Sept. 28, 1868.

26. Ibid., Dec. 3, 1868.

27. SYLVIS, *Life, Speeches,* pp. 229–31.

28. ELLEN DUBOIS, "A New Life: The Development of an American Woman Suffrage Movement, 1860–1869," (Ph.D. diss., Northwestern University, 1975), p. 196.

29. FONER, *Frederick Douglass on Women's Rights,* pp. 33–35.

30. *Revolution,* Sept. 28, 1868.

31. *Workingman's Advocate,* Oct. 1, 8, 15, 1868.

32. *Revolution,* Sept. 7, 1868.

33. Montgomery, *Beyond Equality,* p. 234.

34. New York *World,* Sept. 17, 23, 1868; New York *Tribune,* Sept. 23, 1868; *Revolution,* Sept. 21, 1868; Israel Kugler, "The Woman's Rights Movement and the National Labor Union (1866–1872)," (Ph.D. diss., New York University, 1954), p. 93; Dubois, "A New Life," pp. 206–8.

35. *Proceedings of the Second Session of the National Labor Congress in Convention Assembled at New York City, September 21, 1868* (Philadelphia, 1868), p. 4.

36. Karl Marx and Frederick Engels, *Selected Correspondence, 1845–1895* (New York, 1935), p. 255.

37. *Proceedings of the Second Session of the National Labor Congress,* pp. 8–10.

38. Ibid., p. 39; Kugler, "Woman's Rights Movement," p. 94.

39. Dubois," A New Life," pp. 210–11.

40. *Revolution,* Oct. 1, 1868.

41. *Workingman's Advocate,* Mar. 6, 13, 20, 1869; Sylvis, *Life, Speeches,* pp. 221–22.

42. Philip S. Foner, *Organized Labor and the Black Worker, 1619–1973* (New York, 1974), pp. 23–24.

43. New York *World,* Aug. 17, 1869; *Workingman's Advocate,* Sept. 4, 1869; *Revolution,* Sept. 7, 1869.

44. *Workingman's Advocate,* Sept. 4, 1869.

45. New York *World,* Aug. 17, 1869; Kugler, "Woman's Rights Movement," p. 100; Montgomery, *Beyond Equality,* pp. 398–99.

46. Dubois, "A New Life," p. 272.

47. *Workingman's Advocate,* Sept. 4, 1869.

48. Kugler, "Woman's Rights Movement," p. 193.

49. *Revolution,* Sept. 7, 1869.

50. Foner, *Frederick Douglass on Women's Rights,* p. 30.

51. Parker Pillsbury in *Revolution,* Sept. 7, 1869.

52. *National Anti-Slavery Standard,* Nov. 30, 1869, and reprinted in Philip S. Foner and Ronald L. Lewis, eds., *The Black Worker: A Documentary History from Colonial Times to the Present,* (Philadelphia, 1978), 2:16–17.

53. *Proceedings of the Colored National Labor Convention Held in Washington, D.C., on December 6, 7, 8, 9, 10, 1869* (Washington, D.C., 1870), pp. 43–44, 55–58, and reprinted in Foner and Lewis, *The Black Worker,* pp. 36–39, 49–50. For the story of the Colored National Labor Union, see Foner, *Organized Labor and the Black Worker,* pp. 30–46.

54. *Revolution,* July 25, 1869.

55. Dubois, "A New Life," p. 203.

56. *Revolution,* Aug. 26, 1869.

57. *Workingman's Advocate,* Apr. 23, June 25, Aug. 27, 1870.

58. Andrews and Bliss, *Women in Trade Unions,* p. 88.

59. FONER, *History of the Labor Movement,* 1:387.

60. *New York Times,* Aug. 10, 1871.

Chapter 9: Workingwomen's Associations

1. *New York Times,* Sept. 18, 1868.

2. Ibid., Oct. 14, 1868.

3. Ibid., Nov. 6, 1868.

4. Ibid.

5. Ibid.

6. NANCY F. COTT, *The Bonds of Womanhood* (New Haven, Conn., 1977), p. 232.

7. GEORGE A. STEVENS, *New York Typographical Union No. 6: A Study of a Modern Trade Union and Its Predecessors* (Albany, N.Y., 1912), pp. 422, 427.

8. *The Lily,* Jan. 2, 16, Feb. 1, Mar. 1, 15, May 1, 1854; Larle Ann Porter, "Amelia Bloomer: An Early Iowa Feminist's Sojourn on the Way West," *Annals of Iowa* 41 (1973): 1250-53.

9. *Fincher's Trades' Review,* Feb. 4, 1865; *Revolution,* Oct. 15, 1868; *Nation,* Feb. 11, 1869; Ellen Carroll Dubois, "A New Life: The Developments of the Woman Suffrage Movement, 1860-1869," (Ph.D. diss., Northwestern University, 1975), p. 226.

10. *Report of the Proceedings of the Fifteenth Annual Session of the National Typographical Union, held in the City of Memphis, Tennessee, June 3-7, 1867* (New York, 1867), p. 4.

11. New York *World,* Sept. 20, 27, 1868.

12. *Ibid.,* Sept. 20, 27, 1868; Stevens, *Typographical Union No. 6,* pp. 431-32.

13. New York *World,* Sept. 27, 1868; Stevens, *Typographical Union No. 6,* p. 432.

14. *Revolution,* Mar. 19, 1868; Stevens, *Typographical Union No. 6,* p. 431.

15. *Revolution,* Sept. 10, 1868.

16. Ibid., Sept. 24, Oct. 1, 1868.

17. *Revolution,* Sept. 10, 1868.

18. Ibid., Sept. 24, 1868.

19. Ibid., Oct. 1, 1868.

20. Ibid., Oct. 8, 15, 1868.

21. Ibid., Oct. 22, 1868.

22. Ibid., Oct. 8, 1868.
    Stevens, in his history of Local No. 6, gives the union the credit for initiating the unionization of women printers, but he makes no mention of the previous independent organization of the female typesetters *(Typographical Union No. 6, p. 422).* This is also the viewpoint of Elizabeth Baker, *Technology and Women's Work,* (New York, 1964), p. 116. For a more accurate view, see Dubois, "A New Life," pp. 240-44.

23. Stevens, *Typographical Union No. 6*, pp. 433–34; Dubois, "A New Life," pp. 263–64.

24. Stevens, *Typographical Union No. 6*, pp. 433–34; *New York Times*, Mar. 17, 1869.

25. *Revolution*. Oct. 8, 1868; New York *World*, Feb. 13, 1869.

26. Stevens, *Typographical Union No. 6*, p. 433; Dubois. "A New Life," p. 266.

27. *Workingman's Advocate*, Feb. 13, 20, 1869; New York *World*, Feb. 1, 1869; Alice Henry, *The Trade Union Woman* (New York, 1915), p. 252; Dubois, "A New Life," p. 267.

28. The best account of the conflict and its effects on the Working Women's Association is in Dubois, "A New Life." pp. 246–74.

29. *Revolution*, Oct. 1, 1868.

30. Ibid.

31. Foner, *History of the Labor Movement*, 1:417–22.

32. Edward T. James, Janet Wilson James, and Paul S. Boyer, eds., *Notable American Women, 1607–1950* (Cambridge, Mass., 1971), 1:362.

33. *Revolution*, Oct. 29, Nov. 12, Dec. 10, 1868; Susan B. Anthony to Anna Dickinson, 27 October 1868, Anna Dickinson Papers, Library of Congress; Dubois, "A New Life," pp. 253–56.

34. *Revolution*, July 2, 1869.

35. Dubois, "A New Life," p. 261.

36. Ibid., p. 274.

37. Lynne Masel-Walters, "'Their Rights and Nothing More,' A History of the *Revolution*, 1868–1870," *Journalism Quarterly* 53 (Summer, 1976): 249–51.

38. *New York Times*, May 25, 1869; *Revolution*, May 20, 1869.

39. Dubois. "A New Life," p. 262.

40. Andrews and Bliss, *Women in Trade Unions*, p. 107; Foner, *History of the Labor Movement*, 1:383; *Workingman's Advocate*, May 1, 1869; Eleanor Flexner, *Century of Struggle* (Cambridge, Mass., 1959), pp. 138–39.

41. *Revolution*, Apr. 28, 1870, and reprinted in Rosalyn Baxandall, Linda Gordon, Susan Reverby, eds., *America's Working Women: A Documentary History 1600 to the Present*, (New York, 1976), p. 116.

42. *Workingman's Advocate*, Dec. 2, 1869.

43. Andrews and Bliss, *Women in Trade Unions*, p. 107; Flexner, *Century of Struggle*, pp. 138–39; Horace Greeley and others, *The Great Industries of the United States*, (Hartford, Conn.: 1870), p. 544.

44. The technological changes in the shoe industry may be traced in Blanche K. Hazard, *The Organization of the Boot and Shoe Industry in Massachusetts before 1875* (Cambridge, Mass., 1921), pp. 240–45, and in Alan Dawley, *Class and Community: The Industrial Revolution in Lynn* (Cambridge, Mass., 1977), pp. 92–95.

45. The traditional view of the origins, aims, and composition of the Knights of St. Crispin is Don Lescohier, "The Knights of St. Crispin, 1867–1874: A

Study on Industrial Causes of Trade Unionism," *Bulletin of the University of Wisconsin*, no. 355 (Madison, Wis., 1910). This is effectively challenged in Dawley, *Class and Community*, pp. 144–48.

46. ANDREWS AND BLISS,*Women in Trade Unions*, pp. 108–10; Dawley, *Class and Community*, pp. 143, 176–78.

47. ANDREWS AND BLISS, *Women in Trade Unions*, p. 109.

48. *Baltimore Sun*, Apr. 3, 4, 12, 14, 15, 17, 19, 22, May 12, 1871; *New York Times*, Apr. 19, 20, 25, May 12, 1871.

49. *Lynn Reporter*, Aug. 31, Sept. 1, 2, 1871; Dawley, *Class and Community*, p. 178.

50. *American Workman*, Aug. 7, Dec. 25, 1869, Feb. 25, Apr. 30, July 20, 1870; Andrews and Bliss, *Women in Trade Unions*, pp. 108–9.

51. ANDREWS AND BLISS, *Women in Trade Unions*, p. 109.

52. The resolutions are published in full in Flexner, *Century of Struggle*, p. 140. They also appear in full in Massachusetts, Bureau of Statistics of Labor, *Third Annual Report, (1872)*, pp. 434–36, and in *Lynn Reporter*, May 12, 1872. They are summarized in Dawley, *Class and Community*, pp. 178–79.

53. *Lynn Reporter*, Aug. 10, 17, 24, 1872; Dawley, *Class and Community*. p. 186.

54. LESCHOHIER, "Knights of St. Crispin," pp. 121–24; Andrews and Bliss, *Women in Trade Unions*, p. 109.

55. *Workingman's Advocate*, May 21, Aug. 12, 1870; *Report of Proceedings of the Nineteenth Annual Session of the International Typographical Union Held in Baltimore, Md., June 5, 6, 7 and 8, 1871* (Philadelphia, 1871), pp. 44–47; George A. Tracy, *History of the Typographical Union* (Indianapolis, 1913), pp. 263–64.

56. *Proceedings of the Nineteenth Annual Convention of the International Typographical Union . . . 1871*, p. 68; Stevens, *Typographical Union No. 6*, p. 437.

57. DUBOIS, "A New Life," p. 275; Flexner, *Century of Struggle*, p. 136; *Notable American Women*, 3:478–79.

58. *New York Times*, Oct. 25, 27, 1873.

59. Ibid., Apr. 7, 1872.

60. New York *Daily Graphic*, Oct. 12, 1873.

Chapter 10: The Long Depression

1. LEAH FEDER, *Unemployment Relief in Periods of Depression* (New York, 1936), pp. 38–40, 48; New York Association for Improving the Condition of the Poor, *Thirty-first Annual Report, 1874*, p. 29, and *Thirty-second Annual Report, 1875*, p. 33; Pennsylvania, Bureau of Labor Statistics, *Second Annual Report*, p. 464; Foner, *History of the Labor Movement*, 1:439.

2. New York *Bulletin*, reprinted in Montgomery (Alabama) *Advertiser and Mail*, Nov. 6, 1873.

3. *New York Times*, Dec. 14, 20, 1873; New York *Evening Mail*, Oct. 13, 1873;

Herbert G. Gutman, "Early Effects of the Depression of 1873 upon the Working Classes in New York City" (Master's thesis, Columbia University, 1950), pp. 55–56.

4. New York *Sun,* Nov. 27, 1873.

5. *Chicago Tribune,* Mar. 15, 1874.

6. Ibid., July 2, 1876.

7. *New York Times,* Dec. 20, 1873.

8. *Chicago Tribune,* Dec. 30, 31, 1873, Mar. 29, 1874; *Chicago Inter-Ocean,* Dec. 30, 1873; Kenneth Kann, "Workers' Culture and the Labor Movement in Chicago, 1845–1886" (Ph.D. diss., University of California, Berkeley, 1977), p. 18.

9. Chicago *Daily Tribune,* Dec. 20–23, 1873; *Workingman's Advocate,* Jan. 3, 1874; Feder, *Unemployment Relief,* pp. 51–53; Foner, *History of the Labor Movement,* 2:51–53.

10. HERBERT G. GUTMAN, "The Tompkins Square 'Riot' in New York City on January 13, 1874: A Re-examination of Its Causes and Its Aftermath," *Labor History,* 6 (Winter 1965): 44–48; New York *Sun,* Jan. 14–16, 1874; *New York Times,* Nov. 16, Dec. 12, 1873, Jan. 14–15, 1874; Foner, *History of the Labor Movement,* 1:446–48.

11. New York *Sun,* Oct. 14, 1873; *New York Times,* Dec. 12, 20, 1873.

12. *New York Times,* Mar. 2, 3, 15, Nov. 8, Dec. 3, 5, 1874.

13. New York *World,* Jan. 31, Feb. 21, 1874; New York *Tribune,* Jan. 27, 1874; New York *Herald,* Jan. 30, 31, 1874.

14. New York *Herald,* Jan. 29, 1874.

15. New York *World,* Feb. 4, 1874; New York *Tribune,* Feb. 4, 1874.

16. New York *Herald,* Jan. 30, 1874; New York *World,* Feb. 11, 1874.

17. New York *Tribune,* Feb. 10, 13, 1874; New York *Herald,* Feb. 14, 18, 21, 1874; *New York Times,* Feb. 17, 1874.

18. New York *World,* Feb. 17, 21, 1874; New York *Tribune,* Feb. 17, 24, 27, 1874; Gutman, "Early Effects of the Depression," pp. 133–34.

19. *New York Times,* Nov. 8, Dec. 3, 5, 1874.

20. THOMAS RUSSELL SMITH, *The Cotton Textile Industry of Fall River, Massachusetts* (New York, 1944), pp. 53–71; Sylvia C. Lintner, "A Social History of Fall River, 1859–1879" (Ph.D. diss., Radcliffe College, 1945). pp. 560–64; Philip T. Silvia, Jr., "The Position of Workers in a Textile Community: Fall River in the Early 1880's," *Labor History* 16 (Spring 1975): 230–31.

21. Massachusetts, Bureau of Labor Statistics, *Eleventh Annual Report, (1880),* p. 63; George E. McNeill, *The Labor Movement: The Problem of Today* (New York, 1887), pp. 223–28.

22. Massachusetts, Bureau of Labor Statistics, *Eleventh Annual Report, (1880),* pp. 35–44; Herbert J. Lahne, *The Cotton Mill Worker* (New York, 1944), p. 180; Silvia, "Position of Workers," p. 230.

23. *St. Louis Times,* July 10, 18, 22, Aug. 20, 22, 1876; St. Louis *Missouri Republi-*

can, July 22, 24, Aug. 20, 22, 1876; *Labor Standard,* Aug. 19, 1876; Philip S. Foner, *American Labor Songs of the Nineteenth Century* (Urbana, Ill., 1975), pp. 126–27.

24. The standard work on the Great Strike of 1877 is Robert Bruce, *1877: Year of Violence* (Indianapolis, 1959). A more recent study is Philip S. Foner, *The Grest Labor Uprising of 1877* (New York, 1977).

25. *Baltimore Sun,* July 20, 1877.

26. New York *Sun,* July 20, 1877.

27. RAY V. BROWN, "The Erie Railroad Strike of 1877 in Hornellsville, New York" (Senior thesis, History, Princeton University, 1951), pp. 58–62; *Hornell Times,* July 25, 1877.

28. *Chicago Tribune,* July 27, 1877.

29. *Chicago Times,* July 27, 1877; *Chicago Tribune,* July 27, 1877.

30. Chicago *Inter-Ocean,* July 27, 1877.

31. St. Louis *Missouri Republican,* July 26, 1877. See also David T. Burbank, *The Reign of the Rabble: The St. Louis General Strike of 1877* (New York, 1966), pp. 101–2.

32. *Galveston Daily News,* Aug. 1, 1877.

33. Ibid., Aug. 1, 2, 1877.

34. CHARLES RICHARD WILLIAMS, *The Diary and Letters of Rutherford Burchard Hayes* (Columbus, Ohio, 1924), 5:440.

35. LUCY STONE, "The Strikers and the Mob," *Woman's Journal,* July 28, 1877, p. 236.

36. *Cigar Makers' Official Journal,* January 1876, p. 12; February 1876, pp. 8–9; Andrews and Bliss, *Women in Trade Unions,* pp. 92–93; George E. McNeill, ed., *The Labor Movement: The Problem of Today* (New York, 1887), pp. 585–88.

37. SAMUEL GOMPERS, *Seventy Years of Life and Labor* (New York, 1925), 1:139–42.

38. *New York Times,* Dec. 1, 1877.

39. *Cigar Makers' Official Journal,* November 1877, pp. 3–4; December 1877, pp. 1–2; Andrews and Bliss, *Women in Trade Unions,* p. 93.

40. BERNARD MANDEL, *Samuel Gompers, A Biography* (Yellow Springs, Ohio, 1963), pp. 25–26; *Tobacco Leaf,* quoted in *Cigar Makers' Official Journal.* February 1878, p. 1.

41. BERNARD MANDEL, "The 'Great Uprising' of 1877," *Cigar Makers' Official Journal,* September 1967, pp. 3–5; Gompers, *Seventy Years,* 1:142–44.

42. New York *Herald,* June 18, 1876; *Nineteenth Annual Report, Home for Working Women* (Boston, 1897), copy in Schlesinger Library, Radcliffe College, Cambridge, Mass.

43. *New York Times,* June 2, 1878.

44. U.S., Congress, Senate, *Report of the Committee of the Senate upon the Relations between Labor and Capital and Testimony Taken by the Committee* 1885, 3:6, 28, 75, 452; McNeill, *Labor Movement,* pp. 588–95.

45. ALAN DAWLEY, *Class and Community: The Industrial Revolution in Lynn* (Cambridge, Mass., 1977), pp. 187–88.

46. LIZZIE SWANK HOLMES, "Women Workers of Chicago," *American Federationist* 12 (August 1905): 508-9.

47. *Labor Standard,* Mar. 24, May 5, 12, July 21, 1878, Jan. 4, 1879, Mar. 27, Apr. 20, 1880.

48. *Labor Standard* (New York), July 7, 14, 21, 28, Aug. 4, 11, 18, 25, Sept. 7, 14, 1878, and *Labor Standard* (Paterson), Nov. 23, Dec. 7, 1878. For a picture of the community support for the strikers, see Herbert Gutman, "Class, Status, and Community Power in Nineteenth-Century American Industrial Cities: Paterson, New Jersey: A Case Study," in Herbert Gutman, *Work, Culture, and Society in Industrializing America: Essays in Working-Class and Social History* (New York, 1977), pp. 234–48.

Chapter 11: The Knights of Labor

1. TERENCE V. POWDERLY, *Thirty Years of Labor, 1859–1889* (Columbus, 1890), pp. 534–35; Foner, *History of the Labor Movement,* 1:433–37.

2. HENRY J. BROWNE, *The Catholic Church and the Knights of Labor* (Washington, D.C., 1949), pp. 58–64; Powderly, *Thirty Years of Labor,* pp. 252–57, 359–61.

3. U.S., Department of Labor, Women's Bureau, Bulletin No. 225, *Handbook of Facts on Women Workers,* 1948, p. 1; U.S., Department of Labor, Women's Bureau, Bulletin No. 218, *Women's Occupations through Seven Decades,* 1947), pp. 208–23.

4. ANDREWS AND BLISS, *Women in Trade Unions,* pp. 113–16; Norman J. Ware, *The Labor Movement in the U.S.A., 1860–1895* (New York, 1929) pp. 88–89; Gerald Grob, *Workers and Utopia: A Study of Ideological Conflict in the American Labor Movement, 1865–1900* (Chicago, 1969), pp. 52–55; Philip S. Foner, *History of the Labor Movement in the United States* 2 (New York, 1955): 61.

5. Charlie to Powderly, 25 April, 1887; Powderly to Will C. Bailey, 25 April 1887; John A. Forsythe to Powderly, 24 May 1884; Powderly to Forsythe, 28 May 1884, Terence V. Powderly Papers, Catholic University (hereafter cited as Powderly Papers).

6. ANDREWS AND BLISS, "Women in Trade Unions," pp. 115–16; Foner, *History of the Labor Movement,* 2:61–62; "Report of the General Instructor and Director of Woman's Work," *Proceedings of the General Assembly of the Knights of Labor, 1889,* pp. 4–5.

7. FONER, *History of the Labor Movement,* 2:62; *New York Times,* 8 Sept. 1882; Elizabeth S. Bryant to Powderly, 1 February 1883; Powderly to Bryant, 8 February 1883, Powderly Papers.

8. U.S., Congress, House, *Report No. 447,* 49th Cong., 2d sess., 1887, p. 85; Andrews and Bliss, *Women in Trade Unions,* pp. 130–32; Alan Dawley, *Class*

and Community: The Industrial Revolution in Lynn (Cambridge, Mass., 1977), pp. 189–90.

9. *John Swinton's Paper,* Nov. 29, 1885, Jan. 3, 24, Feb. 28, Apr. 4, Apr. 11, 25, 1886.

10. CLAUDE GOLDIN, "Female Labor Force Participation: The Origin of Black and White Differences, 1870 and 1880," *Journal of Economic History* 37 (March 1977): 87–100.

11. PHILIP S. FONER, *Organized Labor and the Black Worker, 1619–1973* (New York, 1974), pp. 46–50; *Memphis Watchman,* reprinted in New York *Freeman,* Jan. 15, 1871, and in Cleveland *Gazette,* Jan. 22, 1887.

12. FONER, *Organized Labor and the Black Worker,* pp. 56–57; Sidney H. Kessler, "The Negro in the Knights of Labor" (Master's thesis, Columbia University, 1950), pp. 48–54; Kenneth Kann, "The Knights of Labor and the Southern Black Worker," *Labor History* 18 (Winter 1977): 54–55; Melton A. McLaurin, "The Racial Policies of the Knights of Labor and the Organization of Southern Black Workers," *Labor History* 17 (Fall 1976): 575–76; C. R. Alexander to Powderly, 14 October 1886, Powderly Papers.

13. FONER, *Organized Labor and the Black Worker,* pp. 53–55; McLaurin, "Racial Policies of the Knights of Labor," pp. 576–77; *Proceedings of the General Assembly of the Knights of Labor, 1887,* p. 1587; *Report of the International Council of Women Assembled by the National Woman Suffrage Association, Washington, D.C., U.S. of America. Mar. 25 to Apr. 1, 1888* (Washington, D.C., 1888), p. 155; *New York Times,* Sept. 8, 1883.

14. ANDREWS AND BLISS, p. 131; Foner, *History of the Labor Movement,* 2:62.

15. *Progress,* Mar. 26, 1885; *John Swinton's Paper,* June 5, Sept. 13, Oct. 11, 1885; Michael A. Gordon, "The Labor Boycott in New York City, 1880–1886," *Labor History* 16 (Spring 1975): 213–14.

16. *John Swinton's Paper,* Apr. 5, 1885.

17. MELECH EPSTEIN, *Jewish Labor in the U.S.A.: An Industrial, Political and Cultural History of the Jewish Labor Movement* (New York, 1950–53), 1:109; Louis Levine, *The Women Garment Workers,* (New York, 1924), pp. 32, 37–38; New York *Herald,* July 22, 28, 1883; New York *Tribune,* July 22, 1883; *New York Times,* July 22, 23, 28, Aug. 1, 2, 1883.

18. LIZZIE SWANK HOLMES, "Women Workers of Chicago." *American Federationist* 12 (August 1905): 508–9.

19. *Cohoes Daily News,* Mar. 12, 13, Apr. 15, May 14, June 16–17, July 20–23, Aug. 15–16, 1882; Daniel J. Walkowitz, "Working Class Women in the Gilded Age: Factory, Community, and Family Life among Cohoes, New York, Colton Workers," *Journal of Social History.* 5 (Summer, 1972): 486.

20. *New York Times,* Feb. 22, 1885; *Irish World,* Mar. 7, Apr. 4. 1885; Foner, *History of the Labor Movement,* 2:63; Gordon, "The Labor Boycott," p. 212.

21. *Yonkers Statesman,* Feb. 27, Mar. 6, May 15, 22, 1885; *John Swinton's Paper,* June 7, 1885.

22. *John Swinton's Paper,* May 24, 1885; Gordon, "The Labor Boycott," p. 213.

23. *Yonkers Statesman,* Aug. 22, 29, 1885; Foner, *History of the Labor Movement,* 2:64.

24. *New York Times,* June 6, 1886; *Journal of United Labor,* December 1883; *John Swinton's Paper,* Apr. 26, 1885; Gordon, "The Labor Boycott," p. 211; Foner, *History of the Labor Movement,* 2:64; David Montgomery, "Workers' Control of Machine Production in the 19th Century," *Labor History* 17 (Fall 1976): 500.

25. JAMES J. KENNEALLY, "Women and Trade Unions, 1870–1920: The Quandary of the Reformer," *Labor History* 14 (Winter 1973): 44; Powderly to Hayes, 22 December 1889, Powderly Papers.

26. Printed Circular marked "Received Nov 14, 1887," Powderly Papers.

27. *New York Times,* Aug. 31, 1886; *Journal of United Labor,* July 23, 1887; *Journal of the Knights of Labor,* quoted in Edward T. James, "More Corn, Less Hell? A Knights of Labor Glimpse of Mary Elizabeth Lease," *Labor History* 16 (Summer 1975): 408–9.

28. *Proceedings of the General Assembly of the Knights of Labor, 1886,* pp. 163–64, 287–89; Frances Willard, *Glimpses of Fifty Years* (Chicago, 1892), p. 523.

29. *Proceedings of the General Assembly of the Knights of Labor, 1886,* p. 952.

30. *Report of the International Council of Women,* p. 154; Andrews and Bliss, *Women in Trade Unions,* pp. 130–31; interview with Leonora M. Barry Lake in *St. Louis Post-Dispatch,* undated clipping in Leonora M. Barry Lake Folio, Sophia Smith Collection, Smith College Library.

31. Form 74, "Women's Work," File A1-38, Powderly Papers; *Proceedings of the General Assembly of the Knights of Labor, 1888,* p. 14.

32. *New London Telegraph,* Oct. 3, 1888, clipping in letter of L. M. Barry to Powderly, New London, Oct. 4, 1888, Powderly Papers.

33. LENORA M. BARRY to Powderly, 1 March 1888; Barry to Rev. Father McEnroe, 12 March 1888, copy in Powderly Papers; Foner, *History of the Labor Movement,* 2:65.

34. POWDERLY to Barry, 27 February; 23, 29 March; 25 July 1888, Powderly Papers.

35. *Report of the International Council of Women,* pp. 153–56; *Woman's Journal,* Apr. 7, 1888. Copies of several of Barry's speeches to suffrage and temperance conventions are in the Leonora M. Barry Lake Folio, Sophia Smith Collection, Smith College Library.

36. "Report of the General Investigator of Women's Work and Wages," *Proceedings of the General Assembly of the Knights of Labor, 1888,* pp. 9–10.

37. "Report of the General Investigator of Women's Work and Wages," *Proceedings of the General Assembly of the Knights of Labor, 1887,* pp. 1582–84.

38. Ibid., pp. 1581–82.

39. BARRY to Powderly. 15 November 1887. Powderly Papers.

40. *Proceedings of the General Assembly of the Knights of Labor, 1887,* p. 1585; ibid., *1888,* pp. 1, 4.

41. *Proceedings of the General Assembly of the Knights of Labor, 1888,* p. 1.

42. Ibid., p. 2.

43. Ibid., p. 14.

44. "Report of the General Investigator of Women's Work and Wages," *Proceedings of the General Assembly of the Knights of Labor, 1889,* pp. 1–2, 6.

45. BARRY to Powderly, 4 October 1888, 29 December 1888, Powderly Papers.

46. POWDERLY to Barry, 30 November 1889, Powderly Papers.

47. LEONORA BARRY LAKE to General Assembly, Nov. 10, 1890, *Proceedings of the General Assembly of the Knights of Labor, 1890,* p. 6.

48. Ibid., p. 162; Eleanor Flexner, *Century of Struggle* (Cambridge, Mass., 1959), p. 196.

49. FONER, *History of the Labor Movement,* 2:157–71.

50. *New York Times,* May 20. 1886.

51. *Troy Northern Budget,* May 19, 1886.

52. Ibid., May 22, 1886.

53. Ibid., May 20, 1886; *New York Times,* May 20, 21, 1886.

54. *Troy Northern Budget,* May 23, 1886.

55. Ibid., June 6, 1886.

56. Ibid., June 13, 1886.

57. *New York Times,* June 23, 1886.

58. *Troy Northern Budget,* June 25, 26, July 7, 9, 10, 1886.

59. FONER, *Organized Labor and the Black Worker,* pp. 59–61.

60. *New York Times.* Feb. 26, 1897; *Savannah Tribune,* Mar. 10, 1894; *Philadelphia Press,* June 3, 1894; Foner, *Organized Labor and the Black Worker,* pp. 62–63.

61. Chicago *Inter-Ocean,* June 2, 1894.

62. FONER, *Organized Labor and the Black Worker,* pp. 62–63.

63. FONER, *History of the Labor Movement,* 2:168–70.

64. *Journal of United Labor,* Feb. 25, 1885. Nov. 25, 1886, Apr. 30, Dec. 3, 1887, May 2, 9, 1889.

65. Quoted in Andrews and Bliss, *Women in Trade Unions,* p. 126.

66. *Irish World,* July 29, 1882.

67. Reprinted in *John Swinton's Paper,* Oct. 4, 1885.

68. CAROLYN DANIEL McCREESH, "On the Picket Lines: Militant Women Campaign to Organize Garment Workers, 1882–1917" (Ph.D. diss., University of Maryland, 1975), p. 49.

Chapter 12: The American Federation of Labor, 1881–1894

1. For the formation of the Federation of Organized Trades and Labor Unions, see Foner, *History of the Labor Movement,* 1:518–24. For the change to

the American Federation of Labor, see Foner, *History of the Labor Movement,* 2:132–44.

2. FONER, *History of the Labor Movement,* 1:520–21.

3. *Proceedings of the Federation of Organized Trades and Labor Unions, 1882 Convention,* pp. 16, 19, 20, 23; Alice Henry, *Women and the Labor Movement* (New York, 1923), pp. 52–55.

4. *Proceedings of the Federation of Organized Trades and Labor Unions, 1883 Convention,* pp. 13, 15, 19.

5. *Proceedings of the Federation of Organized Trades and Labor Unions, 1885 Convention,* p. 16.

6. *Proceedings of the AFL Convention, 1887,* p. 9.

7. FONER, *History of the Labor Movement,* 2:189–90, Bernard Mandel, *Samuel Gompers, A Biography* (Yellow Springs, Ohio, 1963), pp. 43, 61–70.

8. MARY MEENIN to Chris Evans, 20 June 1892, American Federation of Labor Correspondence, American Federation of Labor Building (hereafter cited as AFL Correspondence).

9. RALPH SCHARNAU, "Elizabeth Morgan, Crusader for Labor Reform," *Labor History* 14 (Summer 1973): 340–41; Foner, *History of the Labor Movement.* 1:475–76.

10. The Illinois state certificate of incorporation, dated December 12, 1888, is in the Thomas J. Morgan Collection, Illinois Historical Survey, University of Illinois, Urbana, Ill.

11. Mrs. Thomas J. Morgan to Gompers, 12 November 1888, AFL Correspondence.

12. Copy of leaflet, "The Aims and Objects of Ladies' Federal Labor Union No. 2703") in AFL Correspondence; *Chicago Recorder,* July 29, 1894.

13. MRS. THOMAS J. MORGAN to Gompers, 20 August 1891, AFL Correspondence; *Chicago Tribune,* Feb. 21, Mar. 9, 1892; Scharnau, "Elizabeth Morgan," pp. 342–43; Ellen M. Ritter, "Elizabeth Morgan: Pioneer Female Labor Agitator," *Central States Speech Journal* 22 (Fall 1971): 242.

14. Quoted in Ritter, "Elizabeth Morgan," p. 243.

15. *Chicago Tribune,* Jan. 26, 1890.

16. The articles appeared in the *Times* between July 30 and August 17, 1888.

17. SCHARNAU, "Elizabeth Morgan," p. 342.

18. *Chicago Herald,* Nov. 3, 1888; *Chicago Times,* Nov. 3, 1888.

19. *Chicago Tribune,* Feb. 21, 25, 1892; *Chicago Herald,* Feb. 21, 25, 1892. Printed circular issued by the Illinois Women's Alliance, Mar. 1, 1893, in AFL Correspondence; Scharnau, "Elizabeth Morgan," pp. 343–44.

20. BESSIE LOUISE PIERCE, *A History of Chicago, 1871–1893* (New York, 1957): 294–95; Scharnau, "Elizabeth Morgan," pp. 344–45.

21. NANCY SCHROM DYE, "The Women's Trade Union League of New York, 1903–1920" (Ph.D. diss., University of Wisconsin, 1974), p. 40; McCreesh, "Picket Lines," pp. 53–56; Grace Dodge, ed., *Thoughts of Busy Girls, Who Have Little Time for Study, Yet Find Much Time for Thinking* (New York, 1892).

22. *The American Hebrew,* Oct. 26, 1888, and reprinted in Morris U. Schappes, "The Political Origins of the United Hebrew Trades, 1888," *Journal of Ethnic Studies* 5 (Spring 1977): 28.

23. EMILY BARROWS, "Trade Union Organization Among Women of Chicago" (Master's thesis, University of Chicago, 1927), pp. 43–44.

24. ALICE HAMILTON, *Exploring the Dangerous Trades: The Autobiography of Alice Hamilton* (Boston, 1953), p. 81.

25. The best study of the origins of the settlement house movement in the United States and its links with the labor movement is Allen F. Davis, *Spearheads for Reform: The Social Settlements and the Progressive Movement, 1890–1914* (New York, 1967). One should, however, also consult the works by settlement house residents such as Jane Addams, *Twenty Years at Hull House* (New York, 1910); Lillian Wald, *The House on Henry Street* (New York, 1915); Mary Simkhovitch, *Neighborhood: My Story of Greenwich House* (New York, 1938); Philip Davis, *And Crown Thy Good* (New York, 1952), and Robert S. Woods, ed., *The City Wilderness: A Settlement Study by the Residents of the South End Boston* (Boston, 1898).

26. BARROWS, "Trade Union Organization," pp. 43–44; Dorothy Rose Blumberg, *Florence Kelley: The Early Years* (New York, 1966), pp. 210–13. For Kelley's correspondence with Engels, see Dorothy Rose Blumberg, "'Dear Mr. Engels': Unpublished Letters, 1884–1894, of Florence Kelley (Wischnewetsky) to Friedrich Engels," *Labor History* 5 (Spring 1964): 105–28.

27. WILLIAM RHINELANDER STEWART, *The Philanthropic Work of Josephine Shaw Lowell* (New York, 1911), pp. 34–37, 357–58; Biographical Notes, "Leonora O'Reilly," undated biographical sketches, file 1, box 1, Leonora O'Reilly Papers, Schlesinger Library, Radcliffe College (hereafter cited as O'Reilly Papers).

28. IDA VAN ETTEN, *The Condition of Women Workers Under the Present Industrial System* (New York, 1890), p. 8; Jacob Andrew Lieberman, "Their Sisters' Keepers: The Women's Hours and Wages Movement in the United States, 1890–1902" (Ph.D. diss., Columbia University, 1971), p. 34; Maude Nathan, *Story of an Epoch-Making Movement* (New York, 1926). pp. 15–16.

29. ALLIS ROSENBERG WOLFE, "Women, Consumerism, and the National Consumers' League in the Progressive Era, 1900–1923," *Labor History* 16 (Summer 1975): 383.

30. New York Association of Working Girls Societies, "New York Association of Working Girls Societies," April 1893, pp. 5–8, copy in box 15, O'Reilly Papers.

31. IDA VAN ETTEN to Gompers, 2 February, 8 June 1891. AFL Correspondence.

32. *Proceedings of the AFL Convention, 1891,* pp. 26–27, 36.

33. HENRY V. JACKSON to Gompers 31 May 1891; John O'Rourke to Gompers, 2 July 1892, AFL Correspondence.

34. LENA ARDNER to Gompers, 23 March 1892; Julia Howard to Gompers, 24 March 1892, AFL Correspondence.

35. Copy of resolutions, dated Feb. 12, 1892, in AFL Correspondence.

36. *Troy Northern Budget,* Jan. 6, 11, 1891.

37. Ibid., Jan. 11, Feb. 1, 1891; *Troy Daily Times,* Jan. 7, 15, 29, 1891.

38. H. J. OGDEN to Gompers, 1 February 1891, AFL Correspondence.

39. DORA SULLIVAN to Gompers, 19 October 1891, AFL Correspondence; *Troy Northern Budget,* Nov. 20, 1891; *Troy Daily Times,* Nov. 23, 1891.

40. MABEL HURD WILLETT, *The Employment of Women in the Clothing Trade,* (New York, 1902), pp. 65, 184; Lillian Wald, *House on Henry Street,* pp. 204–6; McCreesh, "Picket Lines," pp. 66–67; Schappes, "United Hebrew Trades," pp. 15–23, 28.

41. *The Garment Worker* 1 (April 1893): 16–17; *Proceedings of the Third Annual Convention of the United Garment Workers* (Philadelphia, 1892), pp. 3–10; Chas. F. Reichers to Gompers, 26 June 1892, AFL Correspondence, McCreesh, "Picket Lines," pp. 68–70.

42. McCREESH, "Picket Lines," pp. 68–70.

43. JAMES P. HOOLEY to Gompers, 4 October 1891; Joan J. May to Gompers, 22 December 1891, AFL Correspondence.

44. MARY K. O'SULLIVAN, "Autobiography," manuscript in Schlesinger Library, Radcliffe College, Cambridge, Mass., pp. 1–67, 87–88, 98–99.

45. DORA SULLIVAN to Gompers, 19 October, 16 December 1891; 8 January, 18, 26 February, 17 March 1892; Mary E. Kenney to Gompers, Troy, 12 August 1892, AFL Correspondence; Gompers to Dora Sullivan, 4 May 1892; Gompers to AFL Executive Council, 17 November 1891; Gompers to Mamie Mahoney, 24 April 1894, Samuel Gompers Letter Books, Library of Congress.

46. KENNEY to Gompers, 18 May 1892, AFL Correspondence.

47. KENNEY to Gompers, 28 September 1892, AFL Correspondence.

48. MARY KENNEY O'SULLIVAN, "Autobiography," pp. 62–64; McCreesh, "Picket Lines," pp. 62, 69.

49. KENNEY to Gompers, 15 September 1892, AFL Correspondence.

50. GOMPERS to AFL Executive Council, 30 September 1892; Chris Evans to Gompers, 1 October 1892; John B. Lennon to Gompers, 1 October 1892, AFL Correspondence.

51. KENNEY to Gompers, 10 October 1892, AFL Correspondence; *Proceedings of the AFL Convention, 1892,* pp. 17, 30.

52. KENNEY to Gompers, 11 November, 8 December 1892, AFL Correspondence.

53. MRS. T. J. MORGAN to Gompers, 20 August 1891, AFL Correspondence.

54. RAY STANNARD BAKER, quoted in Leo Stein, ed., *Out of the Sweatshop: The Struggle for Industrial Democracy* (New York, 1977), pp. 88–89.

55. *Chicago Daily News,* Aug. 12, 1891; *Chicago Daily Tribune,* Aug. 12, 1891.

56. Chicago Trade and Labor Assembly, *The New Slavery: Investigation into the Sweating System as Applied to the Manufacture of Wearing Apparel, A Report Prepared by Mrs. Thomas J. Morgan* (Chicago, 1891), pp. 9–10, 18–19, 20,

23–24. For a good summary of the pamphlet, see Ritter, "Elizabeth Morgan," pp. 246–50.

57. Mrs. T. J. Morgan to Gompers, 9 June 1891, AFL Correspondence; *Rights of Labor,* Oct. 10, Nov. 17, 1891.

58. Florence Kelley to Henry Demarest Lloyd, 12 June 1891, letter quoted in Blumberg, *Florence Kelley,* p. 130.

59. Morgan to Gompers, 7 April 1892, AFL Correspondence.

60. *Chicago Times,* Apr. 7, 1892.

61. Earl R. Bedner, *A History of Labor Legislation in Illinois* (Chicago, 1929), pp. 153–54, 188, 262–64; Scharnau, "Elizabeth Morgan," pp. 346–48.

62. Morgan to Gompers, 27 January, 21 February, 9 March 1892; 15 March, 2 August 1892, AFL Correspondence; *Chicago Daily Tribune,* Feb. 21, Mar. 9, 1892.

63. *Proceedings of the AFL Convention, 1894,* pp. 31, 45–46; Henry, *Women and the Labor Movement,* p. 54.

64. Morgan to Gompers, 21 November 1892, AFL Correspondence.

65. John F. O'Sullivan to Gompers, Boston, 26 December 1893, AFL Correspondence; Gompers to E. E. Pitt, 29 December 1893, Gompers Letter Books, Library of Congress.

66. Minutes of the Meeting of the AFL Executive Council, N.Y.C., Jan. 13, 1894, AFL Correspondence.

67. Samuel Gompers, *Seventy Years of Life and Labor* (New York, 1925), 1:482.

Chapter 13: The American Federation of Labor, 1894–1900

1. *Proceedings of the AFL Convention, 1893,* p. 19; Foner, *History of the Labor Movement,* 2:235.

2. Gompers to Wm. J. Smith, 28 September 1894, AFL Correspondence.

3. *Garment Worker* 5 (August 1899): 6–7.

4. Wm. Lippman to Gompers, 6 May 1894; Lippman to August McCraith, 16 April 1895, AFL Correspondence.

5. Hannah Parker Kimball to Mary Kenney, Paris, 10 November 1892. AFL Correspondence.

6. John F. O'Sullivan to Gompers, 24 May 1894, AFL Correspondence; Mary Kenney O'Sullivan, "Autobiography," manuscript in Schlesinger Library, Radcliffe College, Cambridge, Mass., pp. 88–92.

7. John F. O'Sullivan to Gompers, 8 June 1894, AFL Correspondence.

8. *Boston Globe,* May 27. June 6, 1894.

9. *Labor Leader,* June 9, 16, Nov. 25, 1894.

10. John F. O'Sullivan to Gompers, 2 November 1894, AFL Correspondence.

11. Mary F. Kenney to Gompers, 28 November 1894, AFL Correspondence.

12. O'Sullivan, "Autobiography," pp. 60–65, 88–95. See also Vida Scudder, *On Journey* (New York, 1937), p. 155.

13. *Far and Near* 39 (January 1894): 41; McCreesh, "Picket Lines," p. 81.

14. *Woman's Journal,* Dec. 20, 1890.

15. Hamilton Wilcox to Gompers, 16 April 1894, AFL Correspondence.

16. *Woman's Journal,* June 8, 1895.

17. Lois Bannister Merk, "Massachusetts and the Woman Suffrage Movement" (Ph.D. diss., Northeastern University, 1961), pp. 273–74, 275, 278, 345, 348, 362–66.

18. Harriette A. Keyser to Gompers, 9 June 1894, enclosing copy of her pamphlet, AFL Correspondence.

19. Susan B. Anthony to Gompers, 14 November 1899, AFL Correspondence.

20. Aileen S. Kraditor, *The Ideas of the Woman Suffrage Movement, 1890–1920* (New York, 1965), pp. 148–49.

21. *Oshkosh Daily Northwestern,* Aug. 5, 1898.

22. Ibid., Aug. 6, 1898.

23. Lee Baxandall et al. "Fur, Logs and Human Lives, The Great Oshkosh Woodworker Strike of 1898," *Green Mountain Quarterly,* no. 3 (May 1976): 29–30. The entire issue is devoted to the strike, and it is the only study of that great struggle.

24. Sarah Crossfield to Gompers, 8 April 1899, AFL Correspondence.

25. Undated newspaper clipping attached to Crossfield to Gompers, 9 October 1899, AFL Correspondence.

26. *General Constitution Governing the Women's International Union Label League of the World,* issued by the Trades' Journal, Muncie, Ind., 1899, pp. 3–4. Copy in AFL Correspondence.

27. L. P. Negele to Gompers, 28 November 1900, AFL Correspondence.

28. J. D. Pierce to Gompers, 11 April 1900, AFL Correspondence.

29. Casper Orebaugh to Gompers, 12 March 1900, AFL Correspondence.

30. W. L. Halcomb to Gompers, 26 January 1901, AFL Correspondence.

31. Keith L. Bryant, Jr., "Kate Barnard, Organized Labor and Social Justice in Oklahoma during the Progressive Era," *Journal of Southern History* 35 (February, 1969): 143–46; Keith L. Bryant, Jr., "The Oklahoma State Federation of Labor during the Age of Reform," *Labor History* 11 (Summer, 1970): 261–63.

32. *Duluth Tribune,* May 9, 1897; *New York Times,* May 10, 1897.

33. *New York Times,* Dec. 5, 6, 13, 1900.

34. *Chicago Daily Tribune,* July 28, 1901; *Chicago Times,* July 28, 1901; *New York Times,* July 29, 1901.

35. *New York Times,* July 29, 1901.

36. Louis Levine, *The Women's Garment Workers* (New York, 1924). pp. 219–20; Mabel Hurd Willett, *The Employment of Women in the Clothing Trade* (New York, 1902), pp. 136–39.

37. LEVINE, *Garment Workers,* pp. 89–93; McCreesh, "Picket Lines," pp. 96–97.

38. LEVINE, *Garment Workers,* pp. 89–109.

39. McCREESH, "Picket Lines," pp. 100–101.

40. "United Laundry Workers, Troy, N.Y., 1900," copy in AFL Correspondence.

41. C. E. NORDECK to Gompers, 15 July 1900, AFL Correspondence.

42. GOMPERS to the Laundry Workers' Union, 8 October 1900, AFL Correspondence.

43. HERMAN ROBINSON to Gompers, 26 November, 3 December 1900, AFL Correspondence.

44. Call to Laundry Workers by Chas. E. Nordeck, General Secretary-Treasurer, Shirt, Waist and Laundry Workers International Union, 3 February 1901, AFL Correspondence.

45. L. H. McCATEER to Gompers, 14 April 1896, AFL Correspondence.

46. McCATEER to Gompers, 21 October 1896, AFL Correspondence.

47. GOMPERS to V. E. St. Cloud, Atlanta. Ga., 4 December 1896, AFL Correspondence.

48. ROBERT HOWARD to Gompers, 26 December 1896, AFL Correspondence.

49. WILL H. WINN to Gompers, 4 December 1896, AFL Correspondence.

50. *New York Times,* Aug. 5, 1877; Ray Marshall, *Labor in the South* (Cambridge, Mass., 1967), p. 81.

51. WILL WINN, "The Negro: His Relations to Southern Industry," *American Federationist* 4 (February 1898): 269–71. For the white chauvinism of AFL organizers in the South, see Foner, *History of the Labor Movement,* 2:358–61.

52. "To All Local Unions Affiliated with the National Union of Textile Workers of America, Lawrence, Mass., Jan. 1, 1899," attached to H. S. Mills to Gompers, 20 February 1899, AFL Correspondence.

53. *Augusta Chronicle,* Nov. 22–24, 1897.

54. *Proceedings of the AFL Convention, 1898,* pp. 10–11.

55. W. H. WINN to Gompers, 19 December 1898, AFL Correspondence.

56. JNO. T. PUGH to Gompers, 14 January 1899, AFL Correspondence.

57. PRINCE W. GREENE to Gompers, 23 January 1899, AFL Correspondence; *Augusta Chronicle,* Jan. 26–30, 1899.

58. GREENE to Gompers, 8, 10, 16 April 1899, AFL Correspondence.

59. *Proceedings of the AFL Convention, 1898,* p. 85; Eva Valesh to Gompers, Minn., 13 November 1896, AFL Correspondence.

60. GOMPERS "To Whom It May Concern," and to Secretary of Trades and Labor Council, Montgomery, Ala., 30 November 1900, Gompers Letter Books, Library of Congress; Elizabeth H. Davidson, *Child Labor Legislation in the Southern Textile States* (Chapel Hill, N.C., 1939), p. 27.

61. IRENE M. ASHBY to Gompers, 17 December 1900, AFL Correspondence; undated clipping, *Birmingham News,* attached to Ashby to Gompers, 17 December 1900, AFL Correspondence.

62. ASHBY to Gompers, 26 December 1900, AFL Correspondence.

63. Gompers to Ashby, 3 January 1900, Gompers Letter Books, Library of Congress; and AFL Correspondence.

64. *Proceedings of the AFL Convention, 1898,* p. 81; Marshall, *Labor in the South,* pp. 80–81.

65. Ashby to Gompers, 11 February 1903, AFL Correspondence. Irene Ashby, "The Fight Against Child Labor in Alabama," *American Federationist* 8 (May 1901): 150–57; Irene Ashby. "Abolish Child Labor," ibid. 9 (January 1902): 19–20; Irene Ashby, "Child Life vs. Dividends," ibid. 9 (May 1902): 215–23; Davidson, *Child Labor,* pp. 25–34, 80–82.

66. Petition, "Cincinnati, Ohio, July 20, 1902," attached to Frank L. Rist to Frank Morrison, 23 July 1900, AFL Correspondence.

67. F. E. Wolfe, *Admission to American Trade Unions* (Baltimore, 1912), p. 85.

68. Morrison to O. Mattie Hill, 6 June 1900; Hill to Morrison, Pontiac, Ill., 12 June 1900; H. M. Eaton to Morrison, Boston, Mass., 20 June 1900, AFL Correspondence.

69. Mary McDowell, "The Story of a Women's Labor Union," *Commons* 7 (January 1903): 1–3; Michael Donnelly, "To Whom It May Concern," Sept. 19, 1902, Mary McDowell Papers, Chicago Historical Society (hereafter cited as McDowell Papers).

70. Michael A. Mulcaire, C.S.C., *The International Brotherhood of Electrical Workers* (Washington, D.C., 1923), pp. 30–31.

71. Gompers to George A. Bottenhausen, Lynn, Mass.. 22 June 1897; Gompers to Henry V. Jackson, Schenectady, N.Y., 22 June 1897, Gompers Letter Books, Library of Congress. I am indebted to Mr. Ted Werntz for calling these letters to my attention.

72. Mulcaire, *Electrical Workers,* p. 31.

73. *Electrical Worker,* December 1897; March 1898; October 1899.

74. *San Antonio Express,* Nov. 5, 1900.

75. Ibid., Nov. 10–13, 14, 15, 25, 30, 1900.

76. Ibid., Nov. 14, 1900; Harold Arthur Shapiro, "The Workers of San Antonio, Texas, 1900–1940" (Ph.D. diss., University of Texas, Austin, 1952), pp. 265–72; Jack Barbash, *Unions and Telephones: The Story of the Communications Workers of America* (New York, 1952), pp. 3–4.

77. *Dallas Times* reprinted in *San Antonio Express,* Dec. 11, 1900.

78. Diary of Leonora O'Reilly, June 24, 1897, O'Reilly Papers.

79. Ibid., June 30. July 6, 1897.

80. Willett, *Employment of Women in the Clothing Trade,* pp. 183–84; Nancy Schrom Dye, "The Women's Trade Union League of New York, 1903–1920" (Ph.D. diss., University of Wisconsin, 1974). pp. 33–34.

Chapter 14: The Turn of the Century

1. *Report of the Industrial Commission on the Relations and Conditions of Capital and Labor Employed in Manufactures and General Business,* 1901, 7:118, 541.

2. CECILE S. NEIDLE, *America's Immigrant Women* (Boston. 1975), pp. 86–87.

3. MARGARY DAVIES, "Woman's Place Is at the Typewriter: The Feminization of the Clerical Labor Force," *Radical America* 8 (July–August 1974): 406. See also Janet Hooks, *Women's Occupations Through Seven Decades*, U.S., Department of Labor, Women's Bureau, *Bulletin No. 218*, 1947, pp. 39–45; Department of Commerce and Labor, Bureau of the Census, *Twelfth Census of the United States, 1900, Special Reports: Occupations*, pp. 7–9; Carl N. Degler, "Revolution Without Ideology: The Changing Place of Women in America," in Robert Jay Lifton, ed., *The Woman in America* (Boston, 1967), p. 196; and Meta Stern Lilienthal, *From Fireside to Factory* (New York, 1916), p. 42.

4. U.S., Department of Commerce and Labor, Bureau of the Census, *Twelfth Census of the United States, 1900, Special Reports: Occupations*, 1901, 19: 630–40; Nancy Schrom Dye, "The Women's Trade Union League of New York, 1903–1920" (Ph.D. diss., University of Wisconsin, 1974), pp. 10–12.

5. DOROTHY RICHARDSON, *The Long Day: The Story of a New York Working Girl* (New York, 1905), pp. 46, 71, 240, 243, 271.

6. MRS. JOHN VAN VORST AND MARIE VAN VORST, *The Woman Who Toils* (New York, 1903), p. 201.

7. Ibid., p. 110.

8. Ibid., pp. 22–26, 27, 33–35, 46, 54, 55.

9. Ibid., pp. 228–29.

10. Ibid., p. 231.

11. Ibid., p. 232.

12. Ibid., pp. 238–39, 267–68, 290–92.

13. CRYSTAL EASTMAN. *Work-Accidents and the Law* (New York, 1910), p. 84; U.S., Congress, Senate, *Woman and Child Wage-Earners in the United States, Senate Document 645*, 61st Cong., 2d sess., 1910, pp. 391–92.

14. LILLIAN R. MATTHEWS, *Women in Trade Unions in San Francisco* (Berkeley, Calif., 1912), p. 11; New York, Assembly, *Report and Testimony of the Special Committee to Investigate Female Labor, Assembly Document No. 97*, 1896, 1:3–4, 30–44, 2:1934–40, 1945–48; Frances Donovan, *The Saleslady* (Chicago, 1929), pp. 27–28; also quoted in Barbara Wertheimer, *We Were There: The Story of Working Women in America* (New York, 1977), p. 239.

15. ELIZABETH BEARDSLEY BUTLER, *Saleswomen in Mercantile Stores, 1909* (New York, 1912), pp. 78, 105–8.

16. *Report and Testimony*, 1:69.

17. BUTLER, *Saleswomen*, pp. 108–9.

18. St. Louis *Post-Dispatch*, Mar. 11, July 3, 1900.

19. MARY VAN KLEECK, "Working Hours of Women Workers," *Charities and Commons* 17 (Oct. 6, 1906): 13, 16.

20. FLORENCE KELLEY, "Industrial Democracy: Women in Trade Unions," *Outlook* 84 (December 1906): 926.

21. JACOB ANDREW LIEBERMAN, "Their Sisters' Keepers: The Women's Hours and Wages Movement in the United States, 1890–1902" (Ph.D. diss., Columbia University, 1971), p. 136.

22. MELECH EPSTEIN, *Jewish Labor in the U.S.A.: An Industrial, Political and Cultural History of the Jewish Labor Movement* (New York, 1950–1953), 1:38–40; Illinois, *Sixth Annual Report of the Factory Inspectors of Illinois, 1899*, p. 10; New York, *Fifteenth Annual Report of the New York Factory Inspectors, 1900*, p. 35; University Settlement Society of New York, *Yearbook* (New York, 1899), p. 11.

23. *Report of the Industrial Commission . . .*, 7:27, 92.

24. LEONORA O'REILLY, "Message to Women Workers," Labor Day, 1898, in O'Reilly Papers.

25. FREDERICK LEWIS ALLEN, *The Big Change: America Transforms Itself, 1900–1950* (New York, 1952), p. 55.

26. DONATA MARY YATES, "Women in Chicago Industries, 1900–1915, A Study of Working Conditions in Factories, Laundries and Restaurants" (Master's thesis, University of Chicago, 1948), p. 16.

27. ELLEN M. HENROTIN, "Organization for Women," *American Federationist*, November 1905, p. 825; Philip S. Foner, *History of the Labor Movement in the United States*, vol. 3, *The Policies and Practices of the American Federation of Labor, 1900–1909* (New York, 1964), p. 18.

28. PAUL F. BRISSENDEN, *Earnings of Factory Workers, 1899 to 1927*, U.S., Department of Labor and Commerce, Bureau of the Census, Monograph 10 (Washington, 1929), pp. 29–30; *Report of the Industrial Commission . . .* 7:27.

29. ELIZABETH BEARDSLEY BUTLER, *Women and the Trades* (New York, 1909), p. 217; National Industrial Conference Board, *Wartime Employment of Women in the Metal Trades* (Boston, 1918), p. 39.

30. MCCREESH, "Picket Lines," p. 119.

31. ROSE COHEN, *Out of the Shadow* (New York, 1918), pp. 23–24.

32. *Hammer and Pen*, February 1902, p. 6, and reprinted in Lieberman, "Their Sisters' Keepers," p. 74.

33. New York, Department of Labor, *Annual Report, 1904*, 2:4; 3:34.

34. U.S., Department of Labor, Women's Bureau, *Negro Women in Industry, Bulletin no. 20*, p. 5.

35. FONER, *History of the Labor Movement*, 3:238–35; Philip S. Foner, *Organized Labor and the Black Worker, 1619–1973* (New York, 1974), pp. 75–80.

36. FONER, *Organized Labor and the Black Worker*, pp. 82–99, 103–7.

37. FANNIE BARRIER WILLIAMS, "The Problem of Employment for Negro Women," *Southern Workman* 32 (September 1903): 402.

38. DONALD KATZMAN, *Seven Days a Week: Women and Domestic Service in Industrializing America* (New York, 1978), pp. 184–87.

39. MARY WHITE OVINGTON, *Half A Man: The Status of the Negro in New York* (New York, 1911), p. 162. Emphasis in original.

40. MARY WHITE OVINGTON, "The Negro Family in New York," *Charities*, Oct. 7, 1905, pp. 133–34.

41. U.S., Department of Commerce and Labor, Bureau of the Census, *Twelfth Census of the United States, 1900* (1901), "Women at Work," table 28, pp. 266–74.

42. W. E. B. Du Bois, *The Philadelphia Negro* (Philadelphia, 1899), p. 323.

43. *Christian Recorder,* Oct. 14, 1900.

44. Du Bois, *The Philadelphia Negro,* p. 175.

45. Brissenden, *Earnings of Factory Workers,* pp. 29–30.

46. *Negro Women in Industry,* U.S. Department of Labor, Womens Bureau *Bulletin No. 20,* p. 5.

47. U.S., Department of Commerce, and Labor, "Women at Work," p. 266.

48. Ovington, "The Negro Family," pp. 132–34.

49. *Independent* 54 (Sept. 18, 1902): 221–22.

Chapter 15: The Socialist Party and Socialist Women

1. Bruce Dancis, "The Socialist Women's Movement in the United States, 1901–1917" (Senior thesis, American Radicalism in the Twentieth Century, University of California, Santa Cruz, 1973), p. 52. A detailed summary of the thesis was published under the title "Socialism and Women in the United States, 1900–1917," *Socialist Revolution* 27 (January–March 1976): 81–144. All references to Dancis are to the thesis.

2. Sally M. Miller, "American Socialist Women and the Second International" (Paper delivered at the ITT Conference, "Women and the Labor Movement," Linz, Austria, September 12–16, 1978), pp. 1–2. Copy in possession of present writer.

3. Karl Marx and Frederick Engels, *The Communist Manifesto* (Chicago, 1954), pp. 48–49.

4. Frederick Engels, *The Origin of the Family, Private Property, and the State* (New York, 1942), p. 50.

5. Ibid., p. 74; Frederick Engels, *The Condition of the Working Class in England* (Stanford, Calif., 1968), p. 145.

6. August Bebel, *Woman and Socialism* (New York, 1910), p. 6.

7. Ibid., pp. 244–45.

8. Quoted in "Foundations of Communist Work Among Women: The German Social Democracy, Part 1: 1875–1900" *Women and Revolution,* Spring 1975, p. 5.

9. Nellie A. Smith in *Colorado Chronicle,* Feb. 19, 1902; *Worker,* Apr. 28, 1901; Ira Kipnis, *The American Socialist Movement. 1897–1912* (New York, 1952), p. 261.

10. Josephine R. Cole in *Los Angeles Socialist,* June 20, 1903; Dancis, "Socialist Women's Movement," p. 23.

11. Dancis, "Socialist Women's Movement," p. 24.

12. Mary E. Garbutt, "Practical Application of Socialism in the Home," *Los Angeles Socialist,* Mar. 19, 1904.

13. "Women in the Party," *Worker,* Apr. 24, 1904; Kipnis, *American Socialist Movement,* pp. 261–62.

14. AILEEN S. KRADITOR, *The Ideas of the Woman Suffrage Movement, 1890–1920* (New York, 1965), pp. 58–59; Dancis, "Socialist Women's Movement," pp. 37–39.

15. For the setbacks to the suffrage movement referred to, see Eleanor Flexner, *Century of Struggle* (Cambridge, Mass., 1959), pp. 240–48.

16. REV. GEORGE W. WOODBEY, *What to Do and How to Do It, or Socialism vs. Capitalism, Wayland's Monthly No. 40* (August 1903), pp. 37–38. For a summary of the pamphlet, see Philip S. Foner, *American Socialism and Black Americans: From the Age of Jackson to World War II* (Westport, Conn., 1977), pp. 155–62.

17. Los Angeles *Common Sense,* Dec. 17, 1904.

18. BESSIE HUGES in *Colorado Chronicle,* Feb. 5, 1902.

19. FONER, *History of the Labor Movement,* 3:369–92.

20. LOUIS LEVINE, *The Women's Garment Workers,* (New York, 1924), pp. 106–7, Joel Seidman, *The Needle Trades* (New York, 1942), p. 96.

21. *Proceedings of the Fourth Annual Convention of the International Ladies' Garment Workers' Union* (Cleveland, 1903), p. 14; Epstein, *Jewish Labor in the U.S.A.,* 1:365.

22. *Proceedings of the Third Annual Convention of the International ILGWU,* New York, 1902, p. 21.

23. Ibid., p. 22.

24. NANCY SCHROM DYE, "The Women's Trade Union League of New York, 1903–1920" (Ph.D. diss., University of Wisconsin, 1974), p. 38.

25. *Proceedings of the Fourth Convention,* pp. 44–46; Epstein, *Jewish Labor,* 1:367–68. The full text of the song, reportedly first sung in eastern Europe, is published in both Yiddish and English in Ruth Rubin, *A Treasury of Jewish Folk Songs* (New York, 1950), pp. 43, 97.

26. MCCREESH, "Picket Lines," p. 102; *Report of Proceedings of the Fourth Convention,* pp. 44–46; Epstein, *Jewish Labor,* 1:367–68.

27. *Proceedings of the Fourth Convention,* pp. 48–52; Helen Marot, *American Labor Unions* (New York, 1914), p. 68.

28. MABEL HURD WILLETT, *The Employment of Women in the Clothing Trade* (New York, 1902), pp. 167–68, 187.

29. *Proceedings of the Twelfth Annual Convention of the UGW,* (Indianapolis, 1903), pp. 40–43; Willett, *Women in the Clothing Trade,* pp. 166–71.

30. ROSE SCHNEIDERMAN, with Lucy Goldthwaite, *All for One* (New York, 1967), pp. 24–40.

31. MARY FIELD PARTON, *The Autobiography of Mother Jones* (Chicago, 1925), pp. 8–9.

32. Ibid., pp. 12–13.

33. Ibid., pp. 30–49.

34. *Cincinnati Chronicle,* July, 1902, pp. 1, 4.

35. FONER, *History of the Labor Movement,* 3:148–49.

36. *International Socialist Review* 1 (1900): 816.

37. Philadelphia *North American,* May 24, 25, 1903.

38. Ibid., June 11, 22, 1903; *Worker,* July 5, 1903.

39. PARTON, *Mother Jones,* pp. 71–72.

40. JOHN SPARGO, *The Bitter Cry of the Children* (New York, 1906), pp. 140–90.

41. Philadelphia *North American,* July 8, 1903; J. Spargo, "Child Slaves of Philadelphia," *Comrade,* August 1903, p. 253.

42. Philadelphia *North American,* July 9, 1903.

43. *New York Times,* July 10, 1903.

44. Ibid., July 11, 1903.

45. PARTON, *Mother Jones,* pp. 76–77.

46. Philadelphia *North American,* July 13, 1903.

47. Ibid., July 15, 1903.

48. *Elizabeth Journal,* reprinted in Philadelphia *North American,* July 17, 1903.

49. Philadelphia *North American,* July 16, 1903.

50. *New York Times,* July 20, 1903.

51. Philadelphia *North American,* July 20, 1903.

52. RUSSELL E. SMITH, "The March of the Mill Children," *Social Service Review* 4 (September 1967): 302; *New York Times,* July 24, 1903.

53. *New York Times,* July 25, 1903; Parton, *Mother Jones,* p. 79.

54. Philadelphia *North American,* July 31, 1903.

55. Ibid., Aug. 4, 1903.

56. Philadelphia *North American,* July 15, Aug. 1, 1903.

57. PARTON, *Mother Jones,* p. 83; Dale Featherling, *Mother Jones, the Miners' Angel* (Carbondale, Ill.. 1971), p. 57.

58. Philadelphia *North American,* July 17, 1903.

Chapter 16: Birth of the National Women's Trade Union League

1. ELEANOR FLEXNER, *Century of Struggle* (Cambridge, Mass., 1959), p. 169.

2. E. J. HUTCHINSON, *Women's Wages* (New York, 1919), pp. 151–54; Allen F. Davis, "The Women's Trade Union League: Origins and Organization," *Labor History* 5 (Winter 1964): 5; McCreesh, "Picket Lines," pp. 139–40.

3. BETTINA EILEEN BERCH, "Industrialization and Working Women in the Nineteenth Century: England, France, and the United States" (Ph.D. diss., University of Wisconsin, Madison, 1976), pp. 297–98; Gladys Meyerand, "Women's Organizations," *Encyclopedia of the Social Sciences* (New York, 1935), 15:465; Benjamim Stolberg, *Tailors' Progress: The Story of a Famous Union and the Men Who Made It* (New York, 1946), p. 61.

4. DOROTHY ROSE BLUMBERG, "'Dear Mr. Engels': Unpublished Letters, 1884–1894, of Florence Kelley (Wischnewetsky) to Friedrich Engels," *Labor History* 5 (Spring 1964): 132.

5. *Annual Report of the National Consumers' League for 1903* (New York, 1903), pp. 6–8, 42–54. The National Consumers' League 12th Annual Report (for the year ending December 3, 1912) contains an Approved List of Factories.

6. *Proceedings of the AFL Convention, 1903*, pp. 22–23.

7. DOROTHY ROSE BLUMBERG, *Florence Kelley: The Making of a Social Pioneer* (New York, 1964), pp. 208–10.

8. PHILIP DAVIS, "The Social Settlement and the Trade Union," *Commons* 1 (April 1904): 142–47.

9. *Weekly Bulletin of the Clothing Trades,* Mar. 24, 1905, p. 2, reprinted in Nancy Schrom Dye, "Creating a Feminist Alliance: Sisterhood and Class Conflict in the New York Women's Trade Union League, 1903–1914," *Feminist Studies* 3 (1975): 25.

10. HELEN MAROT, *American Labor Unions* (New York, 1914), pp. 5–10.

11. *Report of the Industrial Commission on the Relations and Conditions of Capital and Labor Employed in Manufactures and General Business* (Washington, D.C., 1901) 7:60–62, 250.

12. *New York Times,* May 20, 21, 22, 1902; *Worker,* May 20, 1902.

13. IRVING HOWE, *World of Our Fathers* (New York, 1976), pp. 124–25, quoting *Jewish Daily Forward,* June 15, 1902.

14. ANNA STRUNSKY WALLING, ed., *William English Walling: A Symposium* (New York, 1938), pp. 4–8.

15. DAVIS, "Women's Trade Union League," 9–10n. For a general discussion of this interplay, see Arthur Mann, "British Social Thought and American Reformers," *Mississippi Valley Historical Review* 42 (March 1956): 682–92.

16. GLADYS BOONE, *The Women's Trade Union League in Great Britain and the United States of America* (New York, 1942), pp. 20–21.

17. *Women's Union Journal* 13 (1888): 68.

18. HAROLD GOLDMAN, *Emma Paterson* (London, 1974), p. 67.

19. YVONNE KAPP, *Eleanor Marx,* vol. 2, *The Crowded Years* (New York, 1978), p. 85.

20. CHARLES BOOTH, ed., *Labour and Life of the People,* vol. 1 (London, 1889), pp. 435–38; Sidney and Beatrice Webb, *The History of Trade Unionism, 1660–1920* (London, 1919), p. 402.

21. KAPP, *Eleanor Marx,* 2:382–83.

22. London *Times,* July 23, 1880. Also quoted in Lislotte Glage, "Clementine Black: A Study in Social History and Literature" (Paper in preparation for Ph.D., University of Hannover), p. 22.

23. *Women's Trades Union Review* 1 (1891): 14.

24. BOONE, *Women's Trade Union Leagues,* pp. 24–25.

25. Biographical sketch of William English Walling in National Women's Trade Union League Papers, box 1, Library of Congress, Manuscripts Division (hereafter referred to as NWTUL Papers).

26. "Report of the Meeting Held to Organize the Women's Trade Union League," NWTUL Papers, box 1; Samuel Gompers, *Seventy Years of Life and Labor* (New York, 1925), 1:490.

27. "Report of Second Meeting Held to Organize the Women's Trade Union League," NWTUL Papers, box 1.

28. "Report of Third Meeting Held to Organize the Women's Trade Union League," NWTUL Papers, box 1.

29. Minutes of Annual Meeting of the NWTUL, Apr. 18, 1907, NWTUL Papers, box 1.

30. *Constitution of the National Women's Trade Union League of America Adopted in Faneuil Hall, Boston, November 17–19, 1903*, art. 3. The original is in NWTUL Papers, box 25.

31. WILLIAM ENGLISH WALLING to Leonora O'Reilly, 17 December 1903 (with notations in O'Reilly's handwriting), O'Reilly Papers; W. E. Walling to Mary McDowell, 25 November 1903, NWTUL Papers, box 1.

32. *Proceedings of the AFL Convention, 1903,* p. 249; *American Federationist* 10 (December 1903); Mary Kenney O'Sullivan to Alice Henry, n.d., NWTUL Papers, box 28.

33. DAVIS, "Women's Trade Union League," p. 12; "Report of the Annual Meeting, October 7, 1904," NWTUL Papers, box 2.

34. "Report of the Annual Meeting, October 7, 1904," NWTUL Papers, box 2.

Chapter 17: The League Begins Its Work

1. FONER, *History of the Labor Movement,* 3:32–60.

2. Minutes of the First Meeting of the National Executive Board of the NWTUL, Mar. 20, 1904, Boston, NWTUL Papers.

3. Minutes of the National Executive Board, NWTUL, Oct. 7, 1904, NWTUL Papers.

4. Notes from WTUL convention, NWTUL Papers.

5. MARY E. DREIER, *Margaret Dreier Robins: Her Life, Letters, and Work* (New York, 1950), pp. 6–57; Rose Schneiderman, with Lucy Goldthwaite *All for One* (New York, 1967), pp. 78–79.

6. "Secretary's Annual Report to the Women's Trade Union League, 1908," NWTUL Papers.

7. WALTER CHARRIER to Gompers, 1, 8 February, 12 April 1904, AFL Correspondence.

8. RHETTA CHILDE DORR, "The Women Strikers of Troy," *Charities and the Commons* 15 (Nov. 18, 1905): 233–34; *Troy Northern Budget,* Mar. 5, 9, 15, 17, 1905.

9. Minutes of the Executive Board of the Women's Trade Union League of New York, July 28, Aug. 25, Sept. 29, 1905, WTUL of NY Papers, State Labor Library, New York City (hereafter cited as WTUL of NY Papers). Ida

Rauh to Organized Labor and Its Friends, n.d., NWTUL Papers; Dorr, "Women Strikers of Troy," p. 235.

10. GERTRUDE BARNUM to Margaret Dreier Robins, 20 September 1905, NWTUL Papers.

11. *Literary Digest,* Sept. 25, 1905, p. 12.

12. DORR, "Women Strikers of Troy," p. 236.

13. IDA RAUH, "The Troy Strike," NWTUL Papers.

14. DORR, "Women Strikers of Troy," p. 235.

15. Minutes of the Executive Board of the Women's Trade Union League of New York, January 1905, WTUL of NY Papers; Alice Henry, *Women and the Labor Movement* (New York, 1923), p. 116; Nancy Schrom Dye, "The Women's Trade Union League of New York, 1903–1920," (Ph.D. diss., University of Wisconsin, Madison, 1974), pp. 95–96.

16. WILLIAM ENGLISH WALLING to Margaret Dreier, 17 January 1905, NWTUL Papers.

17. Reprinted in U.S., Department of Labor, Women's Bureau, *Toward Better Working Conditions for Women, Women's Bulletin No. 252* 1953, p. 14.

18. *Annual Report of the Women's Trade Union League of New York, 1906–1907,* p. 2; Minutes of the Executive Board of the WTUL of NY, Apr. 26, 1906, WTUL of NY Papers; Dye, "Women's Trade Union League," pp. 97–98.

19. ALICE HENRY, *The Trade Union Woman* (New York, 1915), pp. 45–46.

20. Ibid., pp. 46–50; Barbara Wertheimer, *We Were There: The Story of Working Women in America* (New York, 1977), pp. 215–16.

21. Minutes of the Executive Board of the Women's Trade Union League of New York, Apr. 24, 1907, WTUL of NY Papers; Secretary's Report, Women's Trade Union League of New York, July 25, 1907, WTUL of NY Papers.

22. *Report of the Proceedings of the Convention of the NWTUL, Chicago, 1909,* NWTUL Papers.

23. LEONORA O'REILLY to Gertrude Barnum, 29 December 1905, WTUL of NY Papers; Leonora O'Reilly's Diary, entry for Jan. 1, 1906, O'Reilly Papers; Minutes of the Executive Board Meeting of the WTUL of NY, Jan. 25, 1906, WTUL of NY Papers.

24. ROSE SCHNEIDERMAN, "A Cap-Maker's Story," *Independent* 58 (1905): 935–37; Schneiderman, *All for One,* p. 83.

25. *Life and Labor* 3 (July 1918): 132; (October 1918): 214.

26. WILLIAM ENGLISH WALLING to Mary Dreier, 1 November 1904, 17 January 1905, NWTUL Papers; *Weekly Bulletin of the Clothing Trades* 11 (June 2, 1905); 4, Minutes of the Executive Board Meeting of the WTUL of NY, Dec. 20, 1905, WTUL of NY Papers.

27. McCREESH, "Picket Lines," p. 127.

28. "Trade Unions in Petticoats," *Public Opinion,* vol. 36, no. 9, p. 269.

29. AGNES NESTOR, *Woman's Labor Leader* (Rockford, Ill., 1954), pp. 13–26, 58–60; Agnes Nestor's Diary, June 23, July 17, 1900, Agnes Nestor Papers, Chicago Historical Society.

30. WILLIAM HARD, with Rhetta Childe Dorr, "The Woman's Invasion," *Everybody's Magazine*, December 1908, p. 805.

31. NESTOR, *Woman's Labor Leader*, pp. 66–68.

32. Ibid., pp. 80–81.

33. MARY MCDOWELL, "Woman's Union in Packing House," McDowell Papers; Foner, *History of the Labor Movement*, 3:249–50.

34. Minutes of the First Meeting of the National Executive Board, NWTUL, Mar. 20, 1904, NWTUL Papers; Nestor, *Woman's Labor Leader*, p. 65.

35. JOHN HOWARD KEISER, "John Fitzpatrick and Progressive Unionism" (Ph.D. diss., Northwestern University, 1965), p. 15.

36. FREDERICK D. KERSHNER, JR., "Alice Henry," in Edward T. James, Janet Wilson James, and Paul S. Boyer, eds., *Notable American Women, 1607–1950*, (Cambridge, Mass., 1971), 2:183–84.

37. *Union Labor Advocate* 8 (May 1908): 25–39.

38. *Chicago Herald*, Sept. 12, 1906; *Dallas Laborer*, Sept. 22, 1906.

39. *Hand Book of the Chicago Industrial Exhibit, Brooke's Casino, Wabash and Peck Court, March 11th to 17th* (Chicago, n.d.), pp. 21, 28–30; *Chicago Tribune*, Mar. 17, 1907.

40. *Weekly Bulletin of the Clothing Trade* 11 (Mar. 24, 1905): 3; *Union Labor Advocate* 10 (October 1909): 11; Schneiderman, *All for One*, pp. 77–78.

41. The best treatment of these strikes and the role played by the league in them is Nancy Schrom Dye, "The Women's Trade Union League of New York, 1903–1920" (Ph.D. diss., University of Wisconsin, 1974), pp. 110–55.

42. *Proceedings of the 1904 Convention of the ILGWU*, p. 9; *Annual Report of the Women's Trade Union League of New York, 1907–1908*, p. 15.

43. Minutes of the National Executive Board of the NWTUL, Mar. 26, 1905, NWTUL Papers.

44. PHILIP TAFT, *The AFL in the Time of Gompers* (New York, 1957), pp. 401–3.

45. GOMPERS to Gertrude Barnum, 12 October, 8 November 1905, NWTUL Papers; Samuel Gompers, *Seventy Years of Life and Labor* (New York, 1925), 1:491.

46. JAMES KENNEALLY, "Women and Trade Unions," *Labor History* 14 (Winter 1970): 47; Minutes of the National Board Meeting of the NWTUL, Oct. 4, 1904; Gompers to Gertrude Barnum, 8 November 1905, NWTUL Papers.

47. *Proceedings of the AFL Convention, 1908*, p. 12; *1917*, p. 32; Foner, *History of the Labor Movement*, 3:231–32.

48. MCCREESH, "Picket Lines," pp. 160–61.

49. See Foner, *History of the Labor Movement*, 3:174–218, for a detailed discussion of the effect of craft unionism in retarding organization of the unskilled and semiskilled, and pp. 256–81 for the AFL discriminatory approach to southern and eastern European immigrants. For the latter, see also Melvyn Dubofsky, "Organized Labor and the Immigrant in New York City, 1900–1918," *Labor History* 2 (Spring 1961): 200–209.

50. Minutes of the Meeting of Regular Membership, WTUL of NY, Oct. 28, 1907, WTUL of NY Papers.

51. F. E. WOLFE, *Admission to American Trade Unions* (Baltimore, 1912), pp. 85–86; Sarah Simpson to Gompers, 13 March 1903, AFL Correspondence.

52. WOLFE, *Admission,* pp. 88–92; H. D. Call to Frank Morrison, 14 February 1903, AFL Correspondence; David Brody, *The Butcher Workmen: A Study of Unionization* (Cambridge, Mass., 1964). pp. 41–42.

53. GLADYS BOONE. *The Women's Trade Union League in Great Britain and the United States of America* (New York, 1942), pp. 166–68; Henry, *Women and the Labor Movement,* p. 102; *Report of the Proceedings of the NYWTUL, 4th Conference,* p. 14.

54. P. DOLAN to Gompers, 29 October 1904, AFL Correspondence.

55. BOONE, *Women's Trade Union League,* pp. 166–68; Foner *History of the Labor Movement,* 3:230–31.

56. McCREESH, "Picket Lines," pp. 153–54; Dye, "Women's Trade Union League," pp. 116–17; *Annual Report of the Women's Trade Union League of New York, 1906–1907,* p. 11; Minutes of the Executive Board of the WTUL of NY, Mar. 28, Apr. 24, Sept. 26, 1907, WTUL of NY Papers.

57. McCREESH, "Picket Lines," pp. 155–56.

58. Ibid., p. 157.

59. Ibid., p. 158.

60. FONER, *History of the Labor Movement,* 3:230, 235–39.

61. *Springfield Republican,* June 1, 1905.

62. Ibid., June 9, 1905.

63. Ibid., June 12, 1905.

64. *Annual Report of the Women's Trade Union League of New York, 1907–1908,* p. 5; Foner *History of the Labor Movement,* 3:230n.

Chapter 18: The Waistmakers' Revolt

1. PEARL GOODMAN AND ELIA UELAND, "The Shirtwaist Trade," *Journal of Political Economy* 18 (December 1910): 814–16; Louis Levine, *The Women's Garment Workers* (New York, 1924), pp. 144–48; William Mailly, "The Working Girls' Strike," *Independent* 67 (Dec. 23, 1909): 1416–20.

2. GOODMAN AND UELAND, "The Shirtwaist Trade," pp. 817, 819, 820–25; Woods Hutchinson, "The Hygienic Aspects of the Shirtwaist Strike," *Survey* 23 (Jan. 22, 1910): 541–50; Miriam F. Scott, "The Spirit of the Girl Strikers," *Outlook* 94 (Feb. 19, 1910): 394–95; McCreesh, "Picket Lines," pp. 163–64; Dye, "Women's Trade Union League" p. 160.

3. HUTCHINSON, "Hygienic Aspects," p. 547; Scott, "Spirit of the Girl Strikers," p. 394; Constance D. Leupp, "The Shirtwaist Strike," *Survey* 23 (Dec. 18, 1909): 383–86; Hyman Berman, "Era of the Protocol: A Chapter in the History of the International Ladies' Garment Workers' Union, 1910–1916" (Ph.D. diss., Columbia University, 1956), p. 72; *New York Call,* Dec. 16, 1909.

4. McCREESH, "Picket Lines," pp. 162–63.

5. LEVINE, *Women's Garment Workers,* p. 149; *Proceedings of the Eighth Convention of the ILGWU, 1907* (New York, 1907), p. 30; *Report and Proceedings of the Ninth Convention of the International Ladies' Garment Workers' Union, 1908* (New York, 1908), p. 28; *New York Call,* Aug. 27, 1909; McCreesh, "Picket Lines," p. 166.

6. *New York Call,* Sept. 6, 8, 1909.

7. *New York Call,* Sept. 16, Oct. 12–20, 1909; Sue Ainsley Clark and Edith Wyatt, "The Shirtwaist Makers and Their Strike," *McClure's Magazine* 36 (November 1910): 70–86.

8. *New York Call,* Oct. 22, 1909.

9. BERMAN, "Era of the Protocol." pp. 78–79; *New York Call,* Nov. 25, 1909; *Souvenir History of the Ladies' Waist Makers' Union,* pamphlet in folder 56, n.d., National Women's Trade Union League of America Papers, Schlesinger Library, Radcliffe College, Cambridge, Mass., p. 11; (hereafter cited as NWTUL Papers). *Annual Report of the New York Women's Trade Union League, 1909–1910,* pp. 11–12; Mailly "Working Girls' Strike," p. 1417.

10. Secretary's Report, WTUL of NY, Nov. 11, 1909, WTUL of NY Papers; Dye, "Women's Trade Union League," p. 159.

11. New York *World,* Nov. 23, 1909; *New York Call,* Nov. 23, 1909; Levine, *Women's Garment Workers,* pp. 153–54; Leupp, "Shirtwaist Strike," pp. 383–86; Scott, "Spirit of the Girl Strikers," pp. 392–96; *Souvenir History,* p. 12.

12. McCREESH, "Picket Lines," p. 171.

13. Secretary's Report, Women's Trade Union League of New York, Nov. 17, 1909, WTUL of NY Papers; Dyche, "Strike of the Ladies' Waist Makers of New York," p. 2.

14. MAILLY, "Working Girls' Strike," p. 1419; *New York Call,* Nov. 23, 26, 27, 1909; Charles S. Bernheimer, *The Shirt-Waist Strike: An Investigation Made for the Council and Head Worker of the University Settlement* (New York, 1910), pp. 3–5.

15. MAILLY, "Working Girls' Strike," p. 1419; *New York Call,* Nov. 26–28, 1909; *New York Times,* Dec. 28, 1909; Graham Adams, Jr., *Age of Industrial Violence, 1910–1915* (New York, 1966), p. 106.

16. LEUPP, "Shirtwaist Strike," p. 383; *Annual Report of the Women's Trade Union League of New York. 1909–1910,* p. 14.

17. *New York Call,* Dec. 23, 1909; *New York Times,* Jan. 3, 1910.

18. *New York Times,* Dec. 21, 24, 1909, Jan. 4, 6, 7, 1910; Leupp, "Shirtwaist Strike," p. 384; *New York Call,* Nov. 25, 1909, Jan. 7, 1910; *Souvenir History,* pp. 13–14.

19. MARY CLARK BARNES, "The Strike of the Shirtwaist Makers," *World To-Day* 18 (March 1910): 267.

20. New York *World,* Dec. 4, 12, 1909; Dye, "Women's Trade Union League," p. 165; McCreesh, "Picket Lines," p. 173.

21. *Souvenir History,* pp. 14–15; *New York Call,* Dec. 4, 1909; Theresa Malkiel, *Diary of a Shirtwaist Striker* (New York, 1910), pp. 15, 20–21.

22. *New York Times,* Dec. 17, 1909; Dye, "Women's Trade Union League," pp. 165–66.

23. *New York Times,* Dec. 16, 1909; Minutes of the Regular Meeting of the Women's Trade Union League of New York, Feb. 7, 1910, WTUL of NY Papers; *Annual Report of the Women's Trade Union League of New York, 1909–1910,* p. 14.

24. *New York Times,* Dec. 14, 1909; *Annual Report of the Women's Trade Union League of New York, 1909–1910,* pp. 12–13; Minutes of the Executive Board of the WTUL of NY, Dec. 15, 1909, WTUL of NY Papers.

25. *New York Call,* Dec. 23, 1909; *New York Times,* Dec. 4, 1909.

26. *New York Times,* Dec. 21, 1909.

27. *New York Call,* Dec. 6, 1909; *New York Times,* Dec. 6, 1909; Malkiel. *Diary of a Shirtwaist Striker,* p. 23; *Souvenir History,* pp. 15–16.

28. *Philadelphia Public Ledger,* Feb. 5, 1910.

29. Ibid., Dec. 8, 9, 10, 20, 21, 1909; *Philadelphia Evening Bulletin,* Dec. 9, 10, 20, 21, 1909; McCreesh, "Picket Lines," pp. 174–75.

30. *Philadelphia Evening Bulletin,* Jan. 7, 11, 12, 13, 14, 17, Feb. 1, 5, 1910; *Philadelphia Public Ledger,* Jan. 7, 13, 15, 21, Feb. 3, 1910; Mary Durham to Agnes Nestor, 6 February 1910, Agnes Nestor Papers, Chicago Historical Society.

31. *Philadelphia Evening Bulletin,* Jan. 31, 1910.

32. *Philadelphia Public Ledger,* Jan. 15, 1910; McCreesh, "Picket Lines," p. 175.

33. *Philadelphia Evening Bulletin,* Jan. 11, 1910.

34. Ibid., Jan. 13, 1910.

35. *Philadelphia Public Ledger,* Jan. 15, 1910.

36. Ibid., Jan. 17, 20, 1910.

37. *New York Call,* Dec. 27, 28, 1909; *New York Times,* Dec. 28, 1909.

38. *New York Times,* Dec. 28, 1909; Levine, *Women's Garment Workers,* p. 164; Morris Hillquit, "Speech to the Striking Waist Makers," Jan. 2, 1910, Morris Hillquit Papers, State Historical Society of Wisconsin.

39. Malkiel, *Diary of a Shirtwaist Striker,* p. 55.

40. *New York Times,* Jan. 3, 8, 1910; *New York Call,* Jan. 3, 1910.

41. *Souvenir History,* p. 20; Malkiel, *Diary of a Shirtwaist Striker,* pp. 58–60; *New York Call,* Jan. 3, 1910; Morris Hillquit, speech at Carnegie Hall, Jan. 2, 1910, Morris Hillquit Papers, State Historical Society of Wisconsin.

42. *New York Times,* Dec. 21, 25, 1909, Jan. 4, 5, 6, 11, 1910; Mary Brown Sumner, "The Spirit of the Strikers," *The Survey* 23 (Jan. 22, 1910: 550–55; *New York Call,* Jan. 4, 11, 12, 1910; New York Department of Labor, *Bulletin No. 43,* March 1910, pp. 35–43.

43. *New York Times,* Dec. 28, 1909; Bernheimer, *Shirt-Waist Strike,* pp. 9–10; *Survey* 23 (Jan. 15, 1910): 506.

44. *New York Call,* Dec. 12, 1909.

45. Malkiel, *Diary of a Shirtwaist Striker,* p. 57.

46. Ibid., pp. 28, 45.

47. *New York Call*, Feb. 7, 15, 1910; McCreesh, "Picket Lines," p. 179.

48. *Philadelphia Public Ledger*, Feb. 7, 1910; *Philadelphia Evening Bulletin*, Feb. 8, 1910.

49. BARBARA MARY KLACZYNSKA, "Working Women in Philadelphia, 1900–1930" (Ph.D. diss., Temple University, 1975), pp. 240–41; *Philadelphia Evening Bulletin*, Jan. 18, 1910.

50. MIRIAM F. SCOTT, "What the Women Strikers Won," *Outlook* 95 (July 12, 1910): 480–88; John A. Dyche, *The Strike of the Ladies' Waist Makers* (New York, 1910), p. 2; Berman, "Era of the Protocol," p. 103.

51. MAX KATZMAN to Agnes Nestor, Philadelphia, 17 May 1910, Agnes Nestor Papers, Chicago Historical Society; *Proceedings of the Annual Convention of the ILGWU, 1912*, p. 69; Nancy Schrom Dye, "The Women's Trade Union League of New York, 1903–1920" (Ph.D. diss., University of Wisconsin, Madison, 1974), pp. 178–79.

52. *Survey* 23 (Jan. 29, 1910): 580–81, 620–21.

53. *Horizon* 5 (March 1910): 8–9.

54. Minutes of the Executive Board of the WTUL of NY, Feb. 16, 1910, WTUL of NY Papers, *Proceedings of the Third Biennial Convention of the NWTUL, 1911*, p. 19; Adriana Spadoni, "Italian Working Women in New York," *Colliers'* 44 (Mar. 23, 1912): 122; Frank Edwin Fenton, "Immigrants and Unions: A Case Study, Italians and American Labor, 1870–1920" (Ph.D. diss., Harvard University, 1957), p. 49; Dye, "Women's Trade Union League," p. 277.

55. DYE, "Women's Trade Union League," p. 170.

56. *Annual Report of the Women's Trade Union League of New York, 1909–1910*, p. 11.

57. "Rich and Poor in the Shirtwaist Strike," *Literary Digest*, Jan. 1, 1910, p. 6. Emphasis added.

58. *New York Call*, Dec. 29, 1909. Strike Edition.

59. HELEN MAROT, "A Woman's Strike—An Appreciation of the Shirtwaist Makers of New York." *Proceedings of the Academy of Political Science in the City of New York* (1910): 127–28; Dye, "Women's Trade Union League," p. 171.

60. MARY DURHAM to Agnes Nestor, 6 February 1910, Agnes Nestor Papers, Chicago Historical Society.

61. *Annual Report of the Women's Trade Union League of New York, 1909–1910*, p. 11; Dye, "Women's Trade Union League," (p. 170) does give the impression that the league financed the strike.

62. *Annual Report of the Women's Trade Union League of New York, 1909–1910* and *1910–1911;* Dye, "Women's Trade Union League," pp. 172, 203.

63. Report of Summer Work of the WTUL of NY, Oct. 3, 1910, WTUL of NY Papers; Dye, "Women's Trade Union League," p. 172; "President's Address," pamphlet, 1910, p. 8, file 300, O'Reilly Papers; Samuel M. Gompers, "The Struggle in the Garment Trades—From Misery and Despondency to Betterment and Hope," *American Federationist* 20 (March 1913): 189–90; James J. Kenneally, "Women and Trade Unions, 1870–1920: The Quandary of the Reformer," *Labor History* 14 (Winter 1973): 48.

64. HILLQUIT, "Speech to the Striking Waist Makers," Jan. 2, 1910, Hillquit Papers.

65. *New York Call,* Feb. 6, 1910.

66. WILLIAM M. FEIGENBAUM, "Memories of 1909—The First Dress-Makers' Revolt," *Justice,* Sept. 1, 1933, p. 9.

67. Zilphia Horton Folk Music Collection. Tennessee State Library and Archives, Nashville, Tenn.

Chapter 19: Repercussions of the Garment Workers' Uprising

1. LOUIS LEVINE, *Women's Garment Workers* (New York, 1924), pp. 168; 176; Hyman Berman, "Era of the Protocol: A Chapter in the History of the International Ladies' Garment Workers' Union, 1910–1916" (Ph.D. diss., Columbia University, 1956), pp. 107–108; *New York Call,* July 8, 1910.

2. *Proceedings of the Tenth Annual Convention of the ILGWU, June 6–11, 1910,* pp. 47–48, 71–72; *New York Call,* June 30, 1910; *New York Times,* June 30, 1910; Levine, *Women's Garment Workers,* pp. 180–81.

3. *New York Call,* July 8, 1910; Levine, *Women's Garment Workers,* pp. 172, 181; *Union Labor Advocate* 11 (August 1910): 12; Frank Edwin Fenton, "Immigrants and Unions: A Case Study, Italians and American Labor," 1870–1920" (Ph.D. diss., Harvard University, 1957), pp. 496–97; *Proceedings of the Tenth Annual Convention of the ILGWU,* pp. 49, 57, 94.

4. *New York Call,* July 12, 1910; *New York Times,* July 12, 1910.

5. *New York Times,* July 21, Aug. 12, 13, 14, 1910.

6. *New York Call,* July 15, 1910; Levine, *Women's Garment Workers,* pp. 192–93.

7. HELEN MAROT, "Secretary's Report, July 20, 1910," WTUL of NY Papers. McCreesh, "Picket Lines," pp. 187–88.

8. *New York Call,* July 13, 21, 22, 1910; *New York Times,* July 13, 1910.

9. *Eighth Convention Report of the ILGWU, Report of the President,* pp. 5–6; Berman, "Era of the Protocol," pp. 48–49.

10. *New York Call,* July 28, 1910; Berman, "Era of the Protocol," pp. 126–28.

11. FONER, *History of the Labor Movement,* 2:200.

12. GOMPERS to Abraham Rosenberg, 4 August 1910, AFL Archives.

13. *New York Call,* July 30, Aug. 4, 1910; Levine, *Women's Garment Workers,* pp. 186–91.

14. *New York Times,* Aug. 28, 1900; *New York Call,* Aug. 27, 29, 1910.

15. *New York Times,* Aug. 28, 1910.

16. GRAHAM ADAMS, Jr., *Age of Industrial Violence, 1910–1915* (New York, 1966), pp. 115–16.

17. Reprinted in *Literary Digest,* Sept. 10, 1910, p. 372.

18. *New York Times,* Aug. 29, 31, 1910; *Weekly Bulletin of the Garment Trades* 10 (Sept. 2, 1910): 4.

19. BERMAN, "Era of the Protocol," p. 151; Melvyn Dubofsky, *When Workers Organize: New York City in the Progressive Era,* Amherst, Mass., 1968, pp. 187, 194–95.

20. *New York Call,* Sept. 3, 1910; "The Outcome of the Cloakmakers' Strike," *Outlook* 96 (Sept. 17, 1910): 99–101.

21. *New York Call,* July 4, 1910; Helen Marot, "A Moral in the Cloakmakers' Strike," *Outlook* 96 (Sept. 17, 1910): 99–101.

22. BERMAN, "Era of the Protocol," pp. 152–53; John Laslett, *Labor and the Left* (New York, 1957), chap. 4.

23. *The Ladies' Garment Worker* 1 (Nov. 1, 1910): 2.

24. *Official Report of the Strike Committee of the WTUL of Chicago,* p. 6; McCreesh, "Picket Lines," p. 189.

25. ROBERT NOREN, United Garment Workers, to Emma Stehagen, 9 October 1910, NWTUL Papers, Schlesinger Library, Radcliffe College, Cambridge, Mass.

26. *Official Report of the Strike Committee,* p. 6; McCreesh, "Picket Lines," pp. 189–90.

27. *Official Report of the Strike Committee,* p. 6; McCreesh, "Picket Lines," pp. 190–91; Mary Anderson and Mary N. Winslow, *Woman at Work* (Minneapolis, 1951), p. 38.

28. ANDERSON and Winslow, *Woman at Work,* pp. 38–39.

29. *Official Report of the Strike Committee,* pp. 10–11.

30. Ibid., pp. 13–14; Matthew Josephson, *Sidney Hillman, Statesman of American Labor* (New York, 1952), p. 54.

31. *Life and Labor,* February 1911, p. 52.

32. *Official Report of the Strike Committee,* pp. 15–17.

33. *Chicago Daily Socialist,* Oct. 22–28, 1910; Leo Wolman, *et al., The Clothing Workers of Chicago, 1910–1922* (Chicago, 1925), pp. 26–27; *New York Call,* Nov. 10, 1910; Josephson, *Sidney Hillman,* pp. 41–57.

34. ANNE S. RIVERA, "Clarence Darrow for the Amalgamated," *Advance,* May 1974, p. 12; Alice Henry, "The Hart, Schaffner & Marx Agreement," *Life and Labor* 2 (June 1912): 170–72.

35. McCREESH, "Picket Lines," p. 194.

36. JOSEPHSON, *Sidney Hillman,* pp. 58–60.

37. *New York Call,* June 8, 1911; Levine, *Women's Garment Workers,* pp. 209–12.

38. *New York Call,* Aug. 6, 1911; *Life and Labor,* October 1911, p. 307; Margaret Dreier Robins to Members of the Executive Board, 4 August 1911, NWTUL Papers.

39. *Proceedings of the Eleventh Convention of the ILGWU, Toronto, 1912,* pp. 93–94.

40. McCREESH, "Picket Lines," p. 196.

41. *Public,* Dec. 16, 1910, pp. 1187–88; *Milwaukee Leader,* Dec. 11, 1910.

42. Minutes of the Meetings of the National Executive Board of the NWTUL,

Apr. 17, 18, 19, 1912, O'Reilly Papers; Pauline Newman, "The Story of the Corset Workers Strike in Kalamazoo, Michigan," clipping in O'Reilly Papers; McCreesh, "Picket Lines," pp. 199–200.

43. *Proceedings of the Eleventh Convention of the ILGWU, Toronto, 1912,* pp. 28–29; "Report of an Investigation of the Present Strike at the Kalamazoo Corset Company's Factory, April 17, 1912," O'Reilly Papers; McCreesh, "Picket Lines," p. 200.

44. "Report on an Investigation…"; Leonora O'Reilly, "The Story of Kalamazoo," *Life and Labor* 2 (August 1912): 228–30.

45. *The Ladies' Garment Worker* 5 (October 1914): 87; McCreesh, "Picket Lines," pp. 200–201.

46. *New York Call,* Dec. 22, 1910; Secretary's Report of the WTUL of NY, Dec. 21, 1910, WTUL of NY Papers.

47. NANCY SCHROM DYE, "The Women's Trade Union League of New York, 1903–1920" (Ph.D. diss., University of Wisconsin, Madison, 1974), pp. 180–81.

48. New York, Factory Investigating Commission, *Preliminary Report,* 1915, 2:25, 331.

49. The discussion of the fire is based on reports in the New York *World,* Mar. 26–30, 1911; *New York Call,* Mar. 26–Apr. 8, 1911; New York *Herald,* Mar. 26–27, 1911, and the excellent account of Leo Stein, *The Triangle Fire* (New York, 1962).

50. New York *Tribune* and *New York Call,* reprinted in *Literary Digest,* Jan. 6, 1912, p. 6.

51. *Proceedings of the Third Biennial Convention of the NWTUL, 1911,* p. 18; Nancy Schrom Dye, "The Women's Trade Union League," p. 183.

52. *Proceedings of the ILGWU Convention,* 1912, pp. 53–58; Dye, "Women's Trade Union League," pp. 184–86.

53. *Life and Labor* 2 (December 1912): 357.

54. PHILIP S. FONER, *The Fur and Leather Workers Union* (Newark, N.J., 1950), p. 39.

55. Ibid., pp. 24–26.

56. Ibid., pp. 40–41.

57. Ibid., pp. 39–42; *New York Call,* June 15–22, 1912; *Jewish Daily Forward,* June 15–19, 1912.

58. FONER, *Fur and Leather Workers Union,* pp. 42–43.

59. Ibid., p. 44; *Jewish Daily Forward,* July 7–8, 1912; Rose Blank, "Strike of the Furriers," *Life and Labor* 2 (December 1912): 360–61.

60. FONER, *Fur and Leather Workers Union,* pp. 46–47; Blank, "Strike of the Furriers," p. 360.

61. Quoted in Foner, *Fur and Leather Workers Union,* p. 48.

62. BLANK, "Strike of the Furriers," p. 360.

63. FONER, *Fur and Leather Workers Union,* pp. 44–49; *New York Call,* Aug. 22, 24, 25, Sept. 7, 8, 1912.

64. *Jewish Daily Forward,* Sept. 9, 1912; Foner, *Fur and Leather Workers Union,* pp. 51–52.

65. *New York Call,* Jan. 14, 1913; "Uprising in the Needle Trades in New York," *Life and Labor* 2 (March 1913): 69–70; *New York Times,* Jan. 14, 1913.

66. HARRY BEST, *The Men's Garment Industry of New York and the Strike of 1913* (New York, 1913), pp. 14–15; *New York Call,* June 6, 1912; *Weekly Bulletin* 11 (May 31, 1912): 4; June 7, 1912, p. 4; 12 (Oct. 25, 1912): 1; *Garment Worker* 12 (Nov. 15, 1912): 1.

67. *New York Call,* Dec. 24, 30, 21, 1912; Jan. 5, 6–7, 8–12, 1913; *New York Times,* Jan. 8, 1913; *The Garment Worker* 12 (Jan. 17, 1913): 1; Best, *Men's Garment Industry,* pp. 16–18.

68. *New York Times,* Jan. 4, 1913; *New York Call,* Jan. 3, 14, 18, 23, 1913, and letter of A. Appelberg in ibid., Jan. 22, 1913; *Garment Worker* 12 (Jan. 17, 1913): 1.

69. *New York Call,* Jan. 1, 17, 22, 27, 28, 29, Feb. 3, 7, 10, Mar. 1, 1913; *New York Times,* Jan. 15, 21, 27, 1913; *Garment Worker* 12 (Jan. 24, 1913): 1; ibid. 12 (Jan. 31, 1913): 1–2; Best, *Men's Garment Industry,* p. 23; Letter Books, Feb. 10, 1913, Socialist Party: Local New York, Tamiment Institute Library, New York University.

70. BEST, "Men's Garment Industry," pp. 20–25; *Fiftieth Anniversary Souvenir History of the New York Joint Board of the Amalgamated Clothing Workers of America, 1914–1916* (New York, 1964), pp. 55–57; Dubofsky, *When Workers Organize,* pp. 79–82; *New York Call,* Mar. 9, 12, 13, 1913; *New York Times,* Mar. 2, 13, 1913; *Garment Worker* 12 (Mar. 14, 1913): 1–2; Algernon Lee Scrapbooks, Labor Struggles, 1913, Taminent Institute Library, New York University.

71. ISAAC A. HOURWICH, "The Garment Workers' Strike," *New Review* 1 (Mar. 15, 1913): 426–27.

72. MARTHA BENSLEY BRUERE, "The White Goods Workers Strike," *Life and Labor* 3 (March 1913): 73–75.

73. Ibid., p. 73; New York *World,* Mar. 2, 1913; McCreesh, "Picket Lines," pp. 219–20.

74. "The Unrest in the Garment Trades," *Ladies' Garment Worker,* December 1911, pp. 10–11; May 1912, pp. 7–8; *Proceedings of the ILGWU Convention, 1912,* pp. 78, 88–90; Dye, "Women's Trade Union League," p. 186.

75. ROSE SCHNEIDERMAN, "The White Goods Workers of New York: Their Struggle for Human Conditions," *Life and Labor* 3 (May 1913): 132; Minutes of the Strike Council of the WTUL of NY, Apr. 2, 1911, Sept. 26, 1912, WTUL of NY Papers; Dye, "Women's Trade Union League," p. 187.

76. Minutes of the Strike Council of the WTUL of NY, Apr. 2, 1911; Minutes of the Executive Board, Oct. 24, 1912; Secretary's Report of the WTUL of NY, Aug. 22, 1912, WTUL of NY Papers; "The Stress of the Seasons," *Survey* 29 (Mar. 8, 1913): 806; John A. Dyche, *Strike of the Ladies' Waist Makers, of New York,* New York, 1910, pp. 187–88.

77. *New York Call,* Jan. 7, 1913; "Uprising in the Needle Trades in New York," p. 69.

78. HARRY LANG, *"62," Biography of a Union,* (New York, 1940), pp. 93–99; Minutes of the Executive Board Meeting of Jan. 23, 1913, WTUL of NY Papers, Schneiderman, "White Goods Workers," p. 134.

79. LANG, *"62,"* pp. 101–5; McCreesh, "Picket Lines," p. 221.

80. "The Song of the White Goods Workers," original in NWTUL Papers, Schlesinger Library, Radcliffe College, Cambridge, Mass., and reprinted in McCreesh, "Picket Lines," p. 216.

81. New York *World,* Mar. 2, 1913.

82. Ibid.

83. LEVINE, *Women's Garment Workers,* p. 227; Lang, *"62,"* p. 111; Schneiderman, "White Goods Workers," p. 136.

84. Minutes of the Executive Board of the WTUL of NY, Jan. 23, 1913, WTUL of NY Papers; Helen Marot, "What Can a Union Do for Its Members?" *New York Call,* Jan. 27, 1913; Dye, "Women's Trade Union League," p. 189–90.

85. LEVINE, *Women's Garment Workers,* pp. 229–30; Lang, *"62,"* p. 131; Schneiderman, "White Goods Workers," p. 136; "Report of the New York League to the Biennial Convention of the National Women's Trade Union League," O'Reilly Papers.

    Dye claims that the settlement did not mention either recognition or a preferential shop ("Women's Trade Union League," p. 190). But all other authorities include the preferential shop in the agreement.

86. McCREESH, "Picket Lines," p. 223.

87. *New York Call,* Jan. 16–19, 1913; *New York Times,* Jan. 19, 1913; Levine, *Women's Garment Workers,* pp. 223–26; Berman, "Era of the Protocol," pp. 165–72.

88. DUBOFSKY, *When Workers Organize,* pp. 83–87; Levine, *Women's Garment Workers,* pp. 226–28.

89. LEVINE, *Women's Garment Workers,* pp. 229–31; *Ladies' Garment Worker* 2 (August 1911): 14; McCreesh, "Picket Lines," pp. 225–26.

90. *New York Times,* Mar. 13–14, 1913; Berman, "Era of the Protocol," pp. 194–95; Levine, *Women's Garment Workers,* pp. 219, 235.

91. *Proceedings of the Fourth Biennial Convention of the NWTUL, 1913,* p. 21.

Chapter 20: New Unionism in the Garment Industry

1. JOHN A. DYCHE, *The Strike of the Ladies' Waist Makers of New York,* New York, 1910, p. 191.

2. *Ladies' Garment Worker* 3 (February 1912): 11; Hyman Berman, *op. cit.* pp. 287–88; Jack Hardy, *The Clothing Worker* (New York, 1935), pp. 30–39.

3. McCREESH, "Picket Lines." p. 246.

4. *Ladies' Garment Worker* 5 (April 1914): 16–17; June 1914, p. 25.

5. Ibid., August 1914, pp. 22–23.

6. CHARLES ELBERT ZARETZ, *The Amalgamated Clothing Workers of America* (New York, 1934), pp. 73–90; Earl D. Strong, *The Amalgamated Clothing Workers of America* (Grinnell, Ia., 1940), pp. 2–7.

7. ZARETZ, *Amalgamated Clothing Workers*, pp. 95–96; Leo Wolman et al., *The Clothing Workers of Chicago, 1910–1922* (Chicago, 1922), pp. 76–77; Strong, *Amalgamated Clothing Workers*, pp. 8–10; *Documentary History of the Amalgamated Clothing Workers of America, 1914–1916*, (New York, 1922), pp. 4–6.

8. ZARETZ, *Amalgamated Clothing Workers*, p. 96; Amalgamated Clothing Workers, *The Clothing Workers* (New York, 1932), pp. 74–95; *Documentary History*. pp. 24–25.

9. ZARETZ, *Amalgamated Clothing Workers*, p. 96; Amalgamated Clothing Workers, *Clothing Workers of Chicago*, pp. 74–95.

10. ZARETZ, *Amalgamated Clothing Workers*, p. 97; Matthew Josephson, *Sidney Hillman, Statesman of American Labor* (New York, 1952), pp. 95–97.

11. JOSEPHSON, *Sidney Hillman*, p. 99; McCreesh, "Picket Lines," p. 250.

12. *Garment Worker* 14 (Oct. 23, 1914): 1; Oct. 30, 1914, pp. 1,4; Joel Seidman, *The Needle Trades* (New York, 1942), pp. 115–25; Warren R. Van Tine, *The Making of a Labor Bureaucrat* (Amherst, Mass., 1973), p. 157.

13. Bernard Mandel, *Samuel Gompers: A Biography* (Yellow Springs, Ohio, 1963), p. 166.

14. ZARETZ, *Amalgamated Clothing Workers*, pp. 102–4; *Documentary History*, pp. 74–75.

15. *Documentary History*, pp. 74–75.

16. *Proceedings of the AFL Convention, 1915*, pp. 144–46, 360–61.

17. McCreesh, "Picket Lines," p. 251; Bessie Abramowitz to Sidney Hillman, 20 November 1914, 13 April 1915, Amalgamated Clothing Workers files, Amalgamated Clothing Workers Headquarters. New York City.

18. McCREESH, "Picket Lines." p. 251; Selma Goldblatt to Joseph Schlossberg, 30 November 1915; Schlossberg to Goldblatt, 10 February 1915, Amalgamated Clothing Workers files.

19. McCREESH, "Picket Lines," pp. 251–52; Dorothy Jacobs, "Baltimore Women Workers Were Leaders in Building Up a Strong Organization," *Advance* 1 (July 1917): 6; "Biography of Dorothy Jacobs," Amalgamated Clothing Workers files; Herbert Gutman, "Dorothy Jacobs Bellanca," in Edward T. James, Janet Wilson James, and Paul S. Boyer, eds., *Notable American Women, 1607–1950* (Cambridge, Mass., 1971), 1:124.

20. *Documentary History*, p. 181; *Garment Worker* 15 (Mar. 26, 1915): 1–2; Barbara Wertheimer, *We Were There: The Story of Working Women in America* (New York, 1977), p. 329.

21. *Garment Worker* 14 (May 28, 1915): 1–2.

22. *Proceedings of the AFL Convention, 1915*, pp. 144–46, 360–61; *Garment Worker* 14 (Aug. 27, 1915): 1, 4.

23. ABRAHAM CAHAN to Benjamin Schlesinger, 23 November 1916, Gompers Papers, Wisconsin State Historical Society, cited in Melvyn Dubofsky, "New York City Labor in the Progressive Era: A Study of Organized Labor in an Era of Reform" (Ph.D. diss., University of Rochester, 1960), pp. 302–03.

24. Josephson, *Sidney Hillman,* pp. 116–18.

25. Ibid., pp. 121–23; McCreesh, "Picket Lines," p. 274; Leo Wolman et al., *The Clothing Workers of Chicago,* (Chicago, 1922), pp. 95–98.

26. Josephson, *Sidney Hillman,* pp. 124–25; Leo Wolman et al., *The Clothing Workers of Chicago,* pp. 99–100; McCreesh, "Picket Lines," pp. 274–75.

27. Josephson, *Sidney Hillman,* pp. 125–26; *Proceedings of the Second Biennial Convention of the Amalgamated Clothing Workers of America, Rochester, New York, 1916,* pp. 150–51.

28. Mary "Mother" Jones to Secretary W. B. Wilson, 18 October 1915; Wilson to Jones, October 1915, Conciliation Service, file 313, 121, National Archives, Washington, D.C.; Sidney Hillman to Joseph Schlossberg, 22, 24 October 1915, Amalgamated Clothing Workers files; Mandel, *Gompers,* p. 308, McCreesh, "Picket Lines," pp. 275–76; Josephson, *Sidney Hillman,* pp. 126–28; Melech Epstein, *Jewish Labor in the U.S.A.: An Industrial, Political, and Cultural History of the Jewish Labor Movement* (New York, 1950–1953), 2:252.

29. *New Republic,* Jan. 1, 1916, p. 218; Feb. 19, 1916, pp. 73–74; Mar. 4, 1916, p. 130; Ellen Gates Starr to Gompers, 8 January 1916; Gompers to Starr, 10 February 1916, Amalgamated Clothing Workers files; Benjamin Larger to Gompers, 31 January, 4 October 1916, AFL Correspondence; McCreesh, "Picket Lines," pp. 265–68.

30. Josephson, *Sidney Hillman,* pp. 144–45; Epstein, *Jewish Labor,* 2:51; McCreesh, "Picket Lines," p. 276.

31. Jacobs, "Baltimore Women Workers," p. 6; McCreesh, "Picket Lines," pp. 276–77.

32. Dorothy Jacobs to Sidney Hillman, 30 March 1915, 6 February 1916, Amalgamated Clothing Workers files; McCreesh, "Picket Lines," p. 277.

33. *Proceedings of the Second Biennial Convention of the Amalgamated Clothing Workers, 1916,* p. 193.

34. Dorothy Jacobs to Joseph Schlossberg, 10 September 1916, Amalgamated Clothing Workers files; McCreesh, "Picket Lines," p. 278.

35. General Executive Board to Joint Boards, District Councils, and Local Unions, Oct. 30, 1916, Amalgamated Clothing Workers files; McCreesh, "Picket Lines," p. 279.

36. Dorothy Jacobs to Joseph Schlossberg, 20, 27 July, 13, 20 August, 10, 17 September, 5, 8 November 1916, Amalgamated Clothing Workers files; McCreesh, "Picket Lines," pp. 279–80.

37. *Advance* 1 (Mar. 9, 1917): 1.

38. McCreesh, "Picket Lines," p. 280.

39. Rose Schneiderman, with Lucy Goldthwaite. *All for One* (New York, 1967), pp. 110–12; Emily Barrows, "Trade Union Organization Among Women of Chicago" (Master's thesis, University of Chicago, 1927), pp. 61–69; Nestor, *Woman's Labor Leader* (Rockford, Ill., 1954), p. 163; Wilfred Carsel, *A History of the Chicago Ladies' Garment Workers' Union,* Chicago, 1940, pp. 88–91; McCreesh, "Picket Lines," pp. 280–82.

40. Schneiderman, *All for One,* pp. 113–17; McCreesh, "Picket Lines," pp. 282, 284.

41. *Proceedings of the Thirteenth ILGWU Convention, Philadelphia, 1916,* pp. 27, 48–50.

42. *Ladies' Garment Worker* 7 (March 1916): 20; April 1916, pp. 1–3; June 1916, pp. 12–13; *New York Times,* May 3, 1916; Berman, "Era of the Protocol," pp. 411–15.

43. *Ladies' Garment Worker* 7 (July 1916): 10–11; August 1916, p. 18; September 1916, pp. 18–20; *New York Times,* May 26, 29, June 11, 15, 28, July 19, 1916.

44. *New York Times,* May 27, 29, June 3, 1916; Berman, "Era of the Protocol," pp. 415–16.

45. *New York Times,* Aug. 4, 1916; *Ladies' Garment Cutter* 4 (Aug. 5, 1916): 1–2.

46. *Proceedings of the Thirteenth ILGWU Convention,* p. 12.

47. *Ladies' Garment Worker* 6 (November 1916): 4; Fannia M. Cohn, "Our Educational Work—A Survey" (New York, 1916), pp. 10–11; McCreesh, "Picket Lines," pp. 285–86.

48. *Proceedings of the Thirteenth ILGWU Convention,* p. 27.

49. PHILIP S. FONER, *The Fur and Leather Workers Union* (Newark, N.J., 1950), p. 55.

50. Ibid., pp. 58–60.

51. *Newark* (N.J.) *Times,* April 13–21, 1915; Foner, *Fur and Leather Workers Union,* pp. 56–57.

52. *Fur Worker,* Mar. 13, 20, Apr. 17, 1917.

53. JACOB M. BUDISH AND GEORGE SOULE, *The New Unionism in the Clothing Industry* (New York, 1920), pp. 13–65.

54. SCHNEIDERMAN, *All for One,* pp. 128–30.

55. ROSE SCHNEIDERMAN to Benjamin Schlesinger, 1 December 1916, copy in Rose Schneiderman Papers, Tamiment Institute Library, New York University.

Chapter 21: The Wobblies and the Woman Worker

1. *Proceedings of the First Convention of the Industrial Workers of the World,* New York, 1905, p. 82.

2. Ibid., pp. 3–6.

3. Ibid., pp. 610–14. Other female delegates were Isora Forberg, Evelyn Boehmann, Lilly Levenson, Mary E. Breckon, Rosa Sulway, Julie Mechanic, Mrs. E. C. Cogswell, and Bessie A. Hannan.

4. Originally called the Western Labor Union, its name was changed to American Labor Union in June, 1902. For the history of both the WLU and the ALU, see Foner, *History of the Labor Movement* 3:413–39.

5. *Proceedings, First Convention, IWW,* pp. 39, 167–73, 244–46, 248, 269; Philip S. Foner, *History of the Labor Movement in the United States,* vol. 4, *The Industrial*

Workers of the World, 1905–1917 (New York, 1965), pp. 34–36 (Hereafter cited as Foner, *IWW*.)

6. FONER, *History of the Labor Movement*, 3:231.

7. *Proceedings, First Convention, IWW*, pp. 520, 522.

8. Ibid., p. 462.

9. *Proceedings of the Second Annual Convention of the IWW*, Chicago, 1906, pp. 96–97; Paul Brissenden, *The IWW: A Study of American Syndicalism* (New York, 1920), p. 42.

10. *Proceedings, Second Convention, IWW*, p. 419.

11. "Minutes of the General Advisory Board," *Industrial Union Bulletin*, Mar. 30, 1907; "Minutes of the Local Executive Board," ibid., Jan. 10, 1907, Mar. 30, 1907, Aug. 17, 1907, Sept. 14, 1907, Nov. 9, 1907. See also "Debates in the Ghetto," ibid., May 4, 1907.

12. "General Executive Board," ibid., Nov. 9, 1907; "Still Growing in Portland," ibid., Mar. 30, 1907; "Call for Fifth Convention," *Industrial Worker*, Mar. 19, 1910.

13. ELIZABETH GURLEY FLYNN, *I Speak My Own Piece: Autobiography of "The Rebel Girl"* (New York, 1955), pp. 13–54; Rosalyn Fraad Baxandall, "Elizabeth Gurley Glynn: The Early Years," *Radical America* 8 (January–February 1975): 98.

14. Copy of speech in Elizabeth Gurley Flynn Papers, American Institute for Marxist Studies, New York City.

15. FLYNN, *I Speak My Own Piece*, p. 34: New York *World*, Aug. 23, 1906.

16. Los Angeles *Times*, Mar. 15, 1908.

17. BAXANDALL, "Flynn," p. 100.

18. See, for example, advertisement in *Industrial Worker*, May 20, 1910, p. 2.

19. *Industrial Union Bulletin*, Aug. 3, 1907.

20. *Industrial Worker*, Apr. 22, 1909; *Solidarity*, June 6, 1914; "To Colored Workingmen and Workingwomen," IWW leaflet, Elizabeth Gurley Flynn Collection, Wisconsin State Historical Society; *Voice of Labor*, reprinted in *Solidarity*, June 24, 1911; Foner, *IWW*, pp. 123, 125.

21. *Solidarity*, July 8, 1916.

22. ELIZABETH GURLEY FLYNN, "Women and Socialism," *Solidarity*, May 27, 1911; Foner, *IWW*, pp. 127–28. *One Big Union Monthly*, Sept. 1, 1919, p. 25.

23. ELIZABETH GURLEY FLYNN, "Women in Industry Should Organize," *Industrial Worker*, June 1, 1911. Similar is her article, "Women and Unionism," *Solidarity*, May 27, 1911.

24. *Solidarity*, Nov. 23, 1918.

25. "From a Woman Toiler," *Solidarity*, June 25, 1910.

26. *Industrial Worker*, March 1906, p. 6; August 1906, p. 10; Flynn, *I Speak My Own Piece*, p. 122.

27. SOPHIE VASILIO, "Women in the IWW," *Industrial Union Bulletin*, Apr. 25, 1908, and editor's reply in ibid.

28. *Solidarity*, Sept. 17, 1910; Foner, *IWW*, p. 120.

29. ERNEST GRIFFEATH, "On Free Love and the Home," *Industrial Worker,* June 5, 1913.

30. *Voice of the People,* July 30, 1914; Bill Boyd, "The Girl Out at Work," *Solidarity,* June 29, 1916, Feb. 5, 1921.

31. *Industrial Worker,* Apr. 3, 1913, Dec. 8, 1910, July 12, 1913; *Voice of the People,* Aug. 13, 1914.

32. *Industrial Worker,* Apr. 10, 1913.

33. *Solidarity,* Feb. 8, 1912; "Capitalist Morality," ibid., Sept. 3, 1910; Bill Lloyd, "The Wobbly and the Farmer's Daughter," *Solidarity,* Jan. 1, 1921.

34. "Large Families," *Industrial Worker,* June 1, 1911.

35. *Industrial Worker,* Sept. 28, 1911; "Family Limitation," *Voice of the People,* Nov. 1, 1914; Margaret Sanger, *Autobiography* (New York, 1938), p. 79.

36. FLYNN, *I Speak My Own Piece,* p. 152.

37. JOSEPH R. CONLIN. *Big Bill Haywood and the Radical Union Movement* (Syracuse, N.Y., 1969), pp. 106–7; Mabel Dodge Luahan, *Intimate Memoirs,* vol. 3, *Movers and Shakers* (New York, 1936), pp. 186–88.

38. FLYNN, *I Speak My Own Piece,* p. 84; Ralph Chaplin, *Wobbly: The Rough and Tumble Story of an American Radical* (Chicago, 1978), pp. 112–25.

39. PHILIP S. FONER, *The Case of Joe Hill* (New York, 1965), pp. 25–36.

40. JOYCE L. KORNBLUH, ed., *Rebel Voices: An IWW Anthology* (Ann Arbor, Mich., 1974), p. 138.

41. FLYNN, *I Speak My Own Piece,* pp. 54, 68, 75–77, 103, 108, 140, 323; Foner, *IWW,* pp. 188–89; Baxandall, "Flynn," pp. 102–3.

42. *One Big Union Monthly,* October 1919, p. 39; New York *Tribune,* Feb. 2, 1913; Foner, *IWW,* p. 149.

43. KORNBLUH, *Rebel Voices,* p. 180; Patrick Renshaw, *The Wobblies: The Story of Syndicalism in the United States* (New York, 1967), p. 11, Flynn, *I Speak My Own Piece,* p. 129; Benjamin H. Kizer, "Elizabeth Gurley Flynn," *Pacific Northwest Quarterly* 34 (July 1916): 110–12; Interview with Elizabeth Gurley Flynn, Jan. 31, 1964; *Daily World,* June 30, 1976.

44. *Solidarity.* Jan. 8, 15, 1910.

45. ELIZABETH GURLEY FLYNN, "IWW Call to Women," *Solidarity,* July 31, 1915.

46. *Solidarity,* May 27, 1911; June 28, 1911; Elizabeth Gurley Flynn in ibid., May 27, 1911, and in San Francisco *Bulletin,* Oct. 3, 1914, Elizabeth Gurley Flynn Collection, Wisconsin State Historical Society.

47. CHARLES ASHLEIGH, "Women in the IWW," *Industrial Union Bulletin,* Apr. 25, 1908.

48. ELIZABETH GURLEY FLYNN, "Problems Organizing Women," *Solidarity,* July 15, 1915.

49. "Tenth IWW Convention." *Solidarity,* Dec. 16, 1916.

50. *Solidarity,* Dec. 19, 1914.

51. FONER, *IWW,* pp. 128–29.

52. JANE STREET, "Denver's Rebel Housemaids," *Solidarity,* Apr. 1, 1916.

53. JANE STREET to Mrs. Elmer F. Buse (1917), original in Department of Justice, Record Group, File 1870–28, National Archives, Washington, D.C., and reprinted in Daniel T. Hobby, ed., "We Have Got Results: A Document on the Organization of Domestics in the Progressive Era," *Labor History* 17 (Winter 1976): 103–8.

54. "Housemaids Form Union in Denver," *Solidarity,* Apr. 1, 1916.

55. HOBBY, "We Have Got Results," pp. 104–5.

56. JANE STREET in *Solidarity,* Apr. 1, 1916.

57. *Solidarity,* May 6, 1916.

58. Ibid., Apr. 1, 1916.

59. HOBBY, "We Have Got Results," p. 105.

60. *Solidarity,* Apr. 8, 1916.

61. HOBBY, "We Have Got Results," p. 107.

62. *Solidarity,* Dec. 16, 1916.

63. FONER, *IWW,* pp. 557–58.

64. Ibid., pp. 2, 62–64.

65. FLYNN, "IWW Call to Women," *Solidarity,* July 31, 1915.

Chapter 22: Rebel Women and the Free-Speech Fights

1. *Solidarity,* July 25, 1914; Foner, IWW, pp. 173–74.

2. *Industrial Worker,* Feb. 12, 1910; Foner, *IWW,* p. 175.

3. ELIZABETH GURLEY FLYNN, *I Speak My Own Piece: Autobiography of "The Rebel Girl"* (New York, 1955), pp. 92–94; New York *Call,* Oct. 6, 1909; Foner *IWW,* pp. 175–77.

4. ELIZABETH GURLEY FLYNN, "The Free Speech Fight at Spokane," *International Socialist Review* 10 (December 1909), p. 486; Elizabeth Gurley Flynn, "The Shame of Spokane," ibid., January 1910, pp. 610–19.

5. *Workingman's Paper* (Seattle), Nov. 20, 1909.

6. Ibid., Dec. 4, 1909.

7. Ibid., Jan. 22, 1910.

8. IWW circular, copy in AFL Correspondence; *Solidarity,* Dec. 23, 1909, Feb. 26, July 2, 1910; Foner, *IWW,* pp. 181–82; Benjamin H. Kizer, "Elizabeth Gurley Flynn," *Pacific Northwest Quarterly* 34 (July 1916): 110–12.

9. *Industrial Worker,* Feb. 5, 1910; Flynn, *I Speak My Own Piece,* pp. 97–100.

10. *Solidarity,* Feb. 17, 1912; *Industrial Worker,* Feb. 29, 1912.

11. *Industrial Worker,* Mar. 7, 1912; Oakland *World,* Mar. 23, 1912.

12. *Industrial Worker,* Apr. 25, 1912; Melvyn Dubofsky, *We Shall Be All: A History of the Industrial Workers of the World* (Chicago, 1969), pp. 190–97; Foner, *IWW,* pp. 201–4; Hartwell S. Shippey, "The Shame of San Diego," *Interna-*

tional Socialist Review 10 (March 1912), pp. 718–23; Rosalie Shanks, "The IWW Free Speech Movement in San Diego, 1912," *Journal of San Diego History*, Winter 1973, pp. 25–33.

13. *Industrial Union Bulletin,* Mar. 23, 1907.

14. Ibid., Apr. 13, 1907; *Solidarity,* Mar. 26, 1910.

15. SOMERSET *Reporter,* Jan. 24, 1907; *Industrial Union Bulletin,* Mar. 2, 1907; *Industrial Solidarity,* Mar. 20, 1931.

16. SOMERSET *Reporter,* Jan. 31, Feb. 7, 1907.

17. Ibid., Jan. 24, 1907.

18. Ibid., Feb. 28, 1907.

19. Ibid., Apr. 30, May 8, 1907; *Industrial Union Bulletin,* Apr. 27, Sept. 14, 1907; *Industrial Solidarity,* Mar. 10, 1931; Foner, *IWW,* pp. 86–88.

20. JOSEPH CONLIN, "The Wobblies: A Study of the Industrial Workers of the World, before World War I" (Ph.D. diss., University of Wisconsin, Madison, 1969), p. 145.

21. *Voice of the People,* Sept. 17, 1914.

22. *New York Call,* July 22, Aug. 3, 1909.

23. Ibid., July 16, Aug. 4, 1909; *Solidarity,* Apr. 30, 1910; Paul U. Kellogg, "The McKees Rocks Strike," *Survey,* Aug. 7, 1909, pp. 656–59.

24. Pittsburgh *Leader,* July 15, 1909; *New York Call,* July 22, 1909; Kellogg, "McKees Rocks Strike," p. 665.

25. Pittsburgh *Leader,* July 15, 1909; *New York Call,* July 15, 16, 1909; New York *Tribune,* July 16, 1909; Kellogg, "McKees Rocks Strike," pp. 656–57.

26. FONER, *IWW,* pp. 284, 287–88; New York *Tribune,* July 16, 17, 1909; *New York Call,* July 27, 1909; Louis Duchez, "Victory at McKees Rocks," *International Socialist Review* 10 (October 1909): 289.

27. *Pittsburgh Leader,* July 16, 1909; *New York Call,* July 16, 1909; New York *Tribune,* July 16, 1909; dispatch from Pittsburgh in unnamed paper, dated July 17, 1909, in Eugene V. Debs Clipping Book, No. 2, 1909, Tamiment Institute Library, New York University.

28. DUCHEZ, "Victory at McKees Rocks," p. 289.

29. FONER, *IWW,* pp. 293–94; Duchez, "Victory at McKees Rocks," p. 290; Pittsburgh *Dispatch,* Sept. 3, 1909; *Pittsburgh Leader,* Sept. 9, 1909; *New York Call,* Sept. 7–11, 1909.

30. *New York Call,* Oct. 12, 1909. For an analysis of the McKees Rocks strike that argues that it ended in failure, a conclusion not justified by the evidence presented, see John N. Ingham, "A Strike in the Progressive Era: McKees Rocks, 1909," *Pennsylvania History and Biography* 90 (July 1966): 353–77. Ingham concedes, however, that "the IWW gave the foreigners there [at Pressed Steel] by far the most effective organization they were to have for decades to come" (ibid., p. 374*n*).

31. *Lake County Times,* Jan. 15, Feb. 5, 1910; Donald Griffith Adams, "Foreign-Born Laborers in Indiana" (Master's thesis, University of Indiana, 1911), pp. 15–16; *Solidarity,* Jan. 29, Feb. 5, 1910; Indianapolis *Star,* Jan. 16, 1910.

32. *Lake County Times,* Jan. 19, 26–28, Feb. 4, 1910; *Indianapolis Star,* Jan. 27, 1910; *Solidarity,* Jan. 29, Feb. 5, 1910; Foner, *IWW,* p. 296.

33. *Lake County Times,* Jan. 26–28, Feb. 4, 1910; *Indianapolis Star,* Jan. 27, 1910; *Solidarity,* Feb. 5, 1910; *New York Call,* Feb. 4, 1910; Foner, *IWW,* pp. 298–99.

Chapter 23: The Lawrence Strike

1. U.S., Congress, House, Hearings on Strike in Lawrence, Mass., *House Document No. 671,* 62d Cong., 1st sess., 1912, pp. 458, 460. Maurice B. Dergan, *History of Lawrence, Massachusetts* (Lawrence, Mass., 1924), p. 44; Donald B. Cole, "Lawrence, Massachusetts: 1845–1912" (Ph.D. diss., Harvard University, 1956), p. 35; *Textile Manufacturers Journal,* Mar. 9, 1912, p. 4; Frank Edwin Fenton, "Immigrants and Unions: A Case Study, Italians and American Labor, 1870–1920" (Ph.D. diss., Harvard University, 1957), pp. 320–21.

2. U.S., Bureau of Labor, *Report on Strike of Textile Workers in Lawrence, Massachusetts in 1912,* pp. 19, 76–78; U.S., Department of Commerce and Labor, Bureau of the Census, *Census Monographs,* vol. 10, 1929; Paul F. Brissenden, *Earnings of Factory Workers, 1899 to 1927,* U.S., Bureau of the Census, monograph 10, 1929, pp. 45, 96, 104, 113, 114.

3. Donald B. Cole, *Immigrant City: Lawrence, Massachusetts, 1845–1921* (Chapel Hill, N.C., 1963), pp. 101, 108, 109.

4. U.S., Congress, Senate, *Report on the Strike of the Textile Workers in Lawrence, Massachusetts in 1912. Senate Document No. 870,* 62d Cong., 2d sess., 1912, p. 204.

5. U.S., Bureau of Labor, *Report on Strike of Textile Workers,* pp. 19, 28, 71, 120, 160, 205; Lewis E. Palmer, "A Strike for Four Loaves of Bread," *Survey,* Feb. 3, 1912, pp. 1695–99.

6. U.S., Bureau of Labor, *Report on Strike of Textile Workers,* pp. 22, 88, 119.

7. U.S., Congress, House, *House Document No. 671,* pp. 114–15; *Solidarity,* Mar. 2, 1912; John B. McPherson, "The Lawrence Strike of 1912," *Bulletin of the National Association of Wool Manufacturers* 12 (1912): 236–37.

8. U.S., Bureau of Labor, *Report on Strike of Textile Workers,* pp. 191–204; Dr. Elizabeth Shapleigh, "Occupational Diseases in the Textile Industry," *New York Call,* Dec. 29, 1912.

9. Irving J. Levine, "The Lawrence Strike" (Master's thesis, Columbia University, 1936), p. 35.

10. *Lawrence Evening Tribune,* Dec. 22, 23, 28, 1911; Jan. 4, 12, 1912.

11. Foner, *IWW,* pp. 306–11.

12. Elizabeth Gurley Flynn, "Memories of the Industrial Workers of the World (IWW)," Occasional Paper No. 24 (1977), American Institute for Marxist Studies (New York, 1977), p. 9. The publication is a report of an

address Flynn delivered at Northern Illinois University on November 8, 1962, less than two years before her death.

13. *Lawrence Evening Tribune,* Jan. 17, 1912.

14. *Lawrence Sun,* Jan. 14, 20, Feb. 24, 1912; U.S., Congress, House, *House Document No. 671,* pp. 294–95; Foner, *IWW,* pp. 321–22.

15. "Bread and Roses," by James Oppenheimer, in Joyce L. Kornbluh, ed., *Rebel Voices: An I.W.W. Anthology* (Ann Arbor, Mich., 1964), p. 196.

16. *New York Call,* Feb. 24, 1912; *Lawrence Evening Tribune,* Feb. 24, 1912; Dergan, *History of Lawrence,* p. 173.

17. U.S.. Congress, House, *House Document No. 671,* p. 249.

18. WILLIAM D. HAYWOOD, *Bill Haywood's Book: The Autobiography of William D. Haywood* (New York, 1929), p. 249.

19. *Lawrence Evening Tribune,* Feb. 28, 1912.

20. *Solidarity,* Mar. 2, 1912, July 31, 1915.

21. FRED BEALE, *Proletarian Journey* (New York, 1927), p. 44.

22. *Lawrence Evening Tribune,* Jan. 27, Feb. 16, 1912; Harry Emerson Fosdick, "After the Strike in Lawrence," *Outlook,* June 15, 1912, reprinted in *Solidarity,* July 6, 1912.

23. *Lawrence Evening Tribune,* Jan. 17, 22, Feb. 16, 19, 1912.

24. ELIZABETH GURLEY FLYNN, *I Speak My Own Piece: Autobiography of "The Rebel Girl"* (New York, 1955), p. 122.

25. JAMES P. HEATON, "The Legal Aftermath of the Lawrence Strike," *Survey* 28 (July 6, 1912): 509–10; Vida D. Scudder, "For Justice's Sake," ibid., Apr. 16, 1912, p. 77; Justus Ebert, *The Trial of a New Society* (Cleveland, 1913), p. 42.

26. MARY HEATON VORSE, *Footnote to Folly* (New York, 1935), pp. 13–14.

27. MARY HEATON VORSE, "Elizabeth Gurley Flynn," *Nation,* Feb. 17, 1926, pp. 175–76.

28. FLYNN, "Memories," p. 10.

29. FLYNN, *I Speak My Own Piece,* pp. 125–26.

30. FONER, *IWW,* p. 325.

31. *New York Call,* Mar. 6, 1912; *Lawrence Evening Tribune,* Feb. 10, 18, 1912; Margaret Sanger, *Autobiography* (New York, 1938), p. 81.

32. *New York Call,* Feb. 8, 1912; *Boston American,* Feb. 15, 18, 1912.

33. FONER, *IWW,* p. 326.

34. JOYCE L. KORNBLUH, ed., *Rebel Voices: An IWW Anthology* (Ann Arbor, Mich., 1964), p. 162; Rosalyn Fraad Baxandall, "Elizabeth Gurley Flynn: The Early Years," *Radical America* 8 (January–February 1975): 107.

35. U.S., Congress, House, *House Document No. 671,* pp. 201–8, 249–53, 301–9; *Lawrence Evening Tribune,* Feb. 24, 1912; *Lawrence Sun,* Feb. 25, 1912; *Solidarity,* Mar. 2, 1912; *New York Call,* Mar. 6, 1912.

36. *New York Call,* Feb. 25, 1912; *The Public,* Mar. 1, 1912, p. 202; *Congressional Record,* 62d Cong., 2d sess., pp. 2485–86.

37. LESLIE MARCY AND FREDERICK SUMNER BOYD, "One Big Union Wins," *International Socialist Review* 12 (April 1912): 625.

38. U.S., Congress, House, *House Document No. 671,* p. 302.

39. *Solidarity,* Mar. 16, 1912.

40. *Lawrence Sun,* Mar. 14–15, 1912; *New York Call,* Mar. 14–15, 1912; Foner, *IWW,* pp. 340–42.

41. *Industrial Worker,* July 25, 1912, p. 4.

42. LINDA STERNBERG, "Women Workers and the 1912 Textile Strike in Lawrence, Massachusetts," Paper, Division 3 Project, Hampshire College, Amherst, Mass., Apr. 28, 1975, pp. 74–76.

43. RAY STANNARD BAKER, "Revolutionary Strike," *American Magazine* 74 (May 1912): 30c.

44. MARY HEATON VORSE, "The Troubles at Lawrence," *Harper's Weekly* Mar. 16, 1912, p. 10.

45. STERNBERG, "Women Workers and the 1912 Textile Strike," 112–15.

Chapter 24: Little Falls, Paterson, and Other Struggles

1. Massachusetts, Bureau of Statistics, *13th Annual Report on Strikes and Lockouts for 1912,* 1913, pp. 6–9.

2. *New York Times,* Mar. 25, 1912; *Lawrence Evening Tribune,* Mar. 25, 1912; *American Wool and Cotton Reporter,* Mar. 21, 1912, p. 394; *Textile Manufacturer,* May 25, 1912, p. 146.

3. New York Department of Labor, Reports of the Board of Mediation and Arbitration and Bureau of Labor Statistics, "The Little Falls Textile Workers Dispute," *New York Labor Bulletin* 15 (March 1913): 50–51.

4. New York, Department of Labor, "The Little Falls Textile Workers Dispute," pp. 32–44.

5. New York. Department of Labor, *New York Labor Bulletin* 57 (January 1914): 25–26; New York, Department of Labor, *Annual Report of the Bureau of Labor Statistics: 1912,* 1913, pp. 128–29, 482.

6. *New York Times,* Jan. 4, 1912.

7. *Schenectady Citizen,* Nov. 22, 1912.

8. *New York Times,* Mar. 30, 1912; Josephine Goldmark, "Legislative Gains for Women in 1912," *Survey,* Apr. 13, 1912, pp. 95–96.

9. *Utica Daily Press,* Oct. 16, 1912.

10. *Schenectady Citizen,* Oct. 18, 25, 1912; *Little Falls Journal and Courier,* Nov. 12, Dec. 10, 1912; *New York Call,* Oct. 28, Nov. 12, Dec. 6, 1912; *Syracuse Post Standard,* Oct. 17, 1912. For Lunn, *see* Kenneth E. Hendrickson, Jr., "George R. Lunn and the Socialist Era in Schenectady, 1909–1916," *New York History* 47

(January 1966): 22–40. The best analysis of the role of the Schenectady Socialists in the Little Falls strike, but one that tends to exaggerate the contributions of Mayor Lunn, is Robert E. Snyder, "Between Lawrence and Paterson: The IWW in Little Falls, New York," Paper delivered at Southwest Labor Studies Conference, March 1977.

11. The information on Legere is derived from "My Story," autobiography of Matilda (Rabinowitz) Robbins in the Robbins Papers, Wayne State University, Detroit. Rabinowitz knew Legere and worked with him in the IWW.

12. *Utica Daily Press*, Oct. 23, 1912; *Syracuse Post Standard*, Oct. 24, 1912; *New York Call*, Oct. 24, 1912.

13. *Utica Daily Press*, Oct. 25, 1912.

14. Ibid., Oct. 24, 1912; *Utica Observer*, Oct. 24, 1912; New York *Call*, Oct. 24, 1912; *Little Falls Journal and Courier*, Oct. 29, 1912.

15. *Utica Daily Press*, Oct. 25, 28, 30, 1912; *Schenectady Gazette*, Oct. 26, 1912.

16. *Utica Daily Press*, Oct. 31, Nov. 1, 1912; *Little Falls Journal and Courier*, Nov. 26, Dec. 26. 1912; *Utica Daily Press*, Nov. 2, 1912; *Industrial Worker*, Dec. 28, 1912; William D. Haywood, *Bill Haywood's Book: The Autobiography of William D. Haywood* (New York, 1929), p. 257.

17. "My Story," pp. 42–43, 49.

18. Ibid., pp. 50–51.

19. Ibid., p. 52.

20. *Little Falls Journal and Courier*, Nov. 26, Dec. 26, 1912.

21. PHILIP S. FONER, *Helen Keller: Her Socialist Years* (New York, 1968), pp. 12–14, 32–35; *Little Falls Journal and Courier*, Nov. 19, Dec. 3, 1912.

22. *Little Falls Journal and Courier*, Nov. 19, 26, Dec. 3, 31, 1912; *Utica Daily Press*, Dec. 23, 1912; *Solidarity*, Nov. 23, 1912.

23. *Schenectady Gazette*, Oct. 19, 1912; *Utica Daily Press*, Oct. 22, 1912; *Utica Observer*, Dec. 17, 1912.

24. *Utica Daily Press*, Dec. 17, 1912; *Solidarity*, Dec. 21, 28, 1912; *Industrial Worker*, Dec. 26, 1912; *New York Call*, Dec. 20, 1912.

25. *Utica Daily Press*, Jan. 2–3, 1913; *Utica Observer*, Jan. 3, 1913; *Little Falls Journal and Courier*, Jan. 7, 1913; *New York Call*, Jan. 3, 1913; *Solidarity*, Jan. 11, 1913; Phillips Russell, "The Strike at Little Falls," *International Socialist Review* 13 (December 1912): 455–60.

26. *Industrial Worker*, Jan. 16, 1913.

27. PHILLIPS RUSSELL, "The Fourteen in Jail," *International Socialist Review* 13 (February 1913): 598–99; *Solidarity*, Jan. 18, 25, 1913; Foner, *IWW*, p. 352; Snyder, "Between Lawrence and Paterson," p. 36.

28. *New York Times*, Feb. 26, 1913; Howard Levin, "The Paterson Silk Workers' Strike of 1913," *King's Crown Essays*, Winter 1961–62, p. 45; New Jersey, Bureau of Statistics of Labor and Industry, *Report for 1913*, 1914, p. 188; *Report for 1914* (Camden, N.J., 1915), pp. 26, 127; Gregory Mason, "Industrial War in Paterson," *Outlook* 54 (June 7, 1913): 283–87.

29. W. L. KINKEAD, "Paterson Silk Strike," *Survey* 30 (June 13, 1913): 316; E. Koettgen, "Making Silk," *International Socialist Review* 14 (March 1914): 553–54; New Jersey, Bureau of Statistics of Labor and Industry, *Report for 1914*, 1915, pp. 158–59; Philip Charles Newman, "The IWW in New Jersey, 1912–1913" (Master's thesis, Columbia University, 1954), p. 101; Grace Hutchins, *Labor and Silk* (New York, 1924), pp. 120–21; *Solidarity*, Mar. 15, 1913.

30. ELIZABETH GURLEY FLYNN, "Figures and Facts and Contract Slavery in the Paterson Silk Mills," in *The Pageant of the Paterson Strike* (New York, 1913); William D. Haywood, "The Rip in the Silk Industry," *International Socialist Review* 13 (May 1913): 122–28.

31. *Paterson Press*, Feb. 23, 26, 1912; *New York Call*, Feb. 24, 27, 1912; Philip Newman, "The First IWW Invasion of New Jersey," *Proceedings of the New Jersey Historical Society* 58 (1940): 270–83; Foner, *IWW*, 353–55.

32. *Paterson Press*, Jan. 27–28, Feb. 7, 18, 1913.

33. HAROLD B. DENN, "The History of the Silk Workers in Paterson, New Jersey, With Special Emphasis on Strikes, 1910–1920" (Master's thesis, New York University, 1947), p. 55; *Paterson Press*, Feb. 24, 26, Mar. 4, 1913; Haywood, "Rip in the Silk Industry," p. 783; *Report of the Bureau of Statistics of Labor and Industry of New Jersey for 1913*, p. 185.

34. L. MANNHEIMER, "Darkest New Jersey, How the Paterson Strike Looks to One in the Thick of the Conflict," *Independent* 74 (April–June 1913): 1191–92; *Paterson Press*, Feb. 26, 27, Mar. 1, Apr. 5, 7, 8, 15, June 7, 1913; *New York Call*, Feb. 28, Mar. 4, Apr. 17–19, June 11, 1913; Haywood, "Rip in the Silk Industry," p. 788.

35. HAYWOOD, *Bill Haywood's Book*, p. 267.

36. *Paterson Press*, Mar. 13–14, 19–20, 1913; *New York Call*, Mar. 14, 1913.

37. "The Strike of the Jersey Silk Workers," *Survey*, 30 (Apr. 19, 1913): 81–82; *New York Times*, Apr. 14, May 15, 17, 22, June 4, 21, 1913.

38. *New York Call*, Apr. 20, 22, May 7, 1913; *Paterson Press*, Apr. 18, 19, 22, 1913; *The Education of John Reed: Selected Writings with a Critical Introduction by John Stuart* (New York, 1955), p. 39.

39. GRANVILLE HICKS, *John Reed, The Making of a Revolutionary* (New York, 1936), pp. 100–02; *New York Call*, Apr. 30, 1913; *The Pageant of the Paterson Strike* (New York, 1913).

40. *New York Times*, June 8, 13, 1913; Foner, *IWW*, pp. 366–67.

41. "The End of the Paterson Strike," *Outlook* 104 (1913): 780; New Jersey, Bureau of Statistics of Labor and Industry, *Report for 1913*, pp. 227, 230, 238; *Paterson Press*, June 17, July 25, 1913; *New York Call*, June 20, Aug. 27, 1913; Foner, *IWW*, pp. 367–69.

42. HAROLD S. ROBERTS, *The Rubber Workers* (New York, 1944), pp. 26–37; *New York Call*, Feb. 28, 1913; *Akron Beacon Journal*, Jan. 2, Feb. 12–14, 1913; Foner, *IWW*, pp. 373–75.

43. Akron *Press,* reprinted in Leslie H. March, "800 Percent and the Akron Strike," *International Socialist Review* 13 (April 1913): 719-20.

44. *Akron Beacon Journal,* Feb. 19, 20, 25, Mar. 11, 13, 15, 1913; Roberts, *The Rubber Workers,* p. 44; Foner, *IWW,* pp. 376-79.

45. *Cleveland Socialist,* Apr. 12, 1913; *Akron Beacon Journal,* Mar. 1, 4, 1913; Foner, *IWW,* pp. 382-83.

46. *Detroit Free Press,* Apr. 30, 1913; *Solidarity,* May 3, 1913; *Industrial Worker,* May 15, 1913; Keith Sward, *The Legacy of Henry Ford* (New York, 1948), pp. 47-48; Foner, *IWW,* pp. 384-85.

47. *Detroit Free Press,* May 1, June 17-19, July 21, 1913; Robert W. Dunn, *Labor and Automobiles* (New York, 1928), pp. 125-26, Foner, *IWW,* pp. 386-89.

48. "My Story," p. 59.

49. "From the Notebook of a Labor Organizer," manuscript dated 1929, pp. 14-15, Matilda (Rabinowitz) Robbins Papers, Wayne State University Library, Detroit.

50. Ibid., p. 1.

51. Ibid., pp. 16-17.

52. "My Story," p. 68.

53. Ibid., p. 69.

54. "Reflections of an Organizer," *Solidarity,* Feb. 6, 1917. The article was signed "M.G.R."

55. FONER, *IWW,* pp. 346-49.

56. MELVYN DUBOFSKY, *We Shall Be All: A History of the Industrial Workers of the World* (Chicago, 1969), pp. 154-55, 256-57.

57. FONER, *IWW,* pp. 371-72.

Chapter 25: Wages and Working Conditions

1. VIOLET PIKE, "Women Workers in Factories in New York State," in New York, Factory Investigating Commission, *Preliminary Report,* 1912, 1:294-95.

2. *New York Times,* Mar. 10, 1913.

3. FRANK H. STREIGHTOFF, "Report on the Cost of Living," New York, Factory Investigating Commission, *Fourth Report, 1915,* 1:37-38, 4:1461-1671.

4. Ibid., 2:1-41.

5. Ibid., pp. 41, 101, 215, 245, 257-61, 315-57, 409-11; New York, Factory Investigating Commission, *Third Report* 1914, pp. 40, 42-43; *Fourth Report,* 1:34-36, 2:200.

6. ESTHER PACKARD, "How the Working Girl of New York Lives" and "Living on Six Dollars a Week," *Fourth Report,* 4:1461-1715; Marie S. Orenstein, "How the Working Girl of New York Lives," ibid., pp. 1693-1715; Women's Trade Union League Exhibit, ibid., pp. 1715-16.

7. New York, Factory Investigating Commission, *Preliminary Report* 1912, 3:45–48.

8. Ibid., 3:632–42.

9. New York, Factory Investigating Commission, *Second Report,* 1913, 1:10–16, 124–27, 143–57; 2:759–76.

10. Ibid., 3:1004, 1017.

11. New York, Factory Investigating Commission, *Report, 1913,* 2:439–59.

12. U.S., Bureau of the Census, 1910, *Occupations,* 1911, p. 133.

13. *Independent* 72 (Jan. 25, 1912), pp. 196–200.

14. FLORENCE KELLEOR, *"Out of Work": Study of New York Employment Agencies for Negro Women (also containing data on Philadelphia)* (New York, 1904).

15. ADDIE W. HUNTER, "The Colored Woman's Economic Future," New York *Call,* Feb. 27, 1906.

16. "A Colored Working Girl and Race Prejudice," *Crisis,* April 1916, pp. 32–34, and reprinted in *New York Call,* Apr. 2, 1916.

17. *Philadelphia Public Ledger,* Apr. 3, 1913.

18. *Philadelphia Tribune,* Sept. 21, 1911; Barbara Klaczynska, "Why Women Work: A Comparison of Various Groups—Philadelphia, 1910–1930," *Labor History* 17 (Winter 1976): 85.

19. Washington (State), Industrial Welfare Commission, *First Biennial Report, 1913–1914,* 1915, pp. 10–15.

20. ALICE HAMILTON, "Occupational Conditions and Tuberculosis," *Charities,* May 15, 1906, p. 205.

21. Massachusetts, Commission to Investigate the Inspection of Factories, Workshops, Mercantile Establishments and Other Buildings, 1910. *Hearings, July 1–Nov. 5, 1910,* Typescript, State House Library, Boston, pp. 268–70.

22. U.S., Commission on Industrial Relations, *Final Report,* Washington, D.C., 1916, p. 3.

23. U.S., Commission on Industrial Relations, *Report on the Colorado Strike,* Washington, D.C., 1915, pp. 126–27.

24. *New York Times,* May 25, 1915.

25. U.S., Commission on Industrial Relations, *Final Report,* Washington, D.C., 1916, pp. 34–36.

26. Curry's description of wage rates and working conditions of telephone operators was published by the United States Commission on Industrial Relations in Nelle B. Curry, *Report: Investigation of the Wages and Conditions of Telephone Operating,* Washington, D.C., 1915. Curry's testimony is summarized in Thomas R. Brooks, *Communications Workers of America: The Story of a Union,* New York, 1977, pp. 4–9.

27. U.S., Commission on Industrial Relations, *Final Report,* Washington, D.C., 1916, pp. 36–37; Jack Barbash, *Unions and Telephones: The Story of the Communications Workers of America* (New York, 1953), pp. 5–6.

28. U.S., Commission on Industrial Relations, *Final Report,* Washington, D.C., 1916, pp. 39–40.

Chapter 26: The League, the IWW, and the AFL

1. New York, Department of Labor, *Statistics of Trade Unions in 1914, Bulletin No. 74,* September 1915, p. 21; *Labor Organizations in 1913, Bulletin No. 69,* April 1914, p. 109.
2. SAMUEL GOMPERS, "Working Women Organize," *American Federationist* 21 (March 1914): 232.
3. New York, Factory Investigating Commission, *Third Report,* 1914, pp. 111, 144; *Fourth Report,* 1915, 2:144–56, 165, 224–25, 232, 237, 243, 267–69, 304–12, 337–57, 416.
4. SUE AINSLEY CLARK to Margaret Dreier Robins, April 1912, NWTUL Papers.
5. FONER, *IWW,* pp. 339–40; Mary K. O'Sullivan, "The Labor War at Lawrence," *Survey* 28 (April 1912): 72; Mary Kenney O'Sullivan, Autobiography, n.d., Schlesinger Library, Radcliffe College, Cambridge, Mass.
6. ELIZABETH GLENDOWER EVANS to Margaret Dreier Robins, 25 March 1912, Margaret Dreier Robins Papers, University of Florida, Gainesville, Florida (hereafter cited as Robins Papers).
7. SUE AINSLEY CLARK to Margaret Dreier Robins, April 1912, NWTUL Papers.
8. Minutes of the National Executive Board of the NWTUL, Apr. 17–19, 1912, pp. 2, 15, NWTUL Papers.
9. MARY E. McDOWELL to Mr. Leard (1912); McDowell to Homer D. Call (1912), and May 28, 1912, McDowell Papers.
10. MARGARET DREIER ROBINS to Leonora O'Reilly, 19 July 1911, O'Reilly Papers. *Proceedings of the National Women's Trade Union League Convention, 1911,* p. 4.
11. HOMER D. CALL to Mary E. McDowell, 27 May, 10 June 1912, McDowell Papers; Minutes of the National Executive Board of the NWTUL, Apr. 17–19, 1912, NWTUL Papers.
12. Minutes of the National Executive Board of the NWTUL, Apr. 17–19, 1912, NWTUL Papers; McCreesh, "Picket Lines," p. 212.
13. MARY DREIER ROBINS to Gompers, 3 May 1913, NWTUL Papers.
14. HELEN MAROT to Margaret Dreier Robins, 28 March 1912, NWTUL Papers; Secretary's Report, Women's Trade Union League of New York, Nov. 27, 1912, WTUL of NY Papers; Homer D. Call to Mary E. McDowell, 10 June 1912, McDowell Papers.
15. McCREESH, "Picket Lines," pp. 238–39.
16. Ibid., p. 243.
17. "Training Women in Union Leadership," *Survey,* Dec. 16, 1916, p. 312.

18. VIOLET PIKE, *New World Lessons for Old World People* (New York, 1912), "Lesson Four: A Trade Without a Union" and "Lesson Five: A Trade With a Union." See also Ruth Austin, "Teaching English to Our Foreign Friends," *Life and Labor* 1 (September 1911): 260.

19. MILDRED RANKIN to Margaret Dreier Robins, May (n.d.), Robins Papers.

20. Secretary's Report, *Proceedings of the Fourth Biennial Convention of National Women's Trade Union League of America* (St. Louis, 1913); Josephine F. Pacheco, "NWTUL, AFL, IWW: A Study in Labor and Violence," paper in possession of present writer, p. 15.

21. *Proceedings of the Sixth Biennial Convention of the NWTUL, 1915,* pp. 188–90; Gompers to Margaret Dreier Robins, 31 July 1915, NWTUL Papers.

22. ELIZABETH BRANDEIS, "Labor Legislation," in John R. Commons, et al., *History of Labor in the United States, 1896–1932* (New York, 1918–35), 3:501–39; James T. Patterson, "Mary Dewson and the American Minimum Wage Movement," *Labor History* 5 (Spring 1964): 134–52; Thomas J. Kerr, IV, "The New York Factory Investigating Commission and the Minimum-Wage Movement," ibid. 12 (Summer 1971): 373–91.

23. *Proceedings of the Eighteenth National Convention of the National Association of Manufacturers* (New York, 1913), pp. 71–74; *Twentieth National Convention* (New York, 1915), pp. 126–29.

24. *Proceedings of the AFL Convention, 1912,* p. 231; *1913,* pp. 59–64, 299–300; Samuel Gompers, "The American Labor Movement," *American Federationist* 21 (July 1914): 543–44; "Woman's Work, Rights, and Progress," ibid. 22 (July 1915): 517–19; Samuel Gompers to Abraham I. Elkus, 5 June 1914, Gompers Letter-Books, Library of Congress.

25. "A Living Wage for Women," *Independent* 74 (Apr. 17, 1913): 851; *New York Call,* June 15, 1915; Nancy Schrom Dye, "The Women's Trade Union League of New York, 1903–1920" (Ph.D. diss., University of Wisconsin, 1974), pp. 420–22.

26. "Little Sister" to Leonora O'Reilly, 27 April 1908, O'Reilly Papers.

27. AILEEN S. KRADITOR, *The Ideas of the Woman Suffrage Movement, 1890–1920* (New York, 1965), chap. 6; Ida Husted Harper, ed., *History of Woman Suffrage,* vol. 5, *1900–1920* (New York, 1972), p. 78; *New York Times,* Dec. 31, 1909.

28. ROSE SCHNEIDERMAN, with Lucy Goldthwaite, *All for One* (New York, 1967), pp. 121–22; Margaret Dreier Robins to Leonora O'Reilly, 19 July 1914, O'Reilly Papers; Robin Miller Jacoby, "The Women's Trade Union League and American Feminism," *Feminist Studies* 3 (Fall 1975): 130–31.

29. JACOBY, "Women's Trade Union League," pp. 132–34; Dye, "Women's Trade Union League," p. 360; Mary Beard to Leonora O'Reilly, n.d., O'Reilly Papers.

30. MARGARET HINCHEY to Leonora O'Reilly, n.d., O'Reilly Papers.

31. "Senators vs. Working Women: Miss Rose Schneiderman Replies to New York Senator," in Wage Earners' Suffrage League, New York, O'Reilly Papers; Jacoby, "Women's Trade Union League," p. 133.

32. "Report of the Fifth Biennial Convention," *Life and Labor* 5 (July 1915): 118; *New York Call,* June 2, 1910.

33. LEONORA O'REILLY to Electrical Workers, 19 April 1911, O'Reilly Papers.

34. U.S., Commission on Industrial Relations, *Final Report* Washington, D.C., 1916, pp. 37–38; *New York Times,* May 28, 1915.

35. *New York Times,* May 28, 1915; *American Federationist* 15 (October 1915): 861–62.

36. *New York Times,* Apr. 12, 1916; Barbara Klaczynska, "Why Women Work: A Comparison of Various Groups—Philadelphia, 1910–1930," *Labor History* 17 (Winter 1976): 225–27.

37. *American Federationist* 15: (October 1915): 861–62.

38. LEONORA O'REILLY to Mary Dreier Robins, 31 August 1915, O'Reilly Papers; McCreesh, "Picket Lines," pp. 382–84.

Chapter 27: On the Eve of World War I

1. *New York Call,* June 15, 1915.

2. *Proceedings of the AFL Convention, 1913,* p. 409.

3. JOHN GRAHAM BROOKS, "The Challenge of Unemployment," *The Independent* 81 (Mar. 15, 1915): 383–85.

4. McCREESH, "Picket Lines," pp. 235–36.

5. New York, Department of Labor, *Bulletin No. 69,* March 1915, p. 6; N.Y., Department of Labor, *Bulletin No. 73,* August 1915, p. 2; *Massachusetts Industrial Review,* no. 7 (March 1922).

6. For the story of the IWW and the unemployed, 1913–1915, see Foner, *IWW,* pp. 435–61.

7. J. EDWARD MORGAN, "The Unemployed in San Francisco," *New Review,* April 1914, pp. 193–99.

8. *Solidarity,* Jan. 24, 1915.

9. CAROLYN ASHBAUGH, *Lucy Parsons: American Revolutionary* (Chicago, 1976), pp. 238–39.

10. *Chicago Tribune,* Jan. 18, 1915; Ralph Chaplin, "A Hunger 'Riot' in Chicago," *International Socialist Review* 15 (March 1915): 517–20; Ashbaugh, *Lucy Parsons,* pp. 237–44.

11. FONER, *IWW,* pp. 458–61.

12. McCREESH, "Picket Lines," pp. 235–36.

13. U.S., Bureau of Immigration, *Annual Report of the Commissioner-General of Immigration,* 1913–1919.

14. PHILIP S. FONER, *Organized Labor and the Black Worker, 1619–1973* (New York, 1974), pp. 130–32; *Proceedings of the AFL Convention, 1916,* p. 213.

15. U.S., Department of Labor, Women's Bureau, "Variations in Employment Trends of Women and Men," *Bulletin No. 73,* 1931, pp. vii, 2.

16. Ibid., pp. 34, 37, 55–56, 68, 78.

17. "Women Favored in Making of War Munitions," Cincinnati *Times Star,* May 23, 1917; "Where Women Supplement Men Because of the War," *New York Times,* Dec. 30, 1917. The speaker quoted in the Cincinnati *Times Star* was Arthur L. Humphrey of Wilmerding, Pennsylvania.

18. AMY HEWES, "Women as Munition Makers," *Survey* 37 ("Jan. 6, 1917): 381; *New York Times,* Jan. 5, 1917.

19. HEWES, "Women as Munition Makers," pp. 382–83.

20. "War Orders Bringing Labor More Leisure," *Literary Digest,* Nov. 6, 1915, p. 996; Florence Peterson, "Strikes in the United States, 1880–1936," U.S., Department of Labor, *Bulletin No. 651,* Washington, D.C., 1938, p. 21.

21. *Justice* (Pittsburgh), Jan. 31, Feb. 7, 1914.

22. *Pittsburgh Daily Dispatch,* Apr. 22, 1916; *Pittsburgh Post,* Apr. 23, 1916.

23. *Pittsburgh Daily Dispatch,* Apr. 24, 1916.

24. *Pittsburgh Leader,* Apr. 24, 1916.

25. *Pittsburgh Gazette-Times,* Apr. 25, 1916; *Pittsburgh Daily Dispatch,* Apr. 25, 1916.

26. DIANNE KANITRA, "The Westinghouse Strike of 1916" (Master's thesis, University of Pittsburgh, 1917), p. 15.

27. *Pittsburgh Post,* Apr. 30, 1916.

28. *Pittsburgh Daily Dispatch,* May 2, 1916.

29. Ibid., May 3, 4, 1916; *Pittsburgh Gazette-Times,* May 3, 1916.

30. KANITRA, "Westinghouse Strike," pp. 67–68.

31. *New York Call,* Feb. 27, 1917.

32. *Literary Digest,* Mar. 3, 1917, p. 533.

33. *New York Times,* Feb. 21, 1917; Leslie Marcy, "Food Riots in America," *International Socialist Review* 17 (April 1917): 585.

34. *Philadelphia Press,* Feb. 22, 1917; *New York Times,* Feb. 22, 1917.

35. *New York Times,* Feb. 22, 1917; Philadelphia *North American,* Feb. 21–23, 1917.

36. *Seattle Union Record,* Feb. 27, 1909.

37. Ibid., Dec. 16, 1916.

38. Ibid., Feb. 17, May 26, 1917.

39. Ibid., Mar. 17, 1917.

40. Ibid., July 22, 1916.

41. Ibid., Sept. 2, 1916.

42. Ibid., June 27, 1916.

43. Ibid., Oct. 21, 1916.

44. Ibid., Dec. 16, 1916.

45. Ibid., Dec. 23, 1916.

Bibliography

Manuscript Collections

Amalgamated Clothing Workers Headquarters, New York City
    Amalgamated Clothing Workers Files
American Federation of Labor Archives, American Federation of Labor Building, Washington, D.C.
    American Federation of Labor Correspondence
American Institute for Marxist Studies, New York City
    Elizabeth Gurley Flynn Papers
Radcliffe College, Cambridge, Massachusetts, Arthur and Elizabeth Schlesinger Library on the History of Women in America
    Leonora O'Reilly Papers
    National Women's Trade Union League of America Papers
    Mary K. O'Sullivan, Manuscript Autobiography
    Maude Nathan Scrapbooks
    Harriet H. Robinson Papers
Boston Public Library, Rare Book Room
    Factory Tracts No. 1
Catholic University of America, Washington, D.C.
    Terence V. Powderly Papers
Chicago Historical Society
    Agnes Nestor Papers
    Mary E. McDowell Papers
Illinois Historical Society
    Thomas J. Morgan Papers
State Historical Society of Wisconsin, Madison
    Elizabeth Gurley Flynn Collection
    Morris Hillquit Papers
Smith College Library, Northampton, Massachusetts
    Sophia Smith Collections
    Women in Trade Unions Collection: Leonora M. Barry Lake Folio

Library of Congress, Manuscripts Division, Washington, D.C.
  Samuel Gompers Letter-Books
  National Women's Trade Union League Papers
  Anna Dickinson Papers
National Archives, Washington, D.C.
  Department of Labor Conciliation Service Papers
  Department of Justice, Record Group 60, File 1870-28
New York State Labor Library, New York City
  Women's Trade Union League of New York Papers
Tamiment Institute Library, New York University
  Algernon Lee Scrap Books
  Socialist Party Letter Books
  Eugene V. Debs Clipping Book
  Rose Schneiderman Papers
Tennessee State Library and Archives, Nashville, Tennessee
  Zilphia Horton Folk Music Collection
University of Florida Library, Gainesville, Florida

  Margaret Dreier Robins Papers
Wayne State University Library, Detroit, Michigan
  Matilda (Rabinowitz) Robbins Papers

Unpublished Theses, Dissertations, and Papers

ADAMS, DONALD GRIFFITH, "Foreign-born Laborers in Indiana," M. A. thesis, University of Indiana, 1911.

BARROWS, EMILY, "Trade Union Organization among Women of Chicago," M.A. thesis, University of Chicago, 1927.

BERCH, BETTINA EILEEN, "Industrialization and Working Women in the Nineteenth Century: England, France and the United States," Ph.D. dissertation, University of Wisconsin, Madison, 1976.

BERMAN, HYMAN, "Era of the Protocol: A Chapter of the History of the International Ladies' Garment Workers' Union, 1910–1916," Ph.D. dissertation, Columbia University, 1956.

BORDEN, JOHN, "The Association of Working People of New Castle, Delaware: The First Labor Party of Delaware," M.A. thesis, University of Delaware, 1927.

BROWN, RAY V., "The Erie Railroad Strike of 1877 in Hornellsville, New York," Senior Thesis, History, Princeton University, 1951.

COHEN, MARTIN A., "Jewish Immigrants and American Trade Unions," Ph.D. dissertation, University of Chicago, 1941.

COLE, DONALD B., "Lawrence, Massachusetts: 1845–1912," Ph.D. dissertation, Harvard University, 1956.

CONLIN, JOSEPH, "The Wobblies: A Study of the Industrial Workers of the World before World War I," Ph.D. dissertation, University of Wisconsin, Madison, 1969.

DANCIS, BRUCE, "The Socialist Women's Movement in the United States, 1901–1917," Senior Thesis, University of California, Santa Cruz, June, 1973.

DEGLER, CARL, "Labor in the Economy and Politics of New York City: A Study of the Impact of Early Industrialism," Ph.D. dissertation, Columbia University, 1957.

DENN, HAROLD B., "The History of the Silk Workers in Paterson, New Jersey, with Special Emphasis on Strikes, 1910–1920," M.A. thesis, New York University, 1947.

DUBLIN, THOMAS LOUIS, "Women at Work: The Transformation of Work and Community in Lowell, Massachusetts, 1826–1860," Ph.D. dissertation, Columbia University, 1975.

DUBOFSKY, MELVYN, "New York City Labor in the Progressive Era, 1910–1918, A Study of Organized Labor in an Era of Reform," Ph.D. dissertation, University of Rochester, 1960.

DUBOIS, ELLEN CAROL, "A New Life: The Development of an American Woman Suffrage Movement, 1860–1869," Ph.D. dissertation, Northwestern University, 1975.

DUCATTE, NANCY, "The Shirt and Collar Industry and Kate Mullaney, Troy, N.Y.," undated paper, Library of Trade Union Women's Studies, Cornell University, New York City.

DYE, NANCY SCHROM, "The Women's Trade Union League of New York, 1903–1920," Ph.D. dissertation, University of Wisconsin, Madison, 1974.

FELDMAN, EGAL, "New York Men's Clothing Trade, 1800–1861," Ph.D. dissertation, New York University, 1959.

FENTON, EDWIN, "Immigrants and Unions: A Case Study of Italians and American Labor, 1870–1920," Ph.D. thesis, Harvard University, 1957.

GLAGE, LISLOTTE, "Clementine Black: A Study in Social History and Literature," unpublished paper, in preparation for Ph.D., University of Hannover, Germany.

GUTMAN, HERBERT G., "Early Effects of the Depression of 1873 upon the Working Classes in New York City," M.A. thesis, Columbia University, 1950.

JACOB, KATHERYN ALLAMONG, "The Women of Baltimore Town: A Social History, 1729–1797," M.A. thesis, Georgetown University, 1975.

KANN, KENNETH, "Workers' Culture and the Labor Movement in Chicago, 1845–1886," Ph.D. dissertation, University of California, Berkeley, 1977.

KANITRA, DIANNE, "The Westinghouse Strike of 1916," M.A. thesis, University of Pittsburgh, 1957.

KEISER, JOHN HOWARD, "John Fitzpatrick and Progressive Unionism," Ph.D. dissertation, Northwestern University, 1965.

KESSLER, SIDNEY H., "The Negro in the Knights of Labor," M.A. thesis, Columbia University, 1950.

KUGLER, ISRAEL, "The Women's Rights Movement and the National Labor Union, 1866–1872," Ph.D. dissertation, New York University, 1954.

LAYER, ROBERT G., "Wages, Earnings, and Output in Four Cotton Textile Companies in New England, 1825–1860," Ph.D. dissertation, Harvard University, 1952.

LEVINE, IRVING J., "The Lawrence Strike," M.A. thesis, Columbia University, 1936.

LIEBERMAN, JACOB ANDREW, "Their Sisters' Keepers: The Women's Hours and Wages Movement in the United States, 1890–1925," Ph.D. dissertation, Columbia University, 1971.

LINTNER, SYLVIA C., "A Social History of Fall River, 1859–1879," Ph.D. dissertation, Radcliffe College, 1945.

McCREESH, CAROLYN DANIEL, "On the Picket Lines: Militant Women Campaign to Organize Garment Workers, 1882–1917," Ph.D. dissertation, University of Maryland, 1975.

MAILLOUX, KENNETH FRANK, "The Boston Manufacturing Company of Waltham, Massachusetts, 1813–1848: The First Modern Factory in America," Ph.D. dissertation, Boston University, 1957.

MANGES, FRANCES MAY, "Women Shopkeepers and Artisans in Colonial Philadelphia," Ph.D. dissertation, University of Pennsylvania, 1958.

MERK, LOIS BANNISTER, "Massachusetts and the Woman Suffrage Movement," Ph.D. dissertation, Northeastern University, 1961.

MORRIS, JAMES MATTHEW, "The Road to Trade Unionism: Organized Labor in Cincinnati to 1896," Ph.D. dissertation, University of Cincinnati, 1969.

NEWMAN, PHILIP CHARLES, "The I.W.W. in New Jersey, 1912–1913," M.A. thesis, Columbia University, 1954.

PACHECO, JOSEPHINE F., "NWTUL, AFL, IWW: A Study in Labor and Violence," unpublished paper in possession of author.

SHAPIRO, HAROLD ARTHUR, "The Workers of San Antonio, Texas, 1900–1940," Ph.D. dissertation, University of Texas, Austin, 1952.

SNYDER, ROBERT E., "Between Lawrence and Paterson: The IWW in Little Falls, New York," unpublished paper, Southwest Labor Studies, Conference, March, 1977.

SORAGHAN, CATHERINE V., "History of St. Louis, 1865–1876," M.A. thesis, Washington University, 1936.

STEINBERG, LINDA, "Women Workers and the 1912 Textile Strike in Lawrence, Massachusetts," unpublished paper, Division III Project, Hampshire College, Amherst, Mass., April 28, 1975.

TOWNER, LAWRENCE W., "A Good Master Well Served: A Social History of Servitude in Massachusetts, 1620–1750," Ph.D. dissertation, Northwestern University, 1955.

YATES, DONATA MARY, "Women in Chicago Industries, 1900–1915, A Study of Working Conditions in Factories, Laundries and Restaurants," M.A. thesis, University of Chicago, 1948.

YOUNG, ALFRED F., "Some Thoughts on Mechanic Participation in the American Revolution," unpublished paper presented at the Third Annual Conference in Early American History, Newberry Library, Chicago, Nov. 1, 1974.

Public Documents

Manufacturers of the United States in 1870. A Compendium of the Ninth Census, Washington, D.C., 1872.

U.S. CONGRESS, Senate, *United States Senate (Education and Labor) Committee, Report upon the Relations between Capital and Labor,* Washington, D.C., 1883, vol. 1.

U.S. CONGRESS, *Report of the Industrial Commission on the Relations and Conditions of Capital and Labor Employed in Manufactures and General Business,* Washington, D.C., 1901, vol. 7.

U.S. CONGRESS, Commission on Industrial Relations, *Final Report and Testimony,* Washington, D.C., 1916, vol. 4.

U.S. CONGRESS, Commission on Industrial Relations, *Report on the Colorado Strike,* Washington, D.C., 1915.

U.S. DEPARTMENT OF COMMERCE AND LABOR, Bureau of the Census, *Twelfth Census of the United States,* 1900, vol. 19.

U.S. DEPARTMENT OF COMMERCE AND LABOR, Bureau of the Census, *Thirteenth Census of the United States,* 1910. *Occupations,* Washington, D.C., 1911.

U.S. DEPARTMENT OF COMMERCE AND LABOR, Bureau of Labor, *The Women's Trade Union Movement in Great Britain* by Katherine Graves Busbey. Bulletin No. 83, Washington, D.C., 1909.

U.S. DEPARTMENT OF LABOR, Women's Bureau, *Women's Occupations through Seven Decades.* Bulletin No. 218, Washington, D.C., 1947.

U.S. DEPARTMENT OF LABOR, Women's Bureau, *Handbook of Facts on Women Workers,* Bulletin No. 225, Washington, D.C., 1948.

U.S. DEPARTMENT OF LABOR, Bulletin No. 651, Florence Peterson, *Strikes in the United States, 1880–1936,* Washington, D.C. 1938.

U.S. CONGRESS. "Hearings on Strike in Lawrence, Mass.," 62nd Congress, 1st Session, *House Document No. 671,* Washington, D.C., 1912.

U.S. CONGRESS, "Report on the Strike of the Textile Workers in Lawrence, Massachusetts," 62nd Congress, 2nd Session, *Senate Document No. 870,* Washington, D.C., 1912.

U.S. DEPARTMENT OF COMMERCE AND LABOR, *Tenth Annual Report of the Commissioner of Labor, 1894* ("Strikes and Lockouts"), Washington, D.C., 1895, vol. 1.

NEW YORK, BUREAU OF LABOR STATISTICS, Reports of the Board of Mediation and Arbitration and Bureau of Labor Statistics, "The Little Falls Textile Workers Dispute." *New York Labor Bulletin,* vol. 15, March, 1913, pp. 32–51.

NEW YORK, ASSEMBLY, *Report of the Special Committee of the Assembly to Investigate the Condition of Female Labor in the City of New York,* Albany, 1896, 2 vols.

NEW YORK, FACTORY INVESTIGATING COMMISSION, *Preliminary Report of the Factory Investigating Commission, 1912,* Albany, 1912, 3 vols.

NEW YORK, FACTORY INVESTIGATING COMMISSION, *Second Report of the Factory Investigating Commission, 1913.* Albany, 1913, 4 vols.

NEW YORK, FACTORY INVESTIGATING COMMISSION, *Third Report of the Factory Investigating Commission, 1914.* Albany, 1914.

NEW YORK, FACTORY INVESTIGATING COMMISSION, *Fourth Report of the Factory Investigating Commission, 1915.* Albany, 1915, 4 vols.

NEW YORK, ASSEMBLY, Special Committee to Investigate Female Labor, *Report and Testimony.* Assembly Document No. 97, New York, 1897, vol. 1.

NEW YORK DEPARTMENT OF LABOR, *Annual Reports, 1902–1914.*

NEW YORK, DEPARTMENT OF LABOR, Bureau of Statistics and Information, *Trade Union Statistics in 1913.* Special Bulletin No. 60, Albany, 1914.

NEW YORK, DEPARTMENT OF LABOR, Bureau of Statistics and Information, *Statistics of Trade Unions in 1914,* Bulletin No. 74, Albany, 1915.

NEW YORK, DEPARTMENT OF LABOR, Bureau of Statistics and Information, *Strikes and Lockouts in 1912 and 1913.* Bulletin No. 66, Albany, 1914.

NEW JERSEY, DEPARTMENT OF LABOR, Bureau of Statistics of Labor and Industry, *Report for 1913,* Camden, 1914.

NEW JERSEY, DEPARTMENT OF LABOR, Bureau of Statistics of Labor and Industry, *Report for 1914.* Camden, 1915.

MASSACHUSETTS, GENERAL COURT, Senate, *Senate Document, No. 81,* Boston, 1846.

MASSACHUSETTS, BUREAU OF STATISTICS OF LABOR, *Eleventh Annual Report, 1880* ("Strikes in Massachusetts"), Boston, 1881.

MASSACHUSETTS, BUREAU OF STATISTICS OF LABOR, *Annual Report for 1912* ("Strikes and Lockouts in 1912"), Boston, 1913.

MASSACHUSETTS, COMMISSION TO INVESTIGATE THE INSPECTION OF FACTORIES, WORKSHOPS, MERCANTILE ESTABLISHMENTS, AND OTHER BUILDINGS, 1910, *Hearings, July 1–Nov. 5, 1910,* Typescript, State House Library, Boston.

WASHINGTON, *First Biennial Report of the Industrial Welfare Commission, 1913–1914,* Olympia, 1915.

ILLINOIS, *Sixth Annual Report of the Factory Inspectors of* Illinois, Springfield, 1899.

Organizational Publications and Records

Amalgamated Clothing Workers of America, *Proceedings of the Second Biennial Convention,* Rochester, 1916.

American Federation of Labor, *Proceedings of the Convention,* 1887, 1888, 1891, 1892, 1893, 1898, 1903, 1908, 1912, 1913, 1916.

Colored National Labor Union, *Proceedings of the Annual Convention,* 1869–1871.

Consumers' League of New York City, *Annual Report,* 1892–1910.

Federation of Organized Trades and Labor Unions of the United States and Canada, *Proceedings of the Convention,* 1882,1883.

Industrial Workers of the World, *Proceedings of the First Convention,* 1905.

International Ladies' Garment Workers' Union, *Proceedings of the Convention,* 1900, 1902, 1903, 1908, 1912.

International Typographical Union, *Proceedings of the Convention,* 1871.

Knights of Labor, *Proceedings of the General Assembly,* 1886–1889.

National Consumers' League, *Annual Report,* 1899–1903.

National Labor Union, *Proceedings of the Annual Convention,* 1866–1871.

National Women's Trade Union League, Chicago Industrial Exhibit, *Handbook.* Chicago, 1909.

———, *Proceedings of the Biennial Convention,* 1907–1915.

NEW YORK (CITY), Working Women's Protective Union, *Report,* 1863–1894.

NEW YORK (CITY), Working Women's Society, *Annual Report,* 1893.

———, *Report on the Condition of Working Women in Stores,* 1890.

NEW YORK (STATE), Women's Trade Union League, *Annual Report,* 1906–1912.

Report of the International Council of Women Assembled by National Woman Suffrage Association, Washington, D.C., U.S. of America, Mar. 25 to Apr. 1, 1888, Washington, D.C., 1888.

United Garment Workers, *Proceedings of the Annual Convention,* 1892, 1903.

University Settlement Society of New York, *Yearbook,* 1899.

Women.s International Union Label League of the World, *General Constitution,* 1899.

Newspapers and Magazines

African Repository (New York City)
Akron Beacon Journal
American Citizen (New York City)
American Hebrew, The (Cincinnati)
American Wool and Cotton Reporter (Boston)
American Workman (Boston)
Augusta Chronicle
Balitmore Sun
Bee-Hive (London)
Birmingham News
Boston Advertiser
Boston American
Boston Bee
Boston Chronicle
Boston Courier

Boston Daily Evening Voice
Boston Globe
Boston Gazette
Boston Traveller
Chicago Herald
Chicago Inter-Ocean
Chicago Recorder
Chicago Times
Chicago Tribune
Christian Recorder (Philadelphia)
Cigar Makers' Official Journal (New York City)
Cincinnati Chronicle
Cincinnati Times
Cleveland Socialist
Cohoes Daily News (New York)

Colorado Chronicle (Denver)
Dallas Laborer
Detroit Free Press
Detroit Tribune
Douglass' Monthly (Rochester)
Duluth Tribune
Electrical Worker
Factory Girls' Album (Exeter,
    New Hampshire)
Fincher's Trades' Review (Philadelphia)
Frederick Douglass' Paper (Rochester)
Galveston Daily News
Garment Worker (New York City)
Haverhill Gazette
Horizon (Nashville)
Hornell Times (New York)
Independent, The (New York City)
Independent Chronicle (Boston)
Indianapolis Star
Industrial Solidarity
Industrial Union Bulletin
Industrial Worker (Spokane)
International Socialist Review
    (Girard, Kansas)
Irish World (New York City)
Jackson Daily Clarion
Jewish Daily Forward (New York City)
John Swinton's Paper (New York City)
Journal of the Knights of Labor
Journal of United Labor
Justice (Pittsburgh)
Labor Leader (Boston)
Labor Standard (New York City and
    Paterson)
Ladies' Garment Worker (New York
    City)
Lake County Times (Indiana)
Lawrence Evening Tribune
Lawrence Sun
Leslie's Magazine (New York City)
Life and Labor (New York City)
Literary Digest (New York City)
Little Falls Journal and Courier
    (New York)
London Times
Los Angeles Socialist
Los Angeles Times

Lowell Advertiser
Lowell Offering
Lynn News
Lynn Reporter
Lynn Weekly Reporter
Man (New York City)
Manchester Democrat (New Hampshire)
Manufacturers' and Farmers' Journal
    (Boston)
Maryland Gazette (Baltimore)
Mechanic (Fall River)
Mechanics' Free Press (Philadelphia)
National Gazette (Philadelphia)
National Laborer (Philadelphia)
Newark Daily Advertiser
Newburyport Daily Herald
    (Massachusetts)
New England Offering (Lowell)
New York American
New York Bulletin
New York Call
New York Citizen
New York Daily Graphic
New York Daily Sentinel
New York Evening Mail
New York Evening Post
New York Herald
New York Journal
New York Sun
New York Times
New York Tribune
New York World
Oakland World (California)
One Big Union Monthly
Operatives' Magazine
Oshkosh Daily Northwestern (Wisconsin)
Paterson Courier
Paterson Intelligencer
Paterson Press
Pennsylvanian (Philadelphia)
Philadelphia Evening Bulletin
Philadelphia Evening Post
Philadelphia North American
Philadelphia Public Ledger
Philadelphia Tribune
Pittsburgh Daily Dispatch
Pittsburgh Evening Post

Pittsburgh Gazette-Times
Pittsburgh Journal
Pittsburgh Leader
Pittsburgh Post
Poulson's American Daily Advertiser
   (Philadelphia)
Progress (New York City)
Providence Gazette
Providence Patriot
Revolution (New York City)
Rochester Union and American
San Antonio Express
St. Louis Daily Press
St. Louis Missouri Republican
St. Louis Post-Dispatch
St. Louis Times
Savannah Tribune
Schenectady Citizen (New York)
Solidarity (New Castle, Pa.)
Somerset Reporter (Maine)
Springfield Republican (Massachusetts)

Syracuse Post Standard
Textile Manufacturer
Troy Northern Budget (New York)
Troy Daily Times (New York)
Union Labor Advocate (Chicago)
Utica Daily Press
Utica Observer
Voice of Industry (Lowell)
Voice of the People (New Orleans)
Weekly Bulletin, The (New York City)
Weekly Bulletin of the Clothing Trades
   (New York City)
Weekly Bulletin of the Garment Trades
   (New York City)
Woman's Journal (Boston)
Worker (New York City)
Working Man's Advocate (New York City)
Workingman's Advocate (Chicago)
Workingman's Paper (Seattle)
Yonkers Statesman (New York)
Young America (New York City)

Books

ABBOTT, EDITH, *Women in Industry,* New York, 1910.

ADAMS, CHARLES FRANCIS, ed., *Familiar Letters of John Adams and His Wife Abigail Adams, during the Revolution,* New York, 1876.

ADAMS, GRAHAM, JR., *Age of Industrial Violence, 1910–1915,* New York, 1966.

ADDAMS, JANE, *Twenty Years at Hull House,* New York, 1910.

ALLEN, FREDERICK LEWIS, *The Big Change: America Transforms Itself, 1900–1950,* New York, 1952.

ANDREWS, JOHN B., AND BLISS, HELEN, "History of Women in Trade Unions, 1825 to the Knights of Labor," *Senate Document 645,* 61st Congress, 2nd Session, Washington, D.C., 1911, vol. 10.

ANTHONY, KATHERINE, *Susan B. Anthony: Her Personal History and Her Era,* New York, 1954.

APTHEKER, HERBERT, ed., *A Documentary History of the Negro People in the United States,* New York, 1951.

ARBER, EDWARD, ed., *Travels and Works of Captain John Smith,* Edinburgh, 1910.

ARTHUR, T. S., *The Lady at Home: or Leaves from the Every-Day Book of an American Woman,* Philadelphia, 1847.

ASHBAUGH, CAROLYN, *Lucy Parsons: American Revolutionary,* Chicago, 1976.

BAGNALL, W. R., *Samuel Slater and the Early Development of the Cotton Manufacture in the United States,* Middletown, Conn., 1890.

BAKER, ELIZABETH, *Technology and Women's Work*, New York, 1964.

BARBASH, JACK, *Unions and Telephones: The Story of the Communications Workers of America*, New York, 1953.

BARNES, GILBERT H., AND DUMOND, DWIGHT, eds., *Letters of Theodore Dwight Weld, Angelina Grimké Weld, and Sarah Grimké, 1822–1844*, New York, 1934.

BATCHELDER, SAMUEL, *Introduction and Early Progress of the Cotton Manufacture in the United States*, Boston, 1863.

BAXANDALL, ROSALYN, GORDON, LINDA, AND REVERBY, SUSAN, eds., *America's Working Women: A Documentary History 1600 to the Present*, New York, 1976.

BEALE, FRED, *Proletarian Journey*, New York, 1937.

BEBEL, AUGUST, *Woman and Socialism*, New York, 1910.

BEDNER, EARL R., *A History of Labor Legislation in Illinois*, Chicago, 1929.

BENDER, THOMAS, *Toward an Urban Vision: Ideas and Institutions in Nineteenth Century America*, Lexington, Ky., 1975.

BERLIN, IRA, *Slaves without Masters: The Free Negro in the Ante-Bellum South*, New York, 1974.

BERNHEIMER, CHARLES S., *The Shirt-Waist Strike: An Investigation Made for the Council and Head Worker of the University Settlement*, New York, 1910.

BEST, HARRY, *The Men's Garment Industry of New York and the Strike of 1913*, New York, 1913.

BLUMBERG, DOROTHY ROSE, *Florence Kelley: The Making of a Social Pioneer*, New York, 1964.

BLUMBERG, DOROTHY, *Florence Kelley: The Early Years*, New York, 1966.

BOONE, GLADYS, *The Women's Trade Union League in Great Britain and the United States of America*, New York, 1942.

BOOTH, CHARLES, *Labour and Life of the People*, East London, 1889, vol. 1.

BRADFORD, SARAH E., *Scenes in the Life of Harriet Tubman*, Auburn, N.Y., 1869.

BRISSENDEN, PAUL F., *Earnings of Factory Workers 1899 to 1927*, Washington, D.C., 1929.

———, *The I.W.W.: A Study of American Syndicalism*, New York, 1920.

BROOKS, THOMAS R., *Communications Workers of America: The Story of a Union*, New York, 1977.

BROWNLEE, W. ELLIOT, AND BROWNLEE, MARY M., *Women in the American Economy: A Documentary History, 1675 to 1929*, New Haven and London, 1976.

BRUCE, ROBERT, *1877: Year of Violence*, Indianapolis, 1959.

BUDISH, JACOB M., AND SOULE, GEORGE, *The New Unionism in the Clothing Industry*, New York, 1920.

BURBANK, DAVID T., *The Reign of the Rabble: The St. Louis General Strike of 1877*, New York, 1966.

BURNS, WILLIAM, *Life in New York*, New York, 1851.

BUTLER, ELIZABETH BEARDSLEY, *Saleswomen in Mercantile Stores, 1909*, New York, 1912.

———, *Women and the Trades*, New York, 1909.

CALE, EDGAR BARCLAY, *The Organization of Labor in Philadelphia, 1850-1870*, Philadelphia, 1940.

CALMER, ALAN, *Labor Agitator: The Story of Albert R. Parsons*, New York, 1937.

CAMPBELL, JOHN, *Negro-Mania*, Philadelphia, 1851.

CARROLL, BERNICE A., ed., *Liberating Women's History: Theoretical and Critical Essays*, Urbana, Ill., 1976.

CHAPLIN, RALPH, *Wobbly: The Rough and Tumble Story of an American Radical*, Chicago, 1948.

CLARK, ALICE, *Working Life of Women in the Seventeenth Century*, London, 1919.

CLARK, VICTOR S., *History of Manufacturers in the United States*, vol. 1.

COHEN, ROSE, *Out of the Shadow*, New York, 1918.

COLE, DONALD B., *Immigrant City: Lawrence, Mass., 1845-1921*, Chapel Hill, 1963.

COLEMAN, PETER J., *The Transformation of Rhode Island, 1790-1860*, Providence, 1954.

COMMONS, JOHN R., et al., *History of Labor in the United States*, New York, 1918, vols. 1 & 2; New York, 1935, vol. 3.

COMMONS, JOHN R., et al., eds., *A Documentary History of American Industrial Society*, Cleveland, 1910, vol. 6.

CONLIN, JOSEPH R., *Big Bill Haywood and the Radical Union Movement*, Syracuse, New York, 1969.

CONRAD, EARL, *Harriet Tubman*, Washington, D.C., 1943.

COTT, NANCY F., *The Bonds of Womanhood*, New Haven, Conn., 1977.

CRÈVECOEUR, HECTOR ST. JOHN J., *Letters from an American Farmer*, New York, 1782.

COREA, GENA, *Women's Health Care*, New York, 1977.

CRAFT, WILLIAM, *Running a Thousand Miles for Freedom, or, The Escape of William and Ellen Craft from Slavery*, London, 1860.

DAVIDSON, ELIZABETH H., *Child Labor Legislation in the Southern Textile States*, Chapel Hill, 1939.

DAVIS, ALLEN F., *Spearheads for Reform: The Social Settlements and the Progressive Movement, 1890-1914*, New York, 1967.

DAVIS, ALMOD H., *The Female Preacher, or Memoir of Salome Lincoln, Afterwards the Wife of Elder Junia S. Mowry*, Providence, 1843.

DAVIS, PHILIP, *And Crown Thy Good*, New York, 1952.

DAWLEY, ALAN, *Class and Community: The Industrial Revolution in Lynn*, Cambridge, Mass., 1977.

DELZELL, RUTH, *The Early History of Women Trade Unionists of America*, Chicago, 1919.

DEXTER, ELIZABETH ANTHONY, *Colonial Women of Affairs*, Boston, 1931.

DICKENS, CHARLES, *American Notes*, New York, 1842.

DOUGLAS, ANN, *The Feminization of American Culture*, New York, 1977.

DODGE, GRACE, ed., *Thoughts of Busy Girls Who Have Little Time for Study Yet Find Much Time for Thinking*, New York, 1892.

DONOVAN, FRANCES, *The Saleslady*, Chicago, 1929.

DORGAN, MAURICE B., *History of Lawrence, Mass.*, Lawrence, 1924.

DREIER, MARY E., *Margaret Dreier Robins: Her Life, Letters, and Work*, New York, 1950.

DUBOFSKY, MELVYN, *We Shall Be All: A History of the Industrial Workers of the World*, Chicago, 1969.

———, *When Workers Organize: New York City in the Progressive Era*, Amherst, Mass., 1968.

DU BOIS, W. E. B., *The Philadelphia Negro*, Philadelphia, 1899.

DUNN, ROBERT W., *Labor and Automobiles*, New York, 1928.

EARLE, ALICE, *Colonial Dames and Goodwives*, Boston, 1895.

EBERT, JUSTUS, *The Trial of a New Society*, Cleveland, 1913.

EHRENREICH, BARBARA, AND ENGLISH, DEEDRE, *Witches, Midwives and Nurses: A History of Women Healers*, Oyster Bay, N.Y., 1972.

EISLER, BENITA, ed., *The Lowell Offering: Writings by New England Mill Women (1840–1845)*, Philadelphia and New York, 1978.

ELLET, ELIZABETH, *The Women of the Revolution*, New York, 1950.

ENGELS, FREDERICK, *The Condition of the Working Class in England*, Stanford, Cal., 1968.

———, *The Origin of the Family, Private Property and the State*, New York, 1942.

EPSTEIN, MELECH, *Jewish Labor in the U.S.A.: An Industrial, Political, and Cultural History of the Jewish Labor Movement*, New York, 1950–1953, 2 vols.

ERNST, ROBERT, *Immigrant Life in New York City, 1825–1936*, New York, 1948.

FEDER, LEAH, *Unemployment Relief in Periods of Depression*, New York, 1936.

FEATHERLING, DALE, *Mother Jones, the Miners' Angel*, Carbondale, Ill., 1971.

FLAHERTY, DAVID H., ed., *Essays in the History of Early American Law*, Chapel Hill, 1969.

FLEXNER, ELEANOR, *Century of Struggle*, Cambridge, Mass., 1959.

FLYNN, ELIZABETH GURLEY, *I Speak My Own Piece: Autobiography of the "Rebel Girl,"* New York, 1955.

FONER, PHILIP S., *American Labor Songs of the Nineteenth Century*, Urbana, Ill., 1975.

———, *American Socialism and Black Americans: From the Age of Jackson to World War II*, Westport, Conn., 1977.

———, *The Case of Joe Hill*, New York, 1965.

———, ed., *The Democratic-Republican Societies, 1790–1800: A Documentary Sourcebook of Constitutions, Declarations, Addresses, Resolutions, and Toasts*, Westport, Conn., 1976.

———, ed., *The Factory Girls: A Collection of Writings on Life and Struggles in the New England Factories of the 1840's by the Factory Girls Themselves, and the Story in Their Own Words of the First Trade Unions of Women Workers in the United States*, Urbana, Ill., 1977.

———, ed., *Frederick Douglass on Women's Rights*, Westport, Conn., 1976.

————, *The Fur and Leather Workers Union,* Newark, N.J., 1950.

————, *The Great Labor Uprising of 1877,* New York, 1977.

————, ed., *Helen Keller: Her Socialist Years,* New York, 1968.

————, *History of Black Americans: From Africa to the Emergence of the Cotton Kingdom,* Westport, Conn., 1975.

————, ed., *The Life and Writings of Frederick Douglass,* vol. 5, New York, 1975.

————, *History of the Labor Movement in the United States,* New York, 1947, vol. 1; New York, 1955, vol. 2; New York, 1964, vol. 3; New York, 1965, vol. 4.

————, *Labor and the American Revolution,* Westport, Conn., 1976.

————, ed., *The Letters of Joe Hill,* New York, 1965.

————, *Organized Labor and the Black Worker, 1619–1973,* New York, 1974.

————, ed., *We, the Other People: Alternative Declarations of Independence by Labor Groups, Farmers, Women's Rights Advocates, Socialists, and Blacks, 1829–1975,* Urbana, Ill., 1976.

FONER, PHILIP S., AND LEWIS, RONALD L., eds., *The Black Worker: A Documentary History from Colonial Times to the Present,* Philadelphia, 1978, vol. 2.

FRAZIER, FRANKLIN E., *The Negro Family in the United States,* Chicago, 1969.

GENOVESE, EUGENE D., *Roll, Jordan, Roll: The World the Slaves Made,* New York, 1974.

GINGER, RAY, *The Bending Cross: A Biography of Eugene V. Debs,* New Brunswick, N.J., 1949.

GOLDMAN, HAROLD, *Emma Paterson,* London, 1974.

GOMPERS, SAMUEL, *Seventy Years of Life and Labor,* New York, 1925, vols. 1 and 2.

GREELEY, HORACE, AND OTHERS, *The Great Industries of the United States,* Hartford, Conn., 1870.

GROB, GERALD, *Workers and Utopia: A Study of Ideological Conflict in the American Labor Movement, 1865–1900,* Chicago, 1969.

GROSSMAN, JONATHAN, *William Sylvis, Pioneer of American Labor: A Study of the Labor Movement during the Civil War,* New York, 1945.

GUTMAN, HERBERT, *Work, Culture, and Society in Industrializing America: Essays in Working-Class and Social History,* New York, 1977.

HALL, CLAYTON COLMAN, ed., *Narratives of Early Maryland, 1633–1684,* New York, 1910.

HAMILTON, ALICE, *Exploring the Dangerous Trades: The Autobiography of Alice Hamilton,* Boston, 1953.

HARDY, JACK, *The Clothing Worker,* New York, 1935.

HARLEY, SHARON, AND TERBORG-PENN, ROSALYN, eds., *The Afro-American Woman: Struggles and Images,* Port Washington, N.Y., 1978.

HARPER, IDA HUSTED, ed., *History of Woman Suffrage,* New York, 1972, vol. 5.

HARRIS, DAVID, *Socialist Origins in the United States: American Forerunners of Marx, 1817–1832,* Assen, Holland, 1966.

HAYWOOD, WILLIAM D., *Bill Haywood's Book: The Autobiography of William D. Haywood,* New York, 1929.

HAZARD, BLANCHE K., *The Organization of the Boot and Shoe Industry in Massachusetts before 1875*, Cambridge, Mass., 1921.

HENRETTA, JAMES A., *The Evolution of American Society, 1700–1815*, Lexington, Mass., 1973.

HENRY, ALICE, *The Trade Union Woman*, New York, 1915.

———, *Woman and the Labor Movement*, New York, 1923.

HENSON, JOSIAH, *Father Henson's Story of His Own Life*, New York, 1962.

HICKS, GRANVILLE, *John Reed: The Making of a Revolutionary*, New York, 1936.

HILLQUIT, MORRIS, *Loose Leaves from a Busy Life*, New York, 1934.

HIRSCH, SUSAN E., *Roots of the American Working Class: The Industrialization of Crafts in Newark, 1800–1860*, Philadelphia, 1978.

HOWE, IRVING, *World of Our Fathers*, New York, 1976.

HUTCHINS, GRACE, *Labor and Silk*, New York, 1924.

HUTCHINSON, E. J., *Women's Wages*, New York, 1919.

JERNEGAN, MARCUS W., *Laboring and Dependent Classes in Colonial America*, Chicago, 1931.

JORDAN, WINTHROP D., *White over Black: American Attitudes toward the Negro, 1550–1812*, Chapel Hill, 1968.

JOSEPHSON, HANNAH, *The Golden Threads: New England's Mill Girls and Magnates*, New York, 1949.

JOSEPHSON, MATTHEW, *Sidney Hillman, Statesman of American Labor*, New York, 1952.

KAPP, YVONNE, *Eleanor Marx: The Crowded Years*, New York, 1978.

KATZMAN, DONALD, *Seven Days A Week: Women and Domestic Service in Industrializing America*, New York, 1978.

KELLEOR, FLORENCE, *"Out of Work": Study of New York Employment Agencies for Negro Women (also containing data on Philadelphia)*, New York, 1904.

KIPNIS, IRA, *The American Socialist Movement, 1897–1912*, New York, 1952.

KORNBLUH, JOYCE L., ed., *Rebel Voices: An I.W.W. Anthology*, Ann Arbor, Mich., 1964.

KRADITOR, AILEEN S., *The Ideas of the Woman Suffrage Movement, 1890–1920*, New York, 1965.

———, ed., *Up From the Pedestal: Selected Writings in the Story of American Feminism*, Chicago, 1968.

LANG, HARRY, *"62," Biography of a Union*, New York, 1940.

LARCOM, LUCY, *A New England Girlhood*, Boston, 1890.

LASLETT, JOHN H. M., *Labor and the Left*, New York, 1970.

LAUBER, ALMON W., *Indian Slavery in Colonial Times within the Present Limits of the United States*, New York, 1913.

LEBERGOTT, STANLEY, *Manpower in Economic Growth*, New York, 1964.

LERNER, GERDA, ed., *Black Women in White America: A Documentary History*, New York, 1972.

————, ed., *The Female Experience: An American Documentary,* Indianapolis, 1977.

LESCOHIER, DON, "The Knights of St. Crispin, 1867–1874: A Study in Industrial Causes of Trade Unionism," *Bulletin of the University of Wisconsin, No. 355,* Madison, Wisc., 1910.

LEVINE, LOUIS, *The Women Garment Workers,* New York, 1924.

LITWACK, LEON F., *North of Slavery: The Negro in the Free States, 1790–1860,* Chicago, 1961.

LOSSING, BENSON J., *Pictorial Field-Book of the Revolution,* New York, 1860, vol. 1.

LOWENBERG, BERT JAMES, AND BEGIN, RUTH, eds., *Black Women in Nineteenth Century American Life,* University Park, Pa., 1976.

LUAHAN, MABEL DODGE, *Intimate Memoirs,* New York, 1936, vol. 3.

McNEILL, GEORGE E., *The Labor Movement: The Problem of Today,* New York, 1887.

MALKIEL, THERESA, *Diary of a Shirtwaist Striker,* New York, 1910.

MANDEL, BERNARD, *Samuel Gompers, A Biography,* Yellow Springs, Ohio, 1963.

MAROT, HELEN, *American Labor Unions,* New York, 1914.

MARSHALL, RAY, *Labor in the South,* Cambridge, Mass., 1967.

MARX, KARL, AND ENGELS, FREDERICK, *The Communist Manifesto,* Chicago, 1954.

————, *Selected Correspondence, 1845–1895,* New York, 1935.

MATHEWS, LILLIAN R., *Women in Trade Unions in San Francisco,* Berkeley, Cal., 1912.

MILES, HENRY, *Lowell as It Is and Was,* Lowell, 1845.

MILLER, JOHN C., *Origins of the American Revolution,* Boston, 1943.

MONTGOMERY, DAVID, *Beyond Equality: Labor and the Radical Republicans, 1862–1872,* New York, 1967.

MORRIS, RICHARD B., *Government and Labor in Early America,* New York, 1965.

MORRISON, SAMUEL ELIOT, *Builders of the Bay Colony,* Boston, 1930.

MULCAIRE, MICHAEL A., *The International Brotherhood of Electrical Workers,* Washington, D.C., 1923.

NASH, GARY B., *Red, White and Black: The Peoples of Early America,* Englewood Cliffs, N.J., 1974.

NATHAN, MAUDE, *Story of an Epoch-Making Movement,* New York, 1926.

NATIONAL INDUSTRIAL CONFERENCE BOARD, *Wartime Employment of Women in the Metal Trades,* Boston, 1918.

NEIDLE, CECYLE S., *America's Immigrant Women,* Boston, 1975.

NESTOR, AGNES, *Woman's Labor Leader: An Autobiography of Agnes Nestor,* Rockford, Ill., 1954.

NICOLAY, JOHN G., AND HAY, JOHN, eds., *Complete Works of Abraham Lincoln,* New York, 1915, vol. 5.

PARTON, MARY FIELD, *The Autobiography of Mother Jones,* Chicago, 1925.

PENNY, VIRGINIA, *Five Hundred Employments Adapted to Women,* Philadelphia, 1868.

————, *Think and Act,* Philadelphia, 1869.

PERSONS, CHARLES E., *Labor Laws and Their Enforcement,* New York, 1911.

PESSEN, EDWARD, *Most Uncommon Jacksonians: The Radical Leaders of the Early Labor Movement*, Albany, N.Y., 1967.

PHILLIPS, ULRICH B., *American Negro Slavery*, New York, 1918.

———, ed., "Plantation and Frontier Documents," *Documentary History of American Industrial Society*, Cleveland, 1910, vol. 2.

PIERCE, BESSIE LOUISE, *A History of Chicago, 1871–1893*, New York, 1957, vol. 3.

POWDERLY, TERENCE V., *Thirty Years of Labor, 1859–1889*, Columbus, Ohio, 1890.

QUINT, HOWARD H., *The Forging of American Socialism*, Indianapolis, 1953.

RENSHAW, PATRICK, *The Wobblies: The Story of Syndicalism in the United States*, New York, 1967.

RICHARDSON, DOROTHY, *The Long Day: The Story of a New York Working Girl as Told by Herself*, New York, 1906.

ROBERTS, HAROLD S., *The Rubber Workers*, New York, 1944.

ROBINSON, HARRIET H., *Loom and Spindle: Of Life among the Early Mill Girls*, New York, 1898.

RUBIN, RUTH, *A Treasury of Jewish Folk Songs*, New York, 1950.

RYAN, PAUL, *Womanhood in America*, New York, 1969.

SANGER, MARGARET, *Autobiography*, New York, 1938.

SCHNEIDERMAN, ROSE, WITH GOLDTHWAITE, LUCY, *All for One*, New York, 1967.

SCORESBY, WILLIAM, *American Factories and Their Female Operatives*, London, 1845, repr. New York, 1968.

SCUDDER, VIDA, *Our Journey*, New York, 1937.

SEIDMAN, JOEL, *The Needle Trades*, New York, 1942.

SHLAKMAN, VERA, "Economic History of a Factory Town: A Study of Chicopee, Massachusetts," *Smith College Studies in History*, 20, Northampton, Mass., 1935.

SIEBERT, W. W., *The Underground Railroad from Slavery to Freedom*, New York, 1899.

SIMKHOVITCH, MARY, *Neighborhood, My Story of Greenwich House*, New York, 1938.

SMITH, THOMAS RUSSELL, *The Cotton Textile Industry of Fall River, Massachusetts*, New York, 1944.

SOCHEN, JUNE, *Her Story: A Woman's View of American History, 1660–1880*, New York, 1974.

SPARGO, JOHN, *The Bitter Cry of the Children*, New York, 1906.

SQUIRE, BELLA, *The Woman Movement in America*, Chicago, 1911.

STAROBIN, ROBERT S., *Industrial Slavery in the Old South*, New York, 1970.

STEIN, LEO, *The Triangle Fire*, New York, 1962.

———, ed., *Out of the Sweatshop: The Struggle for Industrial Democracy*, New York, 1977.

STERN, MADELINE B., *We the Women: Career Firsts of Nineteenth Century America*, New York, 1963.

STEVENS, GEORGE A., *New York Typographical Union No. 6: A Study of a Modern Trade Union and its Predecessors*, Albany, N.Y., 1912.

STEWART, WILLIAM RHINELANDER, *The Philanthropic Work of Josephine Shaw Lowell*, New York, 1911.

STILL, WILLIAM, *The Underground Railroad*, Philadelphia, 1872.

STOLBERG, BENJAMIN, *Tailors' Progress: The Story of a Famous Union and the Men Who Made It*, New York, 1946.

STRONG, EARL D., *The Amalgamated Clothing Workers of America*, Grinnell, Iowa, 1940.

SUMNER, HELEN, "History of Women in Industry in the United States," *Report on Condition of Women and Child Wage Earners in the United States, Senate Document No. 645*, 61st Congress, 2nd session, Washington, D.C., 1910–13, vol. 9.

STUART, JOHN, ed., *Education of John Reed, Selected Writings*, New York, 1955.

SWARD, KEITH, *The Legacy of Henry Ford*, New York, 1948.

SYLVIS, JAMES C., *The Life, Speeches, Labors and Essays of William H. Sylvis, Late President of the Iron-Moulders International Union and also of the National Labor Union*, Philadelphia, 1872.

TAFT, PHILIP, *The AFL in the Time of Gompers*, New York, 1957.

TAYLOR, JUNE KING, *Reminiscences of My Life in Camp*, reprinted New York, 1968.

THERNSTROM, STEPHEN, *Poverty and Progress*, Cambridge, Mass., 1964.

TRACY, GEORGE A., *History of the Typographical Union*, Indianapolis, 1913.

VAN HORST, MRS. JOHN, AND VAN HORST, MARIE, *The Woman Who Toils*, New York, 1903.

VAN TINE, WARREN R., *The Making of a Labor Bureaucrat*, Amherst, Mass., 1973.

VINTON, JOHN ADAMS, ed., *Deborah Sampson, The Female Soldier of the American Revolution*, Boston, 1866.

VORSE, MARY HEATON, *Footnote to Folly*, New York, 1935.

WADE, RICHARD, *Slavery in the Cities*, Chicago, 1958.

WALD, LILLIAN, *The House on Henry Street*, New York, 1917.

WALLING, ANNA STRUNSKY, ed., *William English Walling: A Symposium*, New York, 1938.

WARE, CAROLINE F., *The Early New England Cotton Manufacture*, Boston, 1931.

WARE, NORMAN F., *The Industrial Worker, 1840–1860*, Boston and New York, 1924.

———, *The Labor Movement in the U.S.A., 1860–1895*, New York, 1929.

WARNER, SAM BASS, JR., *The Private City*, Philadelphia, 1968.

WEBB, SIDNEY AND BEATRICE, *The History of Trade Unionism, 1660–1920*, London, 1919.

WERTENBAKER, THOMAS J., *Torchbearer of the Revolution*, Princeton, N.J., 1940.

WERTHEIMER, BARBARA, *We Were There: The Story of Working Women in America*, New York, 1977.

WILLARD, FRANCES, *Glimpses of Fifty Years*, Chicago, 1892.

WILLETT, MABEL HURD, *The Employment of Women in the Clothing Trade*, New York, 1902.

WILLIAMS, CHARLES RICHARD, ed., *The Diary and Letters of Rutherford Burchard Hayes*, Columbus, Ohio, 1924.

WINK, ROBIN, *The Negro in Canada,* New Haven, Conn., 1972.

WINSLOW, MARY N., *Woman at Work,* Minneapolis, 1951.

WOLFE, F. E., *Admission to American Trade Unions,* Baltimore, 1912.

WOLMAN, LEO, et al., *The Clothing Workers of Chicago, 1910–1922,* Chicago, 1922.

WOODS, ROBERT S., ed., *The City Wilderness: A Settlement Study by the Residents and Associates of the South End, Boston,* Boston, 1898.

WOODSON, CARTER G., AND GREENE, LORENZO J., *The Negro Wage Earner,* Washington, D.C., 1930; reprinted, New York, 1964.

YOUNG, AGATHA, *The Women and the Crisis,* New York, 1959.

ZARETZ, CHARLES ELBERT, *The Amalgamated Clothing Workers of America,* New York, 1934.

Pamphlets

Address to the People of Philadelphia in the Walnut Street Theatre on the Morning of the Fourth of July, Common Era, 1829, and the Fifty-Fourth year of independence by Frances Wright, New York, 1829.

FLYNN, ELIZABETH GURLEY, "Memories of the Industrial Workers of the World (IWW)," *Occasional Paper No. 24 (1977), American Institute for Marxist Studies,* New York, 1977.

General Report of the Industrial Union with a Statistical Account of the Operations of the Tailoress' Cooperative Store, Philadelphia, 1853.

LAWRENCE, KEN, "Mississippi's First Labor Union," mimeographed pamphlet, Tougaloo, Mississippi, Deep South People's History Project, n.d.

LUTHER, SETH, *An Address on the Origin and Progress of Avarice, and its Deleterious Effects on Human Happiness,* Boston, 1834.

———, *An Address to the Working-Men of New England. . . .,* Boston, 1832.

Pageant of the Paterson Silk Strike, The, New York, 1913.

PIKE, VIOLET, *New World Lessons for Old World People,* New York, 1912.

VAN ETTEN, IDA, *The Condition of Women Workers under the Present Industrial System,* New York, 1890.

WOODBEY, REV. GEORGE W., *What to Do and How to Do It, or Socialism vs. Capitalism, Wayland's Monthly, No. 40,* August, 1903.

Proceedings of the Government and Citizens of Philadelphia on the Reduction of the Hours of Labor, and Increase of Wages, Boston, 1835.

Articles

ABBOT, EDITH, "Harriet Martineau and the Employment of Women in 1836," *Journal of Political Economy* 14(December, 1906): 614–26.

ASHBY, IRENE, "The Fight Against Child Labor in Alabama," *American Federationist* 8(May, 1901): 150–51.

————, "Abolish Child Labor," *American Federationist* 9(January, 1902): 19–20.

————, "Child Life vs. Dividends," *American Federationist* 9(May, 1902): 215–23.

BAKER, RAY STANNARD, "Revolutionary Strike," *American Magazine* 74(May, 1912): 30–35.

BAKER, ROSS K., "Entry of Women into Federal Job World—at a Price," *Smithsonian* 8(July, 1977): 83–85.

BARNES, MARY CLARK, "The Strike of the Shirtwaist Makers," *World-Today* 18(March 1910): 260–70.

BARKER, NANCY JONES, "A Forgotten Feminist: The Early Writings of Ida Husted Harper, 1878–1894," *Indiana Magazine of History,* 73(1977): 79–101.

BARRY, PHILLIPS, "The Fall of the Pemberton Mill," *Bulletin of the Folksong of the North East* 3(Fall, 1931): 16–17.

BAXANDALL, LEE AND ASSOCIATES, "Fur, Log and Human Lives, The Great Oshkosh Woodworker Strike of 1898," *Green Mountain Quarterly* 3(May, 1976). Entire Issue.

BAXANDALL, ROSALYN FRAAD, "Elizabeth Gurley Flynn: The Early Years," *Radical America* 8(Jan–Feb. 1975): 90–102.

BLANK, ROSE, "Strike of the Furriers," *Life and Labor* 2(December, 1912): 360–61.

BLUMBERG, DOROTHY ROSE, "'Dear Mr. Engels': Unpublished Letters, 1884–1894, of Florence Kelley (Wischnewetsky) to Friedrich Engels," *Labor History* 5(Spring, 1964): 105–28.

BROOKS, JOHN GRAHAM, "The Challenge of Unemployment," *The Independent* 81(March 15, 1915): 383–85.

BROWN, JEAN COLLIER, "The Economic Status of Negro Women," *Southern Workmen* 60(October, 1931): 430–31.

BROWNSON, ORESTES S., "The Laboring Classes," *Boston Quarterly Review* 3(July, 1840): 112–15.

BRUERE, MARTHA BENSLEY, "The White Goods Workers Strike," *Life & Labor* 3(March, 1913): 73–75.

BRYANT, KEITH L., JR., "Kate Barnard, Organized Labor and Social Justice in Oklahoma During the Progressive Era," *Journal of Southern History,* 35 (February, 1969): 145–64.

————, "The Oklahoma State Federation of Labor During the Age of Reform," *Labor History,* 11(Summer, 1970): 259–76.

BUHLE, MARI JO, "Socialist Women and the 'Girl Strikers': Chicago, 1910," *Signs* 1(January, 1976): 1047–48.

CHAPLIN, RALPH, "A Hunger 'Riot' in Chicago," *International Socialist Review* 15(March, 1915): 517–20.

CLARK, DEIMUS, "Babes in Bondage: Indentured Irish Children in Philadelphia, in the Nineteenth Century," *Pennsylvania Magazine of History and Biography* 101(October, 1977): 475–86.

CLARK, SUE AINSLEY AND WYATT, EDITH, "The Shirtwaist Makers and Their Strike, *McClure's Magazine* 36(November, 1910): 70–86.

COLEMAN, McALISTER, "All of Which I Saw," *The Progressive* 14(May, 1950): 24–25.

COMETTI, ELIZABETH, "Women and the American Revolution," *New England Quarterly* 20(July, 1947): 329–46.

COTT, NANCY F., "Divorce and the Changing Status of Women in Eighteenth Century Massachusetts," *William & Mary Quarterly,* 3rd Ser., 33(October, 1976): 586–614.

DAVIES, MARGARY, "Woman's Place Is at the Typewriter: The Feminization of the Clerical Labor Force," *Radical America* 8(July–August, 1974): 4–16.

DAVIS, ALLEN F., "The Women's Trade Union League: Origins and Organization," *Labor History* 5(Winter, 1964): 3–17.

DELZELL, RUTH, "1866-Laundry Workers Union, Troy, N.Y.," *Life & Labor* (November, 1912): 333.

DANCIS, BRUCE, "Socialism and Women in the United States, 1900–1917," *Socialist Revolution* 27(January–March, 1976): 81–144.

DAVIS, PHILIP, "The Social Settlement and the Trade Union," *Charities and the Commons* 1(April, 1904): 142–47.

DePAUW, LINDA GRANT, "Land of the Unfree: Legal Limitations on Liberty in Pre-Revolutionary America," *Maryland Historical Magazine* 68(Winter, 1973): 355–68.

DORR, RHETTA CHILDE, "The Women Strikers of Troy," *Charities and the Commons* 15(November 18, 1905): 233–36.

DUBOFSKY, MELVYN, "Organized Labor and the Immigrant in New York City, 1900–1918," *Labor History* 2(Spring, 1961): 182–201.

DUBLIN, THOMAS, "Women, Work and Protest in Early Lowell Mills: 'The Oppressing Hand of Avarice Would Enslave Us,'" *Labor History* 16(Winter, 1975): 99–116.

DUCHEZ, LOUIS, "Victory at McKees Rocks," *International Socialist Review* 10-(October, 1909): 289–300.

DYE, NANCY SCHROM, "Creating a Feminist Alliance: Sisterhood, Feminism or Unionism: The New York Women's Trade Union League and the Labor Movement," *Feminist Studies* 3(Fall, 1975): 111–25.

FLYNN, ELIZABETH GURLEY, "The Shame of Spokane," *International Socialist Review* 11(January, 1910): 610–19.

———, "Women and Unionism," *Solidarity,* May 27, 1911.

———, "I.W.W. Call to Women," *Solidarity,* July 31, 1915.

———, "Problems Organizing Women," *Solidarity,* July 15, 1915.

———, "Women and Socialism," *Solidarity,* May 27, 1915.

———, "Women in Industry Should Organize," *Industrial Worker,* June 1, 1911.

FONER, PHILIP S., "The Battle to End Discrimination Against Negroes on Philadelphia Streetcars (Part I): Background and Beginning of the Battle," *Pennsylvania History* 40(July, 1973): 261–92; (Part II), "The Victory," *Ibid.* (October, 1973): 355–80.

———, "The *Boston Daily Evening Voice:* A Labor Voice for Black Equality, 1864–1867," *Science & Society* 32(Fall, 1974): 304–25.

GERSUNY, CARL, "Seth Luther—The Road from Chepachet," *Rhode Island History* 33(May, 1974): 47–55.

———, "'A Devil in Petticoats,' and Just Cause: Patterns of Punishment in Two New England Textile Factories," *Business History Review* 50(Summer, 1976): 131–52.

———, "Work and Injuries and Adversary Processes in Two New England Textile Mills," *Business History Review* 51(Autumn, 1977): 326–40.

GINGER, RAY, "Labor in a Massachusetts Cotton Mill, 1853–1860," *Business History Review* 28(March, 1954): 67–91.

GITELMAN, HOWARD M., "The Waltham System and the Coming of the Irish," *Labor History* 8(Fall, 1967): 227–53.

GOLDIN, CLAUDE, "Female Labor Force Participation: The Origin of Black and White Differences, 1870 and 1880," *Journal of Economic History* 37(March, 1977): 87–100.

GOLDMARK, JOSEPHINE, "Legislative Gains for Women in 1912," *Survey* 28(April 13, 1912): 95–96.

GOMPERS, SAMUEL, "Woman's Work, Rights, and Progress," *American Federationist* 22(July, 1915): 517–19.

———, "The Struggle in the Garment Trades—From Misery and Despondency to Betterment and Hope," *American Federationist* 20(March, 1913): 189–90.

———, "The American Labor Movement," *American Federationist* 21(July, 1914): 543–44.

———, "Working Women Organize," *American Federationist* 21(March, 1914): 231–34.

GORDON, MICHAEL A., "The Labor Boycott in New York City, 1880–1886," *Labor History* 16(Spring, 1975): 184–229.

GREENE, LORENZO J., "The New England Negro as Seen in Advertisements for Runaway Slaves," *Journal of Negro History* 29(Spring, 1944): 125–46.

GUTMAN, HERBERT G., "The Tompkins Square 'Riot' in New York City on January 13, 1874: A Re-Examination of Its Causes and Its Aftermath," *Labor History* 6(Winter, 1965): 44–70.

HAMILTON, ALICE, "Occupational Conditions and Tuberculosis," *Charities* 16-(May 15, 1906): 205–09.

HARTZ, LOUIS, "Seth Luther: The Story of a Working Class Rebel," *New England Quarterly* 13(September, 1940): 401–18.

HAYWOOD, WILLIAM D., "The Rip in the Silk Industry," *International Socialist Review* 13(May, 1913): 122–28.

HEATON, JAMES P., "The Legal Aftermath of the Lawrence Strike," *Survey* 28-(July 6, 1912): 509–10.

HENDRICKSON, KENNETH E., JR., "George R. Lunn and the Socialist Era in Schenectady, 1909–1916," *New York History* 27(January, 1966): 22–40.

HENROTIN, ELLEN M., "Organization for Women: Its Necessity in Order That They Shall Meet the Modern Method of Collective Bargaining," *American Federationist* 12(November, 1905): 824–27.

HEWES, AMY, "Women as Munition Makers," *Survey* 37(January 6, 1917): 379–85.

HOBBY, DANIEL T., ed., "'We Have Got Results': A Document on the Organization of Domestics in the Progressive Era," *Labor History* 17(Winter, 1976): 103–08.

HOLMES, LIZZIE SWANK, "Women Workers of Chicago," *American Federationist* 12(August, 1905): 508–09.

HOURWICH, ISAAC A., "The Garment Workers' Strike," *The New Review* 1(March 15, 1913): 426–27.

HUTCHINSON, WOODS, "The Hygienic Aspects of the Shirtwaist Strike," *Survey* 23(January 22, 1910): 541–50.

INGHAM, JOHN N., "A Strike in the Progressive Era: McKees Rocks, 1909," *Pennsylvania Magazine of History and Biography* 90(July, 1966): 353–77.

JACOBY, ROBIN MILLER, "The Women's Trade Union League and American Feminism," *Feminist Studies* 3(Fall, 1975): 126–40.

KANN, KENNETH, "The Knights of Labor and the Southern Black Worker," *Labor History* 18(Winter, 1977): 49–70.

KELLEY M. E. J., "Women and the Labor Movement," *North American Review*, 166(March, 1898): 408–17.

KENNEALLY, JAMES, "Women and Trade Unions," *Labor History* 14(Winter, 1973): 42–55.

KERBER, LINDA, "The Republican Mother: Woman and the Enlightenment, An American Perspective," *American Quarterly* 28(Summer, 1976): 43–49.

KERR, THOMAS J., IV, "The New York Factory Investigating Commission and the Minimum-Wage Movement," *Labor History* 12(Summer, 1971): 373–91.

KESSLER-HARRIS, ALICE, "Where Are the Organized Women Workers?" *Feminist Studies* 3(Fall, 1975): 92–110.

KIZER, BENJAMIN H., "Elizabeth Gurley Flynn," *Pacific Northwest Quarterly* 57-(July, 1966): 110–12.

KLACZYNSKA, BARBARA, "Why Women Work: A Comparison of Various Groups—Philadelphia, 1910–1930," *Labor History* 17(Winter, 1976): 73–87.

KOETTGEN, E., "Making Silk," *International Socialist Review* 14(March, 1914): 553–54.

KUGLER, ISRAEL, "The Trade Union Career of Susan B. Anthony," *Labor History* 2(Winter, 1961): 90–100.

KULIK, GARY, "Pawtucket Village and the Strike of 1824: The Origins of Class Conflict in Rhode Island," *Radical History Review* 17(Spring, 1978): 5–39.

LERNER, GERDA, "The Lady and the Mill Girl: Changes in the Status of Women in the Age of Jackson," *American Studies Journal* 4(Spring, 1969): 2–10.

LEUPP, CONSTANCE D., "The Shirtwaist Strike," *Survey* 28(December 18, 1909): 383–86.

LEVIN, HOWARD, "The Paterson Silk Workers' Strike of 1913," *King's Crown Essays* 6(Winter, 1961–62): 30–48.

LINCOLN, JONATHAN TAYLOR, "The Beginning of the Machine Age in New England: Documents Relating to the Introduction of the Power Loom," *Bulletin: Business History Society* 7(June, 1933): 6–20.

LOFTON, WILLISTON H., "Northern Labor and the Negro During the Civil War," *Journal of Negro History* 34(July, 1949): 251–73.

McDONALD, ALLAN, "Lowell: A Commercial Utopia," *New England Quarterly* 10(March, 1937): 37–62.

McDOWELL, MARY, "The Story of a Women's Labor Union," *Charities and the Commons* 7(January, 1903):1–3.

McLAURIN, MELTON A., "The Racial Policies of the Knights of Labor and the Organization of Southern Workers," *Labor History* 17(Fall, 1976): 568–85.

McPHERSON, JOHN B., "The Lawrence Strike of 1912," *Bulletin of the National Association of Wool Manufacturers* 12(1912): 236–37.

MAILLY, WILLIAM, "The Working Girls' Strike," *The Independent* 67(December 23, 1909): 416–20.

MAISEL-WALTERS, LYNN, "'Their Rights and Nothing More,'" A History of the *Revolution*, 1868–1870," *Journalism Quarterly*, 53(Summer, 1976): 242–51.

MAN, ALBON P., JR., "Labor Competition and the New York Draft Riots of 1863," *Journal of Negro History* 36(October, 1951): 375–405.

MANDEL, BERNARD, "The 'Great Uprising' of 1877," *Cigar Makers' Official Journal* (September, 1967): 3–5.

MANN, ARTHUR, "British Social Thought and American Reformers," *Mississippi Valley Historical Review* 42(March, 1956): 682–92.

MANNHEIMER, L., "Darkest New Jersey, How the Paterson Strike Looks to One in the Thick of the Conflict," *The Independent* 74(April–June, 1913): 1191–92.

MARCY, LESLIE H., "800 Percent and the Akron Strike," *International Socialist Review* 13(April, 1913): 19–20.

———, "Food Riots in America," *International Socialist Review* 17(April, 1917): 585–87.

MARCY, LESLIE AND BOYD, FREDERICK SUMNER, "One Big Union Wins," *International Socialist Review* 12(April, 1912): 625–29.

MAROT, HELEN, "A Woman's Strike, An Appreciation of the Shirtwaist Makers of New York," *Proceedings of the Academy of Political Science in the City of New York* (1910): 122–28.

———, "A Moral in the Cloakmakers' Strike," New York *Call* August 7, 1910.

———, "What Can A Union Do For Its Members," New York *Call* January 27, 1913.

MASON, GREGORY, "Industrial War in Paterson," *Outlook* 54(June 7, 1913): 283–87.

MILLER, WILLIAM, "The Effects of the American Revolution on Indentured Servitude, *Pennsylvania History* 7(July, 1940): 131–41.

MONTGOMERY, DAVID, "Workers' Control of Machine Production in the 19th Century," *Labor History* 17(Fall, 1976): 485–509.

Morgan, J. Edward, "The Unemployed in San Francisco," *The New Review* 2(April, 1914): 193–99.

Nettles, Curtis, "British Mercantilism and the Economic Development of the Thirteen Colonies," *Journal of Economic History* 12(Spring, 1952): 105–14.

Newman, Debra L., "Black Women in the Era of the American Revolution in Pennsylvania," *Journal of Negro History* 61(July, 1976): 276–89.

Newman, Philip, "The I.W.W. Invasion of New Jersey," *Proceedings of the New Jersey Historical Society* 58(1940): 270–83.

O'Sullivan, Mary K., "The Labor War at Lawrence," *Survey* 28(April, 1912): 72–74.

Palmer, Lewis E., "A Strike for Four Loaves of Bread," *Survey* 28(February 3, 1912): 1695–99.

Patterson, James T., "Mary Dewson and the American Minimum Wage Movement," *Labor History* 5(Spring, 1964): 134–52.

Porter, Lorle Ann, "Amelia Bloomer: An Early Iowa Feminist's Sojourn On the Way West," *Annals of Iowa* 41(1973): 1242–57.

Rezneck, Samuel, "The Social History of an American Depression, 1837–1843," *American Historical Review* 40(July, 1935): 662–87.

Richardson, Dorothy, "Trade-Union in Petticoats, What the Women Who Work in Chicago Have Done and Are Doing for Themselves Through Their Own Unions," *Leslie's Monthly Magazine* 57(March, 1904): 483–94.

Ritter, Ellen M., "Elizabeth Morgan: Pioneer Female Labor Agitator," *Central States Speech Journal* 22(Fall, 1971): 228–49.

Rosenberg, Carroll Smith, "Beauty, the Beast and the Militant Woman: A Case Study of Sex Roles and Social Stress in Jacksonian America," *American Quarterly* 23(October, 1971): 562–84.

———, "The Hysterical Woman: Sex Roles and the Role Conflict in 19th Century America," *Social Research* 39(Winter 1972): 652–78.

Russell, Phillips, "The Strike at Little Falls," *International Socialist Review* 13-(December, 1912): 455–60.

———, "The Fourteen in Jail," *International Socialist Review*, 13(February, 1913): 895–97.

Schappes, Morris U., "The Political Origins of the United Hebrew Trades of 1888," *Journal of Ethnic Studies* 5(Spring, 1977): 13–44.

Scharnau, Ralph, "Elizabeth Morgan, Crusader for Labor Reform," *Labor History* 14(Summer, 1973): 340–51.

Schlesinger, Elizabeth Bancroft, "Cotton Mather and His Children," *William and Mary Quarterly* 3rd Ser. 10(April, 1953): 165–89.

Schneiderman, Rose, "A Cap-Maker's Story," *Independent* 58(1905): 935–37.

———, "The White Goods Workers of New York: Their Struggle for Human Conditions," *Life and Labor* 3(May, 1913): 132–36.

Scott, Kenneth, "The Slave Insurrection in New York in 1912," *New York Historical Quarterly* 44(Spring, 1961): 133–49.

SCOTT, MIRIAM F., "The Spirit of the Girl Strikers," *Outlook* 94(February 19, 1910): 392–97.

———, "What the Women Strikers Won," *Outlook* 95(July 12, 1910): 480–88.

SHAPLEIGH, DR. ELIZABETH, "Occupational Diseases in the Textile Industry," New York *Call* December 29, 1912.

SILVA, PHILIP T., JR., "The Position of Workers in a Textile Community: Fall River in the Early 1880's," *Labor History* 16(Spring, 1975): 230–48.

SMITH, RUSSELL E., "The March of the Mill Children," *Social Service Review* 41(September, 1967): 298–303.

SPARGO, JOHN, "Child Slaves of Philadelphia," *The Comrade* 2(August, 1903): 253–54.

STEARNS, BERTHA M., ".Early Factory Magazines in New England," *Journal of Economic & 8usiness History* 2(August, 1930): 685–705.

STUCKLEY, JULIA WARD, "The Records of Deborah Sampson Gannett, Woman Soldier of the Revolution," *Prologue* 4(Winter, 1972): 233–41.

SUMNER, MARY BROWN, "The Spirit of the Strikers," *Survey* 23(January 22, 1910): 550–55.

TOWNER, LAWRENCE W., "The Indentures of Boston's Poor Apprentices: 1734–1805," *Publications of the Colonial Society of Massachusetts* 43(1956–63): 417–34.

VAN KLEECK, MARY, "Working Hours of Women Workers," *Charities and the Commons* 17(October 6, 1906): 13–21.

VORSE, MARY HEATON, "Elizabeth Gurley Flynn," *Nation* 102(February 17, 1916): 175–76.

WALKOWITZ, DANIEL J., "Working-Class Women in the Gilded Age: Factory, Community, and Family Life Among Cohoes, New York Cotton Workers," *Journal of Social History,* 5(Summer, 1972): 464–90.

WALLING, WILLIAM ENGLISH, "Field of Organizing for Women Workers," *American Federationist* 12(September, 1905): 625–27.

WAX, DONALD D., "The Image of the Negro in the *Maryland Gazette* 1745–74," *Journalism Quarterly* 13(Spring, 1969): 110–22.

WELTER, BARBARA, "The Cult of True Womanhood, 1820–1860," *American Quarterly* 18(Summer, 1966): 151–74.

WILLIAMSON, HUGH P., "The State Against Celia, A Slave," *Midwest Journal* 8(Spring–Fall, 1956): 408–20.

WINN, WILL, "The Negro: His Relations to Southern Industry," *American Federationist* 4(February, 1898): 269–71.

WOLFE, ALLIS ROSENBERG, "Women, Consumerism, and the National Consumers' League in the Progressive Era, 1900–1923," *Labor History* 16(Summer, 1975): 378–92.

———, "Letters of a Lowell Mill Girl and Friends: 1845–1846," *Labor History* 17(Winter, 1976): 96–102.

YOUNG, LOUISE M., "Woman's Place in American Politics: The Historical Perspective," *Journal of Politics* 38(August, 1976): 295–335.

"Colored Working Girl and Race Prejudice," *The Crisis* 6(April, 1916): 32–34.

"Factory Girl, A," *Lowell Offering* 1(December, 1840): 16–23.

"The Strike of the Lady Shirtwaist Makers," *Survey* 23(November 23, 1909): 228.

"The Shirtwaist Makers' Strike," *Survey* 23(January 15, 1910): 505–06.

"Living Wage for Women, A," *Independent* 74(April 17, 1913): 851–53.

"Uprising in the Needle Trades in New York," *Life & Labor* 2(March, 1913): 69–70.

Index

Ablowitz, Rebecca, 295
Abramowitz, Bessie, 350, 354, 377, 379, 381, 383
Accidents, 91, 462–63
Adams, Abigail, 15–16, 18
Addams, Jane, 219, 220, 227, 299
Address of the National Labor Congress to the Workingmen of the United States, 127
"Address to Working Girls and Women, An," 214
Address to the Working Men of New England, 31–32
Adler, Felix, 220
Afric-American Female Intelligence Society, 107
African Methodist Episcopal Church, 268
African Repository, 164
Akron (Ohio), 452–53
Akron *Press*, 452
Allen, Frederick Lewis, 264
Allies, in National Women's Trade Union League, 300
Altgeld, John Peter, 233
Amalgamated Clothing Workers of America, AFL hostility to, 376–79; factors leading to formation, 368; formation, 376–78; growth, 380–81; ideology, 378; importance of women in, 384; resolution on women adopted, 384–85; role of women in, 378–80, 383–85; role of women in leadership, 383–85; strikes, 381–82
Amalgamated Meat Cutters and Butcher Workmen of North America, 251, 299, 313, 320, 475

American Association for Labor Legislation, 480
American Equal Rights Association, 128
American Federationist, 249, 250, 301, 345
American Federation of Labor (AFL), abandons move to organize workingwomen, 487; advocates equal pay for equal work, 214; affiliates bar women, 214, 319–320, 497; affiliates interested only in skilled workers, 234, 250–51; appoints women organizers, 224, 226, 227, 249; autonomy doctrine of, 320–22; calls for removing women from jobs, 487–88; complaints against antiwomen views in, 306; conflict with National Women's Trade Union League, 479–82, 485–86; craft nature of, 214–15; and domestic servants, 242–43; early approach favorable to women workers, 213–15; effect of depression of 1893 on, 235; endorses woman's suffrage, 237–38, 301; fails to organize women workers, 294; federal labor unions of women in, 222–23; few women delegates at conventions, 301; formation, 213; high dues and initiation fees in, 248, 319; hostility to Consumers' League, 292; ignores needs of workingwomen, 294; increase in membership, 301*n*.; inaugurates move to organize women, 487; inaugurates movement to organize working women, 487; and Jim Crow

AFL (cont'd)
unionism, 320–23; laundry workers
in, 223–24; leaders argue women
unorganizable, 229; National Wom-
en's Trade Union League critical of,
317–23, 472; opposes Amalgamated
Clothing Workers, 377–78, 380–81;
opposes minimum wages for
women, 179–80; pays tribute to
Elizabeth Morgan, 233; position on
women criticized by IWW, 397–98;
racism in, 247, 267; role in formation of National Women's Trade
Union League, 300–301; urges
women to organize, 204; views
women as undermining wages, 496;
women complain cannot join, 250–
51; women organizers, 315, 318
American Industrial Union, 492–93
American Labor Union, 393
American Revolution, 12–19
American Servant Girls' Association,
241–42
American Woman Suffrage Associa-
tion, 177
American Workman, 137, 139
Anarchists, 235, 243
Anchor Federal Labor Union No. 5568,
223
Anderson, Mary, 477
Anthony, Susan B., 56, 128–37, 139,
141, 148, 150–52, 154, 155, 201*n.*,
238, 481
Anti-Women Stenographers' Society,
275–76
Appeal to Reason, 283
Apprentices, 7
Aronovitch, Sadie, 368
Ashby-Macfayden, Irene M., 249–50
Ashleigh, Charles, 405
Association of Waist and Dress Manu-
facturers of New York, 329–31, 335,
337, 338
Association of the Working People of
New Castle, Delaware, 52
Avery, Martha Moore, 300–301
Awl, 90

Bacon, Nathaniel, 12
Bacon's rebellion, 12
Bagley, Sarah G., breaks silence on
Lowell Offering, 60–61; directs
"Female Department," 66–67; elec-
ted president, Lowell Female Labor
Association, 64; elected vice-
president, Lowell Union of As-
sociationists, 69; first woman tele-
graph operator, 80; initiates debate
on *Lowell Offering,* 60–61; leads
ten-hour petition movement, 75–76
Baker, Ray Stannard, 230–31
Ballet dancers, 123
Baltimore, 44–45, 49, 383–84
Baltimore Buttonhole Makers' Union,
379–80, 383–84
Baltimore Sun, 173
Barker, Nellie B., 298
Barnard, Kate, 240–41
Barondess, Joseph, 278, 279
Barry, Leonora M., accomplishments,
207; appeals to men, 204; appointed
head of Department of Woman's
Work, 199; attacked, 200; Director
of Woman's Work, 198–207; early
life, 199–200; marries, 206; opposi-
tion to, 220; resigns, 206–207; on
women's reluctance to join Knights
of Labor, 203–204; work after res-
ignation, 207
Bateman, Mary, 434
Beach, Moses, 119–20, 290
Beal, Fred, 432–33
Beale, St. Justin, 242
Bean, Alice, 477
Beard, Mary, 482, 483
"Beauty of Factory Life," 57–58, 62, 83
Beldner, Sophie, 407*n.*
Bell, Anna Katherine, 492–94
Belmont, Alva, 332–33, 336–38
Benevolent Societies, 49
Berger, Victor, 371, 436
Black, Clementine, 296, 297
Blacklists, 26, 27, 35–36, 74, 79, 158,
218, 303
Black preachers, 94, 96, 105

Black sewing women, 118–19
Black waitresses, 465
Black washerwomen, 10, 104–105, 124–25, 176, 188*n.*
Black women, and Amalgamated Meat Cutters and Butcher Workmen, 313; attacks on during draft riots, 118–19; in Colonial America, 2–6; and Colored National Labor Union, 137–39; description of in South, 269; discriminated against in North, 105–106; as domestic workers, 268–69; excluded from AFL unions, 267; excluded from factories, 105; excluded from unions before Civil War, 106; first union of, 124–25; forced to face discrimination, 464–65; as fugitive slaves, 100–103; and ILGWU, 339–41; in Knights of Labor, 188, 190–92; in slavery, 2–6, 99–107; job discrimination against, 267–69; mainly domestic servants, 463–64; marriage status of as slaves, 4–5; militant tradition of, 107–108; and National Women's Trade Union League, 313, 339–41, 478; occupations, 463; position in South under slavery, 103–104; purchase freedom of relatives, 102–103; role in waistmakers' strike, 339–41; role in War for Independence, 16; as slaves, 2–6, 99–107; strikes, 176; unions, 176, 188; wages, 268; as washerwomen, 10, 104–105, 124–25, 176, 188
Blacks, migration to North, 490; excluded by AFL unions, 267; and National Labor Union, 135; slavery of begins, 2–6; *see also* Black women
Blank, Rose, 363
Bloomer, Amelia Jenks, 144–45
Bloor, Ella Reeve, 48
Boarding-houses, 22–25, 27, 35
Bocchini, Fillipo, 442–45, 448*n.*
Bohemian women, 175–78
Bohm, Ernest, 327
Boot & Shoe Workers' Union, 251

Boston Associates, 22–24
Boston Central Labor Union, 237
Boston Daily Evening Voice, 111, 113, 118, 120–23
Boston Evening Transcript, 35, 42
Boston Globe, 237
Boston Manufacturing Company, 22
Boston Quarterly Review, 58
Boston Trades' Union, 47
Boston Women's Trade Union League, formation, 301; role in garment strike, 372; split in over Lawrence strike, 472–74
Boycotts, 192–93, 224, 228, 294–95
Brandeis, Louis D., 348, 349
Brent, Margaret, 10
Brissenden, Paul, 294–95
British Women's Trade Union League, 295–96
Brooks, James, 129
Brown, Elizabeth, 142
Brown, Julia, 142
Brown, Moses, 20
Brown lung, 82
Brownson, Orestes A., 58–59
Bruere, Henry, 489
Bryant, Elizabeth S., 189
Bryn Mawr College, 332, 334
Bureaus of labor statistics, state, 203
Buse, Mrs. Elmer F., 408

Call, Homer D., 475
Cameron, Andrew C., 125, 130, 136–37
Campbell, Helen, 238
Cap and hatmakers, 168–70
Cardello, Rosa, 433, 434
Carders' Union, 170–71
Carey, Mary A. S., 137, 138, 195
Carey, Matthew, 40, 41, 44–45, 48, 52
Carpet weavers, 194–96
Casey, Josephine, 311, 355, 357, 477
Catholic Church, 185–86, 200
Catt, Carrie Chapman, 277–78
Census statistics, on workingwomen, 1880, 186; 1890, 257; 1900, 257–58

Century of Struggle: The Woman's Rights Movement in the United States, 290

Charriere, Walter, 305–306

Chase, Salmon P., 109

Chicago, 173–76

Chicago Colored Women's Club, 210

Chicago Bindery Workers' Union, 227

Chicago Daily Socialist, 352

Chicago Federation of Labor, 301, 311–16, 322, 351, 353

Chicago Industrial Exhibit, 316

Chicago Inter-Ocean, 175

Chicago News-Record, 233

Chicago Times, 175, 216, 217

Chicago Trade and Labor Assembly, 216, 231, 232

Chicago Tribune, 164–65, 175, 194

Chicago Women's Trade Union League, formation, 301, 311–16, 321; role in men's clothing strike, 351–53

Chicago Working Girls' Clubs, 227

Chicago Working Women's Union, 181–82

Child labor, 20–21, 25–28, 217, 261, 283–89, 307–308, 427–28

Children, strikes of, 29–30, 36–37

"Children's Crusade": *see* "Lawrence Children's Crusade"

Christian Recorder, The, 268

Cigar Makers' International Union, admit women to membership, 127–28, 214; strikes, 177–79; women strikers, 178–79

Cigar Makers' Journal, 178

Cincinnati, 87–88

Cincinnati Enquirer, 88

Cincinnati Post, 392

Citizens' Volunteer Police Association, 453

Citywide federation of women workers, in Philadelphia, 45; in Seattle, 498

Civil Service Act, 189

Civil War, 109–21

Clark, Alice, 7–8

Clark, Sue Hinsley, 472, 474

Clerical work, women in, 258

Cleveland garment strike, 354–56

Cloak, Suit and Shirt Manufacturers' Protective Association, 347

Cloakmakers' Strike, New York (1910), 346–50; (1916), 387–88

Cloth, Hat and Cap Makers' Union, 279–80

Clothing industry, changes in, 39–40

Cluer, John C., 74, 78

Coalition, of trade union and middle-class women, 217–22

Coast Seamen's Journal, 234

Cocheco Manufacturing Company, 26, 30, 32, 153

Cohen, Rose, 266

Cohn, Fannia, 385, 387, 388, 477

Coit, Stanton, 220

Collar, Cuff and Shirt Starchers' Union, 228

Collar girls: *see* Laundry workers

College girls, and women strikers, 331–32, 334

Collins, Jennie, 153

Colonial America, feminists in, 10; role of women in, 8–10; women's legal status in, 10–11; wages of women in, 10

Colored National Labor Union, 137–39

Committee on Female Labor, National Trades' Union, 53–54

Committee on Women's Work, AFL, 222

Common Sense, 275–76

Compulsory education, 217, 249

Condition of Women Workers Under the Present Industrial System, The, 222–23

Connolly, James, 396

Consumers' League: *see* National Consumers' League

Continental Army, 15, 16–18

Cooperative Clothing Store of New York, 89

Co-operative Collar Company, 155–56, 191–92

Cooperatives, 88–89, 116, 155–56, 191–92, 230

Corbin, Margaret, 16

Corset workers, 314, 357–58
Cost of living, demonstrations against, 15–16, 494–95
Coxey's Army, 285
Craft, Ellen, 101–102
Craft, William, 101
Crèvecoeur, Hector St. John de, 4
Crossfield, Sarah, 240
"Cult of True Womanhood," 39
Curry, Nelle B., 467–69

Daly, Margaret, 305, 311, 376
Darlin, Ellen, 93–94
Darrow, Clarence, 227, 230, 354
Daughters of Labor, 189
Daughters of Liberty, 13–15, 19, 158
Daughters of St. Crispin, 97, 156–59, 181, 182, 189, 251
Davis, Allen F., 296
Davis, Philip, 298–99
Day nurseries, 212*n.*
Debs, Eugene V., 132*n.*, 283
Declaration of Independence, 18, 32, 51, 158
Declaration of Sentiments, 72
De Leon, Daniel, 290
Democratic-Republican societies, 49–50
Denison House, 220
Denmark, Constance, 375
Denver Domestic Workers' Industrial Union, 407–11
Department of Woman's Work, Knights of Labor, 198–207
Depressions, of 1837–42, 55; of 1873–79, 159, 163–84; of 1893–97, 234–39; of 1913–14, 487–89
Detroit, 117–18
Detroit Tribune, 117–18
Dewey, Mrs. John, 305
Dewson, Mary, 479
Dickens, Charles, 58
Dickinson, Anna E., 112, 113, 142
Dodge, Grace M., 218
Domestic servants, in IWW, 407–11; letters of, 164–65; unions of, 241–42; 283; 407–11
Domestic system, 18
Donnelly, Michael, 251, 299, 313

Donovan, Frances, 262
Douglas, Charles, 32
Douglas, Stephen A., 96
Douglass, Frederick, 102, 107, 128, 147
Douglass, Lewis H., 147*n.*
Dover (New Hampshire), 26, 30, 32–33
Dover Gazette, 32–33
Draft riots, 118–19, 162, 169
Draper, Alonzo G., 92
Dreier, Margaret: *see* Robins, Margaret Dreier
Dreier, Mary, 310, 327, 331, 482
Dressmakers, 324–25
Driver, Rev. Thomas, 94, 96, 105
Dublin, Thomas, 24, 25, 84
Dubofsky, Melvyn, 456
Du Bois, Ellen Carol, 131, 132*n.*
Du Bois, W. E. B., 268, 341
Dudley, Helena S., 298, 299
Dulany, Daniel, 4
Durham, Mary, 342
Dutcher, Elizabeth, 341
Dyche, John, 317, 347–48, 355, 375
Dye, Nancy Shrom, 361

Eastman, Crystal, 261–62
Eastman, Mehitabel, 56, 71, 72, 75*n.*, 78–79
Eight-hour day, 130, 131, 194, 309, 313, 479, 491–94, 499
Eight Hour Day, 218
Eight-hour law, 263
Emerson, Laura Payne, 417–18
Emerson, Mary, 69
Engels, Frederick, 220, 270–71, 292
England, hours of labor in, 89; increase of women in industry, 296–97; strikes of women workers, 296–97; textile industry, 20–21, 27; women's leagues in, 294–98
English system, 20–21, 27, 57
Equal pay for equal work, AFL and, 214; can benefit men more than women, 214; as device to eliminate women, 320; dim prospects for, 161; during Civil War, 111–12; lack of

Equal pay for equal work (cont'd)
application of, 264–65; voted for by
National Labor Union, 133
Ettor, Joseph J., 430, 431
Evaline, Mary S., 223–24
Evans, Chris, 229
Evans, Elizabeth Glendower, 473
Evans, George Henry, 43–44, 52
Excelsior Labor Club, 195
Excelsior League of Massachusetts,
137

Factories, conditions in, 25–27; rules
in, 26
Factory Girl, 61, 62
Factory girls, and anti-slavery, 68–69;
blacklisted, 74, 79; contribute to relief of Irish famine victims, 69; cordially received by male workers, 72,
75–78; elected officers of New England Workingmen's Association,
74–75; establish magazines, 61–62,
63–64; expose "Beauties of Factory
Life," 62–66, 67; move away from
militancy, 80–81, 82–83; on marriage, 69–70; pioneers for women's
rights, 69–72; poems of, 67–68, 80;
resistance to oppression, 63–64;
unity with male workers, 74–75; *see
also* Female Labor Reform Associations; Lowell Female Labor Reform
Association, Ten-hour Day
Factory Girls' Album, 63–66
"Factory Girls' Association," 35
Factory Girls' Garland, 61
Factory system, attacks on, 31–32;
emergence in textiles, 18, 20–23;
emergence in shoe, 90–91
"Factory Tracts," 67
Factory and Workshop Inspection Act,
233
Fair, Agnes Thecla, 415–16
Fall River (Massachusetts), 170–71,
184
Fall River *Mechanic*, 89
Farley, Harriet, 58–61, 76, 83

Federation of Organized Trades and
Labor Unions of the United States
and Canada, 213
Federation of Union Women and Aux-
iliaries, 498–99
Female Boot and Shoe Binders Soci-
ety, 48
"Female Department," of *Voice of In-
dustry*, 66–67
Female Improvement Society for the
City and County of Philadelphia, 45
Female Industrial Association of New
York, 65–66
Female Labor Reform Association of
Allegheny and Pittsburgh, 64,
76–78, 81–82
Female Labor Reform Association of
Dover, 79
Female Labor Reform Association of
Manchester, 79
Female Labor Reform Association of
Nashua, 79
Female Labor Reform Associations,
achievements, 84; formed in Lowell,
64; constitutions, 64; disappearance,
80–83; *see also* Ten-hour day
Female Society of Lynn and Vicinity
for the Protection of Female Industry, 46–48
Female Umbrella and Parasol Makers,
167–68
Female Union Society of Tailoresses
and Seamstresses of Baltimore,
44–45
Feminists, in Colonial America, 10;
break with abolitionists, 128–29;
look for coalition with labor movement, 129; lose enthusiasm for National Labor Union, 139–40; participate in National Labor Union
conventions, 132–37; praise National Labor Union, 134–35, 151;
split with blacks, 135, 137; and Working Women's Associations, 142–44
Fetjko, Annie, 452
Fincher's Trades' Review, 110–11, 113–
17, 119, 121

Fines, 368
Fitzgerald, Annie, 315, 318
Fitzpatrick, John, 301, 314
Flexner, Eleanor, 290
Flynn, Annie Gurley, 395, 404
Flynn, Elizabeth Gurley, criticizes IWW
    on woman's role, 406–07, 412; early
    life, 395–96; early speeches, 396–97;
    joins IWW, 396, issues call to
    women, 412; marriage, 403–404;
    opposes upper-class women, 404;
    role in free-speech fights, 414–15,
    416; role in Lawrence strike, 432,
    433–36; role in Paterson strike,
    450–58; song dedicated to, 457–58;
    as speaker, 396–97
Flynn, Kathie, 396
Flynn, Tom, 395, 396
Foster, William Z., 417
Four-hour day, 499
Fourier, Charles, 69
Fourth of July, 17–18, 51, 74, 78, 158
Free speech fights, 412–18
Freitas, Mary, 299
French, Samuel J., 419
French-Canadians, 419
Frenette, Edith, 415
Fugitive slaves, 6, 101–103
Fulton, Mary, 82
Fur Worker, 389
Fur Workers (1912 strike), conditions
    leading to, 361–62; general strike
    called, 362–63; limited aid from
    Women's Trade Union League, 363;
    role of women in, 364–65; settle-
    ment, 364–65; victory, 365
Fur Workers (1915 strike), 387

Gallatin, Albert, 20
Galveston Daily News, 176
Gannett, Deborah Simpson, 16–17
Garbatt, Mary, 273
Garment industry, changes in, 243;
    women replace men in, 243
Garment workers, and Knights of
    Labor, 189, 193–94

Garrison, William Lloyd, 102
Gasson, Lena, 369
Gaynor, William, 367–68, 371
General strike, for ten-hour day, 74,
    78
Genovese, Eugene D., 99–100
George, Henry, 287
Germans, in shoe strike, 95
Gersuny, Carl, 28
Gillespie, Mabel, 477
Gilman, Charlotte Perkins, 316, 470
Giovannitti, Arturo, 430, 431
Glasgow, Jesse E., 148, 155, 156
Goff, Mary, 369
Goggins, Catherine, 311–12
Goldblatt, Selma, 379, 383
Golden, John, 420, 472
Goldenberg, Anna, 493, 494
Goldman, Emma, 235, 418
Goldmark, Pauline, 462
Gompers, Samuel, advances reasons
    for small union membership of
    women, 471–72; appeals to laundry
    workers, 245; appoints Mary E.
    Kenney general organizer, 226, 227;
    calls for removal of women from in-
    dustry, 489; critical of report issued
    by Commission on Industrial Rela-
    tions, 484–85; critical of suffrage
    trend in National Women's Trade
    Union League, 485; denounces in-
    junction, 349; invites women dele-
    gates, 222; joins big business leaders
    in National Civic Federation, 283;
    on equal pay for equal work, 214; on
    "Great Uprising" of 1877, 298; op-
    poses Amalgamated Clothing
    Workers, 378, 380, 382; opposes
    minimum wage laws for women,
    479–80; praised, 238; role in strikes,
    327, 348, 364; role in formation of
    National Women's Trade Union
    League, 298–301; sends organizers
    South, 246–47; urges union to or-
    ganize females, 252; urges women
    organizers be appointed, 234
Gould, Jay, 192*n.*

Government employees, unions of, 188–89
Gray, Elizabeth, 65, 66
Gray and Green (publishers), 150–51
Great Labor Uprising of 1877, 173–77
"Great Uprising," 177–79
Greeley, Horace, 69*n.*
Greene, Lorenzo B., 104
Grossman, Herman, 317
Gruening, Martha, 334

Haggerty, Elizabeth, 82
Haley, Margaret, 311
Hamilton, Alice, 219, 465
Hamilton Manufacturing Company, 24, 25, 26, 28*n.*, 60, 83
Hanaflin, Mary, 24, 198–99
Haney, Mary, 477
Hanson, Carrie, 434
Harper, Ida Husted, 132*n.*
Harding, William, 115, 116
Hart, Schaffner & Marx, agreement, 354; strike at, 350, 351, 354
Hartropp, Mary, 241–42
Hayes, John W., 206, 209–10
Hayes, Margaret, 16
Hayes, Rutherford B., 176–77
Haymarket Affair, 207
Haywood, William D., 399, 402–403, 432, 436, 444, 475
Health hazards, 261
Henrotin, Ellen M., 304
Henry, Alice, 314–16, 476
Henry, Maggie, 182
Henry Street Settlement, 220
Hewitt, Mary Susan, 257*n.*
High dues, as device to keep women out of unions, 248, 251
Hill, Joe, 395, 403, 457
Hillman, Sidney, 354, 377, 382, 383
Hillquit, Morris, 335–36, 337, 345
Hinchey, Margaret, 482, 483
Hine, Lewis, 151, 152
Hitchih, Anna, 494
Homes, for working women, 179–81
Homestead strike, 228
Hood, Thomas, 89
Horizon, 341

Hoty, Mary Frances, 189
Hours of work, battle for ten-hour day, 73–79; court decisions on, 486*n*; in England, 57, 79; in 1900, 262–63, 265–66; reduced, 84
Howard, Robert, 246–47
Hull House, 219–20, 227, 230, 292, 295
Hunter, Addie W., 464
Huntington, Joshua, 15
Hutchinson, Anne, 10
Hyde, Beulah H., 416

Illinois Women's Alliance, 217–18, 232
Immigrants, 83–86, 256–57, 315–16, 440–41
Improvement Circles, 57, 60
Indentured servants, 2–3, 15–16, 17
Independent, 463
Independent polical action, 134
Indianapolis Star, 424
Indians, 1–2
Industrial Commission, 256, 266–67, 293–94
Industrial diseases, 465–66
"Industrial Education of Women," 237
Industrial Manifesto, 392–93
Industrial Union Bulletin, 396
Industrial Worker, 401, 402, 405, 447–48
Industrial Workers of the World (IWW), appeals to women; auto workers' strike, 453–54; and black workers, 397; brutal treatment of women members, 415–18; calls for special attention to women, 406–407; and Chinese and Japanese, 397; criticisms of, 455–56; criticizes AFL position on women, 397–98; and domestic servants, 407–11; dues for women, 394–95; formation, 392–94; free speech fights, 412–18; Lawrence strike, 426–29; Little Falls strike, 440–48; male chauvinism in, 457; method of organizing praised, 475; Paterson strike, 448–58; role of wives in strikes, 422–25; role of women in free-speech fights, 412–

18; rubber workers' strike, 452–53; in the South, 454–55; strength among women workers, 456–57; strength on woman question, 412; suffers defeats, 452–55; and unemployed, 488–89; weaknesses in approach to women, 411–12; women's auxiliaries, 399; women members, 399–400; women organizers, 456–57

International Assembly of North America, 125

International Association of Fur Workers of the United States and Canada, 361–62, 365

International Association of Machinists, 493

International Brotherhood of Electrical Workers, 251–54, 469

International Fur Workers' Union, 388–89

International Glove Workers' Union, 394

International Labor Union, 182–84

International Ladies' Garment Workers' Union (ILGWU), absence of women leaders, 78; 278–79; appeals to AFL for aid, 356; approach to women workers, 277–78; appoints women organizers, 387; begins to appoint women to roles in union, 385–86; and black women, 339–41; chartered by AFL, 244; conflicts in, 374–75; formation, 243–44; growth, 373; leaders have little confidence in women, 244; leaders view women as poor union material, 278; leadership ousted, 375; males dominate leadership, 388; opposition in to Protocol of Peace, 374–75; significance of waistmakers' strike for, 344–45; socialists in, 244; stand for woman suffrage, 277–78; strike ends Protocol of Peace, 387–88; women delegates at conventions, 277, 279; and Women's Trade Union League, 317

International Trade Union Label League, 318

International Typographical Union: *see* National Typographical Union

International Workingmen's Association, 164, 166, 169

"Intolerable Acts," 13

Irish, 84, 227, 257n., 280–81, 395–96, 492

Irish Socialist Federation, 396

Ironclad oaths, 171, 181, 303

Iron Molders' Union, 126

Italian Socialist Federation, 430

IWW: *see* Industrial Workers of the World

Jackson (Mississippi), 124–25

Jackson *Daily Clarion,* 124, 125

Jacksonian America, status of women in, 38–39

Jacobs, Dorothy, 379–80, 383–84

Jacques, Abbie, 157

Jessup, William J., 140

Jewish Daily Forward, 348, 363–65, 367

Jewish socialists, 225

Jewish women, boycott Kosher butchers, 294–95; charged with making poor union material, 219, 225, 229

Joan of Arc Assembly, 203, 207–210

Johnbusky, Louisa, 493

Johns, Susie, 142

Johnson, David N., 94

Johnson, Edwin, 177

Johnson, Hiram, 488

Johnson, Jane, 97–98

John Swinton's Paper, 189–90, 196

Jones, Jack Archibald, 403, 414

Jones, Mary Harris (Mother Jones), arrested, 282–83; as United Mine Workers' organizer, 382; at IWW convention, 393; attends rallies of Knights of Labor, 281; breaks with John Mitchell, 283; children die, 280; condemns child labor, 286–87; early life, 280–81; helps organize miners, 281; leads "March of the Mill Children," 283–89; method of organizing, 281–83; organizes wives of miners in strikes, 281–83; role in Chicago strike, 382; works in South-

Jones, Mary Harris (cont'd)
  ern textile mills, 288; what "March
  of Mill Children" accomplished,
  289; works as organizer, 281–83
Journal of United Labor, 211
Journeymen Cordwainers' Union of
  New York City, 86
Journeymen Tailors' Association of St.
  Louis, 110
Journeymen Tailors of New York, 50
Journeymen Tailors' Union of Cleve-
  land, 86
Journeymen Tailors' Union of New
  York, 116

Kalamazoo Corset strike, 357–58
Katzman, David, 268
Kehew, Mary Morton, 299
Keith, Madge, 497–98
Keller, Helen, 445–46
Kelley, Florence, 220, 233, 263, 292,
  304, 479, 491
Kelley, M. B. E., 188
Kenneally, James J., 197
Kenny, Bridget, 494
Keyser, Harrietta A., 238
Knights of Labor (K. of L.), activities
  of women in, 211–12; bar against
  women in, 185–86; black women in,
  188, 190–91, 210; boycotts in, 192–
  93, 196–97; decline, 207, 210–11;
  and equal pay for equal work, 204;
  Department of Woman's Work,
  198–207; formation, 195; government employees in, 188–89; importance of in relation to women workers, 210–11; investigates working
  conditions of women, 201–203; Joan
  of Arc Assembly, 207–10; leadership
  betrays strikes, 209–10; lockouts
  against, 208–10; male chauvinism in,
  204; militancy of women in, 194–96,
  208–209, 212; racism in, 201–210;
  secrecy in, 185; shoeworkers and,
  186–87, 189; strikes, 186–87, 192,
  194–96; Woman's Department,
  198–207; women afraid to join,

203–204; women leaders of, 197–98;
  women's locals in, 187, 198; wom-
  en's occupations in, 188, 189
Knights of St. Crispin, 97, 157–59, 181
Kosher butchers, boycott of, 294–95
Kraditor, Aileen S., 238
Kulik, Gary, 29

Labor Enquirer, 206
Labor Exchanges, 140
"Labor in New York: Its Circum-
  stances, Conditions and Rewards,"
  65
Labor play, America's first, 451
Labor press, 111–13, 121
Labor songs, 26, 35, 57, 115–16, 172,
  183, 184, 345, 370, 403, 404, 408,
  430–31, 451, 457–58, 470, 492–93
Labor Standard, 182
Ladies' Anti-Beef Trust Association,
  294–95
Ladies' Christian Union of New York,
  161
Ladies, Federal Labor Union No.
  2703, 215–18
Ladies' Garment Worker, 375
Ladies' Mechanics' Association of Fall
  River, 19
Ladies' Social Assembly of Olneyville,
  212*n.*
Ladies' Stitching Association, 189
Lady at Home, The, 39
Lady Segar Makers of Providence, 127
LaFollette, Fola, 371
Lake, Leonora M. Barry: *see* Barry,
  Leonora M.
Lake, Oliver R., 206
Lake County Times, 424
Landburg, Dora, 347
Langdon, Emma F., 393
La Pizza, Anna, 431
Larcom, Lucy, 24
Laundresses, 123–25
Laundry workers, in AFL, 223–24,
  228; in Knights of Labor, 207–10;
  national union of, 244–45; in San
  Francisco, 308–309; strikes, 155,

207–10; 223–24, 228, 305–307, 309;
unions shattered in depression, 236
Lawrence (Massachusetts), 426–39
Lawrence, Abbott, 83
Lawrence, Amos, 59
"Lawrence Children's Crusade,"
435–36
Lawrence *Evening Tribune,* 433
Lawrence strike, arrests in, 433; conditions leading to, 426–28; "Children's
Crusade" during, 435–36; early development, 429–30; health condi-
tions, 428; immediate cause, 429;
importance of to women, 438–39;
mass picketing in, 430; police brutal-
ity in, 435–37; premium system,
428; role of Elizabeth Gurley Flynn
in, 432–33; role of women in, 433;
split in Women's Trade Union
League caused by, 472–75; stimu-
lates other strikes, 440; women's role
in, 430–33; victory, 437–38
Lazarus, Emma, 219
Lease, Mary Elizabeth, 198
Legal status, of women in Colonial
America, 10–11
Legere, Benjamin, 442, 445, 448*n.*
Lemlich, Clara, 328, 343, 482, 483
Lennon, John B., 229
Lewis, Augusta, 135, 141, 142, 147–49,
160, 161
Liberator, 102
Lichtman, Charles L., 187
Life and Labor, 314, 479
Lifschitz, Mollie, 369
Limited Suffrage Movement, 485
Lincoln, Abraham, 96, 109, 116–17
Lincoln, Salome, 30–31
Lindstrom, Ellen, 311
Lippard, George, 88
Lippman, William, 236
Liss, Josephine, 433, 434
Literary Digest, 495
Little, Frank, 407
Little Falls strike, children in, 447;
composition of workers in, 442–43;
conditions leading to, 441–43; police

brutality in, 443–44; role of Helen
Keller in, 444–46; role of Helen
Schloss in, 445–46; role of Mathilda
Rabinowitz in, 445–47; role of
women in, 442–48; victory in,
447–48
Little Falls Journal and Courier, 442
Lloyd, Henry Demarest, 227, 230
Local No. 15 (ILGWU), 333–35,
338–39
Local No. 25 (ILGWU), 325–45, 358,
361, 372
Local No. 23, Cloth and Cap Makers'
Union, 280
London, Meyer, 327, 364
Long Day, The, 259, 310
Long Depression, 163–78
Lopez, John, 288–89
Los Angeles Union, 212
Los Angeles Times, 397
Lowell, Francis Cabot, 21–22
Lowell, James Russell, 66
Lowell (Massachusetts), 23–24, 33–35,
56–78, 82–84
Lowell Advertiser, 59, 61, 76
Lowell Courier, 75
Lowell Express, 61
Lowell Female Labor Reform Associa-
tion, compares U.S. and England,
79; constitution, 64; defeats William
Schouler for re-election, 76; forma-
tion, 64; issues "Factory Tracts," 67;
members threatened, with blacklists,
74; participates in anti-slavery activi-
ties, 68; purchases *Voice of Industry,*
66; sponsors "Female Department,"
60; supports ten-hour movement,
75–76, 78
Lowell Female Industrial Reform and
Mutual Aid Society, 81
"Lowell fever," 24
Lowell Offering, 57–61, 69, 75, 83, 219
Lowell System, 23–24, 56–58
Lowell Union of Association, 69
Luther, Seth, 25–26, 31–32, 54
Lynn (Massachusetts), 46–47, 90–97,
157, 159–60, 189

Lynn News, 91–92, 95
Lynn Record, 46–47
Lynn Weekly Reporter, 94

McCateer, L. H., 246
McCreesh, Elizabeth, 356
McDonald, Mary, 132
McDonnell, J. P., 182–84
McDowell, Mary E., 251, 299, 313, 474–75
McEnery, Mary, 477
McEnroe, Father Peter C., 200
McGuire, Peter J., 233
McNamara, Mrs. George T., 498
McNeill, George E., 256
Mahoney, Elizabeth, 477
"Maids Defiance, The," 409
Male Auxiliary, 77–78
Male-female solidarity, 44, 52, 494
Malkiel, Theresa, 338
Maloney, Mary, 254, 279
"Manayunk Working People's Committee," 36
Manchester Democrat, 79
Manchester Female Labor Reform Association, 78–79
Manges, Frances May, 9
Mann, Tom, 249
"March of the Mill Children," 283–89
Marriage relationship, 69–70, 316
Marx, Karl, 133, 270, 271
Marx-Aveling, Eleanor, 297
Marxian Socialists, 182
Mitchell, John, 282, 283
Mitchell, Louisa M., 44
Mittelstadt, Louisa, 475
Molineaux, William, 14
Molly Maguires, 185
Monroe, Sarah, 42
Montgomery, David, 113–14, 196–97
Moore, Fannie, 100
Morgan, Anne, 332
Morgan, Elizabeth Chambers, activity in Illinois Women's Alliance, 217–18; early life, 215; exposes exploitation of child workers, 216–17; hailed by AFL convention, 233; helped by Hull House workers, 220; helps or-

ganize bindery union, 227; in Knights of Labor, 215; in Sovereigns of Industry, 215; leads fight to expose sweatshops, 230–33, nominated for AFL vice-presidency, 233; organizes Federal Labor Union No. 2703, 215; organizes women's unions, 233; testifies before Congressional Committee on sweatshops, 232; works for legislation outlawing sweatshops, 233
Morris, Max, 298, 299
Morrison, Frank, 251, 322
"Mother Jones' Crusaders," 285
"Mother Jones' Industrial Army," 285
Mullaney, Kate, forms Troy Collar Laundry Union, 124; president of cooperative laundry, 155–56; visits Working Women's Association, 155
Massachusetts, legislative committee on ten-hour day, 75–76; ten-hour laws in, 181
Massachusetts State Federation of Labor, 238
Massachusetts Working Women's League, 139, 181
Mechanics' Free Press, 27, 50–51
Men's clothing trade, conditions in, 351–52
Men's Clothing Workers (Chicago strike), causes of, 350–52; role of Chicago Federation of Labor, 351, 353; role of Chicago Women's Trade Union League, 351–52; role of women in, 350–51; sell-out of by United Garment Workers' leadership, 353–54; settlement, 353–54
Middle-Class Reformers, approach to working women, 290–92
Milwaukee, strike of garment workers in, 356
"Mind among the Spindles," 59–60
"Mink Brigade," 343
Minimum wage laws, 480–81
Minimum wages, 479–80
Muller v. Oregon, 304
Munitions industry, 491–94
"Munitions strikes," 491–94

Mutual Fur Protective Association, 362
Myers, Isaac, 138

National American Woman Suffrage
Association, 274, 333, 482
National Association for the Advancement of Colored People, 268
National Association of Colored
Women, 464
National Association of Manufacturers, 479
National Association Opposed to
Woman's Suffrage, 485
National Brotherhood of Electrical
Workers: *see* International Brotherhood of Electrical Workers
National Civic Federation, 283, 348
National Consumers' League, 292,
304, 331, 462, 479, 480, 491
National Equal Rights' League, 54,
200–201, 212, 217, 343
National Industrial Congress, 90, 106
National Industrial Union of Textile
Workers, 419, 443
National Laborer, 48, 52
National Labor Union, adopts progressive approach to women workers, 126–27, 133–34; advocates
equal pay for equal work, 133, 140;
conventions, 130–37, 140, 151, 154;
feminists and, 130–34, 139–40; and
woman's suffrage, 132–34; women
elected officers, 124, 140
National Trades' Union, 31, 32, 53–54,
125
National Trades' Union, 106
National Typographical Union, and
women members, 144, 148, 149,
150, 160–61, 214
National Union of Textile Workers of
America, 245–46, 247–49
National Woman's Suffrage Association, 155, 200–201
National Women's Trade Union
League, AFL provides funds for,
476; allies in, 300; anti-suffrage
forces in, 481–82; battle in, over
AFL, 475–76; and black women,
313, 340–41, 478; Brtitish influence
in formation, 296–98; caught in dilemma, 486; condemns antisuffrage women's groups, 485; conflict in of allies and workingwomen,
310; conflict with AFL, 485–86; constitution, 300; conventions, 304,
373; critical of AFL policies, 317–23;
early objectives, 303–304; factors
leading to formation, 292–94; helps
in strikes of laundry workers, 307;
helps woman suffrage campaign,
482–83; membership provisions,
300; praised for role in waistmakers'
strike, 343; program, 304; publishes
Union Labor Advocate, 314; publishes
Life and Labor, 314; relationship with
AFL, 304, 317–23, 343–44; resents
AFL attitude towards women, 472;
School for Active Workers in the
Labor Movement, 477; supports
minimum wage legislation, 480;
views suffrage as key to organization
of women, 484; views on suffrage for
women, 481–82; yields to AFL, 476;
see also Boston, Chicago, New York
Women Trade Union Leagues
Needle trades: *see* sewing women,
Tailoresses, Waistmakers.
"Needlewomen of New York," 87
Nestor, Agnes, 311–13, 334, 335,
338–39, 396, 476, 477
New England Association of Farmers,
Mechanics, and Other Workingmen,
31–32
New England Labor Reform League,
81
New England Offering, 83
New England Shoemakers' Strike of
1860, 90–97
New England Workingmen's Association, 74, 75*n.*, 78, 81
New Hampshire, laws in, for ten-hour
day, 78–79
New Era of Industry, 72
New York City Woman Suffrage
League's Constitutional Amendment Campaign, 238

New Lowell Offering, 60*n.*
Newman, Pauline, 331, 341–42, 343, 355, 357, 375, 385–86, 387, 477, 482
New Slavery, The, 231
New World Lessons for Old World People, 478
New York *Age,* 339–40, 341
New York *Bulletin,* 163–64
New York Call, 348–49, 360, 365
New York *Daily Graphic,* 161–62
New York *Daily Sentinel,* 43–44, 52
New York *Evening Post,* 50
New York Factory Investigation Commission, 360, 459–63
New York Female Moral Reform Society, 41
New York *Herald,* 33
New York Joint Board of Cloak and Shirt Makers' Unions, 347
New York Parasol and Umbrella Makers' Union, 296
New York State Federation of Labor, 486
New York *Sun,* 119, 121, 167
New York Times, 92, 110, 161, 165, 167, 168, 221, 295, 337, 365, 483, 496
New York Trades' Assembly, 115
New York Typographical Union, 137
New York Weekly Journal, 10
New York Wage Earners' League, 484
New York Women's Trade Union League, assists strikes of women workers, 316–17; favors four-hour day, 499; formation, 301; helps in strikes of women, 307, 308; helps Local No. 25, 326; and ILGWU, 317; praised for role in 1909 strike, 343–44; and shorter hours, 499; role in cloakmakers' strike, 347; role in fur strike, 363–64; role in waistmakers' strike, 327–28, 330–32, 336, 337, 340–41, 342–44; role in white goods' strike, 369–71; and Triangle Fire, 359–60; views men union leaders as enemies of working women, 371–72; workingwomen more important in, 343–44

New York Women's Trade Union League Strike Council, 369
New York Working Women's Labor Union, 139–40, 181
New York Working Women's Society, 221–22
New York *World,* 146–47, 295, 358
Nichols, Thomas, 199, 202
Non-Importation agreements, 14
Nordeck, Charles E., 245
Noren, Robert, 321–22
Norton, Sarah, 154

Olive Leaf and Factory Girls' Repository, 58
One Big Union, 403
Origin of the Family, Private Property and the State, 271
O'Reilly, Leonora, asked to write for *American Federationist,* 485; attacks *The Long Day,* 259, 348; becomes labor organizer, 477; decides to split with male trade unions, 486; early life, 220; exposes conditions of women workers, 461–62; guiding spirit of Local No. 16, 254–55; helps woman suffrage movement, 482; on suffrage as key to unionization of women, 484; on women's wages, 264; role in founding of Women's Trade Union League, 200, 301; role in Kalamazoo strike, 357; role in waistmakers' strike, 333; role in Wage Earners' League, 484*n;* works with Margaret Dreier, 305; works with settlement house workers, 220
O'Reilly, Mary, 199, 211
Oshkosh Daily Northwestern, 239
O'Sullivan, John F., 229, 236, 237
O'Sullivan, Mary E. Kenney, attacks anti-suffrage movement, 485; becomes AFL organizer, 227; campaigns against sweatshops, 230, 233; early life, 226–27; goes to Boston, 236; marries, 237; meets Jane Addams, 227; meets Samuel Gom-

pers, 227; not reappointed AFL organizer, 129–30; organizes Chicago Bindery Workers' Union, 227; organizes for AFL, 228–29; organizes women's unions in Boston during depression, 236–37; organizes shirtwaist workers, 227; role in formation of Women's Trade Union League, 298, 299–300; role in Lawrence strike, 473; starts cooperative, 230; works with League, 311

Out of the Shadow, 266

Ovington, Mary White, 268, 269

"Pageant of the Paterson Strike," 451–52

Panic of 1837, 37, 55; of 1857, 110; of 1873, 159, 163; of 1893, 234, 235

Parsons, Lucy, 393–94, 488, 489

Paterson, Emma Ann, 296

Paterson Association for the Protection of the Working Classes, 36–37

Paterson strike (1912), begins, 449; conditions leading to, 448–49; composition of workers in, 448–49; ends in defeat, 452; Pageant, 451–52; wholesale arrest of strikers, 449–50; violence in, 449

Patterson, Ellen, 114–15

Peers, Emily, 142, 147, 148

Pemberton, Caroline H., 284

Penn, William, 124, 136

Pennsylvania Women's Suffrage Association, 334

Perkins, Frances, 367

Philadelphia, street-car discrimination in, against blacks, 106, 129; waistmakers' strike in, 333–35; 338–39; women workers in, 44–45, 48, 88–89, 105

Philadelphia Benevolent Society, 49*n*.

Philadelphia Evening Bulletin, 86

Philadelphia Negro, The, 268

Philadelphia *North American*, 288, 289

Philadelphia *Public Ledger*, 334–35

Philadelphia Trades' Assembly, 53

Philadelphia Women's Trade Union League, helps organize women workers, 386

Pike, Violet, 336, 478

"Pin money" theory of women working, 257, 472

Pitcher, Molly. *See* Mayes, Margaret.

Pittsburgh Journal, 77, 78, 494

"Pleasures of Factory Life," 60

Poetry, 67–68, 80, 89, 91, 314

Polansky, Esther, 364

Police brutality, 167, 294–95, 326, 327, 330–31, 334, 347, 352, 355, 367, 368, 371–72, 381–82, 435–37, 443–44, 449–50, 452–53

Political Equality League, 332, 336

Powderly, Terence V., 186, 187, 197, 200, 206, 210

Poyntz, Juliet Stuart, 387

Preferential Union shop, 348, 349

Premium system, 428

Printers, women as, 144–48

Problems of Employment for Negro Women, The, 267–68

Prostitutes, strikes of, 421

Prostitution, 41–42, 294, 401–402, 459–60

Protective legislation, for women, 304

"Protocol of Peace," 349–50, 387–88

Providence Gazette, 29

Provident Society, 45

Quartering Act, 13

Question of Women Workers and Women at the Present Time, 272

Quincy, Josiah, 21

Rabinowitz, Matilda, 444–45, 447, 453, 454, 455–56

Racism, in textile industry in South, 247

Radical Republican program of Reconstruction, 129

Railroad Strike of 1877, 173–77

Rauh, Ida, 331, 482

"Rebel Girl, The," 457–58
Red Special, 363
Reed, John, 451
Reichers, Charles F., 226
Reilly, Mary A., 207
Relief and Aid Society, 166
Republican Party, 128, 129, 131, 134
Revolution, 129–55
Richardson, Dorothy, 259
Rights of Labor, 232
Rickert, Thomas, 352–54, 367, 368, 376–78
Robins, Margaret Dreier, angered by AFL, 475; early life, 304–305; elected president of National Women's Trade Union League, 305, 310; helps women financially to become organizers, 477; insists League must retain relations with AFL, 475–76; and Lawrence strike, 474; limits contributions to League, 478–79; on black women members, 340; on trade union opposition to women suffrage, 482; role in Chicago men's clothing strike, 354; role in 1909 waistmakers' strike, 334; writes on "Living Wage," 315
Robins, Raymond, 305
Robinson, Harriet H., 56–57, 69
Rodgers, Elizabeth, 181–82, 197–98, 211
Roosevelt, Eleanor, 305
Roosevelt, Theodore, 285, 286, 371

Sabotage, 409–410
Sage, Mrs. Russell, 120
St. John, Vincent, 402–403, 404, 442, 444
Saleswomen, 171–73, 262
San Antonio *Express,* 253
Sanger, Margaret, 402
Sashon, Rose, 343
Schepps, Mollie, 343
Schlesinger, Benjamin, 375, 385, 390
Schloss, Helen, 445–46
School for Active Workers in Labor Movement, 477

Schouler, William, 58, 61, 75, 76
Scott, Melinda, 311, 319, 343, 361, 386, 499
Scudder, Vida, 298
Schneiderman, Rose, advocates socialist ideas, 476; becomes Socialist, 280; critical of AFL, 487; describes gains of women workers, 373; early life, 280; elected to League executive board, 343; fulltime organizer for ILGWU: helps waistmakers, 326; hired by National American Woman Suffrage Association, 482; meets Dreier sisters, 310; on Triangle Fire, 360; resigns post as ILGWU organizer, 390–91; role in waistmakers' strike, 331–32, 342; role in whitegoods' workers' struggles, 368, 369, 372; role in woman suffrage movement, 482–84; secretary of Cloth and Cap Makers' Union, 280; vice-president Women's Trade Union League, 310
Seamstresses, 39–41, 84–85, 87–89
Seamstresses Association of Cincinnati, 87–88
Seasonal unionism, 224–25
Seattle Union Record, 496, 497
"Second Independence Day," 74
Secrecy, in unions, 158, 185
Seidel, Emil, 356
Self-purchase, of slaves, 102–103
Seneca Falls convention, 72
Settlement house movement, formation, 219–20; helps form unions of women workers, 220, 227, 255, 293; role in formation of National Women's Trade Union League, 298–99, 301; and trade unions, 292–93
Sewing machine, 85, 114, 243
Sewing Girls' Union of Chicago, 140
Sewing Machine Operators' Union, 152
Sewing women, 40–41, 113–18, 119–20
Sewing Women's Protective and Benevolent Union, 114–15, 118

Sex in Industry, 171*n.*

Sexual abuse, of women workers, 357, 421–22, 462

Shackford, Reverend Charles C., 96

Shaw, Anna Howard, 333, 336, 482

Shaw, George Bernard, 330, 402

Shirt-Sewers' Co-operative Union of New York, 87

Shirt, Waist, and Laundry Workers' International Union, 245, 305–307

Shoebinders, 45–48, 90–97, 156–58

Shoe industry, 45–46, 90–91, 156–57

Shore, Samuel, 369, 372

Shurtleff, Robert: *see* Gannett, Deborah Simpson

Shute, Lizzie H., 198, 211

Silver, Clara, 311

Silverman, Hannah, 450

Sisterhood, during 1909 waistmakers' strike, 342–43; and Working Women's Associations, 143–44

Skeffington, Harry, 187

Slater, Samuel, 20–21

Slavery, abolished in North, 17; beginnings, 2–6; growth of, in Cotton Kingdom, 98

Slave codes, 5

Slave rebellions, 6–7

Smith, Charlotte, 189, 213–14

Smith, James McCune, 104

Social Democratic Party, 283

Socialism, as solution to "woman question," 275–76

Socialist Labor Party, 221, 270

Socialist Party of America, debate in, on workingmen, 273–74; leaders not anxious to criticize AFL policies, 277; on woman suffrage, 274–75; position on "woman question," 270; socialism as solution of "woman question," 275–76

Socialist Woman, 272

Solidarity, 400, 401, 405, 407

Somerset Reporter, 420

Sons of Liberty, 13–14, 19, 58

"Song of the Factory Girls," 57

"Song of the White Goods Workers," 370

Southwestern Telegraph & Telephone Company, 252–54

South, strikes of textile workers in, 247, 248, 454–55; textile workers in, 246–49, 454–55

Speed-up, in textile mills, 62–63, 67

Spinner, Francis Elias, 109

Stenographers, 275–76

Stewart, Maria, 106–107

Stirling, Mary, 187, 199, 211

Strain, Father John, 96

Strikebreaking, 136, 150

Stokes, Rose Pastor, 333, 365–66

Stone, Huldah J., 56, 71–72, 73, 75*n.*

Stone, Lucy, 128, 177

Street, Jane, 407–411

Streightoff, Dr. Frank H., 460

Strikes, against black women, 247; auto workers, 453–54; ballet dancers, 123; of black women, 176; box makers, 307–308; carpet weavers, 194–96; children, 29–30, 36–37; cigarmakers, 177–79; cloakmakers (N.Y.), 346–50; corset workers, 314, 357–58; Daughters of St. Crispin, 158; during long depression, 167–71, 173–77; East Hammond, 423–25; first of all women, 43–44; first all-women factory, 30; first of women workers, 29; for eight-hour day, 194; for ten-hour day, 76–78, 82; fur workers, 361–62, 389; 372; garment workers (Cleveland), 354–56; garment workers (Milwaukee), 356; gas workers (London), 297; in 1850s, 84, 90–97; of IWW (419–25); Kimono workers, 372; in Knights of Labor, 176–82, 192, 194–96; lady shoebinders, 48; laundry workers, 155, 207–10, 223–24, 305–307, 309; Lawrence, 426–39; Lynn shoebinders, 47; McKees Rocks, 421–23; matchmakers (London), 296–97; men's clothing workers (Chicago), 350–54, 381–82; men's tailors

Strikes (cont'd)
(N.Y.), 366–68; miners, 281–83; munitions, 491–94; New England shoemakers' of 1860, 90–97; in Paterson, 182–84, 402, 448–58; Polish women, 323; prostitutes, 421; rubber workers, 452–53; shoemakers, 90–97, 186–87; Showhegan, 419–21; in Southern textiles, 247, 248, 454–55; telephone workers, 252–54; textile workers, 28–37, 153, 182–84, 186–87, 283–89, 426–58; in U.S. Steel, 493–94; waistmakers, 324–45; Westinghouse, 492–94; what role of women proves, 494; Wheatland, 411; white goods workers, 368–72; woodworkers, 239–40

Sub-contracting, 324–25

Suffrage movement, 28–29, 131–37, 138, 141, 151, 152, 274, 481–85

Suffragettes, 332–33, 334, 336

Sullivan, Dora, 223, 224, 226, 228

Supreme Court, 304, 313

Survey, 340

Svenson, Hilda, 477

Swank, Lizzie, 181–82, 193–94, 199*n.*, 211, 212

Sweatshop Act, 233

Sweatshops, campaign against, 231–33, 313; conditions in, 231–32; legislation outlawing, 263–64; origins, 230–31, 231*n.*

Sweating system: *see* Sweatshops

Swinton, John, 167, 196

Sylvis, William H., 125, 126–27, 130–137, 156

Tailoresses, 39–45, 87–89, 228

Tailoresses' Industrial Union of Philadelphia, 88–89, 106

Taylor, Susie King, 104

Teachers, 112–13

Telephone operators, 252–54, 258, 316, 467–69

Tenement House system, 178–79

Ten-hour Day, achievements, 84; battle for, 73–79; established for government employees, 74; general strike for, 74, 78; in England, 79; laws for, 78–79, 80, 81–82, 84, 181; Massachusetts legislative investigating committee, 74–76, 78; New Hampshire law, 78–79; petition movement, 75–76; philosophy of, 73

Ten-Hour laws, 78–82, 181

Textile industry, changes in, 170; health hazards, 261–62; in South, 247, 248, 260–61, 450–51; speed-up, 59, 62–63, 67

Textile Manufacturer, 440

Thayer, Reverend Thomas, 58

Thiers, Adolphe, 58

Thomas, Abel C., 58, 61

Thomas, Reverend Charles, 57

Thompson, Flora McDonald, 466–67

Thompson, James P., 415

Tobitt, Anna, 142, 147

Tobitt, William, 147

Tompkins Square riot, 166–67

Torello, Carrie, 450

Townshend Act, 13, 14

Toynbee Hall, 219

Trade unions, increase in membership, 301; leaders hostile to women, 49–54

Train, George Francis, 129–30

Tresca, Carlos, 402, 404

Triangle Fire, 358–60, 367

Triangle Shirtwaist Company, 326, 338, 358–60

Troy (N.Y.), 123–25, 223–24, 305–307

Troy Collar Laundry Union, 124, 134, 155–56, 207

Troy *Northern Budget,* 208

Troy Trades' Assembly, 124, 125

Tubman, Harriet, 103

Twining, Luella, 393

Typographical Society of Philadelphia, 50

Typographical Union, Local No. 6, 145–151

Underground Railroad, 101–103

Unemployment, demonstrations, during long depression, 166–67; during 1913–1914, 487–88

Union label, 240–41, 498

Union Card and Label League of Seattle, 498

Union Labor Advocate, 314–16

Union membership, among women workers, 266–67, 471

Union organizers, increase of women as, 477–78

Unions, exclude blacks, 106; first of industrial women, 56; reject women, 86, 90; number of women in, 266–67, 471; secrecy in, 158, 185; and woman suffragists, 237–38; women afraid to join, 182, 203–204

United Brotherhood of Cloak Makers' Union No. 1, 243

United Brotherhood of Tailors, 376–77

United Cloth and Cap Makers' Union, 380–81*n.*

United Garment Workers, attitude toward women workers, 279; betray Chicago strikers, 353–54; betray New York tailor strikers, 366–68; conflict in, 225, 375–77; emphasizes union label, 225–26; factions in, 375–77; formation, 224–26; indifferent to women workers, 254–55; leadership mainly men, 229; loses members in depression of 1893–1897, 235; split in, 376–77; supported by AFL, 377–78, 380–81; women organize in, 229

United Hebrew Trades, 225, 327, 339, 362, 363, 380

United Laundry Workers of Troy, 244–45

United Men and Women's Trading Society, 44

United Mine Workers of America, 267, 281–83

United States Commission on Industrial Relations, 466–69, 484

United Tailoresses' Society of New York, 42–44

United Textile Workers, 420, 430, 472

Unity, of male and female workers, 74, 78, 90–97

University settlement, 220, 295

Utica Daily Press, 443, 447

Utopian Socialism, 69, 81

Valentine Offering, 67

Valesh, Eva McDonald, 222, 249, 338

Value of the Workingwoman to the State, The, 238

Van Vorst, Bessie, 257, 259–60

Van Vorst, Marie, 257, 259, 260–62

Voice of Industry, 42, 61–62, 65–66, 71, 72, 76, 82

Vorse, Mary Heaton, 434–35, 438–39

Wages, of black women, 268; of cigarmakers, 177; of cloakmakers, 346; in Colonial America, 10; during long depression, 167; in 1830s, 40–41; in 1850s, 85–87; in 1870s, 161–62; in 1880s, 190, 198, 199*m.*, 201–203; in 1900, 259–60, 264; of fur workers, 362; of laundresses, 123–25; in Lawrence mills, 426, in Little Falls, 441; in munitions industry, 491; of shoemakers, 91; of teachers, 112; of telephone operators, 467–68; of textile workers, 25, 441; of waistmakers, 325; of white-goods workers, 368; of women during Civil War, 110; of women workers revealed by N.Y. Factory Investigating Commission, 460–61

Wage slavery, 37, 83, 94

Waistmakers' strike (1909), arrests of strikers, 330–31; beginnings, 326–28; Carnegie Hall meeting, 336–37; composition of strikers, 328–29; conflict between socialists and wealthy women supporters, 337–38; early settlements, 329; effect of, on Women's Trade Union League, 343–44; general strike, 327–28; militancy of women strikers, 330–31; negotiations, 335–36, 337; number of strikers, 328; protracted struggle, 329–30; police brutality, 326; role of black women, 339–41; role of suf-

Waistmakers' strike (cont'd)
frage movement, 332–33; role of
Italian women, 341; settlement in
New York, 338; settlement in
Philadelphia, 338–39; significance
of, 339–41, 344–45; sisterhood dur-
ing, 342–43; wins support of college
women, 331–33; Women's Trade
Union League aids strikers, 340–45
Wald, Lillian, 220, 299
Walling, William English, 295, 298,
300, 301, 303
Walsh, John, 135–36
Waltham System, 24–25, 59
Ware, Norman F., 56, 60
War for Independence, 7, 15–19
Washerwomen, 101, 124–25, 176
Watkins, William J., 119
Wealth against Commonwealth, 227
Weavers' Protective Association,
170–71
Webb, Beatrice, 479
Weld, Theodore, 103–103
Wells, Ida B., 191
Welzenbach, Annie, 433
Wertheimer, Barbara M., 85
Western Home Visitor, 145
Western Union, 192, 244n.
"We Want Bread and Roses, Too,"
430–31
Weyle, Mrs. Walter, 305, 478
What to Do and How to Do It, 275
Wheatland Hopfield strike, 411
Whipple, Frances Harriet, 61
White, Henry, 299
"White lists," 292
White Goods workers, 368–72
White Goods' Workers' Union, 368–69
Whitehead, Myrtle, 477
Whittier, John Greenleaf, 66
Williams, Daniel, 140, 144, 155
Williams, Fannie Barrier, 267–68
Wilson, Elizabeth, 26
Wilson, Joan Hoff, 18
Wilson, Lizzie, 195
Wilson, William B., 382
Wilson, Woodrow, 387, 483, 495
Winn, Will H., 247, 248

Wives, importance of, in standards of
living, 256–57; militant role, 238–
39; organized by Mother Jones,
282–83; role in strikes, 196, 422–25,
466; and union label, 240–41; wages
for, 466–67
Wobblies: *see* Industrial Workers of
the World
Woman's Journal, 238
"Woman Question," 270–71, 275–76
Woman and Socialism, 271–72
Woman's Union Label League, 240
Woman Suffrage, endorsed by AFL,
301; IWW opposes, 405–406; in
1900s, 277–78; in 1890s, 237–38;
Socialist Party and, 274; trade
unions and, 482; working women
not represented in, 274
Woman Suffrage Association, 132, 133
Women Suffrage movement, 128–29,
131–37, 138, 141, 151, 152, 274,
405–406, 482
Woman's Suffrage Party, 482, 483
Women, admitted to Cigar Makers'
union, 127–28; afraid to join unions,
203–204; as apprentices, 7; arrested,
497–98; as artisans, 9–10; demonstrations of, against cost of living,
494–96; devices used to exclude
from unions, 250–51; discriminated
against in work assignments, 265;
eliminated from medical practice,
38; feminists among, 10; in government employment, 109–10; increase
of, in clerical work, 258; increase in
employment during World War I,
490–91; as indentured servants, 2–6;
as labor organizers, 477; legal status
of, 10–11; as midwives, 9; move into
garment trades, 243; number in
unions, 266–67; as printers, 144–48;
protest treatment, 180–81; role during Civil War, 109–21; role during
Great Labor Uprising, 173–79; role
in Amalgamated leadership, 383–
85; role in ILGWU, 385–86; role in
American Revolution, 13–19; role in
Colonial America, 8–10; role in Con-

tinental Army, 16–17; role in Bacon's rebellion, 12; role in Daughters of Liberty, 13–15; role in IWW free speech fights, 414–18; role in Lawrence strike, 430–33, 433–34, 438–39; role in War for Independence, 15–18; significance of Knights of Labor for, 211–12; as slaves, 2–6; unemployment among, 162–64; unemployment demonstrations of, 166–67
Women's Auxiliaries, 399, 498
Women's Cloak Makers' Union, 230
Women's Educational and Industrial Union, 179–80, 299
Women's International Union Label League of the World, 240
Women's Label League, 298
Women's National Industrial League, 213–14
Women's National Trade Union League: *see* National Women's Trade Union League
Women's National Union Label League, 290
Women's National Labor League, 189
Women's Protective and Provident League, 296
Women's rights, 34, 42, 66–67, 69–70, 70–72, 129–32
Women's Trade Union Provident League, 296, 297, 298
Women's Typographical Union, 148–50, 160–61, 196
Woodbridge, Alice L., 220, 221
Worker, 274
Working conditions, in canneries, 462; during long depression, 164–65; in 1870s, 171–76; in 1880s, 190, 198, 199*n.,* 201–203, 230–32; in 1900, 259–63; in laundries, 123–24; in Lawrence, 426–28; of telephone operators, 467–69; in textile mills, 25–27
Working Man's Advocate, 51, 52
Workingman's Advocate, 131–32, 135, 151, 155, 156

Workingmen's Beneficial and Protective Association, 203–204
Working Life of Women in the Seventeenth Century, 7–8
Workingmen of America, 242–43
Working Girls Clubs, 218–19
Working Women's Associations, at National Labor Union conventions, 132, 135; changing composition, 153–55; establish training schools, 150–51; feminists and, 142–44; formation, 140–44, 147; form unions for sewing women, 152; in Boston, 153; middle-class women dominate, 154–55; role in strikebreaking, 150–51; and sisterhood, 143–44
Working Women's Associates (Lynn), 157
Working Women's Clubs, 237
Working Women's Home, 152
Working Women's Improvement Association, 219
Working Women's Protective Union, 120–21, 164, 290
Working Women's Relief Association of Philadelphia, 116
Working Women's Society: *see* New York Working Women's Society
Working Women's Suffrage Association, 140
Working Women's Union of Chicago, 140
Working Women's Union of New York City, 114–16

"Yellow-dog contracts," 171
Young, Alfred P., 13
Young, Ruth, 218
Young, William F., 62
Young Women's Christian Association, 179, 420
Yuganis, Mary, 432

Zetkin, Clara, 272–73
Zuckerman, Florence, 369